C000066322

NOTE ON THE AUTHOR

Warwick Braithwaite (1896-1971) was born in Dunedin, New Zealand. During WWI, he made the dangerous voyage across the world to further his musical studies in piano and composition at the Royal Academy of Music in London.

His ambition was to conduct, so he began his professional career with the remarkable Joseph O'Mara Grand Opera Company. Later he became Music Director for the BBC in Cardiff, where he earned his appointment as the first Musical Director of the National Orchestra of Wales. During WWII he led the Scottish Orchestra through a period of positive growth, and expanded his activities in opera and ballet – first with Vic-Wells, and later with Welsh National Opera, Sadler's Wells, Covent Garden and the Royal Ballet.

Braithwaite worked with all the major British orchestras, and his reputation was enhanced by a large number of radio broadcasts and studio recordings with distinguished artists. Tours took him to every part of the United Kingdom, as well as to New Zealand, Australia, South Africa, Iceland, France, Germany and Italy.

Taken ill during a visit to Australia in 1970, where he was conducting one of his favourite works, *Fidelio*, he returned immediately to London. Braithwaite died in January the following year, leaving a legacy that is only now beginning to be fully appreciated.

THE
GOLDEN
SHORE

An autobiography by

WARWICK BRAITHWAITE

Edited and annotated by

ROGER FLURY

Copyright © 2023 Roger Flury

The moral right of the author has been asserted.

Apart from any fair dealing for the purposes of research or private study,
or criticism or review, as permitted under the Copyright, Designs and Patents
Act 1988, this publication may only be reproduced, stored or transmitted, in
any form or by any means, with the prior permission in writing of the
publishers, or in the case of reprographic reproduction in accordance with
the terms of licences issued by the Copyright Licensing Agency. Enquiries
concerning reproduction outside those terms should be sent to the publishers.

Publication of *The Golden Shore* has been made possible
through the generous support of the Lilburn Trust.

Matador
Unit E2 Airfield Business Park,
Harrison Road, Market Harborough,
Leicestershire. LE16 7UL
Tel: 0116 279 2299
Email: books@troubador.co.uk
Web: www.troubador.co.uk/matador
Twitter: @matadorbooks

ISBN 978 1803135 625

British Library Cataloguing in Publication Data.
A catalogue record for this book is available from the British Library.

Typeset in 10.5pt Minion Pro by Troubador Publishing Ltd, Leicester, UK

Matador is an imprint of Troubador Publishing Ltd

In memory of Peter Downes (1928–2022),
my mentor and friend,
who forgot more than I ever knew,
and taught me more than I can ever remember.

Henry Warwick Braithwaite, 1953.

Lorna Constance Braithwaite, c.1964.

FOREWORD

Warwick Braithwaite, was a conductor of remarkable musicianship and dedication. His career lasted from 1919 to his final performance in Australia in 1970. He was much loved by orchestras, singers and dancers. He was brilliant at steering through the disasters that so often dog opera performances. In his last years he was a kind and encouraging teacher of young singers. He was less popular among music administrators, with whom he often had strong disagreements about matters he considered artistically important.

Conducting what became the National Orchestra of Wales, Warwick frequently presented six or more programmes a week. That workload, and the scale of the repertoire he had to prepare, would have daunted most professionals: he managed it with cheerful stamina. He was an outstanding interpreter of Puccini. The Second World War cut the heart out of his career, as it did the careers of so many other performers. But for that, he would be much better known today. An extensive discography survives him.

In preparing this edition, Roger Flury has assembled a remarkable database which lists every performance our father conducted, giving details of the programmes and the hundreds of artists with whom he worked. It is hoped that this database might, in the future, be made publicly available.

We are both very grateful indeed to Roger for the dedication and meticulous scholarship with which he has edited and given life to Warwick's memoirs.

Rodric Braithwaite
Nicholas Braithwaite

CONTENTS

The Foreword is contributed by Nicholas and Rodric Braithwaite.
The text of all numbered chapters is by Warwick Braithwaite,
abridged and amended by the editor.
The Preface, Bridge Passage, Postlude, Appendices 1–6 and
footnotes are the work of the editor.

CONTENTS

ILLUSTRATIONS

Front cover: *Portrait of Warwick Braithwaite. Conductor, Sadler's Wells Opera.*
Artist: Mitchell, Victor Leonard William. 1964. From Drawings, Paintings and
Prints. Ref: G-482.
Alexander Turnbull Library, Wellington, New Zealand.
Reproduced by permission of Anna Reed (Mitchell Studios, Wellington).

Frontispiece: Portraits of Warwick Braithwaite (1953), and Lorna Braithwaite
(*c.*1964) are from private collections.

The photograph of Warwick and Rewi Braithwaite in New Zealand is
reproduced by courtesy of the family of Fergus Fraser.

The studio portrait of Joseph O'Mara (*c.*1890s) is reproduced by permission of
Special Collections and Archives, Glucksman Library, University of Limerick.

The photograph of the performance of Mendelssohn's *Elijah* in the Dunedin
Town Hall (1947), is reproduced by permission of the Hocken Library,
Dunedin.

Studio portraits of Warwick Braithwaite, Tyrone Guthrie and Frederic
Lamond are reproduced by permission of the National Portrait Gallery,
London.

All other illustrations are from the private collections of the editor and the
Braithwaite family.

Every effort has been made to establish copyright ownership of all images, but
if we have failed to acknowledge copyright, please contact the editor so that a
correction and apology can be made in any subsequent edition.

PREFACE

A SEMINAL FIGURE

An article in the New Zealand journal *Canzona* first sparked my interest in Warwick Braithwaite – a seminal, yet almost forgotten figure in British music.[1] Published in 1996, the article outlined the contents of a significant Braithwaite collection held in the Alexander Turnbull Library's Archive of New Zealand Music. The author was Jill Palmer, who held the post of Music Curator at that institution from 1974 until her retirement in 2012, providing more than a quarter of a century of outstanding service. It seemed that Jill was throwing down the gauntlet to researchers, but it was a challenge that was largely ignored. Braithwaite and his extraordinary contribution to the world of music looked set to be relegated to a footnote in music history.

When I succeeded Jill as Music Curator, it was a time of significant change for both the Alexander Turnbull Library and the National Library of New Zealand, within whose purview it lay.[2] One of those changes, newly reflected in revised position descriptions, was a requirement for curators to undertake research within their own collections. This was something that had always been desirable but which, for a variety of reasons, had always proved easier in theory than in practice. The Braithwaite archive, for which I was now responsible, struck me as a worthy area for research because it appealed on several levels. Here was a New Zealand-born musician who had worked very successfully overseas; a man who was passionately fond of opera, yet someone whose career and achievements – if not completely forgotten – were seriously under-valued.

---

1 Jill Palmer, 'Alexander Turnbull Library: Warwick Braithwaite Collection', *Canzona*, 17/38 (1996), 39–41. *Canzona* is the yearbook of the Composers Association of New Zealand.
2 A detailed description of the role of the Alexander Turnbull Library and its place within the National Library of New Zealand structure can be found at: https://natlib.govt.nz, accessed 20 January 2019.

The Warwick Braithwaite material had been placed with the Archive of New Zealand Music on long-term loan by the conductor's widow, Lorna,[3] but after her death in 1990, the status was changed by her sons Nicholas and Sir Rodric Braithwaite to an outright donation in February 1996. As a result of the research undertaken for this volume, the archive will be considerably expanded thanks to material donated by Braithwaite's sons and further resources acquired by the editor.

The current Braithwaite archive comprises music scores (1910–1967); libretti and short stories under the pseudonyms Atearoa [sic] and Henry Wharton, and articles on music (1932–1965); an unpublished autobiography (written between 1951 and 1956, but covering the period 1896–1956); correspondence (1953–1967); scrapbooks (1928–1953); ephemera (1925–1953); papers relating to opera companies (1937–1938); and some certificates and miscellaneous family papers (1912–1955).

Braithwaite's autobiographical manuscript forms the bulk of his writings and consists of 409 typed pages, recalling events mostly in chronological order. Only a handful of pages of autobiography are in Braithwaite's distinctive hand; the rest were presumably destroyed when the typed version was produced. The unenviable task of transcribing the manuscript was undertaken by Elizabeth Rixon who, with her husband David, ran the semi-professional Slough Opera. It is unlikely that Braithwaite proof-read the typed pages since they contain many errors that he would most certainly have corrected, but it does seem likely that Braithwaite intended his autobiography for publication. A letter of apology from writer and critic Rodney Blumer (later to become editor of *Opera* magazine) for holding onto the manuscript so long, suggests that Braithwaite was tentatively circulating it to colleagues in the music business for their comments.[4] Some of them would have been keen to see how they fared in the conductor's reminiscences, but I suspect that virtually everyone reading the complete manuscript would have concurred with my own assessment that it was unpublishable in its original format. Indeed, my first reaction on reading the manuscript was that some of it was libellous, and that other parts were either unwise or open to misinterpretation. I revisited the autobiography on several occasions, and each time I closed the folder with a mixture of fascination, disappointment and frustration.

The reminiscences of his childhood in Dunedin are charmingly written. His student years and training at the Royal Academy of Music reveal an independent streak and a determination to succeed. Discussion of the tenor and impresario Joseph O'Mara, who gave Braithwaite his first professional break, reveals a true

---

3 Lorna Constance Davies (b. Cardiff, 21 July 1904; d. London, 5 March 1990).
4 Letter from Rodney Milnes Blumer to Warwick Braithwaite, dated 22 August 1967, accompanying the return of Braithwaite's manuscript (private collection).

affection, and this generosity of spirit is found throughout the autobiography when discussing those in the music profession whom he genuinely admired, as well as those working in other fields whose intellect and accomplishments he respected. Above all, it is clear he relished friendship and loyalty.

A different Braithwaite emerges when he joins the BBC and discovers that his ideas do not always match those of his 'betters', and a pattern begins to emerge in each subsequent major position to which he is appointed. As a general rule, the 'honeymoon' period begins happily enough, but as Braithwaite strives to expand, improve or challenge the status quo, we find that communication breaks down, sides are taken and contracts are eventually not renewed. In fairness, it must be said that Braithwaite was usually in the right, but external influences beyond his control such as wars and economic depression, made it difficult for him to see his dreams fulfilled – or, if they *were* fulfilled, then sustained. Smaller and more annoyingly trivial problems seemed to follow him around. Professional jealousies and ignorant, uncooperative management boards surface with alarming regularity. Braithwaite, to his great credit, calls them out fearlessly, but this is not the way to make friends and influence people.

Despite having been resident in Britain since the age of 20, Braithwaite was probably regarded as an outsider in both the country of his birth and in his adopted homeland. He was happy enough to see his New Zealand origins used as a drawcard in Britain, and he was also keen to use his considerable British achievements and reputation to raise his profile on international tours. But he neither looked nor sounded exotic enough for the musical establishment in Britain who were always searching the far horizons for maestros but often failing to see the talent right in front of them. As his memoirs attest, Braithwaite could not contain his anger at such attitudes.

It would be unfair and simplistic to conclude that in Britain, Braithwaite was seen at best as a 'safe pair of hands' or at worst as a trouble-maker. Musicians admired him enormously, and in some cases even wrote to the newspapers to sing his praises. During his final illness, he received affectionate letters and telegrams from singers, répétiteurs, conductors, composers and administrators with whom he had worked over a long period of time.

His relationship with critics blew hot and cold. In Wales and Scotland, his achievements in establishing and developing orchestral professionalism were lauded in print, and his farewell appearances with the National Orchestra of Wales and the Scottish Orchestra exposed a warm generosity of spirit from audiences and critics who recognized what he had achieved against impossible odds. Only occasionally – and usually in London – did a critic take what can only be described as a vindictive dislike to his conducting, finding serious fault in a performance that other critics had simultaneously praised highly.

Braithwaite began his professional career as chorus master, répétiteur and conductor with the O'Mara Grand Opera Company, but established himself nationally as a symphonic conductor, working first in Cardiff and then in Glasgow, and eventually with every major orchestra in Britain. When opera at the highest level beckoned, he unexpectedly found himself conducting for the Sadler's Wells Ballet in London and on tour overseas as a last-minute replacement. The company's founder, Ninette de Valois, had insisted that Braithwaite was the right person for the job in a period of crisis. He, on the other hand, felt unqualified to conduct ballet and did not really enjoy the experience. But nevertheless, his concerns for professional standards and behaviour earned him respect from none other than the company's young prima ballerina, Margot Fonteyn. Her telegrams of gratitude and support can be found in the Archive, and whenever possible, she attended his operatic first nights.

Today, Braithwaite's reputation rests mainly on his work in ballet and opera. In that treacherous terrain he did battle with singers, dancers, managements and critics, yet still had enough energy to climb quite a few peaks in the process, including the British premiere of Prokofiev's *Cinderella* for Sadler's Wells Ballet, the debuts of Victoria de los Angeles and Boris Christoff at Covent Garden, the revivals of *Don Carlos, Falstaff, Die Meistersinger von Nürnberg, La fanciulla del West* for Sadler's Wells Opera, and *I Lombardi, May Night* and *Mefistofele* for Welsh National Opera. These were all works that were rarely, if ever, performed in Britain at that time.

There are some aspects of Braithwaite's career that are not fully revealed in his autobiography, mostly through modesty. Whilst every battle is recounted and relished in detail (especially when hurt pride is involved), the sheer scope of his career, which is breathtaking in its range and depth, is only revealed by a study of his performing schedule. I thought it would be helpful to know exactly where he was for virtually every day of his professional life so that I could check factual information such as dates, places and repertoire, and also gain an understanding of the broader pattern of his life. The performance schedule that I assembled remains a work in progress, and will probably do so for some time. Its length (currently 613 pages) prohibits publishing as an appendix, but it may be possible to share it online in the future. It contains dates, venues, repertoire, performing artists and extracts from press reviews – brilliant, good, indifferent and occasionally bad.

From the schedule we can nevertheless extract some staggering statistics. Over a career lasting more than 50 years, Braithwaite conducted at least 4,000 orchestral concerts and opera performances, the majority of which were broadcast, but rarely preserved, by the BBC. His repertoire consisted of 4,206 works by 1,362 composers. Some of these were repeated many times, making a total of 14,153 items performed. A more detailed analysis shows that he conducted at least 541 performances of 30 operas for Vic-Wells and Sadler's

Wells Opera, 80 performances of 13 operas for Welsh National Opera, 108 performances of eight operas for Covent Garden Opera, and 196 performances of 23 works for Sadler's Wells (Royal) Ballet.

It is almost forgotten that Braithwaite was an early pioneer of the music of Sibelius in Britain. Between 1930 and 1931 he performed all seven symphonies with the National Orchestra of Wales, and during his career he performed 35 of the composer's compositions, from *Valse Triste* in 1924 with the BBC 5WA Station Orchestra in Cardiff, to Symphony no. 7 in 1957 on tour with the Bournemouth Symphony Orchestra in Gloucester's Regal Cinema.[5]

The Performance Schedule shows Braithwaite visiting recording studios frequently between 1931 and 1958. Collectors of vintage recordings will be familiar with his name as conductor for some distinguished singers, notably Isobel Baillie, Gwen Catley, Joan Cross, Kirsten Flagstad, Joan Hammond, Sena Jurinac, Patrice Munsel, Elisabeth Schwarzkopf, Blanche Thebom, Webster Booth, Eugene Conley, Tito Gobbi, Oscar Natzka, Dennis Noble, Nicola Rossi-Lemeni and Paolo Silveri. In addition, he recorded a considerable amount of ballet music, including one of the earliest recordings of excerpts from Prokofiev's *Cinderella* ballet. Between 1938 and 1951 he made 137 sides, mostly for HMV and Columbia. Between 1951 and 1958 Braithwaite recorded mostly ballet excerpts or suites on vinyl for Parlophone (issued in the USA by MGM). Sadly, very little of his major concert repertoire was recorded, the most substantial work being an electrifying 1945 performance of Saint-Saëns' Second Piano Concerto for Decca, with Moura Lympany and the National Symphony Orchestra.[6]

An unexpected, yet welcome, discovery from the schedule has been the occasional appearance of Braithwaite as composer. The Alexander Turnbull Library holds the manuscript scores of thirty compositions ranging from songs, piano sonatas and chamber music to overtures, tone poems, a symphony and a full-length opera. Details of this important collection, and a list of known performances and recordings of his compositions, can be found as an appendix.

Braithwaite was born towards the end of the nineteenth century, and New Zealand was at a considerable remove from Britain. Therefore, it is not surprising that his upbringing was more Victorian than Edwardian. However, despite the social restraints of the time, Braithwaite enjoyed a respectful and loving relationship with his parents. Perhaps the opposition encountered by Joseph and Mary Braithwaite in their desire to wed had led them to adopt a

---

5   A list of Braithwaite's Sibelius repertoire can be found in Appendix 3.
6   A discography of Braithwaite's recordings can be found in Appendix 4.

very slightly more relaxed approach to the upbringing of their own children.[7] Joseph was described in the *Otago Daily Times* obituary notice as displaying 'the finest traits of good citizenship, and, the possessor of a mind cultured and broadened by wide reading. He exerted a considerable amount of influence in the community. He took a great pride in his home life, and his familiar figure will be missed by the public at large.'[8]

He had indeed experienced hardships in his youth and forged his way through life as a businessman, entrepreneur and community leader. He became a city councillor of Dunedin in 1901 and served a one-year term as Mayor, stepping down in 1905. Most importantly, as proprietor of Braithwaite's Book Arcade, he developed a love of literature that was passed onto his son, Warwick.

Joseph and Mary had 16 children (10 boys and 6 girls), of which Henry Warwick Braithwaite was the fourteenth.[9] Three children, Lillian, Sarah and Noel, died before Warwick was born, and two more brothers, Horace and Jack, were victims of war. Joseph and Mary's other children included a successful soprano based in London (Mabel Manson), a footballer who played for New Zealand and won six international caps (John Rewi Fergusson Braithwaite), and a respected city councillor and Mayor of Hamilton (Roderick Alistair MacDonnell Braithwaite). Roderick Braithwaite's son, David Joseph, followed his father by becoming Mayor of Hamilton; and Mabel's son, Willie Braithwaite Manson, saw his promising career as a composer brought to a tragic end at the Battle of the Somme.

Warwick Braithwaite's daughter, Barbara, became a nurse; his eldest son, Rodric, became a distinguished diplomat and author; and his younger son, Nicholas, followed in his father's footsteps to become a distinguished conductor.

Warwick Braithwaite's letters from his mother, Mary, reveal a particularly tender relationship when they were on opposite sides of the world, and it adds an extra poignancy when Braithwaite finds himself orphaned at the outset of his professional career.

---

7   Mary was raised a Catholic; Joseph a member of the Church of England. In a letter to her son Warwick, Mary Braithwaite describes how, as a sixteen-year-old girl she 'gave up my religion and never questioned anything; put all my faith in my husband that he would bring up my children in his faith, which I had embraced. And then straightway to find that my faith had been thrown on stoney ground, [and] for this act I lost father, mother, sisters and brothers and all old friends, and had to live weary, weary years with no faith, no hope.' Letter dated 31 July 1919 (private collection).

8   *Otago Daily Times* (28 March 1917), 7.

9   The Dictionary of New Zealand Biography estimates the number of children born to Joseph and Mary Braithwaite as 16. An article in the Australian newspaper, the *Northern Star* (2 April 1947), gives the total as 22. The largest number of children attributed to Joseph and Mary is 25 (16 boys and 9 girls) of which, we are informed by Dunedin's *The Evening Star* (16 June 1947), that Warwick was the 23rd child. To date, I have verified just 16 births, but it remains a possibility that some births and early deaths were not formally registered.

Braithwaite's writing is lucid, entertaining and fearless. When in battle mode, he writes with all the energy and command of an army general recalling the strategies and outcomes of a great struggle for victory. His wartime experiences as a musician in Britain are fascinating, and his descriptions of the devastating air raids can only have come from someone who struggled to survive them, whilst keeping his family safe and providing a roof over their heads. His memory is occasionally flawed, especially around specific dates or meetings. Where possible I have corrected obvious errors without comment, but occasionally a footnote is required for clarification.

The length of the autobiography has made some pruning necessary and I decided to focus on people and events that directly impacted Braithwaite's life and career. The earliest years are of particular interest because they recall an age long past and a world, which on the surface at least, seemed more innocent and attractive. Those pages, therefore, have survived intact, apart from the removal of some repetition, the logical rearrangement of events, and modest improvements to grammar and spelling.

Some lengthy descriptive passages, such as his excursions in New Zealand, Australia, South Africa and Great Britain, have been retained for their historical interest. The detailed diary of his flight to New Zealand in the early years of trans-world air travel is of more than passing interest to those of us who know only the miseries of long-haul flights in two gigantic hops via Los Angeles or Singapore.

Braithwaite's career ran against the backdrop of some of the twentieth century's most dramatic events including two world wars, the Irish War of Independence, and the Great Depression, all of which impacted his progress as a musician. Some of these are described in depth (e.g., the state of post-war Germany) and it would do a disservice to Braithwaite's descriptive skills to exclude them. Indeed, the cumulative effects of his wartime experiences, including a visit to Belsen and the devastated cities of Berlin and Hamburg, inspire him to write perhaps the single most revelatory sentence in the autobiography:

'I resolved that night, come what may, I would give my whole heart and soul to the better performance of music for the remaining years of my life.'[10]

The major casualties of editorial interference have been Braithwaite's European holiday excursions and his interactions with non-musicians. He was a sociable man, never more at ease than chatting, glass in hand, with friends in clubs or pubs, but most of the people who fascinated him (politicians, businessmen,

---

10 Quoted from Chapter 17.

painters and writers) and whose conversation and opinions he recorded in much detail, are only of passing interest to the core Braithwaite story.

Of more interest, yet sadly neglected by Braithwaite, is any substantial detail about his adult family life. Major events of personal significance, such as his engagement, first marriage, birth of a daughter, divorce, second marriage, and birth of two sons, are hardly touched upon, despite his obvious concern and love for his second wife and all three of his children. His peripatetic lifestyle meant that he travelled alone for long periods at a time, which must have placed a considerable strain on Lorna Braithwaite and the children. Yet he seems almost oblivious to this and describes only the joys of travel, the wonderful sights and, occasionally, the charming women he met along the way. As with many artists, the career came first; everything else came second.

Lorna Braithwaite's letters to her husband reveal a woman preoccupied with domestic issues in general, and financial worries in particular. Her devotion to Warwick shines through in her determination to help him sort out minor problems, and in her concern for his health and general welfare whilst away from home. As her son Nicholas points out, 'she was a woman of immense strength of character'.[11] Not only did she put all her energies into raising a family, she also (when financial worries dominated) began to contribute to *Good Housekeeping* magazine, eventually becoming the much-respected head of the Good Neighbour Service, Baby Expert and Travel Editor sections.

Another aspect of Braithwaite's autobiography that gives cause for regret is the lack of detail about his relationship with that *force majeure* of British musical life, Lilian Baylis. Perhaps the missing pages from the manuscript might have shed some light on this, since they presumably covered his early years with the Vic-Wells Company.[12] Given Braithwaite's colourful recollections of the managers and committees that blighted his professional life in Wales, Scotland, England and Australia, it is probably safe to assume that Baylis would not have been tarred with the same brush. She was respected, admired, and indeed, loved by those who understood her artistic and social mission, and it is not hard to imagine that Braithwaite would have been amongst their number. His anger and resentment were reserved for Tyrone Guthrie who was eventually to be appointed Director – a role that Braithwaite had refused to contemplate.

I mentioned earlier that I had made several attempts to evaluate the manuscript as a research project, but had given up in frustration. The main stumbling block had always been a section about homosexuality which I felt could not be ignored, but which was too offensive to include. On reflection, I came to realize that much of Braithwaite's diatribe on homosexuality was

---

11 Nicholas Braithwaite, *So What Does a Conductor Do?* (N.p.: Nicholas Braithwaite, 2017), 246.

12 Eleven pages are missing from the manuscript held in the Alexander Turnbull Library. See 'Bridge Passage', which attempts to sketch in events between 1931 and 1937.

triggered by his treatment at Covent Garden. Perhaps he felt that there was a 'gay mafia' at work, manipulating appointments by favouring homosexual colleagues over others. It is certainly possible that a staunchly heterosexual man such as Braithwaite would have felt that he was not welcome in that world.

There is no doubt that Braithwaite was very angry over his treatment. He even hinted that he was being blackmailed over a supposed relationship with a woman in the company in an effort to force him from his post. Whatever the truth of the matter, Braithwaite acknowledged that he worked with, and greatly admired, many colleagues whom he presumed, or knew, were homosexual. 'Many of the most truly sweet-natured men I have known are homosexuals,' he wrote.[13] That was not the issue. Unwisely, I think, he went on to write that the apparent surge in homosexuality since WWII was a threat to the survival of humanity. His explanations of the causes of homosexuality, and his suggestions for its treatment and, if possible, eradication, make for uncomfortable reading today. But Braithwaite was only repeating a common opinion of his time that homosexuality was an evil threat to the continuance of the human race, and that it needed to be 'cured'. In fact, his views were very much in tune with others of his generation. According to Sir Thomas Beecham's biographer, Charles Reid, the maestro defined England's two great failings as snobbery and homosexuality. The latter, he held, went on everywhere. 'Everything is controlled by the sods. The country is riddled with homosexuals who are teaching the world how to behave – a spectacle of revolting hypocrisy.'[14] Braithwaite was in good, if misguided, company.[15]

Although I have, in effect, censored this section, I hope that by mentioning it here in some detail, I have thrown a small light on this rather unpleasant corner of the autobiography. For the curious reader, the full text can be consulted (with permission) at the Alexander Turnbull Library. In Braithwaite's defence, I must say that this section feels like an interpolation into the manuscript; possibly an angry self-pitying afterthought brought on by a late-night tipple. If Braithwaite had been afforded the opportunity to revise and proof his manuscript, I like to think that this section would have disappeared. By the time of his death in 1971, public and private attitudes to homosexuality had changed considerably.

As editor of this volume, it has been a priority to retain the authentic 'voice' of the narrator. Braithwaite was not a professional writer, but his text has a natural, attractive and casual tone. Sometimes his use of words seems a

---

13 Henry Warwick Braithwaite, *The Golden Shore* (unpublished manuscript, Wellington, NZ, Alexander Turnbull Library (ATL), MS-Papers-5473), 372.

14 Quoted in Charles Reid, *Thomas Beecham: An Independent Biography* (London: Gollancz, 1962), 239.

15 For a more detailed discussion of homosexuality at Covent Garden during this period see Norman Lebrecht, *Covent Garden; The Untold Story* (London: Simon & Schuster, 2000).

little archaic to the modern reader, but that is all part and parcel of a musician who was raised by a Dunedin bookshop owner within a large and loving late nineteenth– century New Zealand household. Although I was not always able to resist the occasional tweaking of a convoluted sentence or the reordering of the text, I hope that my tampering has not noticeably diminished the presence of the author.

For the sake of conformity, French, German and Italian opera titles are given in the original languages, even though they were performed, for the most part, in English translations. All other titles are given in the standard English form. The use of macrons for words in Māori is now common practice, and for consistency I have applied them to both my own and Braithwaite's texts.

Warwick Braithwaite's story and his magnificent achievements in the world of music deserve to be more widely known, acknowledged and admired. If the publication of this first edition of his autobiography ushers him into the spotlight, my time and effort will have been well spent and fully rewarded.

ACKNOWLEDGEMENTS

My sincere thanks are due, first and foremost, to Sir Rodric and Nicholas Braithwaite. It is they who have the ultimate authority to approve access to the rich material in their father's archive at the Alexander Turnbull Library. They have been extremely generous and helpful at all times, and this volume would simply not exist without their support and encouragement.

My great friend and mentor, Peter Downes, has guided me through my previous books on Mascagni and Puccini, patiently correcting stylistic and factual errors, some of which were so embarrassingly obvious that I shudder to think of them now. Peter has again shared his years of accumulated expertise, and has the added advantage of having met Warwick Braithwaite, whereas I had only seen the maestro in action for a performance of *Faust* at Sadler's Wells in the 1960s. Peter was an 18-year-old office assistant in the Concert Section of the New Zealand Broadcasting Service (NZBS) when Braithwaite made his historic tour with the National Orchestra in 1947. 'He was charismatic and the first celebrity I had ever come across', Peter recalls. 'I was not over-awed by him, but I was thrilled to realize that I, a naïve kid from the country, was actually close to an eminent conductor and could talk to him and watch him rehearse an orchestra. I remember it being whispered that he was a much better conductor than Andersen Tyrer,[16] and the orchestra certainly responded well to him.'[17]

Of the libraries and archives that have played a major role in the creation of this book, I must first acknowledge the management and staff (past and present) of the magnificent Alexander Turnbull Library: Chris Szekely (Chief Librarian), Barbara Lyon (Curator, Ephemera), Marian Minson (Curator, Drawings and Prints), Dr Michael Brown (Curator, Music), Keith McEwing

---

16 The orchestra's first conductor.

17 Quoted from correspondence between Peter Downes and Roger Flury, 7 May 2016, (private collection). Sadly, Peter passed away before the publication of this volume, but he did read most of it. Typical of his modesty, he was embarrassed that the volume was to bear a dedication to him.

(Assistant Curator, Music) and Fiona Oliver (Curator, New Zealand and Pacific Published Collections). I also owe much to the staff of the National Library of New Zealand / Te Puna Mātauranga o Aotearoa: Bill Macnaught (National Librarian), and especially Chris Anderson (Research Services).

The staff at the BBC Cymru Wales Archives in Cardiff provided me with a free car park, a desk and, more importantly, endless coffee, tea and biscuits, as I waded through a complete run of *Radio Times*. My thanks are due to the following BBC Archives staff for their welcome and patience: Edith Hughes, Kevin John, Dr Emma Lile, Andrea Locke and Lona Wharton. The staff at the Local History Collection, Cardiff City Library, were helpful in providing access to newspapers covering Braithwaite's years in that city with the BBC and the National Orchestra of Wales. Working out of a temporary and very cold warehouse made for a trying experience for both staff and clients, and I hope that by now they have found the warm and well-appointed conditions they and their collections so richly deserve.

Others who have provided help and encouragement along the way are: Kathryn Adamson (Royal Academy of Music), Julia Aires (Glyndebourne Productions), Jóhann Heiðar Árnason (Iceland Symphony Orchestra), Jenny Burchell (City Choir, Dunedin), Kristbjörg Clausen (Iceland Symphony Orchestra), Pieter du Plessis (Dunedin Symphony Orchestra), Maggie Gething (Bay of Plenty Symphonia), Lynn Gifford (Canterbury Public Library, Christchurch), Simon Green (Hull Culture and Leisure, Central Reference Library), Christopher Grové (National Film Video and Sound Archives, Pretoria), Michael Hellyer (St Martin-in-the-Fields), Esme James (Bournemouth Symphony Orchestra), Jennifer Jeffrey (Hocken Library, Dunedin), Jo Johnson (London Symphony Orchestra), Sarah Johnston (Ngā Taonga Sound & Vision, Christchurch), Andrew Knowles (The William Alwyn Foundation), Julie Melrose (Islington Heritage Service, London), Amanda Mills (Hocken Library, Dunedin), Graham Muncy (Ralph Vaughan Williams Society), Adam Nagel (City of Birmingham Symphony Orchestra), Lorraine Neilson (Symphony International, Australia), Diarmuid O'Callaghan (Special Collections and Archives, Glucksman Library, University of Limerick), Marilyn Portman (Central City Library, Auckland), Libby Rice (London Symphony Orchestra), Tony Sharkey (Blackpool Central Library), and Adam Wassermann (Opera News, New York).

Individuals who have generously supplied information and encouragement include Rob Barnett, Margaret Batten, Paddy Brennan, Roz Fraser, Ruth and Bob Hellen, Konrad Dryden, Michael Vinten, and my long-time friend and opera expert Roger Beaumont.

Illustrations are acknowledged in the text, but I wish to mention here the excellent help given by Ian Brearey, Digitisation Officer, Royal Academy of Music (London); Dr Oliver Stead, Curator, Drawings, Paintings and Prints, Alexander Turnbull Library (Wellington); Dr Anna Peterson, Curator, Photographs, Hocken Library (Dunedin); Richard Munro, Reprographics, Hocken Collections (Dunedin); Diarmuid O'Callaghan (Special Collections and Archives, Glucksman Library, University of Limerick); and the family of Fergus Fraser, whose autobiography, *My Journey*, was a happy source of some family photographs.

Opportunities to publicly present my research on Warwick Braithwaite have proved extremely helpful in bringing the man and his career into sharp focus. I must thank my friends and colleagues at the International Association of Music Libraries, Archives and Documentation Centres (IAML) for programming a presentation on Warwick Braithwaite during their congress at the National Library of Latvia in Riga on 20 June 2017. Later in the same year, Lana Doyle and Jo Walsh (New Zealand Studies Network) allowed me to speak at greater length in the splendid surroundings of the Piano Gallery of the Royal Academy of Music's Instrument Museum on 24 September. The fact that Braithwaite's sons, Sir Rodric and Nicholas, were in the front row was daunting but immensely gratifying. Most recently, my essay on Warwick Braithwaite was accepted for publication in *The Turnbull Library Record* (2021) to coincide with the fiftieth anniversary of his death.

To the Lilburn Trust, I extend my heartfelt thanks. Without their vision, patience, financial support and encouragement, this volume would certainly have remained unpublished. Hannah Dakin, Beth Archer and the staff at Matador have been generous with advice and practical assistance to make *The Golden Shore* a reality in printed and digital formats. Last, but by no means least, I thank my partner, David Vine, who has shared in this journey every step of the way, offering advice, support, reassurance and copious amounts of musical wisdom.

Roger Flury
Cruckton
Shrewsbury
Shropshire
England

PART I
(1896–1916)

ONE

I REMEMBER,
I REMEMBER

Memory has infinite variations. Why is it that the same brain, poor as it might be in mathematical qualities, can remember happenings quite clearly – the time of day, the perfume of flowers in bloom, the warmth of a hot sun and the happenings of childhood days – yet the same brain often cannot recollect a phone number used only half an hour ago? The answer is a simple one. A child's memories are always major events; a casual phone number is, well, not so important.

To be casual is a sin against humanity. Reflect on that sentence and the reason for many of the world's troubles will become apparent. To live to the full with one's whole mind and body every moment of one's life is the only way to live. When you have nothing to do, better go to sleep and build up your energy for the next full-blooded event!

These remarks are set down as a personal matter in an endeavour to explain the reason for the vividness of certain events in my earliest days.[1]

The words at the beginning of this book, 'I remember, I remember', are the opening lyrics of a song my mother always sang to me, either when I couldn't sleep (the result of too vivid an imagination), or when I was ill. I knew every note and word of that song and was able to write it down from memory long before I ever saw a copy. In fact, I was about fifteen before I set eyes on 'The Golden Shore' by Scott-Gatty.[2] I saw it only once and have never seen it since.

---

1 (Henry) Warwick Braithwaite was born on 9 January 1896 at Dallon Bank, Upper York Place, Dunedin, New Zealand.

2 Sir Alfred Scott-Gatty (1847-1918) held several heraldic offices including Garter at Arms (1904-1918). He was also a popular and prolific composer of songs. *The Golden Shore* was published in London by Boosey & Co., *c.*1880. The text is by 'L.L.B.'

My earliest memories are always connected with music. I was just four when my father, who invariably bought a whole row of seats for every visiting opera company touring New Zealand, bought seats for a performance of *Lohengrin*, and I, at that very young age, was allowed the great privilege of accompanying my elder brother and sister. I can see it all now, even fifty years later – the scenery, the swan getting nearer and nearer, Lohengrin in shining silver armour, the King and the knight on the banks of the Scheldt, and Elsa in a white dress moving from sadness to elation at Lohengrin's advent as her saviour. [3]

I remember that I asked the silly, but quite understandable, question about why the first scene was brought back at the end of the opera. Was it because the audience was so enthusiastic? When I returned home in a complete and stubbornly silent daze, my father, in a perplexed tone of voice, asked me what I wanted to do when I grew up. I replied unhesitatingly, 'I want to be like the man who waved the stick.' Brave little boy – if he only had known!

My father was a stern, but just, man, always in the background and rather remote. Yet his presence was strongly felt by every member of his family. He was never a man to rush his decisions. I was four when he asked me what I wanted to do when I grew up. Perhaps he was startled by the quick and unhesitating answer. Perhaps he expected the usual childlike simpering and shuffling from one foot to another. Whatever it was he expected, the answer was certainly unexpected. I can see his half-amused and doubtful expression to this day. Nothing more was said by him, but my desire became increasingly stronger as similar experiences were added.

There was always music of some kind being performed in our house. All the family used to collect together of an evening and a sing-song was generally started off by my father performing 'O Memory,'[4] followed by my mother (although Irish) singing several Scottish airs. Then duets, trios and finally rounds ended most evenings. Occasionally there were more ambitious musical soirées, aided by friends. Complete operettas such as *The Geisha* and *Dorothy*[5] were given, at least until we grew up. Then the simple nature of that music was substituted for lieder and performances of excerpts from well-known operas.

My first glimpse of Wagner's *Der Ring des Nibelungen* occurred when I was ten years of age. My eldest brother, Percy, presented me with a set of the four vocal scores, and six or seven years later that same brother also gave me the

---

3 Wagner's opera *Lohengrin* was performed in Dunedin by Musgrove's Grand Opera Company on 19 and 23 September 1901. By popular demand, an extra performance was scheduled for 2 October, and special trains were laid on to ensure patrons from further afield could get home after the performance. *Evening Star* (1 Oct. 1901), 5.

4 Most likely the popular vocal trio composed by Henry David Leslie (1822–1896), with words by Lydia Smith which was also published in a version for solo voice and piano.

5 Composed by Sidney Jones (1861–1946) and Alfred Cellier (1844–1891) respectively.

orchestral miniature scores. I imagine I was one of the very few to possess such a treasure in the whole of New Zealand at the time.

But I'm getting ahead of myself. After the *Lohengrin* performance mentioned earlier, my father, having whetted my appetite, retired into his usual cautious huddle. This was a condition that preceded all his decisions, big or small, and I was left to fend musically for myself. Twice in my early life my father delayed his decision as to whether to further my musical education. The second occasion was when, at the age of fifteen, I wanted to study music in London. He thought I was too young to venture out into the cold hard world, and it was not until four years later that I finally made the journey. The visiting examiner of the Royal College of Music and the Royal Academy of Music Associate Board, Dr Shinn (who became a dear friend later on), tried his level best to persuade my father to let me go, but my father was adamant.

Henry Warwick Braithwaite with his nephew, William Braithwaite Manson (r). Dunedin, 1900.

This was not the case of a hard father standing in the way of his 'genius' of a son. My father had many family responsibilities. I was the twentieth of twenty-two children, and my father had been disappointed in some of them.[6] His one desire was that one of his sons should take up music, just as my eldest sister, soprano Mabel Manson, had done. Having eventually made that decision, he saw to it that there was no going back.

How right he was. As a child, I could play the piano before I had a lesson. I played everything in the right keys and with the right harmonies. It is true the tunes and harmonies were simple ones and I had to ferret out, sometimes for hours at a time, the correct harmonies, yet I had what is considered one of the main essentials of a musician, a quick musical ear.

One of my earliest recollections was the rush I used to make, once I was inside St Paul's Church, to get the end seat of the family pew in order to be as near to the organist as possible. Every Sunday was a delight to me because all the time I was learning new tunes. I would hurry home after the service to repeat the tunes on the organ in our big dining room before the rest of my rowdy brothers could disturb me.

---

6 See Appendix 1 for more information on the Braithwaite family.

It was during this time when, as I thought, the hard heart of my father showed no signs of softening, that another sister, Kathleen, who saw my struggles and who was herself learning the piano, started to pass on her musical knowledge to me in the form of short lessons. Perhaps out of sympathy, or the feeling that I picked up everything too quickly for her to cope, both she and my brother Percy espoused my cause with my father. Unfortunately, at about this time, another brother, Cecil (called Jack), a poet of no mean talents, had grievously disappointed my father (but more of this later) and my father, wounded beyond measure in his pride and self-esteem as a good citizen, for the time being washed his hands of the lot of us.

It seemed that I was out of luck, but the family tie (always strong) suddenly became masterful. Kathleen and Percy between them determined I should have lessons and paid for them out of their meagre pocket money. The fat was in the fire, and such a secret could not be kept for very long. I had clandestine lessons once a week for the best part of a term, and one evening the family, all seated at the large table in the dining room, sensed that something unusual was happening.

As a rule, our meals were conducted with a simple ritual. First of all, the children had to be seated, after which father and mother entered, the children standing up as they came in. Grace was then said by my father before we all sat down. But on this day, although we knew our father was home, he had not made the usual joint entrance with our mother. She took her place at one end of the table. We waited, all standing, whispered questionings, Mother flushed and annoyed. Kathleen looked at Percy and I was almost terror struck. Would this mean I was never to have another lesson? Then our father came in.

Although of average height (about 5ft 7in), to my fevered imagination he looked like a giant with his bald head and long white beard. His eyes were very dark brown of a piercing quality and intensity, much like Beecham's.[7] His voice was of a soft quality but on occasion could be hardened. He could mete out punishment and lecture you for your sins in a cold, detached voice, and at those times we all respected and feared him. He was never cruel, but only cruelly just. On this evening we waited for the blow to fall. My father said grace and we sat down. The meal commenced quietly at first, but later the atmosphere thawed. Once again, my father spoke, and in a quiet voice demanded that Percy and Kathleen come to his study in ten minutes' time.

I fled outside and ran to my favourite tree, at the top of which was a little hut built around the big branches. I stayed there until one of my brothers, Neville, told me that my father wanted to speak with me. I had been crying and this

---

7 Sir Thomas Beecham (1879–1961), English impresario, conductor, and a major force in British musical life.

brother (who was, and always has been, the most sympathetic of human beings) cried with me. After this mutual shedding of tears, he suddenly remembered to tell me that I had nothing to worry about as he thought that by the look on the faces of Kathleen and Percy when they came out of our father's study, the decision had gone my way. The sun had come out, the Heavens opened, and I heard the voice of God, unmistakable and kind.

I nearly broke every bone in my body climbing down that tree and rushed to my father's study, but I was waylaid by Kathleen, who whisked me away to the Hall and brushed my clothes and washed my face. Then I knocked timidly at my father's door. I can hear his kindly voice say 'Who is there?' followed by 'Come in.' I burst into tears before him, but I can't remember a word of our interview. I only know that I rushed out, bumping into Kathleen and Percy who carried me to the piano and sat me on the stool and I played every piece of music I knew. Suddenly by my side, with his hand on my shoulder, was my father. There were tears in his eyes too. But all the family was overjoyed. I remember my father afterwards took me for a walk through the spacious Lovers' Walks edging our grounds and talked to me of music and the 'call' to it, the seriousness of music as an art, and the meaning of music to human beings. Many a time, years afterwards, when I was more able to understand, I remembered his words, but I was only seven or eight on this occasion and all I could do was simply drink in the seriousness of them. It was all about music, and that was the only thing I understood much of. Such words as 'calling' to my childlike mind meant God, church, mother, and all the things I really believed in with the fullest strength of my ardent young spirit.

Years before I had been surprised by my mother finding me leaning out of an upstairs window with the big family bible, looking up at the sky, and holding an ardent conversation with God in Heaven. The answer to her question was always the same, 'I am talking to God.' She, sweet soul, used to retire gently and leave me alone. I am wondering what she said to my father though; something about that 'peculiar boy', I imagine. As a result of these things, I confess that I became the favourite child, held in gentle awe by both my father and mother. There was a bond between us that was exceptionally strong, and when my mother died many years afterwards, when I had come to England, I used to dream about her every night and wake up with tears streaming down my face. My father I always thought of with respect, but I loved my mother and every memory I have of her is of some loving and kind action done to me and to others.

I was teased in those days by my brothers, who used to say, 'There's Joseph and Mary (my parents' Christian names), but where is Jesus?', looking at me with half amusement and half something else, which I could not fathom. A bemused jealousy perhaps? Who can say?

*

My first lessons were with the daughter of the language master at Selwyn College, where I was to go eventually some years afterwards.[8] Miss Heinemann was in those days a young woman, handsome and dark in the Jewish style, who, try as she might, could not cure me of an easy-minded laziness. The trouble was, of course, that everything was too easy. Until now I had learnt all my music by ear, but now poor Miss Heinemann had to start right at the beginning, teaching at the other end of the telescope as it were. I had the *vision* of performance through the ear; now I had to learn music through the brain. What a struggle she had! Every now and then she would, through mental exhaustion, sweep me off the piano stool and in desperation play me the piece of music I was learning. Miraculously, and to my cost, I then played it *immediately*. Miss Heinemann would wring her hands in despair. As a punishment, and indeed as it turned out, a solution, she insisted that I write out all my pieces on manuscript. It certainly solved the situation and her idea was a brilliant piece of intuitive reasoning. But such is the resilience of the human mind that this method started me off writing pieces of my own. I can see, after all these years, that although I became at one period a successful concert pianist, this *writing* of music sealed the doom of any eventual success as a soloist. Once interested in music, to strive to be a pianist only seemed to me, despite many years of practising yet to come, to lead to a dead end.

From Miss Heinemann, of blessed memory, I went to a quite remarkable teacher and pianist called Mrs Blanche Levi, who taught me how Chopin should be played. Then, because a sweetheart of mine learnt piano from a rival teacher, Miss Yorston, I persuaded my father to let me go to *her*. This did not last long and neither did the sweetheart.

Next, I was to go to another remarkable musician who summed me up in a minute's interview and who saw I wanted more from music than piano playing. This was Max Scherek,[9] a son of Benno Scherek, the fine concert pianist and, in his later days, manager of the great Teresa Carreño who had been touring Australia and New Zealand about this time.[10] Max didn't bother teaching me piano pieces but asked me to bring my beloved scores of Wagner's *Der Ring des Nibelungen*, and while he sat at one piano and I sat at the other, we went through the four music dramas several times in the course of a few 'lessons'. After the

---

8 Named after George Augustus Selwyn (1809–1878), first Bishop of New Zealand. The school was opened on 15 January 1893.

9 Max Scherek (1884–1949), pianist and teacher who studied in Leipzig. He was a President of the Society of Musicians on several occasions.

10 María Teresa Carreño García de Sena (1853–1917), Venezuelan pianist, singer, composer, and conductor.

Ring we explored the symphonies of Beethoven, Mozart and Haydn, and one day I broached the subject dear to my heart – I wanted to be a conductor. He did not answer for a while, but then said that he could not teach me that. However, if I was serious, he would send me to Sidney Wolf, conductor of the local operatic society and the Dunedin Choral Society.[11] Max was completely selfless, and far from dissuading me, he encouraged me to go to Wolf. Both these men are now dead, and I cannot under-estimate the good they did for me.

Sidney Wolf, in his characteristic way, started me off writing out band parts and playing percussion in the local orchestra. I remember in one operetta I had to play the midnight chimes. I always forgot to count when I got to ten and, more often through desperate nervousness, sounded thirteen or even fourteen, until Wolf transfixed me with a furious glare from his one eye.[12] My father, who always watched every performance I did, would take me to task next morning. I was always nervous of playing before people until cured by my sister Kathleen, who dragged me everywhere and made me play.

It was about this time (aged 15 or 16), when I, who had never been robust, had a serious illness. I caught pneumonia through the silly nonsense of getting terribly hot standing in the orchestra pit of the theatre listening to Puccini's *Madama Butterfly* and, during the interval, taking off a heavy jersey to walk outside in the icy night air and cool down.[13] While convalescing, I can remember Percy looking at me and observing my thin, emaciated body and saying in a languid voice, 'Yes, of course, all musicians are delicate; they've all got to die young.' I was indignant, but secretly scared at the same time because Percy knew a lot, and he was my good big brother.

I did get well and made up my mind to get strong also. I began to go in for every sport. I swam, I played tennis, football, cricket, harriers, rowed, swam rivers and nearly got carried away several times in the fast current. I walked twenty miles a day at weekends. Gradually I made myself tough and have remained so. By the time I left New Zealand to come to London, I was no longer the delicate young boy of my early days.

There are many things I had almost forgotten to tell of my early musical life in far-off Dunedin. During those years of learning the piano I had, like most

---

11 Sidney Ignatius Joseph Wolf (1859-1922), London-born musician who arrived in New Zealand in 1880. He conducted the Dunedin Choral Society from 1914 until his death.

12 Wolf lost an eye in a shooting accident on an ostrich farm in South Africa, c.1878. Historic Cemeteries Conservation Trust of New Zealand, http://www.cemeteries.org.nz/stories/wolfsidney240508.pdf, accessed 7 November 2018.

13 Probably in the winter of 1910, when J.C. Williamson's Grand Opera Company gave performances of *Madama Butterfly* at His Majesty's Theatre, with Bel Sorrel (6 July) and Amy Castles (7 July) in the title role.

other pianists in my hometown, gone in for the Competitions Society prizes.[14] I often scooped the board, no mean task as the standard of playing was very high indeed in those days, but there were two pianists, Kathleen Levi and Vera Moore, who used to run me close and sometimes relegated me to second place. Both of these friends of mine eventually came to London permanently and we have met and talked with much relish about our early days.

I was ever seeking to know more about music. There were two orchestras, an operatic society, a choral society, a male voice choir (Liedertafel), a dramatic society, and about six brass bands, in a town with a population of 65,000 people. All the societies were deadly rivals; if you belonged to one orchestra, you could not, on pain of excommunication, play in the other. The amount of music-making in Dunedin, compared to the size of the town, was colossal. But those were the days when one very largely had to make one's own music. Nearly every household had their musical evenings, and our family competed with others in giving the best. There was no nonsense about such performances; if you did not achieve the required standard, you could not perform, and it was almost a disgrace to be left out.

My father had decreed, as the result of misdemeanours on the part of some of my elder brothers, that the younger members of the family, including myself, must be at home by 9 p.m. This was a blow, as I was beginning to become interested in theatre and musical performances. My poor harassed father! What else could he do? Here again my sympathetic sister Kathleen (ten years older), who was one of the Operatic Society's ballet girls, used to smuggle me in and out of the house via the back stairs. But it did not work for long. My father, ever vigilant, discovered this and for a time put a stop to it. Shortly afterwards, a round-table discussion headed by a deputation consisting of Percy and Kathleen, backed up by my mother, carried the day and I was allowed out for two nights a week which, when my father saw the good of it, was extended to *every* night.

I went to one of the conductors, James Coombs, and begged him to give me lessons.[15] He declined but allowed me to follow his rehearsals with a violin part. I couldn't stand this, so I tried to join a brass band and, for one night every week for two years, I attended rehearsals with an E flat cornet. I then gave this up, and sang in the Cathedral choir, but soon gave that up too.

I blush for shame to tell you that about this time, I seriously studied painting. I could always draw (it was one of my major achievements while at school), but here again, I got tired of drawing cubes and squares in order to learn the fundamentals

---

14 Competitions were, and still are, a major annual activity for young performers in New Zealand. For a talented few, they can provide an important stepping-stone towards a professional career.

15 James Coombs (1856–1940) was conductor of the Dunedin Orchestral Society.

of shading and shape. I packed my sheets of Michelet[16] paper together and one day walked out of Art School, never to return. I am quite sure the Art Master did not regret my loss for one moment, but I felt the disgrace of non-success very keenly. It was not what I wanted. I was seeking some form of creative expression that I had not yet discovered and, unluckily for me, I was beginning to grow up. Time was slipping by. What *did* I want? The answer was not to be found in my surroundings, and once again thoughts of my sister, Mabel Manson, and England, began to take firmer shape in my mind. I had never seen Mabel, who went to England to study singing after she married.[17] When I did meet her in 1916 and heard her sing, I was highly delighted and impressed by the beauty of her voice.

My fears that I would never get anywhere at all musically in New Zealand began to become an obsession with me. I went to my father (I was by this time 17 or 18) and pleaded to be sent to London. He vacillated for weeks and then came out with the most astonishing and crazy idea imaginable. He informed me that he had decided to send me to the Conservatoire at Odessa; in fact, he had already made arrangements for me to go there! I discovered afterwards that the reason was that Benno Scherek had persuaded him that Odessa was the pianists' Mecca, as indeed it might well have been at the time. I got to like the idea after a while then, crash! War between Russia and Austria, and later England, France and Germany, started the 1914–1918 holocaust. Gone were all my hopes in one fell swoop; gone were all my dreams of ever being anything worthwhile musically.

I struggled on for a while trying to hide my bitter disappointment and one day went to my father and told him I wanted to finish any idea of a musical career. I tried to persuade him (and myself) that his book business was the only thing I really wanted to take up. But he was a wise old bird; he acquiesced and I worked for six months unpaid until, one night, coming home late and finding the lights in the drawing room full-on and no one stirring, I went in. There, staring me in the face was a new grand piano with the lid up and with beautiful shining white and black keys gleaming in the glare of electric light. I sat down and played far into the early hours of the morning. All my father said the next day was, 'You look tired, my son; you need not go to work today.'

I never went to 'work' again. Instead, I began to practice with immense fervour and almost insane energy. Behind this terrible and almost frightening burst of crazy intensity was the ever-present notion of having lost much valuable time.

---

16 Michelet was a cheaper type of art paper manufactured in France and considered ideal for drawing with charcoal. Because of its strength, it was also used in book repair.

17 Mabel Braithwaite married local musician William Manson in 1895. She moved from Dunedin to London in 1899 to pursue her singing career, followed in 1900 by her husband and their son, Willie Braithwaite Manson. It is unlikely that Mabel and Warwick had not met in Dunedin, but his tender age at the time would explain his lack of recall later in life. For more information on the Braithwaite family, see Appendix 1.

*

I was blessed with loving, understanding parents and a wonderful home life in an enormous house with lots of brothers and sisters. There was always something happening, as you can well imagine with such a large family who brought all their friends to the house. I can remember at some of our big musical evenings when, for example, we would perform a Gilbert and Sullivan operetta, as many as thirty friends would stay the night, sleeping anywhere and everywhere. The younger members of the family, in those exciting days, were sent to bed comparatively early, but the festivities went on until the early hours of the morning, and I would often be caught half-asleep on the bottom step of the front stairs, straining my ears to hear as much of the performance as possible. I was not interested in the new-fangled experiments in electricity indulged in by my clever brother Neville, who eventually wired up several rooms and successfully lit them with electric light driven by a Pelton wheel, operated entirely by water from a nearby spring.[18] This would be about the year 1906.

My interest in music became a serious matter to my parents, as I never slept on these occasions and such late goings-on took their toll on my nervous system. Frequently I would wake up in the middle of the night, terrified by the shadows cast on my bedroom wall by the branches of the huge macrocarpa trees in the garden. I would shriek out in terror, and generally Percy or one of my older brothers would rush in to calm me down, taking me out on the upstairs veranda to show me the cause of my fright.

My father was an ardent believer in fresh air, cold water, and what he called 'the starvation cure'. All ills, according to him, could be cured by one or a combination of these. We all had to have our cold shower every morning, winter and summer, but an ordinary shower was not enough. My father had cut big holes in the jet and erected a huge tank above the shower. The result was like a waterfall crashing with enormous speed onto our tiny backs. This, not being sufficient at 6 a.m., was followed by races on the dew-covered lawn, stark naked. On the side veranda of our house, my father had installed an open-air gymnasium with handlebars, rings, a vaulting horse and other equipment. Beyond that was a full-sized tennis court surrounded by a high wire netting.

Percy and, I think, Mabel went out one day to collect a wild clematis that used to abound in the New Zealand bush, and planted it to celebrate the birthday of another sister, Lillian. This was a sister I never saw, as she died of

---

18 A late 1870s invention by the American, Lester Allan Pelton (1829–1908), in which water is forced into shaped buckets around the circumference of a wheel, extracting more energy than a traditional water wheel.

pneumonia when she was just 16 years of age.[19] The clematis grew, as it does in New Zealand, until it twined itself around two complete sides of the tennis court, and in spring, the blossom was the delight of the whole countryside. Alas, thirty-one years later, when I went back to New Zealand for the first time after leaving home, the new tenants of our home had cut down all the beautiful trees, and the tennis court with its clematis was gone forever. There were now two houses on our estate, where only one had stood before.

My father's interests were many. Our grounds were set out in as varied a style as possible and showed great originality in conception. How much the ideas could be attributed to my mother I cannot say. The house itself in the early days, when my

Mary and Joseph Braithwaite, 1901.

parents were first married, started by being quite small. Then, as the look in my mother's eye started to set my father afire, the house had of necessity to be enlarged until the front portion, added later, was continued into a higher second storey. There were, I think, twelve bedrooms upstairs with a large hall leading out to the upstairs balcony veranda. This hall was the site of our Christmas tree celebrations.

Every year my father, and later my elder brothers, used to dress up as Father Christmas and just before dawn could be seen by the excited younger members of the family distributing dozens of parcels around the tree. He would then reappear as himself, and a whoop of joy would start a wild scramble for presents. Down below were the huge dining room, drawing room and music room. These were the largest in the house, and behind them, to the rear, were the study, nursery, playroom, kitchen and scullery.

The grounds were a sheer delight. The upper part, closest to the house, contained a lawn with flowerbeds. Two grass terraces led to the lower part of the grounds that consisted of two huge lawns, surrounded by trees of every variety from England. On the extreme edges were the Lovers' Walks, through

---

19 Lillian's death was noted in the newspaper, although her first name was mis-spelled: 'Braithwaite – on the 3rd April, 1894, at her parents' residence, Dallon Bank, Upper York Place, Lilian, the dearly-beloved daughter of Joseph and Mary Braithwaite; in her sixteenth year.' *Otago Daily Times* (4 April 1894), 20. The funeral was announced for 6 April at St Paul's Pro-Cathedral, followed by burial at the Southern Cemetery.

an avenue of trees whose branches formed a canopy. On wedding nights, these avenues were lit by Chinese lanterns, and there was always a procession of guests through them, everyone singing either the wedding march from *Lohengrin* or some other appropriate music. I remember there were two long wooden seats in the Lovers' Walks and it was a tradition that the bridegroom had to carve his and his bride's initials into the wood. No one else was allowed to do this. I wonder where those garden seats are now?

Above and behind our grounds was an elevated portion of ground which belonged to the city, but on which the Corporation allowed my father to plant fruit trees. Beyond this again, and stretching for many miles, was the glorious native bush – a delight to youngsters. Fuchsia trees, which are shrubs in England, grow into big trees in New Zealand, and the yellow-pink thin bark served for many a clandestine 'smoke'. Cut right through this stretch of native bush was the carriageway named The Queen's Drive. The Town Belt, as the bush was called by local people, was situated on the crest of the low hills (probably 800 feet up) surrounding Dunedin, and from many points one could see the city, the harbour and, further beyond the isthmus, the Pacific Ocean with its swirling roar of surf.

Surf bathing in the summer holidays was one of the many delights of every young person in my hometown. Everybody celebrates their Christmas in the height of summer, but at the same time the tired businessman packs up and, with his car and family, goes camping by the big rivers inland or further down to Green Islands by the sea. Our holidays were never spent far from home, as within a few miles, there were many holiday resorts and many unexplored places. If one went on a walking tour inland one always had to carry one's own food and rely on shooting small game for the evening meal. As a boy of fourteen I was an expert in the use of a Winchester Repeater rifle and a small seven-chambered revolver used for shooting rabbits.

So, the halcyon days of youth passed away almost without knowing that there was so much to do.

TWO

THE BRAITHWAITES
OF DUNEDIN

My parents' families migrated to New Zealand in the 1850s. From the little that I was allowed to know about my paternal grandfather, things were not always so easy for my father. On the way out from England my grandmother died and my grandfather married again shortly afterwards. My father hardly knew his mother but appeared to transfer his affections to his stepmother. My grandfather was a 'fast liver'; he made money easily but gambled away several fortunes, and these *were* several as the gold mining craze was at its height about that time. Consequently, my father and his brother John, mere children, had to keep their stepmother in the necessities of life.

When both my uncle and grandfather died (the uncle tragically), my father, Joseph Braithwaite, bore the whole weight of responsibility. He sold newspapers and magazines in the old Arcade (a popular feature of New Zealand cities of that time), eventually establishing his business at the age of fourteen or so, in 1863.[1] From the Arcade he transferred his business to the main street, Princes Street, and until 1922, his book selling shop was a landmark for all to see, for at the entrance was a huge wooden horseshoe at least twenty feet high, on which was printed in huge letters:

BRAITHWAITE'S BOOK ARCADE:
NO-ONE ASKED TO BUY

---

1   Braithwaite's Circulating Library in Farley's Arcade at the corner of High Street and Fleet Street.

15

The entrance to Braithwaite's Book Arcade,
Princes Street, Dunedin, c.1906.

The business was extended and the Arcade became a reality as he bought all the property at the rear as well as several shop frontages. The Arcade went through the main entrance and turned at right angles making a second entrance onto Princes Street about 30 yards further along. Eventually all the other frontages were bought and the business became an emporium where one could buy everything except clothing and food. I think my father's proud boast was 'If we haven't got it in stock, we will get it for you'.

The book department was my father's first love and always remained so. He dabbled in publishing and many were the small books published by Joseph Braithwaite. I have a Braithwaite dictionary to this day. On one occasion, he foolishly turned down an author who later had an enormous sale in this country with the very book that my father had read in manuscript but had not liked. It was a horrifying story by, I think, Richard Marsh, called *The Beetle*.[2]

I used to look forward to the arrival of large white pine cases containing all the latest publications from England (hundreds of duplicate copies), and my delight was to handle these, count them and carry them upstairs to the Wholesale Department where new arrivals were checked and stored. Several

---

2 Richard Marsh (1857–1915) was the pseudonym of the English author born Richard Bernard Heldmann. He is best known for the supernatural thriller novel *The Beetle: A Mystery*, published first as a serial in 1897 and later the same year as a single volume novel.

The Braithwaite family home at Dallon Bank, Upper York Place, Dunedin, c.1900.

of my brothers (there were four of us with only eighteen months between one and the other) used to help on these occasions, but the curious thing about all this was that although many of the sons worked in our father's business, none of them identified sufficiently with it to save it from disaster.

My father began to neglect his commercial business for public life and was an honoured Mayor of Dunedin from 1905 to 1906. He was a member of St Paul's Cathedral Chapter during the period when funds were required for the beautiful new church that now stands on the same site. But the business did not go on by itself as expected, and gradually got into difficulties. In the early days, with no rivals, it was too easy and there was no technique acquired to save the crash when it came. My father, alarmed at the turn of events, saved what he could and turned the business into a limited liability company, but there were many rivals waiting, and destiny was stacked against him. In other words, we as a family were almost in straitened circumstances, and if my father had not sold some of his property at the rear of the business and floated a cinema, we would have been in the soup.[3]

Eventually this cinema became another goldmine, and thus for some

---

3 Presumably the Empire Theatre, whose entrance was in Princes Street, between the two shops occupied by Messrs. Braithwaite (Ltd.). Joseph Braithwaite's obituary states that he had been Chairman of Empire Pictures (Ltd). At the opening in March 1916, musical items were rendered by Messrs William Gemmell *(baritone)* and Warwick Braithwaite *(piano)*. *Otago Daily Times* (4 March 1916), 11.

years the situation was eased. But not for long, as after I had been three years in England, there was nothing beyond a few shares that kept my mother in comparative ease after my father's death. The family became scattered. The beautiful house named Dallon Bank (after my father's home in Cliburn, outside Penrith[4]), was no more, and the businesses were sold. What a tragedy to think that of such a lovely home, and a good and honest house of business, nothing remains but a memory that will soon also disappear. I have still a lingering regret that I might have thrown myself into my father's business and might have kept it alive.

Dallon Bank was never rebuilt, although my father considered several plans submitted by architects.[5] Financial difficulties had set in and the property was thrown into the melting pot in order to save us from bankruptcy. When this happened, not one of our family went near the house and beautiful grounds again. We were ashamed at the turn of events and could not bear to be reminded of it. My mother took it all philosophically; the house, in any case, had become too big to manage. Those were the days when servants began to disappear in New Zealand, never to return. It was easier when the daughters were unmarried and therefore available to help.

My father's decision not to rebuild was a blow felt keenly by the younger members of the family, but there were compensations when we eventually took a home overlooking St Clair beach, with its marvellously white sand and gorgeous surf. Here we revelled in surfboard antics and rivalled one another in swimming out to where the current would take us well away from St Clair and, after a struggle, land us either on what was known as Tomahawk Beach a few miles away, or St Kilda, further along from St Clair. Everything around us became a boy's paradise. In the summer holidays we would arise at 6 a.m. and play tennis before breakfast, swim in the surf and rush back to the house for cream in our porridge and bacon and eggs. Then we were ready to start the day.

*

From the moment my father purchased a Brinsmead grand piano, my days (for several years) were occupied by a most strenuous system of practising. I would rise early in the morning and, on the stroke of nine, go into the Music Room and settle down to a rigorous schedule which nothing could alter:

---

4   Cliburn is a small village situated in the Eden Valley of the county of Westmorland (now Cumbria), halfway between Penrith and Appleby.

5   Dallon Bank and much of its contents had been largely destroyed by fire on the evening of Saturday, 14 April 1911, and the cost of rebuilding the 16-room house was beyond the family resources at this time. *Otago Daily Times* (17 April 1911), 3.

9.00 – 11.00	Left-hand and right-hand finger technique (mostly Czerny and Clementi).
11.00 – 11.15	15-minute break and a walk on the sands.
11.15 – 12.00	Wrist technique, including octave work.
12.00 – 1.00	Passage work from pieces I was working at.
1.00 – 2.00	Lunch.
2.00 – 4.00	Chopin *Études* and Liszt *Transcendental Studies*.
4.00 – 5.00	Repertoire.
5.00 – 9.00	Break.
9.00 – 10.00	Recital to members of family or, on most occasions, to my father.

He would give me a lecture on the meaning of the pieces, and he always believed that every piece of music had an emotional or descriptive basis. His romantic imagination used to run riot, and he certainly gave me the antidote to my preoccupation with technique. My mother didn't want a distraught and overworked son on her hands, so she fed me like a fighting cock. My meals were always ready at the same time, and tasty in the extreme.

Sport was not neglected. I turned out every Saturday as right wing with the Mornington Football Club, and was considered a whirlwind who took risks but pulled off some brilliant shots at goal.[6] On one of these occasions, when up until shortly after half-time neither side had scored and our reputation as champion team was at stake, I could be seen haring down the right wing, heading in the direction of the goal where the ball was loose after a short pass from one of my brothers. With all the determination and speed of a devil-may-care lunatic, I made for that loose ball, kicked at it, and scored a goal. Unfortunately, the opposing fullback also attempted to kick the ball but missed, and with the full force of his boot, broke my shinbone. The crack could be heard all over the field, and the game continued without me. But my goal was the deciding factor and while awaiting an ambulance I felt like Nelson at Trafalgar; victory was ours and from my improvised stretcher news was brought to me of the state of the game. I will never forget my mother's face when the ambulance arrived at our home. I was carried in, and because the journey had been made over rough roads, the two points of the broken bone had jostled one another and given me excruciating pain. I must have looked like Death; indeed, she thought I *was* dead, and took to weeping like any Irish mother would.[7]

My convalescence was fairly rapid, but the Competitions season was near.

---

6 The Mornington Football Club traces its history back to 1894 and is one of the oldest clubs in the region. In the 1960s Mornington merged with Continental (formed in 1957) to become St Kilda–Mornington, but reverted to Mornington in 1985.

7 The injury occurred on 24 May 1913, and was significant enough to make that evening's newspaper. 'A Boy Injured', *Evening Star* (24 May 1913), 6.

In three months, I had to play in the 'Open' pianoforte solo. Broken leg or not, the honour of the Braithwaite family was in jeopardy, so as soon as I could get out of bed I was carried to the piano and did my practice. My brother Neville held my broken leg off the floor for thirty minutes while I practised the competition piece. As time went on, I could get to the piano myself with the aid of crutches and managed to dispense with the selfless service of my brother. I won the competition and was acclaimed a persistent hero, and family honour was gloriously vindicated.

*

Life went on much as usual, but deep down I was becoming dissatisfied. Something inside me (and something I have blessed many times since, when I was apt to become too satisfied with my achievements) told me that all was not as it should be. I still hankered after England; 'home' as we all called it. I knew that what I had achieved in New Zealand could only be a beginning and that I *must*, if I was to be anything at all, come up against the hard life and inevitable struggles in the hub of things – London. Other thoughts and activities also began to force their way into my conscience. Music was not enough. I had grown up absorbed by music, but Life was beginning to knock at the door of my sensibilities.

As one had to make one's own music in such a life of professional backwardness, so one also had to make one's fun and amusements. I was in much demand at the popular 'surprise' parties then in vogue in New Zealand. These parties were primarily friendly, generous and often hilarious. The idea was that one morning you were phoned up by a friend who asked if he or she could come around in the evening with a couple of pals. If the answer was in the affirmative, arrangements were made in which about twenty or so boys and girls and older people (all friends) arrived at your home, complete with food and drink for a celebration. Furniture was cleared away and your house was taken possession of by your friends. Young and middle-aged were all in it and parents relaxed their surveillance.

The first thing that always occurred was to toast the fathers and mothers and the owners of the household, after which, barriers being 'broken' down, fun took on its normal form. Singing, dancing and short recitals, followed in rapid succession. I used to play all the accompaniments and a few piano pieces; silence always being observed during these performances. Someone would give a recitation, or having worked up a little playlet on a scene from Shakespeare, would perform it. Often readings from a new book of poems would be given. One book which tickled me enormously and which some of the details I've remembered to this day. 'Her name was Doreen' is the one line that comes to my mind immediately from *The Sentimental Bloke* by C. J. Dennis, a Melbourne journalist.[8] This book of doggerel poems has been reprinted time and time again. It came out about the year 1916 and I was given a second copy in Sydney during my Tour in 1947. This was a new edition with the original illustrations, all in light pencil; Doreen and Ginger Mick being depicted as lovely little cherubs, and Doreen having delightful feathery wings. The other Australian books I read at this time were *Robbery Under Arms* by Rolf Bolderwood,[9] and *For the Term of his Natural Life*, a story of early convict life in Australia.[10] These books, together with *The Sentimental Bloke*, have become three of Australia's 'classics' and still have an enormous sale.

But to go back to the 'surprise' parties. A nightly round of such parties became the despair of my parents who, although they liked fun themselves, began to see their hopes in their favourite son fading nightly. The deep discontent which I was experiencing at the time led me into all sorts of escapades. I always had a righteous or even a human excuse for such deviations from the path of duty. I remember my first strange feeling of wonder and amazement when I put my arm around a particularly beautiful girl friend. She ran away into the garden, but was eventually cornered by me against a wall. Her eyes were blazing from outraged lack of knowledge, and her bosom was heaving from sharp intakes of breath, but my gaze was suddenly attracted by the shape of her neck and shoulders (a white, almost alabaster-like neck), and well-formed breasts hidden by the flimsy material of her blouse. My stupid wonder increased, and what struck me most was that this was the first time I had ever seen, with my whole being, a vibrant and alive woman. The moment seemed like a year and I kissed her and walked away. I never understood until years afterwards why this pretty girl looked at me with a haughty disdain that was meant to crush me to pieces whenever we met.

Then there was the craze for dancing. We would go anywhere, usually with the same crowd of evenly matched girls and boys. Music certainly began to fade away. Yet not quite, for I met about this time a girl about my own age who, although she also liked fun and games (innocent enough), she liked music better. This girl, tall, fair and beautiful with glorious big blue eyes became my one friend. She and I swore an eternal platonic friendship. We went everywhere together. We did everything together – played tennis, swam, danced – but after all these things were partaken of, there was always a period of critical music making. And when I was inclined to slip from our platonic relationship, she, being wiser than I, gently brought me back to realities. She was a great reader and together we read all the classics: Greek Drama, Shakespeare, Dickens,

8   More accurately *The Songs of a Sentimental Bloke* by Clarence James Dennis (1876–1938).
9   Pseudonym of London-born Australian author Thomas Alexander Browne (1826–1915).
10 Written by English-born Australian novelist and poet, Marcus Andrew Hislop Clarke (1846–1881).

Tennyson, Ibsen, etc. She it was who, at last, when I was about to make the journey to England, suddenly realized she was in love. I was too, but by then all the pent-up longing to continue my career had burst out in a new spurt of energy, and nothing could stand in the way.

Things came to a head between myself and my parents. I swore that unless I could go to England, I would give up music completely. My father now had a reasonable excuse to stop me leaving New Zealand; the war was on and there was danger of German submarines. Although I was under age, I threatened to enlist in the Army, especially as a violinist friend of mine, Leonard Swan, had done so. There were already five of my brothers in the New Zealand army, and three of them had made the landing at Gallipoli. Horace was shot through the head for his pains and died eleven months afterwards, almost completely paralysed. Eric had seen his elder brother struck down and was on the Peninsula for three months afterwards. He was buried alive in a dugout for several days, his hair turning completely white during his incarceration, but he was rescued and sent to England. Cecil, the poet (and incidentally also a tennis champion while Anthony Wilding, *the* New Zealand champion, was out of the country[11]), was killed in France under distressing circumstances too wretched to speak about.[12] Neville, my favourite brother, was transferred to the Royal Army Medical Corps and did valuable work between Gallipoli and Egypt. Percy was an officer training recruits in New Zealand; Rewi eventually came with a draft of New Zealand troops to England, but the very day he was to go to France, the Armistice allowed him a glorious trip around Britain.

I did enlist, but next morning my father phoned the recruiting officer giving my real age and that was that! But now came my chance. To my shame, I told my father that if he would not send me to England, I would go under my own steam. In this plan, my dear mother secretly sought out a concert agent, and it was arranged that I was to give two recitals. All Dunedin was in the know, but although my father pretended to be the one person who had no prior knowledge of it, he came to the recitals because he could not resist it. So, I had all the money I needed for my passage, with enough left over to keep me for a year. My father then 'came clean' and at last threw in his hand. He helped me in every way, and for the last few weeks before my journey, we were all reunited once again.

Of the parting from my home and people, it is too difficult to speak. I can see the ship; I can see my father and mother saying goodbye. As parting gifts, my father presented me with a beautiful fountain pen, and my mother gave me a Kodak folding camera. Holding the paper streamers in both hands as the ship

11 Anthony 'Tony' Frederick Wilding (1883–1915), a former world tennis champion, originally from Christchurch, who was killed in action during World War I.

12 See Appendix 1.

moved off, and the breaking of those streamers which were held at the other end by my father and mother, was a sad and significant event. I never saw my parents again. Now, when I think of the love, kindness, sympathy and help they gave me I still weep tears of sorrow. When I see my own children struggling with their childish problems, I often wonder if I could ever be as good and helpful to them as my own parents were to me. Things have changed. In my young days, family life was stronger. There was no cinema, no wireless, no television. Life was more human and the whole of one's life was bound up in people not things.

Farewell to Dallon Bank, to the Lover's Walks and their canopy of English trees and Chinese lanterns. Farewell to the blossoming red may-trees, to the clematis in bloom around the tennis court, to the profuse rhododendron flowers of all colours, and to the lovely green lawns and dewy morning grass. Farewell to the nooks and corners of a big roomy house, where even a large family could get away from one another if necessary. Farewell to the cable trams going up the hills of Dunedin, to the Town Belt, the Queen's Drive and the native bush. Farewell Pacific Ocean and the whitest of white sand.

PART II
(1916–1922)

THREE

ARRIVAL, TRAGEDY
AND ENLISTMENT

After leaving Dunedin in March 1916 by Inter-Island Steamer, we called in at the North Island port of Gisborne, en route to Auckland. Gisborne had not in those days a deep-water harbour, so a tender had come out to meet us and take off passengers. Who should be on the tender but my friend! She had come with her family to Gisborne, where the ship was now held up for about 24 hours, so I was persuaded to spend the time with her and her parents. The leave-taking afterwards was heart-breaking. I remember that she tried to convince me to stay forever and give up the idea of going away. How could I? How *could* I? That memory is a sacred, but sad, one. For the sake of the continuation of this episode which was to occur 31 years later, I will refer to my friend by the initial 'B'.[1] Suffice it to say that the whirl of life in London completely blotted out, except at rare moments, this poignant affair of my early life.

Arriving at Auckland, I called at the shipping office only to learn that there was no news of my ship for England. I was to travel on the SS *Ionic*,[2] but during the war, dates of arrivals and departures of ships were suppressed, especially as the German raider, the *Emden*, was still prowling around the Indian Ocean.[3] I spent ten days hanging around Auckland all alone in a state of excitement and

---

1 The mysterious 'B' is revealed as Beeban McKnight in Nicholas Braithwaite's autobiography *So what does a conductor do?* (Amazon, 2017).

2 SS *Ionic* (12,352 tons gross) was the second White Star Line steamship to bear the name. Launched in Belfast on 22 May 1903, she could accommodate 688 passengers. She was intended for the UK to NZ route and her maiden voyage was from London to Wellington. The *Ionic* was sold in 1937 and scrapped the same year in Japan.

3 In 1914, the German light cruiser SMS *Emden* captured nearly two dozen ships in the area of the Indian Ocean before being run aground off the Cocos Islands on 9 November the same year.

frustration. My friend from Gisborne joined me for the last few days to keep me company. My memory of this is somewhat hazy, but eventually the *Ionic* arrived and I started on my momentous journey. I travelled second class for £38, and my father had given me a metal container holding fifteen sovereigns for everyday expenses.

The journey normally took six weeks, but to my horror we were only at Cape Town at the end of that time, and it took a further six weeks before the ship berthed at Gravesend Docks in the Thames Estuary.[4] The journey was full of interest, but my sovereigns dwindled until I was almost penniless. I arrived in London with just one shilling in my pocket, but the gods were on my side, for a charming lady had joined the ship at Cape Town and, as I had permission from the captain to practice on the piano in First Class, she being musical, took it upon herself to look after me.

When I arrived at St Pancras railway station, with not a friend in the world to meet me, she offered to convey me by taxi to my sister's house in Cricklewood. This lady, whose name I have now forgotten, lived in the street next to my sister and it was she who gave me my first meal in London, as my sister was not at home at the time. Forlorn and bewildered, I must have presented a miserable face to fellow travellers, and thoughts of me waiting on St Pancras station not knowing where to turn, would have melted the stoniest heart.

I had sent a telegram to my sister from Deal harbour, where the convoy up the Channel stopped for the night before going through the Dover boom the next day. Another telegram was sent from Gravesend asking for my sister to meet me at St Pancras, but again there was no-one there. You can imagine my feelings when I relate that I had never left home on such an adventure before. I had come through a trying journey fraught with great danger. The Captain of the *Ionic* had suffered a terrible strain on the way out to New Zealand and had been taken off the boat on the return journey at Fremantle in West Australia, practically a nervous wreck. The First Mate captained the ship from there onwards. We ran out of potatoes and fresh water on the way from Australia to Cape Town because the ship had to turn southwards halfway across the Indian Ocean to avoid the *Emden*. We were four days at Cape Town taking on coal and provisions, and apart from visiting a friend of my father's, climbing Table Mountain, and hearing a concert at the Town Hall (conducted by Theo Wendt[5]), I did little else.

After Cape Town we called at Dakar, the capital of Senegal, and there took

---

4   The SS *Ionic* docked at Gravesend on 3 July 1916.
5   Theophil Otto Frederick Charles (Theo) Wendt (1874–1951). English-born composer and conductor who was the first conductor of the Cape Town Symphony Orchestra, first musical director of the Broadcasting Organisation and principal conductor of the SABC Symphony Orchestra. Braithwaite later conducted some of his music in Johannesburg.

on a six-inch gun which was erected at the stern of the ship. Things began to look serious, as from Cape Town onwards we had been ordered to wear our lifebelts (or carry them with us all day), and sleep with them on at night.

Dakar was a tremendous change from anything I had ever seen before. We had two days there and saw all there was to see of the town and its inhabitants. A troopship happened to be in the harbour waiting for French native troops from the Cameroons who were being sent to France, and the whole native population had turned out to see these men march to the ship. The colours of the flowing garments of the native women, deep blues, deep reds and spotless whites; the young children, mostly naked, who danced and frolicked at the head of the procession; and the noisy chatter of the natives, all happy and boisterous, was an unforgettable experience.

We were on our way at last and the next port of call was to be London. When we sighted our first whale, everyone thought it was a submarine. It wasn't more than twenty yards from the ship, and as it surfaced, its brown-blue body did indeed look like the hull of a sub. There was a wild scramble for boat stations when the alarm siren sounded, but of course the false alarm only made us more nervous as we got nearer the submarine infested area. Although we were not told so at the time, we went straight from Dakar over to the American coast to join a convoy lane, and from there we made for the English Channel. As the days went on, we fell in with other ships. Destroyers began to flash around us and we got a great kick out of the fact that we were escorted by the famous L class of Jutland fame.[6] These destroyers kept flitting around us until we got to Deal, and then the whole convoy made an early morning dash for the Thames.

My father had always told me of the white cliffs of Dover and the strange emotion he had felt at seeing these bastions of his native land. I felt some of this emotion also. Here was I, a New Zealander, in the land of my parents, my forefathers, and my rightful home. It looked good.

*

On the way from St Pancras railway station by taxi with my benefactress, we probably passed through Regent's Park because I can distinctly remember the profusion of green leaves and flowers (I had always thought London was a stuffy place with nothing else but old dirty buildings!). We passed into Edgeware Road and up Cricklewood Broadway into what was then one of London's newest and most delightful suburbs. My sister, Mabel Manson, lived in St Gabriel's Road.

---

6   A class of 22 Royal Navy destroyers built between 1912 and 1914, some of which were present at the Battle of Jutland.

Mabel Manson, soprano, c.1910.

The name itself sounded beautiful and the houses were all new, but no-one was at home and the excitement of meeting my eldest sister was considerably dampened.[7] I was also looking forward to meeting my nephew, Willie Manson, who had been a King's Scholar at St James' Chapel, London, and who had been left behind for a few years in New Zealand with us while his mother (my sister) pursued her career in England.

Late that first night in London I went around to my sister's house and knocked again at her door. This time Mary, the maid, was in and after thanking my lady from Cape Town, I walked across my sister's threshold. My sister *had* received my telegram from Deal, but she and my brother-in-law had gone out for the evening. I was very upset and could have gone back to New Zealand on the next boat, but the maid, who saw my misery, did her best to give me a much-needed welcome. Later that evening my sister and her husband came home and, although they gave me some sort of a welcome, I felt there was something wrong. It soon came out. Willie, my nephew, had only two weeks earlier gone to France with his regiment, the London Scottish, and was already in the front line at the Somme.

Three days later, early in the morning, I heard my sister screaming most piteously and knew the worst had happened. Willie had been killed instantly on his first venture over the top and on his twentieth birthday, the 1st July 1916. My journey now seemed all in vain. My sister, quite understandably, could not bear to see me walking about while her son, a most gifted musician who had studied at the Royal Academy of Music, was so cruelly cut off from life. I had no-one to talk to about my own grief, for I loved my nephew dearly and we had corresponded regularly. Besides, wasn't I going to the Royal Academy also?

I slunk out of that house of doom and found myself walking around to Teignmouth Road to seek out my Cape Town friend. She kept me there all

---

7   Mabel Manson had left New Zealand for England in 1899. She was 21 years older than Warwick and they were virtual strangers. This may account, in part, for the emotional distance between the two. See Appendix 1.

day and soothed my pent-up feelings, and later that day brought me back to my sister's house where the curtains were already drawn across the windows. I was let in by the maid, who I could see had also been crying, and after a scrappy meal in the kitchen, went quietly up the stairs to my small bedroom – his bedroom. I did not see my sister for several days; she was prostrate with grief. When I did see her, I knew there was no place for me in the house. What was I to do? The war came home to me tragically. In New Zealand we were too far away and it did not really touch our lives to the same extent. Even the death of my brother Horace had not seemed as tragic as my nephew's. Perhaps it was that Horace lived paralysed for eleven months after he was wounded, whereas Willie's death was so very sudden. Whatever the reason, I made up my mind to enlist in the New Zealand forces. I was over military age according to English law and no longer was there anyone to advise me. I was all alone.

I remember walking the streets debating the question. I thought of the sacrifice of my parents, their hopes in me, my brothers already in the army, and the glorious future of music-making which was now smashed at one blow. I was much older than the average music student, having spent too many precious years in New Zealand when I ought to have been in England. It was Mabel who advised my father when I was fifteen not to send me to England as I could learn just as much there as here. If I couldn't go to the Academy why worry about the dangers of war? In my miserable and feverish state of mind I almost welcomed, what seemed to me, certain suicide.

But now my troubles were really about to start. I told my sister I was going to enlist and in no way did she dissuade me. I went to see General Richardson who was a friend of my father and in charge of the New Zealand forces in this country.[8] I told him nothing else but that I wanted to enlist. He, good man that he was, argued with me, trying to put me against it, but it was no use, as I had nothing to go back to. He sent me away asking that I should think it over. I did so, walking around the block of buildings in Southampton Row, and in ten minutes was back before him. He again told me that he couldn't take me in, especially as my parents had sent me over here to study. But when I insisted, he gave me the address of the New Zealand camp at Hornchurch where I was to go and have an examination, and in a matter of a few days I was in khaki. Later I was transferred to Codford on Salisbury Plain, a camp where New Zealand wounded soldiers reported after convalescence. Here I had to train until I was judged fit to go to France.

---

8   Major-General Sir George Spafford Richardson (1868–1938) was at this time New Zealand's military representative in London, commanding all New Zealand troops in the United Kingdom. Ian McGibbon, 'Richardson, George Spafford', Te Ara: The Encyclopedia of New Zealand, https://teara.govt.nz/en/biographies/3r16/richardson-george-spafford, accessed 24 January 2019.

I was already quite proficient as an ordinary soldier because New Zealand, in those days, had Compulsory Military Service and I had done four years as a senior cadet and one year as a Territorial. I was, after a fortnight, ready for the first draft of about fifty men (all veterans, except myself) who paraded before Major Mackenzie. After this gentleman had moved down the line, he stopped before me and said 'Who are you?' I gave him the necessary information, after which he ordered me to step back a pace. To the rest, the adjutant gave the order *right turn, march*, and I was left all by myself, a small figure on a huge parade ground.

What had gone wrong? I asked myself this and many other questions as I slouched back to my hut. The answer, although I didn't know it at the time, was contained in an interview with the adjutant next morning who told me that, apart from other reasons, I was not sufficiently fit enough to take my place with the veterans who had gone off that day. Also, he wished me to organise some sing-songs for the troops during the next fortnight. I suspect now (but did not then) that the hidden hand of General Richardson had something to do with this order, because I was in every fortnightly draft for some months afterwards and the same ridiculous farce was re-enacted. At last, I refused to parade, and although I was still under discipline, I was never charged for insubordination.

After a futile waste of time, six months after my enlistment, I wrote to General Richardson demanding a medical board and, if found fit, to be sent to France or otherwise be discharged to go on with my musical studies. The result was inevitable. Having kept me there for six months and stopped me going to France, they had no option but to declare me unfit for service. It was most amusing, after coming before the medical board the second time, to be asked what I could suggest they should put down on my discharge certificate as a medical reason for discharge. I answered, 'constitutional weariness' and that was it. There was much laughing on both sides and I left the army with some regret, with a medal for services rendered, and discharge pay to the amount of twenty-five pounds, a useful sum those days.

I wrote to my sister asking her to help me find a room, and she put me in touch with Mrs Levi, now in England, who arranged for me to stay in the family of Olive Groves, later a fellow student at the Royal Academy.[9] I cabled my father who sent a typical reply: 'Choose full concert grand for yourself. Pater.' I did so, and bought a boudoir size Steinway.

Now my musical life was to begin (this would be about January 1917). I was

---

9 Olive Alice Groves (1900–1974), English soprano, actor and teacher. She joined Braithwaite in a 1927 BBC broadcast from the 5WA Cardiff studio. She was married to the baritone George Baker and taught at the RAM, where her pupils included Elizabeth Vaughan, Janet Price, Joyce Barker, Margaret Neville and Richard Angas.

fortunate in winning the Goring Thomas Composition Scholarship shortly after my entry to the Royal Academy of Music, and thus relieved my father of any Academy fees for the whole of my three years.[10]

---

10 Arthur Goring Thomas (1850–1892) was a gifted British composer. On 13 July 1892, shortly after his premature death, a concert in which many leading singers of the day participated, was held at St James's Hall, London, to help found a composition scholarship in his memory at the Royal Academy of Music. Braithwaite's scholarship was announced in *The Musical Times*, 59/900 (1 February 1918), 75.

FOUR

IN SEARCH OF MY ROOTS

At the first opportunity for a holiday, I made a pilgrimage to the Lake District in order to find my father's old home, Dallon Bank. I walked from Lancaster to Bowness-on-Windermere on the first day, but had to rest for two further days as both my heels had split open from overdoing it. While in Bowness, I got to know two very sweet young women who, on the third day, rowed me to the head of the Lake so that my heels would have a proper chance to recover. But nothing daunted, I said goodbye to them and continued on my way walking around Grasmere, and made for Coniston (where Ruskin is buried at St Andrew's Church) hoping to reach it before nightfall.[1] I miscalculated my rate of progress very badly and when night came on, I was about eight or ten miles away from my destination. There was nothing else to do but doss down for the night. I had brought with me an army mackintosh sheet and went into the dark woods to settle down under a tree.

The late August night was pitch black and eerie in the extreme. I knew there were no wolves or fierce animals in England, and I also knew there were no robbers, pythons or tigers. But a few hours later I could not bear the eerie hoot of owls, the crackle of broken twigs, the creepy crawling spiders, and the ants. Suddenly my mind switched from England to New Zealand and the night took on possibilities that became terrifying. I imagined hordes of the poisonous katipō and flax spiders were approaching (or waiting until I dropped off to sleep) in order to devour me.[2] I could see the iridescent eyes of numerous animals watching, waiting and blinking with impatience; and it was perishing cold. I packed up, struggled back to the road, and continued to walk, striking matches in order to read the signposts.

---

1 John Ruskin (1819–1900), artist, critic, writer and thinker.
2 The female katipō (Māori for 'night-stinger') is one of only two small venomous spiders in New Zealand. The flax spider is a common non-poisonous jumping spider.

Just as dawn was breaking, I could see ahead the outline of cottages and, as the light grew stronger, the morning sheen of Coniston Water, both of which were a most welcome sight. I sat on a seat by the lake and waited till about 6 a.m. when, from a chimney stack of a nearby cottage, blue smoke began to curl its way upwards. Fortunately, a little notice in the window told me that bed and breakfast was to be had, so I knocked at the door and a bonny wench opened it. I explained that I had walked all through the night, having left Windermere too late, and was on my way to Wastwater, but that I was exceedingly weary and needed some food and a lie down.[3] She at first seemed suspicious, but melted when I nearly fainted on her doorstep. She brought me in and explained that a bed would shortly be available. In the meantime, she would give me a good breakfast.

That was a wonderful breakfast of hot strong tea, two eggs, bacon, and some marvellous ginger cake. She showed me my room and apologetically explained that the occupant of the bed had just gone, would I mind? Did I mind! I snuggled down into warm sheets and didn't wake until 1 p.m. The last thought in my mind before going to sleep was to remember the words of Robbie Burns' poem *The Lass that Made the Bed to Me*. I was grateful.

After lunch I browsed around Coniston, visiting the grave of Ruskin and the little museum that bears his name. I also rowed across the lake to Brantwood, his home. Next morning, I was off early as I had to climb The Old Man of Coniston[4] and continue through the difficult pass to Wastwater. Fortunately, I had brought a compass and a good map, otherwise this day might have ended in complete disaster. After passing around the neck of the 'Old Man', I had sat down to eat my sandwiches and to rest, when, without any warning, the terrible Lakeland mist blotted out everything. Anyone who has experienced this blinding catastrophe will know what I mean. I was inexperienced and completely alone. I sat down and got out the map and compass and calculated the direction, walking with the compass in my hand. To make matters worse a drenching rainstorm began, and continued throughout the day.

I had calculated that if I walked at an even pace in the one direction, skirting obstacles but allowing for any divergences, I would at a certain time strike another pass to the left. My calculations were correct (they were calculations of sheer desperation), and I came on the pass and turned left. I stopped while I then made a further calculation, working out the mileage and time to be taken, and then continued on my way. The storm was still at its height, but by this time I had struck a fairly well-worn track and with my heart singing and almost

---

3 Wastwater is England's deepest lake and lies at the foot of the country's highest peak, Scafell Pike (3,209 ft).

4 The Old Man of Coniston (2,634 ft) is a fell in the Furness Hills, to the west of Coniston village. It is popular with walkers.

bursting with thankfulness, I came to a cottage. Here I became the centre of admiration at what must, in that weather, have seemed a feat such as only the local mountaineers could appreciate. I was on my way shortly afterwards and at about 6 p.m. I arrived at Wastwater and found a little hotel where I went to bed while my clothes were being dried. So, a frightening day's walking ended happily.

Next morning, refreshed and none the worse for my previous day's adventure, I started off along Wastwater (a bleak and bare lake), climbing to Sty Head Pass. From the top of the Sty Head, I located the Tarn (a mere puddle) which proved to be the source of the Derwent. Following this down the mountain and coming to the beautiful Rosthwaite and Seathwaite Valley, I continued alongside the river to Derwentwater. The little villages on the way, with their smithies, shops and tidy cottages, were a delight to the eyes. My excitement mounted as I passed names with the second syllable the same as my own – Blairthwaites, Seathwaites and hundreds of Braithwaites. I had the strong feeling that I had entered the land of my forefathers. They were surely a hardy and romantic race, for didn't their forefathers come to inhabit the mountainous but extremely beautiful Lake District?

The Braithwaites came over from Norway with Harald Hardrada in the eleventh century and, after fighting for their chief, turned their swords into ploughshares. My father was proud of his family tree (unfortunately now lost) which showed a direct line of descent from Hardrada.[5]

At last Keswick was reached and I enjoyed a well-earned rest until morning. In the setting sun, I walked out to Friar's Crag (and to Ruskin's monument[6]) and surveyed the whole extent of the lake. It was like a beautiful scene from a stage play, and in some respects reminded me of stretches of the Wanganui River in New Zealand. In fact, the mountains and streams reminded me very much of New Zealand scenery. It was the undulating hills and sluggish rivers of the South of England I had seen up until then, and I had not been long enough in England to appreciate the beauty of English scenery which, rather like the English character, is all understatement and compromise.

Next morning, I walked out to the little village of Braithwaite, two miles or so from Keswick. Here, in my imagination, was the titular 'keep' and headquarters of the Braithwaite tribe.[7] Its little church, stream and bonny houses, lay nestled in the valley. As I had spent too much time in Braithwaite, I took the train to

---

5 Harald Sigurdsson (c.1015–1066), known as Hardrada (hard ruler), was Harald III, King of Norway from 1046 until his death at the Battle of Stamford Bridge.

6 Situated on the promontory of Friar's Crag and unveiled in 1900.

7 The surname Braithwaite, found in Cumbria and Yorkshire, is derived from the Old Norse words breiðr (broad) and þveit (clearing). *Dictionary of American Family Names*, ed. Patrick Hanks, 3 vols (New York: OUP, 2013).

Penrith, and here I was to be finally disappointed in my search for a village where I had hoped to find Dallon Bank. My information, as it later turned out when I wrote home, was incorrect and I returned to Penrith late at night quite miserable.

The following morning, I was off at 7 a.m. for the longest walk of all, along the long L-shaped Ullswater to Patterdale, and over the Kirkstone Pass to Windermere. Always, in starting off on my walks, and once having got into a settled rhythm, the one theme that sang itself to me was the opening of *Boris Godunov*.[8] But this was a very exhausting walk and after nightfall, about five miles from Windermere, I weakened and caught a bus to Bowness.

So ended my pilgrimage. In less than two weeks I had walked something like one hundred miles and I would not have missed it for anything, despite the fact that the real purpose of my journey was unsuccessful. It wasn't until many years afterwards that I was shown a photograph of my father's home at Cliburn (not far from Penrith). My grandfather was a miller, and the old mill is there to this day. The home is still called Dallon Bank.

---

8 Opera by Modest Mussorgsky which Braithwaite was later to conduct at Covent Garden with Boris Christoff in the title role.

FIVE

FROM STUDENT
TO CONDUCTOR

O f my three years at the Royal Academy of Music there is not much to say. In addition to the Goring Thomas Scholarship already mentioned, I won the Battison Haynes Composition Prize with a quartet, and the Challen Gold Medal in 1917, for pianoforte playing.[1]

The Principal of the Academy (RAM) was Sir Alexander Mackenzie,[2] and my first composition master was Harry Farjeon,[3] brother of Eleanor, Herbert and Jefferson Farjeon. The reason why I went to Harry, apart from the fact that he had been the teacher of my nephew Willie, was that Harry's father was the first editor of the *Otago Daily Times* in Dunedin, my home town, so I was bound to go to him. I could not have wished for a more understanding and helpful master, but somehow it wasn't quite what I wanted. Harry Farjeon was a strange but brilliant man who wrote much pleasant music, but I think that I never really understood him or gained much from his unorthodox methods.

Shortly, I was to plead for a change, but put my foot in it badly. In my

---

1 Two significant prizes. The first was named after Walter Battison Haynes (1859–1900), a professor of harmony and composition at the Royal Academy of Music from 1890 until his death. Braithwaite's award was announced in *The Era*, 24 December 1919, and on page 50 of *The Musical Times* (1 January 1920), but no quartet manuscript from that period has survived. The adjudicator was Sir A.C. Mackenzie. By coincidence, Braithwaite's nephew Willie Manson had won the same prize four years earlier, and the manuscript for his winning composition (two movements of a Piano Trio) has also been lost.

   The Challen Prize was sponsored by the piano manufacturer, Messrs Challen & Co., from 1910 to 1939. Another New Zealander, Janetta McStay, won the prize in 1938.

2 Sir Alexander Campbell Mackenzie (1847–1935), composer, conductor, teacher and administrator.

3 Harry Farjeon (1878–1948), composer and teacher.

interview with the principal, I asked if I could go to Frederick Corder,[4] the master of Arnold Bax, whose music I admired very much. Corder also taught Benjamin Dale, whose Piano Sonata had enjoyed a substantial success.[5] But unfortunately, I had to justify my reasons to the principal and in true New Zealand fashion blurted out the unadulterated truth, which was that I didn't like Farjeon's whole attitude to composition and I didn't like his gentle, fanciful mind. This outraged Sir Alexander, and when Corder was obviously appraised of my reasons, he too was incensed at my audacity. Farjeon had been one of Corder's pupils, so I was in a queer situation, but there was no going back. Harry never once let this change alter his attitude to me. He was always kind and helpful to me in the future, as much as he had been in the past. Corder, on the other hand, appeared to bear me a grudge which I was only able to wear down by a subterfuge, but even then, not with complete success.

For a whole year Corder kept my nose to the grindstone and was determined (or so I have since felt) that if I were to get anywhere, it would only be through the hardest of ways. He nearly succeeded in breaking my spirit and, as far as composition was concerned, would not allow me one iota of an outlet. I only overcame his harshness by composing several sonatas (I think three in all) in two-part counterpoint, and later a three-part contrapuntal sonata. These works were done as exercises to please him and to give me an outlet for my restless desire to compose in the short time at my disposal.

I stuck Corder's harshness, determined to get all I could from a great master. Composition only became of interest when my piano teacher, Hedwig McEwen, the wife of composer John McEwen, spoke about me to her husband. He used to invite me to his house, look at my work, and encourage me in my aspirations to compose.[6]

In almost the first week that I entered the Academy I heard the RAM Quartet consisting of Wolfe Wolfinsohn (1st violin), Joseph Shadwick (2nd violin), Frank Howard (viola), and John Barbirolli (violoncello). At the same time my fellow students included Ethel and Edith Bartlett and Rae Robertson. Ethel Bartlett and Rae Robertson have since become world famous as two-piano recitalists. Paul Beard was also a student there. Paul has been the leader of the BBC orchestra since 1936, and before that he was leader of the Birmingham Municipal Orchestra.

A change came in my attitude towards my career. There was no conducting class at the RAM in those days and, still hankering after my original wishes

---

4 Frederick Corder (1852–1932), composer and teacher.
5 Dale's Piano Sonata in D minor, op. 1, composed between 1902 and 1905.
6 (Sir) John Blackwood McEwen (1868–1948), Scottish composer and teacher. He was Professor of Harmony and Composition at the RAM from 1898 to 1924, and succeeded McKenzie as Principal from 1924 until 1936.

in this respect, I approached Sir Alexander, asking the favour of learning this art. Sir Alexander laughed at me, but again I persisted and asked to have the opportunity of trying my hand at his overture to *The Cricket on the Hearth*.[7] With a twinkle in his merry eye he gave his consent, and my first attempt was almost disastrous. At about this time, Ernest Read (bless him) used to take a few enthusiasts after hours (I was one) and teach them how to read orchestral scores.[8] Later on, I was able to beat correctly for the student orchestra to play through the first movement of Beethoven's Symphony no. 5. What with this, and playing the timpani in the orchestra, I felt I was getting somewhere. I played some piano concertos with the orchestra and worked far into the night at composition. Half way through my three years at the Academy, I decided to live on my own, and cooked my own meals, bought my rations (the war was still on), and even did my own housework. My rooms were in Broadhurst Gardens, South Hampstead, which had fortunately escaped the two Zeppelin raids in the 1914–1918 war, but were eventually demolished during one of Hitler's raids during World War Two.

About this time my sister, who used to sing in opera at the Old Vic,[9] introduced me to that extraordinary being, Lilian Baylis,[10] with whom I was to be associated years afterwards at Sadler's Wells Theatre. My sister and I had met quite a lot during these years, but there were periods when I never went near her and she would often write, upbraiding me for my neglect. I think that time had made her feel a little better towards me, and she now began to wish that I saw more of her. Later she was to give me the tragic news of my father's death and was very kind to me at that period.

It is no good trying to describe my feelings and emotions at the news of my dear father's death.[11] I have said enough to show that towards the end, and just before I left home, my father and I became great friends and I felt conscience-stricken that I had lost so many years when our friendship might have been greater still. The main regret I had was that, beyond winning a few prizes and a scholarship, there was nothing I could show for all his goodness before he died. Perhaps the prizes and the scholarship provided some compensation, for he was a good and really simple man.

As an interlude during this period, I used to go to the Old Vic every

---

7 *The Cricket on the Hearth*, op. 62, is a one-act opera premiered at the Royal Academy of Music on 6 June 1914.

8 Ernest Read (1879–1965), conductor, organist and music educator.

9 The 'Old Vic' was the nickname, acquired sometime in the 1880s, of a theatre in Waterloo Road and the theatrical company that eventually occupied it. It became famous as a training ground for some of the greatest performing artists of the twentieth century.

10 Lilian Mary Baylis (1874–1937), remarkable English theatrical producer and manager.

11 Joseph Braithwaite (b. Cliburn, Westmorland, England, 2 January 1848; d. Dunedin, N.Z., 27 March 1917). See Appendix 1.

Wednesday and Friday when Russell and Sybil Thorndike were regular members of the company.[12] In two seasons, Lilian Baylis produced *all* the Shakespeare plays, and I saw every one of them. I wrote to Baylis, suggesting that the Old Vic company performs one of the Greek tragedies, preferably Sophocles' *Oedipus Rex*. She answered my letter in a very practical way and promised that if I got a £100 guarantee she would fall in with the plan. I set to, and out of my meagre pocket money drew up a circular from which I got the Roneo Company[13] in High Holborn to turn out a hundred copies, and I sent them to everyone I could think of.

The publishers Dent & Co., Gilbert Murray, and a few others answered immediately by sending donations, but the answer to my plea was so disappointing that, after returning the money and thanking those who had answered, I had to write to Baylis confessing my failure. The following season she produced, unaided by a donation, *The Trojan Women* by Euripides, with Sybil Thorndike as Hecuba. I could have strangled her, but the end that I had in mind was achieved, so I had little to grumble about.

At the end of the war my brother Rewi stayed with me for a week, but soon spent the rest of his leave touring Britain and, shortly afterwards, sailed for home. About this time, I had some piano lessons with Myra Hess and Tobias Matthay. Myra Hess was just beginning to strike out on a career which was to prove a worldwide success. I learned the French Horn from one of the greatest horn players this country has known, Friedrich Adolf Borsdorf, the father of four sons, three of whom were fine horn players (the fourth son played the viola). I also learned the clarinet with George Anderson, and the viola with James Lockyer. In this way I was getting a wonderful insight into orchestral technique.

Of course, the Promenade Concerts at the Queen's Hall[14] were attended nightly, and I stood too. Henry J. Wood had given his concerts through the whole of the war period, and even when I was on Salisbury Plain, I got leave once a fortnight and rushed from Codford, arriving (without food) at the Queen's Hall, usually in time for the second item.

Joseph Beecham[15] was giving his seasons of opera in English, first of all at the Aldwych Theatre, and thereafter at Drury Lane where during the war his

---

12 Arthur Russell Thorndike (1885–1972), actor and novelist; his sister, Dame Sybil Thorndike (1882–1976), was a distinguished actor.

13 Roneo (a contraction of Rotary Neostyle), was a trademark used for the inexpensive mimeographic duplicating process that works by forcing ink through a stencil onto paper.

14 The Queen's Hall in Langham Place was opened in 1893 and became London's premier concert venue. It housed the Promenade Concerts from 1895 until the Hall was destroyed by bombing on the night of 10 May 1941.

15 Sir Joseph Beecham (1848–1916), pharmaceutical manufacturer, benefactor, and father of Sir Thomas Beecham (1879-1961), conductor, impresario and a major force in British musical life.

son, Sir Thomas, conducted Wagner's *Die Walküre*. The artists on that occasion were Rosina Buckman,[16] Walter Hyde, Robert Radford and Norman Allin. Later I was to see my first *Tristan and Isolde* with Frank Mullings, Rosina Buckman, Edna Thornton and Norman Allin.

There were no Grand Seasons at Covent Garden's Royal Opera House at that time, and Beecham carried on at Drury Lane, after his father died, with a fine repertoire of operas in English. In addition to Rimsky-Korsakov's version of *Boris Godunov* (which I saw thirteen times from the gallery), I also attended *Louise* (Charpentier); the Mozart productions by Nigel Playfair[17] of *Il Seraglio* and *Le nozze di Figaro*; *Ivan the Terrible* (Rimsky-Korsakov); *Samson and Delilah* (Saint-Saëns) with Frank Mullings and Edna Thornton; and Verdi's *Aida* and *Otello* with Frank Mullings, Miriam Licette *(Desdemona)*, and Rosina Buckman *(Aida)*. I must have seen many other operas under the same regime.

*

My last year at the Royal Academy was saddened by my mother's death, and again I can only say that the suddenness of the news was a terrible shock which I never really got out of my mind. If one believes in strange coincidences, it is curious to recollect that my mother died two years to the day after my father, and of exactly the same cause, a stroke. So, all was over. Never again could I ever write to my parents. I was indeed alone.[18]

Another blow was to follow very soon afterwards. My eldest brother cabled me in very stark terms as follows, 'No more money. You must fend for yourself. Percy.' I draw a veil over the reasons for this sudden blow. Suffice it to say that it was not strictly true, but there was nothing to be done about it at the time.[19] I turned to my sister Mabel for help, but the only advice she could give me was to try for a job as a bus conductor, or work my passage back to New Zealand on a ship. I made no comment of any kind to this cruel advice, but at the time I had had enough of my sister's harshness and made up my mind that the last thing on earth I would do, even if I starved, would be to take her advice ever again.

Then a miracle occurred. I wrote to Arthur Fagge whom I had met at my

---

16 Rosina Buckman (1881–1948), distinguished New Zealand-born soprano.

17 Sir Nigel Ross Playfair (1874–1934), actor, director, impresario.

18 In this paragraph, Braithwaite's recall of events is confused. According to the *Otago Daily Times*, Joseph Braithwaite died from a stroke on 27 March 1917. His wife, Mary, who had since moved to Auckland, suffered a stroke on 30 March 1921 and died in hospital on 1 April 1921. Braithwaite had left the RAM in 1919, and by 1921 was established as a conductor with the touring O'Mara Grand Opera Company.

19 Percy Braithwaite had become Manager of the family business, which was now a limited liability company. Perhaps some financial restraint had been necessary.

sister's home and who was the conductor of the London Choral Society,[20] telling him that I wanted to be a conductor and asking if he could advise me. He was at that moment touring with the Joseph O'Mara Opera Company, and the very day he received my letter, the Chorus Master had been sacked for arriving in an inebriated state. O'Mara sent me a telegram and I joined his company in York.[21] I knew nothing about choral work and had never handled a chorus before in my life. But I did what I could, and after three months I conducted my first opera, Auber's *Fra Diavolo*, a very difficult work to handle well – although I didn't know this until I started to rehearse it.

The reason O'Mara asked me to conduct this opera was that my two colleagues, R.J. Forbes and W.J. Hekker (a Dutchman), thought it beneath them. So, luck was throwing a good weight on my side of the scale. Whether or not this was the real reason didn't much matter, for I threw myself into this new adventure with all the energy of which I was capable. I had already coached the chorus and principals before I knew I was to conduct the performance, so most of the work had been done without the additional excitement and fear of failure.

Joseph O'Mara, tenor and impresario, c.1890s.

© *Special Collections and Archives, Glucksman Library, University of Limerick.*

But I hadn't lost any time during my first three months as coach and chorus master. I was a good pianist in those days and had learned a lot. I never ceased working. All day coaching, looking after off-stage music at night, I would go back to my digs and study the evening's opera and conduct it in my imagination, adding what I had seen the conductors do at certain difficult moments in the score. I must have been an intolerable person those days for I had no time for anything else but music. Work! Work! Work! I suppose I must have worked twelve hours a day. I was always haunted by the fact that I had to make up for lost time, for I was by then 24 years of age.

---

20 Founded in 1903 by Arthur Fagge (1864–1943). Known today as The London Chorus, it has been directed since 1994 by Ronald Corp.

21 The letter from Joseph O'Mara, dated 17 November 1919, states, 'Dear Sir, Your letters received. The most I can offer you as Chorus Master in this Company is Five Pounds per week, and all your Railway expenses will be paid when travelling with the Company. We have Two Conductors at the present time, and for some time to come I do not see any opportunity of you conducting the Orchestra, but should the chance arise, I will give you the Privilege. You can join us next Monday, if the terms are agreeable to you, at the Theatre Royal, York. A line per return will much oblige.' (Private collection).

The great moment of my conducting debut arrived. It took place in the Cork Opera House, a theatre dating from 1855 which had been designed by architect Sir John Benson specifically for opera performance. Located on the banks of the River Lee, the theatre was originally called The Athenaeum, and it was not until 1877 that it officially became the Cork Opera House.

I remember only that the facade was on Classical Greek lines. The stage was roomy enough, and the orchestra pit was the only properly built operatic pit outside Covent Garden. Otherwise, the whole building was then in a shockingly untidy and neglected state.[22]

Of my first performance there is not much to tell that would be of interest to readers, but for myself, naturally, it was the major event of my life.[23] I have often reflected on the question of luck in these matters. After only four years in this country, here I was, at the age of 24, from far-off New Zealand, and not in any way a brilliant student at the RAM, starting off in the career I had always wanted.

What is the force that decides these things? Is it luck only, or partly? I had always worked hard, but I have known many musicians who have worked just as hard, or perhaps even harder. So, what is this strange power within us? Opportunity often knocks in vain. I remember that during my last year at the RAM I was offered the conductorship of the Cape Town Orchestra after Theo Wendt, but I refused it on the grounds that I was not ready for such a job. That was common sense, but I wonder how many young people of my age would have resisted such an offer? I wonder now whether I was right to refuse. Looking back on this, I think that I always had the right sense of proportion in these matters. Yet, accepting a job as chorus master a few months afterwards seems to refute this. Was it because I knew it was now or never, or because I had no choice? These doubts spring to my mind at the moment, but they do not dispose of my original problem: Was it luck or something else?

The will to forge one's way ahead is something that cannot be ignored. I do not mean the capacity to step over the dead bodies of our rivals – that is something quite different and is despicable. No, I mean that combination of urgent earnestness and attention to the smallest detail. The almost pathetic earnestness of purpose cannot fail to enlist the sympathy of others, and attention to details (impossible without hard work) stores up that necessary expertise which makes one ready for every chance as it comes.

---

22 The city of Cork is in the province of Munster, Southwest Ireland. The Cork Opera House was destroyed by fire on 13 December 1955. A new Cork Opera House was opened on 31 October 1965.

23 The performance took place on 24 January 1920 with Evelyn Birks (Zerlina), Edna Penville (Lady Allcash), John Pegg (Fra Diavolo), Wilfred Davies (Lord Allcash), Mr Silverston (Matteo), Joseph Griggen (Giacomo), Mr Locker (Beppo), and Mr Jenkins (Lorenzo). The local critic reported that 'The orchestra, under Mr Warwick Braithwaite, rendered the music with a precision which most happily conveyed the feeling of neatness intended by the author.' Irish Examiner (26 January 1920) 6.

When I said I had no choral experience, I was doing myself an injustice and maligning the memory of a very kindly lady who financed a choral society which consisted of her aristocratic friends. They used to gather at her residence in Portman Square, and although still a student, I was asked by the Principal of the RAM to take on the choir rehearsals. The first work I tackled was Brahms' *Ein Deutsches Requiem* but discovered to my horror that the previous chorus master had taught the singers wrong tempi and allowed them to completely disregard Brahms' dynamics.[24] Being young and enthusiastic (Brahms was my God at the time), I literally tore my hair, squeaking out in my high-pitched voice and in a New Zealand accent, a tirade on the desecration of such noble music. I was highly excited, as too were the astonished ladies and gentlemen of the choir, for my New Zealand accent had put me into a category which they had always regarded as beneath them. I raged on and on, and looked like never stopping. Consequently, their resentment grew until my friend, Lady X, took charge and with evident amusement in her eyes, gave them a pep talk and said something to the effect that at last they were being told something which they should have been told ages ago.[25] Music may be a nice recreation but, for all that, the great works must be taken seriously.

After a break for refreshments, during which my friend took me aside devoting all her precious time to calming me down by asking me about my life and early days, we recommenced the rehearsals. Things went on beautifully after this and I very much regretted saying goodbye to a group of people I had come to regard as my friends, notwithstanding my difficult beginning. I had learned a lot and when I became chorus master of the O'Mara Opera Company, I recalled with gratitude my brief experience with this choir.

My first real lesson in conducting came after the performance of *Fra Diavolo* which, by the way, went quite well. Next morning the clarinet player (also librarian) was very kind to me, saying some very encouraging things. He had one criticism as to my technique. He said, 'Why, when you should be beating 6 (in a slowish 6/8) do you beat two threes? We must have only one downbeat in each bar otherwise those players with bars rests become confused and make wrong entries.' I took this to heart and improved my technique and have never forgotten this sensible piece of advice – there must be one strong downbeat in every bar. I had never had a lesson in conducting from anyone, but only learned by watching my colleagues, and thus had missed one of the most important points of conducting technique.

After *Fra Diavolo*, Joseph O'Mara (to whom I now owed everything) gave

---

24 Possibly Edmund Rogers (1851–1919), composer and organist at St Thomas, Portland Square. He was described as 'a local choral society conductor' in Maggie Humphreys and Robert Evans, *Dictionary of Composers for the Church in Great Britain and Ireland* (London: Mansell, 1997), 291.

25 The identity of 'Lady X' remains a mystery.

me other operas to conduct in quick succession. *Faust, Samson et Dalila, La Juive* and *Roméo et Juliet* were added to my repertoire in a matter of a few weeks, while all the time I was doing my coaching and chorus work. My name, from being in small print as chorus master, was seen to be added in larger print to that of the conductors. I travelled to all the principal towns of Ireland, Scotland and England (but not London) and at the end of my first year had conducted, apart from the above operas, *Lohengrin, Tannhäuser, Rigoletto, II trovatore, Mignon, The Lily of Killarney, The Bohemian Girl, The Puritan's Daughter,* and *The Rose of Castille* (the last three by Balfe).[26]

*

The next two years were very much like the first, but with few new additions to the repertoire, and my old feeling of losing valuable time was beginning to reassert itself. The only excitement outside my work came from the frequent trips to Ireland, where the political situation was becoming more and more dangerous. I was in Cork on the night of 11 December 1920, when the Black-and-Tans[27] burned the City Centre in revenge for the killing of some of their comrades. I was in Dublin in 1921 during the curfew when our performances had to begin at 6 p.m. instead of 8 p.m.[28] On the way to the Gaiety Theatre two British officers walking down Grafton Street were shot in the back and killed. I heard the shots nearby and darted into a shop doorway. Within a few seconds Grafton Street was paraded by Black-and-Tans, in their bluish uniforms and black Berets with drawn Colt revolvers, searching every building. One to whom I spoke, menacing and angry and possibly at the same time scared, threatened to burn Dublin as Cork had been burned. This was the period when, before the curtain went up in the theatre, we still played the English National Anthem, for O'Mara was loyal to the British Crown. But we soon had to stop that. I remember how the gallery used to throw oranges and other harder fruit at

---

26 To this list can be added *Maritana* (Vincent Wallace), *Carmen* (Bizet) and *La traviata* (Verdi), making a total of 17 operas assigned to Braithwaite within his first year.

27 The Royal Irish Constabulary Special Reserve was a force of Temporary Constables recruited to assist the Royal Irish Constabulary during the Irish War of Independence. If the O'Mara Company was in the city at that time, it is likely that the season was abandoned. There are no performance reviews for this period.

28 The O'Mara Company played a long season of 14 operas at the Gaiety Theatre, Dublin, from 20 June to 16 July 1921. The signing of a truce negotiated between de Valera and Lloyd George enabled the curfew to be lifted from 11 July. According to the drama critic, J.J. Ryce, O'Mara had drawn crowds 'of flattering proportions' despite the curfew, and at the tail-end of the season, with normality restored, there was a 'spirit of good cheer' present at the Gaiety Theatre. Robert Goode Hogan and Richard Burnham, *The Years of O'Casey, 1921–1926: A Documentary History* (Newark: University of Delaware Press, 1992), 30–31.

me and the members of the orchestra, on one occasion smashing the leader's precious violin. Personally, the playing of the National Anthem is a tiresome business before an opera and I didn't regret its loss one minute.

I was, if anything, in complete sympathy with the Irish fight for independence. As it turned out, other and more powerful people were also, for the Armistice came early in 1922 on the direct intervention of George V. The Black-and-Tan episode was a discreditable affair, and the previous revolution of 1916 ought to have taught our administration the futility of forceful adherence to the Crown. I am partly Irish, my mother completely so, of Huguenot stock, and Ireland interested me enormously.

While in Ireland I took the trouble to learn as much as I could of Irish aspirations. My friend, Annie Fagin, the harpist, often tried to wean me back to my mother's religion but without any success. *That* was something about Ireland I could not stand. But the aspirations of the Irish people to be Irish was a different matter. I am sure religion played the most important part in this, for Ireland is riddled with its own particular brand of Catholicism which would not allow its people to owe allegiance to a Protestant Crown and country. And why should this be so? As we threw over the domination of the Pope and Italy in Henry VIII's time, why shouldn't the Irish throw over ours?

That is how I looked at the question, but further evidence of the futility of using force was to be seen in the greatness of the men who were put to death after the 1916 rebellion. One has only to read the poems, plays and letters from prison of Pádraig Pearse[29] to realize that the desire for severance from the British Crown was a deep and unalterable reason for existence in the Irish soul. To see Lady Gregory's playlet, *The Rising of the Moon*,[30] during the 1920–1922 period (which I did many times), and its reaction on an audience that was living through a desperate existence, not knowing when one or other of their brothers, sweethearts, fathers and sons were to be dragged out of their beds to be shot as a vengeance for other suchlike murders, was to realize that the ideals of human beings cannot be stifled even by murder – for murder it was without doubt.

I had seen the whole thing grow, from late 1919 until 1922; ambush followed by murder, and murder followed by ambush. Innocent British soldiers,

---

29 Pádraig (Patrick Henry) Pearse (1879–1916), barrister, writer, political activist and one of the leaders of the failed Easter Rising of 1916. He was executed, along with others, but is revered by many as a leading figure in the fight for Irish independence. Arnold Bax, impressed by a meeting with Pearse, composed *In Memoriam* for orchestra shortly after hearing of Pearse's execution.

30 Isabella Augusta, Lady Gregory (1852–1932), playwright and co-founder of the Irish Literary Theatre and the Abbey Theatre. Her play *The Rising of the Moon* was first produced in 1907 and concerns Anglo–Irish tensions seen through an encounter between an Irish police sergeant employed by the English government and an escaped Irish revolutionary disguised as a ballad singer.

English boys from the smiling English counties, shot in the back for vengeance. Young Irish patriots dragged out of their beds in the dead of night and shot without a proper trial. Yet not once was the Opera Company molested or shown any disrespect (except once, later on) and the Irish, say what one will against them, were single-minded and straightforward about their killings. The English soldiers even had to admit that they found their 'enemies' could divorce their minds on occasions from those who administered and those who had to carry out orders.

The legendary figure of Michael Collins (whom I met during his tour of Ireland to explain the terms of the Free State agreement), was the soul of honour and firmness of mind in all his escapades.[31] I learned, shortly after the murder of the two British officers in Grafton Street, that Michael Collins had escaped by doing duty in Paddy Ryan's bar opposite the stage door of the Gaiety, and that the evening before the curfew closed down everything, one of our choristers (himself condemned to death after the 1916 rebellion, but later reprieved) saw him there and had a draught Guinness with him after the opera.

Michael Collins did his duty to Ireland; a duty forced on him by circumstances – and no decent Irishman could resist these circumstances. It was with the utmost horror that I heard he had been shot in the back while mediating between two rival factions in the Civil War which followed. This was an act which will live to the eternal disgrace of the Irish conscience. Michael Collins was a brave and good man and did not deserve to die in such a miserable way. It's no good reminding the Irish of their guilt; they are sorry enough for it as it is, and it will never be forgotten.

The solitary episode in which one of the members of our opera company suffered insult was in a Sunday concert in the Cork Opera House when Collins, Griffith and Dwyer were touring Ireland speaking of the terms they had settled with Lloyd George for a Free State.[32] The Opera House was crowded. It was an Irish Concert with tableaux and national songs. Lyon Mackie,[33] one of our tenors, had begun his group of songs when the audience started an epidemic of sneezing. Irreconcilables in the gallery had thrown down into the stalls little paper bags filled with pepper. Imagine the confusion! Mackie stopped halfway through a song and walked off the stage. Collins and Dwyer harangued the disturbers of the peace with phrases like 'Is this fair play to an artist?' I cleared out of the theatre, and so did most people who didn't want trouble.

---

31 Michael Collins (1890–1922), soldier, politician and a leading figure in the fight for Irish independence during the early years of the twentieth century.

32 Arthur Griffith (1872–1922), Irish politician, writer and founder of the political party Sinn Féin; Seamus (James) Dwyer (1886–1922), Irish businessman and politician.

33 Lyon Mackie (1890–19–?), a leading tenor with the O'Mara company whose roles included Alfredo, Roméo, Turiddu, Faust and the Duke of Mantua.

I didn't like de Valera.[34] I had seen him sometimes in Cork making his way into the back room of a bookshop full of Irish Sinn Féin literature. An enquiry to the shop assistant from me was soon stifled by as dangerous a look in his smiling Irish eyes as possible. De Valera always looked like my idea of an anarchist with his broad black hat, horn rimmed black spectacles, a furtive look, quick nervous movements, and a hard intense look on his face. He had none of the usual *bonhomie* of the average Irish man. Later I couldn't forgive him for becoming the spearhead of revolt against the terms that Michael Collins, Griffith and Dwyer had wrung from the British Government after hard negotiations in London. De Valera had done a lot of thinking during the rebellion, but it was Collins and his group who had done most of the fighting. They had secured an honourable peace at the moment when the Irish rebellion was beginning to crumble from sheer exhaustion. De Valera had stayed at home while Collins and his deputation had gone to London, and the announcement of the terms they brought back was the signal for a sordid schism in the Party, the outcome of which was the elimination of de Valera's one great rival to power. This was what I surmised, whether it be true or not. I was young at the time and followed the whole miserable business to the end.

Joseph O'Mara kept me posted with all the latest news from Ireland and he was affected tremendously at the turn of events. The self-starvation and death of MacSwiney, the Mayor of Cork, was a tragedy which affected O'Mara terribly.[35]

Towards the end of 1922 my feeling of frustration was beginning to affect my work. There was nothing more to learn from touring with O'Mara. The British National Opera Company (BNOC) had just been formed and was to give its first performances in Bradford.[36] I was in Leeds with O'Mara and made the journey to have an interview with Percy Pitt, the Music Director of both Covent Garden and the BNOC. Pitt asked me to join the BNOC as répétiteur at their first Covent Garden season.[37] I broke the news to O'Mara who by that time had begun to look upon me almost as one of his own sons, and indeed I

34 Éamon de Valera (1882–1975), politician and statesman, elected Prime Minister, and Premier of the Republic of Ireland.

35 Terence James MacSwiney (1879–1920), Irish writer and politician who was court-martialled by the British for sedition and confined in Brixton Prison, where he died after a hunger strike lasting 74 days.

36 The BNOC arose in 1922 from the ashes of the Beecham Opera Company which had gone into liquidation two years earlier. The new company flourished on tour and at Covent Garden until 1924, but eventually went into voluntary liquidation in April 1929. It arose again in September of the same year as the Covent Garden English Opera Company, surviving until 1938.

37 The role of an opera répétiteur (from the French verb *répéter* meaning to repeat, go over, learn, or rehearse) is primarily to coach soloists in accordance with the wishes of the conductor. Duties, especially in a small company, may also include training a chorus, taking music rehearsals and prompting the singers during performance. It is often the chosen career path for potential conductors.

have always been grateful for his encouragement and help. O'Mara did his best to persuade me to stay but, as so often since then, my mind was made up and there was no going back. O'Mara and I remained the best of friends for years afterwards until his sudden death in 1927.

Joseph O'Mara was a very great operatic artist. Trained in Milan, performing at La Scala and Covent Garden, he had a brilliant singing career. At the age of well over fifty he was singing principal roles in such operas as *La Juive*, *Tannhäuser*, *Lohengrin*, *Roméo et Juliet* and *Faust*. He threw his passionate nature into all his parts. Canio *(Pagliacci)* and Don José *(Carmen)* were almost terrifying experiences and such was the effect on his audience at the end of these two operas that there was a moment of stupefied silence before applause thundered out. The orchestral players felt this very much, and I, of course, adored his artistry.

The O'Mara Company was handpicked by Joseph and he had the gift (such as Lilian Baylis had) of choosing only those people as members of the Company who were opera crazy and wanted to do little else. Names like Florence Morden *(soprano)*, Mabel Dennis *(contralto)* and Flintoff Moore *(baritone)* are still remembered for their great artistry and singing. There was a large contingent of Irishmen in the company, some escapees from the 1916 rebellion, and Joe's tender heart must have been exercised many times in choosing personnel.

Thea Philips, that great singer, was also a member of the company.[38] Thea's voice was the most natural soprano I have ever heard in the whole of my experience. It was of the purest quality throughout its whole range, and to hear her sing Eily's song 'All Alone' from Benedict's *The Lily of Killarney* was an unforgettable experience. Her Gilda was absolutely supreme, as were indeed her performances of other parts, particularly Leonora in *Il trovatore* and Elsa in *Lohengrin*. The chorus and orchestra were excellent too. The performances of *Tristan und Isolde*, conducted by R.J. Forbes in Liverpool and Manchester during 1922 were more than merely creditable performances, and *La bohème*, *Madama Butterfly* and *Manon Lescaut* could not have been performed better outside Covent Garden.

But another milestone was to be passed and I doffed my hat to my first venture in thankful gratitude.

---

38 Dorothy Jane (Thea) Philips (1892–1960), English soprano and teacher who performed extensively in Britain and Australia.

PART III
(1922–1923)

SIX

THE BRITISH NATIONAL OPERA COMPANY

I now enter the period, beginning in 1922, of which I have the most vivid memories. For the past three years my Steinway Grand had been stored, and I asked my sister to arrange for the sale of it because I had a secret idea in my mind, the substance of which will appear later. I had been having lessons in German and was becoming fairly proficient in that language. I had bought the large full scores of the *Ring*, *Lohengrin* and *Mastersingers* through Mr Balderstone, an amazing personality who lived in Burnley.[1]

I don't suppose anyone will remember him now but Mr Balderstone, whose musical career, I believe, had been ruined by an accident many years previously, used to buy full scores from the publisher Schott of Mainz and sell them to his friends and others. I bought, apart from the above, the Peters Editions of *Tannhäuser*, *Parsifal* and *Tristan* in miniature score, the print of which was still large enough to conduct from. It was during this time that the value of the German mark was beginning to deteriorate so that these scores came to me at a price I could afford. This gave me an idea which I nursed for a long time before carrying out. If scores were cheaper as a result of the deterioration of the German mark, would not living in Germany be relatively cheaper than living in England? I confess that the idea was not repugnant to me and I was determined to go first of all to the Munich Music Festival and stay there for a whole year after my contract with the British National Opera Company (BNOC) and

---

1 John H. Balderstone also encouraged Braithwaite to investigate some of Holst's compositions, especially *Beni Mora*. On 1 October 1921, he wrote to Braithwaite saying 'I have very great hopes of G. Holst, though I do not think he has yet attained his full growth.' Braithwaite gave the first of his 16 performances of *Beni Mora* in a studio broadcast from Cardiff on 9 September 1924. (Letter: Private Collection).

Covent Garden was finished. I badly needed more tuition in conducting and composition, and felt that a year in Munich would put me right.

My sister ran true to style. Although she sold my piano and realized £290 on it, she could have cut off the hand that handed over the money when I announced my intention to go to Germany. She wept at my ingratitude, my disloyalty, both to the memory of her son Willie, and to the country generally. She forbade me to enter her house, and although she later relented, from that moment onwards I was almost a stranger to her.

My twelve weeks[2] at Covent Garden with the BNOC were memorable for the wonderful chance I had of exercising my knowledge of Wagner's major works. The performances of *Der Ring des Nibelungen* (uncut) in English, with artists such as Florence Austral and Beatrice Miranda *(Brünnhilde)*, Agnes Nicholls *(Sieglinde* and *Brünnhilde)*, Walter Hyde *(Loge* and *Siegmund)*, Arthur Jordan and Frank Mullings *(Siegfried)*, Robert Radford *(Hunding)*, Norman Allin *(Hagen)*, and Clarence Whitehill *(Wotan)*, conducted by Albert Coates, Julius Harrison and Eugene Goossens junior, were an eye-opener as to what could be done in England and, with very few exceptions, using British artists.

The repertoire included all Wagner's works from *Lohengrin* to *Parsifal*; all of the 'accepted' works of Puccini then written;[3] all the important Verdi works;[4] some French operas such as Charpentier's *Louise*, Massenet's *Manon*, *The Goldsmith of Toledo* (adapted from the music of Offenbach),[5] and others I may have forgotten;[6] *Boris* and *Coq d'Or* of the Russian composers;[7] and not forgetting the operas of an important and very loveable little man, Mozart.[8] Scenery, costumes and productions were fresh from the Beecham English Opera Company, and that enabled the BNOC to start with a great heritage. Its first season at Covent Garden was a tremendous success. Why? Because an

---

2 The season ran for eight weeks from 1 May to 24 June 1922. Braithwaite includes rehearsals in his calculation.

3 Puccini was still alive in 1922, and the 'accepted works' at the time were *La bohème*, *Tosca*, and *Madama Butterfly*.

4 In fact, only *Aida* was presented in the first BNOC season. *Rigoletto*, *Il trovatore* and *Otello* were added for the remaining three seasons.

5 In the manuscript of his memoirs, Braithwaite recalled (rather dismissively) that Percy Pitt had bought the rights to the opera, 'hoping that it would prove a winner. It didn't and a lot of time was wasted on it.' Warwick Braithwaite, unpublished autobiography, pt 1, ATL Ref.: MS-Papers-5473-1, p. 68.

6 *Carmen*, *Faust*, *Samson et Dalila* were also presented in the first season.

7 No Russian operas were performed by the BNOC. Braithwaite is probably thinking of the Beecham Winter Season (1919–1920) during which *Boris Godunov*, *Le coq d'or*, *Khovanshchina*, and *Prince Igor* were presented.

8 *Die Zauberflöte* was presented in the first season. *Die Entführung aus dem Serail* and *Le nozze di Figaro* were added in the second season.

audience had been built up, people knew what the singers were singing about, and a splendid array of British artists were at hand to interpret the words.

My part as répétiteur in this was quite a small one, and I found it sometimes very hard to settle down as a pianist after three years of conducting. I was no longer interested in playing the piano, and although enthusiastic about it all, my mind would wander at important moments. The chief pleasure I had while with the BNOC was to meet my greatest friend, the conductor Leslie Heward. It was a friendship that lasted for 25 years, until his death in 1943, at the age of 46.[9]

Leslie was a prince among musicians. The ease with which he would digest a new work was the wonder of everyone with whom he came into contact. In addition to this, his lovable character and his loyalty under all circumstances to his friends, endeared him to everyone. I met him for the first time taking the chorus through that intricate 'Quarrel Chorus' at the end of Act II of *Die Meistersinger*. I had been detailed to play for him and, as I entered the chorus room, the rehearsal was in full blast and Leslie was standing up away from the piano, conducting from memory, as indeed he did in all his rehearsal work. He would stop to correct an inner part, and then go on. Anyone knowing this section of the opera will know what a feat that was. But, as I have said, Leslie knew all his work from memory. Off-stage work held no terrors for him. His management of the firework scene from *Louise* was another example of his astounding memory. Everything always went correctly behind the scenes when Leslie was on duty. In those days there were no nights off (or afternoons for that matter) and nobody was any the worse for it. I was privileged to be his second-in-command for off-stage music and he taught me far more than I already knew of that subject. Nothing was left to chance in the correct and split-second technique of off-stage music effects while he was around. Leslie had only joined the BNOC that season and had not worked in opera before, yet he seemed to be the most experienced person on the staff. He was a born leader with his quiet voice, his pale yet deep blue eyes, and his complete certainty of manner backed up by a most gifted musicianship. He was a brilliant pianist and a prolific reader at the piano of new full scores.

Nellie Melba sang with us on a few occasions.[10] She sang Mimì (*La bohème*) with Joseph Hislop as Rodolfo. She was then 61 years of age, but her voice was superlatively fresh and young. The beauty of her voice in Act III and her *Addio!* to Rodolfo brought tears to my eyes. The sheer beauty of tone, blended with

---

9   Leslie Heward (1897–1943), English conductor, pianist and composer. Heward joined the BNOC for the second season, beginning on 26 December 1922 and shared the conducting of *Hänsel und Gretel* with Percy Pitt and Aylmer Buesst. He returned for the two remaining seasons, adding performances of *Madama Butterfly*, *The Perfect Fool* and *Savitri* to his repertoire.

10   Melba and Maggie Teyte sang Mimì during the second season. Melba returned as Mimì in the third season and also sang Marguerite in *Faust*.

pathos, proved completely irresistible to any emotional heart. Beauty of tone has always affected me in that way and, I suppose, always will. Joseph Hislop was, in those days, a most accomplished artist as well, so you can imagine the high standard of the performance.

Some comic things happened which relieved the intensity of one's life. I remember William 'Bill' Boland, a Carl Rosa[11] tenor who was brought in to sing Tristan and Siegfried. Bill possessed a magnificent voice but was never good at memorizing his work. Perhaps it was the management's fault for using him in the first week of his contract to sing such heavy parts. The Carl Rosa had been doing *Siegfried* in a cut version around the same time, so Bill had to learn several pages more for the BNOC. He went quite off the rails in *Siegfried*, singing bits of *Tristan* instead. The role of Tristan was subsequently entrusted to Frank Mullings. Bill went back to the 'Rosa', and that was the last we saw of him.[12]

---

11 The Carl Rosa Opera Company was founded in 1875 by Karl August Nicolaus Rose (1842–1899). The title 'Royal' was conferred by Queen Victoria in 1893.

12 In his defence, it should be pointed out that William Boland was given quite a heavy schedule. In the first BNOC season, he sang the principal tenor roles in *Carmen*, *Madama Butterfly*, *Samson et Dalila*, *Tosca* and *Die Walküre*. In the second season he appeared in *Aida*, *Pagliacci*, *Siegfried* and *Il trovatore*.

SEVEN

MUNICH (1922)

My friend, Leslie Heward, fell in with my idea of going to Munich, and I wrote away for two seats at all the performances. The BNOC season at Covent Garden being over, I went on my way to Germany. I spent a week in Cologne absorbing as much as I could of the language before I moved to Frankfurt, where I had my first insight into German operatic performances. I saw a *Die Meistersinger* and Smetana's *The Bartered Bride* there, and my ideas on opera were almost completely revolutionised. For the first time I was to hear an ensemble company, the result of generations of work. The orchestra numbered 96 and the chorus in Act III of *Die Meistersinger* must have been well over 120. Such enormous forces were overwhelming in their effect, and I began to wonder how it was that in all the moderately sized towns of Germany (150 of them at least), opera had been performed for ten months of the year, while in England we only had eight to ten weeks per year.

Incidentally, why is it that in Germany, France and Italy, the railway stations are very imposing buildings and the amenities (such as the restaurants) reach high standards compared with the British? In Germany, the railway stations are new-looking, imposing buildings, and they generally have three classes of restaurants serving excellent food. The bathrooms and washrooms are always well-appointed. The cloakrooms are arranged, as a rule, so that you put your baggage in on the platform at one end, and are given a coloured ticket which has its own special withdrawal window, generally at the other end and often at the front part of the station building. There is no confusion of people milling around the same window as in most English stations. I am speaking mostly about the year 1922, and things are somewhat better now in England.[1] Railway stations here are utilitarian, yet in Germany and France, and later on in Italy, they look from the outside as if they might easily be cathedrals or theatres. I am thinking particularly of the main station in Milan, which is absolutely magnificent. Rome intends to outdo Milan in this, for the amount of ground set aside for the building of the new station, which I saw when last there in 1949, is colossal.

The opera houses of Germany (and I have seen many) are usually situated in the most magnificent square or avenue of the city and the buildings are imposing, however much one may disagree with their style of architecture. How different from the situation of Covent Garden in London. There have been many schemes to build another opera house of a more imposing nature in London, preferably situated in a well-proportioned square or broad avenue. Unfortunately, up till now the squalor and pinched quarters of the vegetable and fruit market in Covent Garden have held on like grim death to our one claim to cultural fame operatically. Most people, when they walk through the dark streets either from a car park or from the tube station – the women holding their skirts in order to keep them off the wet slimy ground – would be shocked to see the same streets during daytime. The filth, the decayed vegetables, the stench of rotting fruit, onions, potatoes, cabbage leaves, horse dung or nauseating petrol fumes, through which the artists have to plough their way to rehearsals, must be seen to be believed.

At 4.30 p.m. the municipal scavengers get to work, achieving wonders, and by about 5.30 p.m. the 'old lady' has had a wash, put on a clean dress, tidied up the house and pathway outside, and sits down smiling, awaiting her first guest. Smiling? Yes, but an enigmatic one, and at times, with her hand in front of her face, a rude one! There are many people who like this squalor; they think in some mysterious way it is part of opera. To them it would be an unheard-of thing, nay even desecration, either to take the opera house away from Covent Garden or take the market away. They would miss something of the Old Tradition. Of course they would, but has tradition no standards of cleanliness? Apart from this, I don't suppose they know why the dinner interval during the *Ring* at Covent Garden is such a necessity. It is not only a good aid for digestion (both musical and gastronomic), but also a sheer necessity for the scene shifters. Scenery for the Second Act, which cannot be stored in the cramped space of the scene docks on the stage, has to be kept on lorries nearby and brought up Floral Street at the earliest moment possible when the vegetable and other lorries have shaken the filth of the

---

1 Braithwaite is writing his memoir in the 1950s.

market off their tyres. Every difficulty imaginable besets the production staff at Covent Garden because of the cramped space of the stage itself, but the crazy turmoil of the narrow streets outside until 4.30 p.m. adds to these difficulties.[2]

These difficulties did not exist in Germany before the 1939–1945 War. All the opera houses, as pointed out before, were set in imposing surroundings with more than ample space for building and storing scenery, and often with a splendid restaurant in one corner of the building nearby. This was, coming from Covent Garden in 1922, what struck me so forcibly when I travelled through Germany, stopping at various cities on the way. At Munich, the prolific number of operatic buildings was overwhelming. In the whole of England there was but one opera house at that time. In Munich alone there were three – the Residenztheater, used for Mozart; the Hof und Nationaltheater, for grand opera; and the Prinzregententheater, principally for Wagner operas (a little way out, but with a special tramline only used for the opera performances).

The Prinzregententheater was built on the same lines as the Festspielhaus at Bayreuth (which I had not seen yet), and the stage was the latest thing in operatic planning. Built in 1901 and named after Luitpold, Prince Regent of Bavaria,[3] it was intended for performances of Wagner operas simply because Bayreuth was somewhat inaccessible for the Munich aristocracy, and the amenities of Munich for all the year round performances of Wagner were better.[4] This opera house is imposing both outside and inside, but although it was built on the same interior plan as the Festspielhaus to reproduce the miraculous acoustics of the original theatre, it just fell short in this respect. Some people are inclined to exaggerate this failing, but I have heard performances of the same works in both opera houses and can vouch for the excellent acoustics of Munich. Don't misunderstand me on this; the Bayreuth one is better acoustically, but the Munich one is very good also.

---

2   Braithwaite would certainly have been aware of improvements made to the Royal Opera House during the 1960s. He probably also knew of plans to relocate the market but did not live to see it move to a 57-acre site in Nine Elms. The New Covent Garden Market opened on 11 November 1974. Further modernization to the opera house took place in the 1980s, but it was not until 1997–1999 that the most significant reconstruction was undertaken. In 2014, the 'Open Up Project' began, with the aim of improving, amongst other things, the entrances and lobby areas. Despite all these changes, the main auditorium has fortunately retained its splendid atmosphere and familiar horseshoe shape.

3   Prince Luitpold (1821–1912) acted as Regent for 26 years, deposing King Ludwig II (who was controversially declared insane) and acting for Ludwig's legitimate successor, King Otto I, who had already been declared insane and unfit to rule.

4   The Prinzregententheater opened on 21 August 1901 with a performance of Wagner's *Die Meistersinger von Nürnberg*. From 1945 to 1963 it housed the Bavarian State Opera, which had been bombed out of its home at the Hof und Nationaltheater during an air raid on 3 October 1943.

Having arrived at my destination, Munich, I set about finding living quarters. I was very fortunate in locating, after a few misfires, a room with a charming family in a third story flat in Landwehrstraße. This family – father, mother, son and two daughters – made me happy and comfortable, and I stayed with them until I left Munich ten months later. Although it was only four years after the bitter 1914–1918 war, I was never once made to feel embarrassed, although we discussed the war frequently. The father had been in the submarine service and told me with pride that his submarine had got under the boom at Dover and operated in the Channel and later in the Atlantic. I contested this hotly, but he persisted with his contention.[5] We were to hear many such arguments during my stay and it says something for human relationships that I was able to write to them and visit without any embarrassment until about 1935, when Hitler made it impossible for even the kindliest German to discuss anything rationally.

The last time I was in Munich was 1951 and I was passing through with just two hours to spare. I would have liked to look my friends up but, alas, the whole of that district near the railway station had been laid low by bombs. I only hope my friends were spared, as they were such lovable people. It was through them that I got to know the Bavarian and nearby Austrian lakes. Nearly every Sunday morning during that autumn and winter the whole family would arise at 4.30am, catch a train Third Class from the local railway station and with a rucksack bulging with *Wurst*, *Brötchen* and *Bier*, climb to the highest point. Little Hilda, the youngest girl, would usually be the beast of burden on these occasions and when I remonstrated, I was put in my place with a lecture from the father on the *Echte deutsche Familie*[6] training for the young. Little Hilda was only about 12 years of age and was already a great climber, but I thought (and have thought many times since) that the strain for one so young was injudicious to say the least.

Those were happy days. We used to arrive back about 4 p.m., and after a bath and a brush-up I set off for the Hoftheater, the Prinzregenten or the Residenz for an operatic performance. The family rarely came with me on these occasions as they had their Season Tickets which entitled them to so many performances in the year, but not for any Festival performances.

It was useless to sign on to study at the Akademie der Tonkunst immediately

---

5 Braithwaite's host was probably correct. War logs of many German submarines reveal that they 'crossed the [Dover] barrier on the surface almost with impunity and frequently, and when they did become entangled in the nets, freed themselves and continued on their way.' *Net and Boom Defenses*, Ordnance Pamphlet 636A, Navy Department Bureau of Ordnance (Washington, D. C.,1944), 7.

6 The real German family.

I arrived in Munich as the summer holidays were about to commence.[7] There was so much to see and do, and with Leslie Heward, Humphrey Procter-Gregg and Arnold Goldsbrough due to arrive soon, it would have been impossible to work in any case. Until their arrival, I contented myself by becoming familiar with the wonderful museums and picture galleries of Munich and learning something of the history of the place. The surrounding countryside and the upper reaches of the great river Isar (which flows through Munich), were explored as far up and further than Grünwald,[8] with frequent excursions to the Schloss Nymphenburg.[9] Nuremberg was visited several times, and the dwelling of Hans Sachs[10] was entered with almost religious awe, much in the same reverence as the Katharinenkirche,[11] although the latter gave me a feeling of desecration because the church had been stripped of all religious paraphernalia and was at that time used as a concert hall for the performance of choral works.

The old town wall, if one took the trouble to seek it out, was worthwhile looking at. I tried to find the meadow depicted in Act III, Scene 5 of *Die Meistersinger* but, of course, this was an impossibility as it had long since been built over. My visits to the Alte and Neue Pinakothek in Munich were many and regular.[12] The Albrecht Dürer drawings and paintings, satisfying in the extreme, were gazed at many times.

Munich was (and I say *was* quite correctly, for much of it was left in ruins

---

7   The Akademie der Tonkunst (now the Hochschule für Musik und Theater München) is one of the most respected traditional vocational universities in Germany specialising in music and the performing arts. Founded in 1846 as a private institute called the Königliches Conservatorium für Musik, it was transformed in 1867 by King Ludwig II into the Königliche bayerische Musikschule (Royal Bavarian Music School) at the suggestion of Wagner. It was financed privately by Ludwig until it received the status of state institution in 1874. It has since been renamed several times; to the Königliche Akademie der Tonkunst (Royal Academy of the Art of Music), the Staatliche Akademie der Tonkunst (State Academy of Music), the Hochschule für Musik (Munich Music College), and finally the Hochschule für Musik und Theater (University of Music and Performing Arts Munich) in 1998. Its original location, the Odeonsgebäude, was destroyed. 'Hochschule für Musik und Theater München', http://website.musikhochschule-muenchen.de, accessed 23 January 2019.

8   Grünwald (Green Forest) is located approximately 12 km southwest of Munich.

9   Schloss Nymphenburg (Nymphenburg Palace), begun in 1664, was built as the summer residence of the rulers of Bavaria.

10 Hans Sachs (1494-1576), German poet, composer and shoemaker immortalised by Wagner in *Die Meistersinger von Nürnberg*.

11 Katharinenkirche is the setting for Act I of Wagner's *Die Meistersinger von Nürnberg*. Although destroyed by air raids during WWII, some restoration work, undertaken in the 1970s, now enables concerts and other events to be held there.

12 The Alte Pinakothek (1836) is one of the oldest galleries in Europe, and a model for subsequent European museum architecture. The Neue Pinakothek (1853) was founded by King Ludwig I of Bavaria as the first public museum in Europe dedicated exclusively to contemporary art. The building was destroyed in WWII and replaced in 1981. The more recent Pinakothek der Moderne completes the trio of galleries.

after the Second World War) unlike any other German town I had so far visited. Even the railway station was quite different from the usual run of stations in other German cities, and the opera house, situated in the cobbled square by the Residenz, also had a different character of its own. I began to realize that Munich was indeed the capital of Bavaria, which was for many generations a principality with a life completely of its own. At first, I didn't like this divergence from the usual pattern of northern cities, but after a while the higgledy-piggledy charm of the city and its outskirts made a lasting impression on my mind.

My contingent of friends finally arrived from London. I had found them lodgings and we began to drink in our first experiences of German performances of opera and plays at the Schauspielhaus.[13] The first performance Leslie Heward and I saw in 1922 was overwhelming in its impact on our youthful and impressionistic souls. *Der Rosenkavalier* was conducted by Bruno Walter and sung by Lotte Lehmann *(Marschallin)*, Elisabeth Schumann *(Sophie)*, Delia Reinhardt *(Octavian)*, Richard Mayr *(Ochs)*, and a perfect ensemble. The playing from the 120-piece orchestra was superlative. At one moment towards the end of the First Act, during the end of the Marschallin's solo scene when the tone of the orchestra was ravishingly beautiful, both Leslie and I involuntarily pressed one another's arms. This was the only time during the whole performance we were aware of one another, and both of us were in tears. Oh, what a memory, never quite recaptured to the same extent since. We went to every performance at all three opera houses. Pergolesi's *La serva padrona* at the Residenz was another delightful experience. We began to realize that Bruno Walter was the superb artist behind the whole organisation and longed to meet him.

Adrian Boult,[14] who had been a student in Germany, was also in Munich staying at the Park Hotel. Leslie knew him well from his Royal College of Music days, and arranged for Boult to introduce us to Bruno Walter. Not only was Walter a great artist, he was also a most generous-hearted man, and from the first moment he took an interest in both of us, inviting us to all his rehearsals. Such kindness in the middle of a big festival season was appreciated enormously by us young people. I was allowed to sit at the back desk in the sunken orchestra during Walter's conducting of the complete *Ring* cycle. I bless Adrian Boult for that opportunity. The extraordinary thing was that we never seemed to be in the way. There were no silly taboos foisted onto us; we came and went without any finicky official obstruction. We were treated as fellow artists and there were no secrets kept from us. We, of course, never transgressed beyond a certain limit, and were careful to keep out of the way when it was wise to do so.

---

13 The Schauspielhaus, located in Maximilianstraße, was Munich's principal German language theatre.

14 Sir Adrian Boult (1889–1983), distinguished British conductor, associated particularly with the BBC Symphony Orchestra (1930–1950) and the London Philharmonic Orchestra (1950–1959).

A composer little known outside Germany at this time was Hans Pfitzner,[15] whose opera *Palestrina*, had been premiered at the Prinzregententheater in 1917 under Bruno Walter. Later I was to hear *Von deutscher Seele* a 'Romantic Cantata' for choir, organ and orchestra. Another opera of his I liked very much was the earlier work, *Der arme Heinrich*, first performed in Mainz in 1895, but his later works I couldn't bear. Perhaps Pfitzner himself put me off; he was a very intense little man who used to sit with bowed head during rehearsals of his own works in the attitude, I always thought, of complete reverence to the strains of his own genius. Perhaps I was wrong to think so, but the impression of self-pity or self-interest seemed to pervade the atmosphere when he was around.

Walter Braunfels,[16] a composer who wrote an opera to Aristophanes play *The Birds*, was also very evident, as was Erich Korngold, whose *Die tote Stadt* was also produced. I didn't like any of these works; they were harsh and grim musically. I don't think they have stayed the course.[17] But the chief point was that Bruno Walter gave these new works a performance and he was quite right to do so. Braunfels, I was told at the time, expected to get *The Birds* performed in at least fifty opera houses in Germany the following season as a result of Bruno Walter's interest. An operatic composer in Germany, if any good at all, was thus assured of some return for the enormous labour entailed in writing an opera.

Wagner's *Der Ring des Nibelungen* was performed, produced and 'dressed' in an entirely new production with scenery by Leo Pasetti.[18] It was produced by Willi Wirk, who had been at Covent Garden for the German opera seasons for many years before the war and was inordinately proud, among other things, of his command of the English language.[19] When walking from the theatre after rehearsals, Willi would dominate the conversation in execrable English and on one occasion when pointing out proudly the new (in 1922) electrical water power works on the Isar, convulsed us all by telling us how many million horsepowers the plant would develop when working. But his production of the

---

15 Hans Pfitzner (1869-1949), German composer. The opera, *Palestrina*, was to remain his most famous work.

16 Walter Braunfels (1882-1954), German composer, pianist and Director of the Hochschule für Musik Köln (1925-1933 and 1945-1950). Remembered today for his opera, *Die Vögel* (The Birds) which was premiered in 1920 at the Munich Nationaltheater, conducted by Bruno Walter.

17 Despite their initial popularity, none of the mentioned operas has become standard repertoire. They have, however, attracted new interest through performances and commercial recordings since WWII. 'Marietta's Lied' from *Die tote Stadt* has become a popular repertoire piece for sopranos.

18 Leo Pasetti (1889-1937), Russian born, but Munich-based, stage designer who married the distinguished Dutch soprano, Elisabeth Ohms.

19 In his memoirs, Bruno Walter admits to 'no clear recollection of the event' except that Anna von Mildenburg was the stage director. Bruno Walter, *Theme and Variations* (N.Y.: Knopf, 1946), 201. However, Braithwaite's specific recollection of Willi Wirk, does at least suggest his involvement.

Ring was superb and his tremendous confidence and pride in the Prinzregenten stage was fully justified.

The lighting on the stage was, of course, the latest thing imaginable and the two cycloramas (one for full stage, the other for half), were a revelation to all of us in those days. Covent Garden had no such amenity as a cyclorama until about 1933. The lighting bridges at the Prinzregenten were arranged on three levels equidistant from the proscenium; the further from the proscenium the higher they went. On the bridge behind the proscenium were the powerful searchlight-like lamps and also the various lighting machines for cloud effects, lightning, and so on. We could only gaze at these wonders with avidity, realizing how much behind the times the theatres in England were, especially Covent Garden. The other thing which struck us was that in Germany, with the mark crashing down at headlong speed to an infinitesimal worth of its pre-war value, the theatres were still luxuriously subsidized by each state and municipality. Wirk, on one occasion, told us quite frankly that saving money at the expense of operatic perfection would not be tolerated by any section of the population. And so it proved, as I had good reason to experience much later when the mark got to its absolute lowest ebb.

An interesting personality, who I was to meet several times later on, arrived in Munich from Vienna and Salzburg. This was Ethel Smyth,[20] a bundle of energy and forthrightness. She had just come from the Salzburg Festival and whetted all our appetites by her descriptions of the performances she had seen. Almost every day, the Park Hotel would be the gathering place of British musicians in Germany and the artists from the Opera. Boult seemed to know everyone and was always nice about introducing us to the various celebrities. William Henry Bell, Director of the Cape Town Conservatoire, was a wonderfully alive man who came to Munich with his wife and son, and I had found them rooms. Bell was quite a good composer and some years later, when he had retired to live in London, played me his opera *The Rivals* to Sheridan's play. I tried to get it performed at Sadler's Wells but on examination of the full score, found it so atrociously full of mistakes, and the parts (copied by an amateur) quite useless, that we very regretfully decided against a performance. I should say that I was in a minority of one with my colleagues about this.[21]

I remember a delightful trip by motor launch down Starnberger See,

---

20 Ethel Smyth (1858–1944), English composer, writer and suffragette. Braithwaite conducted complete performances and excerpts from her operas *The Boatswain's Mate* and *The Wreckers*.

21 William Henry Bell (1873–1946), prolific English-born composer, organist and lecturer who taught at the Royal Academy of Music and, after 1912, in South Africa. There is no record of any performances of his opera *The Rivals*. However, in 1938 Bell approached Braithwaite for advice over another opera, *The Duenna*, based on Sheridan's play. The music library at the University of Cape Town is named after Bell.

a beautiful lake not far from Munich, with Bell and his family, myself, and Leslie Heward. We had stopped halfway down, attracted by a lovely Bavarian chalet rather like *White Horse Inn*,[22] with a large green lawn in front, and gaily decorated by highly coloured tables and umbrellas. We called in and had a scrumptious tea with large *Kuchen* and *Torte*. The Bells were so entranced with this dream of a place, with its garden overlooking the lake, that they asked me to enquire what it would cost to stay there. With great formality and evident pride, if not a little embarrassment, I spoke in my best German to the waiter. He, not listening at all, but quite likely expecting a certain enquiry after copious cups of tea, answered in perfect English, 'Through the main entrance, along the corridor, and first left.'

*

The time arrived when, one by one, my friends began to depart and I was left alone. Leslie went back to the BNOC, and I entered my name at the Akademie der Tonkunst in Odeonsplatz. I passed the preliminary examination and was taken on by the Director, Siegmund von Hausseger, with whom I studied conducting. My composition teacher was Joseph Haas,[23] a pupil of Max Reger. Bruno Walter also helped me much by making me a voluntary répétiteur at the opera house where I did a lot of coaching, especially at the beginning of the season. Von Hausseger was an excellent teacher of conducting, if a little stiff as a conductor himself, and I got on very well with him. Joseph Haas was a superlative teacher of composition and his 'master class', which I was fortunate enough to join, was extremely interesting. His method, as far as I can now remember, was to take us all through a particular problem in counterpoint, illustrating how he would cope with it in actual composition. We were then set the task of including that problem in a composition of our own, to be produced at the next lesson and submitted to the fire of his criticism. The master class often lasted up to two hours, and time was no object. If necessary, we had to go into another room and rewrite portions of our work in the light of his criticism.

Being a student at the Akademie entitled one to attend all the rehearsals and concerts at the Odeon,[24] the concert hall of Munich, and I heard for the first

---

22 *White Horse Inn* is a later musical comedy, premiered in Berlin in 1930 and composed, principally, by Ralph Benatzky and Robert Stolz.

23 Joseph Haas (1879–1960), German-born composer and teacher. From 1921 he taught at the Akademie für Tonkunst in Munich, becoming a professor there from 1924 to 1950.

24 Sited on the Odeonsplatz, the hall was commissioned by Ludwig I and built between 1826 and 1828. Destroyed by air raids in 1944, and rebuilt in the 1950s, it now houses the Ministry of the Interior (Das Bayerische Staatsministerium des Innern), despite popular moves to restore it as a concert hall.

time all the Richard Strauss tone poems conducted by the composer himself, and all the Bruckner and Mahler symphonies, conducted by Von Hausseger and others.

I had to find a room to practice the piano, and although I was not short of money, I needed to conserve what I had.[25] My landlady put me in touch with a teacher at a kindergarten on the street level of the same building. The teacher, a beautiful Brünnhilde-like German *Fräulein*, offered me the use of her piano for the equivalent of two shillings per day,[26] and also offered to give me conversation in German. So, after the children had gone home, I would use this piano most days and at certain pre-arranged periods have my conversation lessons, some of which were partaken of during long country excursions. Of an evening we would go to a *bierhaus* and join in the innocent fun, typical in Bavaria, of sing-songs, all sitting at long tables and getting more and more warm-hearted as the evening wore on. We were often joined by my landlord and landlady in the evenings. The kindergarten teacher was called Hilde and she was about my own age and beautifully sweet. She was fair, had blue eyes and, as far as I could tell, a perfectly formed figure. She would read Goethe's *Faust* to me and also correct my reading of it. There was something quite motherly about her simple, yet (as it turned out) ardent character, and she always wore blouses with lace which fell in folds from the V-shaped neckband. We were very good friends and what followed many months afterwards on the evening of my departure, was just one of those unaccountable things that defy analysis.

Bruno Walter was nearing the end of his period as Music Director of the Bayerische Staatsoper and I will never forget the occasion of his last appearance. The opera chosen was *Fidelio* and I sat immediately behind him during the performance. The artists were nearly in tears at the end, and when the curtain went up the second time, after some delay, the whole stage was one mass of flowers. Elisabeth Schumann and Lotte Lehmann were weeping unashamedly; the orchestral players threw bouquets of flowers up at him from the orchestral pit, and the audience would not go. The iron curtain came down finally; the lights were put out, but came up again. Bruno Walter appeared for the last time through the little emergency door of the iron curtain, and that was the end. Some years afterwards when I mentioned Munich to him, a look of pain came on his face, for outside the theatre that night an anti-Jewish procession had halted and made a rowdy nuisance of itself during the whole performance.

Walter's successor was Hans Knappertsbusch, a magnificent figure of a man

---

25 Since Braithwaite was no longer receiving financial support from his family, it is likely that he was living on a combination of his savings, the proceeds of the piano sale, wages from the O'Mara company and the BNOC, and the income from private coaching of singers.

26 Two shillings in 1925 had the equivalent purchasing power of £6.48 in 2022, https://www. in2013dollars.com/uk/inflation, accessed 4 March 2022.

and a most hypnotic type of conductor.[27] He was over six-feet tall, with big
pale blue eyes and, in those days, a golden shock of hair on top, but closely
cropped around the back and sides. His first performance was *Die Meistersinger*
with an orchestra enlarged to 140 players, and as usual, the whole performance
was brilliant. I felt however, there was a little constraint on the part of some
of the artists who had only recently been performing with Bruno Walter. This
was inevitable as there was a lot of talk as to Walter's resignation and the fact
that Knappertsbusch was not a Jew and many of the artists were. The tensions
of national feeling were beginning to assert themselves. One evening, I was in
the restaurant opposite the opera house with one of my last remaining English
friends. Seated far back to the rear of the restaurant was a noisy drunken
party of German soldiers in field grey. How menacing it all looked. Near us
was a party of four Americans, including two women. Inevitably the German
officers switched from singing *Die Wacht am Rhein* to *Deutschland uber Alles*,
meanwhile standing up.[28] I didn't want to make any trouble, nor did my friend
Cynthia Cox, a late fellow student at the Royal Academy of Music, so we both
stood up. It was a nuisance, but it was a good tune. Not so the Americans; they
refused, even after being requested to do so by the Germans. In the end they
were thrown out in no gentle manner. Munich did not look such a nice place
from that moment on.

Knappertsbusch requested me to come to an interview and very kindly
pointed out that there were many German students who were entitled to the
position I had at the opera house, and he could not very well refuse them. He
told me he regretted this, but his hands were tied. So, I was only allowed to
attend rehearsals, but even that became difficult after a time. Many of the artists
came to me privately, but I would not take any payment, and it all became more
difficult as time went on.

For a long time afterwards, when nationalistic expressions of opinion on
the Versailles Treaty would crop up in an ordinary discussion, even among
students, I found that the attitude of many Germans began to change towards
me. I remember being refused a student reduction in the price of a seat at the
opera because I was a foreigner. When I thought of the expedient of telling

---

27 Hans Knappertsbusch (1888–1965), distinguished German conductor, famous for his performances
of Wagner, Bruckner and Richard Strauss. He replaced Bruno Walter in October 1922, when that
conductor resigned to undertake extended tours to the USA, London, Amsterdam, Rome and
other centres.

28 *Die Wacht am Rhein* (The Watch on the Rhine), a poem by Max Schneckenburger set to music
by Karl Wilhelm in 1840. During WWI, this song rivalled *Deutschland uber Alles* in popularity
as the unofficial German national anthem. The tune of *Deutschland uber Alles* (Germany above
all) was composed by Franz Josef Haydn in 1797, and adopted by August Heinrich Hoffmann von
Fallersleben in 1841 for his poem *Das Lied der Deutschen*. The song was chosen by the Weimar
Republic as the German national anthem in 1922.

them I was born a New Zealander, the whole attitude changed. To them, being a New Zealander meant I was a national of a Dominion with a grievance. I have to confess that I didn't mind in the least letting them continue in this error. A people who could treat a great artist like Bruno Walter the way they had, deserved all they got.

Towards the Christmas of 1922, I became worried and upset at little things. During those months the Germans were beginning to feel the real pangs of hunger. My landlord had to register even for a mere mouthful of potatoes. When I offered to stand in the long queue, he would not hear of it because I was his guest. Therefore the good man stood for hours for my registration. The police at this time also became difficult. The law about registering *Ausländers* (foreigners) was altered, so whereas it had been enough to have my identity card stamped every three months, I now had to go every week just like other foreigners. The personnel in these places changed from the kindly men I had previously known and passed the time of day with, to a more officious, rough type. Even buying music became almost an act of suspicion. My friends deplored this state of affairs but could do nothing about it.

I had become thoroughly miserable and, although I was receiving great benefit from my lessons at the Academie, my thoughts once more turned to England. All this took time, and I was still to get great benefit from my experiences and to learn many valuable things. Katherine Arkandy, an English singer at the opera, and her husband, took me in hand at this period, and if it had not been for them, I think I would have thrown in the sponge and deserted.[29]

All good things come to their appointed end. I wrote to Percy Pitt at Covent Garden asking if he would let me return to the BNOC once again as a répétiteur. The answer was a telegram asking me to rejoin the company at Covent Garden as soon as possible.

My last day in Munich was spent with Hilde walking through the Grünwald in the snow. It was a glorious day; the river Isar flowed as never before. The silver of the pine trees against the snow; the climbing up to the towers of medieval forts on the banks of the Isar; the copious draughts of Löwenbräu beer; and the half-whispered expressions of our sad thoughts, were things to remember. Again, I was faced with one who desired me to stay, and could not understand why I should want to be on my way. She pleaded with me, but this time with every womanly weapon at her command. She was very attractive, both physically and mentally, and a lovely, generous-hearted companion who

---

29 Katherine Arkandy (1898–1961), soprano. Born Kate Arkend to Latvian parents in Ramsgate, England, she married a German, Henry Julius Hecht. Her distinguished career took her to Budapest and, from 1921, to Munich. She made frequent appearances at Covent Garden throughout the decade, returning to live in England from 1927. She was the mother of distinguished British actress Maxine Audley.

was almost desperate in her desire both to keep me there and to persuade me to succumb to her undoubted charms. What would I have been if, at the moment when I had made up my mind to go back to England, I had taken advantage of her pleading? There are some moments in life when we hang onto a straw, and this for me was one of them. It was the prospect of a career which I hoped one day to carve out for myself. Many times since, I have had a sort of regret that things might have been different, but that's something I have always suppressed.

I saw Hilde again the following year, but the year after that my landlord told me that she was now happily married, and I never saw her again. For many years I kept a little keepsake, in the form of a ring, which she gave me on our last walk through the Grünwald.

EIGHT

THE BRITISH BROADCASTING COMPANY

Back in London I reported to Covent Garden for the 1923 BNOC season, and although not caring any longer for coaching, it was at least a good job and several interesting works were being produced.[1] Holst's *The Perfect Fool* made a great success, but the reason for its subsequent neglect is not hard to find. It has a silly libretto. It all depends on one's sense of humour, but Holst also made insensitive fun of Wagner and Verdi. Several suitors sue for the hand of the Princess. First comes a Troubadour, who sings a skit on Verdi. Next a 'Stranger' who sings to the accompaniment of Wagnerian harmony and silly imitation of alliterative sentences such as one does find in Wagner's libretti. It seemed to me in bad taste, although most of the music was entrancing. The ballet music is well-known and deservedly successful. Holst was a small, kindly man and never came to the rehearsals. Goossens[2] conducted the opera, and Leslie Heward and I were the principal répétiteurs. Holst was the only composer I had met who didn't 'fuss' the conductor by his interfering pressure.

There occurred about this time an event which has changed the face of the world. Wireless entertainment made its bow, and people with homemade crystal sets began to grow in numbers. The British Broadcasting Company

---

1   Braithwaite must have rejoined the BNOC in January 1923, mid-way through its second season.

2   Eugène Goossens (1867–1958), French-born conductor and violinist, best-known perhaps as the father of a talented family of musicians: Sir Eugene *(conductor/composer)*, Marie and Sidonie *(harp)*, Adolphe *(French horn)* and Léon *(oboe)*.

was formed using a room in Marconi House, Aldwych, as a studio.[3] One day an engaging young man called at Covent Garden with some curious-looking engineering and electrical gear, and near the footlights, he placed an odd little instrument with wires attached. I got to know him quite well and was detailed to help him throughout the performance. The man turned out to be Stanton Jeffries, the first Musical Director of the BBC, and that night's performance of *The Magic Flute* went on the air.[4]

It turned out to be one of those chance meetings which bore results undreamed of by either of us. Several times Mr Jefferies brought his magical gear to Covent Garden and we struck up quite a friendship. Later he was to send me an urgent wire to meet with him at 2 Savoy Hill.[5] We were only a few yards from one another. I was at Covent Garden, and yet in those days the BBC people were too busy to walk around the corner or telephone – they just sent telegrams. We met and he put his proposition which was that I should become his assistant at the BBC. I didn't like the idea and went on tour with the BNOC. We played to big houses in all the principal cities and toured the *Ring, Parsifal, Tristan* and *Mastersingers*, as well as other works we had done at Covent Garden, but after a while I began to feel that professionally, I was getting nowhere. By the time we next came to London, I had forgotten all about the BBC, but during a summer tour I began to feel that I really must make a change, so I wired Jefferies to say that if the position was still open, I would take it. The BNOC had packed up for the rest of the summer so I came back to London and entered 2 Savoy Hill as a member of the staff.[6]

My successful interview was with the Director, John Reith, a big tall Scot with an almost terrifying aspect due partly, no doubt, to a war wound on his

---

3 The British Broadcasting Company had been formed on 18 October 1922 by a group of leading wireless manufacturers including Marconi. Daily broadcasting had begun in Marconi's London studio, 2LO, in the Strand, on November 14, 1922. The company was dissolved on 31 December 1926, and the British Broadcasting Corporation was established on 1 January 1927.

4 Braithwaite describes the historic moment in radio broadcasting when, on the evening of 8 January 1923, excerpts from Mozart's *Die Zauberflöte* (performed in English as *The Magic Flute*) were relayed live from Covent Garden. Two days earlier, excerpts from the matinee performance of *Hänsel und Gretel* had been successfully transmitted to selected stations in a test broadcast. According to the *Daily Mail* this was achieved by the 'BNOC in co-operation with the Marconi Telegraphic Company, the Western Electric Company and the Post Office Telegraph Department.' *Daily Mail* (8 January 1923), 6.

5 Dating from 1889, the Savoy Hill building was intended for medical purposes. It became the home of the Institute of Electrical Engineers, which made space available to the BBC in 1923. With the subsequent rapid expansion of broadcasting, the BBC moved to its purpose-built new home at Broadcasting House, Langham Place, in 1932.

6 The fourth (and final) BNOC season ran from 7 January to 16 February 1924, so (although Braithwaite makes no mention of it) the timing of his BBC employment on 28 February 1924 suggests that he may have worked at Covent Garden until the end of the season.

head. But even without this, his eyes could look right through one. I took my place in the big room at the top of the building which served as an office from where artists were toured around the BBC provincial stations. There was a table for the Music Director, Stanton Jefferies. The room also served as a library, and the first music librarian, Frank Hook and his assistant, Miss Wright, worked in such a small area that it could only have been a former lavatory.

Those people who now see the enormous music library at Yalding House would be intrigued at its small beginnings.[7] The size of the little entrance counter and the space behind it at Yalding House would be about the total size of the library at Savoy Hill. Frank Hook and Miss Wright used to work all hours without any assistance in those days, and either Hook or Jefferies invented the clever system whereby baskets of music and band parts, carefully selected into categories like Overtures, Symphonies, Selections, Suites, etc., were circulated to each station in such a way that each basket missed one station alternately. In this way, each station had a new basket of different music every week. This was a brilliant plan and whoever invented it certainly had a flair for organisation.

My first job (fascinating for a while) was another brilliant piece of organisation invented by Jefferies. I had to tour artists around the radio stations, booking hotel accommodation, selecting items, and arranging rail times and tickets. This was a tricky business, for if one was not careful, one would find an artist pushed around to an impossible extent, or put on a train 'in spirit' but still having breakfast at the previous hotel. An even worse error was to leave an artist still singing in one place and with no hope of getting to the next location in time.

In the early days of radio, certain agents would not allow their singers to broadcast, but this was a ridiculous state of affairs and didn't last long. At one 'fell swoop', Jefferies concluded an arrangement with Ibbs & Tillett[8] whereby all their artists (for a 'consideration') were free to accept contracts. Other agents soon fell in with this, and by dint of sheer perseverance, artists such as Clara Butt, Chaliapin and Harry Lauder were to honour us by their presence at the microphone, at enormous fees. This was sound finance as well as extremely good propaganda, and as a result, nothing remained of the opposition.

Some of the first members of the BBC were extremely clever men – Peter Eckersley the brilliant engineer, and his brother Roger; Captain Henry Joseph Round and his new 'breech block' of a microphone; Cecil Lewis the dramatist

---

7 Yalding House, located at 152–156 Great Portland Street, London, housed the BBC's vast central music library and the Third Programme (Radio 3) department from 1952 until 2013. It was subsequently moved to the BBC Archive Centre in Perivale.

8 Robert Leigh Ibbs and John Tillett founded one of the most respected concert agencies in London. After their deaths, John Tillett's widow, Emmie, took the helm. The agency flourished for most of the twentieth century.

and producer (charming); and the most capable of men, Rex Palmer, director of the old 2LO and a singer of no mean attainments (he sang *Elijah* with me later).[9] Kenneth Wright from Manchester joined the London staff about this time and I should think knew more about the early history of the BBC than anyone else.

Jefferies began to overwork himself. He conducted all the orchestral concerts and operas with the 2LO orchestra, and although he had a conductor on his staff (myself) he didn't use me to any extent. I was dying to have a go at the operas which were put down for performance, but with the exception of a repeat performance of a very popular light work by W.H. Bullock, *The Dogs of Devon*, I did no conducting at all. The situation changed however, when Percy Pitt, who had been appointed Musical Director, walked into the studio to hear a rehearsal of *Samson and Delilah*. Pitt came into the office after this in a towering rage, and although Jefferies wasn't the conductor, gave him a terrific trouncing for allowing a rather inexperienced conductor to make such an unholy mess of the music. Actually, I didn't hear the rehearsal, but the little experience I already had of opera gave me an insight into Pitt's anger, for Act Two of *Samson and Delilah* is not such a walkover as some people think.

The inevitable happened. Pitt turned around to me and in the middle of a tirade about tempi etc., pointed at me, telling me that I would have to conduct the operatic part of the programme. I mumbled my excuse (really to soften the blow to Jefferies' *amour-propre*) that I hadn't rehearsed the work. Pitt – I can hear his words now – roared out, 'Rehearsed! What do you want with a rehearsal? You know it backwards!' Secretly I was beside myself with elation, but outwardly took it all very calmly. That evening I did the performance. The two artists were John Collinson and Elsie Suddaby.

Next day Major Corbett-Smith, Director of the Cardiff 5WA station, telephoned Percy Pitt to ask who the conductor was and suggested that, as 5WA needed a Music Director, would he see to it that I was persuaded to take the job. Persuaded? I jumped at it! My enthusiasm for touring artists around the country had spent itself on the barren rocks of time and I was beginning to feel hemmed in by the frustration of office work. There has always been a side of my temperament that enjoyed complex organisational issues, but once I had mastered such intricacy, I had no further use for it.

Reith sent for me, but before that, the aforementioned unfortunate conductor (who had been brought in by Jefferies as his assistant) had been called to Reith's office and we met in the corridor – he returning from, and I going to, an interview. His face was the picture of misery and in answer to my

---

9   Mendelssohn's *Elijah* at Park Hall, Cardiff on 29 March 1929 with Dora Labbette *(soprano)*; Gladys Palmer *(contralto)*; Walter Glynne *(tenor)*; Rex Palmer *(baritone)*; Cardiff Musical Society Chorus; National Orchestra of Wales. Palmer had previously sung excerpts from *Elijah* on 29 January 1928 for a BBC Radio Studio Broadcast from 5WA Cardiff.

query as to what happened, he told me the worst. I was genuinely sorry. Reith told me that I could not be spared from the job of touring artists! There was no-one to take my place. I was crestfallen, but I had a perfect answer. Couldn't the conductor who had, I understand, been dispensed with, be offered the touring job? Reith wouldn't commit himself but I knew that he couldn't refuse. I pointed out that although I was a key man, at the same time I had been eating my heart out for six months because I really had spent all this time away from the practice of music. Pitt added all his weight to my plea, and within a few days I was sitting behind a desk at 39 Park Place, Cardiff, and took my first rehearsal with the orchestra the very next day.[10] From this moment my career restarted. I was equipped as never before for every kind of conducting, and threw my heart and soul into whatever music came my way.

In 1923, the provincial stations were complete entities in their own right. Each station, before simultaneous broadcasting, was equipped to do its own major programmes. Each station, indeed, had something of its own to contribute to the mesh of broadcasting, and wireless sets were not so far advanced or far-reaching as now. The listener had more variety and choice before simultaneous broadcasting took away most of the individuality of the regions. There was much to be said for and against both sides.

In 1929, the complete break-up of the local orchestras to make way for the large BBC Symphony Orchestra in London – ostensibly on the grounds of promoting the highest standard of orchestral playing, but mainly on the grounds of expense – was an expedient that did not reflect any credit on the BBC. This decision was fought against bitterly by the local directors of regions (and of course their conductors) but the weight of London was overwhelming. But this is anticipating, except to draw the moral that many years afterwards, the main provincial stations were to have that decision reversed. But in the meantime, it caused much unhappiness to musicians, and frustration to Regional Directors.

---

10 The BBC Regional Station studio for 5WA Cardiff was originally located above a music shop at 19 Castle Street. The first broadcast was on 13 February 1923, and baritone Mostyn Thomas sang *Dafydd y Garreg Wen*, the first Welsh language song on air. Just over a year later, in March 1924, 5WA moved to larger premises at 39 Park Place.

PART IV
(1923–1931)

NINE

A WELSH ADVENTURE

C ardiff, Wales, rugby, music, male voice choirs; these words are almost like the course of an interview with a psychiatrist. There is so much I could write of my sojourn in Wales that it would fill a book by itself.

Coming from New Zealand, the first thing I did was to go to Cardiff Arms Park. The groundsman showed me the place where Bob Deans was supposed to have scored the equalizing try – a try that was not allowed by the referee in that historic game when Wales defeated New Zealand in 1905 by 3 points to nil (their only defeat).[1] This sporting pilgrimage was repeated in November 1924, when the next all-conquering All Blacks team (which won every match, including the one against Wales at the St Helens ground in Swansea) went with me, in the pouring rain at dead of night with hurricane lamps, to dote over the same spot in silence.[2]

Rugby football; Wales was the place for that! The Newport v Cardiff games; Newport v Gloucester; Llanelli v Aberavon; or Cardiff v Swansea! The crowds; the singing! They say that the 1905 All Blacks, who had done their blood-curdling *haka*[3] before that great game at Arms Park, were spellbound and put

---

1 The Test between the Representative New Zealand Team or 'Originals' and Wales, played on 16 December 1905 in front of 43,000 spectators, is often referred to as one of the sport's greatest matches. It was the only match on that tour that New Zealand lost. Robert George (Bob) Deans (1884–1908) claimed to score a try that would have drawn New Zealand level at 3–3, but was pulled back over the line before the referee could catch up. The try was disallowed.

2 The 1924–1925 All Blacks earned the nickname 'The Invincibles' for obvious reasons.

3 The *haka* is a type of Māori ceremonial dance. It can be confrontational in sporting or battle situations; a sign of welcome to honour guests; a celebration of achievement; or a mark of respect. The most famous example is *Ka Mate*, composed around 1820 by Te Rauparaha, war leader of the Ngāti Toa tribe of the North Island of New Zealand. It was appropriated (not without controversy) by the All Blacks in 1905, and since 2005 has shared its role as the challenge to opposing teams with an equally controversial *haka*, *Kapa o pango*.

off their stride by the fervent singing of the Welsh crowd. Be that as it may, only those who have experienced such mass singing from 40,000 throats have any idea of the thrilling effect on a non-Welshman (or 'a foreigner from across the border', as I was called at certain acrimonious times).

The orchestra at 5WA was not very proficient and I pressed for a better one.[4] This gave me my first experience of the peculiar Welsh problem with which I had to contend, with varying degrees of success, for the next eight years. Wales, orchestrally, didn't really exist in a professional sense, and a number of our players were part-time instrumentalists. I remember one, a plumber by profession, who was always being called away at the most intricate moments to mend somebody's burst pipe. They had never before encountered anyone as single-minded as myself, as far as musical standards were concerned. I literally tore my hair in frustration at the ineptitude and casualness of attitude displayed by some of the players, and the constant defending of National aspirations against the inroads of one who only really wanted good performances. At times it was heart-breaking, but I hadn't striven to forge my way through much worse difficulties, just to be put off by something that patience could overcome. In the long run I think the Welsh musician assessed my work as an honest attempt to give Wales something it had never had before or, very largely, since.

The powers that be who decided these matters at BBC headquarters in London, had given me every assistance in building up a good studio orchestra, and I was glad to know that Percy Pitt brought his weight to bear in this matter. Percy, who has never had his due measure of praise as one of the greatest operatic musicians this country has ever known, became my most ardent supporter in all these matters. In his young days he had been an accompanist of outstanding quality, and although there are many gaps in my knowledge of his career which can better be supplied by others, I got to know his sterling qualities as a musical organiser when he became BBC Music Director. But the work he did as Music Director of the Royal Opera House, Covent Garden and concurrently with the BNOC, is inestimable. Percy spoke several languages fluently (a gift necessary at Covent Garden), and had such an unerring instinct for choosing exactly the right singers, English or foreign, that he was indispensable to that position. He was an excellent conductor, despite the derogatory remarks made by some of the 'young bloods' whom he engaged, and who often were quite unjust in their estimation of his desire for a selfless interpretation of other composers' works. Percy's conducting of *Louise* will always be remembered by those who know. He was always ready to take over any opera at short notice. His knowledge was sound and very deep. During the Grand Seasons he became the friend of

---

4   The Station Orchestra (really just an ensemble in 1924) had been conducted by the Station Director, Arthur Corbett-Smith.

all the foreigners, and one of his greatest friends was Giacomo Puccini. I, of course, learned these facts many years afterwards, especially when, after Percy's sudden death, all his scores were given to the BBC Library and included the full scores of the first editions of Puccini's operas inscribed most affectionately by the composer. I only got to know Percy really intimately during his BBC days. In the BNOC he had been a stern taskmaster, and there was no nonsense about his power over the lives of the 'young fry' of which I was only one. But in the BBC, he became mellower, and we struck up, I am proud to say, a 'man and boy' friendship that lasted until his death in 1932.

I was entrusted with the task of taking over all his projected programmes, and here I was given an insight into Percy's thorough methods. I was sent three big cardboard cases full of programme suggestions. Each item was meticulously described with its timing, keys, and the particular type of music etc., all in Percy's beautiful handwriting. When I came to conduct his programmes, I found that there were no mistakes; the timing was exact to a second, and each item 'came off' in the manner he had described.

I felt, in the few years I had got to know Percy Pitt really well, that he was rather a lonely and perhaps a slightly disappointed man. This was the impression I had. The BNOC had broken up, and another person was Musical Director of The Grand Season at Covent Garden. I suppose, like all operatic musicians, Percy missed the 'paint and the powder' of the opera house more than most because he was the link between the great Melbas of opera (and make no mistake; they *were* great!) and the resurgence of the home product of operas in English. Percy had lost much, but not quite all, of his activities, because apart from the BBC, he conducted at the Old Vic. But after the great days of the Grand Seasons, and the different (but no less) great days of the BNOC, he must have felt the same emotion all of us will surely experience in turn – that of a career fast slowing down. I hope I am not doing my dear friend an injustice in this. I realize most surely that there are others who can supply the gaps in this short tribute to one of the men I have admired so much, and to whom I owe so much.

To continue my years in Cardiff. Shortly after my advent in 1924 as Musical Director of the BBC at 5WA, the Cardiff Musical Society, a choral society of about 170 voices, was beginning to feel that the work of their conductor, T.E. Aylward, was fast becoming less dynamic owing to the inevitable anno domini.[5] Aylward had been one of the wonders and stalwarts of the English tradition of choral singing in Wales. Under his leadership and training, this choir gave some of the most beautifully rendered performances of choral works – and especially of unaccompanied part songs – that I have heard before or since.

---

5 Theodore Edward Aylward (1844-1933), cathedral organist at Llandaff and Chichester, conductor of the Cardiff Musical Society, and chorus-master for the Cardiff Triennial Festival.

The quality of pianissimo that this choir produced was really astounding. Certainly, the acoustics of the old Park Hall had something to do with it, but not entirely. Around 1925, Aylward retired and I was honoured in being chosen as his successor.[6] I threw myself into this entirely new aspect of conducting and succeeded in revitalizing this great choir with some of the energy they had temporarily lost. I came up against an entirely new principle involved in the very make-up of a musical organisation built up on an amateur foundation. Hitherto, I had only conducted professional musicians; now I had to develop a different approach in order to gain the same end, a good performance. That I succeeded in doing so is on record, but I was often driven to desperation by what seemed to me to be a casual attitude on the part of the 'good men and true' of the Committee. I had one great lieutenant and supporter in Raymond Butterworth, the Assistant Chorus Master and the natural leader of the tenor section. Butterworth's championship of most of my new ideas and decisions was full-blooded and forthright. He was a tower of strength.[7]

I remember how I studied Handel's *Messiah* for the first time and realized how humdrum their interpretation of this great tragic and poignant work had become. I set to and made up my mind to extract all the poignancy and drama I possibly could in my preparation of the work. Some of the older choristers, who had been singing the words for years without really knowing what they were singing about, were shocked out of themselves – some to be violently antagonistic, others to be one hundred percent enthusiastic – but in the long run I got my way. My first *Messiah* was a tremendous success and continued to be so in subsequent years.[8]

I tried to get out of the rut of the usual oratorios and performed such works as *Psalmus Hungaricus* (Kodály), *Hymn of Jesus* (Holst), *A Sea Symphony*, *Mass*

---

6 Braithwaite's first concert with the Chorus of the Cardiff Musical Society was Mendelssohn's Symphony no. 2 'Lobgesang' at Park Hall on 15 November 1925, with soloists Dorothy Silk and Rita Mattei *(sopranos)*, and John Coates *(tenor)*. The 5WA Radio Station Orchestra was augmented for the occasion and called the 5WA Symphony Orchestra.

7 Butterworth went on to conduct the choir in several radio broadcasts from 1933 to 1935.

8 Braithwaite conducted Parts II and III of *Messiah* on 15 April 1927, and Part II again on 6 April 1928. His first complete *Messiah* took place in Park Hall on 3 April 1931 with soloists Thea Philips *(soprano)*, Dorothy Clarke *(contralto)*, Ben Williams *(tenor)*, Kenneth Ellis *(bass)*, the Chorus of the Cardiff Musical Society, and the National Orchestra of Wales. The music critic of the *Western Mail and South Wales Echo* reported that 'The *Messiah* was sung as a complete work, with an intelligent appreciation of every meaning of the words and nuance of the music. The whole of the forces moved like an orchestra playing a great symphony, and the oratorio became a poem delineating the great tragedy of Calvary. Opinions may differ on the interpretation of the music, the tempi the conductor adopted, but there can be only one opinion on the beauty of the performance as a whole or on the vocal and orchestral beauty and impressiveness of the whole.... All concerned in an exceptionally beautiful performance are to be congratulated on the success attained under the baton of Mr Braithwaite.' *Western Mail and South Wales Echo* (4 April 1931), 7.

in G, *Toward the Unknown Region* and *Five Mystical Songs* (all by Vaughan Williams), and Elgar's big choral works – *The Kingdom*, *The Apostles*, *The Dream of Gerontius* and *King Olaf*. I wanted to do Wagner's *Das Liebesmahl der Apostel* (*Love Feast of the Apostles*) with several male voice choirs from the outlying districts, but difficulties cropped up which soon put a stop to that. My policy of performing new works in the repertoire gave the committee serious food for thought and the finances of the society began to wear a bedraggled look, but with the aid of the BBC, any crisis was averted for some years.

Cardiff is a city of unusual inequalities. With the squalor and blackness of Tiger Bay and the docks, yet with the most imposing new Civic Centre in Cathays Park, the noble National Museum, and nearby Duke Street and Bute Castle, Cardiff has all the appearance of a capital city.[9] But Cardiff has always been a puzzle to theatrical folk and serious musicians. In my day there wasn't a concert hall worthy of the name. The Park Hall was then a cinema, and Sunday (after a struggle with the Corporation) was the only day for concert giving. The Cory Hall was too small; the only other hall being the Assembly Hall in the City Hall which was (as we discovered some years after) impossible acoustically. Cardiff had little to recommend it for concert giving. Not only in music, but in drama, Cardiff presented almost insoluble problems.

I have thought about this many times. Cardiff is like one of those acoustic blank spots in an otherwise perfect concert hall or opera house: it doesn't matter how one tries to solve the problem, one remains defeated in the end. The reason may well be that the Welsh are right when they call Cardiff a cosmopolitan city. What they really mean is that it is neither Welsh nor English, and has no hard core of enthusiastic, culturally-minded people. Everything died on one's hands in Cardiff. Much as I hate to say this, there is some element of truth about it.[10]

But looking upon it purely from a selfish point of view, I was quite safe, as I was with the 'Mother of All' and it didn't matter much what happened so long as I produced programme after programme for the 'household'.[11]

---

9 Cardiff Town Hall was opened in 1904, and was renamed City Hall when city status was granted in 1905. The National Museum was opened on 21 April 1927 by King George V. The 5WA Station Orchestra was conducted by Sir Henry Walford Davies and Warwick Braithwaite.

10 This is how it must have seemed to Braithwaite at the time. The cultural resurgence of Cardiff in more recent years is demonstrated by its professional opera company; the BBC Symphony Orchestra of Wales; St David's Hall (a concert and conference centre); and most recently, the Millennium Centre at Cardiff Bay, housing opera, theatre, dance, drama, music and arts companies.

11 These domestic references suggest that Braithwaite viewed the BBC as a nurturing, protecting and sheltering environment whose staff were seen as members of its cosy household family, hence the widely-used early nickname for the BBC – 'Auntie'.

TEN

PILGRIMAGE TO BAYREUTH (1924)

The first holiday I had after becoming the Music Director of the Cardiff BBC Station was a return visit to Munich for the Festival, and also to Salzburg. In addition to this, the Wagner Festival of 1924 was on at Bayreuth and I had tickets for the whole repertoire.[1]

My first experience of Bayreuth gave me a tremendous thrill. Here at last I felt I was actually in touch with the great composer himself. Here was a monument (the Festspielhaus) erected in his own lifetime for the performance

Warwick Braithwaite's passport photograph, c.1924.

of his own works – a tribute to his colossal genius and also to his intuitive knowledge of acoustical perfection. The Bayreuth Festspielhaus holds the secret of good theatrical acoustics hidden in the very plan of the building. Wagner intuitively hit upon two fundamental acoustical 'laws' when he sketched the plan of his theatre. The first was what he called the 'mystic gulf' between the singer and audience, created by setting the stage back from the first row of seats, like a picture frame, so that the space between audience and picture frame gave an almost dreamlike quality to the setting. The other revolutionary intuitive discovery was the steep rake

---

1   In fact, this was a momentous occasion as there had been no Wagner Festival since 1914. Bayreuth reopened in 1924 and the season consisted of *Die Meistersinger von Nürnberg* (conducted by Fritz Busch), *Parsifal* (conducted by Karl Muck), and two cycles of *Der Ring des Nibelungen* (conducted by Michael Balling). The Danish-born tenor Lauritz Melchior, made his Bayreuth debut in *Parsifal* and also sang Siegmund.

of the stalls, from the first row set on a level (with the cowl surrounding the orchestra), to the back row.

Both these new ideas assisted acoustics in quite a fantastic way. The 'mystic gulf' allowed the voices to reflect the sound from stage to ceiling, and the steep rake brought the stalls (the further they were from the stage) nearer to the reflecting surfaces of the ceiling, and thus conserved the volume of the sound in a most remarkable way. Why other opera houses built or rebuilt since 1876 (the year of the opening of Bayreuth Festspielhaus) have not followed the same plan is a mystery. I suppose the basic (and base) reason for the building of opera houses in so ornate a style, both inside and out, is to satisfy those who regard the look of the thing as of first importance.

Wagner had a shrewd brain. As he only had the equivalent of £40,000 to spend on the building, he decided quite rightly that the bulk of the money would be spent on the stage, and he has written (in his prose works and the article on Bayreuth) that such a stage must have a height and depth for the perfect performance of his works. The other equally important part of the building was to be the revolutionary idea of the 'sunken orchestra' in which both the conductor and the orchestral players would be completely hidden from the sight of the audience. In this way, nothing would distract from the picture frame idea he had in mind. Whether he, far back in the recesses of his mind, also thought that the huge orchestral forces he employed for the *Ring* would be better subdued by being under the apron stage, is problematic. My contention is that logic and intuition are twin sisters and that it is more often logic that can take 'a wrong turning', whereas intuition seldom does. The auditorium, according to Wagner, was to be a plain building merely to house the audience, but that the stage was to be all-important and the latest thing in mechanical contrivances. The Bayreuth Festspielhaus, with its neat brick half-timbered outside blending with the surrounding trees, and the plain interior with the simple colour design of the ceiling and pillars, is most restful and completely satisfying. One is far more conscious in such a building that one is entering a temple of Art wholly devoted to the performance of music in perfection. The approach to music-making was absolutely simple, and I remember that I was the only member of the audience who wore evening dress – a lesson I learnt for subsequent visits. Alas, today (1951), things have changed somewhat and it is fashionable to 'dress' for performances. In the Twenties, the brochure only made the simple request that 'sporting' clothes should not be worn. To see the great tenor Melchior, who had been studying the *Ring* and *Tristan* in Munich when I was there in 1922, walking about during intervals of the rehearsals in Bavarian costume in the Holy of Holies was an eye-opener.

The great moment arrived when I discovered that visitors were allowed to visit Wagner's home, 'Wahnfried', in the mornings between 11.00 and 12.30.[2] I simply could not believe that this could be true, but it was worth trying. I walked to Richard-Wagner-Straße and there was the beautiful drive leading to the great man's house. I tremulously and, considering my fears, bravely forced myself to walk through the gates, and drove my unwilling limbs by sheer strength of will and purpose up to the steps leading to the front door. The bust of Leopold (the mad king of Bavaria) set at the front of the steps was passed by and at last, my trembling hand pulled the doorbell. Someone opened the door (it was Friedelind[3]) and I murmured the purpose of my visit in formal German. The little girl's eyes twinkled and she showed me into the hall shouting something about 'Grandmother'. I followed the direction of her eyes and saw an old woman with a white lace bonnet, leaning over the balcony above. She said something to the little girl in a small high-pitched voice, and the little girl smiled (eyes still twinkling with evident amusement at my nervousness) and opened the double doors to Wagner's study, and there I was in the most Holy of Holies. The old woman was none other than Cosima.[4]

Nobody else was in that room and I stood still for a while, trying to calm my suppressed excitement. At last, the grand pianoforte caught my attention. This was the now famous piano especially made for Wagner by, I think, Steinway or Bechstein, the lid of which was open.[5] On Wagner's desk was his own score of *Die Meistersinger*, lying open for all the world to see and touch. I turned over the pages of this wonderful score with awe and childish romance. Wagner's handwriting was the clearest and neatest of any composer's I have ever seen, and should be a lesson to some of our contemporary composers. When one remembers that *Die Meistersinger* takes well-nigh five hours to perform and was a 'diversion' between the second and third acts of *Siegfried*, the pure calligraphy shows the same endless painstaking attention to detail and characteristic musical devotion of that great man.

The walls of this study were one mass of shelves packed with thousands of books and hundreds of vocal scores, some of them with Wagner's own

---

2 Wagner's residence, 'Wahnfried' (a compound of the German for delusion and peace), became a museum in 1976. After much refurbishment and redevelopment, it reopened in 2015 as one of three buildings housing the Richard Wagner Museum.

3 Friedelind Wagner (1918–1991), Richard Wagner's granddaughter. Her parents were Siegfried Wagner and his English-born wife Winifred.

4 Cosima Wagner (1837–1930), illegitimate daughter of Franz Liszt. She was married to Hans von Bülow from 1857 until 1870, but began an affair with Richard Wagner in 1863. They were married in 1870. She managed the Bayreuth Festival for 22 years, and is credited with securing its future after Wagner's death.

5 Probably the Bechstein piano, which was a gift from King Ludwig II on Wagner's 51st birthday (1864) and used in the composition of *Die Meistersinger*, *Siegfried* Act 3, *Götterdämmerung* and *Parsifal*. Wagner also owned a Steinway, acquired in 1876.

annotations in pencil on the side of many pages. If Wagner read only half of the books (in many languages), what with his hours spent at composition and his own writings, he must have worked at least twelve hours a day. On his desk were odds and ends like pencils, pens, a rubber and little knick-knacks. I was ready to believe, and indeed *did* believe, that the pens were those used by the Master.

Someone came into the room at this point (it was Siegfried[6]) who perhaps was anxious that I should not stay too long, and who opened the French windows leading to the garden and murmured something about Wagner's grave, pointing to a group of Cyprus trees at the bottom of the garden. I had not realized that Wagner was buried in his own garden, and I could not bring myself to walk towards the grave hidden by the trees. But Siegfried took me by the arm and led me to it. He left me for a few minutes, and I walked around to the head of the marble slab in tremulous emotion. I stood there with bowed head, hardly daring to breathe (how long I could not say), a few feet only from all that remained of the mortal body of one of the greatest composers of all time. Why I cried, God only knows, but I did and copiously. That was the moment in my life wherein I swore utter devotion to my art, in the presence (for his presence was surely there) of a genius who altered the course and history of music in our time.

Before a subsequent visit to Bayreuth the following year, I wrote to Siegfried Wagner's wife, Winifred, telling her I wanted to meet Siegfried. He had been so kind to me on my first visit, but I had been completely inarticulate, as I was too overcome by emotion at the time to address one word of thanks. If I could meet him and perhaps be allowed to come to rehearsals? She wrote a charming postcard to my Bayreuth address, arranging that if I walked up to the Festspielhaus, Siegfried would be waiting for me at a certain time, seated at one of the tables outside the big restaurant during an interval of a rehearsal. I tortured myself with my immodesty and cheek once the arrangement was made, but again found myself up the long avenue and approached the Festspielhaus restaurant. Sure enough, there was Siegfried seated at the table as promised.

Ye Gods! How can I explain my folly? I walked towards Siegfried several times, but each time fear caught me in its terrifying clasp and I turned away. Turned away! I was paralysed, not with fear, but with such a devastating feeling of inferiority that it was no good. Siegfried, who did not help in the slightest, at last got up with a gesture of impatience and strode quickly to the stage door, and my opportunity was lost forever. I sat down in the chair he had vacated and waited until my brain began to work again, looking longingly at the doorway

---

6   Siegfried Wagner (1869–1930), composer, conductor and son of Richard Wagner. He was Artistic Director of the Bayreuth Festival from 1908 to 1930.

through which Siegfried had disappeared. Then slowly but surely, I walked down the hill cursing the weakness of my character.

Siegfried (whom I saw many times afterwards) was a short stocky man with a full face, blue eyes and a baldish head. He used to wear golfing plus-fours and a colourful knitted pullover during these rehearsal periods. Only at performances did I ever see him wearing a lounge jacket. His son Wolfgang, whom I met during the 1951 Festival, is very like him, only not so full in the face.

During that Festival of 1924, I made no further attempt to meet Siegfried because I was so ashamed of my foolishness. However, I was privileged to be taken over the building and stage, as well as into the sunken orchestra, many times. Karl Muck and Franz von Hoesslin as well as Siegfried Wagner were the conductors.[7] Karl Muck was the last of the authentic Wagner conductors, and I well remember the breadth of his readings, especially of *Tristan und Isolde*. The entrance of Tristan in Act One, with the long held note and following chords played broadly by the strings, was an unforgettable experience under his direction.

Melchior was the Tristan and Frida Leider the Isolde; what a pair of mighty Wagnerian singers![8] Perhaps the only other Tristan of that era to reach the stature of Melchior was our own Frank Mullings of the Beecham and BNOC days. Rosina Buckman, the New Zealand dramatic soprano, came very near to the greatness of Frida Leider. This is no exaggeration as only those who witnessed performances by these artists can well verify. Histrionically as well as vocally, the British artists suffered little by comparison. Curiously enough, Melchior and Mullings had much in common. Both were big men and both had similar types of voices, but Mullings was the better musician by a long count. In comparing the two Isoldes, Frida Leider was, by only a small margin, the greater artist than Rosina Buckman. This is an individual matter of taste, for I personally preferred the additional warmth of Leider's voice to Buckman's. But in *Die Walküre*, I preferred Buckman, as her voice in the war-like cry of Brünnhilde was more striking and therefore more appropriate to that role.

One of my minor thrills was to meet a very old gentleman, a Wagner devotee and maniac who had no room in his brain for anybody else's music. He had been present at the first performance of the *Ring* at Bayreuth when Wagner made his famous speech at the end of *Götterdämmerung* in which he said 'at

---

7 Franz von Hoesslin (1885–1946), German conductor who made frequent appearances at Bayreuth throughout the 1920s and 1930s. Karl Muck (1859–1940), German conductor who had been associated with Bayreuth since 1892 and was particularly admired for his performances of *Parsifal* there between 1901 and 1930.

8 Lauritz Melchior (1890–1973), Danish-born tenor who became a U.S. citizen in 1947. His roles at Bayreuth between 1924 and 1931 were Parsifal, Tristan, Siegmund, Siegfried and Tannhäuser. The Berlin-born soprano, Frida Leider (1888–1975), sang Brünnhilde, Kundry and Isolde at Bayreuth between 1928 and 1938.

last you have a true German art.'[9] The old gentleman lived on that memory and could repeat the speech verbatim. I was an ardent listener in my devoted days.

I went to the Bayreuth Festival many times during the next ten years, but discontinued after 1935, not returning until 1951. Hitler had begun to haunt Bayreuth and the attitude of the Festspielhaus people had become too nationalistic. It was about this time when, after Siegfried Wagner had died, there were rumours of a liaison between his widow Winifred and Hitler. From all accounts she had certainly sheltered him many times when he was 'on the run' in the years before 1935, when he used to arrive in the dead of night armed to the teeth against those (imagined or otherwise) who sought his downfall.

Winifred's main task was to keep the festival going when money was scarce, and her friendship with Hitler stood her in good stead when he came into power. Even when Jewish artists had been refused permission to sing at Bayreuth, Winifred called on Hitler's help and he, for as long as he could, assisted her by relaxing the fanatical decrees of his more strident Jew-baiters, much against his own inclinations. Perhaps it was this fact that gave rise to the insistent rumour that Winifred was a strong National Socialist, and which prompted the American military authorities to keep her away from the direction of the festival in 1951. The Management of the festival was taken over by her two sons, Wieland and Wolfgang, so why need she worry? [10] She is perfectly happy to be the central figure of the whole Festival to whom everyone naturally gives obeisance. She has lost none of the privileges that are hers by right.

Winifred Wagner is an English woman, born in Hastings. Her maiden name was Winifred Williams, but she added the surname of Klindworth, the famous German musician who adopted her as a little girl.[11] She went to Bayreuth, met Siegfried, and they instantly became enamoured of one another. By all accounts, she was a beautiful girl and today (1951) she seems to have lost none of her beauty.

Wagner had built an annexe to Wahnfried many years before for Siegfried and his family. This building is to the left of the main house as one goes up the

---

9 Wagner's speech from the stage on the last night of the first complete cycle of *Der Ring des Nibelungen* was improvised and, it seems, imperfectly heard by many present. The official version, published in 1883 states, 'Sie haben jetzt gesehen, was wir können; nun ist es an Ihnen, zu wollen. Und wenn Sie wollen, so haben Sie eine Kunst!' (You have now seen what we can do; now it's up to you to want. And if you want, we have an art!). Some thought he said '…we have a German art.' *Richard Wagner and His World*, ed. Thomas S. Grey (Princeton, N.J.: Princeton University Press, 2009), 407.

10 Wieland Wagner (1917–1966) and Wolfgang Wagner (1919–2010) were appointed joint Directors of the Bayreuth Festival in 1951. On the death of Wieland, Wolfgang became the sole Director until his retirement in 2008.

11 Karl Klindworth (1830–1916), German pianist, conductor, composer, violinist, arranger, publisher and close friend of Richard Wagner.

drive, and as I came away from the sacred precincts of Wagner's study on my first pilgrimage in 1924, the young grandchildren were being unceremoniously called to their midday meal from a spate of noisy skylarking outside the annexe.

ELEVEN

THE NATIONAL ORCHESTRA OF WALES

B ack in Cardiff, things went on in much the same way, but shortly after I was firmly entrenched in the job, I began to have trouble with some of those dissatisfied with me – the 'Welsh Nationalists'.

I really tried hard to find good Welsh compositions to perform, as I was very conscious of my obligation in this matter to Welsh composers. Time and again I had the hateful task of refusing to perform compositions which, although written by Welshmen, were not necessarily good because of that. I discerned two composers who had something to say, and performed pieces by them. Grace Williams[1] had just returned from Vienna and submitted several works to me which I performed when possible. The other composer, who seemed to have a streak of genius, albeit small, was Vincent Thomas of Swansea, the father of Wynford Vaughan-Thomas the BBC commentator.[2] There were other composers who also had performances, and one in particular I remember with pleasure, Maldwyn Price.[3] However, the two most talented composers were Kenneth Harding,[4] Principal Viola with the National Orchestra of Wales who wrote numerous works, all performed later, and a young genius, Daniel Jones[5], who had written suitcases full of works. More about Dan Jones later.

---

1   Grace Mary Williams (1906–1977), Welsh composer.
2   Vincent Thomas (1873–1940), Welsh composer noted particularly for his operas *Enid, Eos and Gwevril*, *A Romance of Spain* and *A Tale of Alsatia*. Braithwaite performed the latter two works in 1928 studio broadcasts from Cardiff for the BBC.
3   Thomas Maldwyn Price (1860–1933), composer and organist who had studied at the Royal Academy of Music.
4   Kenneth Harding (1903–1992), viola player and composer.
5   Daniel Jenkyn Jones (1912–1993), Welsh composer.

On the BBC staff was a talented, genial and friendly man called Reginald Redman – a composer of no mean output.[6] I brought Redman to Cardiff in about 1928 to assist me in my colossal task as conductor of the BBC National Orchestra of Wales (NOW), and the chorus of the Cardiff Musical Society. Redman did much of the donkeywork and was a wonderfully loyal colleague. He became my successor when I was to kick my heels out of Wales some years afterwards.

Now I have to speak of the most important event in the whole musical history of Wales – the formation of the National Orchestra. The idea that Wales should have an orchestra sprang out of decisions made at headquarters that each of the principal stations of the BBC should each have a good-sized orchestra for its own use. This was, in a way, a triumph for the Regional Directors. About that time (1929), the genial and popular musician, Sir Henry Walford Davies, sat on an advisory board to the BBC as well as being Director of the National (Welsh) Council of Music.[7] I believe I am correct in saying that Sir Walford must be given the credit for the suggestion that, as Wales had never had a professional orchestra, it would be serving the purpose of both the BBC and Wales if the orchestra became a public one and not merely a studio one. This was agreed to and the name had to be chosen. Would it be the Welsh Symphony Orchestra? No! There had been an amateur orchestra of that name.[8] My suggestion, The National Orchestra of Wales (abbreviated to NOW), won the day.

A conductor had to be appointed, and it was not a foregone conclusion that because the BBC were paying for the orchestra, the Music Director in Cardiff would become the conductor of the public concerts. I do not know who else put in for the honour, but I imagine my claims were fairly strong under the circumstances. As it turned out, my appointment as conductor was a very convenient measure, otherwise it might have been difficult to satisfy the claims of two different conductors. One would have been haunted by the fear that the studio commitments were taking too much of the players' time, and the other would have been determined to get all the rehearsal he wanted for outside concerts.

In the decision to form an orchestra, Sir Henry managed to keep all controversy away from the Nationalists and wisely decided against making it a public matter. I am not so sure now that it was the best thing to do, for later on when the orchestra was to be thrown away by the BBC (having served its

---

6 Reginald Redman (1892–1972), English conductor and composer.
7 Sir Henry Walford Davies (1869–1941), English composer, conductor, educator and broadcaster. He was Master of the King's Music from 1934 until 1941.
8 Two orchestras that played a significant role in the musical life of Wales were The Welsh Symphony Orchestra (founded by Sir Walford Davies), and Herbert Ware's Orchestra, which appeared in various guises, and broadcast between 1924 and 1944. Neither were professional or full-time.

purpose), and guarantors were asked to come forward, the few people and municipalities who could have saved the orchestra did not do so. More of this sad business later.

Having been appointed conductor by the governing body of the orchestra, consisting of BBC representatives, Sir Henry Walford Davies (for the National Council), Dr (later Sir) Cyril Fox,[9] Curator of the National Museum of Wales, and the Lord Mayor of Cardiff,[10] I had to set about finding players. As I knew all the good Welsh instrumentalists, there was no need for me to spend much time auditioning players in Wales, although I heard anybody who felt they had a chance. I arranged to hear players from as far afield as Glasgow, Manchester, Birmingham and London and travelled to these cities many times during the next three months. The difficulties were enormous and most exasperating. Some

Warwick Braithwaite at the time of his appointment as first conductor of the National Orchestra of Wales, 1928.

people love auditions but when you told them it was for a job in Wales, they turned up their hands in amused horror, despite the fact that it was a permanent job with a paid holiday and only 26 hours per week. As I would not allow the deputy system in the contract under any circumstances, other players laughed at the whole proposition.[11] Who wanted to bury himself in Wales?

Time was pressing on; the first advertised concert was only ten days hence, and I was still without a First Horn and a timpanist. I tried Newcastle, and Edward Clark,[12] the Musical Director at the BBC there, recommended a horn player who I engaged on that recommendation without hearing him. Never will I do that again, for the poor fellow turned out to be incompetent. The advent of the timpanist was a miracle. I was determined I would not have the old studio

---

9   Sir Cyril Fred Fox (1882–1967), English archaeologist who became Director of the National Museum of Wales from 1926.

10 Two Mayors were probably involved: Arthur John Howell (1927) and (Sir) William Richard Williams (1928).

11 It was common practice for orchestral musicians, especially in theatre orchestras, to send a substitute player when, for any reason, they were unable to perform. Conductors have been known to step onto the podium only to be confronted by an orchestra of unfamiliar faces.

12 Thomas Edward Clark (1888–1962), English conductor, music producer for the BBC, devotee of contemporary composers, and a significant contributor to the creation of the BBC Symphony Orchestra. From 1947 to 1955 he was President of the International Society for Contemporary Music.

player, who was deaf anyhow, but two days before, Lionel Falkman,[13] then resident in Cardiff, sent me a note saying he was sending me a young player for audition. He did not exactly recommend the player, as he had only played in a jazz band, but he felt he might turn out to be just the fellow I wanted. I only had half an hour to write out a fiendishly difficult timpani part when the player, Tony Harris, arrived. I gave him my *magnum opus* and left him to get used to it for exactly five minutes, after which I returned to the studio. Then followed the most astounding performance on the part of a timpanist of an unusual, new and difficult timpani concerto that I have ever heard. Tony Harris became a 'star' player and always caused a sensation wherever the orchestra played, for he had the wonderful knack of combining in himself all the percussion parts, and I never had to worry about making an arrangement of the parts for two players. Harris did that himself.

The first concert was a studio broadcast of *L'enfance du Christ* by Berlioz.[14] The orchestra inside the studio consisted of 36 permanent players, but was augmented to 60 for the major outside concerts in Cardiff, and to about 45 in Swansea. I had only regular 'outside' players, so for all practical purposes the size of the orchestra was probably around 60 players. This was the best we could do, and as the BBC footed the bill, it was all that could be reasonably expected. The BBC gave me an allowance of £35 per week for extra players, and by dint of saving on some programmes, I could have a real 'splash' on a programme requiring an enormous orchestra.

The first public concert was a grand affair. Sir Henry Wood was engaged to conduct the first half of the programme, and I did the second.[15] The orchestra was augmented by London players to 75. The concert was given in the Assembly Rooms of the City Hall, Cardiff, which the Corporation gave us without cost for all our Symphony Concerts on Thursday nights and for the popular concerts on Saturday nights.

---

13 Lionel Falkman (1892–1963), violinist and band leader. In Cardiff he conducted the Capitol Cinema Orchestra before moving on to Manchester and London.

14 Performed in English as *The Childhood of Christ*, on 8 April 1928. The artists were Eda Bennie *(soprano)*, Walter Glynne *(tenor)*, Glyn Eastman *(bass-baritone)*, Harry Brindle *(bass)* and The Station Repertory Choir. The orchestra was listed as the 5WA Augmented Station Orchestra, with the formal new name reserved for the first public concert.

15 The NOW made its public debut in the Assembly Room at City Hall on 12 April 1928. Sir Henry Wood conducted *Benvenuto Cellini* Overture (Berlioz); 'In fernem Land' from Wagner's *Lohengrin*; Symphony no. 35, in D, K.385, 'Haffner' (Mozart), Violin concerto no. 1, in G minor (Bruch) and 'Song of the Rhinemaidens' from Wagner's *Götterdämmerung*. In the second half, Braithwaite conducted *Fêtes* (Debussy), 'Wedding Waltz' from Dohnányi's *The Veil of Pierrette*; and *Welsh Rhapsody* (German). Soloists were Marie Wilson *(violin)* and Parry Jones *(tenor)*, both of whom contributed the expected solos with piano accompaniment provided by Hubert Pengelly. The leader of the orchestra was Albert Voorsanger. See Appendix 2 for more information on the orchestra and its fate.

The concert season was for six months, with a concert in the Patti Pavilion at Swansea once a fortnight. The weekly schedule of concerts was as follows:

Monday: Mid-day concert (National Museum of Wales) (free)
Tuesday: Free day.
Wednesday: Mid-day concert (National Museum of Wales) (free)
Thursday: Evening Symphony Concert (City Hall Assembly Rooms)
Friday: Mid-day concert (National Museum of Wales) (free)
Saturday: Mid-day concert (National Museum of Wales) (free)
Saturday: Evening popular Concert (City Hall Assembly Rooms)
Sunday: Popular concert (Park Hall)

In addition to these public concerts, the orchestra undertook all the work required for studio commitments. After the first year, the number of National Museum concerts was found to be too many, so the Friday concert was abandoned and this eased things somewhat. The Monday midday concert was broadcast throughout the whole BBC system for three and a half years (with the exception of the three weeks of holiday in each year) and the fame of the NOW spread far and wide. Finding items for all these programmes, and not repeating one item for at least six weeks, was no small task. I created a system whereby this was possible with a minimum of brain fatigue.

The NOW was launched with a great flourish of trumpets. Wales took it to its warm-hearted and excitable bosom. Eulogistic articles were written by such brilliant columnists as C.B. Rees[16] (now BBC Publicity) and Emrys Jones (later to be one of Northcliffe's young editors). The towns outside Cardiff clamoured for orchestral appearances. We devised a scheme whereby choral societies could hire the orchestra at a nominal cost so that these societies would get the 'feel' of orchestral accompaniment instead of the usual organ. If Wales only knew it, this was the one great opportunity to provide what had been lacking in its musical history – an orchestral foundation to the nation's musical culture. Alas, it was not to be!

The programmes were varied and every type and style of music was given. The mid-day programmes were not just a collection of loose items strung together, but followed a plan which proved most successful. The Monday concert generally included, as its main item, a symphonic poem; the Wednesday concert included a 'classic' symphony of either Mozart, Haydn or early Beethoven; and the Saturday concert was definitely popular, but good, light music. As the Monday mid-day performances were listened to so far afield, these became very important and ambitious. By 1931, I had performed the Sibelius symphonies

---

16 Clifford Burwyn Rees, author and critic.

and other major works of that great composer.[17] The Thursday night Symphony concerts in the City Hall were, of course, the major programmes, and like those of any other public orchestra, generally included a symphony and a concerto. The Saturday night concerts were popular, with sometimes concert performances of complete operas such as *Faust, Hansel and Gretel,* and *Samson and Delilah*.[18] All types of music and composers were called upon, as indeed they had to be, in order to cope with the number of programmes necessary.

*

In the middle of the orchestra's third year, there were ominous rumours of a most disturbing flavour. The audiences had never been big in Cardiff for the Symphony Concerts on Thursdays, and the Museum Concerts were free. The Saturday Popular Concerts were only full when I did operatic programmes, but these cost a lot of money. The Sunday Concerts at the Park Hall were fairly well attended. The 'depression' was on, and unemployment meant empty stomachs and emptier pockets. The Cardiff Musical Society began to get worried about their four concerts a year, and the *Messiah* was the only oratorio that drew a full house.

I was attacked, both in the council of the orchestra and outside, by inane letters in the press about my programmes for the Thursday Concerts. The main theme of the attacks was of course that the programmes were 'too heavy'. E.R. Appleton, the Station Director and Chairman of the Executive Committee, actually advised lightening the programmes to the extent of including Music Hall acts like Layton and Johnstone[19] in my Symphony Programmes! I have his note to the Executive Committee enlarging on the subject to this day. Appleton's main point was that he could not see why humour should be divorced from serious programmes! I agree that the situation was getting desperate, but there was another reason behind the attack, apart from the type of programmes. I searched my heart and mind very thoroughly on the question of symphony programmes and began to mix the types of music (including the Thursday

---

17 For a complete list of all Sibelius compositions performed by Braithwaite with various orchestras, see Appendix 3.

18 The complete Act II of Wagner's *Parsifal* was also given in concert. A feature of the NOW public concerts was the popularity of operatic arias and large excerpts, as well as the Wagner evenings. Complete operas under Braithwaite had already been given public performances by the augmented 5WA Studio Orchestra (*Tannhäuser* and *Lohengrin* [2]), as well as studio performances such as *The Rose of Castille, The Boatswain's Mate, The Bohemian Girl, Carmen, Savitri, Così fan tutte, Les cloches de Corneville,* and *Il trovatore*.

19 Popular African-American entertainers who were persuaded to move to England by Lord and Lady Mountbatten. They broadcast regularly for the BBC and appeared with great success in cabaret and variety. They also made many gramophone recordings.

concerts) with operatic excerpts, but alas, there was little response from the Cardiff people. The attacks from outside were generally of a biased nature. Most of the letters, as usual on these occasions, were signed 'Music Lover' or 'Cymru' or such Welsh designation and could be traced to disappointed Nationalists. But the attacks from inside were more serious.

About this time, some of my players were called to audition for the projected BBC Symphony Orchestra in London, and it was rumoured that in order to finance this orchestra, the regional stations were to be completely depleted of the best players. In other words, the orchestras in the Regions were to be sacked – as they eventually were in early 1930. The Cardiff station was able to hang on to the National Orchestra of Wales because of its outside reputation, but not for long, as the BBC headquarters could not condone a situation whereby all the regions except Wales were denuded of their local studio orchestra. The blow was bound in time to fall on Wales also. The answer to it was finance. The BBC had borne the whole cost of what the Welsh believed was their very own National Orchestra. The salary of the orchestra was £17,000 per year, but on top of this was the expense of artists, conductor, administration, halls, travelling, publicity and printing. A most generous financial gift from the BBC to Wales! Wales and its institutions never paid a penny towards the upkeep of the orchestra.[20] What was the point of the BBC going on with such a venture, especially as it was so easy to prove, in the case of Cardiff, that the orchestra was insufficiently patronized by music lovers to warrant the continuation of pouring out such large sums?

When it was announced that the orchestra was to be disbanded, the Welsh music lover began to search his conscience (and his pocket) as to the reasons. I do not think the average Welshman (by this time very proud of the NOW) ever realized where the money came from for the cost of the orchestra. Questions were asked in Parliament by various Welsh MPs. Letters began to pour into the BBC complaining of the injustice to Wales, but the disintegration went slowly on to the end.

I could only blame the BBC in one respect, and that was the tardy acceptance of the only feasible plan put forward to save the orchestra's existence. This was the suggestion that if Wales supplied a guarantee of £7,000 the BBC would supply the rest; on the face of it, a generous offer on the part of the BBC. But there were 'wheels within wheels' which saw to it that the mechanics of the plan were not oiled.

First of all, the brochure pleading to the Welsh for a financial guarantee was the most inept bit of left-handed English, without any appeal to Welsh sympathies. It was delayed until failure was completely assured. I saw this

---

20 Braithwaite is forgetting that the City Hall and National Museum facilities were provided free; a significant 'contribution' that rendered those venues unavailable for external hire at certain times during the concert season.

coming, but I was still a servant of the BBC as well as conductor of the orchestra, and I could not openly flout the authority of London. But I did the next best thing. I wrote a secret letter to Mrs Snowden (later Lady Snowden) – wife of the financial wizard of the Labour Party and who was one of the Governors of the BBC – for a six months extension in order to give the appeal for funds a reasonable time to ensure success or prove failure. It gave Wales a breathing space and it also gave me time to throw in my lot on this side of the appeal with some ideas of my own. When Mrs Snowden got the six months extension (no-one knew I had written to her), I launched out, after permission was sought and granted by Appleton the Station Director, in a fighting speech during the interval of a crowded Popular Concert at the City Hall, asking that a NOW Music Society of Donors Associates and Guarantors be formed.[21] I had planned the whole thing with great care. All the Press with their correspondents from London and other places were there, and I had hundreds of guarantee forms printed and slipped into the programmes. The atmosphere was positively dynamic; the enthusiasm shattering. Hundreds of forms were delivered to me afterwards with guarantees and donations, and two days afterwards the Press of the whole country acclaimed the idea with great enthusiasm.[22]

This amazing response belied all those who had been foretelling the failure of an appeal, and further strengthened my mind to go 'all out' for it, even if the BBC sacked me. I was caught up in what I had set in motion and there was no stopping me now.[23] On the Monday (22 December), Appleton called me into

21 Advance notice of Braithwaite's speech appeared in the newspaper on the morning of the concert. *Western Mail and South Wales News* (20 December 1930), 9. The content of the speech and the issues raised were well-covered by the newspaper in an Editorial (22 December 1930), 12, and an article (22 December 1930), 9.

22 In a follow-up letter to the *Western Mail*, written on 21 December and published on 23 December 1930, Braithwaite clarifies that the whole scheme is called the 'Welsh National Orchestral Society of Music Lovers, the sole object of which will be to establish the NOW on a permanent financial basis.' The first task was to raise £7,000 in three months so that the orchestra could continue for a further year. Similar societies were to be set up in Swansea, Llanelly (now Llanelli), Bridgend, Neat, Port Talbot, some valley towns, and North Wales.

23 Braithwaite wrote again to the editor of the *Western Mail*, 'Music lovers are reminded that the City Hall concerts present the opportunity, in all likelihood, of witnessing the glorious failure of an organization which has given excellent popular and symphony concerts to the city and contributed to the musical life of the nation with a standard of performance unequalled in the history of orchestral music in the Principality. Such a standard of playing is only possible with an organization continuously playing together, as has been the case with the National Orchestra of Wales, and those who remember the performances and programmes of the past three years will realize how much they are indebted to the men in the orchestra who have worked so hard for the cause of music. I wish to pay my unqualified and wholehearted tribute to those men who have given always of their best, especially during the last few weeks when the fate of the orchestra seems certain, and to wish that the people of Wales will make one last tremendous effort to avert what will be a distressing calamity.' *Western Mail and South Wales News* (23 December 1930), 5.

his room and gave me a dressing down for having made the speech. When I pointed out that he had given me permission to do so he could only stare at me in his cold blue one-eyed way and mutter meaningless phrases about BBC 'servants'. It was then that I knew that he himself was only carrying out orders from someone else. But I also knew in that moment that he was absurdly jealous of the success I had made of my first personal appeal to Wales, whereas his brochure had been received with a complete lack of interest. He even went so far as to persuade the General Council of the Orchestra to pass a resolution as follows: 'The Council decided in the best interests of the NOW the present time is inopportune for making an appeal to the public and resolved that Mr Warwick Braithwaite be advised accordingly.'

Not only this, but a letter from V.H. Goldsmith, the Assistant Controller of the BBC, went further and made the above resolution an order from the BBC to me. In this letter he informed me that the Secretary of the NOW was empowered to make this resolution public if necessary. I challenged him to do so, but, of course, the challenge was ignored. I secretly laughed at their efforts to scare me, because I knew (and they knew) that all I had to do was to reveal the kind of pressure that was being brought to bear upon me to an incredulous public and the fat would have been in the fire. Such a beautiful conflagration that would have been! But there was still a modicum of loyalty within me. It was not the BBC that I had to fend with, but certain short-sighted individuals within the BBC. In all this time never once did anyone in the musical side of the BBC say a word of discouragement. The people who killed the orchestra stone dead were the administration officials. They made all the decisions and they were, with few exceptions, not interested in music in Wales.

During the six months extended period,[24] I interviewed city treasurers, mayors, educational authorities and three of the richest men in the Principality. The Cardiff City Treasurer pointed out that by Statute Law, if Cardiff Corporation could raise the money, and I could get BBC permission and a decision on the financial control of the orchestra, then the Treasurer would press for the guarantee. The BBC refused to have anything to do with the idea, which only confirmed my first impression of unwillingness on their part to help. Without doubt, the BBC wanted the disbandment of the orchestra. A letter to me from the Director General concluded in sympathetic terms and was very encouraging, but he was soon to be appraised of other reasons by certain persons within the BBC as to the real fate worked out for the orchestra.

I made speeches during the interval of every concert, up and down Wales and even organized a 'Flag' day. I formed committees in the bigger centres. Three months before the end, Roger Eckersley came to Cardiff and offered me

---

24 Announced in the *Western Mail and South Wales News* (5 March 1931), 6.

a job at BBC Headquarters (at £100 less than I was already getting), to get me out of the way while the orchestra was slowly strangled to death.[25] I told him in rude language to put his job in the usual unmentionable place reserved for such offers. Sir Walford Davies was asked to approach Howard de Waldon, but whether he did so or not is doubtful.[26]

Sir Walford Davies, one of the instigators of the NOW, who was at the same time Director of the Welsh National Council of Music, had reinstated the defunct amateur Welsh Symphony Orchestra in almost indecent haste and was taking engagements for this orchestra which had previously been undertaken by the NOW.[27] Yet Sir Walford was the man who talked on behalf of me to the heads of the very institutions that might have put the NOW on a firm financial basis. I approached the Marquis of Bute, Lord Tredegar and Lord Plymouth who between them could have helped us out of our trouble, but without success.[28]

We had collected approximately £3,000 by about the fourth month of the appeal, and that was the end.[29] The situation was now hopeless as the players had to be given the required notice. There was nothing more to be done, and the last four concerts were given with a return to dignity. I made the occasion of the very last concert a Benefit for the members of the orchestra, and as I was leaving the building where our high hopes had been so cruelly dashed to the ground, a lot of tearful people bade me goodbye.[30] I turned to a friend saying, 'They came to bury Caesar, not to praise him.' It was a sad ending to a great adventure.

What Wales has lost by the demise of this orchestra is being more fully realized as time goes on, but the Welsh have a habit of moaning, groaning and wallowing in it instead of getting down and moving mountains. The

---

25 Roger Eckersley was Director of Programmes at the BBC from 1924 to 1934, and later Director of Entertainment.

26 Thomas Evelyn Scott-Ellis, 8th Baron Howard de Walden, 4th Baron Seaford (1880–1946), landowner, author, sportsman, and arts patron.

27 Announced as 'The New Philharmonic Orchestra' in the *Western Mail* (10 October 1931). Ronald Harding (conductor), Frank Thomas (leader), Sir Walford Davies (President), and J. McLean (vice-president).

28 John Crichton-Stuart, 4th Marquess of Bute, KT (1881–1947), Scottish peer and, until 1947, owner of Cardiff Castle; Courtenay Charles Evan Morgan, 1st Viscount Tredegar, (1867–1934), British peer; Ivor Miles Windsor-Clive, 2nd Earl of Plymouth PC (1889–1943), politician.

29 There had been two appeals. The first, announced by Braithwaite on 20 December 1930, aimed to carry the orchestra through until March 1931. The second, The National Orchestra of Wales Appeal Fund, announced on 28 March 1931, aimed to raise £14,000, which would be matched by the BBC, and ensure the orchestra's survival until October 1933. It raised just £1,178 9s. 5d., and where possible this was returned to donors. The balance of £465 16s 2d., was distributed to Cardiff charities (£100), the Musicians' Benevolent Fund (£100) and the remainder to members of the orchestra who were losing their employment with the BBC. Braithwaite's figure of about £3,000 probably includes donations to both funds. See also Appendix 2.

30 On 6 October 1931 at City Hall, Cardiff.

Depression is over and gone.[31] Why has Wales not financed an orchestra in more prosperous times? During 1951 I spent two weeks in Swansea and Cardiff and saw something of the Valleys, and there is no longer the terrible problem of unemployment and its accompanying poverty. Yet when a new NOW had been mooted a year before, Cardiff and Swansea Corporations (and perhaps others) had turned the proposition down. The Welsh proudly call themselves a musical nation when they really mean that they do a hell of a lot of singing.[32]

So, was the BBC right to terminate the NOW? On the face of it, yes, except for one thing. While the NOW was kept alive, the BBC could always say that it was really doing something for Welsh musical aspirations and, in time, would have turned the Welsh into a more rounded musical nation. That is where the BBC was really short-sighted, for it struck a blow to a weak, depressed and financially poor nation, when a bigger gesture would have been balm to the soul.

Many people, knowing the history of the NOW, will say that I have not told the whole story. Perhaps I have not, but what is the good of raking up the past? I have deliberately left out certain sordid and unhappy references to those who did so much to kill a great endeavour. What is the point of washing a lot of dirty linen in public? The orchestra has gone, and if it had been wanted strongly enough by the Welsh people, it would have been saved. The six-month extension, and my campaign during those six months, gave ample time to those who could have saved the orchestra. Looking back on it now, I believe the BBC would have relented in their attitude if the desire from Wales had been strongly enough expressed.

Sir Percy Watkins, Secretary of the Welsh Section of the Board of Education (a good friend of mine who was very keen about the NOW), and Dr Tom Jones, Deputy Secretary of the Cabinet, were both approached by Sir Walford Davies during May 1930. But how were they approached? What line of argument or persuasion was taken with them? Sir Percy could have, if he were so moved, persuaded the Board of Education to sponsor a movement in Wales, headed by the Board, giving it its authority and getting a quid pro quo in children's educational circuits for a donation of say £1,000 per year. Sir Percy was, while with me, eager to co-operate. The Cardiff City Treasurer was prepared to press for a scheme of support from the rates and had actually shown me how this could be done by Statute Law.

---

31 Braithwaite is writing in the 1950s. The lack of public support for the NOW can largely be blamed on the Great Depression that began in 1929 and lasted through much of the 1930s. A dramatic fall of 390,000 in the population by 1939 was accompanied by low incomes and everything that comes with lack of work and money. In retrospect, it was not a good time to launch a new professional artistic venture.

32 Braithwaite is railing against the Welsh obsession with male voice choirs and eisteddfods (competitive festivals of literature, music and performance).

These men, faced with a terrifying array of figures, were scared off and had to admit that they alone could not finance the orchestra. Yet all it needed was strength of purpose, resolution and courage to start a movement which would have gathered momentum once the initial plunge had been taken. Why was this never tried?

Then who was behind the decisions of the National Eisteddfod Committee who, once the Llanelli Committee engaged the NOW, saw to it that it never happened again? The visit of the NOW to Llanelli was a scene of amazing enthusiasm. There were two visits; one to the Proclamation Concert, where the audience went literally mad with an almost frightening enthusiasm, and the Eisteddfod itself a year later. There were indeed wheels within wheels here for up until then the London Symphony Orchestra had been engaged year after year. Did the LSO complain to someone at headquarters that they were being superseded in an engagement that they had always undertaken? To Llanelli goes the honour of being the only town to seize on the advent of a national orchestra with enthusiasm. To the LSO, it was merely one engagement of the many, in a year. To the NOW, the Eisteddfod engagement was a gesture of confidence in its future. That confidence was shaken badly by the next Eisteddfod term.

Wales had always been proud of its national aspirations and here was a chance to further the fortunes of its own National orchestra, yet someone deliberately threw away that chance. It was a blow from which the orchestra could never recover. It gave just that sort of ammunition required to seal its doom, and it was given by Welshmen. How could the BBC forgive a Wales that treated its gift in such a callous way? This blow alone took the heart out of the orchestra's most ardent supporters and the full history of that disgraceful bit of sabotage has yet to be written. I only know what happened, but I do not know why. Someone in Wales will know the truth of the matter, and one day I hope it will come out.

What was my plan for the financing of a National Orchestra of Wales? The plan was not a new one; it had been tried with success in other localities. In Wales there were additional sources of revenue which did not exist in other parts of the country. First of all, the bigger towns could contribute sums of money from their rates. This was allowable by Statute Law. By this law the limit of two pence in one pound could be called upon for (I forget the exact wording) public pleasure and amusement. On top of this, each Educational Authority was allowed to spend a sum on Children's Education in Music.

Glamorgan County Council had, I believe, other funds that might be tapped in small areas. The Universities might have been called upon in a small way. Then there was the well-endowed National Council of Music. Perhaps the Arts Council of Great Britain, The Carnegie and Harkness Trusts could have been approached. But the chief thing of all was that some such institution should have launched this fund by coming out boldly with a generous proposition. Once the foundations of sure finance had been laid, the BBC would, in all likelihood, have helped by paying for broadcasts. There was also the question of engagements. Wales badly needed an orchestra for its Choral Societies, its National Opera and its Eisteddfod. The peculiar difficulty of public concerts in Wales could have been overcome.

If New Zealand could have a permanent orchestra of 65 players with its 2 million population in far-flung towns, was it not possible for Wales to have one with its 4 million population in a small compact area? There I must leave the question for the Welsh.[33]

*

In relating my part in the sad affair of the National Orchestra of Wales, I had almost forgotten to mention certain events that were very important in my private life. I had married, but unwisely, and after two years or so this broke up. Several years afterwards, in 1931, I married again and I now have three children – a girl and two boys.[34]

Something that came into my life in Cardiff and had a great impact on my mind was the music of Jean Sibelius. I had, up until 1926, known only pieces like *En Saga* and his little piece, *Valse Triste* (not to be despised by any means). Quite by chance, when

Lorna Constance Davies, c.1928

complaining to Arnold Trowell[35] about the difficulty of finding interesting and 'new' music for the extensive number of concerts I was doing, he advised me to do a Sibelius symphony. I expressed doubts about the composer of *Valse Triste*, but he told me that I would be more than agreeably surprised by the excellence of the bigger works. On his recommendation, I put into the programme the

---

33 In fact, it was left to the BBC, ultimately with stunning results. See Appendix 2 for more information.

34 Braithwaite's first marriage was to Phyllis Greatrex (nee Bain), with whom he had a daughter, Barbara (1924-2001). In 1931 he married Lorna Constance Davies (1904-1990), and they had two sons – Sir Rodric Quentin Braithwaite (1932–), and Nicholas Paul Dallon Braithwaite (1939–). See Appendix 1.

35 Arnold Trowell (1887-1966), New Zealand-born cellist and composer. Braithwaite used Trowell as soloist on 11 occasions between 1927 and 1933, and conducted his symphonic poem *The Waters of Peneois* in Cardiff on 28 November 1929. Trowell performed Elgar's Cello Concerto in the same programme.

Fourth Symphony without even having seen the score. In a few days the schedules were published so there was nothing to do but go through with it. The orchestral players were just as much in a fog as I was, but I persisted until the light began to shed a beam in the dark places.[36] I still think the Fourth Symphony is too bare and stark, but after this first experience, I instinctively knew that a great and original mind had made that music. Quickly after that performance I voraciously devoured his other symphonies, and by the time I left Cardiff, I had conducted most of Sibelius' orchestral works.[37]

Sibelius had cracked wide open the contentions of the 'Twelve Tonists' that the diatonic scale was not only outworn but that it was impossible to write any more tunes in it. Sibelius showed conclusively that if a composer really had something to say, it could still be said in the diatonic. His originality is not in question. He exploited the very opposite style of his early contemporaries Strauss and Schoenberg whose long-winded and Germanistic verboseness followed that of Bruckner, and he gave a new life to composition with his short 'no nonsense' type of themes. Sibelius doesn't explain his tunes in a first movement and endless development way, but simply states that this is all he has to say about this tune. His 'bridge' passages are short and very much to the point. Let us get to the whole point of the movement without any padding. No padding is indeed his watchword, and what a splendid watchword it is after the endless 'composition' of his contemporaries. Sibelius spent his studentship in Germany and it says much for his strength of mind that he shows no Germanic influence in his music. It also says much for the great firm of music publishers, Breitkopf & Härtel, that they published most of his early works and indeed some of his later, more terse, ones.[38]

For a long time, my championship of Sibelius in Cardiff (and Leslie Heward's similar proselytising with the Birmingham Symphony Orchestra) fell on deaf ears. But as we both were quickly conscious of Sibelius' greatness, so in a very short time audiences everywhere began to acclaim him. Neither Heward nor myself were the first conductors to perform the Sibelius symphonies, as Sir

---

36 This first performance in Wales was given at City Hall on 27 November 1930. The newspaper critic wrote, 'The National Orchestra of Wales had been augmented considerably and the work of the Finnish composer was given a careful and successful performance. Mr Warwick Braithwaite and the NOW made a really fine effort and the brooding dreary spirit of the four movements was well expressed.' *Western Mail and South Wales News* (28 November 1930), 9.

37 Braithwaite is justifiably proud of his early advocacy of Sibelius. All seven of the symphonies were performed in Cardiff concerts (within a twelve-month period) in the following order: no. 4 (27 November 1930); no. 2 (22 April 1931); no. 5 (7 May 1931); no. 6 (27 May 1931); no. 3 (10 June 1931); no. 7 (24 June 1931); no. 1 (5 August 1931). See also Appendix 3.

38 Breitkopf & Härtel is also the publisher of the critical edition of *Jean Sibelius Works* whose first volume appeared in 2005, edited by the National Library of Finland and the Sibelius Society of Finland. When completed, the series will contain all the surviving works of the composer.

Henry Wood had done so already during his Promenade concerts but, with few exceptions, these works only had their one performance under Wood. As the public was still engulfed in the Germanic and long-winded composition of the nineteenth century, Sibelius simply did not register with them. Latterly, in my Monday Museum concerts for Cardiff broadcasts over the whole BBC system, I contrived to give one Sibelius piece whenever possible and I am sure that that policy alone began to drive into the minds of the listening public the greatness of the Finnish composer.

When I returned to London and began to conduct once again for the BBC, I had to convince the programme makers that Sibelius was really deserving of a place in their schedules. About this time, Walter Legge (who I was to meet many times afterwards[39]) brought over Robert Kajanus, Sibelius' great friend and conductor of the Helsinki Symphony Orchestra.[40] He was to record several works at the HMV studios in Abbey Road and I was fortunate to be present while this veteran conductor, who had given many of Sibelius' works their first performance, made these recordings. Both Heward and I managed to carry on the work of familiarizing our audiences, either through the BBC or in the concert room, until other conductors quickly made up for lost time.

Some years later, Sir Thomas Beecham began to perform the first and second symphonies and shortly afterwards, pieces like *Tapiola* (that truly great symphonic poem), *Pohjola's Daughter* and many others. Beecham was the champion of the luscious and romantic music of Delius, but once *he* entered the lists in Sibelius' favour, the battle was won. Today, if a conductor wants to win over his audience and bring his concert to a triumphant close, the Sibelius first or second symphonies are among his preferred choices.[41]

Before closing the door on my orchestral experiences in Wales, let me just say that the surrounding country outside Cardiff is surpassingly beautiful. People always smile when one mentions the beauties of South Wales,[42] yet I don't think I have ever seen such small but beautiful gems tucked away in the most unexpected places. At the back of my father-in-law's home is a little ravine called *Coed Garw*, named 'Little Switzerland' which is breathtaking in the spring and summer.[43]

---

39 Walter Legge (1906–1979), legendary classical record producer for EMI.

40 Robert Kajanus (1856–1933), Finnish conductor and prolific composer. In 1930 he recorded Sibelius' Symphonies 1 and 2 for English Columbia in London. Braithwaite is recalling Kajanus' second visit to London (in 1932) to record more Sibelius for HMV, including *Belshazzar's Feast*, *Tapiola*, *Pohjola's Daughter*, and Symphonies nos. 3 and 5.

41 Braithwaite, writing in 1951, might also have added the Fifth Symphony of Sibelius to his list.

42 The landscape of South Wales bears extensive scars of industrial activity, especially mining.

43 This is a valley area surprisingly close to Bettws, Newport, often captured and named by nineteenth and twentieth century artists, photographers and guide book writers as 'Little Switzerland'. The viewpoint at Allt-yr-yn (Alteryn), across the Monmouthshire and Brecon Canal to the wood, Coed Garw and beyond, unfortunately now incorporates the M4 motorway.

The Gower coast has an endless number of fine beaches and striking cliff formations. Many times I walked all over the surrounding country, from St Mellons to Caerphilly and back to Llanishen, in a single day. There were trips across the Severn Estuary on one of Campbell's pleasure steamers[44] to Minehead, and thence by foot, right down the coast through Lynton and Lynmouth, Woolacombe, Combe Martin, Ilfracombe, Barnstaple and Bideford, Charles Kingsley's Westward Ho, and right into Cornwall as far as Harscot, five miles from Bude.

Soon I was to find myself back in London after the strenuous last few months of the NOW, and although I had saved enough money, I was very tired. But, after a few weeks, I was champing at the bit and restless once more to be conducting. My grieving for the National Orchestra of Wales was soon thrown off, and I set about entering the next stage of my career.

---

44 Peter and Alexander Campbell used the White Funnel logo from 1893 for their fleet of paddle steamers using the Bristol Channel.

BRIDGE PASSAGE
(1931–1937)

BY

ROGER FLURY

BRIDGE PASSAGE

(1931-1937)

At this strategic moment in Braithwaite's career, eleven pages of his typed autobiographical manuscript are missing.[1] The gap was noted when the manuscript was deposited at the Alexander Turnbull Library, National Library of New Zealand, and extensive searching within the wider Braithwaite papers and amongst the family, has failed to locate them. So, it falls to the editor to attempt a bridge passage that will link the end of the National Orchestra of Wales experience to the re-establishment of his career in London and beyond. But first, a little more needs to be said about the conductor's time in Cardiff.

Braithwaite was curiously muted in his public comments about the situation with the National Orchestra of Wales. He had done everything asked of him during his tenure – educational concerts, popular programmes, adventurous repertoire, regional touring and the development of a fine ensemble of players. He had promoted the orchestra far and wide, so that its profile was raised within the BBC and amongst the broadcasting audience.[2] Messages praising the NOW were received from as far afield as South Africa, and they were proudly reprinted in the *Radio Times*.[3] A good relationship had also been developed with the editor of the *Western Mail* newspaper, and many column inches had been dedicated to discussing the merits of the orchestra. The steady development of standards, and the expansion of the repertoire heard in Wales, had been charted through the writings of the paper's anonymous reviewer 'Orpheus'. Only when

---

1 Pages 108–118 of the typed manuscript.
2 Among the notable admirers of the orchestra (via radio) was Sir Edward Elgar who, in a letter to Braithwaite quoted in *Western Mail*, wrote: 'I should look forward to meeting your orchestra, which I have heard – in the distance – with the greatest pleasure.' *Western Mail* (10 February 1930), 9.
3 '…the orchestra played the *Men of Harlech*, and played it as I have never heard it before; it was simply glorious.' *Radio Times* (26 April 1929), 679.

things began to look perilous did Braithwaite write letters to the *Western Mail* appealing for the people of Wales to support their orchestra or risk losing it. Out of sheer frustration at the slowness of the authorities to act, he set up his own fundraising campaign, but in the end, no amount of activity could alter the fate of the orchestra. The creation of the large BBC Orchestra in London, ostensibly to improve orchestral playing standards in the capital, had to some extent stripped the regional orchestras of the best players, and all efforts at BBC headquarters were necessarily focussed on the new task ahead.

The last few days of the National Orchestra of Wales in October 1931 must have been difficult for the many players who were shortly to find themselves unemployed. Only eight instrumentalists, plus the fine pianist Hubert Pengelly who had accompanied solo artists in the studio and on the concert platform, were to be retained as the Western Studio Orchestra; others would have to turn to private teaching or seek orchestral work elsewhere. Braithwaite ensured that the orchestra performed with dignity and professionalism, and their last day was captured for posterity on the steps of City Hall, by the *Western Mail* photographer.

The National Museum lunchtime concerts on 3 and 5 October consisted of a request programme and an all-British programme respectively. For the former, Braithwaite selected music by Verdi, Wagner, Edward German, and John Foulds. For the Monday concert on 5 October, broadcast on the National Programme, Braithwaite scheduled an all-British programme with music by Thomas Arne, Elgar and Walton. He conducted his own *Legend for Orchestra 'Hinemoa'*, and then handed over the baton to composer and Assistant Conductor, Reginald Redman, for a performance of Redman's *Nocturne*.

On the same evening, the orchestra broadcast a studio programme (with bass-baritone soloist Glyn Eastman) listed in the newspapers and the *Radio Times* as 'Retrospect; a programme of some of the most popular music played by the National Orchestra of Wales':

Wagner: *Tannhäuser* – Overture
Stanford: *Songs of the Sea* – The Old Superb
Sullivan: *Ivanhoe* – Ho! Jolly Jenkin
Sibelius: *Lemminkäinen Suite, op. 22* – Swan of Tuonela
Bach: *Suite no. 3 in D* – Air (on the G String)
German: *Welsh Rhapsody*

It was an odd programme and hardly lived up to its billing. The works by Bach, Wagner and German had certainly appeared quite often in the orchestra's programming, but the remaining pieces were comparative rarities and could hardly have been considered amongst the most popular music played.

The next day saw the very last subscription concert which, at the suggestion of Braithwaite and the orchestra's many admirers, took the form of a Farewell Benefit Concert for the National Orchestra of Wales, with Louis Levitus *(leader and solo violin)* and Ronald Harding *(cello)*. The works had been selected by Braithwaite from patron submissions to the *Western Mail*, and the final choice was Wagner's overture to *Die Meistersinger von Nürnberg*, Handel's Concerto Grosso op. 3, no. 2 in B flat, Dvořák's Symphony no. 9 'From the New World', the ballet music from Gounod's opera *Faust*, the ever-popular 'Air' from Bach's Suite no. 3 in D, and the crowd-pleasing *Welsh Rhapsody* by Edward German. The anonymous music critic of the *Western Mail* wrote:

In the farewell benefit concert given at the City Hall, Cardiff, on Tuesday night to the National Orchestra of Wales, one of the finest schemes ever designed for the advancement of music in Wales came to nought.

The farewell concert was attended by the biggest and the most enthusiastic audience the orchestra has had in the City Hall, and, although it was referred to as the 'funeral' of the NOW, it was a triumphant conclusion complete with the Oration. The 'baked meats' in the shape of the returns will go to assist the members of the orchestra temporarily – one hopes sincerely – out of employment.

The programme had been arranged on the popular side without departing from the standard of music to which the orchestra, under Mr Warwick Braithwaite, has remained steadfast to the end…and it was in the playing of the 'New World' symphony that the orchestra found itself and demonstrated the results of the work of the past three years. Incidentally, it increased the regrets of the patrons that the skill of ensemble playing has been brought to naught. The orchestra has never played with more finish than they displayed in the Symphony, the lovely second movement reaching as near perfection as an orchestra of the size could hope to attain…

The NOW passes into the category of musical lost opportunities and repeats the experience of the Triennial Festival. But its work has not been in vain, nor is its influence lost on music in Wales.

Western Mail (7 October 1931), 11

The orchestra had really little time to rest on its laurels. The following day (Wednesday 7 October 1931) it gave its final lunchtime concert in the National Museum of Wales. There was just one work, Beethoven's Symphony no. 5 in C minor, op. 67, given more as a gesture of defiance than a valediction.

The Museum Director, Dr Cyril Fox, addressed the audience, thanking Braithwaite for 'the taste and scholarly knowledge of his art', which had resulted in their hearing so wide a range of the finest music. He thanked the orchestra for its magnificent interpretation of those works, and concluded that 'thanks to your united efforts…we have realized in this great national building, that a museum which does not illustrate the art of music is an incomplete home of the Muses.'

In reply, Braithwaite – exuding diplomacy but no doubt by this time battle-weary and bitterly disappointed – spoke of the 'happy relations' that exist between the orchestra, himself, and the people of Wales. His main concern was that their efforts towards the building up of a taste for the best music should not be forgotten, and that the public thirst for music should not be allowed to die. His final comment, at a time when the future for professional music-making in Wales had never looked more bleak, was remarkably prophetic. He sincerely hoped that when times were better, the National Orchestra of Wales would rise again.[4]

Ironically, a newspaper article reported that because many in the audience at the NOW's benefit concert had been unable to obtain programmes, copies autographed by the conductor would be available for sale. Proceeds would increase the funds to be distributed to those players who found themselves unemployed.[5]

There can be little doubt that Braithwaite's contribution to music in Wales, between 1 June 1924 and 7 October 1931, was staggering in its vision and execution. His appointment was not universally welcomed, possibly because of his lack of any connection to Wales, other than by marriage, and he was viewed with suspicion as a man of high-brow tastes.[6] Given the general disconnect between the BBC headquarters and its regional stations throughout this period, the hasty appointment of Braithwaite to Cardiff could be interpreted as simply bridging a gap without much thought to the consequences. It is doubtful that anyone at the BBC had much idea of Braithwaite's potential, and perhaps that explains why his BBC career developed under the radar. Unlike the BBC's 'star' conductors, Braithwaite seldom came under the spotlight and his photograph appeared only rarely in the pages of the *Radio Times*. But from modest beginnings, he applied himself to the development and expansion of the studio orchestra, presenting not only programmes of popular material as required, but adding more 'serious' pieces as a method of expanding tastes and encouraging demand. He was aided to a great extent by the Station Director, E.R. Appleton, and by the determination of Sir Walford Davies, whose dream of a full-sized professional symphony orchestra for Wales provided the much-needed impetus to find a collaborative solution.

Braithwaite had landed, by good fortune, on fertile soil which nurtured his ambition and allowed his abilities as an orchestral conductor to flourish over a

---

4   *Western Mail and South Wales News* (8 October 1931), 11

5   *Western Mail and South Wales News* (10 October 1931), 14.

6   John Davies, *Broadcasting and the BBC in Wales* (Cardiff: University of Wales Press, 1994), 83.

period of seven years. The statistics are impressive, and it is doubtful that any conductor at the time could have matched him for sheer productivity. Between 1924 and 1928, the 5WA Studio Orchestra gave 6,156 performances of 3,058 works by 721 composers. Between 1928 and 1931, the National Orchestra of Wales gave 3,590 performances of 1,178 works by 231 composers.[7]

If it was through a certain amount of luck that Braithwaite found himself at the helm of an orchestra that combined the demands of a busy concert schedule with the requirements of a studio band, it was his own talent and focussed dedication that kept him there – at least until the rug was pulled from beneath his feet by the combined actions of local authorities and the BBC. This act of treachery was aided and abetted by a perfect storm of public indifference in Cardiff, musical politics, and the onset of the Great Depression.

Braithwaite was fortunate in having a series of fine orchestral leaders, beginning with Leonard Busfield who served for the life of the 5WA Studio Orchestra. With the creation of the NOW, Albert Voorsanger took on the role for the first year, and was followed in 1930 by Louis Levitus, who continued on as Leader of the Western Studio Orchestra until the end of 1932. These players not only led the orchestras, but played in various ensembles that helped to fill the broadcasting schedules. So, it was not unusual to find the orchestra performing a lunchtime recital in the National Museum, accompanying a singer in the studio at 3 p.m., and broadcasting a studio concert in the evening followed by the Station Trio traversing a series of Beethoven piano trios. Quite how the players found the time to rehearse and the energy to perform, remains a mystery.

The free concerts at the National Museum had been of great mutual benefit to both organisations, so it was welcome news that the studio ensemble, greatly reduced in size to nine players and renamed the Western Studio Orchestra, would continue to provide lunchtime programmes three times a week, with Braithwaite's assistant, Reginald Redman, taking over the duties of Music Director and conductor.[8]

Just before Braithwaite officially left the employment of the BBC on 31 December 1931 to enter the uncertain world of the free-lance professional musician, he had been called upon to replace an ailing Robert Heger for three concerts with the Scottish Orchestra. Reviews in *The Scotsman* and *The Musical Times*, suggested that Braithwaite had developed into a fine conductor. Taking

---

7   In addition to complete compositions, these statistics include parts of works (e.g., an aria or a movement from a symphony or suite) if performed as a separate item. The *Radio Times* often failed to list programme content, and even if it did, the detail was not always an accurate record of what was played. Playlists of programmes during this period have not been kept in studio archives, but it is reasonable to conclude that totals would have been even higher.

8   See Appendix 2.

on Elgar's Symphony no. 2, a challenging work under any circumstances, but particularly at short notice and without any previous performances under his belt, reaped glowing praise from the critics:

> The chief work for the programme was nothing less than Elgar's second Symphony, which Mr Braithwaite conducted, and the orchestra played, to magnificent effect.
>
> *Musical Times* (1 February 1932), 169.

> Last night Mr Braithwaite gave full play to its magnificence, but never at the cost of clearness. Elgar has ordinarily so much to say in his music that his crowded statement is not always easy to follow. Mr Braithwaite, however, kept everything in proportion. The performance demanded careful listening, but it was worth it, and the Scottish Orchestra played as it always plays under a really good conductor.
>
> *The Scotsman* (15 December 1931), 8.

The circumstances around Braithwaite's engagement for these concerts caused a little embarrassment. Sir Henry Wood had originally been invited to conduct, but for some reason or other had not finalised the arrangement. Robert Heger was brought in to replace him, but was then taken ill, and this led to an invitation for Braithwaite to step in. An unfortunate sequence of events caused a breakdown in communication between the orchestra management and the BBC which resulted in Wood being listed in the *Radio Times* as conductor. Wood was somewhat displeased, but Braithwaite was not perturbed in the least. In fact, although he considered some sections of the orchestra inferior to the NOW, it was a much larger body of musicians with a particularly fine string section (led by Max Jaffa), and he felt that they responded well to his direction. They certainly seemed to enjoy the experience. There was even a whisper that he might be offered a permanent position as Musical Director, but he was to be disappointed. John Barbirolli, George Szell and Aylmer Buesst were each to hold that post throughout the 1930s before Braithwaite was finally given the opportunity to make his mark nine years later, on 9 November 1940.

Fortunately, the links to the BBC and Cardiff were not completely severed with his disheartening return to London in 1932. Four orchestral studio concerts were assigned to him, using some of the section orchestras that were formed within the larger BBC Symphony Orchestra,[9] but even so, his first year of independence must have felt like enforced retirement for a man accustomed

---

9 A system of coding had been introduced, so Braithwaite found himself conducting Sections B, C, D, E or F, depending on the forces required for the broadcast.

to conducting at least 250 concerts in the studio and on the concert platform each year.

An important feature of Braithwaite's time in Cardiff had been the choral contributions provided by various groups such as the 5WA Repertory Chorus, the Lyrian Singers, Lottie Wakelin's Choir and, most importantly, the 5WA Choir (trained by Shapland Dobbs). With these groups he gave studio performances of Mendelssohn's *Elijah* and *Lobgesang*, Debussy's *L'enfant prodigue*, Verdi's *Il trovatore*, Humperdinck's *Hänsel und Gretel*, Saint-Saëns' *Samson et Dalila*, and Bizet's *Carmen*. The first public appearance of the 5WA Choir was at an ambitious concert performance of Wagner's *Lohengrin*, presented in Bristol's Colston Hall on 25 April 1925. This clearly signalled Braithwaite's intentions, not only to expand his orchestra and its activities numerically, but also to test the abilities of his musicians to the limit.

The largest vocal group available to Braithwaite was the Choir of the Cardiff Musical Society. As early as 15 November 1925 the group had taken part in a broadcast concert from Park Hall, performing Mendelssohn's *Lobgesang*. From then, until Braithwaite's last concert with them on 9 December 1934, they performed on 36 occasions. The repertoire was mostly standard for the time – Handel's *Messiah*; Bach's *St Matthew Passion*; Elgar's *The Dream of Gerontius* and *The Kingdom*; Requiems by Verdi and Mozart; Beethoven's Symphony no. 9; and Mendelssohn's *Elijah*, *St Paul* and *Lobgesang*, but there were also some comparative rarities such as Mendelssohn's *Lauda Sion*, Elgar's *The Music Makers* and *The Light of Life*. In addition, the choir performed many smaller choral pieces both interspersed in orchestral concerts and in several a cappella concerts. As a rule, vocal and orchestral excerpts from opera proved extremely popular, especially the all-Wagner programmes.

Braithwaite continued his association with the Choir of the Cardiff Musical Society until 1934, by which time his conducting engagements elsewhere made it impracticable to continue. He was not to return to Wales until 1951, when he entered into a very productive association with the Welsh National Opera.

Hidden amongst the BBC and Cardiff Musical Society engagements for 1932, was an assignment in December to conduct one performance of Mozart's *Così fan tutte* for the Vic-Wells Company at Sadler's Wells. This might almost pass unnoticed, except for the fact that it provided an entrée once again to the world of opera.[10] It was followed in March 1933 by another solitary appearance in the Vic-Wells pit, this time for a performance of Ambroise Thomas' *Mignon*,

---

10 The performance took place at Sadler's Wells on the afternoon of 10 December 1932, and the cast included Joan Cross *(Fiordiligi)*; Winifred Kennard *(Dorabella)*; Nora Sabini *(Despina)*; Morgan Jones *(Ferrando)*; Sumner Austin *(Guglielmo)*; Clive Carey *(Alfonso)*; Clive Carey *(director)*; Owen P. Smyth *(designer)*. This was Braithwaite's debut with the company (possibly replacing Aylmer Buesst, who had conducted the opening night).

which the critic from *The Times* thought had been conducted 'with the right vivacity and lightness'.[11] His engagement book was already looking much healthier, with over thirty scheduled orchestral and choral concerts, enabling him to work again with distinguished artists such as Florence Austral, Heddle Nash, Eileen Joyce, Joan Cross, Cyril Smith, Dora Labbette and Melsa. There were also sixteen more engagements with the Vic-Wells, including *La traviata*, *Otello*, *Tannhäuser* and *Faust*, for which Lilian Baylis offered him ten guineas for three performances per week.[12] Presumably, there was no remuneration for rehearsals.

A surprise development was an invitation to take over direction of the Robert Mayer Concerts for Children, a series which had become a regular feature of concert life in London since 1923. The scheduled conductor, Malcolm Sargent, had been diagnosed with tuberculosis in October 1932, and Braithwaite was asked to take on the season of four concerts at Central Hall, Westminster, between October 1933 and March 1934.

A brief pause in engagements during the August of 1935 allowed Braithwaite to visit the Austrian resort of Zell am See on a walking holiday. He also managed to obtain tickets for some performances at the Salzburg Festival, where Verdi's *Falstaff* was being presented for the first time.[13] The experience was overwhelming and he wrote enthusiastically to his wife Lorna:

> *Falstaff* was the most perfect performance I have ever seen, and Toscanini is the greatest operatic conductor who has ever lived. *Fidelio* was marvellous, but *Falstaff* was unbelievable in its perfection. Jack [Gordon] is completely overcome and feels he can't do it. I on the other hand feel I can and will, so long as rehearsals are well arranged. The Italian singers are much better than the German and a performance of *Figaro* I saw was so bad that I couldn't bear it – I walked out after the first act, went back for the 3rd, but couldn't bring myself to hear the 4th. Weingartner was the conductor – he was just too bad for anything.[14]

The second Glyndebourne Festival took place from 27 May to 29 June 1935, and was intended as a Mozart celebration built around performances of *Così fan Tutte*, *Le nozze di Figaro*, *Die Entführung aus dem Serail* and *Die Zauberflöte*.

---

11 *The Times* (16 March 1933), 12.

12 Letter from Warwick Braithwaite to his wife, Lorna, dated 9 June 1933 (Private collection).

13 This was the first time that Verdi's *Falstaff* had been presented at the Salzburg Festival. The cast for four performances included Mariano Stabile (*Falstaff*), Maria Caniglia or Dusolina Giannini (*Alice*), Edith Mason (*Nannetta*), Angelica Cravcenco (*Quickly*), Mita Vasari (*Meg*), Piero Biasini (*Ford*), Dino Borgioli (*Fenton*), Angelo Badà (*Dr. Caius*), Giuseppe Nessi (*Bardolfo*), Fernando Autori (*Pistola*).

14 Letter to Lorna Braithwaite dated 19 August 1935 (private collection).

Braithwaite's work for Sadler's Wells must have attracted some attention because the Festival Programme lists him as one of the music staff, along with Alberto Erede, Jani Strasser and Edward Renton.[15] The only conductors for the season were Fritz Busch and Hans Oppenheim, so the activities of the music staff were probably limited to vocal coaching and répétiteur work.

Braithwaite conducted four performances of Puccini's *Il Trittico*,[16] performed by students at the Royal Academy of Music in July 1937,[17] and each year, the number of opera engagements at Sadler's Wells steadily increased. Along the way some particularly outstanding performances were favourably acknowledged by the critics, including *Carmen, Die Fledermaus* (1934); *Il barbiere di Siviglia, Fra Diavolo, La traviata, Otello, La bohème* (1935); *Le nozze di Figaro, Falstaff, Die Meistersinger von Nürnberg* (1936); and *Rigoletto, Fidelio* (1937).

In 1936, Braithwaite was made a Fellow of the Royal Academy of Music (FRAM), an award conferred on alumni who have distinguished themselves within the music profession. A new phase in Braithwaite's career was about to begin, as it was, too, for the Vic-Wells Company. The timing was perfect.

As we take up the thread of Braithwaite's own narrative, he has been on the music staff of the Vic-Wells Company since the autumn of 1933. He has conducted a total of 377 performances of 21 operas and been offered, but declined, the post of Director. Happy with his position within the company, and working harmoniously with Musical Director Lawrance Collingwood (a life-long friend) and stage directors Clive Carey, Sumner Austin and Jack Gordon, Braithwaite feared that administrative responsibilities might have had a negative impact on his ability to maintain and develop his conducting career.

---

15 Edward Renton (1912–1975), Scottish-born opera conductor and administrator.

16 Consisting of three one-act operas, *Il tabarro, Suor Angelica* and *Gianni Schicchi*.

17 Braithwaite went on to conduct RAM student performances of Mozart's *Le nozze di Figaro* the following year. Some thirty years later, a letter from Sir Thomas Armstrong suggested that Braithwaite was conducting the Second Orchestra on Mondays for the early months of 1968.

PART V
(1937–1940)

TWELVE

VIC-WELLS I (1937–1939)

I wanted to continue my career as a conductor and knew that the position of Director would quash any idea of that. In my conversation with Lilian Baylis, I suggested Clive Carey as being the most likely person to fill the gap. Clive was offered this position but, as he told me at the time, he, like myself, was too interested in teaching and producing, so he refused it. Baylis obviously knew the end was near[1] and tried hard to find someone to take over the tremendous responsibility.

Tyrone Guthrie had been the Producer of Drama at the Old Vic, but previously had enjoyed great success in the Northern Ireland BBC station as well as making tremendous strides forward as a producer of plays in the West End of London. A forceful, cultured man, he had impressed everyone with whom he came into contact through an original mind of the highest type. Many people had serious doubts as to the wisdom of appointing him Director of the two theatres, as Guthrie's experience had, up until then, been with drama and actors only.[2] As producer at the Old Vic he was superb. I particularly remember one of his earliest productions there – Shakespeare's *As You Like It*.

His amazing gift of remembering even the Christian names in the rank and file of a company stood him in good stead when later he began to try his hand at producing opera. For try his hand

Sir (William) Tyrone Guthrie, photographed in 1947 by Elliott & Fry.
© *National Portrait Gallery, London*

---

1 Lilian Baylis died on 25 November 1937.
2 Guthrie was appointed Director of the Old Vic and Sadler's Wells on 24 February 1939.

he did. The first opera he chose to produce at Sadler's Wells was *La bohème*. I remember one remark of his that gave me some idea of his attitude: 'I intend to take the ham out of opera.' By 'ham' I suppose he meant the traditional little bits of business associated with certain situations in the drama. But actually, it was much deeper than that. Guthrie gave me the impression that he despised the convention of opera altogether. On one occasion, he put words into my mouth, telling *me* that I only liked Italian operas; those operas with blood and thunder in them. Ridiculous! What was really happening was that Guthrie was trying to explain to me his own attitude towards opera. By taking the 'ham' out of opera what he was really saying was that 'I can't bear these melodramatic Italian operas; they are bad drama.' Like a number of clever producers of drama, he thought that he, without any experience or background in opera, could give the operas a completely new lease of life by cutting the 'ham' out to restore them – but to what? It showed an abysmal ignorance of the convention of Grand Opera, and also an abysmal ignorance in the man himself for daring to think that he was the only person who really understood opera.

One has only to look around in the world of opera and delve into the careers of most of the important producers to see that the apprenticeship is a long and arduous one. A producer of opera, unless he wants to fall into the gravest errors of judgement, *must* be a reasonably good musician. If not, there is no doubt that among people who *really* know their business, he will get the 'Oscar' for the most incompetent producer opera has known.

Guthrie struggled on for a long time and, I feel, soon began to repent that he ever had anything to do with opera or operatic artists. Possibly he began to think that operatic artists were a lot of quarrelsome and troublesome children. What he didn't ask himself was 'I wonder if operatic artists were *always* like that?' Or maybe, 'Perhaps they were only like that with *me*.' Of course that was so! Guthrie, in his passion for infusing new life into opera, was asking the artists to do impossibilities. Antics such as running around the stage while singing, do not endear operatic artists to a producer when the perfectly obvious and traditional 'business' was designed to put singers in a fairly reasonable singing position. Singers complained bitterly at all this unnecessary movement, and Guthrie, being a forceful character, insisted (and could do so with impunity because he was the Governor) that his ideas were carried out. The result was inevitably frustration for him, dissatisfaction for the artists, and general unhappiness all round.

I must confess that I was unintelligent enough to sympathise with the artists for the simple reason that musical ensemble was beginning to suffer when Guthrie was the producer. But my 'unintelligence' became of a basic and fundamental kind as far as Guthrie was concerned. Because I disagreed with his ideas of production, I was of a lower order of intelligence, and as he once remarked, 'Ah yes, but you only like the blood and thunder operas. You know the ones with the 'ham' in them.' Much as I admired, and still do admire, the many talents of Guthrie both as a playwright and as a producer in the 'straight' theatre, his remarks to me only convinced me more than ever that the 'workman should stick to his own last'.

Several times in its chequered history, opera in Britain has suffered from the Guthrie type of producer. With opera houses in London and other big cities not having been subsidized for generations (as they have been in most of the continental countries), operatic producers have had little chance to gain experience. At Sadler's Wells there were three producers doing excellent work in the acknowledged operatic tradition. Why Guthrie had to intervene seems a mystery. But perhaps not quite so. I can well understand Guthrie, a producer of great originality in the straight theatre, becoming impatient with some of the conventional movements in our productions and wanting to revitalize them. But he forgot just one thing. There are certain and well-defined limits not experienced, or dreamed of, by straight actors when music, with its strict conventions, is combined with acting. In the world of opera, music, tempi and time signatures are the ruling factors; they simply cannot be ignored or overridden. The producer of plays has just one more difficulty to contend with when he dabbles in opera. That is the stern and unrelenting time element of music, which he *cannot* bend to his own will.

The best operatic producer is the one who realizes this and embraces music to the full. I remember at Sadler's Wells insisting that the final duet between Gilda and Rigoletto, which had previously been cut for years, should be opened up. Previous producers had, in their arrogance, persuaded conductors to make this cut because, as they frequently stated, it was an anti-climax, in the sense that once Gilda was stabbed, she was dead, and that was that. When I pointed out that it was often the case that a stabbed person (you had only to read the daily papers) lived for hours afterwards, the answer was usually, 'Ah yes, but this is the stage, not real life.' This, despite the fact that the most moving music in the whole opera had been sliced out, was the reason put forward, in all seriousness, for this cut. The arrogant producer was not a better judge than Verdi, the genius who selected the libretto and wrote this great final scene! No wonder I had become suspicious of the producer of 'originality'.

Another case in point was the producer who, in his studies, had discovered that Verdi wrote a 'Paris' version of Act II of *La traviata*, in which Germont's aria was shifted to another part of the act, and who insisted on this version being performed despite the fact that Verdi's final thoughts on this matter are published in the Italian version which is now always used. This same producer cut out all the choruses in the gambling scene and changed the names of the characters so as to bring the opera more into line with Dumas' story. Surely there was the hint of a bias, in suchlike veins of opera, towards the literary and non– musical?

The really great producer of opera is the most ardent of men. He sets out with a full understanding of the composer's music and sense of drama, and does his utmost to interpret his production through the composer's eyes. He may find that the meaning of certain orchestral passages escapes him. If he can't think of the right business for these passages, he is sorely tempted to ask for a 'cut' or, as has frequently happened, ask the conductor to speed up these passages. Sometimes he asks for an unnatural pause in the music for a particularly cherished movement on the stage. But the really great operatic producer must, like the conductor, endeavour to interpret the composer's idea. He must seek out the answer to what may be obscure to him, and not, as sometimes happens, impose ideas which are completely false and which must be eked out by the conductor or artist in order to make them at all possible. I have gone into this question more thoroughly in Part Three of my book, *The Conductor's Art*,[3] but cannot insist enough on the correct attitude of the producer.

With some of these 'original' producers the artists have a bad time. Nothing seems right to them. I am not referring to the difficult and swollen-headed artists, but to the normal, sincere and good operatic actor/singer. The whole gist of operatic acting in realistic operas, is to be as natural as possible within the musical conventions inherent in all operas. When an artist is requested to do something which he or she knows is unnatural, the result is more often than not unsuccessful, even though they may endeavour to comply with the producer's wishes to the best of their ability. Here is the crux of the matter. The producer is not the only one with brains. Neither is the conductor for that matter. Whereas the whole training of an operatic artist is to do what he or she is told to do by those in authority, there comes a time when unhappiness and seething discontent become unbearable. Frustration sets in, and neither producers nor artists feel they are getting anywhere.

It was my impression that Guthrie suffered a distinct reverse at Sadler's Wells because of his own attitude towards opera. I am quite aware that a number of people thought otherwise. I am also aware that certain members of the Press, cognisant of Guthrie's great success in the straight theatre, believed he had achieved the same in the operatic sphere. But there were others whose knowledge was of a fundamental kind, who disagreed with almost everything he did. I could not but be impressed by this tall, handsome, cultured and most talented man whose ideas, whatever one may have thought of them, were at least vital and interesting. He knew what he wanted and asked for it in no uncertain voice, and it was a matter of great regret that in the things which

---

3 Warwick Braithwaite, *The Conductor's Art* (London: Williams & Norgate, 1952).

affected me in my work (and often to the detriment of it) there built up between us, a barrier which made it impossible to meet on equal terms. This barrier was strengthened and bolstered up by others who had their own designs on the future management of the company.

As to Guthrie's administrative gifts I cannot say very much. This was a side of his work of which I had very little experience, except that as time went on, he began to listen to the advice of those who were antagonistic towards me. When Guthrie began to do more work outside the two theatres, he would take the advice offered by those people and act on it. The full story cannot be told for several reasons, but certainly not because of any fear of consequences. Those not *au fait* with the seemingly small things which occur in the running of an opera house, cannot possibly understand how far-reaching and eventually all-important those decisions can be, especially if made on wrong premises. To recite a list of grievances, small in themselves, would seem childish. Only those who know what they can mean in an operatic performance would guess their seriousness and the fatal repercussions on one's work.

Guthrie's influence spread far and wide, but one longed for the single-mindedness of Lilian Baylis. Lilian had grown up with the theatre, and she knew what she wanted – an internal growth towards an outward achievement. Guthrie came into something that was ready-made and which had a direction set by the originator of this amazing venture, and like many producers of opera recruited from the ranks of the straight theatre, he wanted to give our venture the stamp of his own originality. Who could blame him? There I leave the subject.

Things went on outwardly as before. The theatre began to flourish and bigger and more important works were produced. Lawrance Collingwood began to build up his reputation as a conductor of Russian operas. *Boris Godunov*, *Eugene Onegin*, *The Snow Maiden* and *Tsar Sultan* were added to the repertoire, and Albert Coates came in for a few guest performances of *La bohème*, *The Snow Maiden* and *Tsar Sultan*. The heyday of achievement was arriving. Ethel Smyth's great opera, *The Wreckers*, enjoyed an enormous success.

The incident of Beecham's advent when he conducted Smyth's *The Boatswain's Mate* and Arthur Benjamin's *The Devil Take Her* (surely a marvellous double bill), was one of the most curious happenings in the whole history of the theatre. Our public was indeed home-grown, for the takings of the Beecham performance was exactly £38, the lowest the theatre had ever experienced and a most unexpected rebuff to the guest conductor idea. John Barbirolli also came and did some fine performances of *Il barbiere di Siviglia*, an opera I was to take over from him later. Stanford Robinson came in for a few performances of *Madama Butterfly*.

The Executive Committee had made a ruling (with which Baylis entirely concurred) that no foreigners were to be allowed admittance, either to the staff of musicians or to the list of singers. We were determined that only a singer's mother tongue would be tolerated, and in this I think we were right.[4] Our whole scheme of things was to build up a tradition of opera in English as well as the equally important task of encouraging operas written by English composers. In other words, we were determined to work out our own operatic salvation in our own way, without interference of any kind from foreigners. In this we were most successful. Every year we hoped to produce an English opera, and this we persisted in until certain English operas became firmly entrenched into the repertoire.

The much-neglected Charles Villiers Stanford would have been pleased at the great success of his last opera *The Travelling Companion*; Ethel Smyth was thrilled by the outstanding success of *The Wreckers*; and Vaughan Williams' *Hugh the Drover* persisted in defying predictions by its continued success. Nicholas Gatty[5] had only a limited success with his *Greysteel*; Collingwood's *Macbeth* had three or more performances, and I remember Joseph Farrington's great performance of the most exacting role of the name part. Holst's *Savitri* was given with another opera, but for some reason didn't stay the course.[6] More than likely, Holst's fondness for Indian legend did not produce an echoing response from our audience. I had conducted *Savitri* many years previously in Cardiff and I was one of the first musicians to read through his original score in about the year 1918 or 1919. The same Mr Balderstone of Burnley, who used to obtain my full scores of Wagner's operas from Germany, brought *Savitri* to me one day. The score was written in pencil and I remember being very enthusiastic about it at the time. I was then with the O'Mara Opera Company and there was no chance of putting on this unknown composer's opera. It was not until I became Music Director of the Welsh radio station that I remembered it and put it down for performance.[7]

This brings me to the projected season of 1939–1940. We all had a fright in the early part of 1938 during the Munich affair. Trenches had already been dug in all the London parks, shelters were being hurriedly built, and private householders were bricking up their garages and porticoes. Gas masks had been issued, but the danger seemed to have passed when Neville Chamberlain came back with his 'peace for our time' speech. We all breathed again.

---

4   It was assumed that the mother tongue of all British and Commonwealth artists was English.

5   Nicholas Comyn Gatty (1874-1946), English composer and nephew of Alfred Scott-Gatty, composer of *The Golden Shore*.

6   *Savitri* was given in a triple bill, with Puccini's *Il tabarro* and *Gianni Schicchi*.

7   Braithwaite conducted the opera on three occasions in Cardiff – a studio broadcast on 1 June 1924 – with Dorothy Silk *(soprano)*. Browning Mummery *(tenor)*, and Joseph Farrington *(baritone)*; another studio broadcast on 8 July 1925 with Eda Bennie, William Heseltine, Andrew Shanks; and a concert performance in City Hall on 14 March 1931 with Megan Thomas, Hubert Eisdell and Joseph Farrington.

THIRTEEN

ITALY AND FRANCE

At various times in my life, I have felt a great need to get away from the narrowing influence of a set routine, and in the year before the war, while I was still at Sadler's Wells, I arranged with Lilian Baylis to have three weeks away from the theatre before Christmas until after the New Year.

At that time, I had become very friendly with Eugenio Clausetti, the London Manager of the Italian music publisher, Ricordi & Co. I expressed a wish to visit Milan and study rehearsal methods at La Scala Opera House, and Clausetti made my visit possible by arranging for Ricordi in Milan to look after me. His father, Carlo Clausetti, did everything possible for me, and every day an ancient Rolls Royce would call at my hotel. The chauffeur would accompany me from my room and, with charming courtesy, seat me beside Carlo, tucking a fur rug around my feet. Carlo, a man of about 70 years who spoke quite good English, would then give me a résumé of the work at La Scala for that morning and escort me into the theatre where the main rehearsal was about to begin. Gino Marinuzzi[1] was the chief conductor – a fiery man with a genius for throwing a tantrum, but a musician of impeccable taste and perfection of style.

The first work I saw rehearsed was an opera by Mulè called *Dafni*.[2] The rehearsal went on far into the night and I was struck by the expertise of all departments, but mostly of the stage staff. The lighting was almost perfect; I could not imagine anything better. The equipment was both modern and lavish. Of course, there was a huge cyclorama (what continental theatre is without one?) which took the lighting from enormous bridges high up above the top of the proscenium. But the most interesting part of the stage was the

---

1   Gino Marinuzzi (1882–1945), distinguished Italian conductor.
2   Giuseppe Mulè (1885–1951), Italian composer and conductor. His opera *Dafni* had been premiered at Rome in 1929. Braithwaite was witnessing rehearsals for the first Milan performances.

lift machinery. To me this was a revelation, particularly in that as far back as 1922 I had, for my own amusement, sketched out a new idea of disposing with the usual wooden rostra used for elevation, by installing three-foot square lifts over the entire stage. These lifts could be set by the electrician to move up or down to certain heights on the turning of a main switch. This machinery had been but lately installed at La Scala and was working when I was there in 1938, and the story of how it came to be installed was told to me by the younger Clausetti. In the beautiful foyer of the Opera House there were about 20 names of hotel keepers and restaurateurs cut into the lovely marble pillars painted in gold, and an appreciative tribute inscribed to their benevolence in 'giving' the funds necessary for the new lift machinery on the stage. Actually, what happened, according to my friend, was that the fascists had decided that the machinery was necessary, and in seeking the financial wherewithal, hit on the brilliant idea that as these hotel keepers and restaurateurs had benefitted by the influx of visitors to La Scala over a long period of years, they ought to give some contribution. In return for this financial contribution, their names were emblazoned in gold lettering on the marble pillars of the foyer.

La Scala Opera House is financed by the Milan Corporation through the simple method of making every other theatre contribute financially to it.[3] Cinemas and variety shows are taxed for this purpose, and the Corporation makes up any deficit. Subsidy is the only way to pay for opera done on such a scale. No opera house worthy of the name can make a profit, and I wonder if it ever occurs to English visitors how the money is found for these great artistic ventures. Returning visitors from Milan speak glowingly of the performances; of the fine orchestra of 100 or more players; of the lavish stage scenery; the chorus and the wonderful artists; yet do they ever ask themselves how this excellence is achieved? The one comment usually is that the Italian nation is *so* musical; even the boys in the street whistle operatic melodies. Of course they do, in the towns where they have had subsidized opera for so many years. Opera is a grandiose art. It cannot be done in the way we attempt it in England. Even at Covent Garden during pre-war years, where a syndicate of private guarantors subsidized a season with foreign singers, the season was curtailed according to the amount of money guaranteed. The seasons at Covent Garden between the two world wars have been a headache to all concerned and have dwindled down to about 8 or 12 weeks. All sorts of last-minute difficulties have occurred to mar the performances. I can remember numerous instances of artists being flown over from Germany or Italy and coming together for the first time at the actual performance. In the years immediately preceding World War II, Covent

---

3   La Scala now receives state funding although, like all arts funding, this has been reduced by the government.

Garden performances were, with few exceptions, flung onto the stage during a hectic period of hurried rehearsals, and for their success they relied on well-known celebrity artists. As the Fascist regimes in Germany and Italy became more truculent, difficulties for us increased.

At La Scala, rehearsals were well organized with nothing left to chance – rather in the same way as rehearsals were then being conducted at Sadler's Wells. In fact, I should say that given a generous subsidy, a more up to date and larger stage and orchestral pit, Sadler's Wells would have, but for the war, progressed to the front rank of opera houses.

Having been invited by John Christie to see the 1938 production of Verdi's *Macbeth* at Glyndebourne (a remarkable production of a big work on a small stage) I was looking forward tremendously to the La Scala performance which opened the season of 1939.[4] On this occasion, the name part was taken by Alexander Sved and he gave a magnificent performance. Sved has a tremendously vital personality and a fine voice. His Macbeth quite astounded me and more so because for some unaccountable reason his appearance at Covent Garden a season or two earlier in *Rigoletto* was not considered a success. I can only think that the reason for this must have been far removed from the question of his own operatic standards, because in that particular season at Covent Garden, some of the operas were inadequately rehearsed. After seeing his great performance in the Milan production of *Macbeth*, I cannot believe that Sved could have sung a bad *Rigoletto*.

The production of *Macbeth* gave La Scala great opportunities for the three big chorus scenes – the Banquet scene, the Scottish scene, and the final storming of Macbeth's stronghold when about 200 men rushed into the castle on the lowering of the drawbridge. It was all so realistic and grand. The singing of the chorus was a great joy, and although their numbers were great, one felt that a true feeling for light and shade and beauty of tone had been the basic training and had become a tradition. The chorus master at that period was well known,

---

4   This reference to John Christie is timely. On 2 June 1939, Braithwaite received an invitation from Christie to join the staff at Glyndebourne for the 1940 season, replacing James Robertson who was going to Canada. Braithwaite was to be the 'English' conductor, to work alongside Fritz Busch (German) and Alberto Erede (Italian), but, according to Christie, he would need to 'stew in our juice' (i.e., absorb the organisational culture) for a year before being allowed to conduct two performances in 1941. Braithwaite's reply, as one of the foremost conductors of opera in English, was understandably cool. He began by praising the Glyndebourne ethos, but feared that the offer of such a position might be seen as a 'step-back from the one I now occupy in the world of music'. His counter-offer was to work incognito for Glyndebourne in 1940, on the understanding that he would be billed as a conductor in 1941. 'I suggest this condition', he writes, 'as a safeguard to my reputation as a conductor at Sadler's Wells and elsewhere, for obvious reasons.' (Private correspondence held by the Braithwaite family). Nothing came of this exchange, and WWII saw the suspension of opera at Glyndebourne after *The Beggar's Opera* in 1940. The house became an evacuee centre for hundreds of London children. Operatic activity resumed in 1946.

not only in Italy, but at the Metropolitan New York, and at Covent Garden as well. A big chorus, of course, can afford to sing pianissimo and even so be heard above a large orchestra. It is the quality of the collective tone which counts in the long run. A small chorus (such as we had at Sadler's Wells) was required to make up in individual sound what it lost in numbers (especially in fortissimo passages) and as a result, the voices tended to develop a hard edge, and the quality of tone in a pianissimo suffered.

I can never understand why Massenet's opera *Werther* has not been a success in England. I saw it first of all in Paris about the year 1920 and was tremendously enthusiastic afterwards. I remember I bought a copy of the score the next day and from memory drew sketches of the stage sets in use at the Opéra-Comique. At that time, I was with the Joseph O'Mara Opera Company, but O'Mara wasn't particularly interested. The performance I saw at La Scala in 1939 gave me one of the greatest operatic thrills I have ever had. The orchestra was conducted by Franco Capuana and the playing was truly perfect; an ensemble like a chamber orchestra and a tone ravishing in its tenderness. Tito Schipa was the tenor, and an American baritone, Frank Valentino, sang Albert. I also heard *La sonnambula* by Bellini, with its delightful plot about a woman who walked in her sleep, resulting in all sorts of complications. The action is set in the Tyrol and the overture starts off with an orchestra behind the curtain echoing the melody of the orchestra in front, which was probably a startling innovation in Bellini's days, but a little childish to modern theatre-goers. The style of Bellini's vocal writing is in the true Italian tradition and the singers taking part were excellent.

I found time while in Milan to visit the Cathedral (of a thousand towers) and on Christmas Eve, out of curiosity, attended the Midnight Mass. Here to me was the solution to some of the strange parading of religious rituals one finds in Italian opera. I can think of many operas where the gorgeous ritual and colours of the Roman Catholic Church were used in operatic scenes, (the first act of the *I gioielli della Madonna*, and first act of *Tosca* are two only). The reason apparently is that religion is part and parcel of everyday life in Italy. At this Midnight Mass, while the service was progressing, the vast space inside the main door of the Cathedral was a hubbub of conversation and seemed like a meeting place for all the young people of Milan. Nobody paid the slightest attention to the service, except those nearest the altar. The crowd was enormous, but I wouldn't say for a moment that it was over-religious; the Mass was just part of their lives and largely taken for granted.

On another occasion I visited the lovely church of S. Maria della Grazia with an Italian student who had lived in London for many years. This friend of mine was keen to show me the architectural beauties of Milan and under his guidance I wasted no time. In the refectory of the church is the famous

Leonardo da Vinci *Last Supper*. When I saw it at first (I confess my complete ignorance) I just didn't believe it was the original. My friend did not come in with me, and when I remarked that I had seen what looked like a copy of the picture, he looked at me more in sorrow than in anger, and with some scorn in his voice said, 'But that *is* the original.' I looked at him, turned on my heel, and went back to the refectory and spent another good hour drinking in what I had so nearly missed.

The next day I visited the Castello del Forza. This huge castle in the middle of Milan, built by the Forza family in the 13th Century, is magnificent. Constructed in reddish stone (rather like Penrith Castle), it covers an immense space. In the summer time I was told the *Fascisti* used to order gala performances of opera in the grounds for the Milanese. An audience of 30,000 often attended, and when *Aida* was performed, the victorious Radamès was brought in on the back of a huge elephant. Among the tributes he presented to the King were real tigers. *Aida* lends itself to such realism.

On Christmas Day, I was invited to Carlo Clausetti's house where I met the members of his family. Eugenio Clausetti and his wife had arrived from London by then and our reunion was especially delightful. I regarded it as both a compliment and a most friendly act to be asked as a guest, and was greeted almost as one of the family. As a rule, Christmas is very much a family festival among Italians. I can remember the old man Clausetti showing me some of his rarest possessions. There were autographed photos of Puccini and Verdi, as well as one of the conductor Arturo Toscanini, which he cherished very much.

The following day Eugenio had arranged a trip to Bergamo by motor car. It was a bright day, but very cold. We travelled along one of the new Via's which Mussolini had built, and turned off it into Bergamo. This very delightful town was chiefly interesting to me for the reason that Donizetti is buried in the church right on the hill overlooking the countryside.[5] On the way back I was immensely amused by passing through the small town of Gorgonzola.[6] We returned to the ordinary roads as the new road, by reason of the icy weather, was a trifle dangerous and Signora Clausetti was expecting a baby in a few months.

New Year's Eve in Milan reminded me very much of the same night in Glasgow. I only know the Scottish Hogmanay in wartime, when restrictions and blackouts make celebrations a little difficult, but even so, Glasgow's New Year's Eve was gay enough. But I was in Milan during New Year's Eve 1938–1939 and it was not only gay but exhilarating as well. No one went to bed at all. Singing crowds paraded the streets in torchlight processions, and bands played all night long. The restaurants and delightful wine shops were open. It was the first night

---

5   Gaetano Donizetti (1797–1848), Italian composer and native of Bergamo. He is buried in the Basilica of Santa Maria Maggiore.

6   Schoolboy humour. Any reference to cheese is always found to be amusing in some circles.

of the La Scala season, and the performance finished at midnight. Everybody spoke to everybody else but, as far as I remember, I didn't notice any inebriation that might have become troublesome.

I came away from Milan with the impression that the Italians seemed to be a naturally graceful race. I had noticed this first of all in the streets. If by accident you were bumped into on a crowded pavement there were profuse and very gracious apologies. Other incidents, too, gave me the same impression that when people are left to themselves and not thinking about dogma, they behave with understanding towards others. It is when people are poisoned by evil slogans that they become inhuman.

I only had one instance of that sort of thing while in Milan. One day Carlo Clausetti couldn't come with me to the La Scala rehearsal, but very kindly gave me a note to Marinuzzi. I presented myself at the rather forbidding, yet imposing, stage entrance, rather like a courtyard, and gave the note to the porter. Don't forget that throughout the country, on all important roads and other public places, Mussolini had erected monuments with the slogan 'Remember Sanctions' in huge stone letters. It was well-known in the theatre that I was an Englishman, and while I was with Clausetti (one of the most honoured figures in the operatic publishing world) everything was alright. But by myself, I began to see the attitude of some of these people change. I am not referring to Marinuzzi of course; he it was who expressed regret at my being kept waiting so long at the stage entrance. I could only get into the theatre by telephoning Clausetti who in turn telephoned Marinuzzi. Clausetti afterwards came to the theatre and stayed with me for the remainder of the rehearsal.

The final memory I have is of the Opera Museum on the upper floor of La Scala. Here one can see models of the first productions of operas at La Scala, the costumes worn by the great Tamagno[7] for *Otello*, programmes of first performances in other countries of Italian works, photographs of all the great singers and musicians and, most wonderful of all, the special room devoted to Verdi, with his piano, desk, manuscripts *and* his top hat and umbrella. I was to go to Milan many times afterwards but this first visit was truly unforgettable.

Back to the imposing railway station, which looked like the west front of a cathedral, I made my way to Lugano where my friend the composer, Hans Wetzler, lived.[8] After spending a glorious day with him amid warm sunshine at Ascona, I took the mountain electric railway to Domodossola in order to catch the connection via Paris and back to London. My passport was stamped no less than four times, including twice by the Italian frontier police – a bunch of fellows who looked self-important and truculent in their feathered hats. I

---

7   Francesco Tamagno (1850–1905), Italian operatic tenor and creator of the title role in Verdi's *Otello* at La Scala, Milan in 1887.

8   Hermann Hans Wetzler (1870–1943), German-American composer.

spent a day and a night in Paris where I met Jack Gordon, one of the producers at Sadler's Wells. I arrived in the late afternoon and called on Jack, who invited me to an early dinner, after which we went to the Opera House. The opera was quite new to me, I've even forgotten its name, and we were sitting in a part of the building which seemed as if we were looking through the wrong end of a telescope. After a while we both decided it wasn't worth the strain and walked around to the Opéra-Comique and saw *Tosca* from the second act onward!

At one time I was a frequent visitor to the Paris Opéra, but I had since given it a wide berth until this night. I don't know what has happened to French operatic performances. Everything seemed in those days (1939), and before that, to be gorgeously produced, but entirely lacking in musical exactness. Probably the lack of any real standard was part and parcel of the deterioration in French public life just before the war. I only went to Paris twice before the war (between 1935 and 1939) and I felt on both these occasions that there was something brewing which was stifling French national life.

The performance of *Tosca* mentioned above was a sad thing to see. Both Tosca and Scarpia, in their big scene in the second act, sang well but ignored the conductor completely. The orchestra played as a number of individuals; each soloist lingered over every juicy phrase in defiance of the rest of the orchestra, and the conductor (who was an excellent and well-known French musician) seemed powerless to exert his authority.

It would be unfair to judge the Opéra-Comique by this one example, but I felt strongly at the time that it was an indication of a breakdown of moral strength. Freedom and independence may be a most desirable thing, but during a performance of opera there are strict and exact limits to individuality.

FOURTEEN

VIC-WELLS II (1939–1940)

Plans for the 1939 season at Sadler's Wells went ahead, although there was still some hesitancy in our deliberations. Instead of choosing four new works for the following season, we chose only three – Wolf-Ferrari's *I quatro rusteghi*, Verdi's *Simon Boccanegra* and, I think, *Sir John in Love*, by Vaughan Williams. The plans were complete and all casting of parts allotted, when a blow fell which was to put an end to Sadler's Wells as I knew it. Baylis' death had been bad enough, but now the war put an end to all our strenuous efforts to reach our goal.[1]

My memory of events about this time seems to be dimmed. What I and my colleagues went through as a result of the declaration of war on Germany is horrible to think about now. My wife, Lorna, was expecting our second son and I had taken on the responsibility of a new house in Hampstead Garden Suburb.[2] As the news got worse, arrangements were made so that when the Government announced a general evacuation from London because of impending air raids, my father-in-law would send a car to London in order to take my wife with the child to Worcester, where her sister was living. Six days before this announcement, on 26 August 1939, our son Nicholas was born, and six days later I carried my wife downstairs into the car. With her father's chauffeur, the nurse and the six-day-old baby, they moved off on their journey. I followed in our own car with the layette basket, a maid, the maid's child, a cat and some luggage.

---

1 The Sadler's Wells premiere of *Sir John in Love* took place on 4 April 1946. The British premieres of *I quatro rusteghi* and *Simon Boccanegra* were eventually given on 7 June 1946 and 27 October 1948 respectively.

2 Lorna and Warwick Braithwaite's house at 23 Linden Lea, London, N.2. remained his permanent residence until his death.

Our cat caused trouble. The poor little thing seemed quite happy for the first few miles, but by the time we got to Tring, I was forced to take action. I stopped at a hat shop and bought an expensive box, cut some holes in it, and placed the cat inside. Despite the luxurious accommodation, it squealed all the way to Worcester. We stopped to have lunch outside Beaconsfield, and while eating food on the wayside, four huge flying boats went over our heads. The war was coming closer!

Arriving at Worcester and seeing my wife and child safely ensconced with her sister, I had to turn back (after a cup of tea) for London. I had a BBC concert the next day and a 10 a.m. rehearsal. It was the first night of the genuine blackout order, and because my car was not equipped with any method of hiding my lights, I was stopped by every enthusiastic, scared and truculent air raid warden from Worcester to London. I arrived home at midnight in the pouring rain, having driven most of the way without lights.

Next morning, I arrived at the BBC Maida Vale studios and was amazed to see Laurance Turner, the orchestra leader, and most of the players outside the entrance reading morning papers. The concert was off and all the London theatres were ordered to close. I drove madly to Sadler's Wells and verified the news. There was to be no more opera during the war – at least not at Sadler's Wells Theatre. There was nothing for it but to go home, pack my belongings and drive once more to Worcester, where I arrived about 6 p.m. in the evening. I had no money, no prospects, and a newly born baby into the bargain. My thoughts at that time were pretty bloody. What was the good of throwing the whole of one's energies into a good cause if the cause itself was to be blown up, like all of us, in the near future? The direst blows were to fall on our country, our people and our institutions, and do what one may, everything was to be annihilated. Here was indeed the abyss. The thoughts were real enough and the blackest days of all were to follow.

I had to work at something and I think this was my salvation. I could not be idle for long, and luck came my way when I visited the Labour Exchange in order to get a job for our maid. Having succeeded in this, as I was leaving the office of the Director, I jokingly mentioned that I was in need of a job myself. He looked at me (his name was Coates, curiously enough, and he was very fond of music[3]) and said 'Are you serious?' I answered that I was most serious. Next morning, I became a company clerk in the Army Medical Board Recruiting Office at 26/- per week. My fall was terrible to behold. From £17 per week, I now received 26 shillings and, as far as I could see, with no prospects of a rise. I was a temporary civil servant. What the doctors made of me is difficult to say, but I was on many occasions entrusted with the eyesight examination entirely

---

3 A reference to both Eric Coates (composer) and Albert Coates (conductor).

on my own. The job was irksome in the extreme and I was longing to get out of it.

Working in the same office was a man who had been a civil servant for 13 years and who had three children. His salary was a disgrace to the country and I began to feel more fed up than ever. About this time, I met one of the temporary clerks, a Worcester man called Glover. During a chance conversation he told me the origin of his name. His forebears were glovers in Worcester, and the name, like many other names such as Carpenter, Heward, Smith, etc., owed its origin to the craft in which his forebears had engaged. One thing led to another and before long he was giving me lessons, mainly during the short luncheon period, on the history of the Worcester guilds. I found this subject of absorbing interest and the idea took shape in my mind of an opera, based on one of the legends of Worcester. I delved into all the books I could find in the public library and took copious notes, which I have to this day, of the Guilds, their rules and their history.

The more I went into the subject the more I could see what a wealth of material was available for an opera, but I knew that one other opera prevented me from carrying out my idea of writing a libretto. My mind turned to Wagner's *Mastersingers*, and the medieval atmosphere of Worcester's past carried me into the vivid atmosphere of Nürnberg as recreated in his opera. Even so, it was worthwhile digging into these things because, apart from keeping me occupied in my leisure moments, it took my mind off other, more serious, considerations.

But not for long. Soon it was apparent, after that Sunday scare (when a single British aeroplane made an unauthorized flight over the East Coast almost at the same time as Chamberlain made his announcement of the declaration of war against Germany) that Hitler had other plans. Weeks went by and nothing happened. Jack Gordon telephoned me with the joyful news that he and one other were prepared to guarantee a limited return of activity to Sadler's Wells. I travelled to London and the Executive Committee met and decided to try one matinée a week and see if the public would respond. Guthrie was asked to come into this, but I believe he washed his hands of it, although he very graciously gave his consent to the Committee 'having a go'. The Governors likewise disassociated themselves from the venture, and the Executive Committee proposed to run it themselves with the small guarantee available.

From one matinée a week, we gave two, and then ventured further, giving one evening performance as well, until in a few weeks' time we were back to our previous schedule. So commenced, in many ways the longest and most extraordinary season since the opening of the theatre. It lasted 14 months and only broke up through a variety of circumstances. The last performance took place on 7 September 1940, on the night of London's first night raid.[4]

*

While I had been working in Worcester, I took the opportunity of going out to Marl Bank, Rainbow Hill, where Edward Elgar had lived and where I had visited him several times while I was in Cardiff. The last time I had been there was during the National Orchestra of Wales days, and Elgar and I had corresponded quite a bit about a concert of his music which I wanted him to conduct in Cardiff. The programme was a hefty one: *Overture 'In the South'*, Violin Concerto, and Symphony no. 2 in E Flat. The correspondence was getting too long-winded and there was something not quite right about it. I felt I had to clinch the matter soon, as the programme people were getting anxious. I asked for an interview and Sir Edward very kindly acquiesced.

I had met Sir Edward at one of the Malvern Shaw Festivals. He was sitting immediately in front of me with George Bernard Shaw and H.G. Wells. I made myself known to him and he introduced me to the other two great people. The play – I forget what it was – commenced and I had no further opportunity of speaking to him. In any case, who was I to mingle with the gods?

I presented myself at Marl Bank, Elgar's lovely house and garden overlooking Worcester, and was ushered into his sitting room with the French doors leading out from the porch into the garden. It was a lovely sunny day, and we talked. First of all, I wanted to fix up the financial details connected with his appearance with the NOW. When it became apparent that he wanted to back out of it, I asked him to give me some sort of a message that would help me in my struggle to keep the orchestra going. But the main impression I have of that interview was the deep gloom that seemed to have taken hold of Elgar about that time. It was only four years before his death, and little music had come from his pen for the few years before. He still complained bitterly about his early struggles and several times mentioned the ingratitude of an unmusical nation in its appreciation of his work. Frankly I was puzzled at his attitude and could see no reason for it at the time.

We had tea and afterwards, with his playful dogs, walked up and down on the lawn in the sunshine. He pointed out with pride, part of the remains of the old Severn Bridge which he had brought to Marl Bank and which I suppose is still there to this day.

The concert in Cardiff was conducted by myself, but the audience was a

---

4   The last evening performance was of Gounod's *Faust*. Braithwaite had conducted a matinée performance of *La bohème* the same day.

small one which, in a sense, bore out Elgar's contention about the attitude to his music – at least in Wales.[5] I still have many letters from Elgar, and when years later I visited his birthplace in Broadheath, Mrs Blake,[6] his daughter, allowed me to see the big collection of Elgar's programmes preserved there. Mine was not among them and I offered to let her have it, but I found I only had one copy and was loath to part with it.

Visiting Marl Bank while in Worcester in 1939, I found many changes. The then tenant appeared to know nothing of Elgar, and I was saddened by the absence of any little bit of evidence that he had ever lived there. No, I was wrong, for in the garden was still the portion of the old bridge; a few pieces of wood were all that remained. I expressed a wish to the lady of the house to let me see Elgar's bedroom – the room where the great man had died and where he had listened for the last time to a recording of some of his works from HMV. I never saw this bedroom in Elgar's lifetime, but with the cheap furniture now in it, I could only reflect (in the gloomiest way) on the transitory nature of life.

The recording referred to was arranged by Fred Gaisberg (one of my oldest friends in this country) and the London Symphony Orchestra with HMV.[7] A landline direct from Abbey Road, London to Marl Bank, Worcester was installed, with a microphone and a loudspeaker. Elgar listened to the rehearsal and although very ill, criticised some points in the playing. Fred Gaisberg, one of the loveliest and most charming of men, told me of these details and how he thought it might cheer Elgar up during his last illness. It was one of the most magnificent gestures ever made to a dying composer. Fred Gaisberg is, alas, no more, nor is W.H. Reed, the leader of the LSO, who was one of Elgar's most intimate friends. Between them, these two men gave Elgar this last enduring happiness.[8]

Willie Reed phoned me up a few days before the Memorial Service held in Worcester Cathedral and very kindly invited me to it. Sometime after this he told me of the sketches Elgar had made for an opera based on a play by Ben Jonson. I

---

5 The programme, given at City Hall, Cardiff on 27 February 1930, substituted *Falstaff* for the Second Symphony. This was one of four all-Elgar concerts given by Braithwaite in Cardiff, and during his BBC employment there, he programmed and conducted Elgar compositions over 250 times. The composer himself guest-conducted two concerts with the NOW in Swansea and Cardiff on 11 and 12 May 1930. The programme on those occasions was *Froissart, Introduction and Allegro, Wand of Youth Suite no. 1, Enigma Variations* and *In the South*. Tenor soloist Heddle Nash contributed excerpts from *The Light of Life* and *King Olaf*. Braithwaite's comments suggest that his disappointment about the fate of the NOW still ran deep.

6 Mrs Carice Irene Elgar Blake (1890-1970).

7 Frederick William Gaisberg (1873-1951), American-born pioneer of the recording industry.

8 This took place on 22 January 1934, and the items being recorded were the 'Triumphal March' and 'Woodland Interlude' from *Caractacus*. Elgar died on 23 February 1934. See Jerrold Northrop Moore, *Edward Elgar: A Creative Life* (OUP, 1984), 821-22.

would dearly love to get hold of these sketches to see if anything could be done with them, as I always believed that Elgar would have loved to have got out of the 'rut' (glorious as it was) of producing oratorio after oratorio.[9] In *Caractacus* and *King Olaf*, there is more than a glimpse of dramatic characterization. During my visit to Broadheath I asked Mrs Blake if the sketches were on view, but as far as I remember the answer was in the negative.[10]

*

Towards the end of the Winter Season at Sadler's Wells, the raid warnings had become more frequent and the fear was ever present in our minds that London would receive the full force of Hitler's malignant hatred. That caused us to at least announce a date for a break in our activities at the theatre.

Guthrie had come back as Director once the season was in full swing and assumed control of everything.[11] But before then the company of artists and representatives from the orchestra began to meet in order to demand a voice in the direction. Meetings were held at which resolutions were passed asking for a fairer share of the takings. It must not be forgotten, in defence of the artists, that they had started this difficult war season entirely on their own and had accepted big reductions in salary on a co-operative basis to keep it going. Guthrie seemed to resist these rightful claims and, from then on, tempers began to get ruffled. Meeting after meeting was held and the more fiery members began to attack Guthrie openly. I remember one remark flung at Guthrie caused him bitterness and anger, and it was quite unnecessary. Someone said, 'If Baylis had been alive such-and-such would not have happened.' Guthrie quite rightly retorted angrily, 'Well Baylis is dead and what are you going to do about that?' Gradually disaffection spread among the artists, and several weakened. Some began to take the easier line of keeping away from meetings altogether. Others went further and worked against their committee by giving Guthrie active support. Guthrie seized the opportunity of 'making hay while the sun shone' and entered into separate agreements with these artists. Soon it became apparent that those who had fought to keep their end up had little chance against a small active body of people who had official support. So, towards August 1940 we all decided in

---

9   A reference to Elgar's sketches for an opera based on Ben Jonson's *The Devil is an Ass*. The work, which was retitled by Elgar as *The Spanish Lady*, was never completed. Dr Percy Young organised the surviving material for recording purposes.

10 The sketches are now held by the British Library. Young's edition of the opera is published by Novello.

11 Guthrie returned on 12 January 1940, having 'given up his film work in order to devote all his energies to Vic-Wells.' Susie Gilbert, *Opera for Everybody* (London, Faber, 2009), 69.

The Old Vic, London, in 1940.

conjunction with Guthrie that the season would end for the time being on Saturday 11th September. Everybody was tired of the wrangling, and a holiday would be an excellent thing. Behind the scenes, arrangements were already in hand for a tour by a much smaller company, but these arrangements were not divulged by Guthrie to the larger committee of artists.

Our last two performances on 7 September 1940 coincided with the first daylight raid on the docks, when hordes of German bombers succeeded in breaking through our defences. From the roof of Sadler's Wells, I saw the end of that raid with the warehouses blazing all along the waterfront. *Tosca* was the afternoon performance (which I had conducted), and *Faust* the evening one, conducted by Collingwood. That night was terrifying, with the whole sky lit up by the flames from the docks. It was also the first of nearly six months of night raids on London. Next morning, I sent my family to Dinas Powys, five miles outside Cardiff, while I awaited what was to come, on my own, in London.

Calling at Sadler's Wells the following Monday, I was told that a smaller company was to tour with Verdi's *La traviata*. I could get little information as to the personnel, but from the few hints that were dropped, I gathered that I was not to be included for the moment.[12]

Two days afterwards, I had a telegram from Joseph Barnes, Manager of the Scottish Orchestra in Glasgow, asking me if I would accept the position of conductor to that honourable and ancient Society known as the Glasgow Choral and Orchestral Union. Seeing no future as yet for me with Sadler's Wells, I wrote to Guthrie telling him of the offer and sought permission to accept. He wrote me a charming letter to the effect that he was glad I had had the offer and, as it was only for three months, he hoped I would rejoin the Sadler's Wells Company later, if they were still in existence.

I had already conducted the Scottish Orchestra for a few concerts during 1931 and looked forward very much to the upcoming season. London was an unhappy place to be, especially at night, as the raids were continuing with redoubled fury. The Scottish season was not to commence until November 9th

---

12 The company toured with an orchestra of five and a chorus of four. Lawrance Collingwood conducted from the piano. Susie Gilbert, *Opera for Everybody* (London, Faber, 2009), 72–73.

1940, so I still had a few weeks in London and experienced the misery of not sleeping in bed (unless it was for a few hours during the day-time).

Before leaving for Scotland, I journeyed to Cardiff and spent a few days with my family, who had been living with my father-in-law during the last few weeks. The arrangement we had made was that I would go on ahead and endeavour to find accommodation for us all in Glasgow. This I did, and eventually after a few weeks, my wife Lorna, and our two boys, Rodric and Nicholas (the latter less than 18 months of age and not yet toddling) had to make the winter trip from Cardiff to Glasgow in an unheated carriage with a small, but very energetic baby, and no restaurant car. Luggage, prams, cot, food and everything necessary for the journey had to be taken, and I met an exhausted mother and a fractious baby at the end of the journey. The train was hours late; they had been travelling all day and were almost beyond caring. We took three rooms in the Shawlands Cross locality, and for the next three months put up with what comfort we were able to secure.

PART VI
(1940–1946)

FIFTEEN

THE SCOTTISH ORCHESTRA

Once in Glasgow, I threw my whole energy into the concerts. My friend Aylmer Buesst had conducted the previous season, and a most difficult one it must have been, with everyone afraid to venture anything. When I arrived to take my first rehearsal, I was genuinely gratified at the high standard of the players. The leader was David McCallum, one of the best principal violinists in the country.[1] The personnel of the orchestra included many well-known names and as a result of the London raids, players were glad enough to leave that city and accept positions with the Scottish.

The whole basis in financing the Scottish was the guarantee system, and to be a guarantor one had to risk at least £5. Glasgow had financed this orchestra for over 50 years. The extraordinary thing was that the season had only been for three months in each year. In a rich city the size of Glasgow this seemed a very niggardly attitude towards orchestral music. But I was not to think about this point for some time yet.

My first season was a success for me personally; the orchestra was very good and the performances at times quite excellent.[2] There were 27 main concerts[3] and my first soloist was that great man and pianist, Scotland's internationally

---

1 David McCallum (1897–1972) went on to lead the LPO, the RPO, and Mantovani's Orchestra. He was the father of actor David McCallum.

2 The consistently excellent reviews support this. At the end of the first season one critic wrote, 'Yesterday's concert...was entirely orchestral, and the full house was in some measure a tribute to Mr Warwick Braithwaite, who was making his last Sunday appearance with the orchestra.' *The Scotsman* (20 January 1941), 3.

3 Braithwaite prepared 27 concerts and conducted 25. Two concerts were guest-conducted by Richard Tauber and Adrian Boult.

Frederic Lamond, pianist,
photographed by Bassano Ltd
in 1919.

© *National Portrait Gallery, London*

famous Frederic Lamond.[4] I was to see much more of Lamond during the next six years.

The audiences, from being half-hearted at the beginning, were getting bigger and bigger, and towards the end of the three-month season, the concerts at St Andrew's Hall were very well attended. The committee was much gratified by a drop in the call on guarantees from 13/6d in the £1 to 7/6d, from the previous season. This was a healthy sign. Orchestral concerts began to be very popular everywhere, and although Scotland was slower than other places, I knew that in a very short time, Scotland would fall into place.

Halfway through the season I wrote to Guthrie suggesting that the Sadler's Wells company should come to Glasgow and do opera once again on a fairly grand scale. I would form a local committee of guarantors and ensure the availability of an orchestra of 65 players. The opera company had been struggling along with an expanded orchestra of twelve players, touring small towns and being generally miserable. Guthrie came up to Glasgow to discuss details, and he and James Easdale, the chairman of the local committee, began to thrash out the difficulties. Easdale called a meeting a few days later and forced the committee to vote for the discontinuation of the whole scheme, because Guthrie's ideas on the cost had been much heavier than Easdale had expected, and there wasn't a dog's chance of getting a guarantee. I asked for three days in which to get commitments of £3,000. This was accepted and I tramped around Glasgow in the pouring rain until, by the evening of the next day, I had more than half that amount. By the time the next meeting was due, Easdale himself was persuaded to guarantee a considerable amount, and I was able to announce that the guarantee fund was successfully subscribed.

After a great deal of trouble, the season of a month was finally on the way. Such was the demand for tickets by the public that the season was a great financial success and the guarantee fund was not called upon. I really had to laugh to myself over this guarantee. I had seen the same sort of thing in Cardiff.

---

4   Frederic Archibald Lamond (1868–1948), pianist, composer and teacher. Other soloists included pianists Noel Mewton-Wood, J. Wight Henderson, Solomon, Clifford Curzon, Benno Moiseiwitsch and eight-year-old wunderkind, Jean Harvey; singers Joan Cross, Noël Eadie, Joan Hammond, Lisa Perli, Eva Turner, Alexander Carmichael, Sir Harry Lauder and Alfred Orda-Wdoczak; violinists David McCallum and Ida Haendel; and cellist Vera Canning.

When chairmen of committees did not want to go to the trouble of getting money for a venture, or perhaps didn't believe in it, the excuse invariably given was that the times were too bad and people had no money. Politically the same thing had happened many times. These men are a menace; the time is never ripe until you make it so. This time I was able to take up the challenge under much better auspices than had existed in Cardiff, and set to with a will. Even so, no-one was more surprised than I when, in less than three days, I had secured the guarantee!

The season got going. Collingwood by then had been appointed Musical Director of the Sadler's Wells Company. A small difficulty arose over the absorption of the twelve players of the Sadler's Wells orchestra into the much bigger 'Scottish'. It was a problem I hadn't thought about until it came crashing onto the horizon. The Scottish Orchestra committee (not the opera committee) insisted, rather foolishly under the circumstances, on its own players retaining the first positions in every case. A lot of bad blood was spilled over this difficulty. Personally, I was innocent of the accusations made against me that I had insisted on placing the Sadler's Wells orchestra in an inferior position, but I found, when the company arrived, a positive rudeness towards me on the part of certain people who ought to have known better. Collingwood was obviously infected, and the long friendship between us at Sadler's Wells itself was endangered. Ironically, when Collingwood got some sort of eye infection, I had to conduct all his operas as well.[5]

Guthrie had asked me before the little season started if I would take the same salary as the other members of the company (£10), which, of course, I was very glad to accept. But in my mind, this meant that when the Glasgow season was over, I would be rejoining the Sadler's Wells company on tour.[6] I took this for granted, but to make sure, I wrote to Guthrie asking for information as to the towns the company was to visit so that I could book rooms. I received no answer until the last week of the opera season, and was flabbergasted by a letter from Guthrie telling me that my services were not required. I was astounded by this most uncalled-for blow. I didn't deserve it. I had done nothing but good for the Sadler's Wells Opera Company and must only conclude, even at this

---

5 The season ran from 10 to 29 March 1941 at the Theatre Royal in Glasgow and continued from 31 March to 5 April at the King's Theatre, Edinburgh. The repertoire was *Madama Butterfly*, *Die Fledermaus*, *Le nozze di Figaro* and *La bohème*, and the conducting was shared between Laurance Collingwood and Braithwaite. Neither *The Glasgow Herald* nor *The Scotsman* reviewed all performances, and daily adverts did not announce the conductors. Performances were in aid of the Glasgow Central War Relief Red Cross Fund, as was a special concert given at Glasgow's Paramount Theatre on 30 March.

6 The Scottish Orchestra season ran from 9 November 1940 to 21 February 1941. Players and conductor had to survive as best they could in the intervening months, hence Braithwaite's disappointment at the lack of an ongoing engagement with the opera company on tour.

distant time, that someone within the company had persistently blackened my character. I feel that Guthrie, left alone, would have been fair in his treatment. If I read his character aright, I felt he thought no less of me because at times swords were crossed. When the members of the company heard that I wasn't being asked to return they were likewise incensed, and I believe every one of them, including orchestra and chorus, signed a petition to Guthrie requesting that I be reinstated. But no. The Director can never go back on his decision and this was the one time that Guthrie's strength of character looked like a pricked balloon. My case was even referred to the Governors, and the letter Guthrie sent me when I first wrote to him about the Scottish Orchestra telling me that I would be rejoining the company, was sent to Geoffrey Toye, one of the Governors. But nothing came of it.

Shortly afterwards Guthrie himself resigned because he was tired of operatic politics, and the new director was someone who ought never to have been offered that position. After five years of mismanagement, wherein many good artists had left out of exasperation, the remaining artists insisted on her resignation.[7] This time the Governors had to acquiesce and, after the war, when the company once more was settled at Sadler's Wells, Clive Carey came back from Australia and became the Director. The building up process commenced all over again.

Here I leave any further reference to Sadler's Wells, except to record that I wrote to the present Music Director in 1948 asking to join the conducting staff once again, but it seems that few of the pre-war people were welcome and the answer was a courteous, but firm 'no'.[8]

*

During the opera season at Glasgow's Theatre Royal, Clydebank had its first taste of air raids on 13 and 14 March, but I had already left Glasgow for Bristol where I was to do a BBC concert. Arriving just outside Bristol after an all-day journey, the second of two devastating raids was in full swing. Our train waited outside at Temple Meads Station from 10.30 p.m. until 4 a.m. All around us we could see the flames and hear the gunfire. As the train moved into the station, we were miserable, exhausted, hungry and a little scared. The all-clear had sounded at midnight, and we had been in that train an extra five and a half hours waiting to move into the station. I will never forget the scenes of devastation on the way from Temple Meads Station to the City Centre – plate glass smashed to millions

7   Braithwaite, hardly an unbiased observer, is referring to the soprano Joan Cross who had sacrificed her own singing career to keep the opera company afloat throughout the war.

8   James Robertson was Music Director of Sadler's Wells from 1946 to 1954. Braithwaite did eventually rejoin Sadler's Wells from 1960 to 1967.

of pieces; bricks and concrete heaped up everywhere; no street lighting and, of course, no taxis or other conveyances.

I had for the first time reserved a room, not at one of the usual hotels (the Royal or the Grand) but, on the advice of one of my sisters-in-law, at a boarding establishment near Victoria Hall, which is at the top of Park Street. By taxi, the journey would have been not more than 20 minutes, but on that night, walking with my heavy suitcase, it would have been more like an hour. I trundled up the lower part of Park Street, but water mains had burst and Park Street was a raging torrent. I turned to the left and again right, finding myself in a narrow parallel lane at the back of the shops. Most of those buildings were on fire or burnt out and the heat was unbearable, but once I had started, I forced my way on until I reached the top of the hill and came out somewhere below the Victoria Rooms. Then I had to find my boarding house, which was in a nearby crescent. There was no street lighting and no-one to ask. I pulled out a box of matches, and with the aid of these, scrutinized the name and number of every home in that crescent. Eventually I came to the last one, about half a mile away from where I had started. By this time my matches were finished, but it was the right address. I pressed the bell, but there was no answer. I pressed it again and again. I was hungry, exhausted, and my limbs were sore from falling over rubble. Eventually, a light showed behind the glass panel and the landlady appeared, looking like Florence Nightingale in curlers. It was by now five 5 a.m. I asked her if she could give me some food as I hadn't eaten since the previous day. She hadn't any food but could give me a biscuit and a glass of milk. I fell into bed and got what sleep I could, but as I had a BBC rehearsal at 10 a.m., it was hopeless.

I was up again at 9 a.m., and after a cup of tea and a bite of bread, I presented myself at the BBC Studio in Whiteladies Road. The rehearsal was delayed until the afternoon as so many of the orchestral players had had their dwellings knocked about by bombs. One bass player, Bert Cockerill, was killed, and Sidonie Goossens and Hyam Greenbaum's flat was hit.[9] Bassoonist, Richard Newton, lost all his clothing and a stock of valuable cane for his reeds. Marie Wilson, a co-leader with Paul Beard, had missed death by a miracle. Almost every member of the orchestra had a tale of distress or miraculous escape to tell.

I began to tell them all how safe we were in Glasgow; that the Glasgow people believed that the configuration of the mountains, and the number of lochs nearby was so confusing to the Germans that Glasgow was comparatively safe. That afternoon, the papers came out with the news that a northern port had suffered a serious raid. I told myself that it might have been Liverpool, not Glasgow. I tried to get through by phone but failed, and I sent a telegram which

---

9 Sidonie Goossens (1899–2004), distinguished harpist and founder member of the BBC Symphony Orchestra. Her first husband, Hyam Greenbaum (1901–1942), was a violinist, composer and music director.

didn't arrive. I was very fearful because not far from Shawlands Cross was a large munitions factory.

I conducted my BBC concert in a whirl – I can't remember to this day what the performance was – and caught the night train back to Glasgow.[10] Sure enough, Glasgow had suffered two raids aimed at the docks, but causing more damage to the tenements. The loss of life was fearful and the Glasgow people were most rudely shocked out of their complacency. My family was safe and I was thankful to be so lucky.

After a few days we had another raid, and this time the Germans were definitely trying for the munitions factory nearby. They seemed to be after me. Then we could hear the scream of three bombs coming down. This was it. My stomach turned inside out. (How many times this happened to me! It may have been good exercise for my anatomy but I never got used to it). I never thought of myself as a coward, but the horrible sound of these screaming bombs was too much for me. It was like being inside a huge dynamo or at the centre of a tornado. My body moved convulsively yet I was rooted to the spot. I think I only uttered one word – "God". Now isn't that strange? I, who as a boy had been in love with belief, yet who from the age of 23 or so had been an agnostic! My wife, who was with me in the sitting room, was almost completely unconcerned except for the safety of our two boys who were sleeping in the next room. When the bombs landed it was on a block of flats only about a hundred yards away. The concussion, or the rush of air, blew in the heavy shutters at the top of a flight of stairs facing the room in which the children slept. We rushed into their bedroom. They were blissfully asleep and looked like angels – perhaps never more so than at that moment.

We left them sleeping and went out in order to see if we could help. The cries and shrieks were pitiful to hear. We brought two women home with us – a mother and her twenty-year-old daughter, both covered in soot. Neither of them was really hurt, but as the older woman was still distraught, we set about being of some practical use. Hot water and soap restored their beauty and hot tea calmed them down. Next morning our landlady gave us a trouncing for bringing these distressed people into her house, because their sooty clothes had made a few marks on her carpet! My wife stayed in our sitting room while I escorted the two women to the Rest Centre not far away. The older woman every now and then would burst into her 'grieving' and I was glad to get her safely fixed up for the night. We never saw them again.

---

10 Braithwaite conducted the BBC Symphony Orchestra at Colston Hall on 14 March. The soloist in Liszt's Piano Concerto no. 1 was Moura Lympany. According to one reviewer, Braithwaite 'secured some vital interpretations in a programme rather more conservative than the type usually associated with him.' *Western Daily Press* (15 March 1941), 3. The programme included the *Hebrides Overture* (Mendelssohn), *Capriol Suite* (Warlock) and *Capriccio espagnol* (Rimsky-Korsakov).

The centre of Glasgow and its immediate surroundings had almost completely escaped. A few drifting landmines had done bad damage here and there, but when I went down to the docks two days later with members of the Sadler's Wells Company, we saw terrible scenes of destruction; whole blocks of tenement flats levelled to the ground, and hundreds of people had been caught unprepared and, of course, killed.

Why the Glasgow people were so complacent about raids was a mystery to me, as earlier on at the beginning of the war, one plane came over and dropped five bombs. One went down the funnel of the cruiser Sussex, but didn't explode; the next hit an underground station near the Clyde and flooded a portion of the line; the third hit the main Post Office; the fourth fell a few yards in front of the City Chambers. I don't remember where the fifth bomb fell, but four bombs could not have had better targets. The underground was out of action for the best part of the next four years. The HMS Sussex, which was full of munitions, had a miraculous escape.[11]

The opera company had escaped altogether although, on the first night, the audience was confined to the theatre.[12] My wife, who was at the theatre, could not get back to Shawlands Cross for hours and went through a great strain. The raids seemed to make very little difference to attendance figures at the Theatre Royal, and by the end of the season there was a good profit. James Easdale had demanded that any profit should go to the Red Cross fund, but when he discovered that the artists had only the small amount of £10 per week, he made a grant out of the profits to the artists, and each one benefitted thereby. They all deserved it.

*

My family came back to London with me and we tried to live once again in our house, despite the ongoing raids. I volunteered as an air raid warden, and my wife would grouse at me because I had to leave her at home under the stairs with the two boys. I had erected an Anderson Shelter in the garage,[13] but what with the floor of the garage being concrete and the shelter being made of corrugated iron, the sound of gunfire and bursting of bombs was amplified to an alarming degree, and my son just would not have it. So, I made a shelter under the stairs

---

11 The HMS *Sussex* did not escape completely. She was in Glasgow Docks for repairs when the bombs struck on 18 September 1940. The resulting fire damage kept her out of service until August 1942. 'HMS Sussex (96)', https://uboat.net/allies/warships/ship/1182.html, accessed 7 January 2019.

12 The 3-week season ran from 10–29 March 1941. Braithwaite refers to the first night of the bombing (13 March), when the opera being performed was *Madama Butterfly*, conducted by Lawrance Collingwood.

13 Named after Sir John Anderson, who commissioned their manufacture, the small metal shelter was intended to be partly sunk in a garden and covered in earth.

where there was a junk cupboard. I had to make a door to prevent the children from falling downstairs, and used to try and keep young Nicholas amused by playing peek-a-boo through the crosspieces of wood.

The raids got steadily worse and I had about 200 yards to walk from my house to the Wardens' Post through showers of shrapnel. I pleaded with the Warden to let me have a tin hat to take home, as the walk up to the Post was positively dangerous. Although there were six to spare, he refused permission. Not to be outdone, by the next raid I put an aluminium cooking pot on my head, much too big for me, with the handle at the back, like the plait of a seventeenth century man o'warsman, and walked into a crowded Post. Roars of laughter greeted my entrance and thereafter the Post Warden relented and gave me a tin hat to take home.

A few nights afterwards, all hell let loose, and while carrying my sleeping youngest out to the garage shelter, a piece of shrapnel missed his darling head by a fraction of an inch and buried itself in the garden. I dug it up the next morning and that decided me. I would not take 'no' for an answer, and I took the family to Paddington Station and saw them off to Cardiff.

The scenes at Paddington Station were indescribable. Thousands of people who had come back to London during the Phoney War period[14] had evidently decided to do the same as me, and the trains were packed to suffocation. What my poor wife went through was bad enough, but at least many others were going through the same misery. Their reward at the other end was, hopefully, a comfortable home and night-time in luxurious beds.

I bought a mattress downstairs and put it outside the stair cupboard. When the raids became unbearable, I would leave the mattress and skulk in the utmost fear under the stairs, my stomach doing its customary tremors at every bomb scream. Life went on like this for weeks, and I envied both the Sadler's Wells Opera Company on tour as well as my family in their comparative safety.

I had saved £250 from my Scottish season, and although I could not pay my bigger debts and got into trouble, the wartime 'moratorium' saved me from serious financial dissolution, although the mental worry was excruciating at times. Soon my savings had all gone and I was really 'on the rocks'. One of my fellow wardens had been buying up abandoned third-class cinemas all over London and had by that time six, mostly dilapidated premises. He offered me a job as 'relief' manager to the whole six. At first, I couldn't bring myself to accept such a job, but later, when my position had become desperate, I took it on. Just imagine, I had to manage a different cinema each day, relieving the resident manager on his day off. I had to deal with mostly poor and uneducated usherettes, standing on their feet from 10 a.m. until 10 p.m. for about 30 shillings per week. I had to count the half

---

14 'Phoney War' is a term – possibly of American origin – that describes the period from 3 September 1939 to 10 May 1940, during which little sign of warlike activity was observed in Britain.

tickets and see that the money was correct and return it to my employer's house every night. I learned for the first time the usefulness of a ready reckoner instead of laboriously counting every eight pence or so. The money always came out right and always to my inexperienced astonishment.

The job was irksome and I hated the conditions under which these usherettes worked. I should have been hard with them when they were lazy or used to slip their boyfriends into the cinema through the back way, but I just couldn't. The climax came when a cashier at one of the outlying cinemas was caught after stealing £7.10s. on her day off. I found that this money was missing, and fancied myself a detective for a few hours without any success. I phoned my employer who asked me to get in touch with the CID. Perhaps the detective knew the type of girls he was questioning but I couldn't stand his methods. The thief was found, but I was determined to leave the business. The type of girl, the long hours and poor pay were enough in my opinion to tempt any villain.

I had stuck this job for six weeks at the magnificent salary of £6.10s per week. The work was unbelievably hard and the duties onerous. I told my employer I didn't like his methods or his job, but he retaliated by begging me to stay with him, even offering me a cinema he had just bought as my very own. This may sound fantastic but I must beg the reader to believe me. He offered me the whole takings of one of his cinemas if I would stay with him. But it was no good; I couldn't bear anything about the job and preferred to starve. I nearly *did* starve, and was in a pitiable situation financially. My house was nearly lost to me, but I fought the people concerned and was able to save it for my family.

At last, a good fairy, in the shape of one of the executive staff of the BBC, heard of my predicament. A delicate situation had meanwhile arisen at the Manchester studio, so I was sent there to clear it up for three months. This carried me on until about three months before my next season with the Scottish.[15] During those fallow three months I did other work such as recording with HMV,[16] so that my financial situation began to take on a more unspotted complexion.

---

15 Between 14 July and 17 December Braithwaite conducted 19 studio concerts with the BBC Northern Orchestra, broadcast from the Manchester studios of the BBC. His second season with the Scottish Orchestra began on 15 November, and so for a month he was working in both Manchester and Glasgow. Also at this time, Braithwaite received a letter dated 13 August 1942 from the Irish composer Frederick May, urging support for the premiere of his substantial work *Songs from Prison*. The first broadcast performance however, was given by Adrian Boult and the BBC Orchestra on 14 December.

16 In fact, Braithwaite began recording for HMV in 1938. The session he is recalling took place on 10 June 1941 at EMI Studio No. 1, Abbey Road, London. The artists were Ann Ziegler *(soprano)* and Webster Booth *(tenor)*, with an unnamed studio orchestra, and the repertoire was 'The Golden Song' and 'The Flower' (Schubert/Clutsam's *Lilac Time*); 'Will you remember?' (Romberg's *Maytime*) and *Love's Garden of Roses* (Haydn Wood).

An excerpt of 'The Sword in the Stone' scene (in short score) from Braithwaite's opera, Pendragon.

It was during this difficult period that I completely finished the sketch of my opera, *Pendragon*, and began to score it, often interrupted by a scared dive under the stairs. The composition of the opera had proceeded fitfully up to the end of Act II, and then interruption after interruption made any further work on it impossible. There had been a lapse of nearly a year before I took it up again, yet curiously enough during this most difficult time, I finished Act III in less than three months. This period for me was quite extraordinary. I would work until midnight, when my ideas would suddenly cease. Next morning, despite bombs and sleepless nights, I would recommence where I left off and write with the utmost ease. As soon as one situation on my imaginary stage was coped with musically, I would be impelled to go on to the next by the over-flowing into my mind of the appropriate music. Personally, I think my first opera is a good one and it should have a performance, but I will do nothing about it. I deliberately kept to a style that I thought most appropriate to the first Arthurian legend of Uther and Igraine, and perhaps I am too afraid of what the modernist will say about it. Be this as it may, the opera is finished, with the exception of the last fifty pages or so of full score.[17]

The raids by this time had become sporadic, and it was possible to live in

---

17 *Pendragon* remains unperformed. See Appendix 5.

one's bed more often. My wife wanted to come back to London, and this was arranged. Our eldest boy, Rodric, had been awarded a scholarship at Bedales School, so he was out of London for most of the time.[18] Glasgow didn't appeal to my wife, so I went there alone for my second season. Again, it was to be a four-month season in Glasgow with more concerts in Inverness, Aberdeen and Dundee, as well as numerous children's concerts. Altogether the number of concerts began to grow.[19] The audiences filled the St Andrew's Hall, and the Edinburgh concerts in the Usher Hall once a fortnight were packed out. Artists such as Solomon, Benno Moiseiwitsch, Clifford Curzon, Ida Haendel, Max Rostal and Myra Hess, appeared with me regularly. To this list was added later, Leff Pouishnoff, Louis Kentner, Julius Isserlis, Colin Horsley (a fellow New Zealander), Moura Lympany and singers such as Eva Turner and Kathleen Ferrier. This second season was a complete financial success and it was obvious to me that the traditional shorter season was out of date. I tried to persuade the slow-minded committee to extend the season, but for the time being I had no success. The seed had been planted though, and was to flower two seasons later.

*

At the end of my second season, I made arrangements to bring the Carl Rosa Opera Company to Glasgow, as Guthrie had refused to repeat the successful Vic-Wells experiment of the previous year. I procured a guarantee of £3,000 which, once again, was not called upon. Several members of the Scottish Orchestra committee were on the opera committee and I was hoping that they would see the urgent wartime need for more music. I think the success of the opera season was convincing enough for some of the committee, notably Charles Rigg, who by now was completely won over to the idea of a six-month orchestra season.[20] But out came the same excuse that the time wasn't ripe for such experiments.

This time I was going to tread more carefully. I had learned something about myself which I could see would always get me into trouble if not kept under control: this was my inability to acknowledge defeat. I had suffered a

---

18 Bedales is an independent co-educational day and boarding school, located in the village of Sleep, near Petersfield, Hampshire.

19 Braithwaite conducted the Scottish Orchestra (now the Royal Scottish National Orchestra) for six seasons. The first three seasons ran from November to March each year; the last three seasons ran from October to April. The approximate number of concerts given in Glasgow, Edinburgh and on tour is as follows: 1940–1941 (25 concerts); 1941–1942 (28 concerts); 1942–1943 (31 concerts); 1943–1944 (85 concerts); 1944–1945 (85 concerts); 1945–1946 (65 concerts). In addition, the orchestra played for seasons of opera given by the Vic-Wells and Carl Rosa companies, oratorio performances by the Glasgow Choral Union, and school concerts.

20 Possibly the baritone Charles D. Rigg, who had broadcast Scottish ballads for the 5SC Glasgow studios of the BBC.

Warwick Braithwaite,
portrait by Howard Coster,
c.1944.

© *National Portrait Gallery, London.*

severe blow with the NOW and another one with Sadler's Wells, all through my persistence and the self-willed confidence that I was right. I knew I was right in every case, but perhaps in fairness to others, I should acknowledge that I didn't always go about things in the right way. The more intensive the opposition, the more insistent my will would become. This time, however, I was no less determined, but far more tactful.

One more completely successful season gave me the ammunition I needed. At several committee meetings I put my case, and put it well; so much so that the committee at last took (for them) the unprecedented decision to have an 'approximate' season of six months during 1943–1944. I won't say that I didn't do a little bit of press work on this occasion but I was very careful to keep my name out of it for the time being. In the 1943–1944 season the number of concerts was exactly doubled in Glasgow to 27 Saturday symphony concerts and 26 Sunday afternoon popular concerts, as well as the usual children's concerts (which were also doubled in number), and concerts on tour. The committee's brochure contained this opening paragraph: 'The Committee's decision to enter upon the adventure of doubling the length of the Concert Season, constitutes an important epoch in the history of the Union…and it is hoped that…frequent and regular attendance at the concerts will ensure that the Committee's enterprise shall be crowned with success!'

I could not help feeling that the committee, or at least the person on the committee (possibly Joseph Barnes[21]) who wrote that opening paragraph, was taking a rather pessimistic view of the future. It was I who had 'entered upon the adventure', not the committee. After all, if I could not ensure the success of a longer season, then I was 'in for it'! Also, it was not the committee that would have to foot the bill if the season was a failure, but the guarantors. This unctuous pessimism annoyed me, and I began to discover a positive dislike shown by the older members of the committee, because they were expected to go to meetings and concerts for six months instead of three. They prophesied more raids, extreme poverty and dreadful unemployment, and it seemed to me they almost hoped for these things to happen so that their 'adventure' and 'enterprise' would prove too much. As it turned out they were wrong. Another thing which I was to see two years later, when I suggested a complete permanent orchestra, was

---

21 Joseph Barnes was both Secretary and Manager of the Choral and Orchestral Union of Glasgow.

the alarm of Joseph Barnes, when he realized that he would have to give up the position of secretary, unless he gave up his solicitor's business. He couldn't do both. But more of that later.

The first six-month season (1943–1944) was therefore an anxious one for me. I worked as never before and conducted *all* the concerts. The millionaire, Sir Daniel Stevenson,[22] gave a donation of £5,000 to the fund, which the committee put aside for the 'general purposes' of the Union. I didn't like the sound of this, as it looked as if this money was going to be locked up and not used as a guarantee for the orchestra. The city corporation gave a cash donation of yet another £5,000 expressly for the concerts, and it looked as if outside the committee there was great faith in the future.

That season, Lamond, as always, led off the series with magnificent performances of the Beethoven Piano Concerto no. 3 and, on the Sunday, the Liszt E flat concerto.[23] Eileen Joyce, Irene Kohler, Jean Pougnet, Eda Kersey, Iso Elinson, Dino Borgioli and others joined our regular list of artists and, as the season neared its last few weeks, there was no doubt as to its financial success. The pessimists were silenced, and the call on guarantors was only five shillings in the pound. I personally felt elated at the undoubted success of this first six-month season, and my optimism was magnificently borne out by this success. However, the committee continued privately to describe the next two longer seasons as 'experimental', even though it was obvious that they had come to stay.

The rest of the story is very much a repetition of the foregoing with one great difference. For a long time, I had experienced difficulty in getting good enough players to come to Glasgow for the six-month season. No player could be tempted to come to Scotland now that the air raids elsewhere had more or less ceased. A six-month orchestral season was almost worse than three months in this respect. There were more concerts than ever. In some weeks when we were on tour in the north of Scotland, I would conduct nine concerts in six days and travel back to Glasgow on my free day. Apart from this, the rehearsals became more arduous than ever, owing to the fact that I had to rehearse every well-known work over and over again because of the gradual decline in the standard of the available players. Other orchestral societies had made their orchestras permanent, and thus attracted better players to their ranks. The

---

22 Sir Daniel Macaulay Stevenson, 1st Baronet (1851 –1944), was a Scottish politician, businessman and philanthropist, and Chancellor of the University of Glasgow from 1934 until his death. His fortune was made in shipbroking and coal exportation.

23 The reviewers in both major newspapers were obviously impressed:
'If the first two concerts at the week-end are any indication, the new and enlarged Scottish Orchestra may very well make musical history during the present season and pave the way for even more ambitious projects.' *The Scotsman* (4 October 1943), 3.
'There is no doubt that this year's Scottish, by their playing in two well-varied programmes, have begun the season with something like distinction.' *The Glasgow Herald* (4 October 1943), 2.

Choral Union was the only first-class society that had not made a move in that direction. When I pointed this out to the committee, the older members again prophesied bankruptcy for all these societies. As time went on, and these orchestras continued in their permanency, a stubborn hard core of resistance to any idea of a permanent orchestra began to reveal itself. The curious thing was that the guarantors themselves, a considerable number of people, actually passed a resolution at one of their meetings, asking that the orchestra should become a permanent one for the following season, and instructed their committee (the Executive) to go ahead and make arrangements for this. They also proposed to form a Scottish Orchestra Society of Music Lovers, a similar body to hold lectures and make propaganda for the orchestra. The Executive Committee gave lip service to this resolution and made a public announcement that they were trying every channel in order to implement such a resolution. Barnes then wrote a long letter to *The Glasgow Herald*, in which he gloomily pointed out how expensive a permanent orchestra would be. I was contacted by the editor who allowed me the privilege of seeing this letter before it got into the paper. I couldn't contain myself any longer, and although I knew it would mean that I would not come back the following season, I wrote a long letter pointing out the possibilities, giving facts and figures.[24]

At last, the atmosphere between myself and certain members of the Executive Committee became strained to such an extent that official business only called us to be polite to one another. It was a matter of great regret to me personally that the chairman and the ex-officio member, Joseph Barnes, began to look at me with distrust, when previously our relations had always been most friendly. Other members of the small committee, Charles Rigg for instance, a bluff 'Honest John', were entirely on my side, but he must have been sadly torn between his loyalty to the committee and his friendship towards me. I began to be most unhappy at the inevitable result of my own forthrightness, and only wished to be away from Scotland. I had done all in my power to persuade the opposition to see the light and establish a permanent orchestra, but was forced to realize that the committee, as it stood, would never budge from their innate opposition to a most desirable thing for musical Scotland.

I had conducted a full schedule of concerts during that last season and had made two suggestions which would have lightened my burden. One of the most desirable innovations was the appointment of a player who would double

---

24 In response to Barnes' letter to *The Glasgow Herald* on 19 April 1946, Braithwaite's letter called for the immediate establishment of a full-time orchestra for an initial period of one year. Any delay in doing this, he claimed, would make it almost impossible to obtain the services of good players. Negative attitudes, and the 'fearsome' financial figures quoted by Mr Barnes, would 'get us nowhere', he concluded. This public squabble would do Braithwaite's position with the Scottish Orchestra no good at all.

as an Orchestral Manager, whose work would be to assist me in little things; who would see to the platform behaviours of the players, see to the seating, the best kind of lighting (very necessary as no-one ever made certain that I had strong enough lighting above my desk), the rounding-up of latecomers onto the platform, touring tickets for the players and booking of hotel accommodation for myself. This suggestion of mine was passed by the Executive Committee, but resisted most strenuously by Joseph Barnes until I had to appear before the committee and insist on the appointment being made without any more delay. The following season, Mr Barnes did not engage this player, so I was left without my manager. The librarian, who already had quite enough to do, took his place but couldn't attend to all the details I thought necessary.

The other suggestion I made was that an assistant should be appointed to conduct some of the children's concerts and a few of the suburban concerts in order that I could be fresher for the main ones. Barnes and a few members of the committee, as far as I can remember, never brought this up at a meeting and I did not get my assistant. These things only served as pinpricks to an already difficult situation and showed me quite plainly that I had nothing to lose by pressing for a permanent orchestra.

I would like to think that the Executive Committee's opposition to the idea was genuinely actuated by serious and sincere motives. In fact, I believe this was so, but there were other motives which I felt began to outweigh this sincerity and which were ingrained as the result of the so-called 'Scottish' orchestra being really a Glasgow orchestra. Barnes began to appeal for funds from other towns, but these other towns were not to have any representation on the committee which formulated the day-to-day policy of the orchestra. Glasgow quite rightly looked upon the 'Scottish' as its own particular affair. Had not Glasgow borne the cost of this orchestra for over fifty years? But what was expedient in the past was no longer so. The previous liability, until the 1943–1944 season, had only been for three months in the year. Now that the orchestra was giving more concerts outside Glasgow than ever before, the whole situation had gradually changed. In practice the Scottish was, in fact, becoming a National Orchestra. Glasgow had no more right to the sole direction any longer, but, and this was the crux of the matter, some of the older members of the committee, including Barnes, could not make a change in their attitude. To them, the Scottish Orchestra would always be, and had always been, a Glasgow orchestra. They resented any move which would take a little of its management from themselves. I am sorry to say that I thought this whole attitude dishonest, were it not for the fact that these members of the committee genuinely thought they were right. They were at best short-sighted. In private, I had heard many derogatory remarks made by members of the committee about Edinburgh's contribution and that town's wish to have a 'say' in the orchestral management. It is true that Edinburgh didn't contribute financially, but on the other hand, it took financial responsibility for concerts given by the orchestra *in* Edinburgh – which after all was fair enough. The Edinburgh concerts were a joy to me, especially as the committee there seemed wider awake to the great future of 'The Scottish'.

When Edinburgh announced its plans for a Festival, they were received with something approaching derision by certain members of the Scottish committee. All I could do was to point out that a permanent orchestra of good players could only benefit from a Scottish Musical Festival, as it would mean engagements. This of course, turned out to be true at first, but the Scottish was eventually not engaged during the Second Festival simply because the playing of this Scottish Orchestra at that time wasn't good enough.[25]

I remember trying very hard to enlist Lord Inverclyde's influence on my behalf.[26] Inverclyde had become the chairman of the Management Committee on which were representatives from contributing towns, and some very lively people they were. On this committee, of course, the Executive also sat. Inverclyde was privately enthusiastic about a permanent orchestra, and in my conversations with him often expressed himself in favour of such a thing. On the other hand, he felt he could not fight against the older members whose experience of running the Scottish Orchestra was spread over a quarter of a century. I prepared a long statement for him, setting out the reasons why a permanent orchestra was necessary. This statement is too long to quote here, but perhaps I may be forgiven if I give some short excerpts from it:

> At the moment the Scottish is recruited almost entirely from 'seaside' players, old men whose playing days are over and women who put their instruments in their cases and never look at them again, or rarely, until the next season commences (an overstatement of course). Other orchestras being on a permanent basis have the first choice of the best available players. With a six-month orchestral season, many players become increasingly restive during the last two weeks and keep asking for time off in order to see about their next job. One player played truant because he wanted the sack in order to get away earlier. Two 1st violinists pretended they were ill (playing in other orchestras for auditions purposes) but came back for their salary on the Friday.

Continuing this statement, I pointed out how these things could have been avoided by having a permanent orchestra. Inverclyde had to be careful not to antagonize his committee, and I began to see that there was little hope in that

---

25 The Scottish Orchestra, conducted by Braithwaite's successor, Walter Susskind, had performed at the inaugural Edinburgh Festival in 1947.

26 John Alan Burns, 4th Baron Inverclyde, KStJ (1897–1957).

direction. But several new men of quite a different stamp came on the bigger committee and began to voice the wishes of the vast majority of the guarantors. Two in particular, George Singleton, the owner of the Cosmo Cinema and Dr Tom Honeyman, the Director of the Art Gallery, came out in the open together with Mr Charles Rigg and stood up in no uncertain fashion against the solid wall of prejudice and modest tradition within the committee itself. These men, along with others, set the ball rolling, and two years after I had kicked my heels of Glasgow, the permanent National Scottish Orchestra came into being. I was sorry to hear that the guarantor scheme had been dropped, as I always felt that the private interest of thousands of individuals who are guarantors is a firm foundation for enthusiastic audiences.

Well, there is the history of my part in this affair as seen through my eyes. I don't pretend that I have given anyone else's point of view; that would be presumption on my part. The various personalities engaged in this internal struggle all had their reasons for their views. I had, at times, given angry expression privately to my disappointment at what had seemed a stonewalling attitude on the part of some of the members of the executive and management committees. I had liked all these men without exception, but could not understand the stoical opposition to what seemed an excellent thing in itself. My going perhaps focussed public attention on the controversy, and probably gave stimulus to a growing determination to see that the seed I had planted would flower into bloom. So, I cannot complain.

To the end, the committee fought the issue, and on the occasion of my last concert with the Scottish at St Andrew's Hall, a message was sent to me from the chairman of the committee telling me that I was not to mention in my final speech, the subject of a permanent orchestra. This was like a red rag to a bull, and in a semi-humorous speech, I told the audience that I had been asked not to mention the topic on which I was about to speak. The audience roared with laughter, and I kept up this byplay for a short while and then burst into my theme with the vigour of a prophet. I carried the audience with me in a tremendous sweep of enthusiasm, and I believe to this day that my farewell speech marked the beginning of the permanent orchestra in Scotland.[27]

Looking back over those last three seasons with the Scottish I wonder what

---

27 The concert took place on 6 April 1946 and was reviewed in both *The Scotsman* and *The Glasgow Herald* two days later. The latter newspaper dwelt in some detail on Braithwaite's speech: 'At the close of a brilliant and enthusiastic plebiscite evening…Warwick Braithwaite, responding to an ovation from the delighted audience, thanked the players for their splendid co-operation during a very heavy season, and regretted deeply the breaking up of "this fine association of six months." He declared – "This is our home and we want to stay. It is a great shame, after we have worked so faithfully, that we must disband at the height of our powers. We must all work to secure as soon as possible a permanent orchestra." This part of his speech was warmly applauded from all parts of the house.' *Glasgow Herald* (8 April 1946), 2.

else I could have done. I realize I must have been a thorn in the side of those committee members antagonistic to my ideas. Had I meddled in something that should have been left to the slow processes of another half-century's enterprise and experiment? I can only pose the question, 'When is the right moment to make a forward move?' I answer my own question by saying that I can only formulate the theory that times were better in 1945 for a new move to be made. St Andrew's Hall and the Usher Hall had been full for all our concerts. That was the moment.

While this struggle lasted it brought me only pain, and it took a long time for me to eradicate the impression left on my mind. A permanent orchestra will certainly bring other (and more difficult) problems to solve, and its creation does not mean that it will go on automatically without a lot of heart-searching, particularly on the financial side, but at least it will solve musical problems and standards, and that is the most important thing of all.

The creation of a permanent orchestra is only the beginning. I know as well as anyone that a permanent orchestra must work hard in order to retain what has already been won. For some years to come, the Scottish Orchestra has missionary work to do before it will have built up a secure future.

*

Before I leave the subject of Glasgow, I must pay tribute to some members of the Glasgow Art Club,[28] who were the friendliest men I met in that city; the kind of men who seem to sanctify the very air we breathe. Alex Lindsay stands out in my mind for sheer downright kindness and helpfulness, and I must also mention Sandy Proudfoot who, in one sentence, can bring a rarefied atmosphere to a gathering. There was Charles McCartney, with his puckish sense of humour and, at the same time, penetrating intellectual wit. There was also Tom Honeyman, a staunch supporter of a permanent Scottish orchestra. He found time in his busy life as Director of the Glasgow Art Gallery to study numerous allied problems. He is simple and direct in his speech, straight to the point: no flowery or meaningless phrases. His work as Director of the Kelvingrove Art Gallery is known everywhere in Great Britain where artists foregather. I believe Tom started as a doctor of medicine but became interested in artists. I first got to know of him through reading his book about that fine Scottish artist, Leslie Hunter, who Tom championed when he was comparatively unknown. Now, almost anything of Hunter's will fetch a high price. Dr Honeyman had

---

28 The Glasgow Art Club was founded in 1867, and since 1893 it has occupied two Georgian houses in Bath Street. It is a private members' club and a popular meeting place for active or retired artists and those with an interest in the arts. 'The Glasgow Art Club: Established 1867', http://glasgowartclub. co.uk, accessed 7 January 2019.

the amazing achievement to his credit that he had made the public definitely conscious of the need to get to know the great works of art.

He also gives an important place to music and enlists the interest of all lovers of artistic pursuits. In this he has been assisted by that remarkable character, Dr Henry Farmer, who has become an expert on the subject of early music and musical instruments. Honeyman never missed a symphony concert at St Andrew's Hall and was one of the chief subscribers of the Citizens Theatre. Tom is a practical man in the best sense of the word; half idealist, half realist, with both feet firmly planted on this earth. He believes that as art galleries and museums are subsidized, so too should the Scottish orchestra, as a permanent national orchestra for Scotland. He is not only content to have the wherewithal for *his* work, but also wants to see music given its rightful place, and he has been of great encouragement to me in my campaign for a permanent orchestra for Scotland.

About the same time as I met Dr Honeyman, I met that electric bundle of galvanized nervosity and brilliance, Patrick Dollan (now Sir Patrick Dollan) and his sweet and equally brilliant wife, Agnes. Those were astounding days. I was a frequent visitor to the City Chambers where I was always sure of a welcome from Pat (as he was then to his friends), even when he was in the midst of a busy day. I have never met a man who could do so many things all at once, and who had the business of being Lord Provost of an immense city like Glasgow absolutely at his fingertips. I have never met a man who could so quickly switch from one subject to another in a few seconds, or could make a speech that would lift one to spheres of the highest endeavour. He had the gift of being able to put people completely at their ease when meeting other people poles apart. He had boundless energy. In particular, I remember the last day of my first wartime season of concerts, when he gave a dinner to the committee of the Scottish Orchestra, the Directors of the Art Gallery, and newspaper men and others likely to be interested in a permanent orchestra. He did all he could to arouse interest. On that day he made three speeches on the subject of a permanent Scottish orchestra – one at the luncheon, another brilliant one at the end of the final concert (when he suggested that all Scotland should become guarantors of the orchestra by putting a farthing on the rates), and later at the supper given to the orchestra, in order to clinch the matter with the committee. So far, his suggestion has not been taken up, but it is bound to follow in due course that all opposition to a permanent orchestra will fade away, and Scotland will gain immeasurably. I was completely captivated by the drive of this man and he honoured me by a friendship which has never dimmed even though, to my regret, our paths have diverged.

Quite the most outstanding musician in Glasgow was, of course, Frederic Lamond. I don't say this because he was a Glasgow man and the best pianist

Glasgow had produced, but because Lamond was a great musician judged by any standards, and amongst the first rank pianists in that Lion's Den – the continent of Europe. Lamond should have written his memoirs. I had often asked him to do so as he has memories of the greatest musicians of the nineteenth century that are of the utmost importance to all of us today. He knew Liszt, Tchaikovsky, Brahms – to name just three of the giants. He met and knew many lesser giants as well. The two wars interfered with his career to some extent. Being British, his international status suffered somewhat, and the Second World War brought him back to Glasgow a disappointed man, because he missed the many and varied opportunities of working with, and meeting, the numerous friends he had made in Europe.

He and I always enjoyed working together. I liked his broad musical outlook and admired his great knowledge, not only of pianoforte music, but of operatic and orchestral music as well. Some of the most delightful moments before and after rehearsals were spent in his company. At the time of writing this, Lamond is, I think, 76 years of age, and the number of concerts he gives, and the amount of travelling he still does in order to play concerts all over the country, is absolutely colossal. To quote only one instance: he played two Brahms concertos with the Scottish Orchestra on the Saturday night and Sunday afternoon; travelled to London on Monday and played at the Albert Hall on Tuesday; and on Wednesday he travelled to Holland and gave about six recitals a week, as well as playing concertos. Lamond is tough, like all Scots of the last generation. At the same time, I feel that in any continental country such an artist would have been given a stipend to live on, so that he could cut down on some of the unnecessary work he had to do. But perhaps Lamond wants to go on working as hard as ever. Well, he shows no sign of weariness or lack of vitality, and his memory is as bright as ever.

Another musician (and good fellow) is Ian Whyte, Musical Director of the BBC in Scotland at its headquarters in Glasgow.[29] One always felt welcome at his house, and his enjoyment of music was inexhaustible. He would frequently sit down at his Bechstein piano and play for hours, even after a heavy day at the studio. On those privileged occasions one could not but admire the beauty and ease of his playing. He had a great sense of humour also and would frequently improvise a long and intricate pianoforte piece, taking off the idiosyncrasies of some celebrity. He once did this on the occasion of an Art Club dinner at which I was the honoured guest. Ian was a very amusing and brilliant musician who did great things for Scottish folk music. I remember once being shown a huge cabinet in his room, crammed full of arrangements he had made of old Scottish

---

29 Ian Whyte (1901-1960), Scottish composer and conductor, was the BBC's Director of Scottish Music (1935-1946) and Principal Conductor of the BBC Scottish Orchestra (1946-1960).

melodies. His own compositions are considerable as well, and Ian seems to have packed several lives into his young life.

As I am attempting to write about interesting characters rather than professional people, I feel I must mention one of the happiest and best characters it has been my privilege to know in Glasgow. He was not known to the general public and was rarely seen by them. His position was considered a lowly one, probably with a salary to match, yet without him the Scottish Orchestra would have ceased to function. His four sons were in the forces; he had been in the Great War. He spoke about his boys and loved them like the old warhorse he was. His wife must have been a wonderful woman because her name was always on his lips. He had been the attendant of the Scottish Orchestra for over 25 years and coped with all difficulties, even though he had more than twice the amount of work to do when the season was extended to six months. He was still expected to shift all the instruments and baggage in the most out-of-date and slow method as of yore (an open lorry drawn by a horse) when a covered-in motor wagon would do the job in half the time from door to door. Jock Watt was getting no younger, but no-one would have known it by the look of his chubby face and bright blue eyes, and I felt that his work could be eased considerably. Jock had known every conductor of the Scottish intimately during those 25 years. He was a man of infinite tact and of a sterling character; good natured and generous to a fault. The tale is told that when Sir Landon Ronald was knighted and came to St Andrew's Hall for his first rehearsal, he insisted on shaking hands first of all with 'Watty' (the nickname Jock Watt was known by) and when Jock called him Sir Landon, he (Ronald) took him severely to task and told Jock to call him by the name he knew all the orchestral players called him by – 'Landy'. I worked with Jock for six years and I never knew him to be bad tempered. Nor was he put out by the Glasgow weather, which is a dangerous thing for an uncovered wagon full of instruments and boxes of band parts.

It is seldom that musicians and businessmen become fast friends, yet I can count some of my most pleasant hours in Glasgow in the company of businessmen of all kinds. Most of them would tease me for my fondness for classical music, but all of them followed my doings in Scotland with great interest. I find the Glasgow businessman a many-sided creature. His fondness for racy stories and recounting interesting reminiscences is inexhaustible.

Before I left Glasgow, a dinner was given to me by all my closest friends at the Art Club, all of whom had stood by me during my last season, when I was in despair and, at the same time, very much overworked. At this dinner, speeches were made of a most warm nature in which, not unashamedly, a few tears escaped from the eyes of some of the speakers. When my turn came, my heart was almost too full to speak, but I somehow managed to thank them all for the kindness they had bestowed on me. Later a *quaich* was given to me with the signatures of all my friends engraved upon it as a parting gift.[30]

*

I was quite determined that my last view of Scotland was not going to be an acrimonious one. In a flash of intuition, I knew I believed in the goodness of the Scottish people and my many friends up and down the country. Although I had suffered a severe blow from the few, I was not going to let that blow be the lasting impression I would take away with me. So, I brought my daughter Barbara up to Glasgow for the last few remaining days of my 1945–1946 season, and planned a trip to the Hebrides before going back to London.[31] The war was over and I had to begin all over again.

---

30 A *quaich* is a traditional shallow Scottish drinking cup, originally carved from wood. Today it is usually made from silver, but its original significance as a mark of hospitality, friendship and trust still applies. This cup was accompanied by the following note: 'To Warwick Braithwaite. One evening, a few of your friends in The Art Club were discussing the affairs of the world – as usual! The subject of music was raised and general regret was expressed that you were no longer with us. We would like you to know this, and the happy suggestion was made that we convey it to you in the form of a "Quaich" – a loving cup – with our signatures engraved around it, to express our deep appreciation of you as Conductor of The Scottish Orchestra, and as a fellow member of the Glasgow Art Club. That you may enjoy many years of prosperity is the sincere wish of us all – Arthur R. Anderson, John L. Adam, W. Baird-Taylor, Gordon Carr, H. Adam Crawford, C. Davenport, Charles Fraser, Robert Gray, J.M. MacCormick, W. Charles Macartney, Wm. H. MacLellan, Angus Robertson, Andrew F. Shanks, Philip B. Simons, James G. Speirs, David Traill, James Taylor Thomson, John W. Weir, Robert Whyte.

31 Barbara was 22 years of age at the time of this trip.

SIXTEEN

WARTIME REMINISCENCES AND SOME PERSONALITIES

CONSTANT LAMBERT – LESLIE HEWARD – E.J. MOERAN

By early 1944, we had been untroubled by raids, and life was beginning to be possible once again.[1] Then one June night, about 10.30 p.m., the air throbbed with what we all thought was the noise of hundreds of planes dropping their bombs. There was only one difference; as we followed the course of these planes, a curious tell-tale flame came, as we thought, from the rear of the fuselage. We would see the flame disappear and then hear first of all the scream of what we took to be the bomb falling, followed by the noise of the explosion. The siren had gone at 10.30 p.m., and although there was a lull around midnight, and another lull about 4 a.m., the all-clear was not given till 6.06 a.m. A few minutes after that the warning siren went off again. Wardens on duty were worn out by the length of the long warning period. Next night the same thing happened, and Mr Morrison, M.P.,[2] announced that the raiders were pilotless planes. Again, my family had to leave London.

I again stayed on, not because of any real need to do so, but because between seasons with the Scottish Orchestra, I had to be prepared for any

---

1 This chapter begins with the period between April and 7 November 1944, when as usual he returned to London between Scottish Orchestra seasons. These months were packed with a heavy schedule of engagements with other orchestras.

2 Herbert Stanley Morrison, Baron Morrison of Lambeth (1880–1965), was Home Secretary from 4 October 1940 to 23 May 1945 in the Labour coalition government.

conducting dates that were offered. Although the 'flying bomb' troubled us every day, and at periods every night, for some weeks to come, life went on much as usual. I much admired the uplifting morale of the ordinary London folk, such as shop girls, typists and bus conductors, who carried on their business in an almost fatalistic mood. Many a time one would, in the middle of the day, be walking along the street and hear the throbbing noise of a flying bomb overhead. With plate glass in every shop, the danger of shattered fragments was very great.

Stephen Williams[3] met me one day at the 'Gluepot' (i.e., The George, on the corner of Mortimer and Great Portland Streets),[4] and was highly amused at the sight of two men carrying a huge window of plate glass across Regent Street while a flying bomb was travelling overhead. On another occasion, while talking with a group of friends in the Gluepot, including Stephen Williams, C.B. Rees, 'Spike' Hughes, Constant Lambert and others, we were physically shaken by a bomb which came down behind Charlotte Street (where Betty Lutyens lived).[5] In a few minutes, Betty herself appeared with Edward Clark, both having had a terrifying experience. The bomb had cracked their walls and blown them across their living room.

I was talking to a man one night who said that he had remained in his sitting room throughout every raid. When his home was hit, all that seemed to happen was that his refrigerator slid through the wall from the kitchen and deposited itself immediately in front of him. He didn't hear a sound and was untouched. That this is a true story I have no doubt at all, as I saw with my own eyes a very apt illustration of the vagaries of blast. One day, during the summer of 1940, walking along the Garden Suburb Market Place, a bomb from an enemy plane came screaming down about half a mile away. Walking in front of me, about 100 yards away, was a young woman dressed in a thin print dress. To her embarrassment, the air blast tore off her thin dress completely, and quite wisely she took refuge in a children's clothing shop. The strange thing about this incident was that neither the young lady, nor the plate glass windows in the vicinity, were in the slightest degree damaged.

Another incident is worth telling for both its humour and strangeness. During the early days of the raids, before the night raids became intolerable, we had a lot of reconnoitring at night-time by enemy planes. Our guns didn't fire for a few weeks, and the relief when they did was felt by all London people. On one occasion, when I was returning from a concert in which I accompanied

---

3 Stephen Williams (1908–1994), journalist, broadcaster, producer and pioneer of Radio Luxembourg. *The Times* (28 November 1994), 21.

4 Established in 1677, the pub was nicknamed 'The Gluepot' by Sir Thomas Beecham. He claimed his orchestral musicians were often late for rehearsals because they were stuck there.

5 Elisabeth Lutyens (1906–1983), English composer, married to Edward Clark.

Ruth Naylor in some songs,[6] I had to take refuge in a house as things were beginning to get 'hot'. The household consisted of an old man (a retired banker), and his frail wife. Both of them were well over 70 years of age. Outside in their garden they had an Anderson Shelter, correctly buried half under the soil. When I asked them why they didn't use it, the two dears told me with outraged pride that Hitler wasn't going to drive them from the sitting room they loved, nor were they going to alter the routine they had always kept up with their pet canary of covering the cage for the night with a piece of cloth.

A few nights later a land mine came down in their district, and the following morning I went around to see how they had fared. The nearer I got to their house the more I feared for them. As it turned out, their home was one which escaped complete destruction, although it was no longer fit to live in. Pinned onto the lintel of the front door was a notice 'Please come to the back door'. I did, and found those two people occupied with picking up bits and pieces they treasured and packing them into suitcases. I saw the canary's cage, the lower part of which had been strengthened with glass, shattered to atoms. When I enquired what had happened to the canary, they told a fantastic story. The blast had shattered the cage, and the canary had apparently disintegrated. In the morning, they were back at the house retrieving odds and ends, and commiserating with each other about the loss of their beloved pet, when a blackbird flew onto the window sill and chirruped joyously. It was their soot-covered canary, which had miraculously escaped. These two old people went to live with their son-in-law not so far away from their shattered house, but were bombed once again. They escaped a second time, but only because the son-in-law insisted that they took refuge in the Anderson Shelter.

Life was far from pleasant during these terrible raids, but we endeavoured to keep going by clinging to the usual routine and traditions of civilized life. One of the things that helped was attending innumerable parties. Any excuse was good enough, and the screaming of nearby bombs seldom halted conversation for more than a few seconds. I remember one party in particular, given by Stephen Williams and his wife, Diane. Their parties were always well-arranged affairs. Stephen went to immense trouble in choosing his guests, and as a rule wrote verses to a well-known tune in which he humorously took off each guest one by one. Pat Mannick and Stephen would give duets from Gilbert and Sullivan operas, and on one occasion the actor, Donald Wolfit, sang an aria in the best style. Flora Robson, on a different occasion, showed her talent for parties and enjoyment.

It was through Stephen Williams that I was asked by Guy Schofield, Editor

---

6   Ruth Naylor (1908–1976), Australian-born soprano performing with the Vic-Wells Company. Braithwaite conducted her on at least 75 occasions between 1933 and 1940 in roles such as Gilda, Violetta, Micaëla, Musetta, Mimì, Marguerite, Nedda, Adele and the Queen of the Night.

of the *Evening News* in 1946, to organize a concert for the Musicians Benevolent Fund.[7] The *Evening News* went to the utmost trouble and expense to make the concert a great success, and all the proceeds of a full Royal Albert Hall went to the fund. I made up a programme of English works:

> Purcell: *Trumpet Voluntary*[8]
> Bax: *Tintagel*
> Vaughan Williams: *Hugh the Drover* – Song of the Road
> Arne: *Alfred* – Rule Britannia (arranged by Humphrey Searle)
> Elgar: Violoncello Concerto
> Vaughan Williams: *London Symphony* (conducted by the composer)
> Lambert: *The Rio Grande* (conducted by the composer)
>
> Artists: Guilhermina Suggia *(cello)*; Roland Dyson *(trumpet)*; Arthur Carron *(tenor)*; with the Goldsmiths Choral Union and London Symphony Orchestra;
> Ralph Vaughan Williams, Constant Lambert and Warwick Braithwaite *(conductors)*.

The London Symphony Orchestra had been engaged, and there were two rehearsals. I had asked the players to give one rehearsal free, but not only was it against their principles, they also pointed out that orchestral musicians did not benefit in any way from that fund, because it was specifically established to aid musicians *other than* orchestral players. Nevertheless, the sight of Vaughan Williams conducting his *A London Symphony*, made a striking impression at the concert.

I had tried to secure Pablo Casals to play the Elgar Violoncello Concerto, and *The Evening News* offered to send a Lancaster plane to southern France to bring him to London and take him back, with a fee of 600 guineas. He was to stay at the Dorchester Hotel free of expense to him, but Casals had made it known that he would never play in England again for political reasons, and all our tempting offers, sent through a mutual friend, were to no avail. Madame Guilhermina Suggia (the subject of Augustus John's famous painting), agreed to play the work and gave a magnificent performance.[9] We got on well together

---

7 In 2014, the fund adopted the name Help Musicians UK. 'Help Musicians UK', https://www.helpmusicians.org.uk, accessed 7 January 2019.

8 Misattributed for many years to Henry Purcell, this is now known, correctly, as *The Prince of Denmark's March* by Jeremiah Clarke.

9 Guilhermina Suggia (1885–1950), Portuguese cellist. A review of the concert in *The Times* suggests that Suggia '...was helped in this mellow performance by the understanding of Mr Warwick Braithwaite who conducted it.' *The Times* (7 November 1946), 6.

and I was very impressed with her interpretation of Elgar's great work. Her early death was a great shock to the world of music.

I asked composer Humphrey Searle[10] to rescore Arne's *Rule Britannia* in such a way that, commencing from the first verse in Arne's own simple orchestration, gradually the full orchestra would be brought in, bringing the last chorus to a great climax. This proved a success, and both Arthur Carron and the Goldsmiths Choir came in for tremendous applause.

Constant Lambert conducted his own *Rio Grande* magnificently.[11] I had always liked and tremendously admired Constant. I was, professionally at least, one of his oldest and, might I say, best friends. We first met at Sadler's Wells in 1932 when he was in the process of making his amazing career as composer, conductor, and writer on musical subjects. He only conducted ballet at Sadler's Wells, not trying his hand at opera until Beecham's 1936–1937 Winter Season at Covent Garden, where he conducted three performances of Puccini's *Manon Lescaut*. We had always liked one another and had the same viewpoints on quite a variety of musical subjects. His book, *Music Ho!*, was a great success, and has recently been reprinted in the Penguin series.[12] His newspaper articles on music were eagerly read and discussed by most musicians throughout the country. He would cross swords fearlessly with such giants as Ernest Newman and others when he disagreed with them.

Constant Lambert,
composer and conductor.

Constant possessed the greatest musical integrity of any musician I have ever known, with possibly the exception of Leslie Heward, and it is not altogether strange that he and Leslie were also very great friends. Both were highly intelligent and extraordinarily gifted musicians.

Constant's compositions were not many; in fact, I believe that his life may have been saddened by the spectre of inspiration partly drying up, or coming on him at all too rare intervals. Whether it was this, or the fact that he burned himself out conducting too much ballet and, in the war years, playing his own two-piano versions of the ballet repertoire virtually every night, will never

10 Humphrey Searle (1915–1982), English composer and writer.

11 Constant Lambert (1905–1951), British composer, writer and conductor (especially of ballet).

12 *Music Ho! A Study of Music in Decline*, was originally published by Faber & Faber in 1934. The third edition was published in paperback by Penguin in 1948.

be known. It was evident to all his friends that something had happened to him, and the end might easily have been brought about by the mysterious workings of the spirit, dampened in the last few years by the body. A series of disappointments can make carnage of a sensitive soul, and Constant was sensitive to a degree. Yet I have never met a musician with such a marvellous wit. A brilliant conversationalist with a sense of wit is a wonderful combination, and Constant had both these attributes. I was in Austria during August 1951 when, quite by chance, I read in a newspaper that Constant had died suddenly, and it was such a shock that the rest of my holiday was completely ruined.

I am anticipating the years somewhat, but although it would be easier for me to give a year-by-year history of things which the music lover could put into a diary, my thoughts are different. Both Constant Lambert and Leslie Heward died at the same young age of forty-six. Leslie died during 1943 and Constant in 1951.

Leslie Heward, conductor.

I had met Leslie Heward many times during my Cardiff days, and we kept up a desultory correspondence. When in London for conferences at the BBC, it would so happen that Leslie would also be there from Birmingham, and we would more or less continue where we had left off, and the intervening weeks or months would disappear. The years only drew us more together, and our lack of opportunities to meet made little difference to our friendship. But, on occasion, he was beginning to show signs of that moroseness which grew on him rapidly in the years to follow and which, as time went on, he strove to stifle in the vicious cycle of alcohol. Heaven alone knows that I would not, and indeed could not, say anything of a derogatory nature about one of the most brilliant and most lovable musicians of our time; a loyal friend under all circumstances, and a man of great integrity of character.

Things had become steadily worse with Leslie's health, and it was apparent to everyone that all was not well. Fundamentally, his health created the unhappiness that made him do things of which he was often ashamed afterwards. He wanted to get away from this country, to start afresh somewhere, but always there would creep back into his mind a love for his own land.

Leslie was born in Littletown, Liversedge, in the county of Yorkshire, yet he had none of that well-known awkwardness one often meets in a Yorkshire person. There was nothing dour, narrow-minded or selfish in his nature. He was the soul of generosity, warm-hearted and cultured. His gifts as a musician were almost Mozart-like. He certainly had Mozart's gift of instant realization of the most difficult musical problems. He was a fine pianist who seldom practised, but whose facility of technique was astounding, and whose memory was remarkable for its accuracy. All this and more I have hinted at earlier, but it needs to be said many times. So, why was it that Heward, in a practical sense, never really came into his own? One could think of all sorts of reasons, but perhaps the truest is that Heward was doomed never to get his true recognition, except from those who knew him intimately.

Leslie would never give lip service to any idea or person. On many occasions he would appear, after conducting a concert, dressed in an old cap and mac, and would go around to the nearest pub for a drink with his friends. Many important people would drop around to the green room and find either he was gone, or dressed more like a working man, eager to get away. I can, but don't need to, defend this behaviour. More often than not, the inane and tiresome remarks from well-meaning guarantors and others who visit green rooms can be soul-destroying in the extreme and are often very annoying. Leslie suffered fools very impatiently, yet he was the kindest man I have ever known. All this may have mitigated against him reaching the highest conducting position in the country, for there could have been no other reasons why a man of such great musical gifts should become finally so unhappy about himself.

Sometime during 1939, Heward had made contacts with the Canadian Broadcasting Corporation and planned a tour of that country conducting at various towns. He came back via the USA and arrived in this country just before war was declared. It was then that he had a terrible collapse of health and went to a nursing home for a long time. Tuberculosis had been suspected and found active. After his sojourn in the nursing home, Heward looked well and seemed completely cured. However, we all noticed that he would not eat sufficient good food, so we tried to trick him into having a proper meal, but invariably he became annoyed by our efforts.

I remember on one occasion during the recording sessions of Jack Moeran's symphony, which he recorded for the British Council with the Hallé Orchestra in Manchester, another friend and I scoured the town for a big juicy steak (a difficult enough thing during the war and still more difficult after it), and arranged with the proprietor of the London Oyster Bar to have it ready at a certain time. We persuaded Leslie, as cleverly as we could, to come with us. He did so, but as soon as he saw what was going on, he turned on his heel at the entrance and petulantly left us, after calling us a few wicked names. We were absolutely flabbergasted and stood there in a whirl of doubt, anger and surprise. But this was serious and we knew it. My friend, who adored Leslie, nearly broke down and I was left doing my best to comfort him. That was the only time, during the years I had known him, that Leslie failed to apologise for his behaviour.

At last Leslie's health once again broke down, and he was sent to St Christopher's Hospital, just outside Brighton. But the week before that, he stayed with me in London, where my wife and I gave up our rations of eggs, butter and bacon in an endeavour to make him eat. My wife tried her best and practically stood over Leslie during breakfast in order to see that he ate properly. He fiddled with his food and did his best to eat out of politeness, but that week was almost a nightmare.

Leslie brought presents for everybody. He gave a party at the Café Royal on the occasion of Maggie Teyte's birthday.[13] That morning he had cashed several cheques that he had received for conducting, amounting to at least £200, but later that evening he had to borrow £35 to pay the bill. This sounds incredible, but it is true. Was it perhaps that Leslie knew he had not long to live?

Some days later he went into hospital for an operation, and after a few weeks, he was back home and soon conducting again. But not for long. Almost his last engagement was with the BBC Orchestra, and the players in that orchestra can today speak of the great performance he conducted of Berlioz's *Symphonie fantastique* at Bedford, where the orchestra had its temporary home during the war. Back he went to hospital for the last time. There was no question of another operation; rest was prescribed. I saw him several times in hospital, and the change in his weight was pitiful to behold. The doctors humoured him by letting him eat and drink whatever he fancied. Eventually, he was sent home, but was too weak to stand or move, and spent the last weeks in bed attended by his wife, Leonore. Again, I went to see him, but although his intellect was still strong, his energy had gone.

One day after seeing Leslie, Joan Hammond[14] and I felt something more should be done, and from Brighton we phoned Lord Horder,[15] a friend of Leslie's, and asked him to go to his aid. Horder asked to be put in touch with Leslie's doctor, and later phoned both Joan and myself to report that there was nothing he could do, and it would only be a matter of a few days before Leslie would be no more. After returning to London, I telephoned Leslie's oldest and best friend, Arnold Goldsbrough,[16] and together we went up to Birmingham to see if we could do anything for Leonore. We spent a whole day with Leslie, coming back to London late that night. Early next morning, Arnold phoned me with the news that Leslie Heward had passed away. We both met at Paddington

---

13 Dame Maggie Teyte (1888-1976), English operatic soprano, renowned also for her interpretation of French art song.

14 Dame Joan Hammond (1912–1996), New Zealand-born, Australian operatic soprano. Braithwaite conducted her in *Aida*, *La traviata*, *Madama Butterfly* and *Tosca* for Carl Rosa, Covent Garden and Welsh National Opera. He also made 17 recordings with her for HMV and Columbia, as well as numerous radio broadcasts and concerts.

15 Thomas Jeeves Horder, 1st Baron Horder, GCVO (1871–1955), distinguished English physician.

16 Arnold Goldsbrough (1892–1964), English keyboard player, conductor and teacher.

and took the earliest train we could. There was nothing much we could do except to try and comfort Leonore and, as I had to return to London for an engagement, Arnold stayed on and made all the necessary arrangements. A few days afterwards most of Leslie's friends went to Birmingham for the funeral.

One pitiful incident occurred just before the funeral. Leonore asked Arnold, Humphrey Procter-Gregg[17] and myself to see Leslie for the last time. It was curious that this was the only time the four of us had been together since 1922 in Munich, and the one moment when we three together realized how much Leslie meant to us. We knew we were losing our best friend – a most lovable character and a man with a generosity of soul, and of such brilliance, that we would never encounter again.

A little book was published later, edited by musicologist Eric Blom, in which several of Heward's friends wrote their appreciations.[18] I was asked to contribute to this but I could not bring myself to put pen to paper. I have asked myself many times since, why I – who regarded Leslie as not only a beloved friend but whom I admired more than anyone else – neglected to add my contribution. But the question is still unanswered and will always remain so.

Leslie Heward did not compose a great deal of music, but what he did write was finely put together. His best orchestral work was called *Quodlibet*, a piece of most unusual construction in which five short phrases, dealt with in five sections, became one long tune in the last movement. At one time Leslie and Proctor-Gregg collaborated on an opera on the subject of Ibsen's *Peer Gynt*, but it remained unfinished. There were a number of beautiful songs and several odds and ends, but his output was not big enough to warrant serious consideration as a composer. Yet all that I have seen of his music is unquestionably worthwhile.

The mention of Moeran's symphony brings me to another sad history. E. J. Moeran (or Jack to his friends), a great admirer of Leslie Heward, led a curious life.[19] He would hide himself, either in Kenmare or near Hereford, for weeks at a time when actually composing, and so long as his mind was occupied in that way, no harm ever came to him. Jack and I were also good friends and I performed his works as soon as they came to hand. His Symphony in G minor[20] remains one of the most outstanding and original works since Walton's Symphony. It is dedicated to Sir Hamilton Harty, another great Irishman and one whom I met when he conducted *Figaro* with the BNOC at Covent Garden

17 Humphrey Procter-Gregg (1895–1980), English teacher and composer.

18 *Leslie Heward 1897–1943: a memorial volume*, edited by Eric Blom (London: Dent, 1944). Blom's own contribution to the volume relates how Warwick Braithwaite and Arnold Goldsbrough visited him on the day of Heward's death and asked him 'to get these tributes together'.

19 E(rnest) J(ohn) Smeed Moeran (1894–1950), English composer.

20 Braithwaite conducted Moeran's Symphony in G Minor on at least six occasions in Glasgow, Sydney and Johannesburg.

E.J. Moeran, composer.

during the 1922–1923 season. Harty was the conductor of the Hallé concerts for many years and I will never forget his renderings of Berlioz in particular.

Jack Moeran was a brilliant conversationalist and a boon companion with a most generous nature, but in-between composing he would have long bouts of drinking. Much as one admired him, one simply could not always be patient when Jack got into a dithering state, as he did frequently. Many would be the times in Manchester when Pat Ryan[21] and I would half-carry Jack from the 'Haunch of Venison' up the hill to London Road Station to await his train to Hereford. One's enjoyment of his company was spoiled so many times by this incredible weakness. Jack could not hold his drink and, as he was a big fellow, all too frequently one would be saddled with a 15-stone lump of helpless flesh.

But that was not the real Jack, and all his friends knew it. He married Peers Coetmore who, sweet person that she is, managed for a while to pull him together.[22] But the old habits grew to alarming proportions, and his frequent absences from home drove Peers to reconsider the whole basis of their life together. Peers sold up her flat and went on an extensive tour of New Zealand, Australia and South Africa in 1950–1951, and it was during that time Jack died a tragic death. Let it not be thought that Peers' absence was a contributing cause. She had done all she could, and put up with the utmost any woman could be expected to cope with, and that's all there is to it. But Moeran's compositions stand on their own merits, particularly the Symphony in G minor [23] (1934–1937), the Sinfonietta (1944), and the Cello Sonata in A minor (1947). His memory is held in very high esteem by all his friends.

As the war began to near its end, the flying bomb bases were captured and, with a sigh of relief, Londoners began to travel back to their homes. Herbert Morrison announced that the danger was past, but one Friday night there was an isolated explosion somewhere in London followed by a curious 'whoosh' sort of sound. I wrote to my wife and told her to wait for a while. Two days later, another huge explosion was heard. It was given out that the first explosion was a gasometer. I didn't believe it, and the second explosion proved that we were

---

21 Pat Ryan, close friend of Moeran and principal clarinet with the Hallé Orchestra (1939–1958).
22 Peers Coetmore (1905–1976), English cellist who married Moeran in 1945. His Cello Concerto and Cello Sonata are dedicated to her.
23 Braithwaite conducted Moeran's Sinfonietta in Glasgow, Edinburgh and Christchurch (New Zealand).

in for some other devilish nonsense from Hitler. Sure enough, it was the rocket bomb.[24] This really was the last straw. Hitler's V-2 was raining down on us. The 'whoosh' was explained by the fact that the bomb travelled faster than sound, and that the noise of its passage through the air came after the explosion.

My friend C.B. Rees and his wife Margery had a miraculous escape from the Sunday morning bomb. They lived at Kew, and the bomb landed at the end of their street, about 100 yards away. The ceiling of their bedroom came down on them and most of the furniture was destroyed. The shock, especially to C.B.'s wife, was a terrible one. The house on which the bomb fell was completely obliterated, along with its inhabitants. C.B. told me that only the night before, the husband of the family had been telling him of the number of escapes he had had from bombs all through the war, and that he believed he had a charmed life.

The nearest V-2 to my house was only about a mile away as the crow flies, and fell in soft earth behind the Hampstead Public Library, making a crater big enough for a public building. A mile away may seem as good as a miss, but one has only to realize that a small deviation of the bomb's flight would have altered its course, and our house could easily have been the target. We were lucky, and suffered only superficial damage during the whole war. I had seen tragic happenings all over London, and the number of people rendered homeless and those injured and killed, made me thank my lucky stars that my family had escaped. Hitler and his crowd were murderously inclined. They made war on the helpless, on women and children and they deserved all they got in the end. Evidently the great advance of science has not meant an equivalent advance in civilization.

---

24 The first V-2 rocket bomb to be directed at London was launched from The Hague on 8 September 1944, killing three people in Chiswick and injuring a further 19. For several weeks, the British Government claimed that gas mains were the cause of continuing explosions. Finally, on 10 November 1944, Churchill announced that Britain had been under enemy rocket attack.

SEVENTEEN

HAMBURG, BELSEN AND BERLIN (1945)

It can never be possible to remember all the incidents of such a fantastic dream; a dream in which so many things happened that, even now, I find myself forgetting their order and character in a haze of half-belief.

It was during August 1945, three months after World War II had ended, that Walter Legge[1] asked me to conduct three weeks of Opera in Hamburg with Sadler's Wells artists and the Hamburg Philharmonic State Orchestra.[2] I proceeded to ENSA HQ at Drury Lane Theatre for the business of being fitted with a uniform,[3] and later went to a Wellcome Institute to be inoculated. All things completed at last, I stepped into a Dakota plane bound for Hamburg.

At the Hamburg Aerodrome, I had tea in the restaurant overlooking the field where our Dakota was resting like some strange giant bird with its wings outstretched. Lots of men in uniform, all very quiet and tired. We had left our homes at 5 a.m., and it was now 11 a.m.

Frank Lynas, the ENSA official, came beaming into the restaurant and within a few minutes we had left the airfield and were driving to Hamburg

---

1 Walter Legge (1906–1979), English record producer and founder of the Philharmonia Orchestra. During, and immediately after WWII, Legge was involved in the musical work of the Entertainments National Service Association (ENSA), and from 1941, took charge of a newly formed Music Division. In 1953 he married the distinguished soprano Elisabeth Schwarzkopf (1915–2006).

2 Braithwaite's visit to Germany took place in the gap before his final season with the Scottish Orchestra. He conducted a concert with the LPO and pianist Colin Horsley in Bristol on 7 August 1945 and must have arrived in Hamburg about ten days later to prepare for the opera season. By his own calculation, he was away for five weeks.

3 Civilian artists working for ENSA were required to wear a special uniform to differentiate them from other service personnel, even after the war.

through one of the worst bombed areas. Thousands of flats and large buildings had been reduced to rubble. What a dreadful sight! What a commentary on our age! This was new to me then, but I was to see much more later.

The Hamburg Opera House stage, which survived the bombings, was of modern design with the sunken stage to a depth of 45 feet, with side stages as well, so that little time was needed for scene changes. There were two huge canvas sky cycloramas that surrounded the entire stage. One was transparent so that lantern slide scenery could be projected from behind, thus saving money on expensive sets. However, although the stage survived and the theatre staff were still employed, the auditorium itself was in ruins. The only other available theatre, the Schauspielhaus, needed to be altered to cope with opera instead of the usual drama performances, and extensive changes needed to be made to the orchestra pit in order to accommodate sixty-seven players. This was simply and efficiently done by Herr Schultz's competent carpenters.

Herr Schultz was a remarkable man who did everything possible for the ultimate success of our season. His staff were thrilled at the idea of opera in the Schauspielhaus and gave us every assistance. The expertise and speed with which they changed scenery was quite amazing. A great deal of this co-operation came as a result of Captain Budd's excellent methods of dealing with the staff under his direction. Budd was in complete control of the theatre on behalf of ENSA, and he had organized the staff most excellently, employing scene painters and getting the 'canvas' (it was really made of paper of a thick texture) and the wood from elsewhere. The Staatsoper loaned the Sadler's Wells Company scenery and band parts for four of our operas, as none of these things arrived in time for our season of three weeks. Everything Captain Budd promised one could be sure of having, from transport to rehearsal rooms.

At the Staatsoper there was one person who seemed, by her tact and knowledge of operatic administration, to keep everything together in that mere shell of a building. I refer to Frau Hart, the Secretary of the Director (Intendant). Frau Hart spoke no English at all, but she always guessed what one wanted. On the numerous occasions when I was in a difficulty about, for instance, a vocal score of *La bohème* or a répétiteur for rehearsals, she would overcome any objection from whatever quarter it came, and everything was smoothed over. We would have liked to help these people; they needed help. Their buildings were destroyed; they had no money to get opera going again, and were grateful to us as the only people to help them. Frau Hart was most anxious to hear some of our performances, but of course this was forbidden, because the performances were for British troops only. We had to refuse requests from the German opera people many times. There were ways of getting around these prohibitions and I did so several times. Frau Hart was worth her weight in gold for the invaluable help she gave us.

Our scenery hadn't arrived for *La bohème* and this was required for the opening night. What were we to do? Eric Bass, the Sadler's Wells stage manager, was at his wits end to put scenery together for the performance. Frau Hart was telephoned and the answer came back. 'Yes, we have a set of scenery not destroyed during the raids.' Next morning at 9 a.m., a huge covered wagon full of scenery and properties, plus a lighting expert from the opera house, arrived at the Schauspielhaus. The workmen who brought the scenery had been loading it on the wagon from 6 a.m.

The Staatsoper stage designer came also. He spoke perfect English, and brought with him all his scenery designs exquisitely drawn to scale and in eight bound books with photographs. These proved infinitely interesting to Powell Lloyd and Eric Bass, who gazed in wonder at the order and efficiency of the Hamburg Opera House staff. The scenery had, of course, to be adapted to suit the smaller stage of the Schauspielhaus, and both the Sadler's Wells producer and the stage manager spent hours with the Staatsoper people adjusting the scenery for our purpose. The co-operation given by these Hamburg Opera House people was a good example of human beings working together in harmony on an interesting problem. In between orchestral rehearsals, I would also spend part of my time with these people during lighting rehearsals, and enjoyed every minute of it.

On one occasion, we had to borrow scenery for our performance of *Rigoletto*. Eric Bass told me that he had seen some of it, and the woodwork was in very bad condition as a result of storing. Herr Schultz looked at it and promised that in a few hours, the scenery would be restored to its original state. He was as good as his word, for I met Eric that evening in a state of wonderment and praise for the good workmanship of Herr Schultz's men. The *Rigoletto* scenery was really lovely and the performances were every bit in keeping with the sets.

Warwick Braithwaite with fellow conductor Eugen Jochum in Hamburg, 1945.

The Hamburg Philharmonic had been promised to play for the performances, but instead I was presented with a ragged collection of the dregs of Hamburg's instrumentalists. After an hour's rehearsal, I called the leader aside and told him that I would not rehearse any more. He entirely agreed with me, and Frank Lynas and I scoured Hamburg for the correct military authority who could make a decision on the matter. After three days, and with the most forceful help of Majors Black and Lawrence, and after protracted negotiations with the Philharmonic people, we eventually secured the prominent players.

The Hamburg Philharmonic Orchestra is 120 strong. Up until 1943, when the Staatsoper had been bombed (the iron safety curtain saved the stage), the City of Hamburg subsidized opera to the extent of one and a quarter million marks per year, and the organization had a staff of 600, inclusive of all departments.[4] The Philharmonic Orchestra is the opera orchestra as well. The standard of ensemble playing was exceedingly high and rehearsals were a joy.

Great conductors like Karl Muck and Gustav Mahler had been associated with this orchestra for many years. The conductor during 1945 was Eugen Jochum – a most interesting and vital personality.[5] At the time of my visit, the orchestra gave only three symphony concerts each week, the same programme being repeated three times. On the days of the concerts there were no rehearsals. The orchestra rehearsed Monday, Tuesday and Wednesday (Thursday was a free day), and then performed the three concerts on Friday, Saturday and Sunday. Eugen Jochum was much loved by the Hamburg audiences. He was then about 44 years of age, but looked older. He had been through difficult times during the war, and owed a great debt of gratitude to Army Welfare for reorganising the concerts and bringing the scattered players of the Philharmonic together again. He was deeply conscious of this debt.

On the official Army Welfare side, Major Black undertook some difficult tasks for us so that we were enabled to give of our best. He was strongly backed up by Colonel Lawrence when necessary, and between these two most friendly officers, everything went well. But this tribute would be half-hearted if I didn't mention in a general way the many kindnesses showered on us by all officers at that time in Hamburg. I remember arriving in the city without a towel, but Captain 'Peter' Grimes soon got me one from somewhere (we christened him after the principal character in Britten's opera).

The rehearsals went beautifully, for we had sixty-seven members of the Hamburg Philharmonic Opera Orchestra. The operas performed by the Sadler's Wells Opera Company were *La bohème*, *Madama Butterfly*, *The Bartered Bride*, *Così fan tutte*, *Rigoletto*, and *Le nozze di Figaro*. The first performance (*La bohème*) was magnificent.

Robert Ainsworth[6] had come over to help take some of the operas off my shoulders, so I arranged for him to do *The Bartered Bride* (Ainsworth died a few years later at a comparatively young age). My friend John Barbirolli had arrived and wanted four orchestral rehearsals for his performances of *Butterfly*!

---

4   The current Staatsoper was opened on 15 October 1955.
5   Eugen Jochum (1902-1987), German conductor who succeeded Karl Böhm as Musical Director of the Hamburg Opera and Philharmonic Orchestra (1934-1949). He subsequently became the first Musical Director of the Bavarian Radio Symphony Orchestra (1949-1961).
6   Robert Ainsworth (1901-1947), Chorus Master and conductor at Covent Garden from 1935-1939, and married to contralto Muriel Brunskill.

This problem was surmounted eventually, and again, Major Black, with infinite wisdom and tact, smoothed over all difficulties with the orchestra. I conducted *Bohème*, *Così*, and *Rigoletto*, but later took over *The Bartered Bride*, *Figaro* and one *Butterfly*. The performances were very good, particularly *Bohème*, and Barbirolli had two excellent performances of *Butterfly*. We played Sundays as well, so we had very little rest and the work was hard.

The only time I got near to disappointment with the playing of the Hamburg Philharmonic Orchestra was at the first rehearsal of *Rigoletto*. Technically the playing was good, but dramatically it lacked force and character. Such a thing is not unusual with an orchestra, particularly a German one, when performing Italian works, especially Verdi. At my second rehearsal I worked hard and insisted on more attention to the dramatic elements in the score. I remember completely using up my vocabulary of dramatic expressions in German in order to rouse the players to the highest pitch of musical nuance. I succeeded, particularly in the music of the last act, in getting what I wanted, and at the performance they excelled themselves. When the last note had been played and the full tragedy of *Rigoletto* had unfolded, there was an uncanny silence from our audience. Suddenly the most vociferous applause burst out, and I was informed afterwards by many people, that some difficulty was experienced in getting the soldiers out of the theatre, such had been their tremendous enthusiasm. On the stage and in the orchestra, we were conscious of the rapt attention during all four acts of the opera, and felt we had made a very good impression. The male chorus on this occasion gave a magnificent performance, almost like the pre-war days at Sadler's Wells. There were, of course, many of the experienced members of Sadler's Wells Chorus with us, and these singers (mainly Welsh) were a tower of strength.

The enthusiasm of the ordinary Tommy was something one must experience to believe. They filled the theatre every night with one exception, and that was the second performance of *Così*. I think this opera, which dealt with the infidelity of sweethearts left behind by their soldier lovers, was perhaps a doubtful choice. The production was a beautiful one and the artists excellent; quite the best thing the Sadler's Wells company did.

The make-up artist, loaned by the Staatsoper in Hamburg, did a remarkable piece of work to John Hargreave's face and I have never seen such an effective characterisation of Rigoletto as on this occasion. Rigoletto looked half-mad, yet tender in all the scenes with Gilda, and fiercely eloquent, almost to grandeur in the scenes with Marullo.

One morning at about midday, I met John Barbirolli and Walter Legge in the Atlantic Bar to introduce them to Major Black, so that we could discuss the rehearsal difficulties. I was standing in the middle of the room, and was attracted by a very young and jolly party of two women and four men at a nearby table.

One member of the party, Mary, invited me for lunch with her companions, and we talked of music, a subject she and her friends seemed to know a lot about. It was well past the lunch hour by the time we all filed into the restaurant. I had also been invited to join the War Correspondents at the opera that evening in their box, and did so for a short time. I reciprocated by inviting everyone to a *Così fan tutte* orchestral rehearsal the next morning.

Mary also came to the rehearsal, and afterwards we wended our way to the Atlantic Hotel where we met more of her friends.[7] Lunch over, Mary walked with me part of the way to my hotel. The sun was warm, and we talked of music and I babbled a lot of nonsense about painting. We said goodbye and half-promised to write to one another. She went off to Berlin, and Hamburg became a duller city. I did have several letters from Berlin describing her experiences, and then one Sunday she suddenly walked into the Schauspielhaus. She talked about Berlin, the city of displaced people; refugees from the Russian occupied zone; a doomed city and a doomed people, where the stench of death pervaded the air, every building a shambles. She talked about young children dying of hunger, and graves being dug now, because later the people would not have the strength to do it. Berlin seemed strangely fascinating and movingly beautiful in a tragic way.

Mary stayed in Hamburg for eight days, and that first night we went to *Figaro*, conducted by Walter Susskind, which was most enjoyable.[8] The next day Parry Jones, Mary and I went to Belsen Camp No.1. We bumped our way by Jeep out of stricken Hamburg to the Autobahn. Even on one of these great motoring roads built all over Germany by order of Hitler, there were signs of bomb damage, with huge craters filled in by Royal Engineers. Our driver was both impatient and muddle-headed, and missed a turning that would have taken two hours off our journey time.

We eventually arrived at Belsen (now taken over by the British) and passed several lone graves of German soldiers with their helmets stuck on the top of a bit of wood, and flowers over the graves. But we were to see worse things than that at Belsen. Our jeep turned into the camp, past the blocks of administrative buildings. We passed groups of Jewish women who were displaced nationals of Hungary, Poland and other countries. I was told later that all these women had been sterilized.

Our jeep stopped in one of the squares at the back of a main set of buildings which housed the Red Cross staff, and we eventually found the British Royal Army Medical Corps officer with whom Mary had become great friends when

---

7 The identity of Mary is never fully revealed, but there is a strong suggestion that this relationship was more than just professional.

8 Walter Susskind (1913–1980), Czech-born, British conductor who succeeded Braithwaite as Musical Director of the Scottish Orchestra.

earlier she had spent three weeks at Belsen with the Red Cross. He was a dear fellow, about 50, and had seen horror enough to put 20 years onto his age. Mary suddenly turned at the sound of a voice and gave a huge affectionate hug to a sweet little Hungarian girl she had known during her earlier visit. All the girls in the camp had a number tattooed on their arms – a sign that the Germans considered them fit to work. The unstamped ones perished.[9]

Then came the journey to Camp No.1, the notorious Concentration Camp. I had undertaken the journey with mixed feelings, and now that we were on our way, I tried to discover reasons why the Germans had behaved with such bestiality. Belsen is set in one of nature's fairest spots. Trees abound and the countryside is pleasant. Why did the Germans choose such a beautiful spot? We turned out of the main gate and followed the car in front along an improvised road in very bad condition. Dust was rising in clouds as we passed groups of displaced persons, mostly Jewish men and women. We turned in through a gate, past a British sentry and a few miserable wooden huts marked *Bade – Männer – Frauen*, and other huts which were used as stores. Soon we came to the end of these huts, all now deserted, and to the entrance proper of Camp No.1.

This camp was entirely surrounded by a high barbed wire fence, and outside the entrance the British had erected two huge wooden placards on either side, one in English,[10] the other in German. The English one said:

> THIS IS THE SITE OF
> THE INFAMOUS BELSEN
> CONCENTRATION CAMP
> Liberated by the British on 15 April 1945.
> -----------------------------
> 10,000 UNBURIED DEAD WERE FOUND HERE,
> ANOTHER 13,000 HAVE SINCE DIED.
> ALL OF THEM VICTIMS OF THE
> GERMAN NEW ORDER IN EUROPE,
> AND AN EXAMPLE OF NAZI KULTUR.

Passing through the barbed wire gate we came to a sea of huts destroyed by the British flame-throwing tanks. We left our trucks and stood beside the pitiful little pieces of human evidence, such as odd shoes and bits of clothing still left

---

9   Tattoos to identify those fit for work were used only in Auschwitz. The women that Braithwaite describes had probably been transferred to Belsen from there. 'Tattoos and Numbers: The System of Identifying Prisoners at Auschwitz', *Holocaust Encyclopedia*, https://www.ushmm.org/wlc/en/article.php?ModuleId=10007056, accessed 23 January 2019.

10 The layout of the text is confirmed from photographs of the period. The American Holocaust Museum now calculates the total number of deaths between 1940 and 1945 in the Bergen-Belsen concentration camp complex at approximately 50,000.

lying about. All so inexpressibly sad and silent, but so eloquent. We rejoined our trucks and went still further into this weird underworld. The British had burned all the huts, so all that remained were the Watch Towers (about ten of them), and the items that could not be burned.

We came to the women's quarters among the trees, and stopped for a while at one of the huge mounds of earth and sand piled above the graves of thousands of unknown dead, for the Germans destroyed records of these victims. Some people had erected wooden boards with inscriptions in Hebrew on them – pitiful reminders that the majority of these unknown dead were Jewish. I was silent but drank in these sights deeply. I felt ill and disquieted; the experience was too much for me, and I could not eat the refreshments that had been provided for us. We promised to bring some Sadler's Wells artists two days later to give a concert for the displaced persons. Farewell was said of our kindly hosts, and we started for Hamburg, 89 kilometres away.

The journey back was uneventful, except for one bad skid, and we arrived in Hamburg about 8 p.m. That night, after meeting many friends at the Atlantic, we supped together and later went to the Garrison Officers Mess to meet other friends. Parry Jones[11] was there and a delightful evening was spent by all of us. Parry was most entertaining, and he was at the top of his form. An interesting personality joined us in Colonel de Beer,[12] who was in Hamburg to trace the church bells which the Germans had stolen from France and Belgium.[13]

I had already seen the bells during two trips up the harbour by launch to the submarine pens. The pens had fifteen feet of solid concrete above them as a protection against bombing. We were overawed by the immensity of these huge constructions. At the side entrance, a big notice told us that these pens were gas and bomb proof, but the Germans were too hopeful. There were several submarines sunken and submerged by a bomb which blew open the outside sea doors and smashed all the glass and woodwork at the rear of the pen. Such protection as they had, availed them nothing.

On the day of our promised concert, eighteen of us in a huge army lorry started off, taking the shortest route through Zoltan and Bergen. On arrival

---

11 Parry Jones (1891–1963), Welsh tenor. He performed with Warwick Braithwaite on at least 50 occasions, between 1925 and 1951, including the inaugural concert of the National Orchestra of Wales on 12 April 1928.

12 Joseph C. E. de Beer (1887–1953), Belgian museum curator and art historian.

13 'Following the German surrender, thousands of surviving church bells filled an area in Hamburg harbour the size of an American football field. In summer 1945, the British MFAA began the arduous task of sorting and identifying each object. De Beer arrived in Hamburg as soon as possible with the Commission's inventory and photographs in hand, an invaluable tool which over time restored the sound of chimes to many of Belgium's churches.' *The Monuments Men Foundation*, https://www.monumentsmenfoundation.org, accessed 7 January 2019.

at Aspinall's headquarters I met Leo Genn,[14] who was there with the Crimes Commission. He told us we would see Josef Kramer and Irma Grese.[15] Kramer was handcuffed to his prison doctor; Grese looked like a typical German Fraulein, rather striking in a cold, relentless way. We went back to the Red Cross HQ to give the concert, which took place in a big Kino[16] and was absolutely full. The artists were Linda Parker, Edith Coates, Arthur Servant, and Ronald Stear, with Walter Susskind at the piano. They gave of their best, and were much appreciated by the audience.

After the concert we went out to the concentration camp. The artists were deeply moved and were taken to the graves of the 13,000 people buried by the Red Cross. Each grave had a piece of wood over it with the name of the dead person on it. These graves were well tended, with orderly arrangements of the reddish sand, abounding with flowers. A melancholy sight, but infinitely easier to look at than the mounds of the anonymous dead left by the Germans.

Very soon we started for Hamburg in a Red Cross truck, arriving at the hotel where a farewell party was being given for the Sadler's Wells Opera Company.

The next night I had to conduct *The Bartered Bride*, and during lunch that day at the Atlantic Hotel, I met Hubert Greenslade at the entrance. He had just come from Berlin, where he had arranged for me to conduct and rehearse the Deutsches Opernhaus orchestra for the following week. This was good news, and that night *The Bartered Bride* went with a swing. The audience was very enthusiastic and the Philharmonic Orchestra came in for tremendous applause at the end of the opera. I made some eulogistic remarks about the standard of their work and the spirit of co-operation they had shown. The Leader presented me with a lovely souvenir in the form of a book of the 100-year history of the Orchestra, signed by every member of the present personnel.

On Sunday 23 September, two buses called for the Sadler's Wells Company and I saw them off to Detmold, promising to meet them again at the end of my Berlin week. I packed at midnight and slept until 7 a.m. The sun was already warm; it was a lovely day. I said goodbye to the staff at the Hotel and sent home some presents, which never arrived.

Mary and I were seated together in the plane, the door was shut, the engines started and we glided along the runway. It was a beautiful day and the countryside below looked beautiful as well. After an hour's travelling, we passed over Lake Wannsee and the plane began to descend to Gatow, the airfield used

---

14 Leo John Genn (1905–1978), British actor and barrister who was part of the British unit that investigated war crimes at Belsen, and later was an assistant prosecutor at the trial for Belsen in Lüneburg, Germany.

15 Kramer was camp Commandant, and Grese was warden of the women's section of Belsen-Bergen. Both were executed for war crimes on 13 December 1945.

16 A colloquial term for cinema.

by the British.[17] Mary was whisked away to the Am Zoo Hotel by her friends and I, in a fine car, to the ENSA Headquarters where Major Harrington met me and gave me lunch, and then by another car to the rehearsal at the Theater an des Westens with the opera orchestra.

Here we were in Berlin, and I was on my way to the Theater an des Westens where an orchestra of 95 players awaited me for rehearsal. Major Harrington's transport driver, Sue, drove me through shattered Berlin. The rehearsal passed off well and I made good friends immediately. We then trailed back to the Am Zoo Hotel, but Sue called on me at 6 p.m. to take me to a reception given by Admiral Parry (of River Plate fame). He gave a magnificent party in the Kaiser Allee. I much admired the character and personality of Admiral Parry, who spoke of his Graf Spee adventure in such a modest fashion. Apparently, his ship had run out of ammunition, but nevertheless he still pursued the German ship. I met a high-ranking Russian Officer at this party, as well as the son of Cyril Rootham, the composer, who spoke Russian very well and acted as a most efficient interpreter.[18] It was interesting to hear the views of the Russians on art and music.

Next day, after the rehearsal, Mary told me that a friend had arranged for a car to call at 2.30 p.m., to visit Berlin's devastated centre. Geoffrey, her friend, was courteous, kind, and most efficient as a guide. We toured through the so-called Russian Zone and visited the Kanzlei,[19] the marble building erected by the Nazi Party. We ascended the stairs to the many offices lately occupied by the Ministry of Culture. Curiously enough, although there was lots of evidence of various adjutants and Ministries, there was no evidence in the offices we saw of Goebbels. I picked up a report of the Berlin Theatres, which I still have, among the millions of papers scattered about these offices. Several sheets of Hitler's own personal notepaper, marked 'Adolph Hitler (München)' in gold lettering, found their way into my hands. Iron Crosses and Ribbons were laying out everywhere. We spent some time in the rooms where thousands of gifts to Hitler from grateful German people were housed. All these papers and gifts were scattered about in the most shameful disorder. We walked through Hitler's huge reception room, with his outsize desk, and also through the room where he held his ambassadorial levees with their ugly, gross chandeliers. The whole building was fantastic in its shrieking marble ugliness, almost as if the Nazi Party were afraid that the world would not believe that this cancer could live forever.

---

17 RAF base in the district of Gatow in south-western Berlin.

18 Jasper St John Rootham (1910–1990), was in Berlin where his fluency in Russian involved him in negotiations with the Soviet army ahead of the Potsdam Conference.

19 The New Reich Chancellery, designed for Hitler by Albert Speer, was opened in 1939 and severely damaged in 1945. The ruins were eventually demolished by the Soviet occupation forces.

From here we went to the old Reichstag building, where tradition had been trampled in the dust. The only commentary I can make on this tragedy is that from the floor right up to the ceiling, on every wall, were names of Russian soldiers written in white, blue, red, brown, black, orange chalks. From a short distance, walls looked as if a huge embroidery design had been painted on them. One can imagine the feelings that had motivated the Russian soldiers. I was told that when the Russian siege of Berlin commenced, they brought 22,000 guns to bear on the city, and it certainly looked like it. The huge pillars of the Reichstag building in the Entrance Hall were cracked and split, and the dome had fallen in and shattered on the floor. We left this tragic building where, at the entrance, the colossal statue of Barbarossa (in beautiful bronze), had been toppled over onto one side by the Russians.

It felt good to be in the sunshine. There were about 200 people in the Tiergarten being taken away in buses and lorries because they were participating in black market transactions; poor humans, trying to sell watches for cigarettes – the only currency that existed in Berlin at that time. We regained our car and slowly motored around the Reichstag, looking at the stumps of trees which had been sawn off for firewood by a desperate people seeking winter warmth. We passed the shelters where Hitler and Eva Braun had been burned after committing suicide.

From the Reichstag, we went to two Railway Stations where we witnessed the pitiful, sordid, shameful, melancholy and miserable lot of refugees. No words can describe the absolute hopelessness of these termini, where the dregs of humanity had congregated. Long queues of human beings, with no hope left of anything; undernourished, without destinations or any sane ideas as to their ultimate aim in life; children whose eyes were sunken like dead people; mothers, with babies vainly sucking at their breasts; groups and families held together by despair; and people with their last belongings strapped together with rope or string. Some heavenly agency had dispensed mugs of tea, but only those strong enough to push their way through to the canteen could get a cup. Others had made wood fires and boiled some liquid outside the station. The last dregs of hopelessness. Dante's Inferno illustrated by some fantastic genius of an artist might describe it, but words cannot. I wanted to see more, but the eyes of those people, with their mute appeal, burned right through to my innermost conscience.

On the way back we passed the Canal, whose foul stench seemed a fitting commentary on what I had just seen. I was told that on average there were, at that time, 250 suicides a day in Berlin. What else could one expect? A canal was as good a place as any.

That night I went to a performance of Beethoven's *Fidelio* conducted by my friend Robert Heger. Beethoven has made the only fitting commentary on such a situation. I wept more tears during the first act of Beethoven's opera than I had ever before. The scene where the prisoners are let out of their prison by the orders of a kindly jailer, and when they collect together in the courtyard and sing of the sun and freedom, is one of the most moving moments in the whole of opera. The most poignant moment of all is when the aged prisoner prays to the Almighty for strength and hope. It was so moving on this occasion that my tears could not be kept back. Then the dungeon scene in which Leonora helps to dig the grave of her husband, could almost have taken place in Belsen or Auschwitz. One wonders if Beethoven might not have been a clairvoyant. *Fidelio* was too real and near to us for tranquillity. I couldn't see Heger afterwards because my emotions were too acute; an evening too moving and expressive to be entirely happy.

Sleep would have been welcome that night. I went to bed in my room, but visions of what I had seen passed through my brain. How low had this nation fallen. I was standing once again upstairs in the ruins of the Chancellery where all the stationery and papers of Hitler's secretaries were scattered everywhere. In one room I was knee-deep in Iron Crosses and Ribbons. Outside the room, in a long passage, there were thousands of Ribbons, and I also found ten or twelve Iron Crosses of the 1918 and 1938 years. While rummaging among this fantastic rubble, a German military policeman came up to me in a furtive way, taking out of his pocket an Iron Cross wrapped in tissue paper. He wanted five cigarettes for it. He didn't speak a word, but just held the Iron Cross in one hand while the five fingers of his other hand were held up, and the motion of puffing indicated without doubt what he wanted. I would have no truck with such business. He seemed oblivious to the horror and tragedy of the downfall of a great nation.

If we in this country regard the Victoria Cross as the greatest honour a soldier can earn by his bravery, then the German people regarded their Iron Cross as a similar symbol and reward. For a member of the Wehrmacht to barter such a symbol for five cigarettes was the most devastating commentary on the downfall of a great nation, humiliated into the dust. Which reminds me, I was ankle deep in dust both in the Kanzlei and the Reichstag. My uniform was covered in dust because we had crawled through rubble and girders at the top of the Chancellery, a most nerve-racking experience. As one came outside the door of the Reichstag, one was offered souvenirs and postcards in exchange for cigarettes.

I can never forget the simple humans who hung about the station waiting for as long as eight or more hours for a mug of tea or for a ticket for the one train a day. These people lived at the station until their turn came to get a ticket which would take them into the British Zone. Many died of starvation or cold. There was no drinking water. The canal was near, only a few yards away, but one dare not drink the water because it was infected and had to be boiled before being consumed. These people had the patience borne of hopeless despair. Only a miracle could save them from death, but even if that miracle happened, there was no enthusiasm because the future held little hope. Like the buildings in Berlin, these displaced people were hollow and empty.

One saw evidence everywhere of the fierce battle for Berlin; tanks and cars upturned and guns blown up and rusted; electric overhead wires hanging down like weeping willows; stunted tree trunks; bomb craters filled with filth; great holes in the road where the underground had been blown up; churches smashed and their towers peppered with gunfire. The Staatsoper, Schiller and Lessing Theatres had been blitzed, and the Charlottenburg Opera House damaged beyond repair. German army lorries and tanks stood abandoned at almost every street corner. What incredible devastation! Yet there were a few places more or less intact. The Rundfunk, where Joyce[20] gave his nightly talks to Britain, still survived on the outskirts of the city. The Hotel Savoy, where I stayed, was undamaged, but without hot water. The Hotel Adlon was a shambles. The Russian Army had taken complete revenge for Stalingrad, Kharkov and Leningrad; the Germans were suffering in full measure for the bestialities inflicted on Russian prisoners at places like Auschwitz where, I was told, 30,000 Russians were tormented and buried alive in huge pits.

Having seen Belsen, and having studied facts and figures as to the number of Jews gassed and tormented to death, one could only conclude that the Germans were reaping the harvest of a dastardly regime which they, in the majority, hailed vociferously. No mercy should be shewn them, but cruelty (as practised by their regime), should not be meted out by us.

My rehearsals with the Deutsche Opera House Orchestra, a fine body of 95 players, were a wonderful antidote to these harrowing sights of shell-pitted Berlin. I made good friends with these men, who struck me as being musicians first and Germans afterwards. Music was the one sane thing in Germany at that time, and at my rehearsals I could speak to them in their own language, and we met on purely artistic grounds. They gave of their best and the rehearsals went smoothly. One strange thing struck me at the time with the German orchestral players; they were entirely unfamiliar with Russian music. The rehearsal of Tchaikovsky's *Francesca da Rimini* and the dances from Borodin's *Prince Igor* were not entirely easy, but after a while they played this music magnificently. The explanation was simple. No Russian music had been played in Germany for many years.

On my second morning's rehearsal, Robert Heger, who had at one time conducted the Scottish Orchestra, came to see me. He told me of his work in

---

20 William Brooke Joyce (1906–1946), better known as Lord Haw-Haw, was an American-born broadcaster of propaganda during WWII. He was convicted of high treason and executed on 3 January 1946.

Berlin and of the concerts he conducted. There was quite a lot of music being performed in Berlin, and the Berlin Philharmonic Orchestra had been brought back to strength and performed regularly. Heger and I spoke of mutual friends of ours in Glasgow and I promised to convey messages to them. Heger very kindly invited me to revisit Berlin and conduct concerts with his orchestra. This I gladly consented to do but could not get permission from the authorities to take advantage of his offer.

That evening, which by an unkind fate proved to be my last in Berlin, was spent with friends who came to my hotel for supper. The conversation turned on art, music and the future of our civilization; indeed, the future of this world of ours was the one topic of serious conversation in Hamburg or Berlin at that time. One had only to mention the Atom Bomb to start a spate of gloomy prophecies. Gloomy or not, there is a key to it somewhere. I had often remarked that it took a major war, with millions of people cruelly done to death, to give artists their chance of pitiful material to paint. It had taken the same to allow me to conduct the Hamburg Philharmonic, the Deutsches Opernhaus Orchestra, and to accept an offer to conduct the Berlin Philharmonic. What is wrong with human beings? One day we must be able to use our energies and brains to the full in peaceful things. Until that day comes, there will always be fighting caused by the maldistribution of the wealth of this world, and we will always behave like badly brought up children. These and other arguments were invariably used during these discussions, and the consensus of opinion was that our civilization would be obliterated and give way to a new era. I believe in the everlasting power of the human soul as mirrored by artists, musicians and poets. *That* will never be killed. If it dies in one place, it will spring up elsewhere. I often thought of Thornton Wilder's play, *The Skin of our Teeth*,[21] as a truer prophecy than most people believed. In this play, Wilder preaches the same theory that there will always be a few people left after a cataclysm of destruction who will preserve the key which will take man on to the next era. I wonder if it is worthwhile. When every advance in science made during *this* civilization can be used for evil as well as good, what is the purpose of advancement? The whole of this argument can be summed up in the invention of the scientific arch-destroyer of life – the Atom Bomb.

Karel Čapek's play *R.U.R.* was, in its essence, another prophecy rapidly coming true.[22] We never learn. The United States Government have withheld the secret of the atom bomb. But are they big enough to destroy it and the factories? Are they big enough to renounce the power over other people which it gives? I very much doubt it, and there you have the key to universal destruction sooner or later.

---

21 Pulitzer Prize-winning play, premiered in New Haven, Connecticut on 15 October 1942.

22 *Rossumovi univerzální roboti* (Rossum's Universal Robots), written in 1920, was one of the earliest literary introductions to the concept of robotic creatures.

These and many other arguments pervaded the discussions among most of my acquaintances while I was in Germany, and on this occasion, we went far into the night speculating on the future of mankind. My friends went back to their hotel leaving me to my own gloomy reflections. I resolved that night, come what may, I would give my whole heart and soul to the better performance of music for the remaining years of my life.

It had been obvious to me for some time that people all over the world were clinging to the arts more strongly than ever. One saw the tremendous growth in attendances at concerts as one aspect of this. Can this be the key that will open up a new evaluation of our present civilization? Are human beings at last becoming tired and angry at the eternal fighting? Did they see, in that struggle, the answer to their destruction? Or their continuation? It may have been. If so, World War II will not have been fought in vain. But will the next generation gather anything about this from their elders? There is a futile gap between parents and children which, in most cases, is the fault of the parents who have forgotten their own youthful aspirations. The first sign of a descent into the abyss.

Sleep came at last, and the next day was to be full of disappointment. I was telephoned early by Major Harrington's secretary to say that London had decided I was to be sent back by plane that day as originally planned, to commence rehearsals in Glasgow on the first of October with my orchestra, the 'Scottish'. It was indeed a mournful blow, as I was announced to conduct a concert on the Sunday with the Deutsche Opera House Orchestra. This engagement had originally been planned to help out ENSA, who had to find another conductor for the one originally announced. Now they had to find yet *another* conductor to replace me. That morning I called the orchestra together at 9.30 a.m. and did my final rehearsal of the symphony programme I was to have conducted, so that at least I was preparing the orchestra well for the conductor who would ultimately do the concert. The players paid me the tribute of being disappointed when they heard I was to go. We had had five splendid rehearsals and a fine spirit of co-operation had existed between us. I was loath to say goodbye, and left them with the issue still in doubt, as Major Harrington wasn't sure up to the last moment if weather conditions would allow an air-lift from Berlin.

My friends came to the theatre and we all went along to the Hotel Am Zoo for a final parting drink. I jokingly offered Major Harrington all sorts of bribes to arrange for me to miss that plane, but although he had done everything to make my stay in Berlin as pleasant as possible, he was staunch and true when it came to orders from his superior officers. I was high priority No. 3, so the case on my behalf fizzled out. At the airfield the officials really saw to it that I was put on that plane and, with my luggage on board, we were soon in the air.

The journey back from Hamburg to Croydon was much more interesting than the outward flight, for the weather was perfect. We had a very agreeable navigator on board who came through the cabin with maps, and talked to each passenger in turn, showing exactly where we were and the route we had taken, or were about to take. It was also very interesting to see the countryside below as we got nearer Holland. Huge forts every few miles lined the border with Germany. The way the land is parcelled out in long strips for the purpose of agriculture, and the towns and villages, all set out in straight lines, was monotonous in its regularity. As we passed over the Zuyder Zee, the sun was shining brightly and one could see the distant coastline. A few minutes later we were over The Wash and flying over typical English towns and villages. Here, the thing that impressed me was the entire absence of regularity. The layout of the roads and towns was a joy to see. Instead of dozens of straight strips of land, there were graceful curves and irregular patterns. The towns had a personality about them entirely absent from those in Holland. The English method seems to fly in the face of utility, and I got much more pleasure looking at our countryside with its apparent lack of orderly layout. Each building site was different from the other, and the solidarity of the buildings was in great contrast to the Dutch style. I felt suddenly warmed by these differences and thought that perhaps this was a sign of our independence of spirit and an inner freedom from a compulsion which one sees so much of on the continent. Of course, this isn't quite the right explanation. The Dutch are a free people, and the land, being uniformly flat, may be responsible for this parcelling of which one sees so much.

The plane landed at Croydon[23] just as the sun was setting. We were home again. The unfailing courtesy of the officials at Croydon made me feel good, and no time was wasted. A bus was waiting, and the hale and hearty driver seemed to exude the English character. Within a few hours of leaving Berlin, we were being driven across London towards the West End. I had no regrets now; London seemed so large and friendly.

Arriving eventually in Glasgow felt like coming back to an old friend. Having been away so long, the friend was there, things were the same, and people were as kind. My rehearsals with the Scottish Orchestra were scheduled to commence on Monday, 1st October, but owing to a terrible mishap on the

---

23 Probably on 30 September 1945. Braithwaite was scheduled to begin rehearsals for his final season with the Scottish Orchestra on 1 October. The first concert of the season was on 6 October and the *Glasgow Herald* critic wrote, 'Mr Braithwaite, who was received with special warmth when he first appeared, had a formidable task in welding this largely new combination of players into a responsive unit for performance, and he and the players are due great credit for the remarkable spontaneity that prevailed. The vitality of *Romeo & Juliet* and the Spanish rhapsody [*España*] could have been secured only from an orchestra that is already very alert. A series of fine concerts may confidently be looked forward to in the season just begun.' *The Glasgow Herald* (8 October 1945), 4.

line and my train having to crawl the first part of the journey, I was four hours late in Glasgow – too late for the first rehearsal and too tired for the afternoon. So, by an irony of fate, if I had done that concert in Berlin, I would not have commenced my rehearsals any earlier than I did.

That was the end of my extraordinarily interesting five weeks in Germany. A doomed country, or a peasant nation for the next fifty years? Who knows? The German people are strong, vital and industrious, but it was the policy of the Nazi Party to go down fighting. In doing so, they have brought down the whole German people with them. It will take generations of hard work and bitter experiences to bring the new generations any real happiness. One may well argue that the populace had the regime it deserved. This is problematic and requires further investigation. A few machine guns can cower any populace, and the Nazis had the machine guns plus a devilish propaganda machine. Goebbels and Hitler between them were the fiendish architects of this sorrowful downfall of a nation, and I believe it will probably take three generations to eradicate the ill effects.

EIGHTEEN

HAMBURG POSTSCRIPT

A VISIT TO 'THE CATACOMBS'

An unforgettable experience of quite another kind was a visit to the air raid shelter beneath the square opposite my hotel in Hamburg. The inhabitants of this shelter were not allowed to leave between 11 p.m. and dawn. The iron gate below was kept locked with a German policeman in charge. The gate was opened for us and this policeman took us in tow. He was most solicitous that we should see all, and took us from room to room, each one hotter than the last. The stench was awful and the steam arising from perspiring bodies was thick with a greasy smell. Most people were asleep on benches in all sorts of attitudes. Soldiers, just released from Prisoner of War camps, spent a night there before tramping to some other destination, weary and footsore; they just fell asleep where they were. Their boots were worn to tatters; uniforms torn to pieces, faded and full of dust. What a pitiful sight; babies whimpering to themselves; their mothers endeavouring to quieten them; young men lolling about, eyes and ears wide open for any trouble; and other people intercepting us, hoping for cigarettes. How glad I was to suggest getting out of this Hell.

It was a bitter experience, and these people had been going through this since 1943, when Hamburg had its three major raids on three nights.[1] Each raid lasted only 20 minutes, but more than 30,000 people were killed as a result. On the way to the Atlantic Hotel, one passed five or six bombed buildings with

---

1 Three major attacks on Hamburg, each using more than 770 aircraft, took place in late July 1943. The operation, which destroyed most of the city, was codenamed 'Gomorrah'. The death toll was 42,600, with 37,000 injured. Noble Frankland and Charles Webster, *The Strategic Air Offensive Against Germany, 1939–1945, Volume II: Endeavour, Part 4* (London: Her Majesty's Stationery Office,1961), 260–261.

huge black crosses painted on them. These indicated that there were hundreds of buried dead who were never heard of again.

One may well ask if any resentment was felt against the RAF and Flying Fortress crews. Of course, there must have been, but I found in conversation with sensible Germans that they were thankful they had not experienced the Atom bomb. They clung to the belief that England suffered as badly, and I did not have the heart to disillusion them.

There were many deep shelters, including one under the station which, I was told, held 30,000 people. I didn't try to find out if this was true. I only saw one surface shelter, and that was a private one. In 1945, any civilian caught on the streets after curfew, was taken away to prison by the British Military Police, working in conjunction with the German police. If they tried to escape, they were shot, not necessarily fatally, but the risk was great. There were many incidents of such shootings, and it reminded one forcibly that a state of acute tension existed in occupied Germany, and it would probably get steadily worse as conditions deteriorated in winter.

I felt our troops would go through many difficult times when called upon to decide between their feelings for common humanity and King's Regulations. I didn't envy them their situation but I believe the British soldier, who did all he could to help the ordinary German (as long as he behaved), would eventually cope with every new aspect of relations between the two nationalities.

BROADCASTING TO THE FORCES

There was a splendid group of Army men running the British Forces Network (BFN) Radio Station in Hamburg. This was situated in the Musikhalle Hamburg building[2] and I much admired the way Trevor Harvey[3] coped with the vast amount of work which broadcasting to the Forces entailed. Trevor was Musical Director of this organisation and, speaking perfect German, he got the utmost co-operation from everyone. He combined a firm manner with unruffled courtesy.

It was at Broadcasting House, Hamburg, that I met the composer Edmund Rubbra once again. Edmund and his colleagues (I've forgotten their names) had been touring the British Zone, playing to troops for some months.[4] Their

---

2 Now the Laeiszhalle, and home to the Hamburg Philharmonic and Hamburg Symphony Orchestras.

3 Trevor Harvey (1911-1989), English conductor and critic. He was assistant Chorus Master at the BBC (1935-1942), Associate Conductor of the Henry Wood Promenade Concerts (1949-1952), conductor of the British Youth Symphony Orchestra (1960-1972), and much-respected contributor of reviews to *Gramophone* magazine.

4 At the request of the War Office, Rubbra formed a piano trio with violinist Joshua Glazier and cellist William Pleeth to perform for the troops.

programme, or at least the one I heard, included Rubbra's *Phantasy* for two violins and piano, a work that I quite liked and which was performed to a very high standard. The instrumental pieces were interspersed with two groups of songs sung by a fine baritone singer called Rabin.[5] Edmund couldn't come to our operatic performances as he and his party were fully occupied playing to troops.

I met Eric Maschwitz[6] later in Glasgow and asked him how the BFN organisation started. He very kindly sent me a most interesting letter on this point which I insert in full:

Dear Braithwaite,

Just in case we don't get a chance to chat, herewith are a few details about BFN and how it started.

It all originated with the Field Broadcasting Unit of 21st Army Group, which operated three little 1kW mobile stations up near the front line, the Unit being commanded by Major John Macmillan (before the War with IBC in commercial radio) under myself who was Chief Broadcasting Officer with 21 A.G. We followed the advance over the Rhine and into Germany, keeping an eye open for high-power stations to commandeer as we realized that as soon as peace came, our little tiny stations which merely relayed the BBC and covered about a twenty-mile radius, would be useless for covering the Occupation Zone and undertaking the important morale job of interesting the troops and keeping them from worrying about home, release dates, etc.

The obvious transmitter was the 100kW one at Hamburg, connected with the up-to-date German Broadcasting House in the centre of the city, but we had rivals in the field – the Information Control organisation, whose job was to broadcast to the German people. In the race into Hamburg, they just beat us, taking over both studios and transmitter, so we found ourselves without anything. Hearing of another 100kW station at Norden, near Emden on the North Sea coast, we sent off a reconnaissance party and managed to seize it intact with its crew of German technicians. At the same time in Hamburg, Macmillan and I commandeered the Musikhalle in the Karlluck Platz by the simple method of writing on an envelope that we had requisitioned it, and sticking the envelope on the door. Here was a huge concert building with two concert halls – one a 2,000-seater with an organ, the other a 300-seater capable of being turned into an excellent all-purpose studio.

By having the concert hall under our roof, we automatically acquired some sort of control over the Hamburg Philharmonic Orchestra which, though managed by Major Tommy Lambert of the Information Control Unit, could only give performances in our hall. We quickly arranged that if

---

5   Samuel Rabin (1903-1991), English sculptor, artist, teacher, singer, wrestler and Olympic bronze medallist.

6   Eric Maschwitz (1901-1969), English entertainer, writer, lyricist, broadcaster and broadcasting executive.

they could have the hall on Wednesdays for public concerts to the Germans, they should give a repeat show on Saturdays for Allied troops, which we should be allowed to broadcast. They did some of their rehearsing in the Hall, and some on the stage of the Opera House, the auditorium of which had been burned out in one of our raids.

Now we had a station at Norden and studios at Hamburg miles apart. How could we join them by landline to bring the output of the studios to the transmitter? The German telephone system was in a mess and it took days of hard work before we had chased up the right circuits, persuaded Signals to repair repeater stations, etc., and the first blessed sound came through.

The BFN programme began officially on 29 July. We called it a network then, although Norden was the only station working, to be followed in two weeks by a second station down south in the Ruhr, and after another two months by a third in Berlin. Norden is, of course, the BFN station heard at home here, on 455 metres, formerly the wavelength of the German station at Cologne. I managed to get 455 metres for us at a wavelength conference in Paris in June, when we and the Americans were fighting over the allocation of the old German wavelengths for our various forces and Propaganda services. By sticking to my guns, I managed to get a very good wavelength with a clear channel. BFN is operated still by No. 1 Field Broadcasting Unit.

Only four of the personnel had had any connection with broadcasting before they came to us – Macmillan, the C.O., Sgt. Gordon Crier (BBC producer), Sgt. Alan Clark (BBC receptionist) and Sgt. Dickinson (BBC engineer). We got the loan of two or three professional broadcasters from the Canadians, but the rest were trained by us. If you listen to the stations you will, no doubt, be amazed at the skill with which these youngsters act as announcers, producers, balancers, script writers, etc., and the punctuality and excellent quality of the programmes, all after six months in the game and working with more or less home-made materials. Our chief engineer, Capt. Shepherd, was a civil servant before the War and acquired all his engineering knowledge in the Army (signals).

The Hamburg Philharmonic you know all about. When we first started it up, Eugen Jochum, its own conductor, was away in the American Zone and the orchestra was being directed by Albert Bittner of Essen (not a very likeable man),[7] the protégé of the former *Gauleiter*.[8] Certain key players

---

7 Albert Bittner (1900–1980), German conductor who had worked at Berlin, Graz (where he joined the Nazi Party), Oldenburg, Gera and Essen (1936–1943). After Hamburg, he became Music Director at the Opera House in Braunschweig (1945–1955). He later taught at the Hochschule für Musik und Theater Hamburg.

8 Probably Karl Kaufmann (1900–1965), who was *Gauleiter* of Hamburg (i.e., head of the Nazi Party, and government of Hamburg) from 1933 until 1945. The *Gauleiter* was directly appointed by Hitler and answerable only to him. In practice, Hitler interfered little in the affairs of the local leaders and their power was almost absolute.

were also missing in concentration camps, etc. The return of Jochum made a big difference to the orchestra which now attracts 2,000 British troops every week. It's odd to think that for many of these chaps, Jochum will be the only conductor they know.

One of the great pleasures of Hamburg was the presence there of so many beautiful Bechstein pianos. At Broadcasting House alone, we had four concert grands of such an exquisite quality that when Solomon came out to do a series of recitals, he spent half a day darting from piano to piano trying to make up his mind which to demand for his performance. Hamburg is of course the site of the largest Bechstein factory; in every large house or flat throughout the city there seems to be a Bechstein piano of unusual beauty.

As broadcasters, we were helped from the start by the co-operative attitude of visiting musicians, such as Barbirolli, Solomon, Parry Jones, yourself and others. This was partly due to ENSA – with whom we always kept a close and friendly liaison – having convinced them that as far as the Occupation troops were concerned, BFN was the finest publicity vehicle for ENSA entertainment. The fact that we eventually got Trevor Harvey as our Director of Music helped enormously; he tackled the job like a Trojan. He could have got a Class B release and gone back to the BBC,[9] but he wrote and told Boult that he thought it important to stay for a year or so and received the Maestro's blessing in reply.

I look back to the few visits I made to Broadcasting House with great pleasure. Trevor Harvey was most helpful on all occasions and, as the Philharmonic Orchestra held its rehearsals in the Main Hall, I had invaluable opportunities to study Eugen Jochum's work.

The Hamburg Philharmonic Orchestra includes approximately 70 string players, and the beauty and wealth of tone which these fine players produced was a joy to hear. I remember on one occasion the programme included Vaughan Williams' *Fantasia on a Theme by Thomas Tallis* for double string orchestra and solo quartet of strings. I thought Jochum's tempi somewhat fast, and this work can suffer some sort of queer transformation if taken too fast. I didn't really enjoy the performance from that point of view, but the glorious tone of those string players was a revelation. I had never heard such warmth from any other orchestra. The other main item was a symphony by Bruckner (the one with the four tubas).[10] This I thought, with the exception of the scherzo, tiresome. I

---

9 A 'Class B' release applied to service personnel who had been in pre-war occupations which were now considered vital to the reconstruction of Britain. Those who were granted this early discharge were expected to work for their reconstruction employer only, or else risk recall to the Forces.

10 Anton Bruckner's Symphony no. 7 in E major employs four Wagner tubas in the 'Adagio' and 'Finale'.

can't listen to these works without feeling that the composer tried to make up for his quietness and modest kind of life, by producing long and terribly self-conscious works. One finds beautiful themes start each movement but they are so chewed up and bandied about that one wishes the composer had torn up most of his development sections. But of course, the Germans and Austrians love Bruckner and dislike Elgar, so there is something in the claim that all music is fundamentally nationalistic.

Brahms was born in Hamburg and I had looked forward to seeing his house, but alas it had been destroyed during one of those raids I spoke of earlier. The Hamburgers years ago erected a colossal statue to him in the foyer of the Musikhalle (the Concert Hall).[11] This statue is carved out of marble, and rests on a turntable which can be turned to face any direction. I could never understand the reason for this.

The Musikhalle itself is an acoustically good and comfortable concert hall, capable of holding about 2,000 people.[12] The German audiences I saw there looked both well-dressed and very well-nourished, even though this was only four months after the war. Saturday afternoon concerts were for British troops and always full and, as a rule, they were broadcast to the Forces.

The German orchestras I came into contact with had one player who looked after the arrangements, such as rehearsals and other matters. This player in German orchestras is called the Inspector. The Inspector also attends to discipline and carries out the wishes of the conductor in regard to times of rehearsals and finding extra players when necessary. Usually there are three leaders or concertmasters who share the work of leading.

One of the most interesting Germans I met was the librarian and conductor's assistant of the Hamburg Philharmonic Orchestra. An exquisitely dressed little man with most polished manners; kindly, helpful and entirely sympathetic towards our efforts to produce a good season of opera. This was George Manzau, a non-playing member of the orchestra. He looked after the conductors most efficiently. He made me a beautiful baton case including four very light batons, and took it upon his shoulders to seat the orchestra, attend all rehearsals, and generally advise guest conductors as to German methods of placing the players for operatic performances. In England, as a rule, the string players are on the left and front of the conductor, and the wind players on the right (dividing the sheep from the goats). In Germany, the strings are grouped around the centre of the orchestral well; firsts on the left of the conductor, seconds immediately in front, violas on his right, and cellos and basses behind the second violins.

---

11 The marble sculpture is located in the Brahms Foyer and is the work of Leipzig artist Max Klinger.

12 The building was funded by shipping magnate Carl Laeisz and opened in 1908. It was known as Laeiszhalle until 1933, when it became the Musikhalle Hamburg. Since 2005, it has again been called Laeiszhalle.

The flutes, oboes, clarinets and horns are seated behind the first violins, and the trumpets, trombones and percussion behind the violas to the right of the conductor, thus keeping the woodwind and horn players together and the brass players at the other end of the orchestra. There is something very good about this arrangement because the blend of the instruments seems more mellow. I was very impressed by the tone of the trumpets and trombones. These instruments in German orchestras have a wide bell and the players use the large bore instruments. The result is less brilliant but more satisfying. The general technical excellence of the woodwind players was of a very high quality.

*

Since having returned home, I have been asked many times about the condition of the German people and their attitude towards Britain. I can only give my impressions of the people I met in the towns that I visited.

From all accounts, Hamburg was never a Nazi stronghold, and I was told that the last time Hitler had been there he was given a very frosty reception. This might have been true, as Hamburg is a great port, and a city where all nationalities meet. Of the many people I spoke to, most disavowed all sympathy with the Nazi Party; but most of these people were musicians, artists and theatre people. My impression was different when I met a few, and saw many, of the well-dressed and well-nourished Germans who constituted the bulk of the audience that frequented the Musikhalle. Here there seemed to be an impregnable barrier, and I rarely had an opportunity of finding out what these people really thought about the war. They were untouched by it and were resentful towards the British troops. Don't forget that for several years the German people had all Europe at their feet, and moreover, all the produce and wares that had been stolen from other countries. I was amazed at the standard of dress exhibited by the women, who all seemed to have silk stockings.

That was in Hamburg. In Berlin it was entirely different, and I saw no evidence of well-dressed people. Everything was drab. The photographs one saw in the English press of super well-dressed Berlin women were a surprise to me. Maybe I didn't just see them in the streets. In Hamburg there were portions of the residential area untouched by bombs, and there was a very great contrast between the well-dressed and the drab. Berlin had not escaped anywhere, and it was overrun by refugees as well.

I was often asked why the orchestras were so good and generally had such large personnel. During the war, right up to 1943, the German orchestras were untouched. Even after that, only very few young members were taken, and only for munitions work. I have in my possession a *Deutsches Theaterjahrbuch* of 1943, in which the name of every theatre, opera house and their personnel is given in detail. In the larger towns the orchestras were frequently 140 strong. A full list of the opera houses subsidized by the Corporations contained names of all the administration officials. In the front of this book were the portraits of Hitler, Goebbels, Göring and many others who were President and Vice Presidents of the Ministry of Culture. After these pages came a short list of those who had died as a result of raids or in the Forces. There were surprisingly few names, and among them very few musicians or singers. The Nazi Party knew that they could not make big inroads into the musical life of Germany; music and the theatre were the only pleasures left to the German people. So, the reason for the high standard of the orchestra is apparent.

Just before I left Hamburg, I was told that 300 more musicians were to be auditioned with a view to forming a new orchestra. This has been done and I had great pleasure in conducting the superb Sinfonieorchester des Norddeutschen Rundfunks[13] during the Sadler's Wells Ballet tour of 1949.

From the information I gleaned from various sources, most opera houses in Germany had been bombed, and one completely destroyed. In Berlin, the Staatsoper, the Krolloper and the Charlottenburg were shattered. The Staatsoper was a magnificent building with a huge stage. The walls were still left but the inside was a mass of twisted girders. The only opera house left standing was the one in which I rehearsed – the Theater an des Westens – which, by some trick of fate, had only a slightly damaged roof. In Munich, the Hoftheater was smashed and the little Residenztheater damaged almost beyond repair. No one seemed to know anything about the Prinzregententheater in Munich, an opera house whose stage is one of the finest in Europe, and a replica of the Bayreuth Festspielhaus.[14] I was told that Hanover, Cologne, Braunswig, Dresden, Leipzig, Nuremberg, Augsburg and the Vienna Opera House were all destroyed, but it was a great pity because the allied occupation armies would have found their task easier if some of these theatres had escaped.

---

13 Known in English as the North German Radio Symphony Orchestra. From 1945–1947, its chief conductor was Hans Schmidt-Isserstedt.

14 The Prinzregententheater did suffer some damage, but was still able to accommodate the homeless Bavarian State Opera from 1944 to 1963. It was repaired in 1958 and fully renovated in 1988.

NINETEEN

SOME MORE PERSONALITIES

During the five or six years before the war, I had become interested in world politics and joined the Left Book Club.[1] In the early days of this organisation I became Chairman of the London Musicians Section, but found the meetings, held in a sub-basement chamber of the Shaftesbury Hotel in Seven Dials, too frequent and dull.

It was Edward Clark who first introduced me to the Left Book Club, and on the committee I found some old friends of mine – Arnold Goldsbrough[2] and Alan Bush.[3] Alan in those days had grown a fine bushy beard which went well with his didactic and forthright manner in debate. I confess I felt out of it and quite uncomfortable during my short period of chairmanship, and at times was incensed by the rough views expressed by 'comrade' this or 'comrade' that. It was not that I didn't feel very exercised in my heart about the unfortunate ones, but that the bloodcurdling views expressed by the more militant members

---

1 The Left Book Club (LBC) was one of the first book clubs in the UK. Founded by Stafford Cripps, Victor Gollancz and John Strachey, it aimed to 'help in the struggle for world peace and against fascism'. At its peak, it had a membership of 57,000, but ceased publishing in 1948. The Left Book Club was relaunched in 2015. 'Left Book Club', https://en.wikipedia.org/wiki/Left_Book_Club#cite_note-16, accessed 10 February 2019.

2 Arnold Goldsbrough (1892-1964), English organist, harpsichordist, and conductor who, in 1948, founded his own orchestra for the performance of early music. This eventually became the English Chamber Orchestra.

3 Alan Bush (1900-1995). British composer, pianist, conductor, teacher and political activist. A committed communist, his uncompromising political beliefs were often reflected in his music. He composed prolifically, but struggled for recognition from the British musical establishment, which largely ignored his works. Rachel O'Higgins, 'Profile of Alan Bush', *Alan Bush Music Trust*, http://www.alanbushtrust.org.uk/profile.asp?room=Profile, accessed 10 February 2019.

shocked me almost beyond measure. What struck me then, and has impressed itself more and more on my mind the older I become, was the complete inability on the part of these comrades to see anyone else's point of view. This is no new aspect of the human race. The dyed-in-the-wool conservatives or capitalist conservatives are all tarred with the same brush. They are all alike, left and right. No real progress will be made in political freedom until both sides fully understand the circumstances which have helped to form opinion. Killing off your opponent will decide very little; they tried that after the French Revolution.

I experienced a lot of verbal killing off in that section of the Left Book Club, but it did not stop me from reading the best of the enormous output from the publishers Gollancz & Co. The war put a stop to the club, as far as I know, but I had finished with it much earlier. What finally decided me was the performance of *Belshazzar* by Handel for which Randall Swingler[4] wrote a new libretto. I had consented to conduct this, but when I read the new libretto, I jumped sky high. I had long arguments with both Alan Bush and Edward Clark and expressed my extreme displeasure and distaste in being connected with such an unwarranted travesty of the original. Handel would have torn that libretto up in a towering rage if he had read it. The libretto was left wing propaganda of a most virulent sort. This I didn't object to so much, but to have it foisted onto Handel's music was in the worst possible taste. God forbid that all these old works should be mishandled in this way by a cultural committee of the Left, and then restored later by a cultural committee of the Right when politics changed. The whole thing was foolish. I was persuaded much against my will to conduct these performances, but I swore I would be careful not to get so entangled in future.[5]

Perhaps my friends thought me wrong in not throwing everything I possessed into the melting pot, but I had a lot to lose by doing so, and although my politics are of a leftish variety, no-one would take on my responsibilities if I lost all I had gained. I have been able to separate my work from politics, and no amount of persuasion on my friends' part, with their specious arguments, has deviated me from that point of view. Christian Darnton,[6] that brilliant intellect and fine composer, who is completely sincere in his belief in communism, has

---

4   Randall Swingler (1909-1967), English poet, novelist, playwright, critic, flautist and librettist who joined the Communist Party in 1934.

5   Handel's *Belshazzar* was presented at the New Scala Theatre, under the auspices of 'London Co-Operative Societies' from 16–21 May 1938. Soloists were May Blyth (*Nitocris*), Parry Jones (*Belshazzar*), Tom Williams (*Cyrus*), Trevor Anthony (*Daniel*) and Roderick Jones (*Gobrias*). A massed choir of 300 was accompanied by the augmented Boyd Neel String Orchestra, conducted by Braithwaite. The stage director was Alan Bush. A review in the *Musical Times* declared 'The Boyd Neel String Orchestra, supplemented with excellent wood-wind, brass and an electrically amplified harpsichord (not a happy device), showed a fitting sense of co-operation under the spirited direction of Mr Warwick Braithwaite.' *Musical Times* (June 1938), 465.

6   Philip Christian Darnton (1905-1981), English composer of German descent.

not even been able to draw me into the fold, however much I admire his powers of persuasion. My beliefs belong to myself, and at the moment I am not disposed to believe they are more important than the artistic struggle for existence.

Christian Darnton is an extraordinary personality – a man with a very clear brain which can be turned to any subject, reducing it to its fundamental essentials. Whilst with him, and basking in the scintillating beam of the intellect, I always found that any arguments would completely disintegrate and I would invariably end up convinced against my will. Christian's music is just like himself – clear and transparent but of an intellectual quality one finds in all the great composers. His Third Symphony, which I performed in Glasgow during the 1944–1945 season was a great success yet, for some reason, this has not been heard of again. His Pianoforte Concerto played by Adolf Hallis at a contemporary music concert (one of a series given by the BBC in Broadcasting House under my direction in 1935), is also a magnificently brilliant and interesting work but again, for some obscure reason, has not been heard of since.[7] Another symphony he wrote, and which I was privileged to hear played by the composer at the piano, was in my humble opinion one of the outstanding works I had seen about that period.[8] Christian told me that, being dissatisfied with it for some reason, he tore it up. I hope this is not true and is only an expression that composers sometimes use when a work is tucked away for future revision. But knowing Christian, I am afraid that this symphony has been lost to us.

The biggest and most remarkable work that Darnton has written so far is his opera *Celestial Roundabout*,[9] written to a libretto by Randall Swingler. I have had the opportunity of going through this work and was greatly impressed by Christian's complete grasp of the operatic convention. The end of the first act is most original and moving. This work was written, along with the other works, for the Arts Council, but for some reason was not ever considered. It didn't even get so far as to be studied by every member of the board entrusted with selecting the best works sent in. There is some hidden reason for this and I am wondering if Christian's political beliefs have anything to do with it. It seems to me that a musical work must be judged on its merits alone and not turned down because of the political beliefs expressed by the librettist, however much the composer

---

7   Braithwaite conducted Darnton's *Piano Concerto* with the BBC Orchestra Section D (29 November 1935), and two more works during his tenure with the Scottish Orchestra: *Stalingrad (overture)* (19 December 1943) and *Symphony no. 3* (31 March 1945). The symphony and the concerto were premieres.

8   Possibly *Symphony no. 2 'Anagram'* (1939-1940) which survives as incomplete piano and short scores, http://www.musicweb-international.com/darnton/darnton.htm#Works, accessed 23 May 2022.

9   Perhaps a working title for Darnton's only opera, *Fantasy Fair* (1949-1951). Extracts performed in concert (1953).

may believe in them. The terms of the Arts Council opera scheme were that the libretto was to be submitted first of all, after which the composer, should his libretto be approved, was asked to go ahead with the music. I can well imagine that if the judges read Randall Swingler's libretto, some of them would have, in this witch-hunting age, smelt danger to the state! On the other hand, when one thinks of the poor libretti of many popular operas, one realizes how important the music can be in the final count. Of the operas chosen by this aforesaid committee, one, *Wat Tyler* by Alan Bush has already had its first performance, not in this country, but in Germany in a German translation.[10] One other, *John Socman* by George Lloyd, was performed by the Carl Rosa Opera Company in Bristol[11] and elsewhere. The remaining works by Karl Rankl, Arthur Benjamin, Berthold Goldschmidt and Lennox Berkeley have not been performed.[12] I hope and trust that Darnton's opera will be performed soon, probably not in this country, but in all likelihood on the continent.

A composer not known to the public at large was my great friend Ricardo Blamey Lafone.[13] Blamey, as his friends called him, was Financial Councillor to the Argentine Embassy for many years. His mother was an English woman who had married an Argentinian. He was a relative of General Blamey, the commander of the Australian Army. Blamey had been in London for many years and gave delightful dinner parties at his beautifully furnished house in Montpelier Square. Everything in that house was of the very best quality and taste. He chose his guests carefully, and the food was prepared superbly and served by a quiet and trained man servant. Blamey Lafone had studied composition in this country with Benjamin Dale, the Warden of the Royal Academy of Music. He has written four major orchestral works scored for an immense orchestra, and several smaller works, among them the charming ballet *Acis and Galatea*, the last work he wrote.

One of the reasons his compositions are not widely known was that Blamey was most particular about the number of rehearsals and the constitution of the orchestra. If he considered that his work was not to have enough rehearsals, he would refuse permission, even at the last moment, for its performance. If there were not enough string players, he would also refuse permission. His four major works were: *Andalgalá* (1931), a suite of delightful music depicting native life; *Escenas Catamarqueñas* (1934), another suite, again of refreshing music,

---

10 First staged in Leipzig on 6 September 1953.

11 Premiered at the Bristol Hippodrome on 15 May 1951, with Redvers Llewellyn, Ruth Packer, John Myrddin, Gita Denise and Tudor Davies. The conductor was Arthur Hammond.

12 *A Tale of Two Cities* (Arthur Benjamin), *Deirdre of the Sorrows* (Karl Rankl), *Beatrice Cenci* (Berthold Goldschmidt), *Nelson* (Lennox Berkeley). Only Rankl's opera remains unperformed, although excerpts were broadcast by the BBC.

13 Ricardo Blamey Lafone (1880–1946), Argentine composer, lawyer, diplomat, and teacher.

superbly scored; *El Ombú* (1937), a symphonic poem of surprising originality after W.F. Hudson's story of that name; and *Juvenilia* (1936), another symphonic poem magnificently scored, comprising scenes from school days, again after a well-known story by an Argentine author. These big works were difficult, but quite different both harmonically and melodically from any works I had ever heard up to that time.

I conducted many of Blamey's works, and I was not the only one to do so. My friend Richard Austin, son of my earlier friend of the BNOC days, Frederic Austin, had also conducted them. Aylmer Buesst and Sir Adrian Boult have also conducted some of them. Blamey's works gave me a curiously personal pleasure. Maybe it was because of the happy, yet poignant, harmonics and unexpected modulations, with rhythms almost, yet not quite, Spanish in character. As the BBC have all Blamey's scores and parts in their library, I can recommend musicians to their study. One movement of the Suite *Escenas Catamarqueñas*, called 'Doña Elena baila la Cueca' (Aunt Elena Dances the Queca),[14] is most intriguing and delightful, both rhythmically and harmonically. The last movement of the same suite is called 'Domingo de Carnaval' and its melodies are both original and entrancing.

Blamey was a delightful companion with a most sensitive nature, and a man with tremendous knowledge on all subjects both cultural and worldly. Alas, his life was to end in complete tragedy. Blamey had stuck it out in London during all the raids. The only concession he made to Hitler was to shift his dining room from the first floor to the basement, so that his dinner parties could go on much as usual. When the war was over, Blamey decided that he should go to Buenos Aires for a long-delayed trip home. I had dinner with him on the Tuesday, and he explained that he had changed his date of departure because some friends had booked on another plane and he thought it would be nice to travel together. He told me he did not really want to go as he feared uncertainty about the future. Peron was in power and Blamey, although very guarded in his remarks and opinions on such matters, was not altogether happy about things. I phoned him a few hours before he left on the Friday, and his voice over the phone was most miserable. He was 62 years of age, but a fine-looking man with a noble head. My brother-in-law, a reporter on a Sunday newspaper, was staying with me at the time.

On the Saturday evening about 6 p.m. he arrived home and quite casually informed me that there had been another air crash. I was working at the time and, without much interest, asked where the crash was. He said at Bathurst

---

14 Cueca is a family of musical styles and associated dances from Argentina, Chile and Bolivia. The cueca has held the status of a national dance in Chile since 1979. 'Cueca', *National Library of Chile : Memoria Chilena*, http://www.memoriachilena.cl/602/w3-article-3510.html, accessed 23 January 2019.

Aerodrome in North West Africa. I pricked up my ears at this and asked him if he had a list of names of the passengers. He reeled off several names, then stopped at one, adding that he could not quite make out the name. I asked if it was Blamey Lafone, and my brother quite excitedly said that certainly was the name. Could he use my phone to tell the office? I was dumbfounded and struck to the heart that such a wonderfully sincere character, on his first plane journey, should be so suddenly and tragically done to death. I pulled myself together and phoned his housekeeper, who naturally collapsed at the other end. I phoned the Ambassador who exclaimed, 'Good God!' I then immediately sent a cable to his brother in Buenos Aires, informing him of the tragedy. The plane had burst into flames on take-off, and all that was left of my friend were his eye glasses, which were returned to London and identified by his housekeeper. His brother wrote me a long letter and told me that it would have been Blamey's wish that all his music and books should be mine, and he arranged with the Ambassador for me to go through everything and dispose of them in the best way I could. I arranged that one set of scores and parts should go to the BBC, and this was all arranged with Blamey's sister, who lived in England. The other set of scores and parts went to the Academie Nacional in Buenos Aires.[15] I wrote an appreciation of Blamey which was printed in *The Times* and published a week after the tragedy.[16] So, one of the most lovable, sensitive and cultured friends I have ever had, was no more. Blamey had intended, on this trip to his home town, to arrange a tour for me through the Argentine with, if possible, some performances at the famous Teatro Colón. My disappointment was nothing to the sorrow I felt at his death.

I have only spoken about Vaughan Williams quite incidentally, on the occasion of the big concert at the Albert Hall attended by Queen Mary and Princess Margaret. I spoke only of his conducting of the London Symphony Orchestra, but I had met Vaughan Williams many times before this and had often been in correspondence with him over various matters, mainly connected with his own compositions. The music of Vaughan Williams seemed to echo, in some mysterious way, the intrinsic atmosphere and colour of both the English character and countryside. But, apart from the use of traditional folk tunes in his early works, which at one time seemed to threaten to be his permanent method of composition, there has crept into his work of late years a much deeper feeling, almost a longing after holiness which only becomes apparent on occasions in the early works. I speak particularly of the Fifth Symphony, which exudes a depth and spirituality in music hardly ever reached before, except by the greatest of all composers. This seems to spring from an inward happiness

---

15 Academia Nacional de Bellas Artes (National Academy of Fine Arts), founded in 1936.
16 Braithwaite contributed an obituary for *The Times* (24 September 1946), 7.

and a depth of human understanding rare among contemporary composers. Vaughan Williams has put himself into these works, yet I have never met a man who is so delightfully unselfconscious and who can enjoy a comic situation. I wouldn't go so far as to say which is the real man, the conversationalist or the composer.

The story is told that the composer/conductor Julius Harrison[17] once pointed out the excellence of his hearing-aid, and suggested to Vaughan Williams that he should have one too. Vaughan Williams replied that it may be quite an excellent gadget, but he could see its many disadvantages as well. When pressed for an example, he suggested that a visit to a lavatory might sound like an avalanche. I cannot vouch for the truth of this story, but if it is true, it shows an almost Rabelaisian sense of humour.

Another incidence of Vaughan Williams' wit was given to me after the first performance of his opera *The Pilgrim's Progress*. It was a great night; all musical London was at Covent Garden, and interspersed among the audience were many bishops and other clerics. At the party given afterwards in the foyer, attended by a number of notables including a few of these clerical gentlemen, Vaughan Williams took me aside and, with a distressed twinkle in his eye, asked me to stand by him 'for God's sake' as he had been 'pursued by Bishops all the evening.' And he meant it! So, there is an imp somewhere in Vaughan Williams' make up.

One other incident, often quoted, occurred many years ago during a rehearsal of a then new work at the Queens Hall. The conductor turned to Vaughan Williams and pointed out a clash in the melody and harmony which sounded completely wrong, and asked him if he should conduct it. Vaughan Williams' reply was characteristic; 'It sounds wrong and possibly is wrong, but that's what I wrote.'

I only met the Dutch composer Bernard van Dieren once, and this was on the occasion of a Contemporary Music Concert at the BBC when I conducted his *Anjou* (comedy overture).[18] There was some hitch about the provision of a full score of this work which no one seemed to be able to fathom. The concert day was getting nearer and still I had no score, so I went to see van Dieren who was living in St John's Wood. When I called one afternoon it was to find him in bed seriously ill; he died a fortnight later. He had a negative photograph of the overture: that is, the notes were white on a black page, and all the pages were quite stiff and bound loosely together by thin wire. I struggled along with this score two days before the performance and, at the final rehearsal, van Dieren

---

17 Julius Harrison (1885–1963), English composer, conductor and teacher.

18 Bernard van Dieren (1887–1936), Dutch composer, critic and author, who spent much of his working life in England. Braithwaite conducted van Dieren's overture *Anjou* with the BBC Orchestra on 29 November 1935.

appeared looking at death's door, which of course, was unhappily the case. He stood by me and angrily whispered various instructions in my ear during the course of the rehearsal. Nothing really satisfied him, and on one occasion, where he had written some very high notes for two trumpets at the extreme of their compass and marked them pianissimo, he burst out with, 'Trumpets you are not playing pianissimo!' Ernest Hall, probably the greatest exponent on that instrument in England, quietly remarked that no trumpet player could possibly cope with those high notes pianissimo. The composer was adamant. It was all very difficult and I called an interval in the rehearsal so that we could try to pacify him. At the resumption, van Dieren insisted on another run through the overture, which we had already spent more time on than we should have. There were other difficult works on the programme as well, so then it was the turn of the orchestra to protest. Several players got up and actually refused to play the work again. It was a most difficult and painful scene for me, for the composer, and for Edward Clark, who was responsible for the programme.

In the evening *Anjou* went very well, and van Dieren heard it at his home. The orchestra really gave of their best, but I don't think van Dieren was ever satisfied and another performance was scheduled later, but by that time the composer had died.[19]

Edward Clark, whom I have mentioned several times, was in charge of the Contemporary Concerts given by the BBC, and was (in 1923) Musical Director at the BBC station at Newcastle. It was during that period that I got to know him very well. All the Musical Directors, including myself, used to meet every three months at a conference at Headquarters. There we used to air our grievances and unravel the outstanding musical troubles of our regions. Edward had studied composition with Arnold Schoenberg, among others, and took up conducting as a career later. I remember a series of programmes he did at the Queen's Hall with the LSO, shortly after the First World War. The programmes were always interesting and his meticulous knowledge of these works was quite amazing. Clark could remember the keys, words and music of most Richard Strauss, Wolf and other lieder composers. This knowledge was positively encyclopaedic, and he could give details of most modern orchestral works at a moment's notice. As a programme builder he was invaluable to the BBC. Music of our time was entirely safe in his hands. His own programmes were a perfect combination of various styles in music. A Strauss waltz would be surprisingly sandwiched in between items of a much rarer quality. As a conductor, Edward combined a most lucid technique with a beauty of bodily movement and stance yet, for some reason that I cannot understand, he gradually became neglected by those

19 A van Dieren Memorial Concert was broadcast from the BBC on 9 April 1937. *Anjou* was conducted by Constant Lambert.

in power. The last concert I saw him conduct was of contemporary music at Covent Garden, which included two short orchestral pieces by Elisabeth Lutyens. I had not seen Edward conduct for a long time and was most impressed by his work. His work in the BBC appeared to be excellent, and it was he who dealt with Toscanini before the War and arranged his programmes with him. Edward was largely responsible for the outstanding performances given by the BBC Symphony Orchestra with such works as Berg's *Wozzeck*, Schoenberg's *Gurrelieder* and Hindemith's *Mathis der Maler*. Internal difficulties over the last series of programmes given by Toscanini caused Edward to resign from the BBC, and I believe his decision, although made in quite understandable circumstances, was perhaps somewhat hasty. The clash of temperaments which occurred at that time was only a momentary thing, and resigning may not have been the best answer. Still, there it was. Edward has paid for his decision and the BBC has lost a great musical mind. Edward has thrown in his lot with the International Society for Contemporary Music, for whom he has worked untiringly.

At the time of writing (1952) there are a number of twelve-tone composers who are beginning to make their mark on the public's ears. Humphrey Searle and Elisabeth Lutyens, both convinced twelve-tonists, are beginning to get performances. Racine Fricker, a brilliant modernist, has streaked across the sky of orchestral events. Alan Rawsthorne produces a major work at least once a year and is now accepted as one of the best of our up-and-coming young composers. John Gardner,[20] one of my colleagues at Covent Garden, has caused quite a sensation with his First Symphony, the last movement of which is quite breathtaking in its virility. All these composers I count as friends.

Daniel Jones, whom I first met in Swansea about 1929, is perhaps the most brilliant of them all.[21] When I first met him, he was a young boy of fifteen. His father brought him to me, along with a suitcase of least 200 works in manuscript, all of them beautifully written and interesting, if somewhat wayward in structure. As far as I could tell, Dan was completely self-taught. The works he then showed included big orchestral scores, perfectly scored; quartets and quintets for various instrumental combinations, and a few dramatic scenes for voice and orchestra. Already his knowledge at that young age surpassed that of many a fully-grown and experienced musician. I advised his father to send him immediately to the Royal Academy of Music, but unfortunately his father was determined that Daniel would pass his matriculation and later B.Sc., so he did not get to the RAM until several years afterwards. Dan won the

20 John Linton Gardner (1917–2011), English composer, répétiteur and lecturer.
21 Daniel Jenkyn Jones (1912–1993), prolific Welsh composer whose works include seven completed string quartets and thirteen symphonies. His Symphony no. 8 (1972) is dedicated to Warwick Braithwaite, as is his youthful Sonata no. XVII in B major, op. 249 (score dated 7 October 1931).

Mendelssohn Scholarship and since then has written an enormous number of compositions. Already he has three symphonies to his credit, all of them works of outstanding quality and achievement. Nothing will tempt Dan to leave his beloved Swansea where he lives at the moment, and at the comparatively young age of 36, he is already known as a composer of well-balanced originality. Like all men of great intellectual brilliance, Dan is a great raconteur and a vigorous conversationalist. Blessed with a strong constitution and good health, he is also a boon companion and never seems to tire during his hospitable nights of enjoyment.

One of Dan's great friends is another outstanding genius, Dylan Thomas, the poet. Dylan is also full of vitality. The story is told (how true it is I can't tell), that on the occasion of his first engagement at the BBC Cardiff studio where he was to read some of his poems, he was nowhere to be found. Someone from the Cardiff studio phoned London, and London got in touch with Dylan who had completely forgotten the broadcast. He was hurried to a London studio and the reading was sent to Cardiff by landline. The day was saved. Any other person would have been struck off the BBC list, but not Dylan. I first met him during work on the London Philharmonic Orchestra film, *Battle for Music*.[22] I was engaged for this film as one of the conductors, and after some of the sessions we used to relax at one of the well-known night clubs in Soho. On one occasion, the sight of Dylan and Cecil Gray,[23] the composer and musicologist (also a friend of mine), entering this club arm in arm, hilariously greeting everyone and dancing together cheek to cheek in imitation of some of the gliding couples in the small floor area, created anything but a mild sensation.

Those were the days when I met many of the literary men of the BBC. One of these was Geoffrey Bridson, whose play *Aaron's Field* has become very well known.[24] Geoffrey was a very likeable man, and his plays and radio presentations were most interesting. Louis MacNeice, shy, sensitive and very accomplished, has made some of the most important contributions to the Third Programme of the BBC, as well as to the literary world.[25] His new translations of Goethe's *Faust* and of some of the Greek classics, are worthy to take their place among the greatest translations of all time. Spike Hughes, a delightful companion and the son of composer Herbert Hughes, possesses a penetrating sense of humour and a great ability as a writer and critic.[26] Whenever one meets him, he always seems to be smiling his way through life.

---

22 *Battle for Music* (1943) is a dramatised documentary, directed by Donald Taylor, about the trials of the LPO during World War II.
23 Cecil Gray (1895–1951), Scottish music critic, writer and composer.
24 Douglas Geoffrey Bridson (1910–1980), radio producer and author.
25 Frederick Louis MacNeice (1907–1963), Irish poet, dramatist and translator.
26 Patrick Cairns 'Spike' Hughes (1908–1987), British jazz musician, composer, writer and journalist.

Edward J. Dent, that doyen of operatic libretti translators, is still to be seen at every first night either at Sadler's Wells or Covent Garden.[27] Dent was a governor of Sadler's Wells before the War, and we used his new translations when producing an opera at that theatre, even though they would sometimes create occasional and embarrassing difficulties for us.

One of the earliest BBC playwrights and producers was that extraordinary wayward genius, Ivor McClure.[28] Ivor became the first producer of the Cardiff 5WA Region and wrote the first short thrillers ever produced by the BBC. I don't remember how many plays of this sort McClure wrote, but there must have been dozens, and I wrote incidental music for them.[29] Ivor was a real character, and as well as being the BBC producer, he and his wife were Bentley racing drivers. Once, Ivor drove me from Cardiff to London to watch the All Blacks play England at Twickenham in 1925.[30] When we totted up the mileage and time, we found we had done an average of over 50 miles an hour; a most hair-raising journey, throughout which Ivor laughed from beginning to end.

That rather saturnine, undemonstrative but quietly witty man, John Ireland[31] still persists in looking and feeling (in 1952) as young as ever. In the early years of World War II, John used to frequent the Gluepot near the Queen's Hall, and although not even then a young man, used to stand up against the bar with my other younger friends – Constant Lambert, Alan Rawsthorne, Christian Darnton, Leslie Heward, Hubert Foss, C.B. Rees, Stephen Williams and a host of others. Willie Walton[32] sometimes called in and later most of us would adjourn to what was left of Paganini's for lunch, which generally lasted till 4 p.m. John's quiet wit and sparkling small eyes enlivened the proceedings. He and Constant Lambert would keep a party very much alive. It wasn't exactly what John said, but the way he spoke that more often than not left all of us convulsed. Sometimes it would be a complaint, delivered in a miserable voice, that his music was never played, yet on one of these occasions the BBC Proms had devoted a whole night to his compositions! I once reproached him for not producing a large major orchestral composition, and I even guaranteed to give it at least three performances while I was with the Scottish Orchestra. To this John parried with, 'All composers are writing symphonies these days and I won't do it even for a guarantee of £1,000.' I answered, 'Well, write a sinfonietta.' 'No', said John, 'They' (meaning, I suppose, the public), 'expect more than that from me.' So that was that!

---

27 Edward Joseph Dent (1876–1957), British author, academic, translator and librettist.

28 Ivor Herbert McClure (1890–1981), playwright, producer, pilot and adventurer.

29 The location of these scores is unknown.

30 3 January 1925 at Twickenham. Score: England 11, New Zealand 17.

31 John Nicholson Ireland (1879–1962), English composer and teacher.

32 Sir William Turner Walton (1902–1983), English composer.

Quite recently I brought up the subject again but with just a little success. He seemed to be thinking that it might be worthwhile, but I wonder! When one remembers the outstanding success of his tone poems *Mai Dun* and *Forgotten Rite*, and his genius for effective orchestration, one hopes he will get down to the problem. His early Piano Concerto still gives me the utmost pleasure, especially the end of the slow movement. John Ireland is an original, and a composer using beautiful sounds.

PART VII
(1946–1948)

TWENTY

FLYING ACROSS
THE WORLD

After I left the Scottish Orchestra in April 1946, and with my German experiences behind me, the business of freelancing and building up my concert connections occupied all my attention. Harold Holt[1] gave me several concerts at the Albert Hall with the London Symphony Orchestra, and gradually my engagement book began to look healthier. H.B. Phillips, the Director of the Carl Rosa Opera Company, asked me to do three guest performances per week with them, and it was at the end of this period that a project I had been working on for some time took on a more definite shape.[2]

Several months earlier at the Savage Club,[3] I had met a Mr Longman, who represented the firm which made electrical equipment for the Australian Broadcasting Commission. During the course of our conversations, I spoke to him of my ambition to go to New Zealand to see my people. I knew I could not afford to do so on my own, and I asked Mr Longman if he could help me. Then began a series of events quite fortuitous for me. Mr Longman introduced me to 'Bill' Bearup,[4] the ABC representative in London, at Australia House, and in a few days, a cable came from Sydney inviting me

---

1 Harold Holt (1885-1953), South African-born son of a Jewish diamond merchant. From the 1920s to the 1950s he was one of the leading impresarios in London.

2 During this period Braithwaite conducted *Les contes d'Hoffmann* and *La bohème* on tour for Carl Rosa, three concerts at the Royal Albert Hall, a concert in the Festival of the International Society for Contemporary Music, nine studio concerts with various BBC orchestras around the country, and 16 recordings for HMV and Columbia.

3 An exclusive 'gentlemen's club', founded in London in 1857.

4 Thomas William Bearup (1897-1980). In 1946, Bearup was posted to London as the ABC's Overseas Representative and he held this position until his retirement from the ABC in 1962.

to Australia for a three-month tour conducting in all the important towns in that country.

The first step of getting to New Zealand was made miraculously easy for me but the second, of squeezing an offer from the New Zealand Broadcasting Service, was much more difficult. I asked Harold Holt to handle the whole affair and he did so most successfully; the only difficulty appeared to be with the New Zealand people. The ABC contract was fixed up with the utmost speed and in a truly business-like manner, but the New Zealand part of the journey became so protracted that I began to fear it would never come to fruition. I decided to let some of my brothers in New Zealand handle the affair.

My eldest brother, Percy, contacted Arthur Manning, assistant editor of the Evening Star (a Dunedin newspaper), and he most cleverly created publicity about myself and the fact that I was going to conduct with the ABC in Australia. The New Zealand Broadcasting Service officials left their offer so late that public opinion in New Zealand began to be expressed openly. This reluctance to make an offer had an element of unfairness and intrigue behind it. My name had been put forward some years previously as a possible conductor for the orchestra. Percy had wanted me to put in for the position in those earlier days, but I had no intention whatsoever of leaving London. I now took the trouble of writing to Andersen Tyrer,[5] the pianist who, caught by the war while in New Zealand, became the first conductor of the new government-subsidized National Orchestra. I told him that my intention was only to visit New Zealand for a short period in order to see my family whom I had not seen for 31 years. If, at the same time, I could do some conducting, no-one would be better pleased than myself. To this letter Tyrer made no reply. The hand of friendship that I extended was thus rudely ignored. I was not going to take this lying down, so I then wrote a letter to the Prime Minister along the same lines. One of my other brothers, Rewi, who had been the election agent for Fred Jones, the Minister of Broadcasting, also took a hand. Between the lot of them, the offer to conduct in my native country was at last granted, and I travelled down to Poole to catch the flying boat for Sydney. My son, Rodric, was at Bedales, not too far away, and we spent my last night in England at the BOAC Hotel in that town. The last sight I had of Rodric was his figure standing on the pier as the plane was taxiing over the water.

TRAVEL DIARY

23 March 1947

Thus, in the early hours of the morning, after the most fearful English winter

---

5 Andersen Tyrer (1893–1962), English concert pianist and founding conductor of the National Orchestra of the New Zealand Broadcasting Service from 1947 to 1950.

in living memory, the comfortable flying boat took off from a very rough sea, but once in the air, flew wondrously smoothly. I gave up my seat to a child who was sitting away from its parents, but by doing so got a window seat. The aircraft was most comfortable (the Hythe class of flying boat) and so solidly built that it could withstand the fiercest of storms.[6] The lounge was a spacious compartment in the middle of the fuselage, with large windows on either side giving views of the land below. Upstairs was a compartment with three beds.

Soon we were at 10,000 feet, passing clouds, and at 11.30 a.m. we were in the port of Marseilles in brilliant sunshine having a nice cup of tea. Off again, we were over the blue Mediterranean, and on over Sardinia (Sicily), through the Strait of Bonifacio, and our first night was spent at Augusta[7] where we arrived at 4.30 p.m. On the way we saw Mount Etna which was, at that time, smouldering for our benefit. Augusta is subtropical. I and a few of the passengers went into the town, which seemed to consist of only one long street. Women were lounging in their doorways, the streets were dirty, and the usual tourist trade of nylons and other goods was in full swing. The hotel we stayed at had been commandeered by the RAF and was most comfortable.

24 March 1947

Next morning, I was up at 6 a.m. The sun was hot and I wanted to bathe in the blue water of the Mediterranean, but I couldn't, because my vaccination had not quite healed. We left Augusta at 9.50 a.m. The ultramarine sea was calm and we crossed the Mediterranean to the African Coast. We passed Benghazi, Tobruk and Sidi Barrani. There were many signs of the recent war; emergency landing fields almost obliterated but still discernible. Desert everywhere and not a blade of grass. We could see sunken vessels in Tobruk harbour.[8] The pyramids were circled and the plane dipped its wing to the Sphinx. Suddenly, after hours of desert, we were over that wonderful belt of the Nile irrigation territory. To come suddenly upon green cultivation stretching as far as the eye could see on both sides of the Nile, was a most refreshing sight. Then to descend onto the Nile itself was thrilling; the ancient waterway of the Pharaohs, mentioned in the Bible and countless histories of Egypt. It almost seemed to me that I had come to a home I once knew, and a river I had once

---

6 From 1942 onwards, the British Overseas Airways Corporation (BOAC) obtained decommissioned Sunderland Mark III transport planes and converted them into Hythe class commercial flying boats. With room for up to 24 passengers, including sleeping berths for 16, the service from Poole to Australia, New Zealand, Hong Kong, Shanghai and Tokyo began in 1946 and took 206 flying hours.

7 Augusta is a Sicilian town in the province of Syracuse.

8 During the siege of Tobruk (from 10 April to 27 November 1941), a total of 62 ships were destroyed or damaged. Frank Harrison, *Tobruk: The Great Siege Reassessed* (London: Brockhampton Press, 1999), 228.

boated on, for there was something familiar about the whole thing. Yet, of course, I had never been there before.

The Nile is one of the most publicised rivers in the world, and from childhood I had seen pictures of the native boats plying their traffic on this river. Always in the background are the Pyramids and the Sphinx, Egypt's ancient monuments and a reminder of its ancient civilization.

The population of Cairo is reputed to be three million, and I can well believe it, for such a sprawling mass of humanity could mean nought else.[9] I had a look at the Opera House where Verdi's *Aida* was first performed.[10] It is a squat building but excellently built for its purpose. Outside they were hanging tapestries over the entrance in order to lessen the heat inside. There was no opera during that visit, but a company from the Comédie-Française was giving several plays.

We were whisked away to Shepheard's Hotel, where we were to spend the night. My brothers had told me much about Shepheard's during the 1914–1918 War, and as a hotel it certainly lived up to its reputation.[11] It was a most imposing building in the quasi-Persian style. Anything could be had day and night and the hotel never closed. Tall Nubians were the major-domos and looked most attractive in their flowing white robes. At the entrance Hall were legions of attendants all dressed in uniforms of many colours. Shepheard's had been newly decorated and looked clean and fresh inside, but one could not get a thing done without having to tip at an exorbitant rate.

25 March 1947

Next morning, we left Cairo, and the plane was in the air by 9 a.m. We passed over the Suez Canal and the Defence memorial,[12] then nothing else but desert and white sand for hours. By this time, I found that my winter clothing became unbearable (don't forget that only two days before I was caught in the grip of

---

9   In 1947 the population of Cairo was 2,090,654. By 1950, this had risen to 2,494,000. The estimated population in 2017 is 19,486,000.

10 On 24 December 1871 at the Khedivial Opera House. The theatre was destroyed by fire in 1971, and a new opera house, part of Cairo's National Cultural Centre, opened in 1988.

11 Shepheard's Hotel – owned by Samuel Shepheard and generally considered one of the world's great hotels – was burnt down during the anti-British riots of January 1952. A new Shepheard Hotel, owned by various corporate groups, but honouring the Shepheard name, was opened in 1957 on a site nearby. The Egyptian General Company for Tourism & Hotels (EGOTH) owns the land and hotel buildings. 'Shepheard Hotel', http://www.shepheard-hotel.com/history.html, accessed 22 January 2019.

12 The Suez Canal Defence Monument at Gebel Maryam on the shore of Lake Timsah, Ismailia, Egypt, was designed by the French architect Michel Roux-Spitz with Raymond Delamarre, a sculptor and medallist. Constructed between 1926 and 1930 to commemorate the defence of the Suez Canal by the Western Allies during WWI from the threat of the Turkish Ottoman Army's attempts to seize control of the Suez Canal.

an icy English winter), and I changed into much lighter material. Soon we were over the Dead Sea, and then, Jerusalem. Shortly afterwards we came lower and flew around the traditional site of the Garden of Eden. From the air we could see the Euphrates with its dozens of outlets to the sea, and came lower still over many villages and much cultivation. We arrived at Basra on the Euphrates and refuelled. Huge date plantations everywhere. We made a perfect landing at night at the island of Bahrain. Went up to the market next morning to buy an Eversharp pencil, but the outrageous price of 30 rupees was too much. The minaret in Bahrain is very beautiful with mosaic decoration up the walls. The local Sheik is very rich in oil royalties. He has a beautiful palace and a harem with 14 wives.

26 March 1947
We left at 10 a.m. and were soon over the Persian Gulf. All the way along in the shallow water one could see the fishing traps. Over the Persian Gulf there are many sandy islands on which people (mostly fishermen) live in mud huts. We arrived over Karachi about 4.30 p.m. local time and landed. Here we were taken to a beautifully appointed Rest Station with a fine restaurant. An Indian servant for each person did our washing beautifully.

27 March 1947
A new crew took over the flying boat and at 1.30 a.m. we took off for Calcutta. The seats had meantime been converted into fairly comfortable beds, but it was too noisy and exciting for sleep. Up at 6 a.m. and a hearty breakfast. Passed over well-cultivated but difficult country. Very hot. Came down on the river at Calcutta. Stayed on the BOAC official houseboat for half an hour. After having our passports stamped and being passed by the Health Authorities, we were off again. Over the Ganges, a river with many openings to the sea. Over the Bay of Bengal at about 7,500 feet in glorious weather.

Rangoon, our next stop, had been badly bombed by both the Japanese and later by the British.[13] The Burmese peasants live in rush plaited huts. Went to a Burmese Arts and Crafts Exhibition and saw performance of the Burmese Sword Dancers. Later went to a Burmese theatre performance which seemed to go on all night. The orchestra was a most interesting collection of instruments. The principal member was a solitary gong player, completely surrounded by tuned gongs; the large drums of different pitches were played by others, as were cymbals, clappers made of split bamboo, and a wind instrument that sounded like a cross between a raucous oboe and bagpipes. All the players were expert,

---

13 Rangoon is the colonial name for Yangon, capital of the Yangon Region of Myanmar, formerly known as Burma.

and the audience seemed enraptured but didn't applaud. The ensemble kept perfect time with the dancing. Small children were also part of the audience and, at that late hour, gazed longingly at the performance.

Mr Campbell, one of the passengers, took me to his club, and after a wonderful meal I got back to the hotel at 2.30 a.m.

28 March 1947

Up again at 5.15 a.m. Joined the plane and we took off for Singapore. Over Penang we ran into rain and climbed to 13,000 feet. For some reason the food we took on at Rangoon wasn't so good. We arrived in Singapore at 4 p.m. and went straight to the wonderful Raffles Hotel. Terribly expensive. Town a sink of iniquity. Saw the Southern Cross in the night sky for the first time since I was a boy in New Zealand. It was too hot to sleep.

29 March 1947

Left Singapore at 10.30 a.m. and soon ran into the first bit of bad weather we had struck so far. Several people were sick. Clouds and rainstorms. Still warm at 12,000 ft. Ate a hearty lunch. Came down at Surabaya (Dutch East Indies) at 3.30 p.m.[14] Harbour full of wrecks. Lots of bombing. Went to Orange Hotel and changed traveller's cheques (7/6d) for four guilders. Went to a club for supper where I saw some very lovely women, all in European dress, who seemed well-to-do. Dutch soldiers everywhere making a nuisance of themselves with the native population. Very hot; couldn't sleep. No running water in hotel; Dutch blew up pumping station.

30 March 1947

Off at 7 a.m. for Port Darwin in Australia. Fighting was still going on with Indonesia. Passed over Bali and dozens of smaller islands, some with extinct volcanoes. Thought of Joseph Conrad quite a lot.

Over the so-called treacherous Timor Sea, we had perfect weather. Plane was steady; almost seemed stationary. Soon we ran into storms and lightning half an hour from Darwin, but landed beautifully. We were all very excited. Here we were in Australia at last, among our own folk. On the way to the hotel, we passed many houses built on poles at least three feet from the ground, and after supper we walked outside. Insects of all sorts were buzzing. Birds made noises like catcalls. Butterflies with a six-inch wing span would suddenly fly at our faces. Went to the ABC radio station which had opened only three weeks earlier. They phoned through to Sydney. Sent cable home. Changed money. Hotel very good. Nice staff; no tipping! It was good to hear English spoken – even Australian style. Several of the inhabitants fraternized with us, and looked at us as if we had come from Mars.

---

14 Now the capital of Jawa Timur, Indonesia.

31 March 1947

Up at 3.30 a.m.; took off at 5 a.m. Pitch black so went to sleep until breakfast. Over the Gulf of Carpentaria.[15] Slept again over miles of desert country. Came down at Bowen on the east coast of Australia. Bowen is a one street town with a small jetty, and is not too far from the Barrier Reef. I would have liked to stop there, but we were herded into the plane which taxied over the water for a long time, and suddenly turned back and stopped. We were told that we would take off 12 hours later, so we had the rest of the day in Bowen where the heat was stifling. There wasn't much to do so we ambled about, and what with the heat and the disappointment, got into a fair amount of nonsensical trouble. It was my first taste of Australian whisky, and having had a few of those, we discovered that the girl behind the bar had a bottle of King George V whisky tucked away in the refrigerator.[16] It was like a breath of good old Scotland. Far from excusing myself, my friend and I finished it. The gods looked after us and we duly presented ourselves at the jetty at midnight and rather unsteadily greeted the crew as we stepped into the plane.

We were off on our last lap. Sleep claimed me for a while, and then someone wakened me as we flew over Brisbane and Newcastle, both lit up with twinkling lights. It was a wonderful sight in the clear night sky.

1 April 1947

More sleep, and as dawn came up, we were approaching Sydney. We arrived at Rose Bay at 6 a.m., gliding over the immense bridge and skimming over the water to come to rest at the end of a marvellously interesting journey of nine days.[17]

The BOAC is a most efficient company. Everything went to schedule, and the crew during those nine days were most helpful and kind. The immense amount of organisation required at each port of call, shows an organising genius on someone's part. Nothing went wrong. Times of arriving and departure were kept strictly to the minute, with the exception of the last lap. The servicing of the plane (or planes, because we did change planes at one point, although it

---

15 An inlet of the Arafura Sea on the northern coast of Queensland and the Northern Territory, covering some 300,000 km².

16 John Walker & Sons' King George V whisky commemorates the granting of the Royal Warrant on 1 January 1934. It is created using whiskies from distilleries that were operating during George's twenty-five-year reign (1910–1936), some of which no longer exist. 'John Walker & Sons Exclusive Blends', https://www.johnniewalker.com/en/our-whisky/john-walker-and-sons/king-george-v, accessed 10 January 2019.

17 From 1938, passenger seaplane flights to and from London began and terminated in Sydney Harbour on Rose Bay, making it the city's first international airport, and what is now Rose Bay Water Airport. Kim Hanna, *Rose Bay Airport*, Dictionary of Sydney, 2014, http://dictionaryofsydney.org/entry/rose_bay_airport, accessed 22 January 2019.

was difficult to tell at first as they were so alike), proceeded in a most efficient manner. The air hostess in each port looked after our welfare with unfailing courtesy. There was never any slipping up in the booking of rooms or meals. I take off my hat to the BOAC. It is a splendid organisation.

TWENTY-ONE

AUSTRALIA AND THE ABC

The ABC officials were at Rose Bay in full force. Roy Lamb, the Federal Concert Manager, who became my friend from the beginning, had managed everything. The publicity of the ABC was something to wonder at. The Sydney newspapers were there, but Roy Lamb saw to it that as soon as I had passed through Customs, I was whisked away to the Australia Hotel for breakfast.

At 11 a.m. the press representatives were admitted to a room at the hotel and, over a cup of tea, I was the centre of a battery of cameras and a bombardment of questions as to the state of music in Britain and the severe winter we had gone through. When I produced a photograph of the frozen sea at Whitstable Bay during February 1947, few of the reporters present took in the significance of it, and the photo was never used by them.

Next, I had an interview with the General Manager of ABC, Charles Moses. He was a tall, handsome, urbane and hospitable man and seemed to me ideal for the position he held. He exuded confidence and a feeling of friendliness which always pervaded the atmosphere whenever he was present. In his room, which I was to see several times while in Sydney, he introduced me to most of the heads of his staff and talked about the tour I was to do. After that I was flung into a round of interviews, broadcasts, and photographs. Before I knew where I was, I found myself at the Sydney Horse Show, presenting the first prize to a young agricultural student who was to tour the farms of New Zealand for three months.

Arriving back at the centre of the city, Roy Lamb invited me (at about midnight) to a little restaurant in an underground station and asked me if I would like a steak. I was so ravenous I could have eaten a horse. But a steak! I hadn't tasted one since 1939. Could I have an egg on top? Certainly! Could I have, perhaps, two? Why certainly; as many as you like! When the steak came

223

it lapped over the sides of the plate. On top were two big yellow 'eyes' looking at me and smiling at my surprise. I hadn't had food like this for years. I tucked in, but alas, I couldn't eat more than one third of that lovely steak. My capacity for food had diminished as a result of the belt tightening process during the war, and I looked at my host who, I could tell, had been waiting for some such thing to happen. He told me that all artists who came out to Australia after the war had experienced the same sort of thing. It took me over five weeks before I could eat meat as I used to.

I weighed only 10 stone 10 lbs when I left England, but by the time I returned six months later, I had put on 20 lbs, despite the fact that I had been rehearsing, conducting and (in the heat of Australia) perspiring copiously. I had travelled thousands of miles and led a strenuous physical and mental life, so I think this is a good illustration of the lack of protein which all classes in England suffered during the war and, indeed, more so after.

I had been settled in a private hotel in Parramatta, about thirty minutes by electric train outside Sydney, as all hotels in the city were full with visitors to the famous Horse Show. I went back that night tired, but thrilled, with my first day in Australia. The air was so light and fresh, and the atmosphere so dry, that one felt physically lighter and on top form. It was the beginning of April, which is the middle of Autumn in Australia, and the temperature was about the same as the height of summer in the south of England. No wonder Australians always feel chilly in England and complain incessantly about the damp atmosphere.

I slept from 1 a.m. until about 9 a.m., and awakened as fresh as if I had led a quiet and normal life. The air and the sun were irresistible and believe it or not, I was entirely refreshed and eager to start another day. I have often wondered since whether having been born under the Southern Cross, and having lived my first 19 years there, caused my body and mind once again to respond to the earlier routine into which I was born. It's an interesting theory and having been back in England since 1948 (four years), part of this energy and freshness having somewhat disappeared, I am inclined to think there is something in it. Be this as it may, the period of ten months that I spent on the other side of the world, was one of great activity for me. I was never tired, nor could the longest air journey (Perth to Brisbane via Adelaide, Melbourne and Sydney) daunt me. I used to step out of the plane as if I had taken only a short bus ride.

Roy Lamb called on me and we had breakfast together. He outlined the details of my tour and took me into town, where I received the tickets for my journey to Melbourne. I then went out to Bondi Beach and, later in the afternoon, paid a visit to my widowed brother-in-law, William Manson.

In the early days of gramophone recording, Will Manson had been quite an important figure, along with Louis Sterling (now Sir Louis), Will Gaisberg and his brother Fred. Will Manson's chief 'baby' had been the now forgotten

Zonophone label – a popular and cheap adjunct of HMV which at one time swept the market. Later, Will became the manager of the HMV English Branch, but after his son (my nephew Willie) was killed at the Somme battle in 1916, Will and Mabel did not stay long in England. In 1925, he went to Australia to open up a new HMV factory.[1] Mabel died shortly afterwards, and if anyone died of a broken heart it was my sister.[2] Life was never the same after her son died. She was buried at South Head Cemetery and Will and I went there the next day to see her grave. It was a sad business.

Walking past the other graves I came across the resting place of George Lambert, the great Australian painter and the father of Constant Lambert. I wrote Constant that night to tell him that his father's grave was tidy and well kept. Later when I returned to England, I gave him a fuller description of the locality which in many ways is a wonderful spot, right on the South head of the entrance to the harbour, facing the quiet Pacific Ocean.

After a few days in Sydney, I travelled to Melbourne by rail. What a journey! It was very hot and at the change of trains at Albany, on the border between the state of New South Wales and Victoria, a ridiculous mistake happened. I was apparently booked to travel by the celebrated Blue Train, but unfortunately no-one had briefed me in Sydney that there were two trains. So, I leisurely sat down in the ordinary train and, as the Blue Train was pulling out, suddenly realized, too late, that I should have been on it. The difference, of course, is that the Blue is a luxury train and for such a long journey almost a necessity. My annoyance and chagrin did not last long, for soon I was travelling through Ned Kelly country. What memories that name brought to my mind. When I was a child in New Zealand, I had read about Kelly the bandit; the man who invented a metal shield of armour for his head and vulnerable parts of his body and who defied the police of two States for many years.

Ned Kelly was one of three brothers who became bandits as the result of early misdemeanours. He was surrounded in a shack, and no mercy was shown him. The police, armed with rifles, simply waited until hunger forced Kelly to surrender. But as no chances were to be taken, he was shot without mercy. Kelly's life was serialized in dozens of boys' papers in Australia and New Zealand, and he inevitably became the dashing hero of many escapades, mostly invented by writers who ought to have known better. I am quite sure Ned Kelly had many

---

1 Will Manson transferred to Sydney in December 1925 to be the General Manager of a Gramophone Company Ltd office and pressing plant which opened in the suburb of Erskineville, on 18 January 1926. Both HMV and the lower-priced Zonophone labels were to be pressed here for distribution throughout Australasia. (Peter Downes, pers. comm.).

2 Mabel Manson died from a Cerebral Haemorrhage in Sydney on 14 June 1928 (Register No. NSW 1928/10576). Her husband William (Will) was to die in Sydney on 19 August 1953 (Register No. NSW 1953/17100). (Peter Downes, pers. comm.).

excellent qualities, but the fact remains that he put himself outside the law and was ruthless in his crimes.

On the way through this wild country there was much evidence of soil erosion. The appalling sight of the breaking up of soil and the cavities this left, even on flat land, was quite horrifying. To imagine flesh falling away and disappearing from a human body will give some idea of the terrible aspect of the earth divided by this evil. I was told that the lack of trees and too little water caused this deterioration. The torrential rainstorms tear away the earth, and with nothing to stop this process, the earth begins to crumble and disintegrate. Little ravines stretching for miles had been formed, and the banks eroded by this process would gradually crumble until the small ravine became a bigger one. And so the process went on.

*

Arriving in Melbourne the publicity machine of the ABC was again working at full pressure. I was photographed in company with some platelayers on the railway line. They were big hefty fellows who could have crushed me with the utmost ease. I was photographed with the engine driver, and eventually escaped to my hotel and went straight to bed. Next morning, I met the Melbourne Symphony Orchestra and commenced rehearsals. Here I was to have a most agreeable surprise. The quality of this orchestra in all departments was unbelievably excellent. The strings were excellent technicians with a ravishing tone. The orchestra numbered 95 players, and all of them good. I remember particularly their accompaniment of Lorna Sydney[3] in Wagner's *Wesendonck Lieder* and the terrific climax at the end of the Second Symphony of Sibelius. The concert was repeated three times to full houses.

In Melbourne I met Sir Bernard Heinze, a remarkable man who conducted the orchestra and held at the same time the Chair of Music at the University. Heinze was a self-made musician, and although he has been out of Australia often, he is at the same time, an Australian musical product. He was born there and is one of the few Australians to reach the highest position entirely by his own efforts. Australia has been doing the same thing as England by ignoring its own talent and importing 'names', usually foreigners. Heinze may not be an entirely English name, but Bernard is a real, proper and cultured Australian.[4] I take off my hat and salute a good son of Australia. I saw him conduct several times. He reminds me somewhat of Malcolm Sargent – the same quick and responsive style, the same slim and willowy appearance and, in conversation, the same quick and

---

3 Lorna Sydney Smith (later Baroness von Ronacher) (1910–1974), was an Australian mezzo-soprano.

4 Sir Bernard Thomas Heinze (1894–1982), Australian conductor and administrator. In 1949 he became the first Australian to be knighted for services to music.

witty mind. There the resemblance ends, not altogether to Bernard's disadvantage.[5]

During those ten days in Melbourne, so many things happened to me, but by far the most remarkable coincidence concerned my own family. When I was a boy in New Zealand before the 1914–1918 war, I used to correspond with two of my cousins (two young girls) whose name was the same as my mother's maiden name, Bellett. I, of course, had never met them as I never went to Australia while I was in New Zealand. I had not corresponded with them in the 33 years between 1914 and 1947, but as I was in Melbourne, I thought I would look them

Caricature of Warwick Braithwaite by 'Prior' (1947).

up. I soon realized that to find them was a hopeless task, as of course they had both married and I had no idea of their surnames. One day I walked along Burke Street in order to choose a bank where I could send money to London. I walked into the most imposing bank building in Burke Street and went up to the foreign draft counter. The long business of filling in forms was completed, and the young woman behind the counter asked me to wait for a few minutes while she had the form countersigned by a senior official. I wasn't kept waiting more than two minutes when she returned with a young man of about 35 years. He put his hand across the counter and said, 'My name is Jim Bellett. We are cousins.' This Jim Bellett was a brother of my two cousins. I didn't even know there *was* a brother. So, through him, I met my two pen correspondents for the first time. When it is realized that Melbourne has a population of over one million, and at least a hundred banks, this coincidence shows how small the world is.

Another charming coincidence occurred when the hotel boy came up to my room to tell me that Mr Braithwaite wished to see me. What could this be? I went downstairs and there in the lounge was a man in his late seventies, who rose to greet me. He asked me if I was the son of Joseph Braithwaite of Dunedin. I answered in the affirmative. He then slowly produced an old letter from his pocket and asked me to read it. As soon as I looked at the envelope, I knew that it was my father's handwriting. Inside, was a letter written in 1900 to this Mr Braithwaite from my father, who wrote to him on the occasion of his father's death fighting with the Australian Horse during the South African war.[6] It was quite touching, and the old man was in tears. The letter was typical of my

---

5   One senses that Sargent did not rank highly in Braithwaite's opinion.
6   The Australian Commonwealth Horse was a mounted infantry unit of the Australian Army, formed in 1902 for action in the Conacher Second Boer War.

father's character. It told this son that his father had died for King, Country and Empire. I asked my visitor if I could have the letter but, quite understandably, he would not give it to me. A most touching scene. I met the daughter of this Mr Braithwaite, a young woman called Nancy, a very good violinist, and we had a very pleasant time together at their home in St Kilda.[7]

Rudy Himmer,[8] the Music Director of the ABC in Melbourne, invited Lorna Sydney and I to his house in the middle of a blue gum forest outside Melbourne called The Dandenongs. Rudy brewed his own beer and a very strong brew it was. What with that and the 'Billy' tea and the steaks done in the forest over a grill in the open, life took on a real colonial flavour. To live in the open like this, with the weather comfortably hot, was just what I had longed for. Rudy's estate was delightful and relaxing; right in the bush and far from the city. The Australian bird varieties were a continual source of wonder. The Lyrebird, which cunningly imitates the calls of other birds, was everywhere. The brilliant red feathered parakeets were shrieking in almost every branch. All this, and the sunshine, conspired to make that day one of the most memorable. Rudy and his wife were the most hospitable people I met in a land where hospitality is written in capital letters.

Dr John Heath and his wife Eileen were the other two darling people of whom I have only the most tender memories.[9] They lived in a small church, which they have turned into a home, on the outskirts of Melbourne. Eileen was a very fine painter, and the 'body of the Kirk' was both her studio and sitting room. Many were the times we would go back there after a concert or a night out on the town, to relax and talk about all sorts of things. John held the position of Dentistry Professor, and lectured at Melbourne University. He told me of the amazing expedition of which he was a member, when, in 1926, they penetrated beyond Alice Springs right up to Hermannsburg in order to study the history and traditions of the Aranda tribe of Aboriginals. He showed me hundreds of coloured plates he had taken of the amazing country and I have in

---

7   Nancy Francis Braithwaite had been a violin student at the University of Melbourne Conservatorium of Music and was mentioned many times in Australian newspapers as a promising and talented artist. She became a member of the Melbourne Symphony Orchestra. Her father (who visited Warwick Braithwaite at the hotel) was Henry (Harry) Wharton Braithwaite.

8   Rudolf Himmer had previously been Controller of Celebrity Concerts for the ABC.

9   John Samuel Robert Heath (Sam) (1893–1970) artist, sportsman, philosopher, dentist and epicurean. 'Reared among the Plymouth Brethren, [John] Heath senior had enlisted as a medical orderly in the Great War, became a freethinker, trained as a dentist (he owned the first x-ray machine in Australia), dabbled in Aboriginal anthropology, and, under the influence of his friend Max Meldrum, became a moderately well-known artist. His home, a converted Presbyterian Church, was an oasis in the cultural desert of Oakleigh. Heath himself exemplified… the talented, versatile, high-minded, unorthodox outsider.' *The Australian Academy of the Humanities Annual Report 2014–15; Francis Barrymore (Barry) Smith 1932–2015,* https://www.humanities.org.au/wp-content/uploads/2017/04/AAH-Obit-Smith-2015.pdf, accessed 23 May 2022.

my possession, a seed pod of a tree which existed a million years ago in Egypt, but had been discovered in the interior of Australia.

John asked me if I would come on a new expedition, which was going to the same territory during the middle of June 1947, and supervise the making of gramophone records of the Aranda tribe singing folksongs. I cabled the New Zealand Broadcasting Service for permission to delay my arrival by ten days. The answer was no; but more of this later. It was a great disappointment, as John had arranged for me to get back to Sydney by plane from Broken Hill, the famous mining town in the interior. So, an opportunity that comes only once in a lifetime was spoiled by the same element of intrigue that was almost to ruin my New Zealand tour.

It was John Heath who introduced me to the paintings of Namatjira, most famous of the Aboriginal painters.[10] The history of this amazing genius is a source of continual wonder to me. Namatjira had been one of the 'boys' who helped during one of the earlier expeditions. He carried paint boxes, canvases and other paraphernalia around while the official painter did his work. He began to try his hand in an imitative way, and it was Rex Battarbee who saw that there was a gift here of a most extraordinary kind.[11] Namatjira was given a few lessons by Mr Battarbee, and he is today one of Australia's most famous artists. The extraordinary thing about Namatjira's paintings is his complete grasp of the principle of perspective. His feeling for the peculiar colour of the Australian landscape was then something quite new and original. I saw several of his paintings in Perth, and I consider them of the highest class. I brought back with me a volume containing 12 reproductions which I showed to several artists at the Savage Club in London, and they all expressed great satisfaction at the quality of the painting.

I visited the Melbourne Savage Club one midday, and as the entrance is below the rooms of the club itself, I felt a little uncomfortable about walking upstairs all alone and unannounced. As I was hesitating, two men came downstairs. Then there occurred one of those simple coincidences which made life in Australia very pleasant for me. The commissionaire spoke to one of the men and immediately he shook my hand in a most friendly fashion. He was the son-in-law of my old friend, conductor Aylmer Buesst. Needless to say, the Melbourne Savage Club opened its doors to me in the usual wholehearted Australian style. Other old friends came in, such as Horace Stevens the famous baritone, for many years a popular singer of oratorio in England.[12] The other was Fred Collier, BNOC baritone of the 1922–1924 seasons, well-known for his singing of Klingsor in Wagner's *Parsifal*.[13]

---

10 Albert (Elea) Namatjira (1902–1959), Aboriginal artist.

11 Reginald Ernest (Rex) Battarbee (1893–1973), Australian artist and teacher of Albert Namatjira.

12 Horace Ernest Stevens (1876–1950), Australian bass-baritone.

13 Frederick Redmond Collier (1885–1964), Australian bass-baritone.

Another old friend with whom I renewed an acquaintanceship in Melbourne was Thea Philips, one of the loveliest soprano singers I have ever known.[14] A fine Melba-like voice, Thea did her first operatic performance with me as far back as 1921/1922 in the part of Lily in *The Lily of Killarney*.[15] Later she became a principal soprano with Beecham. The lovely story is told of her first performance of the soprano part in *Messiah* with Sir Thomas Beecham conducting *his* first performance during the thirties. Sir Thomas' tempi were unusually faster than others, but Thea had learned the usual tempi with an acknowledged coach. At the rehearsal she slipped up once or twice and Sir Thomas became a bit testy as a result. Thea told him that she would be alright at the performance. When she walked into the Green Room at the Queen's Hall next night, she reassured Sir Thomas that she had taken *Messiah* to bed with her, working far into the night. Sir Thomas unhesitatingly replied, 'Oh! We can expect then an immaculate conception?'

I also met another soprano of the BNOC days, Gertrude Johnson, who had started a school for opera in Melbourne.[16] Florence Austral was also back in Australia and I met her several times in Sydney.[17] All these singers needed was a permanent opera company to keep them fully occupied. Most of them had retired from singing through the lack of an opera organization to replace the BNOC after it went into liquidation in 1928. There was little left for the 'big' operatic singers to do in England. I also made a firm friend in William Herbert, a tenor who eventually came to London and has since made a great success here.[18]

Rudy Himmer and John Heath were members of the Melbourne Wine Growers Society. I was invited to several of their sessions, usually in the middle of the day. It was quite comical to see the seriousness of their attitude towards wine vintages. The ritual was that every member would bring his own particular vintage, but with the label removed. Solemnly the bottle was passed around and a taste would be taken of each one by every member. Then there would be a pause while the taster searched his memory and prepared to pass a verdict as to where the wine came from and what year it was bottled! Considering the hundreds of wines produced in Australia and the dozens of wineries, this was no easy matter, although we had many a laugh over the terrible mistakes made.

---

14 Dorothy Jane (Thea) Philips (1892–1960), English-born soprano and teacher.

15 Presumably with the O'Mara Company.

16 Gertrude Emily Johnson (1894–1973), Australian soprano and founder of the National Theatre in Melbourne.

17 Florence Mary Austral (1892–1968), Australian soprano.

18 William Scott Herbert (1920–1975), Australian tenor and teacher, remembered particularly for his oratorio performances.

I was to see Melbourne several times again, but only as I was passing through from other towns. My last hour or so was spent in the beautiful Botanic Gardens. Four things impressed me about Melbourne: the wide streets and the perfectly laid out town; the main road to St Hilda, which I am sure is the most beautifully laid out road in the world; John Heath's home-cum-chapel; and pineapples at 1s 6d when they were 30 shillings in London.

*

I had suggested to the ABC that to travel Australia by train during my tour was going to be tiresome, and with true Australian hospitality, they arranged for me to travel everywhere by the most efficient Australian Airlines. Air travel in Australia is both popular and absolutely comfortable. When I was there (in 1947) the two big airlines, Trans Australia Airlines (TAA[19]), and Australian National Airways (ANA), used the American Lockheed Constellation aircraft. Flying is the solution to the enormous distances in Australia. To go from Melbourne to Perth took three days and nights by train; by Constellation aircraft it took about 13 hours non-stop.

My concerts with the Melbourne Symphony Orchestra were a great success and I was loath to leave such an excellent body of players. But the tour was on, and I flew to Sydney, where I stayed for three weeks. The Sydney Symphony Orchestra (SSO) of 87 players was another agreeable surprise. I use the word 'surprise' because, like most musicians in England, I had been led to believe that I could not expect much of a standard from Australian orchestras. The opposite was the case. The Sydney Symphony Orchestra appeared to me much more of an efficient machine than the Melbourne Symphony Orchestra, and I think that perhaps this feeling comes about by the air of complete confidence and efficiency which is so apparent in dealings with the orchestra and its officials. Sydney itself is faster (like London), and a most efficient town, whereas Melbourne is slower, more comfortable (expressed admirably by the German word *gemütlich*) and the people are quieter. The Melbourne strings produced a ravishingly beautiful tone. The Sydney strings struck me as being more brilliant. I did five concerts in Sydney, all of which were packed out, and the playing of the orchestra was superb. Moeran's Symphony in G Minor was played three times and created great interest; Lorna Sydney sang several arias; and the orchestra's first oboe, Horace Green, played Rutland Boughton's Concerto superbly. But I don't think that the people of Sydney showed great enthusiasm for English music. The *Tallis Fantasia* of Vaughan Williams, however, was played superbly by the Sydney

---

19 Trans Australia Airlines was formed in 1946, and renamed Australian Airlines in 1986. It merged with Qantas in September 1992.

strings and was the most successful piece in the concert. Neville Cardus gave it a special notice.[20] The playing of the orchestra in Mozart's 'Haffner' Symphony was spoken of as the best since the time Beecham conducted the SSO some years previously.

What struck me very forcibly with the SSO (and all the Australian orchestras), was the vitality of their rehearsing. There was never a sign of that damnable lassitude and 'couldn't care less' attitude that sometimes creeps into rehearsals with English orchestras. Indeed, the Australian players frequently asked me to go over a particularly difficult movement again and again.

While in Sydney I was present at the Anzac Day Procession on 25 April. No-one in England, who has not seen this celebration, can possibly imagine what an astonishing affair it is.[21] From dawn, the various contingents gather together, and the procession starts about 9 a.m., reaching the centre of Sydney about 10 a.m., and goes on for hours. The private celebrations go on well into the night. Men from every Australian regiment, with banners and placards showing their regimental names and numbers, parade with a jollity hard to imagine in a similar affair over here. Veterans from the 1914–1918 War march in a group by themselves. There is laughter and very little parade ground discipline. Men from New Zealand are included, and everybody turns out for the Parade. Hughes, the famous 1914–1918 War Australian Premier, stood in Martin Place from 8 a.m. until about 2 p.m., and as the groups passed by, they gave him a special cheer.[22]

After Sydney, my next visit was to Adelaide. I had always longed to see this city, especially as so many of my operatic friends had come from there and I had already heard so much about it. Ruth Naylor and Arnold Matters studied at the Adelaide School of Music, and both were with me at Sadler's Wells. The journey by plane was of course via Melbourne, and after leaving that city, we were soon over the marvellous vineyards which seemed to stretch for hundreds of miles into the interior. Adelaide itself is a well laid-out city, and I particularly remember the number of buildings with verandas all around the upper floors. My hotel was one such building, and after a meal, one could stroll right around the veranda on all sides.

The Adelaide orchestra was quite good although somewhat smaller than their Sydney and Melbourne colleagues. The ABC officials were kindness itself. John Heath had arranged with a friend of his at Adelaide University that I

---

20 Neville Cardus (1888–1975), English writer on cricket and music, resident in Sydney in the 1940s and writing for the *Sydney Morning Herald*.

21 According to the front page of the *Sydney Morning Herald* (26 April 1947), approximately 200,000 people lined the streets, and at least 50,000 participated in the march.

22 William Morris 'Billy' Hughes, (1862–1952), seventh Prime Minister of Australia (1915–1923), and the longest serving Parliamentarian (51 years, 213 days).

should see the film taken of the 1926 Expedition,[23] which showed in detail some of the most lifelike animal dances of the aboriginal. One in particular, which I will never forget, was the Emu dance, in which three natives moved and controlled their bodies in exact imitation of these graceful yet somewhat ungainly birds.

It was at Adelaide that I met Rudi Büring, proprietor of the famous Quelltaler Estate, and a visit to him at his office resulted in a tour of one of his wineries.[24] Here I was entertained right royally and only tore myself away when I could no longer taste the difference between one hock and another. By this time, I was simply pining for a breath of sea air and through the kindness of a friend, I was taken out on the Sunday to a seaside resort. Roy Lamb, who had come to Adelaide, was one of the members of this small party which eventually ended up in the home of a friend. After one of the concerts, Roy and myself with Lorna Sydney, were the guests of Mrs Connally and her charming husband. Their home was a little outside Adelaide and situated in lovely grounds. Mrs Connolly was an active member of the Adelaide Symphony Orchestra Committee and both she and her husband were splendid hosts.

On to Perth; a non-stop flight of eleven hours, which took us over the Great Australian Bight.[25] The pilot came through to talk about the various places of interest.[26] I pointed to a large lake coloured blue on the map and asked him to show it to me through the window. He pointed to a large circular white sanded basin and said, 'There it is; they haven't had water there for seven years.' The 'lake' did not exist, and would not until the rains came. He also told me about the epidemic of millions of tiny mice, no bigger than a thumbnail, that get into every nook and cranny of up-country houses during periods of dry weather. That, and white ants, was the reason why most of the homes were built on piles.

An amusing incident occurred in the plane. There was a middle-aged lady sitting next to me who didn't eat any food, but drank at least a dozen of the tiny bottles of spirits. Eventually she became talkative and asked me if I would have a 'pile ile'. I couldn't understand what she meant, but after translating in my mind all the possible things I could think of into drink, I realized she meant Pale Ale, which I gladly accepted.

---

23 'Scenes of Aboriginal Life', was the title of a film documenting the Board for Anthropological Research expedition to Wilenga and Ooldea, South Australia, during 7–21 May 1926. 'Films Recorded During the Board for Anthropological Research Expeditions, 1926–1966', http://archives. samuseum.sa.gov.au/aa346/AA346-09.htm, accessed 10 January 2019.

24 Adolph Wilhelm Rudolph (Rudi) Büring (1872–1950) became managing director of his father's wine business from 1934–1950. He was an accomplished artist, and designed all the bottle labels for Quelltaler wines.

25 A large open bay off the central and western portions of the southern coastline of mainland Australia.

26 The First Officer would have been delegated to fly the plane in place of the captain!

We arrived at Perth after dark. Perth is one of the most beautifully situated cities in the whole of Australia. The Swan River, broad and beautiful, flows through the town to the sea a few miles away. The University (free) is situated in a lovely park not far from the centre of the town and must be an ideal spot for the students to work. My hotel, The Esplanade, was facing the river with a broad green sward in between, and in every way was most delightful. The friendliness of the birds was most touching; every morning one of the fantails used to follow me on my walks, and when I sat down on a seat by the river it used to perch on my shoulder. Both in Australia and New Zealand the birds seem to have little fear of humans. The koala, that pretty cuddly animal, never runs away and will allow itself to be carried about, putting its paws around one's neck, just like a baby. Inside the hotel was a big photograph of another aspect of wild Australian life. It was a photograph of a huge python which had swallowed an old kangaroo. Caught in the act, or shortly afterwards, the photographer was able to dispatch it easily. An old male kangaroo is the largest of that ungainly and peculiar animal, and I was told they could grow to five or six feet in height.

The Perth Orchestra in 1947 was the least good of the Australian orchestras. I was very disappointed and wrote Charles Moses to this effect. Perth is by the Indian Ocean and the nearest big town to Adelaide, which is 11 hours away by fast plane. That it takes the same time to cross the Atlantic gives an idea of the distance. I remember suggesting that Perth should be paid particular attention by the ABC because of this almost complete separation from the other big centres. Later this orchestra was made into a permanent one by the ABC and conditions are bound to be better now.[27] While in Perth I was taken by car through the wild country outside the city. We went as far as the new dam which had been built only a few years previously.[28] I was introduced also to the grasstree – a stunted sort of tree or palm which is about the size of a man with what looks like, from a distance, a shock of hair on a well-shaped head.[29]

Claudio Arrau was the soloist at the Perth Concert.[30] This fine pianist

27 In 1950, the Perth Symphony Orchestra evolved into the West Australian Symphony Orchestra and was still flourishing in 2017 under the Musical Directorship of Asher Fisch. A new Perth Symphony Orchestra was formed in 2011 as a not-for-profit professional orchestra.

28 The construction of the Canning Dam started in 1933 and was the State's biggest public works project during the Great Depression. Opened in 1940, it cost more than £1 million. 'Canning Dam', https://www.perthhillsarmadale.com.au/canning-dam, accessed 23 May 2022.

29 Members of the genus *Xanthorrhoea* are also known as grasstrees. The form of the plant resembles a tree, with very long and bunched, grass-like, leaves that emerge from a central base.

30 Claudio Arrau (1903–1991), Chilean pianist considered one of the greatest of the twentieth century. This concert was not part of Warwick Braithwaite's tour, but he replaced the scheduled conductor, William Cade (1883–1957), founding conductor of the Adelaide Symphony Orchestra. A critic wrote, 'Warwick Braithwaite impressed as a man of personality with a comprehensive outlook on music whose meticulous care of detail leads on to a realisation of the full pictorial value of the work in hand.' *West Australian* (19 May 1947), 13.

created quite a stir while in Australia and he played the Liszt E flat Concerto with a brilliance only equalled by the Italian Michelangeli, with whom I had performed the same concerto at the Royal Albert Hall some months earlier.[31]

From Perth I did the marathon plane journey to Brisbane, via Adelaide, Melbourne and Sydney – a distance of nearly 3,000 miles. From Perth our plane came down at Kalgoorlie, the famous mining town which, from the air, appeared to be just a big factory with a forest of chimneys. The next stop was an outlandish place called Forest where, as far as I could see, there was not one tree.[32] While waiting to refuel, I wandered about the many scraggy buildings on the aerodrome. Here I met my first aboriginal; he was a big lanky fellow who was throwing boomerangs just for fun, and for ten Player's cigarettes he gave me a demonstration in this fascinating art. One of his boomerangs just skimmed over the ground in a wide circle and returned right to his feet.

From Adelaide we flew to Melbourne (where I spent the night), and the next day we flew to the capital of Australia. Canberra is on a plateau and the temperature can be unusually cold compared to other parts of Australia. We then flew on to Sydney, where we changed planes for Brisbane. A tropical storm close to our destination forced us to land at an emergency field midway between Sydney and Brisbane. Several hours later, we arrived safely and I was whisked away to my hotel. The building was of an unusual type, with large landings on each of its four floors, onto which all the bedroom doors opened. The heat was terrific, and at one end of the landing was a veranda where guests who were unable to sleep could sit about and read while sipping cool drinks. I had purchased some Passion Fruit and ate several. I paid for it the next day!

In the morning Mr Farnsworth,[33] the ABC Musical Director, came to see me and we went together to the magnificent Town Hall where I met the Queensland Symphony Orchestra. This was a smaller orchestra (about 50 players) but excellent. The soloist in the Bax Violin Concerto was Ernest Llewellyn, a magnificent violinist. Llewellyn had a string quartet, subsidized by the Queensland Government, which did guest work in the outlying towns. The press was again enthusiastic as they had been in the other Australian towns.

From Brisbane I went back to Adelaide and thence to Sydney, where I spent a week tidying up things such as Income Tax and fees. I had come to the end of

---

31 The concert with pianist Arturo Benedetti Michelangeli and the London Symphony Orchestra had taken place in the Royal Albert Hall, London, on 15 December 1946. The programme also included the Overture to *L'Italiana in Algeri* (Rossini), *Variations symphoniques* (Franck) and *Symphonie fantastique* (Berlioz).

32 Braithwaite's mis-spelling of Forrest (population 18 in 2006) accounts for his surprise at the lack of trees. Named after Sir John Forrest, the explorer who became the first Premier of Western Australia, the airstrip was an important fuel stop on the service between Perth and Adelaide.

33 John Farnsworth Hall (1899-1987), Australian conductor and violinist, appointed the first resident conductor of the Queensland Symphony Orchestra in 1947.

a delightful three-month tour and had loved every moment of it: the picnics up the Hawkesbury River with Will Manson; listening to birds like the kookaburra and parakeet; visiting Brisbane Zoo, where I saw koalas, kangaroos and the platypus; trips to Manly Beach, Bondi and Coogee; the party at Palm Beach, near Sydney where Charles Moses and I vied with one another as to who could drink more of the excellent Jamaica Rum; the meeting with my good friend Kubelík,[34] who followed me as guest conductor with the ABC orchestras; and the Boyd Neel Orchestra, led by Frederick Grinke,[35] which was also in Australia at the same time, and had a tremendous success.

I had the opportunity of watching the wood chopping competition at the Sydney Horse Show. Expert axemen from all over Australia take part in these strenuous contests in which it is considered slow to cut through a trunk of a tree in less than 55 seconds. Charles Moses, amongst his many accomplishments, is one of the best axemen in New South Wales.

But the most thrilling thing for me was to meet Alfred Hill,[36] the New Zealand (and Australian) composer who had written that most popular song, *Waiata Poi*, sung thousands of times by Rosina Buckman and many times by my sister Mabel. I met him in Sydney, where he was with the ABC in an advising capacity, and found him to be a charming, but forthright, character.

I had first seen Alfred Hill when I was 13 years of age. His opera *A Moorish Maid* had been produced by the Dunedin Operatic Society in 1908, with Rosina Buckman especially engaged for the leading role, and Alfred Hill conducting. I was the 'call boy'. Hill has written many compositions including string quartets, one of which, the *Māori*, had quite a success.[37] His cantata *Hinemoa*, to the Māori legend of the same name, is charming in a simple and naive way. His Māori orchestral pieces are worth performance, especially the *Māori Rhapsody*. I revere his name as the first New Zealand composer and hope we will meet again.

---

34 Rafael Kubelík (1914-1996), distinguished Bohemian-born, Swiss-naturalized conductor who spent most of his professional life in exile, performing with major orchestras and opera companies in North America, England and Germany.

35 Frederick Grinke (1911-1987), Canadian violinist and teacher, who was Concertmaster of the Boyd Neel Orchestra (1937-1947), and Professor at the Royal Academy of Music (1939-1978). He played concertos with Braithwaite in 1934 and 1950.

36 Alfred Francis Hill (1869-1960), Australian/New Zealand composer, conductor and teacher. His works include 13 symphonies, 17 string quartets, five concertos, eight operas, and 72 pieces for piano.

37 Braithwaite could have been referring to either the first or second of Hill's string quartets, but current practice is to label String Quartet no. 1 in B-flat, 'Māori', and String Quartet no. 2 in G minor, 'A Māori Legend in 4 Scenes'.

TWENTY-TWO

NEW ZEALAND AND THE NZBS

The days were becoming fewer and, as I had to catch the flying boat at midnight for New Zealand on 10 June 1947, Roy Lamb and I spent the evening together. I was then driven to Rose Bay and boarded the magnificent, modern, two-story flying boat. I slept part of the night but I was too excited as dawn came up. At last, about 8 a.m. Australian time, I had a glimpse of my own land. After flying the length and breadth of Australia over desert and sandy wastes, I was now flying over Ninety Mile Beach and later, over the green pastures of Auckland Province. Everywhere there were trees, green grass and rivers. The plane came down on the waters of Auckland Harbour, and I was back in the country of my birth which I had not revisited for thirty-one years.

Who would be there to meet me? None other than my youngest brother, Roderick.[1] I saw him on the other side of the barrier but couldn't quite recognize him. When I did, I cried to myself. The Customs officials got me through as quickly as they could, and then came the quiet and controlled handshakes with Roderick, as if the occasion was quite an ordinary one.

When reading the following pages, I would beg the reader to put himself in my place. I had left home when I was 19, and had experienced an uphill struggle from the moment I arrived in England. Every now and then at odd moments, I would dream of my home, Dallon Bank. I would think of the times I and my brothers and sisters had enjoyed together. It was a happy childhood in ideal surroundings, with the Pacific Ocean, the Harbour, Lake Logan and the

---

1 Roderick Braithwaite (1901–1963), the youngest of Joseph and Mary's children, served as mayor of Hamilton between 1953 and 1959. His wife, Kathleen Braithwaite (née Arey), was a city councillor from 1962 to 1974, including a period as deputy mayor. See Appendix 1.

native bush, all contributing their quota towards a boy's life. There was yachting, boating, swimming, walking, climbing, and adventure galore.

In England I had been pitchforked immediately into an unaccustomed life for a shy and somewhat backward youth, and I had to work my way through a maze of new and unusual aspects of living. I had come through and hung on, and never given up the struggle, but always at the back of my mind was the conviction that I was not cut out for life in Britain. However, there was no going back, and I put myself into the thick of the battle which, in no small measure, gave me the necessary strength and determination to survive. But here I was about to revisit scenes of my childhood.

During the last few days in Australia, and on the flight across the sea to Auckland, I began to wonder whether I had been wise to make this trip. Would I disappoint my family, or would they now seem so different after our long separation? Had I grown too far away from them? Would they seem to me culturally backward, uncouth or rough? Would they resent my air of superiority? Not that I in any way felt superior, but quite naturally and understandably I had become very English. I was a Pommy![2]

Well, I have to relate that my fears were completely groundless. I was overjoyed to find that my brothers had kept very much abreast of the times both politically, culturally and as human beings. They were a continual solace to me during difficult moments caused through the stupidity of a few people in the New Zealand Broadcasting Service (NZBS) who should have known better. But more of that later.

Roderick had brought his car up from Hamilton, about 80 miles from Auckland, and after meeting Colin Trim, the IYA Station Director, and conferring with a few other officials in Auckland, Roderick and I started on our way to his home through some delightful country. We passed along the banks of the magnificent Waikato River, the scene of many historic battles with Māori; through Cambridge (a very English-looking town with beech and oak trees in abundance); through the mining town of Huntly; and arrived in Hamilton where I received a most warm-hearted welcome from Roderick's wife and family. The young children (two boys and a girl), had decorated the entrance hall with flowers and a huge 'Welcome Home' banner. All very touching.

That evening I put through a long-distance call to Rewi[3] in Dunedin and, by an arrangement with the Telephone Service, our line was connected to another

---

2   A slang term used in Australia, South Africa and New Zealand to describe English people. The term can be regarded as affectionate or offensive.

3   John Rewi Ferguson Braithwaite (1897–1987) and his wife, Dorothy, lived at St Clair. See Appendix 1 for more family information.

brother, also in Dunedin, but right across the harbour.[4] Four brothers were all talking to one another for the first time after 31 years, and it was most thrilling, even though all we could talk about were trivialities.

Next morning, we made a trip to the Kaimai Ranges on the top of which, and surrounded by a mass of New Zealand bush, lived another brother, Neville,[5] who had married a schoolteacher. He was the first New Zealander to build his own radio set (about the year 1922) and his own studio, but it was later taken over by the Government when broadcasting in New Zealand became nationalized. At the time I saw him, he had a big transmitting set with which he talked to amateurs all over the world. He is unfortunately cursed with an incurable illness (disseminated sclerosis[6]), and although he is extraordinarily optimistic about it, such an illness at the moment baffles scientists and doctors alike. I wrote to a doctor friend in Harley Street asking if he could suggest anything, but the answer was an unhappy one.

Later that night the National Orchestra was to broadcast from Auckland Town Hall, so Roderick and his family left me alone while I listened to the radio. My feelings on hearing this magnificent orchestra in 1947 are hard to describe. When I was a boy in New Zealand, there simply wasn't an orchestra of a high enough standard to compare with what the rest of the cultural world already possessed. The amateur orchestras of 1912 Dunedin were the Philharmonic and the Orchestral Society, but they were only a collection of enthusiastic amateurs who practised once a week and gave three concerts a year, much like the amateur orchestral societies up and down Britain. But here was something quite new, and the fantastic change from those pre-war days of amateurism to a fully-fledged professional National Orchestra was one of the major achievements of the Labour Government in New Zealand.

The National Orchestra was formed shortly after the Second World War, and consisted of 65 first-rate players chosen from the length and breadth of the land.[7] Each district contributed its quota of players, who were engaged on a full New Zealand Broadcasting Service (NZBS) contract, and during the 'off' concert season, each section became the studio orchestra of the big broadcasting stations of Auckland, Wellington (Headquarters), Christchurch and Dunedin. During the concert season of six month's duration, the players travelled to Wellington to commence rehearsals, and then toured from there to

---

4 Percy Braithwaite was living in Dunedin at this time.
5 Neville Douglas Braithwaite (1893–1959).
6 More commonly known as multiple sclerosis.
7 The orchestra gave its first performance on Thursday 6 March 1947 in the Wellington Town Hall. The programme consisted of *Overture 'Carnival'* (Dvořák), Symphony no. 2 in D (Brahms), *A Shropshire Lad* (Butterworth), *Romanian Rhapsody no. 1* (Enescu), 'Prelude and Liebestod' from *Tristan und Isolde* (Wagner), and *Till Eulenspiegel* (Richard Strauss). The Leader was Vincent Aspey, and the conductor was Andersen Tyrer.

the four major cities where they gave several symphony concerts, and visited the smaller towns like Gisborne and Napier en route. The programme I heard that night at my brother's house included *Till Eulenspiegel* (Strauss) and the Fifth Symphony of Tchaikovsky. The opening horn tune in the Richard Strauss tone poem was superbly performed by a young player who was, as I heard afterwards, practically self-taught. This was something I had not expected and it was indeed a tremendous revelation to me. My emotions got the better of me and I was glad my brother and his family had shown such understanding when they left me alone in the other room.

*

Next morning Roderick had planned a trip to see the thermal wonders of Rotorua, and I can report that this fantastic region lived up to its reputation. To see hot water gurgling from everywhere and anywhere was positively awe-inspiring. A jet of scalding steam would suddenly appear in the main street, which Māori would then encircle with stones as a precaution. In the Māori churchyard, jets of steam would unexpectedly gush out of stone coffins. It must be like living in an inferno. I walked to the edge of the lake where, on one side, scalding hot water gushed up from the depths, but a little further on, just a few feet away, the normal cold-water lake would create a bank of resistance. One could catch a fish in the cold part of the lake, take out its innards, and row to the hot water and cook it. This is not an exaggeration; I've seen it done.

Potatoes, meat, puddings, hams and fish are all cooked by this method, and never over a fire; milk is sterilized and water for tea is also boiled in this way. The Māori name for the wonderful and weird district known to us as the Hot Lakes District is Whakarewarewa and comprises an area of about four square miles. There are several geysers, the most famous being Pōhutu and The Prince of Wales Feathers, the latter named because it gives out a feathery gush of scalding water and steam about 40 feet high. A tribe of Māori own this district and it is amusing to see the little Māori children having their morning bath in one of the cooler pools. One of the most fantastic sights is a boiling mud pool into which liquid mud gurgles and pops just like porridge in an immense pot.

Rotorua itself is the little township on the edge of this inferno, in which there is an enormous bath house or sanatorium with every kind of medicinal water known to science and to which rheumatic sufferers from all over the world take the cures.[8]

---

8   Opened in 1907, the Tudor-style bathhouse and spa offered, at its height, 60,000 to 80,000 baths annually and about 30,000 special treatments. The spa closed in 1949 and the iconic building has since been used for many purposes, most recently as an art gallery and museum.

One of the loveliest and most entrancing sights just outside Ōhinemutu[9] is a place called Fairy Springs.[10] This is a spring of pure transparent water which gushes through priceless volcanic black glass on the bottom of the pool and where the trout come to spawn. The depth of this wide pool is perhaps ten feet, yet such is the transparency of the water that it looks only about six inches deep. The larger males escort their females from the lake up the mile length stream, and there is a pathway by the side where this journey can be observed. I thought I would touch one of the trout (because they are quite tame at this time) but a male quickly and angrily rushed at my outstretched hand.

A few miles further on is Tikitere, a region of escaping steam jets and cauldrons.[11] One part is called 'Bacon and Eggs' as it emits a sizzling noise just like a huge pan of that delectable morning dish.

As everyone knows, the great Tarawera eruption of 1886 destroyed the famous Pink and White Terraces. These were huge steps of pink and white deposits which varied in height from a few inches to 12 feet, and which had formed over thousands of years. The White Terrace surpassed its sister in both size and loveliness. It was said to look like white alabaster, but tinged with a faint salmon colour. From all accounts, in the sunshine it glittered with the varied colours of an opal. Each terrace was a wall which held water the colour of which was a lovely blue. A geyser on the hillside above the Terraces was responsible for the deposits which had formed them.

In 1885 a certain Josiah Martin, during a photographic tour, took the first exact measurements of the White Terrace.[12] The formation covered about 20 acres. Its height was 82 feet and the frontage was almost 800 feet. The crater of the geyser had a diameter of 240 feet and was generally full of azure blue water, with the unfathomable funnel 15 feet wide. The gush of the geyser was intermittent but it could throw up water with fresh deposits of a siliceous substance to a height of 60 or 70 feet. The Pink Terrace was of a smaller area, about five and a half acres, the surface smooth as enamel and of a pale pink colour. The water

---

9   A lakeside Māori village close to Rotorua and home to the Ngāti Whakaue tribe. The site was chosen for its abundant geothermal energy.

10 Now incorporated into Rainbow Springs Nature Park.

11 Dubbed 'Hell's Gate' by George Bernard Shaw after a visit in 1934.

12 Josiah Martin (1843–1916) was a New Zealand teacher and photographer who captured the eruption of Mt Tarawera on camera. Braithwaite's measurements of the terraces are most likely to be drawn from Ferdinand von Hochstetter's topographic and geological survey of the Lake Rotomahana area in 1859. Von Hochstetter states that the Pink Terrace descended about 72ft over a distance of about 330ft. The Pink Terrace started at the top with a width of 246–328ft and the bottom layers were about 89ft wide. Tourists preferred to bathe in the upper Pink Terrace pools due to their clarity and the range of temperature and depths. Ferdinand von Hochstetter, *New Zealand: its physical geography, geology, and natural history: with special reference to the results of government expeditions in the provinces of Auckland and Nelson*; translated by Edward Sauter (Stuttgart: J.G. Cotta, 1867), 389–435.

flowed gently over the rim, and again quoting from a contemporary description, 'one might stand on the edge and look far down into its azure depths, a spectacle stretched out below, matched only by the coral forest in the shimmer of a placid sea. The baths on the terrace were shallow, but sensuously luxurious, imparting a peculiar smoothness to the skin.'

The surroundings of the Pink and White Terraces, which extended with other thermal phenomena over a stretch of a hundred miles, must have been one of the greatest wonders of the world, and the terrible eruption of Mt Tarawera destroyed this extraordinarily beautiful and wonderful freak of nature.[13] My father used to tell us children of this eruption, and the story has always remained in my memory. At the time, the people of New Zealand were thankful that no big town had sprung up in this district as the death toll would have been much greater. The 'signs and portents of something unusual happening' were noticed by Josiah Martin, who reported a year earlier (1885) that a sort of tidal wave travelled across Lake Tarawera. In a district where such things were almost a daily occurrence this was not much thought of at the time. Mr Martin also witnessed and reported a bigger than usual eruption from the great cauldron behind the White Terrace. Just immediately before the eruption of Tarawera, local Māori reported a phantom canoe passing over the lake, and they believed that Tūhoto Ariki, the tribal priest of Te Wairoa, had cursed their tribe for profiteering from the natural wonders of the area. A neighbouring volcano, Mount Ruapehu, showed evidence of unusual activity in the unprecedented eruption of steam from its crater. South of Lake Taupo, 80 miles away, rumblings had been heard, and similar rumblings were heard at the coastal towns of Tauranga and Gisborne the night before the eruption.

A party of tourists the day previously had gone through the usual routine when visiting the Terraces, and that night all had gone to bed tired and happy in Joseph McRae's hotel in Te Wairoa. At 1 a.m. in the dead of night, people were shaken out of their beds by the earthquake and continuous rumblings. At about 1.40 a.m., the great explosion occurred.

The curious thing about this eruption was the great and terrifying electrical storm that took place at the same time. During the night, a violent atmospheric disturbance was set up, creating a tornado which tore through the nearby forests, uprooting huge trees in its path. Subsequently the air became charged with pungent gases which were smelt as far away as Gisborne. The owner of the Rotomahana Hotel at Te Wairoa, Joseph McRae, had this to say about that night:

---

13 For many years the terraces were thought to have been destroyed, but a survey in 2017 suggested that they may still exist underground. This has yet to be proven. Eleanor Ainge Roy, 'Lost natural wonder in New Zealand may be found, say researchers', https://www.theguardian.com/world/2017/jun/12/lost-natural-wonder-in-new-zealand-may-be-found-say-researchers, accessed 22 January 2019.

About two minutes to one [the earth] began to shake and shook for about an hour before the eruption broke out. When this was first seen it was just like a small cloud on the mountain, shot with flashes of lightning of great brilliancy. Apparently, the mountains had three craters, and flames of fire were shooting up fully a thousand feet high. We returned to the hotel and shortly after, what seemed to be heavy hailstones came pouring on the roof. This was succeeded by a fall of heavy stones, fire balls and mud, the latter falling after the manner of rain.[14]

There is no need to say more, except that one side of Mt Tarawera blew out and buried villages. The Pink and White Terraces, forests and Lake Rotomahana disappeared.[15] Other lakes were formed further away. I have in front of me this moment, photographs of villages before and after the eruption, with the latter looking like Hiroshima after the atom bomb. The Tikitapu Forest was completely destroyed, and the total loss of life was 147 Māori and six Europeans.[16] Most of the deaths were caused by houses and the *whares* (native houses) collapsing under the weight of mud and stones deposited on them.

*

In Auckland I had a minor surprise when Colin Trim informed me that James Shelley,[17] the New Zealand Director of Broadcasting, wanted to see me in Wellington. So, the next day I flew to Wellington and was booked at the St George's Hotel. As the air passage and the hotel booking had been made by the New Zealand Broadcasting Service, I awaited a call to the interview. I was at the hotel two days and still no message came from Mr Shelley. At last, I phoned up and suggested I came around to see him that morning. I will pass over the reception I was given, except to say that here was I, a New Zealander, in my country for the first time in 31 years, and made to feel like a stranger and interloper. Shelley deliberately tried his utmost to 'smoke me out' but I hadn't come all that way to stand for this.[18]

---

14 McRae's statement, of which this is an abridged version, appeared in the *New Zealand Herald* (12 June 1886), 5.

15 The geography of Lake Rotomahana was substantially altered by the eruption of Mount Tarawera. More recent (2018) information can be found at: https://www.frontiersin.org/articles/10.3389/feart.2018.00205/full, accessed 4 March 2022.

16 Most reference sources estimate the death toll at about 120.

17 Hotel St George is a landmark art-deco building in Wellington. Opened in 1930, it was originally one of the city's finest hotels with a distinguished clientele. Its fame now rests on the fact that the Beatles stayed there in 1964. The building has since been a university hostel and is now (2017) a backpacker, student and long-term accommodation facility.

18 'Smoke me out' is a slang term meaning to make a place so uncomfortable that the person will leave.

In an interview with the Concert Manager, John Proudfoot,[19] I was asked for my list of chosen repertoire. I told him that I had sent typed programme lists six months earlier by airmail, and on looking through a pile of papers nearly a foot high on his desk, he came across them. They had been there all that time, and it was evident that someone had gone through them, for certain works had a cross against them and others a tick. I discovered afterwards that the cross meant that the NZBS library did not possess scores or parts of these works. I was livid with rage, and Proudfoot explained that he had only just been appointed to his present position and that he was not responsible. This I was ready to believe, as I found John Proudfoot an extremely nice fellow. He asked me to make up four programmes, which I did, but even so I had to beg some works from the ABC Library in Sydney. If the then Managing Director, on receipt of my original programmes, had asked me to bring scores and parts with me, I could have done so, just as I had done for the ABC in Australia.

But there was a certain gentleman in the NZBS who had set out to sabotage my tour from the very beginning. He seized on any pretext to do so. First of all, the programme mess-up. The next thing was that, as Eugene Goossens was passing through Auckland on his way to take up his position with the Sydney Symphony Orchestra, he called Goossens (whilst I was already in the country) and gave him my first concert without so much as contacting me. The crowning insult was to ask me to talk on the radio to New Zealand listeners about my programmes, and to be told immediately afterwards that Goossens was doing my first concert, even though my name was already on the posters all over the town.

Proudfoot had also been instructed to tell me that Andersen Tyrer, the conductor of the orchestra, insisted on playing a concerto at every one of my concerts. This was the last straw. I simply turned around to dear old John and, in a quiet voice, asked him to book my passage next morning back to England. John's face blanched at this calm announcement and he begged me to reconsider it. I made it quite clear that there was no point in reconsidering it, and went over again the several things that had, or had not, been done which showed quite plainly that someone behind the scenes was deliberately putting difficulties in my way, with the object of upsetting my tour. I asked him if that was so, and he had to acknowledge that there was no other explanation for the various shortcomings and deliberate sabotage. Further than that he could not go, but both of us knew who the evil genius was.

19 John William Proudfoot (1914–1998).

I told Proudfoot that if he could arrange an interview with Fred Jones,[20] the Minister of Broadcasting, in the morning, I would put the whole case to him in an endeavour to clear up the situation. If I did not succeed, I would leave New Zealand immediately. John then phoned Fred Jones and an interview was arranged for the next morning. I also told Proudfoot that Gene Goossens was one of my old colleagues in England (where we first met as far back as 1922 at Covent Garden), and if I had been asked, I would of course have consented immediately to him doing my first concert. But the way in which the whole thing had been misarranged, and the lack of tact shown by Shelley and someone else, was nothing less than insulting. John and I talked far into the night about this and other things.

At 11 a.m. next morning I went up to Parliament Buildings for the interview with Fred Jones. I outlined in brief all the events leading up to the present impasse and told him, without any equivocation, that I would not have Andersen Tyrer on any of my programmes. He asked me why, and I told him. When I arrived in Auckland to confer with other NZBS officials, one of them asked me if I would like to meet Tyrer. I replied that I would be delighted to do so. All Tyrer had to do was to walk exactly fifteen yards to the hall in which I was sitting. The aforesaid official was away some time, far longer than the simple situation warranted. At last, he returned and in a very embarrassed manner told me that Tyrer would not come. I then said in a jocular tone of voice, 'Well, If Mahomet won't come to the mountain, the mountain must go to Mahomet', and I walked the fifteen yards and met Tyrer.

I was told many weeks later by the same NZBS official that Tyrer made some sort of coarse remark to him about me. It was a very miserable business and does not bear dwelling on. Fred Jones was in a difficult position and there was little he could say, but I think he handled the whole situation with great tact. I intimated that my own mind was made up and, although it went very much against the grain, I would not alter it. That night Proudfoot came to the hotel and told me that the NZBS had given way and I was to go back to Auckland and take over after Goossens had done his concert. That night the Music Teachers Association gave me a reception in the Banqueting Hall of the hotel. The Mayor of Wellington[21] was there, along with Fred Jones, the music teachers of Wellington, and my nephew Jack (a son of Percy). The NZBS was

---

20 Frederick Jones (1884–1966), Dunedin-born Labour politician who held the posts of Minister of Defence (1935–1949) and Minister of Broadcasting (1944–1949). Erik Olssen and Shawn Ryan, 'Jones, Frederick', Dictionary of New Zealand Biography, first published in 1998., Te Ara – The Encyclopedia of New Zealand, https://teara.govt.nz/en/biographies/4j8/jones-frederick, accessed 11 January 2019.

21 Sir William Appleton (1889–1958), Mayor of Wellington from 1944 to 1950.

represented by a minor official; neither Shelley nor William Yates[22] was present. The mayor made a charming speech, as did Fred Jones and Charles Bryant, the President of the Association. I made a suitable reply, saying how glad I was to be back in the land of my birth, of course making no reference whatsoever to events behind the scenes. Then happened one of the traditions peculiar to New Zealand. There must have been at least 150 people at that reception, and they formed into a huge queue, each one shaking hands with me in turn. My arm afterwards was quite sore, but it was a simple and charming scene.

After paying my respects to several relatives, I was off to Auckland by air. Next morning, I renewed my acquaintanceship with Eugene Goossens. I hadn't seen him for many years, although I had often had musical dealings with the rest of his family: Sidonie and Marie (brilliant harpists) and Léon (world famous oboe player). Eugene had been in the USA for the last fifteen years or so, and made rare trips back to London during that time, usually when his seasons of concerts with American orchestras were over. The first occasion when I met Gene was with the BNOC at Covent Garden in 1922, when I and others played the *Parsifal* bells behind the scenes. Goossens was on top of a very high ladder taking the beat through a peephole. It was all hands on deck in those days. Goossens's father and grandfather were also conductors, but it is curious how music so seldom runs through from one generation to another, at least to the extent that it has in the Goossens family.[23]

The Music Teachers Association had sent a telegram to Goossens protesting that he had taken over my advertised concert, but as he explained to me when me met, the NZBS had sent a radio cable to his ship when he was on his way from Honolulu to Auckland and had asked him to conduct a concert. He had readily consented and had known nothing about the situation. I would have done the same thing under the circumstances. It was nice meeting Gene again, especially as I was able to give him news of his brother and sisters who had played with me just before I left London.

While waiting for Goossens to finish his tenure of office with the orchestra, my mind went back to the expedition to Alice Springs in Australia and for which I had unsuccessfully wired the NZBS for permission to accompany. Here was I kicking my heels for the ten days I could have been with the expedition. Not that it was any comfort to me, for I couldn't have known the programme situation was so bad with the NZBS, and if I had gone on this expedition there would have been a dreadful last-minute scramble to find music even for one

---

22 William Yates (1898–1969) was to succeed James Shelley as Director of Broadcasting from 1949 to 1958.

23 At the time of writing, Braithwaite could not have foreseen that his son, Nicholas, would indeed follow in his footsteps with great success. He was, however, proudly sitting in the auditorium for Nicholas' operatic conducting debut with Welsh National Opera on 8 October 1966.

symphony concert, without the aid of the ABC library.

The Boyd Neel Orchestra had also arrived in New Zealand about the same time and I was to meet them all once again. We alternated in the same public halls all through Australia and New Zealand. One night I would give a concert, and the next Boyd Neel would give one, so we saw a lot of one another.

My first concert in Auckland was a tremendous success. The public in New Zealand is a conscious one. They are so modest about themselves that they simply will not believe anyone from New Zealand could possibly be at the top of his profession in England. At the end of the concert the audience would not go, and crowded around the platform, bringing me back time and time again. The orchestra joined in this ovation as well. This was most gratifying to me because, at the first rehearsal, I had detected, from some of the players, obstinate and obstructive tactics which would have annoyed someone with less patience than I. As it was, I was able to break down this attitude by the exercise of tact and persuasion. The truth came out later without me trying to find out the reason. The orchestra had been told by one unkindly antagonistic that I was a fourth-rate conductor and had been forced upon them. Some players even went so far as to tell me that this same person had tried to persuade them to refuse to tour with me. But the normal inquisitiveness of man was too strong, even for these players, and they stayed on just to see if I could conduct. From the end of the first rehearsal, I won over the orchestra completely.

My first concert was not an easy one for the orchestra. The first half of the programme opened without an overture, and consisted of only one work, Beethoven's Symphony no. 3 'Eroica'. It tested orchestra and audience alike, but it worked.[24] At the end of the concert the applause just wouldn't stop, so I repeated Weber's *Oberon Overture* as an encore. The press next morning gave the orchestra and myself the most glowing notices. It was a triumphant beginning to my tour and such scenes were to be repeated in all the other towns.

The news leaked out that I had refused to have Andersen Tyrer as a soloist, but only one

Warwick Braithwaite portrait from an NZBS concert programme in 1947.

---

24 Braithwaite was known for his unpredictable programme building. The second half of this concert, in the Auckland Town Hall on 4 July 1947, consisted of the 'Overture' to Weber's *Oberon*, Mozart's *Eine kleine Nachtmusik*, the 'Nocturne' and 'Scherzo' from Mendelssohn's *A Midsummer Night's Dream* and the 'Polovtsian Dances' from Borodin's *Prince Igor*.

paper, obviously 'inspired', referred to this matter. That was the end of that. Colin Horsley was also touring in New Zealand and I asked that he might play a concerto with me. There was some opposition to this from the NZBS but it was short-lived, and Horsley appeared with me later in one of the Dunedin concerts.[25] From the moment the press had hailed me as an artistic conductor I had no further trouble of any kind, and the rest of the tour went most successfully.

While in Auckland I looked up a friend of my boyhood days, Leonard Swan the violinist.[26] He had left Dunedin and was now the head of a well-known firm of chartered accountants. He invited me to the Auckland Yachting Club where another charming New Zealand tradition manifested itself. Each member had a locker in which he kept his own personal property, including bottles of whatever the owner fancied. In Len's case this was whisky and he brought out his bottle. The ritual was as follows (and it happened in private houses wherever I went): the host handed his bottle to a guest who became the host for the first round; he filled everybody's glass as if he were the host, and then his own, and replaced the bottle in front of the real host who, for the second round, handed his bottle to another guest and so on. It seemed to me to be a most friendly way of entertaining and has some subtlety about it.

*

From Auckland I went to Wellington by air and rehearsed in the Town Hall. The same story of enthusiasm could be told about this concert, and the hall was booked out. It was in Wellington that I met Sir Bernard Freyberg, the Governor General of New Zealand, who not only came to the concert but held a reception for me in the interval.[27] Both he and Lady Freyberg were most charming and friendly. Sir Bernard earned a Distinguished Service Order (DSO) at Gallipoli during the landings in April 1915. He swam during the night from a ship several miles out, with combustible material tied to his head, landed alone on a beach, collected wood for a bonfire and set it alight to create a diversion from the main landing. When one thinks of the hazards of such a daring and heroic deed of a man quite alone, and with the

---

25 Colin Robert Horsley (1920–2012), a New Zealand pianist and teacher based in the United Kingdom, performed the Schumann Piano Concerto with Braithwaite on 23 July 1947 at the Dunedin Town Hall.

26 A brief account of Leonard Swan's violin playing in the Dunedin Competitions of 1915 appeared in the *Otago Daily Times* (23 September 1915): 'Mr Swan had opened well, and with dramatic expression. He had produced a nice broad tone, and his playing had been of artistic quality.'

27 Bernard Cyril Freyberg (1889–1963), British-born soldier who served as the 7th Governor-General of New Zealand from 1946 to 1952.

beaches full of barbed wire (for the Turks had had ample warning of our coming through War Office and Admiralty stupidity), one can well believe that this honour, and the Victoria Cross which followed, were well earned. Sir Bernard's promotion was only a question of time, and later he rapidly climbed to the position of General and continued his heroic deeds as leader of the New Zealand forces in World War II, staying in Crete until the very last moment, and receiving further wounds as a result. This is the story as I had been told it.

An evening at the Wellington Savage Club included Sir Bernard and myself as guests. He was, of course, the principal guest, but he insisted on me being beside him, and as we walked through the ranks of the members, he held my arm and presented me as if I were the honoured guest. I won't forget this charming action as it was the one thing which killed any further nonsense from any quarter during my tour.

Also, while in Wellington, I met once again after 31 years, other relatives from a different branch of the family. Percy had married in his young days into a famous old whaling family called Howell, and old man Howell being a prolific child getter, there was a numerous progeny.[28] Percy's wife, May, was very fair although her mother had been full-blooded Māori. Unfortunately, she and Percy had quarrelled and she went to Wellington and married a rich lawyer called Ellison. They had a child called Mura,[29] and when Ellison died, May returned to Dunedin. Soon the old romance broke out again and they married. Sad to relate, May died 8 years later of an incurable illness, and Mura the child went back to Wellington to live with other relatives. Mura and I had been playmates and had always liked one another. She had married Bernard Johns, a well-known architect in Wellington.[30] I sought them out in their lovely house in one of the beautiful bays of Wellington Harbour, and what a greeting I had from them! Bernard was full of fun and vitality. Many were the hilarious parties we had together and with other relations.

From Wellington, I flew across Cook Strait to Christchurch and then to Dunedin. While the plane was over the Straits I looked out for whales, as this was the season when they swim through the Straits to warmer climes. During this period the whalers catch them easily, and tinned whale is quite a delicacy in New Zealand.[31]

---

28 Percy Macdonell Braithwaite (1876–1959) married Ethel May Ellison on 31 July 1906. Ethel May died in 1915.

29 Hinemura Gertude Lois Johns (1900–1989).

30 Bernard Winton Johns (1902–1982) married Hinemura in 1933.

31 Hunting whales in New Zealand waters was made illegal in 1978. Jock Phillips, 'Whaling', Te Ara – the Encyclopedia of New Zealand, http://www.TeAra.govt.nz/en/whaling, accessed 11 January 2019.

The plane skirted the wonderful Kaikoura Mountains at the head of the South Island, and then the more wonderful snow-capped Southern Alps came into view. This group of very high mountains, with Mt Cook as the giant, is one of the most awe-inspiring sights in the whole of New Zealand.[32] At the foot of these mountains, which extend for over 40 miles, commence the Canterbury Plains on which the famous Canterbury lamb is reared. From the air one gets a marvellous view of the flatlands, with straight roads stretching for miles into the interior. The plane stopped in Christchurch for a few minutes in order to let down and take up passengers, and at last I was on my way to my home town of Dunedin.

*

How can I describe my feelings as the plane approached Otago Harbour at the base of which nestles Dunedin? The sun was shining, there wasn't a cloud to be seen; the sea was a vivid blue and the land was a deep green. My face was glued to the plane window. At last, we were flying down to the harbour itself, and I could make out the bays where I swam and boated as a boy. Soon we were flying over the town itself, over my own home and over the Boys High School nearby, and on to the enormous airfield on the Taieri Plain. My tears could not be restrained; memory upon memory crowded into my brain. I could see the lines of surf where the Pacific Ocean rollers rushed onto the beaches at St Clair and St Kilda. It was too much for me.

Shortly the plane came down on the airfield and taxied up to the tarmac in front of the control tower.[33] I could see a group of people standing there, and I recognized three of my brothers, Percy, Eric and Rewi. The plane came to rest and everyone got out before me. Then I stepped onto the tarmac and was hugged and patted on the back by my brothers. I was then introduced to the 4YA Director and the Mayor of Dunedin (a charming man[34]), before being taken by car, through scenes of childhood, to Wain's Hotel in the centre of the city.

After more introductions, Percy, Eric, Rewi and myself walked arm in arm from Wain's Hotel, up Princes Street, followed by a number of friends and other relations. The first pilgrimage was made to the site where my father's Book Arcade had been. We stood arm in arm in the road outside this building,

---

32 Since 1998, the mountain has been known as Aoraki/Mount Cook, to incorporate its historic Māori name.

33 Until the opening of the larger Dunedin Airport in 1962, flights landed at the Taieri Aerodrome, now home to the Otago Aero Club.

34 Sir Donald Charles Cameron (1877–1962), Mayor of Dunedin from 1944 to 1950. He was knighted in 1948 and also received the freedom of the City of Edinburgh the following year.

and gazed in silence at the place where my father had worked and built up his business. There wasn't a vestige of the Arcade left, the whole area having been split up into a series of small shops.

Next morning, we made two more pilgrimages. The first was to our old home Dallon Bank, but alas the grounds had been tampered with. The trees were all cut down, there were no Lovers' Walks, no clematis, and no tennis court. Nothing remained except another house built on the foundations of the old, and another one built where the tennis court had been.[35] It was inexpressibly sad for all of us.

The second pilgrimage was to my parents' grave where I left a wreath. It had come on to snow and it was just as well, for our emotions were beginning to get the better of us, and the cold prevented us from staying too long. That afternoon, the Mayor gave me a reception at the Town Hall, first privately in the Mayor's Parlour, and later in the council chambers. Hundreds of people could not get in and were disappointed. The doors were left open so that the people outside could hear the speeches. In the little private reception, the Mayor spoke a few words of welcome and asked me to speak. By this time my heart was so full that I broke down and wept. My brother Percy pulled me together and as I was walking with him to the bigger reception, whispered fiercely in my ear, 'If you don't pull yourself together, I'll break your blasted neck.' That did the trick, and from then on, with the exception of a few seconds during my speech, I managed to keep my emotions under control.

I hope that the reader will understand a little of what I was going through in those days. At this reception was Mr Scherek (my last professor), along with some of my brothers' other relations and old friends of the family. It was for me a very touching and emotional affair. Mr Cameron, the Mayor, spoke of my father who was Mayor of Dunedin in 1905–1906, and Max Scherek spoke of his memories of me as his pupil. There were other speeches of course, including one by Mary Martin, the representative of the Music Teachers Association.[36] My immediate relations returned with me to the Mayor's Parlour for tea, and I was very glad just to be quiet among friends.

I had been asked by Arthur Manning, sub-editor of the *Evening Star* newspaper, what I planned to do while in Dunedin. One of the things I wanted to do was to travel up the cable car from the centre of the city to the track where

---

35 Dallon Bank had been damaged by fire in 1911. The salvaged part of the house was put up for sale, and the land was divided into two lots.

36 Mary Annie Martin (1896–1988), writer on music, broadcaster, and one of Otago University's first Bachelor of Music graduates. She was the first woman lecturer in the Music Department and helped found the Dunedin Chamber Music Society. In 1965 she was New Zealand president of the Federation of Societies of Registered Music Teachers. For 20 years, until 1965, the initials 'M.M' were carried by the principal reports of Dunedin concerts in the *Otago Daily Times*, including a review of Braithwaite's 1947 concert.

I, my father and others used to jump off while the car was still going, and from there we would walk home down through the bush to Dallon Bank past a clump of eucalyptus trees. This had been arranged for me, and the Corporation put a cable tram at my disposal at 10 a.m. one morning. With all my available relations and family friends, and with the old retired gripman[37] as guide, we travelled up Rattray Street to Māori Hill and, at the track leading to Dallon Bank, I and my brothers, with a few sprightly friends, jumped off at the appropriate spot. It was childishly thrilling and I was much beholden to the City Authorities for giving me this privilege.

On the way back via Arthur Street, I visited my first school,[38] and before I climbed the dozens of steps leading to the school buildings, I suddenly remembered the old Tuck Shop at the corner where I used to buy liquorice strips. I bounded over the road and went into the shop asking for Mrs Bonacci, and although she was no longer there, I bought a dozen liquorice strips because they still sold them to the present generation. I suppose it must have been 40 years since I had been to that shop.

Memories of childhood proved to be stronger and more accurate than those of a more mature age. At Arthur Street School the pupils were paraded in front of me, and after making a speech about what my first school had done for me in life, I whispered to the headmaster about giving the pupils a half-holiday. He agreed and I became a greater hero in their eyes than before. One little girl held my hand all the way back to the waiting car, and as I kissed her, she put her hand into the pocket of her pinny and held out a penny for 'Uncle Warwick', as I had been so kind as to give her a half-holiday. She insisted that I took the penny and I still have it today.

Perhaps these foregoing incidents are not particularly interesting to the reader but the human aspect, apart from a recitation of small and unimportant events, are things to ponder over. The fact that the Corporation put a cable car at my disposal was just such a thing which proves the sensitivity of the people in that far-off land; the gripman, who came out of retirement to act as guide, simply because he remembered my father and two sons who travelled up and down on his tram; the little child who gave me her penny as a gift; the headmaster who gave the children a half-holiday in my honour; these things are beautifully human. Where else in the world would this have happened? On the way by cable car, I passed the Christian Brothers School where, as boys, we heard all manner of epithets flung at us by the sons of Roman Catholic families who had been told that my mother had sinned in marrying my father,

---

37 The person who starts and stops the cable car by pulling the lever to engage and disengage the car from the moving cable.

38 Dunedin's longest established school, which moved to the Arthur Street site in 1877. The buildings were replaced in the 1960s.

a Protestant. We passed St Joseph's Cathedral, where my father and mother had been first married in the vestry, followed by a second ceremony in the Anglican (St Paul's) vestry. I had yet to appear before the Dunedin audiences as a conductor but the days before my appearance were a series of pilgrimages of a most personal kind.

The greatest surprise in Dunedin was a magnificent concert hall, by far the most perfect acoustically that I had experienced anywhere in Australia and New Zealand. The capacity is 2,300, and the platform is roomy, with well-graded steps. The organ at the back is, I believe, one of the best and biggest in the Southern Hemisphere. The curious thing about the Dunedin Town Hall is that, although it is very big, the acoustics are just as good when rehearsing as later at the concert. I met the architect while in Dunedin, and asked him how he had managed this phenomenon. He just replied by saying all he was concerned with was to plan a good hall. Whether this was modesty or poking a bit of fun I never found out, as he was a most reticent man. The hall itself was paid for out of the Municipal profits from the New Zealand and South Seas International Exhibition held from 1926 to 1927, and it has cost the ratepayers absolutely nothing.

My two orchestral concerts were tremendous occasions. The hall was completely full, with many hundreds standing. Colin Horsley, the excellent pianist, played the Schumann Pianoforte Concerto at the first concert. The enthusiasm was unbelievably intense, and as usual I had to give an encore at each concert as well as make a speech. My relations were elated at the successful outcome, and for them the two concerts were great occasions. The press gave glowing accounts, and let me say that the New Zealand press notices are really worth preserving.[39] For one thing, because newsprint comes from Canada, the newspapers have as much paper as they need. Music critics can spread themselves and are encouraged to study their subject and express themselves at great length without having to compromise.

After my last concert,[40] my brother Rewi and a good friend of his, planned a trip to Lake Wakatipu, one of the most glorious lakes in New Zealand, about 107 miles from Dunedin. We started off at 5 a.m. and, as it was quite dark for many miles, I slept in the back of the car. As daylight came, we began to pass through Gore, Milton and other small towns. Milton is beautifully situated in

---

39 'Our high hopes of Mr Braithwaite as a conductor have been fully justified and exceeded. The programme had obviously been carefully prepared, and the conductor was able to draw from the orchestra exactly what he wished with the simplest means and without exaggerated gestures. There was subtlety and refinement about his interpretations, though, when occasion demanded, as in the *Capriccio espagnol*, he could throw discretion to the winds and indulge in a glorious vulgarity... Mr Braithwaite and the orchestra were given a great and well-deserved ovation such as has seldom been known in the Dunedin Town Hall.' *Otago Daily Times* (24 July 1947).

40 On 29 July 1947.

the plains between the great Taieri River, Lake Waihola and the rising ground leading to Central Otago. Soon we were at Kingston, at the southern end of the lake. In the old days (when I was a boy), one had to take a steamer from Kingston to the beautiful lakeside town of Queenstown, but some years ago a very fine road had been built by the Labour government. Although one misses the wonderful view from the steamer of the mountain chain called The Remarkables (so-called because of their remarkably craggy shape), the journey time is more than halved by road.

Lake Wakatipu is one of the most beautiful lakes in New Zealand and is 50 miles long. Queenstown nestles in a bend of the lake, and what with the ideal situation, the blue colour of the water, the mountain ranges tipped with snow, and the beauty of the surrounding country, one is loath to tear oneself away. I sent a cable home to my family expressing the useless wish that they could have been with me.

The journey back was through the deep Kawarau Gorge, where about two hundred feet below the road the Kawarau River flows and crashes over huge falls. The road follows the course of the river through mighty ravines and 'cuts' in the rock for many miles. Vista after vista opened up before us until the road dipped down to the fruit growing district of Central Otago. Here we passed through the almost derelict gold mining towns of Alexandra, Roxburgh and others. Further on, after one left the fruit growing district (how much of our family's money was sunk in this district!), one found oneself in a curious barren desert-like locality; sand everywhere, and wasteland. Soon we were to reach the famous gold-mining town of Cromwell, where the biggest river in New Zealand, the Clutha, roars its way through the town.[41] The Clutha doesn't look very big, but is very deep and fast-flowing, and I am told that the amount of water which flows under the Cromwell Bridge is the highest of any river in the world. The head of Lake Wakatipu is called Paradise, and there is a particular kind of bird which is not found anywhere else in New Zealand, which for want of a better name is called Paradise Duck.[42] We arrived back in Dunedin late at night, very tired but comfortably happy and elated by the glorious scenery.

On the Sunday, my brother Percy arranged a family reunion at Portobello, one of the bays in Otago Harbour. Family members came from all over the South Island and there were about 50 people, including great nephews and nieces with their parents. Relatives from the North Island were not there, because of the great distances they would have had to travel.

---

41 The Clutha River / Mata-Au is New Zealand's largest river by volume, and the second longest after the North Island's Waikato River. The construction of the Clyde Dam in the 1990s flooded the old town centre which lay at the confluence of the Clutha and Kawarau Rivers. A new site for Cromwell's commercial centre was found on nearby higher ground.

42 *Tadorna variegata* (or Paradise Shelduck).

The last thing I did in Dunedin was to phone my family. It was 5.30 p.m. when I phoned and 6.30 a.m. the same day in London. When my little boy, Nicholas, came to the phone (it was the day after his birthday) all he could say was, 'Hullo Daddy. I'm very tired. I'm going straight back to bed!' That's all he thought of a phone call of 12,000 miles.

I was to return to Dunedin for a final choral concert of Mendelssohn's *Elijah* on the 50th anniversary of the choir's first performance of that work, when my sister Mabel sang the soprano part.[43] But more of this later.

*

From Dunedin I flew to Christchurch for two concerts, and during the weekend between, a party from the orchestra invited me to Arthur's Pass. This spot was right in the midst of the Alps and at the base of the famous Ōtira Gorge where the electric railway comes out of the five-mile-long tunnel. We left in a hired car driven by one of the violinists of the orchestra, a player who had been one of the violinists of the London Philharmonic Orchestra and also had toured with that orchestra, with myself as conductor, during the war in England.[44] The wonderful mountain scenery right in the mid-country of the Alps was again breathtaking. For hours we travelled along one of the completely straight roads from Christchurch to the mountainous region, and by nightfall we arrived at Arthur's Pass and set to make ourselves comfortable in one of the Government tourist 'shacks' which are at the disposal of those touring that district. As it was during the middle of winter, we had the whole glorious country to ourselves.

Arthur's Pass is the only way through from the Plains to the West Coast, and the overhanging mountains connecting with the beautiful New Zealand bush was a lovely sight. Surrounded by these enormously high mountains (Mt. Cook is over 12,000 ft. high[45]), one has the uncomfortable feeling of being the smallest of God's creatures. We caught an electric train the next day through the tunnel, just to be able to say we had used it, and arrived at the first station on the other side. After sampling a few pints of West Coast beer, we headed back to Arthur's Pass where we climbed to a nearby waterfall whose course had been recently altered by an earthquake.

---

43 The performance took place on 14 December 1897 in Garrison Hall. Mabel Manson was one of several sopranos to share the solos in that performance. Her husband William was also listed as a soloist.

44 Presumably Alex Sylvester Lindsay (1919–1974), distinguished NZ-born violinist, conductor and founder of the Lindsay String Orchestra.

45 At the time of Braithwaite's visit in 1947, Aoraki/Mount Cook was 12,349 ft high (3,764 metres). By 2014, rockslides and erosion had reduced the figure to 12,218 feet (3,724 metres). 'Otago-led study revises height of Aoraki/Mt Cook', https://www.otago.ac.nz/news/news/otago062651.html, accessed 22 January 2019.

That night the stock of coal ran out and, as it was perishing cold, we were at our wits end to know how to keep ourselves warm. We walked through the main street looking for a shop where we could buy wood, but as it was Sunday and wintertime, the few stores were closed. We met a government ranger and asked him where we could get fuel of some sort. He told us of the coal trucks which came through the Ōtira tunnel from Westport on the West Coast. Because it was Sunday, they were lying in the railway sidings until Monday morning, when they would be hauled to Christchurch. We asked him why he told us such tantalizing news, but he didn't answer. His face broke into a broad grin and he went on his way. Later, when it was really dark, a car was manoeuvred up to one of those coal trucks, and one strong male climbed onto the truck while two others held a big sack open to receive manna in the form of big black lumps – enough coal to keep a fire going for a week. So, we didn't freeze that night.

Next morning, we had to leave for Christchurch at 5 a.m. to arrive in time for the orchestral rehearsal at 2 p.m. We had eaten all our food, and by the time daylight came we were cold and ravenously hungry. Passing over the dry bed of a river, we noticed a wooden shack in a clump of trees about 200 yards from the road. We tooted the horn and, in a few seconds, someone opened a door. The owner was our friend, the ranger. We explained about the food situation and he invited all of us to a breakfast of eggs and bacon with tea, bread, butter and marmalade. A most fortuitous meeting! I asked the ranger how he liked living all by himself in such a remote part of the country. He told me that he once went for a fortnight's holiday to Christchurch, but the city frightened him with its noise, its mad car drivers and the absence of mountains (Christchurch is called the city of the plains), and he left after a week to return to his mountain home.

We had to motor over a very high mountain road before the descent to the plains, but when we arrived at this pass it was impossible to proceed any further. I was becoming most anxious and at last phoned up the Christchurch Municipal Offices, asking that a road clearance bulldozer be sent out. They couldn't understand at the other end, as they informed me that the road had already been cleared the night before. I shouted down the phone at them and at last they realized that the road was impassable again. There was only one thing to do, and that was to wait until the road men arrived. We went a few miles back to the only hotel in the area and drowned our sorrows as best we could for a couple of hours. Arriving once again at the pass we found that the roadmen had done a good job, and we got up to the highest point partly by leaving the driver in the car and pushing and laying bits of trees in order that the tyres could get a grip. At last we were over, and we began to make headway on the other side.

Our troubles were not over though, as someone had miscalculated the amount of petrol required for the journey. Again, we stopped while two of the party walked about three miles to the only garage in the area and arrived back in a horse driven cart. By this time, I was really alarmed. I phoned the NZBS office in Christchurch saying that we had had bad luck and might be an hour late. As it was, we arrived in Christchurch with ample time to spare and all passed off according to schedule. It was an exciting weekend among beautiful mountains, but if the snowfall had been heavier on the pass, we could have been stuck for days.

The Christchurch concerts were a great success but the less said about the Civic Hall the better. Christchurch is the 'English' town of New Zealand and prides itself on its cultural activities, yet the Civic Hall (it is called a theatre) would be a disgrace to a town one quarter the size. I said so at a Civic Reception given in my honour, and exhorted the Mayor and Municipality to do something about it. Apparently, they had been trying to do something about it for years, but certain business interests, who owned the property, had managed to block any new building. I heard afterwards that, as a result of my speeches on the subject, the whole question was raised once again but how far it has progressed, I can't say at this moment.[46]

A few days afterwards, I was on my way to Wellington by plane for my final concert with the National Orchestra. As it was the last concert of the season, the Governor and his charming wife were there and gave a reception during the interval in which I was very glad to renew my acquaintance with two such lovely people. The concert was a terrific success and the cheering at the end was a most sincere farewell from my own countrymen. I made a speech in which I praised the playing of the orchestra, and gave due measures of praise to the Government and the NZBS officials for the magnificent way in which the orchestra was run.

While in Wellington I saw Lord Montgomery who was touring New Zealand at the time. I had seen him earlier in Dunedin when we stayed at Wain's Hotel, and Fred Jones introduced me. I was surprised that he was not as tall as I had imagined. During a polite exchange, and after Fred Jones had introduced me as a conductor 'well-known in England', Lord Montgomery said, 'Conductor! Ah yes! I only know Sir Malcolm Sargent!' I wonder how low my stock went down that moment.

In Christchurch, the orchestra gave me a farewell party, organized by that indefatigable manager of the orchestra, Lionel 'Slim' Somerville, who had also shepherded me everywhere during the tour. He was a delightful fellow, full of

---

46 The Civic Theatre was opened on 17 March 1928 and demolished in 1983. The Christchurch Town Hall arts complex opened in 1972 on the banks of the Avon River overlooking Victoria Square. Significant damage sustained during the February 2011 earthquake caused its closure, but rebuilding and improvements have been undertaken and it reopened in 2019. 'New addition to Town Hall strikes right chord', http://www.scoop.co.nz/stories/AK1806/S00638/new-addition-to-town-hall-strikes-right-chord.htm, accessed 22 January 2019.

Dunedin Choral Society Incorporated performing 'Elijah', 1947.
Dunedin Choral Society Incorporated Papers, MS-2086/039,
Hocken Collections, Uare Taoka o Hākena, University of Otago.

amazing energy and when necessary, politely tactful. I had always wanted one of the famous Kaiapoi rugs, one of which I had taken to England in 1914 and subsequently lost.[47] The players presented me with one of these. Montgomery was also given one during his tour, and I was told that these two rugs were among the last to be produced by this famous firm.

After the final concert with the national orchestra, I went back to Dunedin for the *Elijah* concert with the Dunedin Choral Society.[48] Some of the older members of this choir remembered my father and all the circumstances of his life. It was very touching to hear the nice way they spoke of him.

One day at Wain's Hotel I was summoned over the Tannoy system with a message to say that a woman wanted to see me in the hall. I jumped up with

47 Founded in 1878, the Kaiapoi Woollen Manufacturing Company exported woollen goods, including the famous travel rug. Mergers and takeovers eventually sealed its fate and the factory closed in 1978, exactly a century later.

48 On 27 August 1947 with Dora Drake *(soprano)*, Mary Pratt *(mezzo)*; Alfred Walmsley *(tenor)*; Bryan Drake *(baritone)*; Dunedin Choral Society; Augmented 4YA Orchestra (leader: Ethel Wallace); Douglas Palmer *(organ)*. The reviews were enthusiastic:

'For the third time in recent weeks our Town Hall has been filled to capacity for concerts where Mr Warwick Braithwaite has been the conductor. This is a great tribute to a fellow-countryman, paid not from a sense of duty, but from a recognition of his outstanding qualities as conductor and musician.' *Otago Daily Times* 28 Aug 1947.

'Last night's performance was on a large scale and probably the most satisfying heard in this city for a number of years....Mr Braithwaite preserved a brisk tempo throughout and brought out the full dramatic beauty of the score without any extravagant speeding up of the music.' *Evening Star* 28 Aug 1947

alacrity and went downstairs. In the hall was an elderly lady who greeted me as if I were a long-lost son. My oldest brother Percy, who was with me, knew her immediately. She had come to tell me such a story connected with my mother, that only then did I realize why there was still such a strong anti-Catholic feeling shown by my brothers. This is the story.

When my father was courting my mother (then 15 years old), he came to an arrangement with her father that he would not see her for six months. During that time, he went to Alexandra in Central Otago to stay with the father and mother of this lady who had come to see me. While my father was away, my mother's parents did everything they could to persuade their daughter to have nothing further to do with my father. Strong and stern parental pressure was brought to bear upon my mother to promise never to see my father again. My mother would not give way and the climax was reached when physical persuasion was tried. One night, so the story goes, my mother defiantly upbraided her parents and then a scene developed which today seems unbelievable. My mother was tied naked to a bedpost and unmercifully beaten by her father with a leather strap. But such is the way of things, her spirit was far from broken. In the middle of the night my mother stole out of the house, went to a nearby field where she knew there was a horse, and rode bareback through the night from Dunedin to Alexandra, a distance of nearly 80 miles. She arrived exhausted the next day, but safe. This decided my father. He brought her back to Dunedin a few days afterwards (not to her father's house) and he himself went to her father and told him in no uncertain terms what he thought of him. The outcome of it all was that he wrung a most unwilling consent to the marriage. The lady who told me this story was prepared to verify every word of it. My brother, Percy, already knew the story, but it had never been told to the younger members of the family. My mother was tough.[49]

While in Dunedin for the second time, I stayed with my brother Rewi and roamed among the sandhills of St Clair and St Hilda where, as a boy, I had known every nook and cranny. The wonderful surf of the Pacific Ocean looked the same to me, and the pure white sand gleamed in the morning sun. It was delightful but also sad, for I was going to leave this lovely place soon, possibly never to return.

Once more farewell to lovely Dunedin, the Pacific Ocean; a memory of Dallon Bank (no more Lover's Walks); farewell to the clematis around the tennis

---

49 Sir Rodric Braithwaite holds moving correspondence between Joseph and Mary dating from the time of their courtship. Mary later wrote to Warwick in England recalling the conflict between her strict Catholic upbringing and potential marriage to a non-Catholic. At one point, her father wanted her forcibly locked away in a convent to prevent the marriage to Joseph. Letter from Mary to Warwick, 31 July 1919 (private collection).

court; farewell to the cable trams, the Town Belt and Queen's Drive; farewell to the memory I had of my beautiful home. Rewi, with his wife and three children, saw me off. I'll never forget the look on his face. His eyes searched mine long and lovingly. I turned and walked to the plane, more miserable than I had ever felt in my whole life.

Back in Wellington, I took a few days to fix up Income Tax, renew my passport, and be injected for Yellow Fever. Why Yellow Fever? That is a story of one more venture.

Before I had left England, the baritone Redvers Llewellyn,[50] who had been in Johannesburg during the War, told me that John Connell, the Music Director of that city, needed a conductor for the oncoming season from September through until February. I had written to Connell, and during the Australian and New Zealand tour, letters had passed between us. It was arranged that I should arrive in Johannesburg around 20th September. As there was a 'belt' of Yellow Fever between Egypt and the Sudan, no passenger, even by plane, could do the journey unless he had been injected as a precaution.

This was a difficult matter in far off New Zealand. When I wrote to Fred Jones, MP for Broadcasting in New Zealand, to arrange for serum, he regretfully declined to do anything about it. This was a serious blow, for without the serum my visit to South Africa was off. While in Dunedin for the last time, I met my old friend Ernest Drake, the celebrated New Zealand singing teacher.[51] Ernest phoned a doctor friend living opposite who came over to get particulars from me, and, through the New Zealand National Health Service, he sent a cable to the School of Tropical Diseases in Euston Road, London, who sent out the required serum by BOAC.[52] This doctor also arranged for a colleague in Wellington to inject me with it. Sending out serum by BOAC was quite a tricky business as it had to be kept frozen all through the tropics. I was injected in Wellington under the Health Service, and as I had paid Income Tax and Social Welfare tax, the whole procedure cost exactly 10 shillings. Under the Health Scheme, 7/6d was returned to me, and so the next stage of my world tour was settled.

My last few days in Wellington were spent with relatives, after which time I flew to Auckland via Palmerston North, skirting Mount Egmont (a second

---

50 Thomas Redvers Llewellyn (1901–1976), Welsh baritone and one of the major British operatic baritones of his generation. Between 1934–1948, he performed over 140 times with Braithwaite, mostly at Sadler's Wells. Together, they also recorded arias by Bizet, Gounod, Verdi and Wagner for HMV.

51 Ernest Winfred Drake (1890–1958), Tasmanian-born tenor, teacher and conductor; father of Dunedin-born baritone Bryan Drake (1925–2001).

52 British Overseas Airways Corporation was a state-owned airline operating under that name from 1940 until its merger with British European Airways (BEA) to form British Airways in 1974.

edition of Mount Fujiyama[53]) with its perfectly shaped snow-capped cone and crater. Far away to the right, the twin volcanoes Ruapehu and Ngāuruhoe, could be seen. Ruapehu, dormant for many years, had only recently become active, and bearing in mind the events preceding the Tarawera of 1886, I couldn't help wondering if this might be a repeat of something similar.

Arriving at Auckland for just one night with my old friend Leonard Swan, I then took the train to Hamilton. I had promised to conduct the local orchestra when my contract was over, as my brother Roderick was the Chairman of the Committee. Another pleasant coincidence happened after the rehearsal, when I received a phone call from Ian Coster, the London columnist and friend of mine, who was in Hamilton for two weeks to see his elderly mother.[54] Before and after the concert we were able to spend some time together, and I was to see him once again, for a fleeting moment, in Singapore some weeks later when our paths happily crossed.

The orchestral concert at Hamilton was a pleasant affair, and afterwards I visited Tūrangawaewae Marae, whose meeting house was adorned with the most beautiful Māori carving I had ever seen. There were many relics of the great Māori tribes, including several Māori axes. These axes were war weapons cut out of solid New Zealand greenstone, a jade-like stone, which is now rarely found and is no longer allowed to be sent out of the country. Up until about 90 years ago it was thought that the Māori carvings were only interesting designs of a decorative nature, but it has since been proved beyond doubt, especially by the painstaking and brilliant work of Ettie Rout[55] in her book *Māori Symbolism*, that the Māori carvings are records of the great migration of the early Māori from Hawaiki, the original land shrouded in complete mystery, to Aotearoa, the 'long white cloud', (i.e. New Zealand), across the immense Pacific Ocean.[56]

After spending a few more days with Roderick and being presented with

---

53 Now commonly known as Mount Fuji, it is the tallest peak in Japan. The similarity to the shape of Mount Taranaki (or Mount Egmont) allowed it to be used as a substitute for Fuji in some scenes of the 2003 film, *The Last Samurai*.

54 (Charles) Ian Dillwyn Coster (1903–1955), Royal Marine, writer, theatre critic and journalist.

55 Ettie Annie Rout (1877–1936), Tasmanian-born New Zealander, known for her work on sexually transmitted infections among servicemen during the First World War. Her interest in Māori culture resulted in the book *Māori Symbolism: Being an Account of the Origin, Migration and Culture of the New Zealand Māori as Recorded in Certain Sacred Legends* (Kegan Paul, 1926).

56 Hawaiki is the traditional Māori place of origin. The first Māori are said to have sailed to New Zealand from Hawaiki, and in Māori mythology Hawaiki is the place where Io, the supreme being, created the world and its first people. It is the place from which each person comes, and it is where each will return after death. Te Ahukaramū Charles Royal, 'Hawaiki', Te Ara – the Encyclopedia of New Zealand, http://www.TeAra.govt.nz/en/hawaiki, accessed 11 January 2019.

the Key of Hamilton[57] in a charming ceremony presided over by the Mayor, I went to Tauranga (Zane Grey's tunny fishing haunt[58]), and conducted another local orchestra. This was the orchestra in which my brother Neville's doctor played the double bass. This was no ordinary double bass, as it was made in New Zealand out of wood from the famous Kauri tree.[59] It was a beautiful instrument with a deep resonant tone. The Kauri, a coniferous tree peculiar to New Zealand which attains a height of over 100 feet, is one of the wonders of the country. The wood is straight grained, easily worked, and susceptible to a high polish, so it is ideal for stringed instruments.

The doctor brought my brother Neville and his wife to Tauranga from the Kaimai mountain range, and we were all together for a few days. The concert itself was amusing but quite pleasant. Afterwards, we adjourned to the doctor's house where a real New Zealand party went on into the early hours of the morning. I said goodbye to Tauranga, after spending the next day fishing outside the harbour, and repaired to Neville's home in the mountains. The Tauranga Orchestra presented me with a set of beautiful coffee spoons with the handles made from the wonderfully coloured Paua shell. This is a shell rather like the mussel shell found in England, but which is a mixture of the most vivid blue and green colour. Once more farewells were taken of Neville and his wife at their lone bungalow on Mount Kaimai, after which Roderick motored me back to Hamilton, where I was to spend my last night in New Zealand.

But before relating the rest of the journey, I will recall to the reader my girl sweetheart 'B' mentioned in the first few pages of this book. I had met everyone else I had wanted to meet while in New Zealand, but try as I may, I couldn't find the friend of my boyhood days. I had set enquiries afoot in all directions. I had even advertised in the Gisborne daily paper for a whole week asking 'B' to get into touch with me, but all to no avail. It was my one disappointment and at last I gave up the attempt. When I returned to London I asked my brother, Percy, to keep on making an effort to find my friend. About six months after my return (December 1948), my brother wrote to say he had quite by accident met 'B's sister in Wellington. Now that I had an address, we have corresponded with one another regularly but, alas, I have never seen her again.

---

57 Warwick Braithwaite was the first person to be awarded the highest civic honour of Freedom Holder of the City. It was awarded by Roderick Braithwaite (then a city councillor and later mayor of Hamilton) and Mayor Harold Caro. *Waikato Times* (9 September 1947).

58 Zane Grey (1872–1939), American writer of popular adventure novels. An enthusiastic fisherman, he travelled widely, visiting New Zealand four times between 1926 and 1933.

59 *Agathis australis* can attain heights of 130 feet with trunk diameters over 15 feet.

TWENTY-THREE

SOUTH AFRICA
AND THE SABC

From Auckland I caught the flying boat to Sydney where the Australian Broadcasting Corporation had arranged accommodation for me. My last day was spent with Roy Lamb, Ewart Chapple and others. An old friend of my wife's was Secretary of the Musicians' Club, and a final party was given in my honour in the club premises. Later we were invited to a private party, and as my flight was scheduled to leave at midnight, Roy Lamb saw to it that I was there in time. Hilarious and joyous farewells were taken at the airport, and then I was off on my first hop of the journey to Port Darwin.

At Darwin, a fellow passenger and I asked a taxi driver to show us the bomb damage done by Japanese planes. People in Britain don't realize how badly Darwin was hit; at least two-thirds of the town was laid in ruins, and I can well understand Mr Curtin's desire to get the Australian soldiers to their own country.[1] Later that evening my fellow passenger and I went to an Australian-style Rodeo show where Aboriginal and Australian cowboys vied with one another to see who could stay the longest on some of the wildest horses that I've ever seen. An Aboriginal won the chief event. Coming back very late, we passed tennis courts brilliantly illuminated by huge electric lamps, where the local people played until the early hours of the morning. It's too hot for daytime tennis in Darwin.

There is no need to go into the rest of the journey in detail as it was exactly

---

1 John Joseph Ambrose Curtin (1885–1945), Prime Minister of Australia (1941-1945). Curtin insisted that Australian troops, en route from the Middle East to the Dutch East Indies but deflected by Churchill to Burma, should be recalled to defend their own country against the Japanese. 'Crisis at Home and Abroad', http://john.curtin.edu.au/manofpeace/crisis.html, accessed 11 January 2019.

the reverse of the journey out, but at Rangoon I made a pilgrimage to the Golden Pagoda and, with several fellow passengers, took off my shoes to walk through the immense area of the Pagoda.[2] It came on to rain, and coupled with the mess left by the pigeons, you can imagine the state of our feet. The Golden Pagoda is one of the biggest in the world and is full of shrines to Buddha.

On to Calcutta, Karachi, Bahrain, over Jerusalem again, and then the Suez Canal came once more into sight. Down to the Nile and to Shepheard's Hotel to await my plane from Rome. I was ten days in Cairo because of a bit of bad organisation, and another problem had originated in New Zealand where my traveller's cheques had not been made negotiable in Egypt. I was in a real jam this time; no one would change my cheques, and the situation had become really desperate. At last, I managed to persuade a clerk of Barclays Bank in Cairo (who had steadfastly refused to change the cheques for days), to eventually cash them. In the transaction I lost a pound but it was worth it.

As I had several more days to wait, I planned out my sightseeing carefully. First, I visited the Egyptian Museum to view the fabulous collection from Tutankhamun's tomb. The sarcophagi, five in number, made to enclose one another around the original tomb, were all of pure gold. The funerary goods buried with the king were to the number of many hundreds.[3]

Another visit was to the Muhammad Ali Mosque on the one hill on the outskirts of Cairo. This is a noble and magnificent building in which, hanging from the very high ceiling outside, are hundreds of glass chandeliers, from which hang glass strips that tinkle away prettily in the slightest breeze. From the outside, the Pyramids in the Valley of the Kings could be seen. I was shown everything by a very handsome, tall and dusky Nubian guide who spoke absolutely perfect English.

The comedy of the airlift to Johannesburg was beginning to wear thin, so I went to the BOAC office and placed my case in the hands of a very efficient official who persuaded the original agency to refund my passage money. That night I was one of the passengers in a York plane[4] bound for Johannesburg.

The journey from Cairo began at 1 a.m., and I slept until daylight. We came down at Khartoum, passed over Omdurman, and later stopped at Nairobi where we stayed the night at a lovely hotel. I missed the opportunity of going out to

---

2 Rangoon (now Yangon) was the former capital city of Burma (now Myanmar). In 2005 the capital was moved from Yangon to Nay Pyi Taw.

3 5,398 items were found in the tomb, including a solid gold coffin, face mask, thrones, archery bows, trumpets, a lotus chalice, food, wine, sandals, and fresh linen underwear. Howard Carter took ten years to catalogue the items. A.R. Williams, 'King Tut: The Teen Whose Death Rocked Egypt', https://news.nationalgeographic.com/2015/11/151124-tut-biography-egypt-tomb-archaeology, accessed 11 January 2019.

4 A plane developed by the British aviation company, Avro, during WWII, for military, and later civilian, purposes.

the game reserve, which was only a few miles outside the town. Next morning, we were off early and came down at Salisbury[5] for refuelling. Our next stop was Johannesburg.

I had sent a wire to John Connell[6] from Cairo and expected someone to be at the Johannesburg Airport to meet me, but much to my surprise there was no-one. What had gone wrong? I phoned the City Chambers but no-one knew where Connell was. I travelled to the centre of the city by the airline bus and on the way thought that perhaps someone was sure to meet me at the terminus. But again, no-one was there to greet me. I phoned this person and that person, but no-one knew where Connell was to be found. The clerk at the terminus tried various people for me and at last, after nearly an hour of phoning, the sister of John Connell's secretary arrived at the airline office full of apologies. By chance she had found the telegram at Connell's office when she went there during a reception that night at the City Hall.

I was taken to the Carlton Hotel, quite the biggest hotel in Johannesburg, and by the time my luggage was in my room and I had changed, John Connell turned up with some friends. John was quite nonchalant about the inconvenience caused me, and in a merry mood, we all went into the dining room and partook of a hearty meal.

*

As I had a few days before my first concert, I asked Connell to arrange a trip to Kruger National Park.[7] This was done and John loaned me his cine camera for the trip. Everything was arranged through the Transvaal Railway and I set off at night time to Nelspruit, arriving early next morning. I had tickets for everything, including a shave and bath at a very nice hotel, as well as a very good breakfast. At 9 a.m. (the time stated on the ticket) a beautiful Buick car with its African driver was waiting for me outside the hotel. From Nelspruit we drove through wild country right into 'darkest Africa', passing kraals[8] and other Zulu and Bantu habitations. I managed to photograph a party of Zulu young men in full tribal feathers practising throwing their spears.

Our first stop was at the Government rest camp called Pretoriuskop. As we arrived about three hours before nightfall, my driver took me out to see if there were any lions about. I was extraordinarily lucky as within thirty minutes

5 Salisbury was renamed Harare in 1982, and is the capital of Zimbabwe (formerly Rhodesia).
6 John Connell (1891–1955), Scottish organist who founded the Johannesburg Municipal Orchestra and became conductor of the Johannesburg Philharmonic and Choral Society. He retained these positions until his retirement in 1950.
7 The first National Park in South Africa, opened to the public in 1926.
8 A traditional African village of huts, typically enclosed by a fence.

of leaving the rest camp, I saw a pride of six lions basking in the afternoon sun. It was an opportunity not to be missed and I took photos of them through the windscreen. There is a stern rule that no-one is allowed to get out of a car in the Reserve, but I had to get a good series of shots at my first pride of lions, so I opened the door of the car, keeping my right elbow against the open door in case of accidents. It was just as well, for the lions weren't more than 25 yards away and the nearest one must have got my scent, for he made a definite move in my direction. I quickly got back to my seat, but I had secured a very good film of the lions. We saw some secretary birds, warthogs, many wildebeests and zebra and, as night came on, we turned back to Pretoriuskop. We had the next two days before us so we knew we would see as much as we wanted.

The rest camps provided at several selected places in the park were excellently run, with little huts made of brick and, in some cases, shaped like a native hut. At Pretoriuskop there were hot and cold showers and quite a good restaurant and store. Actually, the amenities of civilization were ever present, which is quite wonderful when one considers Johannesburg is about 300 miles away.

The Kruger National Park is 220 miles long by an average of 40 miles wide. It is wild, scraggy country with mainly small trees sparsely dotted in the grassland. Every now and then one comes across huge, but flat, rock formations where perhaps, under a tree in the hot midday sun, one might find a pride of resting lions. They look for all the world like huge tortoiseshell pussycats – benign and harmless. A curious thing I noticed was the tendency, even in the wild, for a lion every now and then to stretch his legs and walk up and down just as he does in a zoo, as if he were impatiently waiting for something. He puts his nose in the air and looks around as if surveying his undisputed kingdom. He is the only wild animal that flatly refuses to take the slightest notice of human beings in motor cars. All the other animals appear scared and run away to a safe distance.

I was told that a pride of lions, when hunting, is directed by the lioness who sends the males off to scare game by their full-throated roar, right into her path where she is waiting to pounce on them. She is the first to satisfy her hunger, and next the cubs, after which the male has his fill. If the victim is a wildebeest or some other huge animal, the lions, having had their fill, relinquish the carcass to the vultures who have been circling around in the early dawn awaiting their turn. Again, this is a strict ritual of feeding, for the king of the vultures is served by his bodyguard – others being kept away – after which the young are given titbits such as kidneys and liver. Then when all this is over, the rabble make one riotous dive for what's left of the animal and, before a few minutes are gone, nothing is left but the bones. The vultures fly off and the miserable jackals slink in for anything that might be left, chewing the bones for the succulent marrow inside.

Next morning, my driver and I were away on our trip through the Reserve. We came across the hippopotami lolling in the deep water of the pool in the river that flows through the Reserve. I took some delightful colour films of these lazy animals. We passed herds of zebra, giraffe, wildebeest and later, big troops of baboons. These animals are really comic because they are so like human beings in their ways. Towards nightfall the leader, generally a huge male, goes off scouting for shelter. He shouts at his lieutenants and beckons them with his arm when he has found a likely group of trees, and the lieutenants chivvy the rest of the tribe so that they all quickly move towards shelter. It is amusing to see the young babies playing amongst themselves, just like human children, and being smacked on their little behinds by their mothers and fathers. Within a few minutes of chattering and scratching, the whole troop of perhaps fifty or sixty baboons is in the treetops.

Towards 4 p.m. we came to Skukuza Rest Camp. Here we found a lively party including Robert Taylor, the film star, dressed in a garish suit of many colours. He was on a tour of the game reserve at the same time as myself. He looks exactly the same in real life as he does in his films: short, wiry, extremely healthy, and with an air of no-nonsense about him. I think he seemed glad to be away from the atrocious amount of attention he was receiving in the towns.

Skukuza is the main rest camp and also the headquarters of the warden of the Game Reserve. It is quite a little township on its own with good buildings including a post office, stores, and a fine collection of round huts used by travellers for the night. We were off early next morning and continued on our way to the last rest camp, Malelane. Here I was to meet a New Zealander, one of the rangers in charge of Malelane, a Mr James, who had come to South Africa many years ago and settled in the Game Reserve for good. He invited me to stay with him and his wife when I told him I would be coming back before I left for England in January. Although the Reserve was shut during that period, he would get permission for me to enter. This he eventually did and I will tell of my second trip in its right place later.

We crossed the river after leaving Malelane and left the Reserve behind us. As there was no drink to be had in the Reserve, I asked my driver to stop at the nearest village outside. He did so, and just as I was lamenting to the barman that I had seen almost everything except elephants, a man rushed into the bar giving us the news that a herd had been sighted in the Reserve. We rushed to our cars and took a rough track down to the river, and there on the other side was the herd of magnificent elephants slowly moving through the trees, stripping the bark and, with their heads, uprooting huge trees to eat the soft bark from their roots. I took a few feet of film, but as the sun was already going down, they proved of no use. I was out of luck, and this was the only time my film proved to be a failure. We left as the elephants moved out of sight and continued on our way, driving through the darkness to Nelspruit where I stayed for the night after partaking of a lovely dinner with my Afrikaans driver. Next morning, I was on my way to Johannesburg and to work.

I was in Johannesburg as conductor of the City Orchestra from September 20th 1947, until the end of January 1948.[9] The orchestra was put together by John Connell who auditioned players in London, Brussels, Paris and Amsterdam.[10] The personnel was therefore very mixed. The solo woodwind, mainly young Dutchmen, were fantastically good and there was hardly one player in the orchestra who did not attain a very high standard of performance. It was a real joy to conduct for such players, but there was just one chink in the armour. Connell was always at a great disadvantage with such players who knew that in Johannesburg they could not be replaced because there was no pool of players to call upon. The only other orchestra in Johannesburg was the SABC Orchestra (also a very fine orchestra), and as they also had a permanent contract, John Connell had little choice in the replacing of a difficult instrumentalist. Sometimes he had to wait for months to arrange for another replacement from Europe, and then only after he himself had made a rushed journey by air and personally visited three capitals in order to appoint the player required. It was a difficult position for him and I felt this difficulty keenly. But a conductor cannot give way even under these circumstances. What tact could do I tried, but eventually I had to lay down the law as far as I could. The players respected me, and as a result I seldom had any real difficulty.

John Connell was one of the most amazing organisers I have ever met. Out of nothing, and by force of personality alone, he made Johannesburg a musical city. John had his faults, but in one thing he had *never* faltered, and that was in furthering the musical life of Johannesburg. People may forget (but they would be wrong to do so) that John Connell arrived in Johannesburg when there was no music happening of any worth. He built up a series of concerts, an orchestra recruited from the best European centres and seasons of opera which Johannesburg had only previously experienced from a few touring companies. He had persuaded the Johannesburg Corporation in some miraculous way known only to himself, to subsidize an orchestra and

---

9 Braithwaite's first concert in South Africa was on 7 October 1947 and his last was on 27 January 1948. He conducted 26 concerts with the Johannesburg City Orchestra, and a further nine concerts combined with the South African Broadcasting Corporation Symphony Orchestra.

10 In 1946, the newly-formed City Orchestra took over the formal civic role of the Johannesburg Symphony Orchestra. The JSO continued to make itself available to accompany young concerto soloists, choirs, charity work, perform rare and difficult works, and give concerts for non-European audiences. Pamela Tancsik, 'Tracing Joseph Trauneck: The Wanderings of a Persecuted Man', *Fontes Artis Musicae*, 56/ 2 (2009), 115–137.

an operatic season, as well as buying a site on which to one day build an opera house and a concert hall.

Connell had but one great rival, a monopoly and an octopus in the form of the African Consolidated Theatres.[11] This is an organisation which owns *all* the African Theatres and will buy out any opposition, cultural or otherwise. It was started by Schlesinger and Stodel, and in the usual way of such things, these partners bought their way to a position where they owned not only the African Theatres but also the principal hotels and restaurants right through South Africa. What a monument to business acumen! But Connell was a tough Scot and had a wonderful way with businessmen. He also had a wonderful way with the Afrikaners, even growing a beard at one time in order to show his sympathy with the bearded Voortrekkers.[12]

Talking about beards, I have one. While looking out of the railway carriage window waiting for the train to move off from Johannesburg station, a rowdy bunch of Voortrekkers saluted me, evidently thinking I was one of themselves!

The amount of work John Connell got through was positively heroic, and Johannesburg must surely recognize him one day as the greatest influence in music that the city has ever had. One of his many activities was the giving of Grand Opera seasons in Johannesburg and Pretoria. He was brave enough to do such works as *Salome* (by Richard Strauss) with mostly local talent. There was nothing he wouldn't have a shot at, and it is to his everlasting credit that Johannesburg was being talked about in European capitals as another centre of music.

Of my stay in Johannesburg there is little to mention, except the series of concerts I conducted both with the City Orchestra and the combined South African Broadcasting Corporation (SABC) and City Orchestras. I did all Beethoven's symphonies including the 'Choral', and during the course of that four months, most of the well-known great works, as well as several modern ones. One concert at the SABC was devoted to South African composers including a symphony by Van Wyck; a tone poem by Gideon Fagan; some songs by my old friend Theo Wendt (sung by Betsy de la Porte, who used to be a member of the Sadler's Wells Opera before the war, and who is once again settled in Johannesburg); and an overture by Gilbert Harris, an Englishman who had

---

11 Founded in 1913 by Isadore William Schlesinger (1871–1949) and Harry Stodel (1868–1951). Between 1920 and 1960 virtually no-one could play the cities without the support and involvement of ACT, or at least utilizing their facilities. 'African Consolidated Theatres', http://esat.sun.ac.za/index.php?title=African_Consolidated_Theatres, accessed 11 January 2019.

12 The Voortrekkers (Afrikaans and Dutch for *pioneers*, literally 'those in front who pull'; or 'fore-trekkers') were Boer pastoralists from the frontiers of the Cape Colony who migrated eastwards due to grievances with the then-British colonial administration. 'An Introduction to the Great Trek', http://www.voortrekker-history.co.za/index.php, accessed 22 January 2019.

been in Johannesburg for fifteen years.[13] Adolph Hallis, that magnificent pianist now teaching in Johannesburg, also played with me.[14]

I had been staying at the Carlton Hotel, a sumptuous but very expensive hotel, and with the help of friends, I was able to rent a good, but very small, flat facing Johannesburg Park and thus defeat the drain on my finances entailed by living in an African Theatres Hotel.

Joan Hammond toured South Africa while I was there, and I had great pleasure in having her in one of my programmes.[15] She had enormous success everywhere she went, and I was privileged to be one of the few guests at a little farewell party before she flew to the USA for a concert tour.

I met an old friend in Johannesburg, John van Zyl, who had been at the RAM with me in London. John now teaches singing in Johannesburg, and shortly after I arrived there, he phoned me, and together with Joan Hammond and a few other friends, we went out to the home of Leo Quayle[16] at a delightful 'oasis' called Springs, between Pretoria and Johannesburg. This delicious spot, situated in the middle of scraggy country, is indeed an oasis, for suddenly we were plunged into a small area of green grass, lovely trees and bathing pools. Flowers of all kinds were in profusion and I will never forget the kindness of my host. Leo Quayle visited me two years later in London and brought with him over 10,000 feet of colour film mainly of South Africa and Southern Rhodesia, together with his own projector. It was an amazing record of his own trips all over the southern part of Africa.

From Springs we continued on our way to Pretoria. It was a week before the famous Jacaranda Festival, and Pretoria was a mass of pale blue blooms at this time. I took films of the Union Buildings[17] on the top of the hill overlooking Pretoria, and General Smuts' house[18] at the bottom of the gardens overlooking, and in front of, the immense building. There were flowers everywhere. The Jacaranda, which grows in Australia, and northern New Zealand as well, is a large flowering tree, the blooms being rather like wisteria. In Pretoria, all the avenues, and most private gardens, are planted with these lovely trees and, as

---

13 Arnold van Wyck (1916–1983); Gideon Fagan (1904–1980); Theo Wendt 1900–1951); Gilbert Harris (1900–?).

14 Adolph Hallis (1896–1987), South African pianist and teacher. He performed Khachaturian's Piano Concerto in Johannesburg on 21 November 1947. Hallis had previously worked with Braithwaite playing Liszt's *Totentanz* with the National Orchestra of Wales in 1928, and the first performance in England of Christian Darnton's Piano concerto in 1935 with the BBC Orchestra.

15 Joan Hammond performed a concert of arias by Mozart, Weber, Giordano, Verdi and Puccini with combined orchestras in Johannesburg on 19 October 1947.

16 Leo Quayle (1918–2005), South African conductor and lecturer.

17 The Union Buildings form the official seat of the South African government and also house the offices of the president of South Africa.

18 Now a museum.

a result of the temperature of Pretoria being much hotter than Johannesburg (which is 6,000 ft. above sea level), these trees, and many others, make a wonderful blaze of colour during the end of September.

I made so many friends during my stay in Johannesburg that it would require a volume on its own to recount all my doings, but I must mention two who were to accompany me on my second trip to the Game Reserve, Lottie and George Wilson. Lottie was the principal viola player with the SABC orchestra and George, her husband, the manager of a mine on the outskirts of Johannesburg. George is one of Scotland's most versatile sons. Lottie, an Afrikaner and one of the most beautiful women I met in Johannesburg, is also an exceptionally fine viola player. We all had very good times together and I was loath to leave Johannesburg because of them. Gilbert Harris, the composer, was also the librarian of the SABC and both he and his wife Barbara, together with the Wilsons, became my most intimate friends.

Towards December, when the temperature of Johannesburg begins to rise uncomfortably, the concerts took place in Johannesburg Park – a proceeding I didn't care for very much. John Connell tried his hardest to persuade me to stay on until February for the Opera Season, but I wanted to end my wanderings. Thoughts began to bring my home nearer; I had been away for eleven months. I decided to phone my family on New Years' Eve and had booked the line from 7 p.m. at the flat of Gilbert Harris. I waited and waited but no call came through. I was mad with rage. About 10 p.m. I went around to the main telephone exchange, but as far as I could tell, all the telephone operators were away 'first footing'.[19] I waited until midnight and went to bed absolutely disconsolate.

Next morning, I again went to the Telephone Exchange and insisted on seeing the head man. I told him that not only I, but my family in London, had been kept up half the night waiting for the inebriated telephonists in Johannesburg to come to their senses, but he had little to say except that the Cape Town radio telephone beam had blown down. I found later, through a source that I cannot disclose, that this was not true. Be that as it may, the exchange made amends by putting through a priority call within a few hours. So, I had a talk with my family and told them I was already booked to travel in the SS *Durban Castle* arriving at Southampton towards the end of February. I had done 63,000 miles by air during the first six months of my tour and decided not to tempt providence any longer. Hence my return by train to Cape Town, and boat from there.

---

19 The Hogmanay tradition of 'first footing' (i.e., the 'first foot' in the house after midnight) is still common across Scotland. To ensure good luck for the house the 'first foot' should be a dark male, and he should bring with him symbolic pieces of coal, shortbread, salt, black bun and a wee dram of whisky. Ben Johnson, 'The History of Hogmanay', https://www.historic-uk.com/HistoryUK/HistoryofScotland/The-History-of-Hogmanay, accessed 11 January 2019.

*

My last few days in Johannesburg were a round of farewell parties, visits to the famous and very luxurious Royal Golfing Club and Country Club, and, of course, the most exciting three days in the Kruger National Park. George and Lottie Wilson came with me and we motored down from Johannesburg leaving at 5 a.m., taking all our food with us. The distance is more than 300 miles over roads mostly of red sand, corrugated by the action of wind and rain. Miles from anywhere we had a breakdown, but George, being an expert mechanic, put things right in less than an hour. But it was *so* hot! We arrived at Nelspruit around midday, freshened up, and were off again on the same route my Afrikaner driver had taken the previous September. We reached Pretoriuskop[20] later that afternoon, and I enquired of the manager if my New Zealand friend, Mr James, had arranged for our passage through to the Malelane Private Camp, but there seemed to be a hitch somewhere, so we stayed that night at the rest camp. Before going to bed we spent the last few hours of daylight motoring along the tracks through the jungle in the hope of seeing some lions. We found many elephant tracks and uprooted trees, and we even came across a huge notice 'Beware of Elephants' but, beyond a few zebra and springbok and smaller animals, we were out of luck.

Next morning the manager of Pretoriuskop told me that word had come through from the warden at Skukuza[21] that we were allowed to proceed. We packed up, and in a short time were on our way. We rushed the journey a bit, getting to Skukuza by midday, but saw a few giraffe, zebra, wildebeest, baboons, warthogs and hippos on the way. After lunch we were off again to Malelane where we were directed to Mr James' house and there met his delightful wife. Sitting on the verandah, completely enclosed by very fine metal gauze to keep out mosquitos, we had our tiffin[22] and were regaled with some hair-raising adventure stories from Mr James.

Every camp in the park is equipped with a radio set on a low wavelength which is in touch with headquarters at Skukuza. About 7 p.m. each ranger turns on his set and makes his report to the warden. It was very nice to hear the warden asking if Mr Braithwaite's party had arrived safely. Mr James then received instructions from the warden to go out that night and patrol his area in order to trace the whereabouts of an old killer-lion. Imagine what an opportunity this was for us. Mr James saw the look of enquiry in our faces and invited us to accompany him. When night came, our host rose from his chair,

---

20 A rest camp near the Numbi gate entry to the South-West Kruger National Park.

21 The largest rest camp, and administrative HQ, of Kruger National Park.

22 Tiffin is an Indian-British term for a snack of some kind, either a light mid-day meal or afternoon tea.

said goodbye to his wife, and got out his huge Buick car equipped with a high-powered detachable searchlight which can be held in the palm of one hand. I sat next to him with my finger on the searchlight switch, while Lottie and George sat in the rear. We were out for about three hours, but during that period we didn't meet the 'killer' lion. We did, however, come across a lioness with three cubs, who lolled ahead of the car (which had slowed down to a walking pace) and eventually, after a few hundred yards, turned off into the thick undergrowth. When we came up to the place where the lioness and cubs had gone off the track, I shone the searchlight and saw four pairs of eyes blinking at us from just a few yards away. In a trice they disappeared. During the rest of this night journey we only saw some startled wildcats and other varieties; the 'killer' lion was nowhere to be seen, although on one occasion we heard the roar from several lions – a roar which always precedes a kill. It was too dangerous to get out of the car, especially as we were conscious of being watched by dozens of eyes in the darkness, and the slightest false move on our part might have proved fatal.

We got back around midnight and Mr James, who seemed loath to part with our company, regaled us with his adventure stories right into the early hours of the morning. Next day we were up early and once again off into the jungle by car. I had two more reels of colour film left, and again, although we didn't see any lions, I was able to take pictures of some magnificent giraffes, some of them about 18ft in height.

Just before returning for lunch, Mr James suddenly stopped the car and whispered to us to be absolutely silent. Soon a huge pack of wild dogs crossed the road in front of us. They all stopped, just like one man (or one dog), and gave us a long stare. I quickly got my camera working and took several feet of film. Mr James assured us that this particular pack had not been seen for at least a year and that we were extraordinarily lucky. These wild dogs, with their warm brown colour with black markings, are terribly ferocious and only hunt in packs. Mr James told us that when chasing a springbok or the more common, but very fast, impala (a sort of lithesome antelope), they gradually wear down the harassed animal by biting lumps of flesh from it until it sinks down exhausted. Then it is torn to pieces. The film I took of these dogs turned out to be the most successful shot of all. Later that day we saw many tribes of baboons chattering away, quite unconcerned by our presence.

A flight of vultures was overhead, and one of the young black workers in the park came rushing out of the jungle to tell me that there was a 'kill' going on (in daylight), just a few hundred yards off the road. Mr James gave this boy a dressing-down for leaving his lorry, but afterwards told us that such a thing happened frequently. The boys often tried to scare off the lions at a kill in order the secure the meal for themselves. The native Bantu, Zulu and others used to walk through the Reserve completely unprotected. One day we saw a native walking through the lion country, followed a few yards behind by his woman who was carrying a child of not more than three months. We saw three other natives later on, still further inside the jungle, and they seemed quite unconcerned as to the terrors of wildlife. Actually, the only animals that would have attacked them were lions and buffalo; most other animals being scared of humans unless cornered. Even the warthog – that ugly, ferocious and dangerous-looking animal – sheers off with his tail completely erect when he sees a human.

The wild buffalo is both a cunning and ferocious killer; in fact, he seems to take delight in killing humans just for the fun of it. A buffalo hunter needs to know the favourite trick of the animal, which is to double-back in a wide circle and wait for the hunter to pass. He then charges from behind. If the hunter is inexperienced, the consequences can be fatal.

At the crack of dawn, we were off on our homeward journey. George wanted to go back another way, through some particularly beautiful country. Certainly, this deviation was worth it, until we came to a very steep hill climb over a moderately high mountain. It had rained the night before (one of those torrential downpours). When we came to the steep hill climb, we found a bus and six or seven cars completely bogged down and stranded. George was all for making a rush at the hill and getting over by sheer speed. So, in company with willing helpers from the other cars, we collected stones, branches of trees and whatever we could lay our hands on, so as to strengthen the sea of mud before us. Lottie and I left George to drive the car and he backed it about a hundred yards down the hill, and gathering speed, went for it with a tremendous spirit. But the car not only got stuck, but the branches got helplessly entangled in the wheels, and it took us another hour to free them. We gave it up as hopeless and turned back. We stayed the night at a hotel and arrived in Johannesburg the next day, tired but happy. It had been a wonderful trip and has remained a most entrancing memory.

A few days later I was on the train to Cape Town where I was to stay with my friend Albert Coates.[23] Normally I would have had twenty-six hours in Cape Town, but Mother Nature intervened during the night with one of her downpours which washed away about a mile of the railway line and a low-lying bridge a few miles outside Beaufort West, about halfway to Cape Town. We were stuck in this town for exactly twenty-four hours. I wired Coates and some other friends who were expecting to meet me, but as no-one knew how long the delay would be, I couldn't tell them much.

Beaufort West is a small town, but fortunately it is also one of the few towns that contains big railway workshops. The population was one hundred

---

23 Albert Coates (1882–1953), distinguished English conductor and composer who worked internationally. In 1946 he settled in South Africa, conducting in Johannesburg and Cape Town.

percent Afrikaans speaking. The bridge building crew went out about 10 p.m. (we arrived at Beaufort West at midnight) and by noon the next day they had returned to Beaufort West after having completed their job in about twenty-six hours. I continued the journey through the Great and Little Karoo deserts, to Cape Town. I only had time to get my luggage through the customs and see the few friends who had found out the time of arrival of my train. Then, together with three other travellers who were also delayed, we boarded the *Durban Castle*, which had waited an extra three hours.

The journey home to England was quite uneventful, with the exception of the life on the sea itself. Very soon after leaving Cape Town we ran into tropical weather. The sea abounded in marine life; schools of whales, dolphins, porpoises and flying fish disported themselves for our benefit. The most exciting sight was a terrific battle between a giant electric stingray and several sharks. The ray shot out of the water to a height of about twenty feet, and landed on the heads of the sharks with a most resounding smack. This went on several times but as our ship sailed on, we could not see the outcome of the battle. The giant electric stingray is an enormous square shaped fish with a long tail and to see it flying out of the water at such a height was an astounding sight.

We stayed at Madeira in the Canary Islands for one night and threw shillings at the boys who dived from the deck of the ship, retrieving every coin we threw in the water. The temperature began to get lower as we approached the Bay of Biscay, and in a few days, we could see Cape Finisterre. Before long we were ploughing our way up the English Channel, heavy overcoats and thick underclothes on. We docked at Southampton, but I had so much with me which I had brought from Johannesburg, that by the time I cleared Customs, I missed the boat train to London. I phoned my wife and asked her to borrow £10, as I was coming by car and all my money had gone on Customs charges. So, I arrived home after eleven months of touring, having travelled nearly 72,000 miles. The whole family was at home – my two boys, my wife, and Barbara, my daughter – and, as I unloaded my trunks, I handed out the various presents I had bought for them. Now that I was back in London, I took several hundred feet of film of my youngest son, but within a fortnight I was to get a rude shock. Burglars broke into the house and the only thing they took was my treasured Cine Kodak. What a blow!

*

I have not said much about my concerts with the Johannesburg City Orchestra. There were generally two concerts per week, with one at Pretoria once a fortnight. The Tuesday night concert was the main symphony programme and, on the Sunday, we presented a shorter popular concert. Throughout my four months I conducted all these concerts and occasionally a choral work. There were two performances of *Messiah* – one in the Afrikaans language, the other in English. The English performance, conducted by me and sung by a choir made up mostly of Afrikaners, was not so good. John Connell conducted the other performance and he very kindly played the organ obbligato for my performance. I think the members of the choir showed less interest when they had to sing in English.

This question of the rivalry between the English and the Afrikaners was always present in Johannesburg, as in the rest of the Union. I remember meeting a most cultured and very beautiful Afrikaans lady, a successful barrister, and as long as we kept to cultural subjects, she was most charming. We only crossed swords once, and that was when I brought up the subject of English composers into our conversation, for she dismissed our composers contemptuously. When I expostulated at this unreasonable attitude (and I was instancing such composers as Purcell, Elgar, Vaughan Williams, Walton and Britten), she confessed that she detested anything English. I couldn't let this go without a challenge, and it transpired that two of her uncles were 'treated brutally' by the British during the South African War. She also gave me a description of the awful happenings in the concentration camps during that same war, when thousands of prisoners (including women and children), died of typhus. I was shocked at this, as in my history books there was no mention of concentration camps.[24]

John Connell, by his tact and complete selfless devotion to the cause of music in Johannesburg, had managed to keep politics out of his dealings with the Afrikaans musicians, and whereas I would at, times, question some of his decisions relative to the standard of many of their artists, I soon learnt the difficult position he was in. I remember in particular an article in a Sunday newspaper, written by an amateur critic – a woman who was anti-British and pro-Afrikaans, and who had become interested in an Afrikaans local conductor. She had the temerity to write a scurrilous article attacking me personally, and professionally. I was so incensed by the antagonistic tone of this article that I consulted a Johannesburg solicitor about it. Connell, although sympathetic, advised me to ignore it, but I felt I could not. The solicitor wrote to the Editor of the paper who disavowed all responsibility for the opinions expressed by the writer, and I felt forced to take an action against this woman. Connell pointed out that even if I won the case, he would have to clean up the mess when I had gone, so in the end I did nothing about it. If such an article had been written

---

24 27,927 persons died in the white camps; 20,000 died in the black camps. For more information on this period, see 'Women and Children in White Concentration Camps during the Anglo-Boer War, 1900–1902' and 'Black Concentration Camps during the Anglo-Boer War 2, 1900–1902', South African History Online, http://www.sahistory.org.za, accessed 11 January 2019.

in an English newspaper, I would have received a verdict against the writer and thousands of pounds in damages. Of that there was no doubt.

Other articles were written by columnists which showed me pretty clearly that Connell had always been in a difficult position. I had not yet conducted the orchestra when an article came out in the *Johannesburg Sunday Times* protesting about the cost of a guest conductor and mentioning details of the probable salary (not far wrong either). Apart from these pinpricks, I had a very good press with such phrases as 'British Conductor given ovation at City Concert', 'Concert of rare quality', and 'Conductor adds to his Prestige'. In fact, I don't think I had a bad concert review all the time I wielded the baton in Johannesburg, but at the end the wolves – in the shape of local people with axes to grind – were waiting to tear me to pieces. These people were determined to leave no stone unturned in wrecking all that Connell had done. I believe, eventually, although I don't know the full story, John Connell was forced to resign some years later, and I can well imagine his feelings towards these people with their ingratitude and unfairness. From all accounts, the opera season which he built up has now been abandoned and is no more, and his dynamic personality is sadly missed in other matters. Politics may have triumphed.

Connell was a Scot not an Afrikaner, but he kept clear of politics, and I pay my highest tribute to him, not only because he was a great host, but for his pertinacity and disinterested work in a difficult situation. He *made* Municipal Johannesburg and whatever happens in the future, he will be remembered as a gleaming meteor across the sky of Johannesburg's cultural life.

Johannesburg, in 1947–1948, was a difficult city.[25] Only sixty years ago it was a crazy mining town – crazy in the sense that fortunes were made and lost in a few days. Financiers were tumbling over one another to seize their chances of diamonds, gold and coal. Only people who were after these commodities were tolerated in its early life. Mines changed hands with lightning speed; shares were often bought for very little and, in a few hours or days, soared to fantastic, undreamt-of heights. Natives were herded into the mines to work for next to nothing. Labour was too cheap, and the white man soon began to regard the native as his own particular, and virtually unpaid, beast of burden – just as he is today, with the exception that he is housed in huge camps near the mines and paid a little more. With such cheap labour, is it any wonder that the shareholders became fabulously rich and, as a result, the present generation is living in luxury? In the main, all the rich diamond mines in goldfields have been pegged out and today it is the share-pushing and share-conscious public that derives its living from the mines. Gone are the old pioneering days when men were men and worked with their own hands, thus building up their own

---

25 Braithwaite is writing in 1956.

fortunes. Today all Johannesburg becomes nervous and shaken when shares go down a few pence. The barometer of Johannesburg life, social as well as cultural, is the price of shares. The whole outlook of life there is influenced by the share lists. The result has been that to live in Johannesburg is like living in a huge stock exchange where, on all sides, the conversation is concerned with little other than the price of shares or how much someone made or lost in a transaction. The glint of triumph would come into the eyes of friends of mine when they would announce that a week ago, they had bought so many hundred shares at such and such a price, and today they were worth so much more. This called for a celebration, and more often than not the gain is wiped out temporarily by throwing a great party. And what parties they were, even if temporarily someone's shares had gone down. A party on such an occasion was necessary to get one out of the gloom of disappointment. Then for days the financial columns would be scanned in fear and trembling. If the crisis blew over, another party would be on the way. From fear to elation and then to fear and forgetfulness.

Sensible people kept out of this racket, but only by making sure of gilt-edged securities of other less frustrating occupations. I was told on good authority that there are so many diamonds in the Transvaal and other parts of South Africa, that if they were all mined, everybody could have a bracelet for next to nothing. I was also told that the fabulously rich Oppenheimer monopoly deliberately keeps down production because of the fictitious value of diamonds.[26] One story, which I have good reason to know is true, is that in one spot in South Africa owned by Oppenheimer, there are several square acres covered with two feet of concrete and patrolled by armed guards because of the wealth of diamonds underneath which will not be mined for many years to come.

There are other problems too. There is an element of national strife in the town. The Jews are disliked by an ignorant section of both Afrikaners and English. The Afrikaners also hate the 'usurping' English. The British seemed to me to be the only calm and untroubled section of the community, and they just got on with a job of work. It was my impression that, on the whole, they took much more interest in cultural activities and really tried to weld the warring elements together for this purpose. But the Afrikaner stood aloof, and not for the right reasons.

---

26 Sir Ernest Oppenheimer (1880–1957), German-born diamond and gold mining entrepreneur, financier and philanthropist, who controlled De Beers and founded the Anglo-American Corporation of South Africa. He was succeeded by his son, Harry Frederick Oppenheimer (1908–2000), a prominent South African businessman, industrialist and philanthropist. Harry Oppenheimer was often ranked as one of the wealthiest people in the world. Marilyn Berger, 'Harry Oppenheimer, 91, South African Industrialist, Dies, https://www.nytimes.com/2000/08/21/business/harry-oppenheimer-91-south-african-industrialist-dies.html, accessed 4 March 2022.

Such was my impression of the unusual situation in Johannesburg. I cannot vouch for the absolute overall accuracy of this impression; as a guest I could only see what I was allowed to see. But there was something in what I *felt* while I was there. The only people who really became friendly and hospitable towards me were the British, or the men and women of mixed marriages (British and Afrikaans). Other friends, notably Adolph Hallis, Betsy de la Porte and John van Zyl, who had spent many years of their youth in London were, of course quite different and understood the British, with all their mixture of good and bad points.

Despite these good people, the warring elements caused me to become depressed during the last few weeks of my contract, and although John Connell wanted me to stay on for the opera season, I just couldn't bring myself to put up with all the nonsense. I could have extended my stay, but I knew if I stayed any longer, I would become embroiled in personal controversy with Afrikaner musicians or their columnists, and I thought it was not worthwhile. I was very sorry to leave Connell like that, especially after he had been such a stalwart upholder of the dignity of music as a cultural element in a difficult city.

PART VIII
(1948–1952)

TWENTY-FOUR

BIZET, BALLET AND BORIS

B ack in London, I had to rebuild my freelance conducting connections. How soon I had been forgotten! This was a good tonic for me; a correction to any over-estimation of my reputation and career. I had conducted the London Philharmonic all over England and Scotland during the war; the London Symphony Orchestra in London immediately after the war; the BBC regional orchestras in all the main centres as well as in studio programmes, and also the BBC Symphony Orchestra. At the Albert Hall I had done a few concerts, but the thing I didn't like was the everlasting sight of myself not daring to go too far from my telephone.

A fair estimation of the value of my work as a conductor could be summed up in the sentence 'very good, experienced and sincere in his approach to this work.' My operatic reputation was nearly second to none among the British conductors, and it has been said of me that I had a special talent for coping with the hazards of stage performances. As an accompanist in concert work with singers I was well known to be excellent. The recording companies called on me on numerous occasions (and still do), when they required a conductor who was both experienced and, by universal consent within the profession, also knew his job.

In the first six months after my world tour, I had a thin time of it, even though I had written to most of the people who mattered in that respect. There was no publicity value in the great success of my tour. No one wanted to know about such far off places, and I was struck dumb by such lack of interest. The great musical experience I had been through when I had conducted over 59 symphony concerts with 11 different orchestras meant nothing. My tour, beyond memories and experiences, meant absolutely nothing musically to either the public at large or musical organisations. I might just as well have stayed at home. The sense of achievement I had as a result of an amazing tour was rudely shaken by perhaps the most insular musical people on this globe.

I battered at all musical doors but few were opened. I asked myself innumerable times during this period of my life what was the point of working hard and sincerely if, at the very time when the ordinary businessman was safe and secure (financially at least), I had little or nothing, and had to start all over again? Then I saw an article by Tom Russell, a late viola player with my old National Orchestra of Wales who had since become the Manager of the London Philharmonic Orchestra, who wrote that British conductors had been found wanting, and from then onwards only foreigners were to be engaged. I saw red. The LPO had climbed up to fame on the backs of English conductors like Leslie Heward, Constant Lambert, Basil Cameron and myself during the war, when we were quite good enough for them. I wrote Russell a sharp letter of rebuke, but as far as I remember his answer was quite unsatisfactory. Far be it for me to wish to decry the work of other men, even foreigners, but surely there is a limit to the passing over of our men in favour of men with foreign names.

During the war, and indeed during the LPO tours afterwards – all with British conductors – the musical public had filled our concert halls, and surely this was good enough? It's worth noting too that this had been done under the most atrocious conditions with lack of proper rehearsal. The public had been successfully weaned off men with foreign names who were, in some mysterious way, supposed to be the only ones with the know-how of conducting. The little coteries of longhaired devotees of Herr or Signor so-and-so had largely disappeared from our concert halls, but now the red carpet was to be put down once again and the LPO was the first orchestra to buy one.

But there was no red carpet for the home-grown conductor; he had to do his work without any pre-publicity or especial mark of respect or discipline. I remember the incident of a certain foreign refugee musician who had very little conducting experience and not much talent, who, without even asking for it, had himself billed as 'The Great ...', and here followed the surname only. When I saw this, I knew the worst and despaired of the British entrepreneur. The Victorian days had come back again; the days of German opera in the Italian language; the halcyon days of the foreign name in our municipal programmes. Could this happen in *their* own countries? There was no reciprocity, and never will be so long as our musical nation places its own musicians last.[1]

I have often asked myself whether only a musician trained on the

---

1 Braithwaite's thoughts on the list of conductors at the helm of Britain's major orchestras in 2021 might have been interesting: Joshua Bell (ASMF); Kirill Karabits (Bournemouth SO); Bramwell Tovey (BBC Concert O); Sakari Oramo (BBC Symphony); Omer Meir Wellber (BBC Philharmonic); Thomas Dausgaard (BBC Scottish); Mirga Gržinyte-Tyla (CBSO); Mark Elder (Hallé); Edward Gardner (LPO); Simon Rattle (LSO); Santtu-Matias Rouvali (Philharmonia); Ryan Bancroft (BBC National Orchestra of Wales); Domingo Hindoyan (Royal Liverpool Philharmonic) Vasily Petrenko (Royal Philharmonic); Thomas Søndergård (Royal Scottish); Daniele Rustioni (Ulster O).

continent is worth his salt. Are foreigners more colourful than we are? Have they more personality? The truly great ones excepted, do we really want a 'Schwarz', 'Blamenkind' or 'Festalori' permanently with us?[2] Isn't it rather that the committee members or governors of our musical societies, generally very excellent people in themselves, are picked for their places in society and are rarely able to judge between the merits of two musicians? But they can, as a rule, be impressed by foreign names. It is easy to be impressed by a phrase such as 'I was conductor of Wiesbaden' etc., or even to mention some big towns. But they forget to mention in what *capacity* they worked in the big towns. Be that as it may, and leaving myself out of it altogether, there are some very talented and first-class British conductors eating their hearts out in this country. I leave the answer to others; not because I have no answer, but because it is impossible to discuss this subject when it so dearly concerns myself.

In 1945, Karl Rankl was appointed Musical Director of the first subsidized opera company in the history of England.[3] Many were critical of this appointment[4] and questions were even asked in Parliament. But a well-known firm of music publishers was backing the whole venture financially, so the Covent Garden Trust took no notice of these criticisms.[5] The only answer given was a private one to myself by one of the Trust, who said that Rankl was the only conductor of operatic experience in the country to take on the job. What a farce of a statement. I don't wish to imply that Karl Rankl knew *nothing* about opera, but rather to point out the implication that no Britisher knew *anything* about opera. Rankl stuck to London for five years, but it was soon apparent that he had little experience of the big works he conducted; either that, or he was a bad conductor and a poor artist. When the Opera House was taken out of the hands of the aforementioned music publisher, Rankl resigned. The reasons

Karl Rankl, conductor.

---

2 Braithwaite is inventing surnames whilst hinting at real figures.

3 Karl Rankl (1898–1968), Austrian-born conductor whose appointment as music director of the Covent Garden Opera Company in 1946 was highly controversial, but who nevertheless established a company of largely British artists which laid the foundations of the present Royal Opera.

4 Notably, Sir Thomas Beecham.

5 The music publisher, Boosey & Hawkes, had purchased a five-year lease of the Royal Opera House in 1944, rescuing it from becoming a permanent dance hall and providing a venue for opera and ballet. At the end of this period, the building was subject to a compulsory purchase order by the Ministry of Works under a Labour Government led by Clement Attlee.

for his resignation are not so shrouded in mystery as some people think, but the inside history of this must remain cloistered for some time.[6] That Rankl was no Music Director was apparent to every member of the Covent Garden staff, but as to why he didn't appear to *try* to be Music Director is a mystery. That no Englishman was to have the opportunity of doing what Rankl had the opportunity to do – but failed – was a fantastic example of the inability of our Trusts and Boards to accurately assess values.

Why Rankl conducted every first night, took most rehearsals, and gave little or no time to the organisation of the musical side of the Opera House (which simply grew up higgledy-piggledy) can only be explained by his desire to appear before the public in as favourable a light as possible. Maybe it was for that reason that even he was not allowed to exercise his authority as Music Director within the inner councils of the Opera House. Signs were not wanting that this was the reason for his overbearing manner, his cruelty to young singers and his backing out of undertakings given, even after due discussion, to his colleagues. But what a chance he had to establish the first subsidized opera house in the history of London, and to put the artistic and administrative organisation of it on the highest plane.

The fact of the matter was that Rankl did not know the English operatic scene. He was woefully oblivious of the opera companies that had done yeoman service in the past. He was ignorant of the many British operatic artists who had been kicking their heels doing nothing since before the war. Like all foreigners ignorant of the history of operatic endeavour in this country, he must have decided to start afresh and exclude experienced people. Why were experienced artists and musicians kept out? Was it some kind of fear that held him, and others, from bringing in obviously experienced people? To answer this question, I must continue my own autobiography as I was intrinsically mixed up in the whole question of Covent Garden.

After building up my freelance connections once again during the years after the war, I had written to David Webster,[7] the Administrator of Covent Garden, when I heard that opera was to recommence at that ancient and venerable institution, and offered my services in a conducting capacity. I never had a reply, but six months afterwards, (sometime in 1946), I was telephoned by Webster's secretary asking if I would come to Covent Garden for an interview.

---

6   Rankl's limitations as a conductor, his difficult relationships with staff and artists, and his declining reputation with critics and audiences led to his 'resignation' in 1951. The following year he began a successful five-year tenure as conductor of the Scottish National Orchestra, ironically the position that Braithwaite had held from 1940–1946. The story is told in more depth in Norman Lebrecht, *Covent Garden: the untold story: dispatches from the English culture war, 1945–2000* (London; Simon & Schuster, 2000).

7   Sir David Webster (1903–1971), chief executive of the Royal Opera House, Covent Garden from 1945 to 1970.

I enquired of the secretary as to who the interview was with. She replied that Rankl, Webster, Lambert and Buesst would be there 'to hear me'. I sat up at this! To *hear* me! She gave me the choice of several days, and I chose the following Wednesday. But just to make sure, I asked her what they might want to *hear*? Then came the real blow to my esteem. 'Aren't you the singer, Warwick Braithwaite?' she asked. I kept calm and informed her that I was well-known as a conductor, but that if she liked I would come and sing in my conductor's voice to the learned gentlemen concerned. Of course, she was full of the most cringing apologies, and that was that.

When I met Constant Lambert the same day and told him of this conversation, he nearly had a fit. I can still see the tears rolling down his cheeks when he begged me to walk on the stage of Covent Garden the following day with a copy of *Carmen* and sing 'The Flower Song'. I began to see the funny side of it at last. This incident was a scandal but I didn't use it in any way. Lambert wanted me to give the story to the press, and mutual press friends of ours were simply dying to use the story. I am glad I didn't.

Shortly afterwards, in March 1947, I went on my World Tour and arrived home in February 1948. Sometime in July 1948 I was telephoned again by Rankl's secretary and asked if I would come to lunch. Such was the leakage of information, that I had already been warned that there was a possibility I would be asked to join the Covent Garden music staff. Rankl and I met, and I was given the choice of conducting either *Carmen*, *Boris Godunov*, *Der Rosenkavalier* or *The Magic Flute*, but as no guarantee was given me as to production rehearsals, I thought *Carmen* was the best choice. I was allowed a full orchestral rehearsal and a preliminary piano rehearsal. I found many of the tempi atrociously wrong, and certain peculiar pauses and slight alterations which had been put in by Rankl (he had conducted every performance up to then). There was no time to bring the work back to its original shape, but I did what I could. As it turns out, the whole company still talk of that performance as being by far the best they have ever done. The performance went without a hitch, and David Webster came around to see me during the second interval and told me without any hesitation that I would certainly be with the company the following season.[8] He also told me a very significant thing as well. He said that Rankl had admitted I could conduct alright, but he didn't like my tempi! I was to find out to my cost very soon that this was going to cause trouble. Rankl could not bear anyone else taking over a work he had conducted and altering, even in the slightest degree, his own interpretation. This ridiculous brand of

---

8   In a letter to his son Nicholas, dated 23 July 1970, Braithwaite recalls that he had replaced Peter Gellhorn as the conductor of *Le Contes d'Hoffman* for Carl Rosa in 1947. Gellhorn had been appointed Rankl's assistant at Covent Garden, and he put in a good word for Braithwaite to David Webster. This would account for the invitation in 1948 on his return from the international tour.

fear (or selfishness) was to mark the start of a life of misery for me later on. But I am anticipating.

*

What feelings I had when I stood on the Covent Garden rostrum; a place which, as a lad of 23, I had only viewed from a distance! To tread the boards of the stage where I had worked as a répétiteur in 1922 with the British National Opera Company; to wander through the auditorium when it was empty; to meet some of the old hands of the stage like Mr Ballard (Chief Machinist) and Sydney Cheney, (Chief Electrician); to go up to the 'flies' and wander around; all these things were, to me, the completion of a full circle of experience. No one in the present company would have understood my feelings, so I didn't reveal them. Even if I had, they would probably have thought I was a sentimental fool. But I had something to be sentimental about.

A couple of weeks later I had my interview with the General Administrator, David Webster. Imagine my surprise when he told me that the Sadler's Wells Ballet were losing their conductor and they had the Edinburgh Festival during September followed by a tour of Paris, Düsseldorf and Hamburg.[9] Would I

Dame Ninette de Valois, founder of the Royal Ballet.

help them out until a new conductor was appointed? I asked about opera, and David Webster promised me I would conduct opera as soon as the new man was found for ballet.[10] I then protested that I had never conducted ballet, except on one occasion at Sadler's Wells when Constant had an important outside engagement. Miss Ninette de Valois[11] also remembered that isolated occasion and she had always felt I was naturally a ballet conductor. In fact, then it was that I remembered Miss de Valois had tried to secure my services during the latter part of the war, but I had in all honesty refused the offer. This was different; here I was to be at Covent Garden with the distinct understanding that

---

9   In 1946, the Sadler's Wells Ballet became the resident ballet company of the newly reopened Royal Opera House in Covent Garden.

10 A notice in *The Stage* announced that 'Warwick Braithwaite has joined the musical staff of Covent Garden Opera, filling one of the vacancies caused by the recent resignations of Hugo Rignold, Geoffrey Corbett and Reginald Goodall.' *The Stage* 12 Aug 1948: 6.

11 Dame Ninette de Valois (1898–2001), founder of the Royal Ballet company.

I would go over to opera as soon as the new ballet conductor was found. I was not 'naturally' a ballet conductor and I had some misgivings about it, but when it was put to me by David Webster that I would be helping them out of a great difficulty, I reluctantly consented.

On the other hand, this was something new for me, and I always liked breaking new ground. Ballet was the only aspect of conducting I had never done before – with the one exception already mentioned. I had conducted all kinds of music including symphonies, operas, oratorios, concertos, and even in my early BBC days, light opera and revue. Now I was to add something quite new.

I found the ballet company a most delightful troupe to work with. The company was well-organised: they did what they were told by those in authority. They worked very hard indeed and deserved their great success. I found the principals – Margot Fonteyn, Moira Shearer, Beryl Grey, Pamela May and the numerous young ballerinas – most willing to help me all they could. If I made a mistake in tempi (which I often did in the early days), they were most sympathetic and understanding. The principal men, Michael Soames, Robert Helpmann, Frederick Ashton, Léonide Rassine, Alexander Grant[12] and others too numerous to mention, were hard-working, delightful companions on the various tours we did, and everybody made me feel absolutely happy. No wonder in such an atmosphere I was able to learn how to accommodate myself quickly to the especial difficulties of balletic art. Immersed in learning more than a dozen ballets in a week's rehearsal for the Edinburgh Festival, I had no time to think of other things, and with the congenial atmosphere and the invaluable help of Joseph Shadwick, the leader of the Covent Garden Orchestra (who knew more about ballet than anyone), I think I made a fairly useful debut in my new line of business. In the fortnight at Edinburgh, I went through the fire every night and emerged in a better state of mind than my fears had allowed.

After Edinburgh I did a week at the Davis Theatre, Croydon and the following week I was in Paris with the company at the Théâtre des Champs Elysées. Here, things weren't so comfortable, and on one occasion I threw the only other tantrum in my life. It was all so silly, but nevertheless serious at the time, that I wonder now why I made such a ridiculous fuss. The details don't matter now, but with Constant Lambert looking on (I had begged de Valois to ask him to go to Paris with me), I put on my hat and coat and angrily made for the stage door and a return to London. Luckily for me, de Valois met me and, in some magical way, stopped the tornado that was going on in my mind. She persuaded me to go back and, like a lamb, I swallowed my feelings. After a break, I continued rehearsing. I can still see Margot Fonteyn, Beryl Grey and

---

12 Alexander Grant (1925–2011), distinguished New Zealand-born dancer.

a few others of the company gazing at me in a way approaching admiration. Afterwards, Margot told me that she was positively delighted to see me show such temperament, as no-one had ever done it before and everything was too much accepted in the company.

From Paris, where our reception was a bit lukewarm (possibly because we were at the theatre of the ballet company of that city, and they had not been invited to Covent Garden when visiting London), we travelled to Düsseldorf. Here we completely captivated the German audience. It was the same at Hamburg, where we had the finest orchestra in Europe to play with, the NWDR Symphony Orchestra.[13]

While in Hamburg my many friends from the Philharmonic Orchestra came to see me. Herr Mangan, the elegant librarian, presented me with yet another set of batons, and I was invited by my pianist, Eugen Jochum, to the final rehearsal of Fürtwangler's Second Symphony, conducted by the composer. Jochum and I followed the whole rehearsal from a manuscript full score. I met Fürtwangler after the rehearsal and it was interesting to see the way he would listen, but say very little. The most eloquent part of Fürtwangler was his deep set pale blue eyes, dreamy yet intense. I found the Second Symphony a most interesting and vital work, and I wonder that Fürtwangler doesn't have it performed over here.[14]

I visited the Staatsoper, which I had not seen since the end of the war, and found all the rubble cleared away from the auditorium and seats for 600 people on the stage itself where, in the meantime, opera is still being performed. I also met Herr Schulz, the Stage Manager of the Deutsches Schauspielhaus where, with the Sadler's Wells Opera, I had performed in those three months after the War. Herr Schulz brought me a parcel, and in it was some laundry that I had failed to collect three years earlier! Altogether my second visit to Hamburg brought many happy memories back again, and after seeing Herr Ruch, the Intendant of the Opera, with Jochum, I left happier still in the knowledge that I had been promised some performances during the following season.

Back to London, where there was still no ballet conductor to take my place. In the meantime, I began to feel that Rankl had become impatient that I had not been available for opera. In fact, he said so on one occasion, remarking that whenever he wanted me, I was always with the ballet. Yet when I was released

---

13 The orchestra of the German radio broadcaster, Nordwestdeutscher Rundfunk (NWDR), was founded in 1945. After the NWDR's splitting into Norddeutscher Rundfunk and Westdeutscher Rundfunk in 1955/56, the orchestra was renamed the NDR Sinfonieorchester. It is now called the NDR Elbphilharmonie Orchester.

14 A compact disc recording of Fürtwangler's Symphony no. 2 was made by the BBC Symphony Orchestra conducted by Alfred Walter, at the BBC Maida Vale Studio, London, on 23–24 January 1992. The performance was issued on the Marco Polo label.

from the ballet, he found another excuse not to use me; he felt I would not do the operas he had done in exactly the same way. When I pointed out that this was too much to expect of any conductor, he replied that Gellhorn (his assistant),[15] managed to do this quite well.

At last, I suggested to David Webster that Robert Irving[16] should be approached for the ballet conducting position. It took a long time for this to happen, but I knew that Irving was very keen about ballet. Before this happened, I had been pecking away at both Rankl and Webster about conducting opera. Rankl then gave me a real armful. He gave me a performance of *Die Meistersinger* and *Aida* in the same week. That was the week I did five performances, including three of ballet as well. Of course, I had no orchestral rehearsals for the two operas. By this time, I was determined to show Rankl that I could do work even without orchestral rehearsal, and although I was both angry and nervous about doing such a thing at Covent Garden of all places, *Die Meistersinger* was a triumph for me and the press gave me extraordinarily good notices, whereas Rankl had had some indifferent ones and a few bad ones.[17] *Aida* went the same way, and this did not improve the situation between Rankl and myself.

My next tour with the ballet was to Florence for the May Festival,[18] and I suggested to David Webster that after the season I should leave the ballet company for good. Irving had taken over Prokofiev's *Cinderella*, of which I had done the first performances, and I felt that I had done all that could have been expected of me. So, for the last few weeks of the season, I acted the part of disinterested onlooker.

The only disagreeable thing which occurred while I was with the ballet company was an incident with Massine[19] who came for a few guest performances. At the rehearsal of the Rossini-Respighi ballet *La boutique fantasque*, I had taken the 'Tarantella' at our usual pace, but he asked me to slow it down for him and Danilova, who was the other guest. This I did at the performance, but apparently it was a bit too slow. Possibly I wanted to err on the right side and stuck to the tempo which I had set at the beginning. It wasn't my tempo but the tempo Massine asked for at the sketchy rehearsal that morning.

I confess that this business of changing tempi for particular dancers has always worried me, because it seems so unmusical. A piece of music has a

---

15 Peter Gellhorn (1912–2004), German-born conductor, composer and pianist.

16 Robert Irving (1913–1991), English conductor, associated mostly with ballet.

17 '...the performance as a whole was most pleasurable. The conductor, Warwick Braithwaite, gave his singers time to breathe and to spread themselves in their parts, and each member of the company now seems to know what Wagner expects of him, musically and dramatically.' *The Times* (23 February 1949), 6.

18 This was the twelfth Maggio Musicale Fiorentino. Sadler's Wells Ballet performed eight times over a ten-day period (20-30 May 1949). The repertoire included Prokofiev's *Cinderella*.

19 Léonide Massine (1896-1979), Russian choreographer and ballet dancer.

tempo which is inherent in the work itself, and when a dancer asks me to alter this fundamental tempo, my whole idea of tempo can become fogged. Perhaps that happened on this occasion, but I am sure that Massine thought I had done it on purpose because he insisted someone else conduct for him. David Webster commiserated, pointing out that it was not worth bothering about. After that incident, and the way Massine reacted, I thought him a little rat and not worth thinking about. Danilova on the other hand, was always charming and took infinite pains to show me her way of doing things. Apart from this little incident with Massine, I had a delightful eight months with the ballet company, and we have remained friends since. I usually go to their first nights and several of them, especially Margot, come to my first nights of an opera.

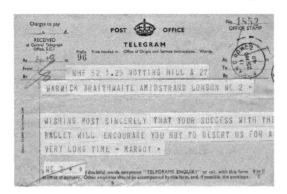

Telegram from Dame Margot Fonteyn,
25 November 1948.

I had wonderful memories of the last tour to Florence with the Ballet. We were to perform in the Teatro Comunale, and on the first night of the festival, we were guests of the Intendant, Signor Volto, at a performance of Monteverdi's *Orfeo*. Princess Margaret was touring Italy at the time and was to be present. All Florence was in a state of excitement to see our princess, and every woman in Florence who could borrow, buy, steal or pay for a beautiful evening gown was there. I have never seen such a mass of beautiful frocks and colours – or women who could wear their clothes as if they were part of them. As Princess Margaret came in, she walked through ranks of admiring and beautifully dressed young women who had come to show her how Florentine society could dress. The gasp of astonishment when the princess appeared in a glorious, yet perfectly simple, white evening dress, walking with a most queenly tread, was a tribute to her undoubted success. It was an unforgettable royal entry, and every woman present felt the impact of Princess Margaret's personality.

I had made the journey by plane to Florence via Milan. We were too high over the Alps and came down in Milan too quickly. The outcome was that I became deaf for two days, and Robert Irving took over my rehearsals. The performances themselves were good, and as usual Sadler's Wells Ballet had a great success. As far as I was concerned, every leisure moment of the three weeks in Florence was filled by visiting the Pitti Palace and seeing what I could of the art treasures of that city. I also took the fast electric train to Rome, and although I only had a day and a half, I mapped out my sightseeing so that I made the most of the short time at my disposal.

I had not been to Rome before. The journey down the banks of the Arno River, where there were still scars left by the Allies' march through Italy, recalled the horrors of the last war. In Rome I didn't waste any time. On arrival I fixed up a room near the site of the new railway terminus and started off for St Peter's and the Vatican. I could only find time to walk through the basilica and took in very quickly the dimensions and marks on the floor which are purported to show how much bigger St Peter's was than any other church. From there I went into the Vatican. I knew I couldn't see everything so I chose the Sistine Chapel and the several rooms containing the Raphael paintings. The Sistine Chapel I estimated would take me 30 minutes, but I was there at least one and a half hours and wanted to stay even longer. What struck me as so wonderful, apart from the ceiling paintings, were the perspective paintings of the cornices of the ceiling arches. These are not architectural pieces but painted cornices and the lifelike and real shape in perspective is most deceiving. I may be wrong, but I thought I could even detect shadows, and yet when I walked a few yards to the other side with my eyes on a particular arch, I thought the shadow disappeared. The difference of style between the ceiling paintings and the wall behind where the altar would be, was most marked. But one must remember that the ceiling was painted when Michelangelo was a young man, and the wall when he was an old man. It was not so much a change of style as the difference between youth and old age. The Raphael rooms were simply entrancing. To see these paintings after having studied them from copies was like coming out of a hothouse into the fresh air. I spent all the rest of that afternoon in the Vatican gardens.

Next morning, I was up early and spent hours wandering about the Forum, after which I climbed the various levels of the Colosseum. The Arch of Constantine is one of the wonders of Rome; it looks as if it might have been built only a few years ago, such is its state of preservation. I saw as much of Rome as I could, except for the Victor Emmanuel II Monument. The colossal size of this is its chief virtue, but for the rest it looks like an outsize wedding cake. But I would be doing the Italians an injustice if I didn't pay respect to the generosity of their tribute to the man who welded the Italian republics into one nation. It may not be beautiful as a monument, but the gratitude is overflowing in its immensity.[20]

I was loath to leave Rome as there was so much to see, and after one more walk through the Forum, peopling it in my imagination with Caesar, Brutus,

---

20 Had Braithwaite visited the monument he would have discovered that it housed a museum and the tomb of an unknown soldier from WWI.

Cassius and the like, I hurried to the station. I think I got every ounce out of my short visit but it has whetted my appetite for a longer stay in the 'Eternal City'.[21]

Back in Florence I attended a party given in honour of Sadler's Wells Ballet at a villa overlooking the city. I was further entranced by the millions of fireflies which flitted about in the trees below. I had never seen fireflies before, and indeed scarcely believed they really existed. But to see millions of them alight as soon as night came on was simply delightful and fairylike.

I spent a few days in Switzerland on the way home, taking in three days of walking from Montreux to Lausanne, and arrived back in London, happy in the knowledge that I was to go over to opera completely the following season.[22]

---

21 Rome was first called 'The Eternal City' (in Latin, Urbs Aeterna) by the Roman poet Tibullus in the 1st century BC.

22 Braithwaite fails to mention that in a churchyard at Vevey, near Lausanne, he came across the graves of three NZ servicemen, and offered to contact their families to reassure them that the graves were well-maintained. *Gisborne Herald* (17 March 1949).

TWENTY-FIVE

COVENT GARDEN EXPOSED; BAYREUTH REVISITED

September 1949 came along and Covent Garden rehearsals commenced in earnest. I was to do *Boris Godunov* with Boris Christoff who, so he told me, had been a schoolteacher in Sofia and gave it up for opera. When he came to us, he had been performing in opera for just three years.[1]

The version of *Boris* that Rankl had done at Covent Garden the previous season was one of the original versions, and although I wanted to do the Rimsky-Korsakov version, after a lot of argument – the biggest of which was that there was not time to learn a new version with a different translation and with Rimsky's musical alterations – we adhered to tradition.[2] But someone had blundered, because when Christoff arrived he went into a Chaliapinesque rage and refused to sing the original version. I was faced with a problem and, after consultation with David Webster, I thought of the expedient of having the few pages of the Rimsky Korsakov version which concern Boris, photographed and inserted in the score and parts. So *that* difficulty was bridged over quite easily, although the hotchpotch was not by any means desirable. Christoff caused us still further trouble by refusing to make entrances at the places

---

1 Boris Christoff (1914–1993), Bulgarian bass and one of the finest artists of his generation. Christoff had made his operatic debut as Colline in *La bohème* at Reggio Calabria on 12 March 1946.

2 During the previous season's new production of *Boris Godunov*, the title role had been sung by Paolo Silveri. It was also the occasion of Peter Brook's directorial debut with the company. Mussorgsky's opera exists in an original (1869) and revised (1872) version. Other composers, notably Rimsky-Korsakov and Shostakovich produced 'improved' versions, and these were performed for much of the twentieth century. Mussorgsky's 1872 version has returned to favour in recent decades.

in our production settled upon by the producer, and wanted all manner of alterations in the position of the stage properties to suit himself. In many ways I could sympathise with Christoff as he had learnt the Rimsky version, and had performed *Boris* on the continent with very much the same orthodox scenery in vogue for most productions of that work. An appearance for him at Covent Garden, en route to the Metropolitan, was of the utmost importance and he was determined to fight the Covent Garden producer, Peter Brook, every step of the way. There was a time, about four days before the performance, when it looked like it would have to be cancelled. Christoff was adamant and Nowakowski,[3] a Polish bass already with the company was asked to stand by. I did the whole of the last orchestra rehearsal of the Nursery scene with Christoff and at the end of it, although David Webster congratulated me on having come through the whole beastly affair with credit and without losing my composure, I expressed the hope that I would never have to do so again.[4]

This vexed question of Mussorgsky's *Boris Godunov* is a tiresome one. Let me say at the outset that there is no question of Mussorgsky's genius or originality, but the question that looms very large in the theatre is the practicability of the original version. The musicologist will find all the places where Rimsky-Korsakov has changed Mussorgsky's modulations, some quite unnecessarily, and will fill pages of vitriolic condemnation of these changes. If it were a case of sheer vandalism and unwarranted interference with a composer's work, I would agree with the musicologist. But there are so many places in the original where the wayward originality of the composer makes all sorts of impractical difficulties in performance, and however much time one spends in getting the composer's ideas to fit practical situations, every now and then a performer finds he or she is really up against it. To take one instance only: at the end of the revolutionary scene when the large chorus, soldiers and horses have to be got off the stage, Mussorgsky only gives the poor producer four bars to do so. If the chorus begins to leave sooner, there are difficulties of ensemble in the final few bars. Rimsky has elongated the exit music for eight bars without in any way damaging the original and, with his practical sense of the theatre, has solved a situation that in the original was well-nigh impossible on a big stage.

The fact of the matter is that the opera *Boris Godunov* has been a success since Chaliapin did the Rimsky version, and every production of Mussorgsky's

---

3   Marian Nowakowski (1912–2000), Polish bass. He performed with Braithwaite on at least 17 occasions between 1944 and 1950, including *La bohème*, *Die Meistersinger* and *Aida* at Covent Garden, concerts with the Scottish Orchestra, and song recordings with the LSO.

4   'Indeed, after Mr Christoff, the next honour goes to Mr Warwick Braithwaite for a very taut and dramatic reading of this long and ramificatory score.' *The Times* (21 November 1949), 7. The author and critic Harold Rosenthal wrote, '…Braithwaite really distinguished himself in the pit.' Harold Rosenthal, *Two Centuries of Opera at Covent Garden* (London: Putnam, 1958), 597.

original, despite a few eulogistic notices from musicologists, begins to lose its audience. With all his originality, Mussorgsky could have stepped down occasionally to meet the practicalities of the opera house. The fact is that he did not. Rimsky-Korsakov has been called every kind of name for his version, but anyone can read his preface to the final scene of his second version to understand the time, trouble and sincerity with which he undertook the revision. Rimsky-Korsakov was a busy composer himself, and his labour of friendship and love meant valuable time taken from his own periods of work. He orchestrated the 600 pages from beginning to end, and a man does not take on such a colossal task, unpaid, unless he is doing a labour of love.

Where would *Khovanshchina* be if Rimsky-Korsakov hadn't scored it for full orchestra? Mussorgsky left this work mainly in piano sketches. Rimsky has rescued it for the opera house by considerable expenditure of valuable time lost to himself.

The solution of this vexed question of *Boris* may be in the use of the Shostakovich version which I tried to get for the opera house in 1960.[5] From all accounts, Shostakovich's version is mainly a reorchestration with few, if any, deviations from the composer's own version. Until this is heard I would ask musicologists, purists and others to refrain from their condemnation of Rimsky-Korsakov.

The other work I was to conduct that season was Massenet's *Manon*. Like many British musicians, I had been warned off Massenet by listening too much to musicologists and university professors. It was with a feeling of treading an unknown musical country that I commenced studying *Manon* – not that I didn't know Massenet's music, but I was less familiar with his operas. I had always adored *Werther*, and *Thaïs* had appealed to me many years ago in Paris with Jeritza in the title role,[6] but such is the power of insidious propaganda that Massenet's operas were tucked away in the recesses of my mind as works to be looked at some time or other.

It was with real joy that I rediscovered *Manon* for myself. A more complete operatic composer than Massenet does not exist. The test of an operatic composer is that every dramatic situation on the stage should call forth appropriate music. The tender lyrical moments must tell; the poignant moments must strike to the heart; all variations of mood must be reflected in the music. The test is how well the composer copes musically with these infinite variations. Massenet comes out of them all with flying colours, and if only the artists concerned would study the music deeply enough, they would find everything there. Massenet

---

5   Shostakovich's version, based on a conflation by Pavel Lamm of Mussorgsky's two versions, was commissioned by the Bolshoi Theatre in 1949. Due to the German invasion of Russia, the premiere was delayed until 1959.

6   Maria Jeritza (1887–1982), distinguished Czech soprano.

has a subtlety of phrasing that is quite entrancing, and if very sensitive folk decry some banal moments in his operas, let them think of that most sensitive composer, Debussy, who admired Massenet's music endlessly. If you don't like banalities in Massenet's music, turn to Verdi, and see how wretched they can sound. Even at his worst, Massenet is a very accomplished composer. By some subtle touch of orchestral alchemy, he can make an ordinary tune sound full of grace; he can sing about the most ordinary things, and he can infuse beauty into wretchedness. But by far his greatest achievement is the way he uses his material. Nothing is forgotten. The 'Moonlight' music, tender and nostalgic, of the first scene of *Werther* can become the basis of the tragedy of the final scene. The 'Méditation' in *Thaïs* can become the vehicle of the impassioned final duet. Don't despise the 'Méditation'; it says what it is supposed to say, no more. But in the last scene, the composer bends this tune to his own accomplished will and things we never dreamed of inherent in such a contemplative piece become the background of the tremendously exciting ecstasy of the last few pages of the score. It is my ambition to conduct a well-rehearsed performance of *Thaïs* one day. I am convinced that this will never happen, because the fashion at Covent Garden is to bring over a foreign conductor, and for Massenet it will certainly be a Frenchman.[7] I once heard *Manon* at the Opéra-Comique. It was conducted by a well-known French conductor, and it was no more like Massenet than *Charley's Aunt*.[8]

My first Manon was Elisabeth Schwarzkopf,[9] who gave the part a most beautiful and original interpretation. Miss Schwarzkopf had the wonderful gift of a most sensitive artistry, and by her movements and facial expression she was enabled to suggest the young romantic and clever little girl of the story. As well as this, she had a remarkable gift of musical memory and was a very fast learner. Sometimes I used to wish she wasn't so conscious of her gift of quick study.

The Des Grieux was that strange wayward tenor, Walter Midgley.[10] Midgely could do the most amazing things vocally and there is no doubt he was, in his

---

7 Braithwaite did conduct two studio performances of excerpts from *Thaïs* for broadcast on the BBC Home Service. The first took place on 7 January 1951 with Joan Hammond, Marion Studholme, Elizabeth Eriksson, Barbara Howitt and Marko Rothmuller. The second was on 27 April 1952 with Hammond, Sheila Rex and Dennis Noble. On both occasions he conducted the BBC Opera Orchestra.

8 *Charley's Aunt*, a farce in three acts by Brandon Thomas. It broke all records with an original London run of 1,466 performances from 1893 to 1896.

9 Elisabeth Schwarzkopf (1915–2006), German soprano and teacher, considered one of the greatest artists of the twentieth century. She was particularly admired for her performances of lieder, Viennese operetta, and the operas of Mozart and Richard Strauss.

10 Walter Midgley (1912–1980), English tenor who sang leading roles at the Royal Opera House from 1948 to 1953, including 11 performances with Braithwaite. They worked together again in a performance of *La bohème* for Welsh National Opera on 5 May 1959.

peculiar way, worth his weight in gold to our opera house. But alas he would not listen or learn from anyone. I was responsible in a small measure for his return to Covent Garden and I suppose David Webster thought that because I had tackled difficult foreign artists and succeeded where others failed, I would be just the man for Midgley. I was just the man alright, but in another way.

It was a great pity, for Midgley sang very well. Curiously enough during the early performances of *Manon*, I only had one point of difference with him and that was the last cadence of the well-known 'Dream Song' in Act Two. Midgley wanted to rewrite Massenet's ending, mainly because he had heard some tenor do it that way on a gramophone record. When I pointed out that it was not Massenet's ending, and that it was a bad thing to imitate the faults of others, things quietened down a bit. The following season the point came up again, as well as other foolish ideas. This time Midgley insisted, with little grace, that he must have his way or else! I think that David Webster and others did their utmost to placate him.

I had him for *Madama Butterfly* and *Tosca* too. Again, he wanted to pull Puccini's music about in the same sort of way. At last, the Opera House was faced with finding another tenor, but in the meantime there was only one thing to do, and that was to ask me to give up *Tosca*, which I did. *Manon*, by that time, was out of the repertoire, and another tenor[11] did Pinkerton in *Butterfly*, so that by giving up *Tosca*, Midgley and I never crossed one another's path again. My replacement conductor suffered in the same way, and when Midgley tried to tell David Webster which conductors he should have for the following season, that was the end of him.

Before I leave this affair, let me clear up the issue between soloists and conductors. There is no question in a conductor's mind as to the importance of the operatic soloist, who has to perform a most difficult task. The singer must not only perform everything from memory, but must act as well *and* remember exactly where to be at any given moment on the stage. By a system of elaborate and very often arduous rehearsals, the artist, both with the producer and the conductor, together and separately, goes through the role, and before the final rehearsal all doubtful points are cleared up. Differences of opinion do come about, and little friendly arguments and discussions occur, until either one or the other compromises or is won over by convincing reasons as to the correct interpretation. When an artist makes a mistake in the staging during performance the conductor, if he is any good at all, covers up the awkward moment because he knows by experience that such mistakes are quite unintentional. A conductor will often give way when an artist wants

---

11 James Johnston (1903–1991), Belfast-born, lyric tenor who had a very successful career in leading roles at Sadler's Wells and Covent Garden.

to do something unusual, as long as it is artistic and beautiful. Music can be stretched at the right moments without harm to the composer. As a rule, most artists ask the question 'Can I do such and such a thing at this point?' The conductor looks at the score, sizes up the possibilities and, if it doesn't offend good taste or alter the composer's clear intention, he gives permission. Most artists regard the conductor as the person who, by experience, knows what is possible and what is not. The conductor has to control perhaps 96 or so instrumentalists at the same time and, depending on the intricacy of the accompaniment, is the only one able to decide any deviation from the normal. These problems usually sort themselves out, but the more serious deviations from the composer's own notation are quite a different matter. I am not a purist by any means, but one thing I cannot tolerate is the placing of oneself above the composer. To take the case once again of the last bar of the 'Dream Song' in Act II of *Manon*. Massenet has written an entrancing and sensitive harmonic suspension, falling down in a cadence of great charm. To alter this to the most ordinary 'perfect' cadence is robbing the composer, and the public, of one of the subtleties of composition.

It doesn't take much imagination to realize that Midgley was doing himself out of a most beautiful cadence. I pleaded with him in vain; I tried cajolery and I tried tact. I sat down at the piano and showed him the difference between the two endings, but he was adamant. I tried trick conducting: that is to say, I wilfully deceived the singer (who wasn't looking at me in any case), and sometimes, without him knowing it, gained my point. But he had a friend in the audience, especially charged with watching for this moment, and it all blew up again. Midgley eventually began to sing so quietly that he couldn't be heard above the pianissimo of the orchestra, and again there was trouble. The outcome of this and indeed, of any similar contretemps, is always fatal to the interests of a singer. An orchestra begins to groan when a singer of such a wayward nature begins to open his mouth.

How different to the really great artist Ludwig Weber, for whom I conducted three performances of *Boris*.[12] Here was an artist of worldwide experience and repute whose respect for the composer was absolutely sincere. Weber is perhaps today (1952), the greatest of all operatic basses. His performance of Gurnemanz in *Parsifal* at Bayreuth last year was entirely superb. Yet I never experienced one moment of trouble either at rehearsal or performance. Anything he suggested was always inherent in the composer's music.

Victoria de los Angeles, who did several performances of *Manon* and superb performances of *Madama Butterfly* and *La bohème* with me, was in the

---

12 Ludwig Weber (1899–1974), Austrian bass, noted for his Wagnerian roles. He was a regular at Bayreuth from 1951 to 1962.

same category.[13] Schwarzkopf again, was superbly conscious of the composer's music. Even Paolo Silveri, who sang Escamillo with me, and was inclined to try his hand at anything, always toed the line when the composer's ideas were pointed out to him.

All these artists have a respect for the conductor's work and they realize, one and all, that the conductor has made a study of these questions and has spent all his conducting life dealing with them. The conductor is the teacher, and artists can learn much from him. This is not to say that a conductor doesn't learn a lot from a great artist. Of course he does, and such learning is added to the sum total of his store of knowledge.

*

My advent at Covent Garden had turned out to be very successful. The press gave me very good notices, and all in particular mentioned that I produced good sounds from the orchestra and allowed the artists to sing their music and express themselves with a degree of artistic freedom. This was not a surprise to me, as this side of my conducting was already well known before I went to Covent Garden. I knew that I had a feeling and an understanding for music and drama, but difficulties of an internal nature cropped up which made me despondent.

I began to fret about never being able to discuss my problems with Rankl. Works were allotted to me, and rehearsals planned, without any consultation whatsoever. I would find that I was committed to an opera with an already-decided cast, and often with inadequate rehearsals allocated to me. I tried to beat down the secrecy by suggesting a weekly meeting of the conductors and key members of the staff. For a while, after much agitation, such meetings did take place, but not before everything had already been arranged. Time was wasted in extraneous matters not connected with either my own problems or musical matters other than Rankl's own rehearsals. I would wait until all these matters were decided upon and then, as a rule, Rankl would dismiss the gathering, usually with the excuse that he was due for a rehearsal. I begged Rankl to give me some of the German operas, but he always used the old excuse that he was late for a rehearsal to avoid discussing the matter.

Gellhorn was in charge of the rehearsal sheet. In effect this meant that after Rankl had demanded his rehearsals and Gellhorn put down his own, there was very little time left for me. If I tried to anticipate this state of things by sending

---

13 Victoria de los Ángeles (1923–2005), Catalan operatic soprano and recitalist, remembered for her magnificent recordings, including *La bohème, La vida breve, Manon, Werther, Faust, Carmen, La traviata, Suor Angelica,* and *Madama Butterfly.*

in my list of rehearsals in good time, excuses were made that, because of Rankl's rehearsals (which were *assumed* to have priority), my rehearsals were either cut down or omitted altogether.

I struggled along under these circumstances against tremendous odds, and continually drew upon my knack of getting good performances without adequate rehearsals. But occasionally I would 'slip up' in a musical sense, and keep things together between orchestra and singer by doing violence to my own musical feelings. On one such occasion, during a performance of Act 1 of *La bohème* with de los Angeles – of which the only rehearsal was done at a hall in North London without scenery, props, or the Marcello (who was required for one of Rankl's rehearsals) – I held on to a note for the sake of the soprano, who was making her first appearance at Covent Garden and who had not seen the stage or the scenery. Lord Harewood, in the magazine *Opera*, complained that I made a pause out of a *tenuto*. Already feeling sore about the inadequate rehearsal for such an artist as de los Angeles, I did what I had never done before – I wrote to Harewood pointing out that when a single rehearsal is of such a scrappy nature, the conductor is forced to play safe and simply keep singer and orchestra together. I had a reply from Harewood's assistant, Harold Rosenthal, who went so far as to say that he thoroughly sympathised with my situation. When Harewood eventually replied, he simply pointed out that a critic was not concerned with the lack of rehearsal; all he was concerned with was what he heard as a member of the audience. The reply was not altogether unexpected and there was no answer to it.

I once more tried to break down the internal frustration I was experiencing inside the Opera House, but I could see that the 'Magic Circle' (as I christened it) in which only Rankl, Gellhorn and Rankl's secretary, Patrick Terry, were admitted, was of such a secret nature that the more I struggled against it the more trouble I brought upon myself. I really felt an outsider and believe I was deliberately left outside discussions which were vital to me. The General Administrator, David Webster, was very nice and confessed that everything was not as it should be, and promised to make alterations which would clarify matters. I believe he really *did* try, but he was in a predicament because Rankl was, after all, the Musical Director, and had been appointed as such by the Covent Garden Trust.

The last attempt which David Webster made to help me was over the production of *Butterfly*. Rankl's name was, as usual, down for the first performance. Under the circumstances, I had come to accept this situation as being irrevocable, and I looked about for other crumbs in the season's list of operas. At a reception given to the Ballet company, which had returned from its first triumphant tour of America, David Webster took me aside and told me that I would be conducting *Butterfly*. Rankl's secretary, Terry, in the most unctuous manner, congratulated me on the news, as if I had never conducted *Butterfly* before![14]

The next morning Terry phoned me at home and announced, in a sepulchral tone, that I would not be conducting *Butterfly*, but that Rankl would. Strange goings on! I had nothing to say, but sat down and wrote a short letter to David Webster in which I posed the enigma: 'The Administrator says I am conducting *Butterfly*, but Rankl's secretary says I am not. Where am I?' Four days later, David Webster sent for me and announced that I was certainly going to conduct *Butterfly*, but to say nothing about it for 48 hours. Two evenings later, I was listening to a performance of *Der Rosenkavalier* conducted by Gellhorn and, by accident, ran into both Rankl and Terry. Terry whispered into my ear that he was so glad I was to conduct *Butterfly*, but by that time I couldn't have cared less!

I met Rankl in the Foyer during the interval. He, with perfect mid-European charm, invited me to drink with him and spoke about working together much more in the future. All futile empty trash, for he saw to it that we never had the smallest opportunity of ever getting together. The whole thing was most sickening and I am sure this, and other suchlike frustrations, were responsible for a minor physical breakdown which hit me some months later. I thought I was tough, and I really believe I am, but continual frustration is bound to have an effect on one's physique. Everything is connected in the body and I am only glad that a minor attack of varicose veins in my right leg was the only uncomfortable result of the frustration I had gone through.

I remember seeing David Webster by accident one day and he asked me how I was getting on. I answered in a non-committal fashion and I remember he enjoined me to see that I got the rehearsals I needed. A vain hope! In case the reader may think I am inclined to overstress my needs, let me repeat that virtually every opera I conducted at Covent Garden was unrehearsed (perhaps with the exception of *Butterfly*, whose rehearsals were originally arranged for Rankl), and by that, I mean I hardly ever had uninterrupted or complete rehearsals. This is no exaggeration. For *Tosca* I never had the Scarpia, Tosca and Cavaradossi together before the final orchestral rehearsal. I never saw the choirboys until the dress rehearsal, and their scene with the Sacristan is a difficult one. When I took over *Aida* from Goodall, I had just one orchestral rehearsal. Rankl came to me on that occasion and told me that I must not take the March in the Triumphal Scene so fast, whereas before, it had been a dirge! As the personnel of the orchestra and the chorus changed slightly from season to season, one orchestra rehearsal of three hours for a work like *Carmen*, for

---

14 Braithwaite had conducted *Madama Butterfly* on at least 30 occasions prior to this incident, and went on to conduct another 40 performances during the rest of his career.

instance, was quite inadequate. Both *Carmen* and *Aida* take three hours in performance and I couldn't get through rehearsals for these works in the three hours allotted. *La bohème* was easier, although difficult orchestrally, but three hours only allowed me to clear up a few points. There was no question of me giving the works my own individual stamp; I had just to get through! This I didn't mind if I had some compensation, such as adding a new work to the repertoire. I think the best work I did was when we changed to the Rimsky-Korsakov version of *Boris*. Here I had fairly adequate rehearsal and proved that I could do well. *Butterfly* was quite adequate and *Tosca* would have been fine if the tenor had rehearsed with me. Repeated requests to Rankl to let me do some of the German composers' works met with the blank refusal already spoken of.

My third season opened even more miserably. Various operas which I was to conduct were scheduled to have their only orchestral rehearsal as many as three weeks before the performance. I don't know who managed this schedule, but if it was Webster, then my outspoken comments proved my undoing. From that moment I had lost the day, and when I expressed my annoyance and criticism to someone outside the company, I did myself an injustice because this same person became a member of the Covent Garden Trust about that time, and I presume our conversation was repeated to David Webster. So I carried on doing my work with a very heavy heart. Signs were not wanting that Webster had lost confidence in me and I had only to wait for the blow to fall. I had lost something of my eagerness. I had attended rehearsals punctually and had given of my best. I was on the best of terms with the artists, orchestra and chorus and with most of the musical staff. A conductor must be obeyed musically, but an order in an opera house can best be made as a request on the basis of a musical brotherhood.

That season I had done more performances than either Rankl or Gellhorn, but when this was publicised in Harewood's magazine, *Opera*, it was the signal for some changes in the conducting of certain operas. The following season Rankl took both *Carmen* and *La bohème* away from me. *Carmen* was eventually taken over by Erich Kleiber,[15] but when I enquired why *La bohème* was taken from me I was told that Rankl had decided I conducted it badly.

In this I know I am on dangerous ground; dangerous in the sense that if I disagree with this verdict and give reasons for it, the reader may draw the conclusion that I am entirely lacking in self-criticism. When I took over *La bohème* in my first season, I found that Rankl's interpretation was entirely un-

---

15 Erich Kleiber (1890–1956), Austrian-born conductor, considered one the finest of the twentieth century. He appeared as guest conductor at Covent Garden during Rankl's last season and remained until 1952. Hopes were high that Kleiber (or possibly Beecham, Kempe or Pritchard), would succeed Rankl, but no decision was made until 1954 when it was announced that Rafael Kubelík would become Music Director. Kubelík held the post from 1955 until 1958.

Italian and un-vocal. Several points he had missed which even a novice could have avoided. These were musical errors, so when I took over this work all these matters were corrected and *La bohème* took on its own proper shape. Rankl told me that my opening of Act II was too fast and should have been beaten in two. What right had he to tell me how I should do the work? None! He simply could not bear the thought of someone on the music staff at Covent Garden having their own ideas.

My interpretations of *La bohème*, *Tosca* and *Madama Butterfly* were amply verified by the Italian conductor, my friend Franco Capuana, who has been a guest at Covent Garden this present season.[16] Capuana's interpretations of these works have been close to my own in all the details that matter. Rankl completely ignored, or didn't take the trouble to find out, that I had gone to the fountainhead many times in my life to hear these and other works in the country of their origin. I went to Milan for Italian operas, Paris for French operas: Berlin, Cologne, Leipzig, Frankfurt, Nuremberg, Bayreuth and Munich for German works: and Vienna for a mixture of all. I didn't waste time in these places and I only went to them very largely to listen to opera and take notes. I learnt these works that way. Rankl probably had only learnt Italian works in Germany, where tempi in such works as a general rule are much slower.

In all the above, the reader can be assured I am telling the absolute truth. At Covent Garden I fell badly between a Musical Director who feared for his reputation and position, and an Administrator who was in a difficult situation. The cry went up within the Trust, headed by Harewood, that Covent Garden must hire an Italian conductor for Italian works. I believe Capuana was asked to do the first production of *Tosca* but could not. I had to do it, and received very good notices from the press. The following season Capuana was engaged but he was allocated even less rehearsal time than I had, and every opera he did was well-nigh a disgrace to the opera house. *Tosca* had such notices as 'why did Capuana bulldoze his way through this opera?' I knew the reasons, which naturally gave me a sympathetic satisfaction, proving conclusively that no conductor can pull off a work without adequate rehearsal. I could do it even better than Capuana because, for one thing, I knew the singers, chorus, and orchestra and the general lay of the operatic land, and could speak to my artists in their own language. Capuana could not speak a word of English. I am not decrying Capuana's gifts in saying this because I know his work at La Scala, where I have heard him many times, and I admire his grasp of the operas he conducts. But no conductor can make bricks without straw, and the lack of straw affected Capuana's work at Covent Garden to his detriment much more than mine.

---

16 Braithwaite is writing in 1952. He shared conducting of the seven performances of *La bohème* with Franco Capuana, who also led performances of *Il trovatore*, *Madama Butterfly*, *Tosca* and *Rigoletto* in the same 1951–1952 season.

David Webster, probably alarmed at signs of dissatisfaction among the musical and production staff over the poor schedule of rehearsals and the bad management in the order of operas to be performed at the beginning of the 1950–1951 season, called a meeting of those affected. A description of the discussion at this meeting is most revealing, and I am sure he never realized, until then, the strength of the dissatisfaction among his staff. At this meeting, presided over by Webster, were the following key members of the staff: Karl Rankl, myself, Peter Gellhorn, Patrick Terry, Cliff Clifford (stage manager), Henry Robinson (stage director), John Sullivan (scene production), Douglas Robinson (chorus master), Christopher West (resident producer). We had been asked by Webster to work out our own ideas as to how the opening of the season could be better planned.

I had worked out my own scheme and so had West, and we found them almost identical when they were compared. I had tried to get the others together to present a considered plan to David Webster but everyone seemed unwilling, or afraid, to do so. It didn't really matter as things turned out because David Webster didn't ask us for our plans. It was evident that everyone (except Rankl) had thought about the situation along the same lines, which proved conclusively to everybody (except Rankl) that the objections raised to the original schedule were sensible.

David Webster opened the proceedings by making a most extraordinary speech. He began by trying to prove, among other things, that rehearsals in an opera house such as Covent Garden could not reach the standard of La Scala (this was directed at me); that the Box Office dictated the standard; and that conductors wished for more rehearsals for their own personal satisfaction and pleasure! We were all dumbfounded by such a philistine statement, intended, I am sure, to hit us straight between the eyes and bludgeon all the fight out of us.

After these opening comments, Webster declared the meeting open. He asked for one of us to start off and, for a few seconds, no-one answered. But, as I had suffered most by the bad arrangements, I delivered myself of a few choice words, pointing out that to do an opera with the only orchestral rehearsal scheduled three weeks before the performance was not even allowing an opera half a chance of ever achieving a modicum of standard. I instanced *Manon* (orchestral rehearsal three weeks before performance), *Aida* (two weeks before), *Butterfly* (ten days before), and pointed out that to do a work that was new to the repertoire on the opening night of the season, meant that none of the other works could be rehearsed properly. There was only six hours a day for rehearsal, and with eleven other works to be got on to the stage with, in the case of some operas, new singers, new choristers and new personnel in every department of the orchestra, was madness. I finished my talk by using some strong words such as 'flinging on operas in this way was bad for the opera house and got us nowhere.'

Everybody (except Rankl) said more or less the same thing in turn. The Chorus Master told the meeting that he had often been alarmed at the way he sometimes had to send the chorus onto the stage only half-rehearsed. He blamed the new work (*The Flying Dutchman* – Rankl's production) at the beginning of the season for this state of affairs. On the musical side there was no doubt that if eleven operas were to be put into the repertoire in two weeks, a new production made it impossible for adequate rehearsal to be given to these. From everyone present this fact alone was of the utmost importance, and it had happened the previous season, when *Boris* and *The Olympians* had also put everything else out of joint. Webster had promised at the time that it wouldn't happen again, but it did with a vengeance.

Webster countered all these complaints by again pointing out that the box office was the most important thing in the opera house. Rankl and Terry supported David Webster to the full. Why? Let us take Rankl's position first of all. He had been criticised unmercifully in the press for nearly every performance he had done. He had the full support of David Webster for his policy of grabbing all the rehearsal time. He had been 'sitting pretty' all through and did not exert himself to see that I had enough rehearsal. David Webster had overridden him about Kleiber and also about who was to conduct *Butterfly*, and as a result his position was very precarious. He was a much more disappointed man than I was, and he resigned shortly afterwards from an intolerable position.

Patrick Terry, who had not the slightest idea of operatic standards, but who was first and foremost an office-seeker, was bound to support his superiors. I do not blame him for this, but another aspect of his intrusion into our affairs was solely actuated by his quite mistaken advocacy of Reginald Goodall and, as a result, his enmity (perhaps too strong a word) towards me. It didn't matter to Terry who was the better conductor. That is where friendship can be a foolish thing. Goodall will never be a *better* conductor because of this friendship; the seed of Goodall's faults are in his own peculiar nature. This applies to us all, for all of us have our faults which can, in the same way, spring to varying extents from our own natures. I am not blind to this obvious fact.

Peter Gellhorn, on the other hand, whether in the light of subsequent events or not, was entirely sincere in his opinions on these matters and presented his case with a clarity I very much envied. The stage and production staff were likewise quite open about their complaints as well. In fact, there was no doubt that we presented a formidable and almost unanswerable case, but the most we got from David Webster was the promise to consider our views. Gellhorn assured me that David Webster was the sort of person who would solve the problems in his own way. I only hoped so, but I feared that I had been too outspoken.

In the light of the above remarks and the description I have given of that momentous meeting, the things which happened to me from then on are very interesting and I will relate them without any bias or comment on my part, leaving the reader to draw whatever conclusions may be drawn. I will have to give the official reasons for these successive blows to my reputation, but I will not make any comment on them either.

The first thing that happened was that David Webster attended the final rehearsal of *Tosca* and complained that in some places the orchestra was too loud for Midgley's voice. Three weeks later Midgley complained to Webster, without saying a word to me, that I had (from my hospital bed[17]) written to him pointing out some of the places in *Tosca* which would improve his performance if he looked at them. This letter was couched in the most tactful and friendly language and I still have a copy of it before me as I write. Only a megalomaniac would have objected to such a letter. When I returned to Covent Garden eight days after the operation, I was asked if I would give up *Tosca* in view of the difficult situation which had arisen over Midgley. This I did,[18] but I was not asked to conduct this work again after Midgley left the company until 12 months later.[19] Rankl had conducted one performance and refused to conduct another one while Midgley was in the cast. Gellhorn was then asked to do the rest of them, even after Midgley had left. In other words, the management took me out of *Tosca*.

Joan Hammond, who had been doing *Aida* with me during the season, phoned me up when she read in the papers that I was forced to take a week's rest because my left leg had not completely healed up, and I had conducted too soon after the operation. She said she was worried about doing *Aida* with Rankl because of lack of rehearsal. Would I conduct it just this once if she could get David Webster's permission? I was agreeable. She phoned me later saying that she had spoken to David Webster and asked me to offer to do it. I phoned David Webster immediately but my well-intentioned offer seemed to offend him quite needlessly.[20]

The next event of vital importance to me was that Vaughan Williams' opera *The Pilgrim's Progress* was to be performed. I was sure that Rankl would not want to do this, so I wrote to Vaughan Williams and asked if, when considering a conductor for his work, he would remember me. His reply was that this was the first time he had heard I was at Covent Garden, but that sometime ago, in

---

17 Braithwaite was in hospital for a minor operation, presumably for varicose veins.

18 A discrete notice appeared in *The Times*: 'Warwick Braithwaite, conductor at the Royal Opera, Covent Garden, has recently undergone a slight operation on his foot, and because of the need for rest, he will not conduct *Tosca* on Monday. His place will be taken by Mr Karl Rankl.' *The Times* (9 December 1950), 4.

19 On 6 February 1952, the day King George VI died, and consequently the performance was cancelled.

20 Braithwaite conducted Joan Hammond in *Aida* for three performances in 1951 (4, 14 January, 27 April). The January performance is presumably the one to which Hammond is referring.

consultation with David Webster, he expressed the wish that (as he put it), he didn't want any of the 'heads' to do it. David Webster had the chance then of giving me a new work by pointing out that I was the only British conductor at Covent Garden, but he didn't. Vaughan Williams then asked for a young man, and in his letter to me wrote that the young man was coming to see him that day.[21] I showed this letter to David Webster who blandly said that Vaughan Williams wanted a 'young man' to conduct his work and that was that.

Operas came and went and my spirit began to fail me, but I think I kept on going, in spite of these kicks, fairly well. I was determined not to let my work suffer. The next blow came when I returned from a holiday to Bayreuth and Salzburg. So far, David Webster had never let me know at the end of one season if I was to come back the following season, so I did not worry over much when I heard nothing before I went on holiday. Many artists had heard nothing too, but all those whose services were being dispensed with had been forewarned as early as the previous February. So, rightly or wrongly, I assumed that things had blown over and I hoped the following season would settle down into one happier than the last.

*

On the 6th of August I went with my wife and youngest boy Nicholas to Austria.[22] We were going to spend a week in Walchsee for Nicholas to improve swimming, and the following week, travel to Bayreuth and back to Salzburg and then to Hallstatt[23] where our oldest son, Rodric (with the British Army in Vienna), would join us for a few days.

All proceeded according to plan. I sent a postcard to Miss Keen, David Webster's secretary, giving an address in Bayreuth in case Covent Garden wished to get in touch with me. We had decided to travel via Basle and the Inn Valley to Innsbruck, and then on to Walchsee. As it turned out we were too tired and sleepy to see much of the Inn Valley. The week in Walchsee was wonderful for Nicky who boated, swam and made loads of friends. We disported ourselves at the local *Waldfest* (Festival in the Woods) where the local band, and another from a nearby village, ploughed their way through Tyrolean tunes and marches. Nothing seemed to happen for hours in the boiling sun except an enormous

---

21 The opera was conducted by Leonard Hancock (1921–1999). He was perhaps better known as a répétiteur, teacher and translator, married first to soprano Iris Kells and later to soprano Catherine Wilson.

22 Nicholas Paul Dallon Braithwaite was born on 26 August 1939. See Appendix 1.

23 Hallstatt is a small village in the district of Gmunden, situated on Hallstätter See. It is part of the Dachstein/Salzkammergut Cultural Landscape, one of the World Heritage Sites in Austria since 1997.

amount of drinking of schnapps and beer by young and old alike. We got tired of this boring affair and went back to our hotel. The festivities went on far into the next morning and it seemed as if all the drunken couples in the neighbourhood congregated under our window until dawn, gurgling away like turtle doves. Occasionally, a woman would shriek and run for her life, followed by another's determined footsteps.

We started off for Bayreuth early in the morning and arrived there at about 6 p.m. Our luggage had gone astray, and we decided to eat near the station and await the next train. Looking for a medium-priced restaurant we got into conversation with one of the choristers of the Festspiele, and she accompanied us to a restaurant where we met one of the viola players of the orchestra. With him was one of the flower maidens in *Parsifal*. We were very tired and hungry, but the food we were offered was too much for us. Our luggage was still on its way, so we went to our rooms and slept soundly.

Next morning, we visited the Wagner Exhibition with the high-sounding title *Wagner in the World*. It was a most interesting collection of manuscripts, photographs, programmes and translations, along with an array of all kinds of Wagneriana. One of the most interesting exhibits was a Japanese translation of *The Ring of the Nibelung*. Photographs of the productions of Wagner's music dramas in the most important opera houses of the world gave me a good idea of what the same thing means to other people. The full score of Wagner's overture *Rule Britannia* was also on view.[24] I knew this overture had been written but could never get a score. It had been lost for many years and had turned up in an old collection of manuscripts quite recently. Wagner, in one of his letters has said that the first four bars of *Rule Britannia* summed up the character of the British race. Perhaps this is a statement the musicologists might discuss at some length. Certainly, there is a decisiveness about those first four bars which possibly indicated a forthrightness in the British character as Wagner found it in his day.

Ludwig Weber and his accomplished wife met me at the stage door of the Festspielhaus, and Frau Weber took charge of Nicholas for that day and the next, so that my wife and I could go to the performances of *Parsifal* and *Die Meistersinger*. As we didn't have tickets for the latter, Herr Weber took me into Wolfgang Wagner's office and introduced me. Winifred Wagner, a very handsome woman showing no signs of her age, spoke to me for quite a while and I reminded her of the day when I had the good fortune to have seen Cosima Wagner. Naturally she couldn't remember the circumstances, but made appropriate conversation nevertheless. Wolfgang gave me two

---

24 A concert overture in D major, composed by Wagner in 1837, and possibly intended to raise much-needed funds from England. Following a few performances conducted by Wagner, the work was, until recently, heard only in a version edited by Felix Mottl.

tickets for *Die Meistersinger*, so we decided to stay the extra day. I met Walter Legge once again (the HMV director of continental recording) who was in Bayreuth supervising the recording of *Die Meistersinger*. He told me that he had got most of it and was to try for the Second Act that following evening.[25] Schwarzkopf was the Eva, and Hans Hopf (who had sung Radamès with me at Covent Garden), was the Walther. Victoria Sladen was at the festival as well, and we all had a very jolly supper together after the show.[26] Sylvia Fisher was also there, so I was told, but we could not find her.[27] Hans Knappertsbusch, from my Munich days, was the conductor of *Parsifal* and gave a most beautiful rendering of Wagner's score.

Die Meistersinger was a bit of a disappointment to me. I don't think Karajan was the best conductor for this very German work. With thoughts and memories of Bruno Walter, Karl Muck and others to guide me, I felt that Karajan was the kind of man imbued with a desire to hurry the tempi, especially in the scene between Eva and Sachs in Act Two. The musical beauty of this scene was glossed over and I began to suspect that a recording atmosphere had crept in. The power of the full chorus, especially during the 'Wachet auf!' chorale and at the end of the opera, was simply overwhelming. The Bayreuth chorus is chosen from the best choristers throughout Germany and numbers about 100 members. In addition, Bayreuth, especially for *Die Meistersinger* performances, contributes another big chorus quota. The Bayreuth municipality gives financial backing to the festival and looks upon it as an honour to do so.

Frederick Dalberg was the Pogner.[28] He came to us at Covent Garden the following season and proved a real asset to our Company. His King Mark in the performances during May 1952 were, by a long way, head and shoulders above the performances of the other artists in the cast. Dalberg, born in England, is a South African who went to Munich many years before the war, and after the war continued singing in Western Germany. He apparently made up his mind that a change was a good thing and he came to London. This has proved to be of great advantage to us, for whatever role Dalberg performs he brings great experience, thought and artistry to it.

25 Legge was successful in his efforts. The recording was issued on five Columbia LPs, and has been reissued many times on compact disc.

26 Victoria Sladen (1910-1999), English soprano. She had performed with Braithwaite at a concert in Glasgow with the LPO on 7 September 1944, and with Sadler's Wells in Hamburg during September 1945, where she sang in *The Bartered Bride*.

27 Sylvia Fisher (1910-1996), Australian soprano who despite a long and very distinguished career in Great Britain, performed only once with Braithwaite. The occasion was a radio programme, with the BBC Symphony Orchestra, in the series *Ring Up the Curtain!: Selections from Operas by Beethoven and Mozart*. It was introduced by Spike Hughes and broadcast on 4 April 1949.

28 Frederick Dalberg (1908-1988), English-born, South African bass who, in addition to his Wagnerian repertoire, also created roles in operas by Britten, Tippet and Walton.

I was invited to sit in the sunken orchestra once again by some of the players and, as there was a seat vacant at the back of the first violins, I was very tempted to do so. But it meant leaving my wife alone, so I very regretfully refused the offer. I was once again most impressed by the roominess of the sunken orchestra pit and wondered if we would ever have such a thing at Covent Garden at some time in the dim future.

From Bayreuth, after visiting Wahnfried once again,[29] we travelled to Salzburg where we intended to see *Wozzeck*. Alban Berg's music drama had been played complete on two occasions at BBC concerts conducted by Sir Adrian Boult in London, and it was good to hear it now as a staged work.[30] Kleiber was to conduct it at Covent Garden the following season and I had promised to bring back some notes on the production for some members of our staff. As it turned out, Covent Garden used the same scene designer as Salzburg did, and therefore my notes were not needed. Karl Böhm was the conductor and Christel Goltz the Marie.[31] She did it subsequently at Covent Garden in very much her own way. Goltz has been criticised for giving this character a 'sluttish' interpretation, but I personally thought it was interesting to say the least.

My reactions to Alban Berg's music drama are very mixed. The enormous cerebral technique of the composer is a continual wonder to me. There is not a bar of music which could be omitted, and the intensity of it is amazing. I bought a score and spent the following week studying it. After attending all the rehearsals and seeing several performances later at Covent Garden, I feel qualified to offer my own opinion of the work for what it is worth.

The sincerity of the composer is not in question. Berg's music is ideally suited to Georg Büchner's sordid and half-mad play. As to whether Berg could have written suitable music to a more rational play is open to question. The fundamental criticism I make is that nowhere does the music illustrate what the characters are feeling in their hearts. Most of the music is illustrative of deeds, not feelings, with the one exception, and that is the interlude between the last two scenes. But one has to wait until the end for this, and it is a long time to wait. I doubt whether the labelling of certain parts of the music into variations, passacaglia, fugue, etc., serves any useful purpose, except to prove how clever the composer is. The *sprechstimme* and *sprechgesang*, in which Berg writes pitched notes but puts a cross line through the stems to indicate that the singer is to almost speak the lines somewhere near the pitch indicated, is not entirely successful and I doubt whether operatic singers thank him for it,

---

29 Braithwaite had previously visited Wagner's house, Wahnfried, in 1924.

30 Boult had conducted performances of *Wozzeck* on 14 March 1934 (Queen's Hall) and 16 March 1949 (Royal Albert Hall).

31 Christel Goltz (1912-2008), a leading dramatic soprano of her generation, particularly associated with the operas of Richard Strauss.

or even really understand it. In the scene where Marie reads a passage from the Bible, she commences, solo, a theme used in a fugue by the orchestra. This theme is supposed to be half sung (*sprechgesang*) but unless the singer *sings* it in the correct pitch the following fugal counterpoint of the orchestra becomes meaningless.

The powerful effect of the work is undeniable but I don't feel, even yet, as if I can make up my mind as to the permanent value of *Wozzeck* as a stage musical work. The only thing I can say with certainty is that I don't think it can be followed by similar works, or that it in any way sets a new road for others to follow in opera. It is in a sense, a dead end.

Next morning, we were off to Hallstatt for the meeting with Rodric, who was coming from Vienna. We arrived at our hotel on the other side of the lake, which could only be reached by rowing boat. The guard at the little railway halt blew a small horn which was answered by the boatman on the other side, and through the dark we knew we were rowed to our destination. The boats on the lake are all of the gondola type, heavy and propelled by the same kind of large oar used by Venetian gondoliers.

A few days after our arrival we ascended the mountain above us and then descended right into the bowels of the earth on an excursion to the ancient Roman salt mines. Various types of salt were pointed out to us, and we were rushed at breakneck speed by electric trolley, sitting astride packed like sardines, men and women holding onto one another tightly. Concern for our own safety was no respecter of persons and we alighted at the exit, miles further on, in a slightly embarrassed state. Nicky told me afterwards that he was scared to death on the trolley, but he showed no signs of it at the time. Good lad!

The miners have a way of getting to a lower level using a system of wooden chutes. With a miner acting as the brakeman, you slide down a wooden chute on your behind, and when it levels out at the bottom, you come to a stop amid shrieks of laughter.

In Hallstatt itself was the church burial ground where, apparently, the coffins are dug up after twelve years as there is only limited space for the dead. The bones are deposited in a large hall where the skulls are marked with the names and dates of the dead person and arranged in orderly rows. Of course, Nicky took a photo of this eerie place!

With the arrival of Rodric, the next two days were taken up with talking, after which he left again for Vienna, and the following day we made for London. Travelling via the same route by which we had arrived, we were now able to take in the beauty of the Inn Valley which was very much worth the long way home.

TWENTY-SIX

COVENT GARDEN UNRAVELLED

I had a concert with the BBC at the start of September 1951, and only after this did I begin to worry about Covent Garden.[1] There was no letter from the opera house and I made several attempts to get in touch with Webster, but weeks went by and still I had not heard a word. I met several artists who told me that they had only just received their letter of contract, so again I was not unduly worried. But by the end of September, I still hadn't heard from David Webster and I began to get alarmed.

I wrote to William Walton asking him if he knew what was happening. Walton was a member of the Trust, although for most of the past two years he had been in Capri busy writing his opera.[2] I had received an offer of two weeks with the Welsh National Opera, but I had to keep them waiting until I heard from Webster. Walton advised me to accept this offer, but I didn't altogether like the sound of this. In previous years I would have received my contract from Covent Garden by this time. I knew this coming season was to commence later, especially as the festival season had finished much later than usual.[3] More letters and phone calls to Covent Garden elicited nothing of a concrete nature. I heard the rumour that five guest conductors were coming to Covent Garden. This

---

1   In fact, there were two studio concerts (1 and 2 September 1951) with the BBC Opera Orchestra. The first was of music by Granados, Lalo, Blamey Lafone and Chabrier, with New Zealand violinist Alan Loveday as soloist in three movements from Lalo's *Symphonie espagnole*. The second programme featured music by Domenico Scarlatti (probably the Scarlatti-Tommasini suite *The Good-humoured Ladies*), and Debussy.
2   Walton's *Troilus and Cressida* was premiered at Covent Garden on 3 December 1954.
3   The 1951–1952 Season commenced on 22 October.

didn't help matters. What would be found for me with such a bevy of guests?[4]

I eventually saw David Webster who informed me that my contract was to be of a different sort this season. He offered me a retaining salary with a promise of appearances at Covent Garden and a certain number of touring dates. This amounted to one performance of *La bohème*,[5] and about nine performances on the tour. So, because of the delay, I was faced with signing this contract whether I liked it or not. I have searched my mind and heart for reasons. I have heard every performance of the operas I used to conduct, conducted by others, and I, with all the modesty in the world, fail to see what advantage Covent Garden would gain by the change.

The reason I suffered a reversal of fortune at Covent Garden was, I am convinced, because I had been fearless in pointing out the lack of proper musical organisation. Whatever had driven Rankl to insist on conducting every first night and to neglect dealing with the daily problems of the organisation, will perhaps never be known. Fundamentally, I believe Rankl's appointment was the first mistake, and it would have been much better if a Briton had been appointed instead, even if (as was said at the time in answer to wide but quite ridiculous criticisms), that there was no-one in Britain experienced enough for the job.

Leaving out the question as to who should be Musical Director at Covent Garden, the fact remains that Rankl had been appointed. How did he carry out his job? This is the whole crux of my endless criticisms of the lack of proper musical organisation. In my book *The Conductor's Art*,[6] I dealt with this question fairly exhaustively and hypothetically, but Covent Garden was in my mind when I outlined the essentials of operatic musical organisation. In that treatise I did not pretend that what I was advocating could not be improved upon, but it was an attempt to give a lead to anyone who might be prepared to learn. At least the attempt was fair and sincere and I could not do more than that. I feel sure that Rankl either set himself against having experienced men by his side, or he did not know the recent history of operatic endeavour in this country.

I was only engaged *to conduct* at Covent Garden, not to be Musical Director. It was therefore not my intention to interfere in any way with the musical administration, and such ideas were far removed from my thoughts. It was only when I realized that lack of organisation was responsible for any inequalities in my performances, and that things over which I had no control were making it difficult for me to do my work well, that I began to ask for some kind of co-operation from Rankl and his assistants. I pointed out that a conductor should

---

4   In addition to Gellhorn, Braithwaite, Kleiber, Barbirolli and Krauss (who had all appeared in the previous season), the 'guests' were Capuana, Beecham, Britten, Tauský and Goodall.

5   On 21 February 1952.

6   Warwick Braithwaite, *The Conductor's Art* (London: Williams and Norgate, 1952).

have some say in the casting and rehearsal of his allocated operas, otherwise how could he be responsible for a standard which, by the public and critics, was attributed to him? When I pointed out this obvious flaw, I began to find myself up against this curious stonewalling 'Magic Circle'. The high priority of rehearsal which Rankl allocated to himself was out of all proportion and thoroughly detrimental to the other operas. My contention was that the public paid their money for my operas as well as his.

What became apparent very soon was that Rankl, with all his rehearsals (which he persisted in to the very end of his tenure of office), did not succeed in giving better performances than I, even with the inadequate rehearsals I was allowed. Frequently, as it turned out, I would be allotted the weakest of the répétiteurs for my rehearsals, and the artists I needed were often required at the same time by Rankl (and he always insisted on his priority). My life was made a misery, and it was while I was trying to make sure that each conductor was given his fair share of rehearsal time that I began to feel opposition stiffen. I can attribute all my troubles to this, and to my keenness to do good performances. Under the circumstances I may have been *too* keen. Such a thought is a terrible comment on the whole unsatisfactory situation.

When Rankl left, we all thought that things would improve. The hullabaloo set up during the previous seasons about the poor performances done by Rankl, must be what influenced the Trust to take the opportunity of his resignation to make a clean sweep. Rankl was out; I had given a certain amount of trouble, was I to be out? I think so! Instead of realizing that I had a legitimate grouse, desired work under better circumstances, and should be given a chance to prove what I could do, a quite different line was taken. I am certain that my fearless criticism was looked upon as disloyalty, and once certain types smell such a thing, their hands go up in horror. I will never learn the lesson.

Three of the guest conductors (Beecham, Barbirolli and Britten), were British, and they were only guests in the sense that they were responsible for just one or two works. But the three foreigners (Capuana, Kleiber and Krauss) took over more opera than the designation 'guest' would warrant – and to the tune of many thousands of pounds of taxpayer money. Financing opera is quite allowable, and thank goodness for Mr Aneurin Bevan who was responsible for the relevant statute. But did Mr Bevan, or his party, really mean that this money should be used for the employment of foreign conductors and singers to the detriment of the British ones? I doubt it. In some cases, it may be true to say that there is no artist in the country capable of filling a role, but in the vast majority of cases, the wool is being pulled over the minister's eyes.

Why has Hilde Zadek, from the Vienna Opera House, been in this country for months at a time singing *Tosca* and *Aida*, when we have two British sopranos who are just as good, if not better. Joan Hammond has sung a few performances of *Aida* and given the best performances of the role at Covent Garden since the theatre reopened. She is also a very good Tosca and should be ideal for Turandot. Her operatic repertoire doesn't end there by any means. She is a splendid Butterfly, Leonore and Violetta, and could sing most roles suited to her voice. She has a big public following as well, yet for reasons best known to himself, the Administrator passes her over for an artist from Vienna who is no better. There have been several instances of this kind of thing.

What are the reasons for denying the most experienced British operatic artists their rightful place in this great national operatic venture? I don't want to give the impression that there are hordes of British artists who have been kept out of Covent Garden. To be fair, I have to admit that Covent Garden has been the proving ground of many young artists who have shown their worth. However, there are several notable artists who have been overlooked, and also some young artists who were, during Rankl's regime, treated very badly or injudiciously.

For my own part, I am adept at self-criticism. I've done it all my life. Looking back over the three main positions I have held before that of conductor at Covent Garden, I began to observe very soon that the ending of each position looked very much alike. But looking somewhat closer I realize that each position had quite different problems. With the National Orchestra of Wales (NOW) I was fighting a foregone conclusion that the orchestra had to go, despite my fight to keep it alive. With Sadler's Wells there was the clash with Tyrone Guthrie. With the Scottish Orchestra it was a clash between myself and the committee on the important question of a permanent orchestra. With Covent Garden, as I see it, I fell primarily between the claims of the Music Director, who never gave me a reasonable chance, and my own insistence on a better organization which would have given me the chance I needed.

After several months of waiting and wondering whether David Webster would approach me for the 1952–1953 season, I wrote to him on 26 August, saying that as I had not heard to the contrary, I had held myself free and would he let me know if I was required. By 15 October I had still received no reply. He had asked me by phone on 26 August to conduct for the Melba film made in conjunction with Patrice Munsel and the Covent Garden Orchestra; the reason apparently being that he would only consent to a Covent Garden conductor taking part in the session.[7] I thought, in my foolishness, that the latter directive

---

7   The film *Melba*, a 1953 biopic of the life of Dame Nellie Melba, was directed by Lewis Milestone for Horizon Pictures. The title role was played by American coloratura soprano Patrice Munsel, supported by a fine cast including Sybil Thorndyke, Robert Morley, Martita Hunt, Alec Clunes, Theodore Bikel, John Justin and John McCallum. The film score was composed by Arthur Benjamin and conducted by Muir Mathieson. Braithwaite conducted all the 'classical' items with the Orchestra of the Royal Opera House, Covent Garden. The musical soundtrack was recorded in August 1952 and issued by RCA Victor and HMV the following year.

from the Covent Garden Administrator meant by implication that I was still to be one of next season's conductors. But after waiting from 26 August till 15 October for a reply to my letter, I was forced to come to the conclusion that this was all poppycock.

PART IX
(1952–1956)

TWENTY-SEVEN

A MEETING WITH
SIBELIUS (1952)

I had always believed – and acted on my belief – that as far as possible, a conductor should try and absorb the circumstances and surroundings from which a great composer derives his inspiration. In this respect I had been to Mozart's house in Salzburg, to Wahnfried for Wagner, to Hereford for Elgar, to Milan and Florence for Verdi and Puccini. But just to go places is not enough. In studying Wagner, I delved into the *Völsunga Saga* before reading his *Der Ring des Nibelungen*.

When I first started to conduct Sibelius, I commenced reading the *Kalevala*, the Finnish national saga, in Kirby's translation.[1] Afterwards, names such as *Tapiola*, *Tuonela*, *Pohjola* and *Lemminkäinen* began to have some meaning. For many years I had wanted to go to Finland, but circumstances had always prevented me. I had wanted to meet Sibelius, but it looked as if I would never have time to do so. A happy circumstance, the result of a Finlander reading my book *The Conductor's Art*, and presenting a copy to Jussi Jalas,[2] ended in an invitation to stay with this man for the second Sibelius Festival in Helsinki during the week of June 7th 1952. Even at the last moment the trip didn't look like coming off, but through the lifting of passport visa regulations during the festival and later the Olympic Games, I experienced no delay and was able to buy an air ticket one day and travel the next.

---

1 William Forsell Kirby (1844–1912), English entomologist and folklorist, whose translation of *Kalevala* from the Finnish was an influence on the writings of J.R.R. Tolkien. P.E. Bragg. 'Biographies of Phasmatologists – 4. William Forsell Kirby', *Phasmid Studies*, 16/1 (2007), 5–10, http://biostor.org/reference/202019, accessed 20 February 2019.

2 Armas Jussi Veikko Jalas (orig. Blomstedt) (1908–1985), Finnish conductor, composer and son-in-law of Sibelius. He changed his surname to Jalas in 1943.

The journey by plane is only about 8 hours, and after leaving Copenhagen the plane flew over the Swedish coast with its maze of inland lakes. Shortly after reaching the Gulf of Finland, the plane flew over the Archipelago Sea.[3] Soon afterwards, we came down at Helsinki aerodrome. I arrived at one o'clock in the morning, but it was still light. Never having experienced such a thing before, the journey by car through countryside, and later the streets of Helsinki in the half-light, was entrancing. People believe that the birds go to bed at sunset and awake at sunrise, but in Finland during summer, as there is no night or dawn, the birds adjust as sensibly as human beings.

In a few hours I was up again and my host, Mr Aarne Liukkonen, showed me the sights of Helsinki. From the tower of the Torni Hotel he pointed out an island, only 15 miles away, leased after the Russo-Finnish War to the Russian Government for 50 years. A visit to the wonderful children's hospital, of which the Finns are very proud, followed during the course of many visits that morning. My host's flat was immediately behind the Parliament, a building of pink granite with one side completely graced by Grecian pillars. An imposing building, but not entirely to my liking.

In the afternoon I met Jussi Jalas, the conductor of both opera and symphony concerts. Mr Jalas gave a most interesting lecture in English on the modern composers of Finland. During the interval I met his wife, one of Sibelius' daughters (Margaret), and as all these people spoke English, conversation became pleasant and easy. Olin Downes,[4] the American critic, was also of the party, and he seemed to know of the many performances of Sibelius' symphonies which I had done in the past. Downes is the American counterpart of our Cecil Gray and has been a Sibelius apostle for many years. His well-known book on the composer is now almost a classic. Of the works I heard on tape at this lecture recital, the two composers, Pylkkänen and Klami, were exceedingly good.[5] Klami, in particular, should be better known in England; his overture *The Cobbler on the Heath* (1936) is a first-class composition. Pylkkänen was represented by a radio opera called *The Wolf's Bride*,[6] and here again one felt he was a first-rate talent.

That evening, Ormandy was rehearsing for the final orchestral concert, and I had a good opportunity to study the conductor at work.[7] Later that evening,

---

3   Braithwaite would have flown over an area which, since 1983, has been designated Archipelago National Park (Saaristomeren kansallispuisto).

4   Edwin Olin Downes (1886–1955), American music critic of *The New York Times* and champion of Sibelius.

5   Tauno Kullervo Pylkkänen (1918–1980) and Uuno (Kalervo) Klami (1900–1961), Finnish composers.

6   The radio opera, *Sudenmorsian*, was awarded the Prix Italia in 1950.

7   Eugene Ormandy (1899-1985), Hungarian-born conductor, known for his long tenure with the Philadelphia Orchestra.

Jussi Jalas met me with my host at the Musician's Club, and we talked and discussed music far into the northern night hours. The following day I was a guest at the final concert and the dinner reception given by the Municipality in the old and magnificent Town Hall. Every Finnish musician of note was there; Kilpinen the writer of many fine songs was present.[8] In his young days, he had been the subject of a magnificently sculptured head by the Finnish sculptor Kalervo Kallio.[9] Kilpinen, who must be well over 60, is a fine-looking man with a shock of white hair. In the granite he looks out on the world as fearlessly as he does in the flesh.

Similä, the conductor, was also there. [10] During the Festival, Similä had conducted the Symphony no. 4 of Sibelius, and I was privileged to follow the performance from a tape recording at the Finnish Radio Studios. I was tremendously impressed; it had the stamp of complete understanding of this difficult work. I had never before heard the slow movement rendered with such complete and deep feeling.

While in Helsinki, and in conversation about this symphony with many musicians who were in close touch with Sibelius, I was given a clue to the strangeness of its idiom that made, so far as I am concerned, many points immediately clear and full of meaning. The slow movement is a musical picture of the agony in Gethsemane. The last movement is a musical picture of the Judgement of Pilate, and the three oboe repetitions of the theme on the last page of the full score represent the denials of Peter and the cock crow. Thinking over this explanation of the symphony, many other points fell into line with the story of Christ. The first movement might easily depict the journey through the night of Joseph and Mary and the tremendous impact on the future of the world by the birth of Jesus; the trumpet and trombone figure which occurs six bars after letter C in the score, might easily depict the edict of Herod that the first-born son should be slain; the flight through the night is depicted after letter E to letter I; and the fear of discovery with the new-born hope can be heard in the little oboe and clarinet theme towards the end of the movement. The scherzo which follows might depict the boyhood of Jesus, with the gradual changes to manhood. The fierce gesture of the new theme (but arising out of the original theme) could depict the expulsion of the money changers from the Temple. The sorrow of the third movement is undeniable, and the anticipation of the opening of the last movement is prophetic of the rabble who demanded the death of Jesus. The intrusion of this phrase has been an enigma to musicians the world over. I vouch for the correctness of this theory, but if the work is viewed

---

8   Yrjö Henrik Kilpinen (1892–1959), Finnish composer.
9   Niilo Kalervo Kallio (1909–1969), Finnish sculptor; son of the fourth President of Finland, Kyösti Kallio.
10 Martti Similä (1898–1958), Finnish conductor.

with the life of Jesus in mind, many difficulties in the understanding of the work will disappear. I must add, however, that Sibelius would be the first to deny any connection with the above theory.

At the dinner reception after the last concert, Jussi Jalas introduced me to the eldest daughter of Sibelius, Mrs Paloheimo,[11] who promised that she would arrange for me to visit the great man either the following morning or the next. I wasn't very hopeful as I knew that few people had been accorded that privilege and it was rather far out in the country. In any case, I did not want to push myself forward or intrude upon Sibelius' retirement.

That day I had met Professor Soini[12] the director of the opera house. Soini is a man of 60 years but most virile and still sings such roles as Scarpia or Rigoletto at the Helsinki Opera. The evening before I left for England, he had invited me to his country house built on the shores of a beautiful lake, about 70 miles from Helsinki. Here we enjoyed a rare occasion of hospitality in the true Finnish style. Soini lives there almost like a legendary lord and his hospitality is most generous. His son-in-law drove me over rough sandy roads which the rain had turned into a surface of corrugated quagmire. His car was a new English one and broke down under the strain, but apparently this was only an exhibition of English temperament and eventually we arrived safe, if somewhat sore.

On the Saturday morning, I was warned to stand by at 3 p.m., as Eva Paloheimo had learned that the impossible was about to happen and Sibelius was expecting me. I had brought my copies of the Second and Fourth Symphonies and it was my hope that if ever I saw the Master, I would take them with me and be so bold as to ask him to autograph them. At last I was on my way by car with Mrs Paloheimo. We turned out of Helsinki and were soon into the country, passing the ancient site of the original capital, Helsingfors. Turning off the main road, we came to a narrow track just wide enough for our car, and there before us was the wood in which the villa, Ainola, could be seen. The villa itself is on an eminence[13] and our car came to rest outside the front entrance. Mrs Paloheimo led the way and soon we were inside the main room of Sibelius' house. In this room was a grand piano but very few books. Through a wide arch was another big room. In a moment a big, tall, bald man strode into the room. It was Sibelius. I was told he was 86, but this man looked about 50 and the picture of health. Broad, upright and with a sprightly step, he swept into the room. Introductions were hardly necessary because he knew of me already and could tell me exactly what (either by wireless or other means) I had done.[14] He knew

---

11 Eva Paloheimo (1893-1978).

12 Oiva Soini (1893–1971), Finnish baritone, teacher and Director of the National Opera in Helsinki.

13 In the sense of rising ground.

14 For a complete list of Sibelius works performed under Braithwaite's direction, see Appendix 3.

of my Cardiff days when I had, up till 1931, conducted many of his works,[15] and he mentioned a concert I had conducted quite recently with the BBC Scottish Orchestra of his Third Symphony. I was to discover that he followed music in England very closely and knew most of the young composers' works. One might have expected a man of 86 to have been rather slow in his reactions. Most men I have known of that age had slowed up both physically and mentally, but Sibelius showed no signs of slowing up. Indeed, his brain seemed as active as a man in his prime, his bodily movements were quick and strong, and the only sign of any physical ailment was to be seen in his hands which shook rather badly. But even this he laughed at.

We sat around a table in the corner by the grand piano in the big reception room while coffee and cognac were served. The conversation was dominated by Sibelius who spoke of Vaughan Williams and his symphonies, which he admired very much. I mentioned that Vaughan Williams had written another symphony – the Seventh – and that all musical England was expecting it with great interest. I didn't ask any foolish questions about his own Eighth Symphony[16] but I did enquire about the opera he wrote many years ago and which has not been released. His answer was both humorous and final. The name of the opera is *The Maiden in the Tower*, and all Sibelius would say about it was, 'She is now in the tower' and as far as he was concerned, 'would never leave it.'[17]

Suddenly, halfway through our conversation, Sibelius got up and strode across the room, picking up a box of cigars which he brought back to me. I didn't accept one, but lit his for him. I then pulled out my box cigarette making machine and proceeded to make a cigarette. He was immensely impressed by this, so I made another in illustration of the excellence and celerity of this little invention. He handled it like a young boy with a new toy and suggested that his great grandchildren would be most interested to possess such a machine. I promised to send him one. I tell this incident as an illustration of Sibelius' interest in the ordinary things of life. I felt that I would be wrong to talk about his music; God knows he must have been bored with the amount of fawning that is indulged in by visitors from abroad. We met as human beings, and music was incidental to our conversation. I think that was why our conversation rattled along quite merrily.

However, he mentioned his days in Birmingham with Granville Bantock, and the time in Manchester when he conducted the Hallé orchestra; he spoke

---

15 Braithwaite conducted 99 performances of 29 different works by Sibelius in Cardiff.

16 Now presumed to have perished in a bonfire that Sibelius and his wife made of his manuscripts in 1945. Supposed fragments have been found, lasting just a few minutes.

17 The opera had been performed just twice in Helsinki in 1896 before it was withdrawn for revision. Nevertheless, Sibelius conducted the overture of the opera in April 1900, at his concert in Turku. The opera has now been published, performed and recorded.

with pleasure of Sir Henry Wood's great work at the Queen's Hall; he spoke of Rubbra and how much he admired his Fifth Symphony, the records of which had just been presented to him by The British Council.[18] He had listened to this work that very morning, and felt that Rubbra was a most serious and important composer. He called Elgar the aristocrat of composers.

I had been there for one and a half hours, and Mrs Paloheimo very wisely suggested that the time had come for us to depart. Sibelius kept up a running fire of conversation right to the end, even as we were at the front door, and like the excellent host he is, waved to us as we entered the car. So, my visit was at an end.

Back in Helsinki I began to think of the greatness of this man Sibelius. As a personality, as a world figure, he is head and shoulders above all other musicians of Finland. There is a breadth of vision and brain power that has made him one of the greatest figures in the musical world. Even his works with a programmatic base, such as *The Swan of Tuonela, Tapiola, En Saga, Pohjola's Daughter, Nightride and Sunrise*, live as music first, and programme music afterwards. The ancient Finnish saga, *Kalevala*, has been the source of inspiration for many of his works, but never have these legends been allowed to interfere with his marvellous sense of musical construction. Incidentally, Jussi Jalas had told me the previous evening that Sibelius writes music every morning, but will not allow the rest of the world to see it.

I took the opportunity of visiting the Art Gallery and saw the Kalevala paintings of Gallen-Kallela[19] the greatest modern painter and great friend of Sibelius, and I can well understand the influence the great artist had on the composer. The picture of Lemminkäinen's body by the shores of the black river of death, Tuonela, with the white swan in the background and his mother looking up in anguished and pathetic pain, is one of the most striking and original paintings I have ever seen.[20] The Sibelius tone poem *Tuonela*, full of dark pity and sorrow, is a musical picture of this foreboding tragedy. To see this painting and then to hear Sibelius' tone poem will give the listener a much deeper insight into its meaning.

There is no doubt in my mind that Sibelius has been strongly influenced by dramatic ideas, and even though he would quite rightly deny such influence, I for one hold to my own opinion on this matter. I have always felt that the first

18 This recording of Rubbra's Symphony no. 5 in B flat, op. 63 was sponsored by the British Council and recorded by EMI in No. 1 Studio, Abbey Road, London, on 14 and 15 December 1950. The Hallé Orchestra was conducted by Sir John Barbirolli. It was the first of Rubbra's symphonies to be recorded, and the composer was present at the sessions.

19 Akseli Gallen-Kallela (1865–1931), Finnish painter, best known for his illustrations of the Kalevala.

20 *Lemminkäisen äiti* (Lemminkäinen's Mother), painted in 1897, is located in Helsinki's Ateneum, one of the three museums forming the Finnish National Gallery.

movement of the Fifth Symphony is a musical picture of the tragedy within a beehive. This may sound quite ridiculous, but consider the sadness of the bassoon solo (the old Queen moaning over her lot); and consider the amount of buzzing that gradually reaches a terrific climax until the joyful flight out of the hive of the new Queen and her followers at the end of the movement. If this idea seems odd to purists, let me say at once that it is only thrown off as an unimportant flick of the imagination and can make no difference whatsoever to my appreciation of the greatness of this symphony. In the interpretation of works, a musician may think of many ideas which may give help to his understanding, especially when the particular work in question may be obscure or the construction difficult to understand. The fact that the composer had no such idea makes very little difference. The last movement of Vaughan Williams' Sixth Symphony has been spoken of as a musical illustration of the dead world of Hiroshima after the atomic bomb fell. On the other hand, this movement might well be an illustration of the vast and silent region of the South Pole to the lone human beholder. It does no harm to think of music on these lines. Great composers are very much in touch with the world, but most composers hesitate to give titles to their 'absolute' compositions. Who wants to undress oneself in public?

The popular picture of Sibelius living by the lake and ponds of Finland is somewhat inaccurate. His villa is not far from one of the main country roads. There is no lake nearby, or not so near that he can walk out and view the changing colours of the scene.[21] Villa Ainola, as stated earlier, is in the middle of a small wood of beech trees and pines. All around are fields under cultivation. The front of the wood which encloses the estate is surrounded by a hedge of laurel about five feet high, planted many years ago, so Mrs Paloheimo told me, by Mrs Sibelius. On some of the tree trunks about 20 feet from the ground are little nesting boxes – a most charming sight. The visit to Sibelius was the climax of four days of strenuous comings and goings, and back in England I was glad of a few days' rest.

Finally, one little anecdote given to me by Jussi Jalas from Sibelius' wild youth. The favourite restaurant where Sibelius, Gallen-Kallela, Kajanus and Järnefelt[22] used to foregather and drink in a comradely fashion, discussing music and art far into the night, is called Kämp. The famous painting by Gallen-Kallela called *Symposion* depicts three men at a table with half-filled glasses and empty bottles, looking out on the world with ecstatic eyes. A fourth figure, lying head down on the table, is already very far gone. This man's face is not seen and I did

---

21 Braithwaite's visit was too brief to have noticed the proximity of Lake Tuusulanjärvi.
22 Edvard Armas Järnefelt (1869–1958), Finnish conductor and composer. Braithwaite conducted *Berceuse* 16 times, *Danse* (suite) on one occasion, and *Praeludium* more than 30 times.

not find out who he was.[23] Altogether the painting is a remarkable portrait of three very great men. The story I tell is that after one of those evenings, Sibelius arrived home a little the worse for wear, and his wife told him he could go back where he came from. Sibelius turned and did go back to Kämp's and, on the way, the following well-known tune, later to make its bow as the *Musette* in the *King Christian II Suite*, came to his mind with Mrs Sibelius' injunction, 'You can go back to Kämp's again' ringing in his ears. Jussi Jalas wrote it out on an envelope for me with the Finnish words and an English translation, and here it is:

The other well-known story about the same restaurant has been told with many variations with reference to Sibelius and Kajanus, but Jussi Jalas vouches for the correctness of this version. It is the story of these two, along with Järnefelt, who were imbibing. Kajanus, who was to leave on a two-day lecture tour, was called to the phone by a waiter (I have used that same phone several times while in Helsinki). Kajanus finished his phone call and, forgetting about the other two, went off without saying goodbye. Three evenings later he came into the restaurant and Sibelius and Järnefelt were there again. Sibelius turned to Kajanus as he entered the restaurant and said, 'That was a long telephone call.'

The point about repeating these anecdotes is to show that the prevalent idea of Sibelius as being a grim person is not entirely correct. A man and his music are not always a reflection of one another. Klami, the composer of the overture *The Cobbler on the Heath* – one of the wittiest compositions I have ever heard – is reported, by those who know him well, to be a very solemn person with apparently little sense of humour and certainly little gaiety.

After having seen the Helsinki Art Gallery with its collection of the art of Finnish painters and sculptors, I wonder why these are not better known in this country. Gallen-Kallela in particular, with his Kalevala paintings shows an originality of style and colour which strikes one immediately as something far removed from Western European painting, much in the same way that the music of Sibelius is different from that of other Western European composers. Even considered apart from Gallen-Kallela's choice of Kalevala subjects, his paintings show the imprint of a forceful personality and an original mind. The wonderful 1897 portrait entitled *Tytön pää, Pikku Anna* (Head of a Girl, Little Anna) in the Ateneum in Helsinki is most striking and should be seen by

---

23 Oskar Merikanto (1868–1924), Finnish pianist, organist, conductor and composer. The other men in the painting are (l to r) Akseli Gallen-Kallela, Robert Kajanus and Jean Sibelius. There are two versions of this painting; Braithwaite's description matches the second version.

everybody. The Kalevala triptych, depicting Aino, entitled *Aino-aru* (painted in 1891), is a glorious riot of colour, but colour applied in quite a new way.

Edelfelt[24] and Eero Järnefelt[25] (brother of Mrs Sibelius), are also very fine painters. The sculptor Wäinö Aaltonen[26] is a man to be reckoned with. The already mentioned Kalervo Kallio's fine granite bust of the composer Kilpinen, is one of the most masterful sculptures of a most masterful face. An exhibition of Finnish artists is long overdue in London.[27]

---

24 Albert Gustaf Aristides Edelfelt (1854–1905), Finnish painter, among the first to achieve international fame.

25 Erik (Eero) Nikolai Järnefelt (1863–1937), Finnish painter and art professor.

26 Wäinö Valdemar Aaltonen (1894–1966), Finnish artist and leading sculptor.

27 Braithwaite would have been delighted to know that the centenary of Finnish independence was celebrated with a number of art events in London in 2017, including an exhibition at the National Gallery which united all of Gallen-Kallela's Lake Keitele landscapes.

TWENTY-EIGHT

WORLD TRAVELS

Having left Covent Garden in June 1952 after the events already described, I heard that the New Zealand Broadcasting Service was looking for a guest conductor to fill the season after my friend Michael Bowles[1] had left, and a new Musical Director was appointed. After what I thought was a quite an unnecessary interview at the BBC (considering that I was already well known to the NZBS), I was offered the position to conduct the New Zealand National Symphony Orchestra for a period of one whole season, from March to November 1953. After some deep thought I decided it would be a good thing to leave London for a while, and I made plans for a journey to New Zealand via New York and San Francisco, and thence across the Pacific Ocean to Auckland.

The first time I had returned to New Zealand was in 1947, and I had travelled via the Middle East. Now I decided it would be a good opportunity to see both New York and San Francisco for the first time. I was in New York in January 1953 and, through an enterprising sister-in-law, I was able to meet nearly everybody I wanted to.[2] I called on Rudolf Bing, who had left the Edinburgh Festival two or three years earlier, and who had taken on the difficult job of administrator of

---

1   Michael Andrew Bowles (1909–1998), Irish conductor and composer, who became the first permanent conductor of the National Orchestra of the New Zealand Broadcasting Service (1950–1953), having been warmly recommended by the English conductor Sir Adrian Boult, who was an uncle-in-law. 'Michael Bowles', *The Contemporary Music Centre, Ireland*, https://www.cmc.ie/composers/michael-bowles, accessed 23 January 2019.

2   On that occasion, Braithwaite was invited to broadcast a talk for WNYC (New York Public Radio), aired on 27 January 1953 in their series *Speaking of Music*. The audio can be heard at https://www.wnyc.org/story/warwick-braithwaite, accessed 23 May 2022.

the Metropolitan Opera House, New York.[3] I went to several performances at this opera house and renewed my acquaintance with some of the singers I had recorded with in London.

Blanche Thebom[4] was at that time singing the part of Fiordiligi in *Così fan tutte* and I went around to the dressing room with Bing to see her. Eugene Conley[5] was also singing at this period at the Metropolitan Opera in *La bohème*, *Madama Butterfly* and *Tosca*. We spent many moments of his spare time together in which his wife Winifred Heidt,[6] a very fine Carmen, also participated. Moura Lympany, as bright as ever, with her husband, came to a few cocktail parties. Ethel Bartlett and Rae Robertson were also in New York, and I had great pleasure in renewing acquaintance with them as I had not seen much of them since our RAM days together.

I'm not sure whether it was then, or later on my second visit in December 1953, that I renewed acquaintance with Alec Templeton.[7] Alec had fallen on his feet very squarely since my Cardiff days. He was blind from birth, but an excellent pianist and composer of light songs and clever little piano pieces. About this time, he was very much in demand at parties and tours throughout the country. He had made money with his recordings and now lived in a beautiful town 50 miles from New York. He had a car, a manservant, and a wealthy wife who was of the utmost help to him. He remembered with pleasure, enthusiasm, and not without flashes of humour, his days at the BBC studios at Cardiff.

The musical life of New York I found quite fascinating. Some of the performances at the Metropolitan were really fine: others were not up to the standard achieved already by Covent Garden, and I found the tone of the brass in the orchestra almost unbearable. But, apart from this, there was nothing much wrong with the musical organisation of the Met, and I felt in this respect that Covent Garden had much to learn. I liked most of the productions I saw, especially *Carmen* and *Così fan tutte*. John Brownlee as Don Alfonso in *Così* was an example of how to sing easily and more gracefully on the stage. In regard

---

3 Sir Rudolf Bing (1902–1997), Austrian-born, British opera manager, notably remembered as the General Manager of the Metropolitan Opera in New York from 1950 to 1972.

4 Blanche Thebom (1915–2010), American mezzo-soprano. In 1950, she recorded songs and arias with Braithwaite and the LSO for RCA in EMI's Abbey Road Studios.

5 Eugene Conley (1908–1981), American operatic tenor who in 1950 recorded an album of arias for Decca with Braithwaite and the New Symphony Orchestra of London. He also conducted Conley and Elisabeth Schwarzkopf in *La bohème* at Covent Garden in 1949.

6 Mezzo-soprano Winifred Heidt recorded arias for Decca/London by Bizet and Saint-Saëns, conducted by Braithwaite on 11 September 1950. Neither these, nor a duet from *Il trovatore* with her husband, were released, probably for technical reasons.

7 Alec Andrew Templeton (1910–1963), Welsh composer, pianist and satirist, resident in the USA from 1936. Braithwaite had conducted one of his works, *Village Dance*, for a Cardiff radio broadcast on 2 June 1927.

to the production of *Carmen*, this was by our own producer, Tyrone Guthrie, and many aspects of it were excellent, particularly the final act. The entrance of Don José in this act was full of the feeling of poignant drama, and the stabbing of Carmen was most convincingly done.

But for me, it was Toscanini's rehearsals with the NBC orchestra that were the most interesting part of musical life in New York. A manager at the NBC was kind enough to allow me to be one of the very few privileged people to attend these rehearsals, which were usually held on Saturday mornings at Carnegie Hall – the concerts being on a Sunday. Toscanini would have been about 85 then and, as far as I could tell, showed no diminution of his powers, either physically or musically. At both the rehearsals I attended there was the inevitable moment when he tore strips off the players (apparently a regular thing at all rehearsals), but otherwise the rehearsals came to a tranquil end, with everybody, including the players, very happy. I spoke to a number of musicians during the recess and they talked about the old man with great reverence.

I remember a most humorous and ridiculous incident at one of Toscanini's performances. An elderly lady came around to the lobby behind the platform and tackled the leader of the orchestra, demanding her money back because he had worn a tie pin which caught the light and shone in her eyes. She was most vociferous in her complaint. You should have seen the leader's face – indignation, dismay and then mirth, lighting up his features in turn.

I also heard the New York Philharmonic Orchestra conducted by Georg Szell, whom I followed as conductor of the Scottish Orchestra. The main piece in this performance was the Sibelius Second Symphony. I found again that the brass section of this orchestra was raucous in the extreme, and it made me long for the golden tone of our London orchestras. What struck me as the chief difference between the London or Vienna orchestras and those in New York was, with the latter, the feeling of efficiency which pervaded their performances. But on the other hand, they lacked the velvety tone which is ever present with European orchestras. After the Sibelius, which opened the concert, I left Carnegie Hall, not being able to stand any more of the kind of tone produced by the brass.[8] I found this same kind of brassy playing with the Boston and Philadelphia orchestras as well. I know that most brass players in American orchestras use the splendid Conn[9] instruments yet somehow, they didn't produce the round golden tone of the English and European players on instruments reputed to be not as good. This was one of the criticisms which the Boston Orchestra had at the 1956 Edinburgh Festival, so it wasn't imagination on my part.

---

8 Braithwaite is going for dramatic effect here. In fact, the Sibelius symphony was the last item on the programme at both concerts on 15 and 16 January.

9 Charles Gerard Conn (1844-1931), American band instrument manufacturer, entrepreneur and politician.

Through my sister-in-law, who arranged many of my appointments in a most efficient style, I met Mr Judson of Columbia Artists.[10] Mr Judson was the most important musical agent in all America. I had what appeared to be a most gratifying interview with him, and he promised that when I came back to the States for five weeks from November 2nd to December 12th 1953, I should conduct, under his management, four concerts at Buffalo, Seattle, Minneapolis and San Francisco. He gave me a letter to Howard Skinner, manager of the San Francisco Orchestra and Opera House, so that I could meet him when passing through that city on my way by plane across the Pacific to New Zealand. All went well in San Francisco. I met the manager of the orchestra and was invited to a symphony concert conducted by Victor de Sabata at the Opera House. De Sabata, at this, his first concert with the San Francisco Orchestra, was an enormous success.[11] It was a brilliant concert and the orchestra, I thought, was superb.

The next afternoon I left San Francisco by BOAC for my journey across the Pacific, and arrived at Honolulu that evening. We were taken out to a very nice hotel near Waikiki beach for a magnificent supper and given a most attentive time by BOAC officials. At about one o'clock in the morning we started off for Kanton Island airport where we arrived at 6 a.m.and refuelled. It was very warm, even at that early hour, and leaving the sleeping bunk for the airport building in our dressing gowns was quite pleasant. We had early morning coffee, and after about an hour were in the air again for Nadi Airport in Fiji. We came down there again for refuelling and were treated to a most pleasing lunch.

*

The last lap of the journey was to Auckland, New Zealand, where we arrived at 6 p.m. on 31 January 1953. There, of course, was my youngest brother, Roderick, and his family waiting with my old friend Len Swan. I spent two days with my brother in Hamilton and then went back to Auckland where Len Swan was waiting for me, and we were off the next day on his launch for ten days of cruising in the Hauraki gulf. What a cruise! There were five of us, and Len's launch (a 38-footer) was completely self-contained. The run up from Auckland yacht harbour to Kawau Island took us the best part of six hours, and we arrived at the little inlet where most launches and yachts dropped anchor. The inlet was the entrance to the place where the third Governor of New Zealand, Sir George

---

10 Arthur Leon Judson (1881–1975), Ohio-born leading artists' manager who also managed the New York Philharmonic and Philadelphia Orchestra.

11 On 29 January 1953.

Grey,[12] had built his summer retreat. This mansion, largely made of Kauri wood, had been turned into a hotel many years ago. Several annexes had been built onto the original home, and the Auckland yachting fraternity made it one of their ports of call on their sailing holidays.

Sir George Grey, now known only for his Māori Grammar and his translations of Māori mythology, had brought all sorts of unusual animals and birds to Kawau Island. At one time there were monkeys on the island but these had to be destroyed because they became a danger to human beings. The only animal that thrived was the wallaby.[13]

From Kawau we went along the Coromandel Coast and landed at Coromandel itself. This had been a thriving gold mining town in the 1880s. One could tell how thriving it must have been by the size of the huge post office building and the remains of innumerable derelict pubs. There was only one pub left operating and Len Swan knew the proprietor well. We stayed for the best part of the day, drinking one another's health. The proprietor gave me two souvenirs to take away, but Len Swan still has them – a walking stick made of spider wood, and a bottle made during George V's reign by one of the English brewers. It was a very beautiful bottle made of blue glass with the head of the monarch impressed on it.

After a few more days of sailing into the bays of the Coromandel we turned back for Auckland. I needed to go to Wellington for consultations with the programme department of the NZBS, but before that I had a few more days with my brother Roderick (who eventually became the Mayor of Hamilton). Knowing that I would be unlikely to have any free time in my schedule for the next nine months, I suggested we see as many of the sights of the North Island as possible in the few days at my disposal. So, we decided to visit Rotorua and the Waitomo Caves. I had noticed somewhere on the route from Auckland, the neglected monument to Rewi Maniapoto,[14] the redoubtable warrior chief who fought against the British during the Māori wars. He it was who, when called upon to surrender, shouted out he would fight for ever, for ever and forever! The monument, which is also his grave, appeared to be utterly neglected, contributing to my opinion that New Zealanders neglect anything historical or worthy of preservation. The Māori fought against the British fiercely and

---

12 Sir George Grey (1812-1898), soldier, explorer, colonial governor and premier who took a scholarly interest in Māori language and culture. He served twice as Governor of New Zealand (1845–1853 and 1861–1868), and was Premier from 1877 to 1879.

13 The Pōhutukawa Trust New Zealand is now humanely eradicating the remaining wallabies from the island to enable ecological restoration. *The Pohutukawa Trust New Zealand*, http://pohutukawatrust.kiwi, accessed 23 January 2019.

14 The Rewi Maniapoto Memorial and Reserve is at Kihikihi, a small town in the Waikato region, 22 miles south of Hamilton. A major renovation took place in 1990, and the site was further improved in 2012. Since July 2016, the Memorial and Reserve is now a Grade 1 listed heritage site.

uncompromisingly, sometimes with brutal ferocity and at other times with an almost old-world gallantry. Rewi Maniapoto, the fiercest of all the chiefs, and a man who had thoughts of uniting all the tribes of the King Country, was one of the most nationalistic of them all. He tried to rid Aotearoa (New Zealand) of the white man forever. Who would blame him, and who could not understand his ferocity?

We British are too apt to think of ourselves as God's messengers, and the rightful owners of a country, particularly if the opposition have dark skin and lack the comforts of our civilization. There have been enlightened white people of British stock who tried to understand the Māori and his very fine culture, tribal organisation, health and family laws. Sir George Grey, Samuel Marsden[15] and Bishop Selwyn[16] did their utmost to bring about a fuller understanding between the two races. Sir George Grey went to enormous trouble and learned the Māori language, but by far his most important contribution was his translation of the very fine legends of the Māori. I remember, as a small boy, hearing my father read the superb legend of *Hinemoa*. Actually, this legend is one of the tales which make up, with others, the latter part of the book translated by Grey, and it doesn't come into the category of the mythological system told by the Māori as to the origin of Heaven, Earth, the World and Man. But *Hinemoa* makes very pleasant reading and can rival in structure and form similar love stories of other civilizations.

Those tourists who go to Rotorua and visit the little island in the middle of the lake, can still see to this day where Hinemoa rested in a pool of warm water after her long swim from the mainland. This pool is called Hinemoa's Bath. A knowledge of the legend would be a great help in appreciating the simplicity of the Māori mind in such things. Every Māori knows the story of Hinemoa and the fact that it is such a tender story of human love, and occurred in such idyllic and natural surroundings, speaks volumes for the preservation of this relic in exactly the same untouched state as it was on the day that Hinemoa performed her epic swim.[17]

Sir George Grey was appointed Governor of New Zealand by the British

---

15 Samuel Marsden (1765-1838), Yorkshire-born Anglican minister, missionary and magistrate.

16 George Augustus Selwyn (1809-1878), English missionary, consecrated Bishop of New Zealand in 1841.

17 Braithwaite composed two Māori-inspired works for orchestra. *Auē – Māori tone picture* (1931) was premiered by the National Orchestra of Wales on 8 September 1931 in a studio programme called *Folk-Music of Many Lands*. It was subsequently performed by the Sadler's Wells Orchestra, the Welsh Concert Orchestra and the Scottish Orchestra. Another composition, *Legend*, sometimes called *Hinemoa* (1931), was premiered at a lunchtime concert in the National Museum of Wales by the National Orchestra of Wales on 5 October 1931. It was most recently performed and broadcast in a performance by the Ulster Orchestra conducted by Nicholas Braithwaite on 19 August 2015 at Ulster Hall, Belfast.

Government in 1845, and when he arrived in New Zealand there was rebellion and war between the two races. The Māori had contended in arms against the British with considerable success, so that the Governor must have had his hands full from the moment he arrived in the country. He soon saw that if he was to fully understand the grievances of the Māori chiefs and make treaties with them, he would have to dispense with both the European and Māori Christian interpreters, as he felt strongly that he was not enabled to understand fully these grievances in the honest, but garbled, versions of these translators. So, he set out to learn the language, and for eight years gave what spare time he could to this object. During the course of learning the Māori language, he began to realize that in the speeches and letters of the Māori chiefs there were constant references to ancient poems and proverbs, or that the chiefs made allusions to an ancient system of mythology, and in the translation of these the interpreters were most at fault. No publication existed of these poems, proverbs and mythologies, and the chiefs used quotations from these in all of their speeches. Sir George Grey felt it his duty, if he was to hold unrestricted discussions with the Māori, that he must acquaint himself with this side of Māori culture and history. He worked unceasingly at this self-imposed task, and when travelling from island to island, he insisted on being accompanied by his native tutors. Having collected and written down these poems, proverbs, chants, religious songs and mythologies, his work was then lost when Government House was destroyed by fire.[18] He recommended his labours all over again, and this gives us some idea of the industry of this man, and the extent of the debt the Māori and British in New Zealand owe to him. I must also pay tribute to the wonderful work of Sir George Grey in translating and publishing his *Polynesian mythology and ancient traditional history of the New Zealand race, as furnished by their priests and chiefs*.[19] One of the most interesting points which Sir George Grey makes is that, at the time he translated these works, they had prevailed among the Māori race for centuries. There have been several translators of these works since, but Sir George Grey was the first man who, having heard them from the lips of the Māori chiefs themselves, wrote them down for the rest of the world to read.

My trip to Rotorua included a return visit to Fairy Springs,[20] and from there it was only a short distance to the enclosed area where the thermal activity proceeds. This is what most people think of when the name Rotorua is mentioned, for here is the Devil's Cauldron incarnate. There are very hot geysers, boiling mud pools, hot springs, warm pools, and little holes in the

---

18 In 1848.

19 Published in London by John Murray (1855). Much of the information contained in this section must have been drawn from Grey's writings.

20 Braithwaite had previously visited Rotorua in 1947.

ground from which hot steam spouts incessantly. There are other small holes where the Māori women sink their pots full of raw meat or vegetables and thus cook their meals at no cost whatsoever. The smell of sulphur pervades everything, but I didn't find it excessive or unpleasant. People suffering from all sorts of complaints go to Rotorua where there are both enclosed and open-air baths of varying temperatures, and different kinds of waters for the cure of various ills. The whole of this district, underneath the crust of earth of varying thicknesses, is no doubt one vast thermal region. On Lake Rotorua one can catch a trout and row a few yards to another portion of the lake and cook it in very hot water.

Another site near Rotorua is called Geyser Valley.[21] Here enormous jets of steam from about ten holes belch their roaring mass out continuously. They can be heard miles away. At one time the New Zealand government tried to harness these jets to make electricity, and spent enormous sums on experimentation without discovering that 'wet' steam could not be used unless it was 'dried', and so far, no method has been discovered to do this. Why this steam has not been used for central heating I don't know. The steam belches forth with enormous power, and there would be no need for pumping stations as the force of the steam provides its own motive power.[22]

The Waitomo Caves system is one of the most beautiful wonders of the world; a veritable fairyland of extraordinary beauty. To visit the largest cavern, known as the Glow-worm Cave, we were taken in a boat by a guide, complete silence being necessary as the boat proceeded slowly through the cave. Above our heads were millions of glow-worms, shining brightly like a super Milky Way on a perfect starry night. It is an experience, the beauty of which one can never forget. I was most strangely moved by this wonder and only can say that everyone should see it, and until they do, they have not seen real beauty in most magical surroundings. By the way, the Government has built a super hotel right on the spot, and there is no doubt that everything is done to make the tourist comfortable.

Much had changed in New Zealand with the organization of the orchestra, and this time I had no troubles such as I had experienced during the period of Musical Directorship in 1947. In fact, relations with the NZBS were quite different, and I was asked to stay on with the orchestra during the Queen's tour

---

21 Part of the Wairakei Geothermal Field. In 1958 this became the location of the Wairakei power station, the first of its type (wet steam) in the world.

22 Geothermal power now supplies approximately 20% of New Zealand's electricity, https://www. nzgeothermal.org.nz/geothermal-in-nz/what-is-geothermal/, accessed 23 May 2022.

of New Zealand, through Christmas 1953 and until August 1954[23].

In the holiday period November–December 1953 I spent five weeks in New York. While there, my old friend, Dylan Thomas, collapsed and died.[24] I tried to get to the hospital, but every difficulty was put in my way and I felt powerless to do anything but just wait. My friend Philip Wittenberg, who incidentally raised funds for Dylan's wife and family,[25] told me some of the circumstances of Dylan's last days, and I had to be content with this sort of second-hand news of Dylan's sinking. It was all very sad and gave me a bad shock. My affairs musically in New York came to nothing and I left for New Zealand having accomplished nothing beyond making very many dear friends.

The Royal Tour was about to commence when I returned to New Zealand, and at the beginning was marred by that terrible railway disaster when Mount Ruapehu disgorged its crater lake and washed away a railway bridge just before the Wellington to Auckland night express was crossing.[26] Many lives were lost. The Queen's Christmas Message to the Commonwealth dealt most sympathetically with this disaster and must have given great solace to those bereaved. The Royal Tour progressed despite this tragedy and New Zealanders gave the Queen and the Duke of Edinburgh a tremendous reception everywhere.

One of the reasons I was happy to stay in New Zealand for so long was because the Royal Concert was to be given in my own home town Dunedin in that very beautiful and lovely Town Hall auditorium, and it was a great delight for me to arrange a programme that I hoped the Queen would appreciate. I knew, as Her Royal Highness the Princess Elizabeth, she had heard *Hansel und Gretel* at Sadler's Wells when she was quite a child, and I had a specially selected choir from all the girls' schools in Dunedin to sing the chorus parts. The concert was a very great success, and I believe both the Queen and the Duke of

---

23 Musically, not everything went according to plan. Braithwaite avoids mention of a Dunedin performance of Dyson's *The Canterbury Pilgrims* in September 1953, which was sabotaged by poor preparation. He walked out of the final rehearsal, but reluctantly conducted the performance. The whole debacle is covered by Joy Tonks in *The New Zealand Symphony Orchestra: The First Forty Years* (Auckland: Reed Methuen, 1986) pages 57-59.

24 Dylan Thomas died on 9 November 1953 in St Vincent's Hospital, New York.

25 Philip Wittenberg (1895-1987) was a distinguished Manhattan lawyer who acted as Treasurer for a fund to assist Dylan Thomas' widow and children. The Dylan Thomas Fund Committee consisted of W.H. Auden, Marianne Moore, E.E. Cummings, Wallace Stevens, Arthur Miller, Tennessee Williams and Thornton Wilder.

26 On 24 December a North Island main trunk express plunged off the Tangiwai bridge into the Whangaehu River. The bridge had been fatally weakened by a lahar from Mt Ruapehu's crater lake. Of the 285 people on board, 151 were killed. This was New Zealand's worst rail disaster. 'Tangiwai railway disaster', Ministry for Cultural and Heritage, https://nzhistory.govt.nz/culture/the-tangiwai-railway-disaster, updated 7 August 2014, accessed 14 January 2019.

Edinburgh were pleased with the programme.[27] In my conversation with Her Majesty after the concert,[28] I was quite astounded to find that she remembered she had met my brother Roderick, Mayor of Hamilton, and knew that my father had been one of Dunedin's mayors.

*

After the Royal Tour ended, I was back in Wellington in order to make up the programmes of the next season. Then I set out on a voyage to find out if New Zealand was as scenically beautiful as I had always been told as a child. I left Wellington by the small steamer which goes over to Picton, a small town at the base of the Marlborough Sounds in the northern tip of the South Island. As we came through Tory Channel to enter the Queen Charlotte Sound, one could see the tremendous tidal current gurgling its way between the high rocks of the entrance. I felt that even a very slight miscalculation on the part of the helmsman could easily get the little steamer into trouble, but we arrived safely at Picton and from there I travelled in a rickety train to Nelson and stayed at the Nelson Hotel for the night.

Next morning, I caught a bus which was to take me down the Buller Gorge, one of the reportedly major scenic wonders of the South Island. Thus commenced a succession of great scenic panoramas which were revealed to me for a whole fortnight. The Buller Gorge defies description. For hours I travelled down a road high above the Buller River, through the most awe-inspiring mountain scenery with the green coloured river below. Former settlements, which had been thriving towns in the heyday of gold mining, now lay virtually derelict, often with only one pub remaining, whereas before there were fifty. But those solitary pubs were very proud of their gold mining days with, in many instances, photographs of the dancing girls, typical of all rough old mining communities of the 1860's.

After reaching Westport, I caught a bus to Greymouth down the magnificent coastal road and stayed the night, before travelling to Hokitika and on to the Franz Josef Glacier. This glacier is fairly easy to access if you don't mind walking from the nearest road for about a mile over the rocky bed of the remains of the glacial river, and from there one could (if transport was possible) visit many glaciers within a radius of 18 miles or so. The great Tasman Glacier is only a few

---

27 Braithwaite fails to mention that he had been awarded the Queen Elizabeth II Coronation Medal in June 1953, along with other notable New Zealanders.

28 There were Royal Concerts in Auckland (25 December 1953) and Dunedin (26 January 1954). At the first, he shared the conducting with Horace Hollinrake (1904–1955), but at the second, which had a more substantial programme, he was the sole conductor. It was after this concert that Braithwaite was presented to the royal visitors.

miles away from the Franz Josef.[29] From the admirable Franz Josef Hotel, I flew over Mount Cook to Queenstown on Lake Wakatipu and spent several days there. I caught the steamer to the head of the lake to a place called Paradise[30] (it almost was) and thence by bus to the Dart Valley. I had never seen anything so grandiose, so magnificent as this panorama of great mountains and valleys, and in such a perfect setting.

From Queenstown I was intent on making the long, arduous, but the most gratifying, trip by bus via Lumsden, past Lakes Te Anau and Manapouri, and on to Cascade Creek Tourist Camp, where I spent the night. The following morning, I was off by the tourist bus through the amazing Eglinton Valley of awe-inspiring New Zealand beech trees, and on to the Homer Tunnel, cut through solid rock for about two miles.

Another bus took me to Milford Sound, and here was the climax I had hoped for. Everything that had gone before was as nothing compared to the grandeur, the enormity, the design of its most wonderful waterway. The Milford Sound is a fiord, but also much more. The fiord winds its ten miles to the open sea, but one passes the most immense mountains, the sides of which precipitate themselves sheer into the sea. The mountains are heavily wooded with New Zealand trees; there are many waterfalls, and the great Bowen Falls has water which is blown back by the wind and never reaches the sea!

I called on the manager of the new Government Tourist Hotel at Milford Sound. He is a relative of mine through marriage, and I was able to see this most up-to-date hotel whose enormous windows offer a vista right down to one of the famous landmarks – the mountains called Lion's Head. It came on to rain about this time and from that moment it never stopped until I got out of the mountainous district. On the way back, the little streams we had passed over earlier, had become raging torrents and on approaching the Homer Tunnel, one could see hundreds of waterfalls tearing down the sides of the huge mountains.

It was an unforgettable trip and I was glad I had done it. The most amazing thing about it was that, whereas it had been raining nearly all the time I was on the West Coast, on the other side of the Alps the whole countryside was bone dry. There was just no more rain left. Central Otago was in the grip of a bad drought, and during the journey down the Kawarau Gorge and then into Central Otago, the burnt-up state of the country was lamentable to behold. Water was being provided to residents from water wagons and there seemed no

---

29 New Zealand glaciers, including the famous Fox and Franz Josef Glaciers, have been in retreat since 1890, despite occasional shorter periods of advance. Both glaciers are currently more than 2.5 km (1.6 miles) shorter than a century ago.

30 Braithwaite had mentioned Paradise on his previous visit in 1947, but presumably had not visited it on that occasion.

end to the drought. Yet only ten miles away on the West Coast, the rain never stopped. But this perpetual rain was responsible for some of the great glories of the New Zealand scenery, the roaring torrents, waterfalls and the wonderfully lush growth of New Zealand forests.

*

After this trip of two weeks,[31] I was back in Wellington and hard at work preparing for the Promenade Concerts in the four big cities during March and April 1954, and also preparing for the concert season proper, which commenced at the end of March in Wellington. I carried through all concerts, not missing one engagement, until the next conductor, James Robertson, arrived at the end of August. I saw a little of James during my last week in New Zealand and gave him my opinion of certain matters dealing with the musical side of life in New Zealand.

The season with the National Orchestra produced some interesting performances. I tried, in my programmes, to give as comprehensive a selection of music to each of the big centres as possible. I was worried about Dunedin because attendances had fallen off during the previous two seasons before I took over. I had gone to the trouble of studying my predecessor's programmes with the attendances of each concert and found that, although Dunedin had been given some very good programmes of the very highest value, the musical public seemed to be indifferent. My predecessor, Michael Bowles, had done his very best for my home town, but somehow the Dunedin musical folk stayed away. I gave this problem a great deal of thought, and two considerations influenced me to try other types of programmes. The first consideration was the seeming advantage I had of being 'local boy made good'. I was to receive a shock to my self-esteem in this respect, as it made not the slightest difference. Dunedin people would fall back on the most puerile excuses as to why they stayed away. The programmes had on one hand been too highbrow and on the other too lowbrow. I thought it worth trying to attract more of the 'lowbrows' by including fairly light music. By light music I mean music by Massenet among others, and some of the Russian composers; all of it bright and brilliantly orchestrated. But the result was disappointing, and attendance hardly improved in any way. I was the recipient of scurrilous letters on the one hand from university professors complaining that I was underestimating their intelligence, and on the other from 'lowbrows' who said the performances were too classical! There was no way of satisfying the smug Dunedin concertgoers. The 'university brethren' boycotted the concerts and the ordinary citizens had lost touch with the concert going habit anyway.

---

31 Braithwaite's trip must have occurred in February 1954. That was the only period in his schedule that would allow for a two-week holiday.

*

Whilst touring in New Zealand during 1954, I had conducted some performances of opera with an organisation calling itself the National Opera of Australia, and managed (or mis-managed) by a curious woman, Mrs Clarice Lorenz.[32] This lady, who appeared to think that I was the answer to all her troubles, offered me a contract for two years as Artistic and Musical Director. I confess that the headed notepaper of this organization, with its galaxy of important names from the New South Wales Government downwards, and the experience of working with a fine body of Australian singers, led me to believe that there was a possibility of great future things with them. But when I arrived in Sydney and sat at my office table, the real truth as to the parlous state of the organization and its muddle and debt, became only too apparent. I very quickly found out three things. Firstly, Mrs Lorenz's word could not be trusted; secondly, there was already a mountain of debt and no hope of ever paying it off; and thirdly, Mrs Lorenz continued to plan elaborate and expensive seasons with absolutely *no* hope of ever financing them. Managers and accountants one after another had left because they could get no business satisfaction from her. Other men on the committee had endeavoured to extricate themselves from the worst results of her lack of business acumen, but had been forced out by a body of men who, for some reason, stuck to her through thick and thin. When I took over there was, as far as one could ever find out, a supposed debt of £45,000. The debt was much bigger than this if it was added to the many comparatively small debts which certain well-wishers to the cause of opera in Australia had waived for the time being.

I planned to do six operas for the seven-week season in Sydney, all of a popular nature – *Die Fledermaus*, *Il trovatore*, *Rigoletto*, *Madama Butterfly*, *La traviata*, and *La bohème*. A more popular choice of repertoire would be impossible to find. My job was to cast the operas, find the scenic designers, and ensure that no new sets would be made unless they were practical from an operatic point of view. They must also be produced as cheaply as possible. I was on the tail of the scenic designers all the time and had the utmost co-operation from them. When the set models were passed by me, the next step was to arrange payment to the designers, and after that, initiate the construction of the sets and payment for same. Now the fun commenced in earnest. Designer after designer declined to go any further with his work until I could guarantee payment. Try as I might I could not nail Mrs Lorenz down to a firm contract for these men. At

32 Clarice Maude Lorenz (1906-1981). Her National Opera of Australia toured several works around New Zealand during April and May 1954. Braithwaite conducted some performances of Gounod's *Faust*, and on 1 May, Mrs Lorenz announced that Warwick Braithwaite would be the Artistic Director of the company from August 1955. Had Braithwaite known that the company returned to Sydney leaving £1800 in unpaid bills, he might well have resisted the offer.

last, I refused to sign any letter from the National Opera to any firm or designer in which a promise to pay any sum of money was involved. This was a very wise precaution as far as I was concerned as it kept my nose clean. I had attracted some very talented designers around me and had accepted the designs subject to financial arrangements being completed by Mrs Lorenz. Hereafter followed the most expert wriggling, humbuggery and hornswoggling by this lady that it has ever been my misfortune to see. It was most distressing to see these artists trying to get their due from this most untrustworthy woman. Finally, I was amazed at her cruel guile and sordid prevarication, and my heart sank more and more when I was at last forced to realize that the whole organisation of the National Opera of Australia was a complete farce.

After having done what I could in advance planning and complete casting, I left the financial arrangements in Mrs Lorenz's hands. I caught the MS *Neptunia* from Sydney on 29 October so that I would be back in London for Christmas with my family. The fare for this trip had already been paid by the New Zealand Government, and it was arranged with Mrs Lorenz in our preliminary talks in New Zealand that I should make this trip (which cost her nothing), and that she should pay my airfare back to Sydney in the New Year (1955). Having promised to be back at the earliest date in the New Year, I arrived in Sydney on January 12th.

While in London, my uneasy feeling about my contract began to assume importance and came to a head when I received a cable from a stooge accountant to the effect that the National Opera Australia would only pay £100 towards my fare. I immediately sent an air mail letter pointing out that although the NOA was honour-bound to pay my fare, I would pay the residue out of deductions from my salary spread over a year. This was consented to and the fare was paid for in Sydney (actually it wasn't, although I didn't know at the time, and this is one more of the unpaid debts of the NOA). I left London on 7 January by the *Monarch Brae* and arrived in New York the next day.[33] My birthday (9 January) was spent with my two sisters-in-law and I left that night for San Francisco and then across the Pacific by Qantas.

Arriving in Sydney, and having to wait for over an hour while the authorities found the port doctor, I came out to the general enclosure to be met by a new publicity NOA official. The previous one, like many before her, had left owing to the completely stultifying conditions under which she had to work. I then went back to my old flat at Martin Hall, and no sooner was I ensconced there than the phone rang and the indefatigable Hon. Director (Mrs Lorenz) was speaking. All was honeyed and sugary and she offered to come along to my flat in order to talk over a few details about the forthcoming season. She brought with her a bottle of rum and over many sips of this delectable beverage we settled some

---

33 Possibly a BOAC 'Monarch' flight which operated a regular overnight service from London to New York.

points which were urgent. Next morning, I was at the office and surprise after surprise was in store for me.

First, Nicholson & Co (the Ricordi agents) had refused to supply vocal scores and orchestral parts for all the operas because of an unsettled debt of £780 for past seasons. Second, no theatre management would let Mrs Lorenz have their theatre because of the tottering financial position. One theatre management after another refused, unless the rent was paid in cash in advance. I was sent on stooge-like missions by Mrs Lorenz to various managements, all with the same result. The J.C. Williamson organization was very courteous to me personally, and indeed sympathised with my predicament. Third, the buying of materials for the costumes went through the same pattern of frustration. The designer would find the right material one day, but because of delays in guaranteeing payment, the same material would be sold elsewhere. Fourth, the wardrobe mistress (who had been with the company in New Zealand) had resigned, and nothing would persuade her to rejoin the Company. She was a first-rate wardrobe mistress, and although another was found, she could not cope with all the work. Mrs Lorenz very grandly told her to get helpers, and this poor woman fell into the trap. None of the helpers were paid and fell away, and with the season only a few weeks away the situation was chaotic. Fifth, at the end of my second week, the stooge accountant informed me that one third of my salary had been deducted, and was to be deducted every week. With PAYE,[34] it was impossible to live on this amount. All I had been promised was that the rest of my airfare (and this was purely a voluntary gesture on my part) would be deducted over a year. This would have meant about £2.10s. per week over a year. Naturally I was incensed by their disgraceful procedure and protested vigorously.

Letter after letter passed between Mrs Lorenz and myself, and I threatened to resign in a week's time unless this state of affairs was rectified. In a subsequent interview with Mrs Lorenz, I offered to step up my contribution to six pounds per week. This was accepted but her stooge accountant tried a fast one over me by suggesting that I be a party to diddling the Income Tax by declaring my salary to be lower than it was. I would not consent to this and took steps to safeguard myself by seeking legal advice. Finally, I had to be content with losing more of my salary than I wished, but I made up my mind that I would take action at a time and in such a manner when and where it would hurt most. In the meantime, the worst theatre in Sydney was engaged, but only after the rent was paid in advance and a further sum lodged with the theatre management against the expenses of staff and the costs of getting in and out. This theatre had a stage that was entirely inadequate but which had an apron stage – a compensation

---

34 The Pay As You Earn (PAYE) system is a method of paying income tax and national insurance contributions.

only when the curtain was up. The chorus dressing rooms were non-existent and a space under the stage was divided by hessian material – one side for men and the other for women. No water closets or basins could be installed because of lack of money, and how this loyal body of men and women carried on under these circumstances is something incredible to believe. But carry on they did, and a great deal of the artistic success of this sad season of seven weeks was solely through the loyalty of these choristers and the virile assistance of the principals.

The climax came when Mrs Lorenz insisted on sacking a singer I had engaged for the part of Gilda in *Rigoletto*. I hadn't heard this soprano since I conducted the Sadler's Wells Opera in Hamburg (nine years previously), but no other Gilda was available. Mrs Lorenz had heard this singer fairly recently (whereas I hadn't) but had waited with devilish cunning for the moment when she could make me look incompetent. The whole process was a dirty example of intrigue. After this I wrote to Mrs Lorenz officially resigning from the NOA to take effect at the end of the season, four weeks hence.

At no time did I give any indication to the outside world that anything was amiss, but an interfering friend of mine (who had suffered from Mrs Lorenz most cruelly) tipped off the press. The fat was really in the fire. The Australian press must be experienced to be believed – a pack of wolves would be more humane. Once they get their noses on the trail, they never leave the ground. I was phoned up every morning at seven o'clock by a reporter on *The Sun* newspaper pleading for a break. Then the blow fell. A young reporter, set on by that arch-wolf Frank Packer,[35] the editor-owner of the *Sydney Herald*, came to the theatre during the first performance of *La traviata*. He insisted that I had a story to give Australia, but I denied I had resigned and would not budge from my attitude. At the end of the performance, however, I was told of the disgraceful behaviour of Mrs Lorenz in the front of the house. She was very much the worse for drink and started shrieking out to the Australian Broadcasting Commission (ABC) officials and the reporters that I could have the company if I wanted it. Apparently, this kind of thing had been going on all through the performance. The only inkling I had of this was during the Second Act, when I was handed an almost indecipherable note from Mrs Lorenz asking me to leave the conductor's desk to attend a Press Conference. I went on quite calmly and absolutely unruffled, thinking that Mrs Lorenz was either mad or completely drunk. Both suppositions vied with one another as to first place.

After the performance, Roy Lamb of the ABC asked me to go to Mrs Lorenz and 'put your arms around her and beg forgiveness.' This decided me and I brought several people back to my flat including the young reporter aforementioned. We discussed the whole matter until the early hours of the

---

35 Sir Douglas Frank Hewson Packer (1906–1974), Australian media proprietor.

morning, and a press statement was decided upon. This was phoned through to the Night Editor and that finished one whole day of incredible happenings.

The whole sordid business gathered momentum during the last few weeks. More press statements were given, including one from Mrs Lorenz saying that I had not resigned. Meetings with the committee presided over by Mrs Lorenz led to nothing. I had a plan which Robin Lovejoy[36] and I had worked out and which we were prepared to submit to the committee. Indeed, we were asked by them to do so. It would have saved the whole situation, and it included the removal of Mrs Lorenz as Hon. Managing Director, and substituting a triumvirate including the Chairman of the Committee, Lovejoy and myself. Although this was an interim suggestion only, it was doomed to failure from the start. The committee by now only included Mrs Lorenz's male stooges – most other disinterested parties having either resigned or simply stayed away. Instead of discussing our plan, in which the Triumvirate was only one part of a much more precise list of reforms, these men shouted at Robin and myself like enraged parrots. The irony of it all was that we had been asked by the Chairman of the committee to give our views, but this was not to be, and we both left the meeting knowing full well that our scheme would never be discussed. It was also very apparent to me that anyone who tried to get things right with the working of the NOA would, sooner or later, be manoeuvred into a position by Mrs Lorenz so that a resignation was the only honourable outcome. If anyone questioned her methods, the walls closed in and the only hope of retaining any sanity was to break out. One very gratifying thing to me personally was the absolute solidarity of the choristers, the principals and the orchestra. The choristers and principals (with one exception), resigned in a body when my resignation was eventually accepted by Mrs Lorenz and her committee. The members of the orchestra sent me a letter, signed by every member, in which they all identified themselves with my action. Of course, there were backsliders, but in a company of seventy or eighty people, there were only three of these.

It was most amusing to see the wriggling of these three people. They had learnt quite a lot from Mrs Lorenz's methods and imitated them very well. There was a musician, an Austrian refugee, who had settled in New Zealand, and who mostly by intrigue got himself under Mrs Lorenz's aegis as a coach and eventually as a conductor.[37] He made a great show of conducting from memory, knowing full well that such a thing can be used for propaganda purposes with simple folk to the extinction of a full appraisement of a real talent for operatic

---

36 Robin Casper Lovejoy (1923-1985), Australian actor, director and theatre designer.

37 Unmistakably Georg Tintner (1917-1999). This uncharacteristic outburst of anger and jealousy towards a fellow conductor suggests the depth of feeling that Braithwaite still held about his treatment by Mrs Lorenz. For a different perspective on this period see Tanya Buchdahl Tintner's excellent biography *Out of Time: The Vexed Life of Georg Tintner* (Crawley, W.A.: University of Western Australia, 2011).

conducting. He was also a sly intriguer and gentle-voiced to boot. He was a vegetarian and used to eat nuts. When he played piano for my rehearsals he played haltingly and badly; when he played for himself it was a different matter. This gentleman waited until he saw which way the cat jumped and allied himself with Mrs Lorenz unreservedly in the end.

To finish the description of this sordid business, Mrs Lorenz staged a nervous breakdown and did not appear in public for a few days, while all the time having indignant meetings with her sycophants at home. Pressure from some source was brought to bear on Frank Packer of the *Sydney Herald*, and the campaign against Mrs Lorenz was called off mysteriously. This was nothing new, as such things had happened before, and one could believe that there must have been some sort of blackmail operating around the corner that made this possible. I had lunch one day with Eugene Goossens who told me that Mrs Lorenz owed him £150 for conducting during the previous season. When I asked him why he had allowed her to get away with this he replied that he would insist on getting his money somehow. Well, he didn't and I am now wondering why. The Income Tax authorities found evidence of crooked dealing (so I was told by an official of the Income Tax Department) but didn't sue Mrs Lorenz. When I told this official of my predicament and that I had to get back to London but had absolutely no money, I was given the utmost consideration by him and my PAYE rebate was more than enough to pay my fare.

My impression was that everybody outside the aegis of the NOA knew of the double-dealing propensities of Mrs Lorenz, but that nobody wanted to start proceedings against her. The artists, chorus and orchestra saw the season through, but for the last three weeks received either no payment, or only payment in dribs and drabs. Later some of the artists were asked to appear at concerts organised by Mrs Lorenz in order to make enough money to pay their back salaries. Of course, they were asked to sing for nothing. None of them complied with these overtures.

As to Mrs Lorenz, one aspect of the whole affair was the extraordinary power she seemed to wield in certain official quarters. This power was certainly not the result of belief in her as an opera organiser. The best brains, both financial and artistic in Sydney, had, after experiencing her slap-happy methods, cut themselves adrift from her mismanagement, yet a number of men who knew nothing about opera or opera management supported her through thick and thin. They condoned her mistakes and there was no gaff that these men would not stomach. She should have been put into the bankruptcy court, yet no one would sue her and start proceedings. Equity[38] in Sydney threatened all sorts of actions, but these were suddenly dropped. Why? What secret power

---

38 Presumably Actors Equity, now a member of the Media, Entertainment & Arts Alliance.

did this curious woman possess? Those who knew that opera in Sydney could not progress under such mis-management would stare blankly and shut their mouths if they were asked to start a campaign to get rid of her. So, I suppose Sydney opera enthusiasts have got what they deserve.[39]

*

Having arrived back in London in July 1955 practically penniless, I was most anxious about the immediate future. But after a few days at home, bewildered at the lack of engagements, I happened to meet an old friend[40] who was employed by Associated-Rediffusion[41] and who thought I was the very man for his series of programmes. I was contracted to do one television programme a fortnight, but unfortunately my friend's programmes were cancelled at the last moment. The company had an orchestra and myself on their hands, so we did a lot of background music recording instead, thus working out our contract.

Once again, I was asked by the Welsh National Opera to participate in a two-week season of popular repertoire given in Swansea.[42] I was also asked to conduct the work to be performed during their visit to Sadler's Wells in July 1956. This was Verdi's fourth opera, *I Lombardi*, and I was agreeably surprised at the strength of the work and tried very hard to make it the great success it was. I felt I was really making this Welsh chorus sing with care and nuance, and the critics in London lauded our efforts up to the skies.[43]

After the Cardiff Season of two weeks in October 1956, I was offered an engagement of four weeks in Reykjavík, Iceland, to conduct performances of *Il trovatore*, and a symphony concert with the National Symphony Orchestra

---

39 History suggests that things turned out well enough. The Australian Opera Company (1956–1957) became the Elizabethan Theatre Trust Opera Company (1957–1970), The Australian Opera (1970–1996) and finally Opera Australia (1996–).

40 Possibly Boris Ford (1917–1998), who briefly held the post of first head of schools broadcasting (1957–1958). Associated-Rediffusion shouldered some of the losses from Associated Television, and this caused the cancellation of many of their 'artistic' projects and a concentration on light entertainment and variety.

41 Associated-Rediffusion began television transmission for London and parts of the surrounding counties, on weekdays between 22 September 1955 and 29 July 1968. Weekend independent transmissions were supplied by Associated Television (ATV).

42 At the Empire Theatre, Swansea. Braithwaite conducted *Il trovatore* and *La bohème* on 16 and 17 April 1956 respectively.

43 The performances of *I Lombardi* on 16 and 21 July 1956 were greeted with fine reviews: 'The opera is well cast and well played by the Bournemouth Symphony Orchestra under Mr Braithwaite, who skilfully equates accompaniment with interpretation.' *The Times* (17 July 1956), 5. 'I wish that I could write at length about a vivid performance of Verdi's early *I Lombardi* conducted by Warwick Braithwaite...It was not merely distinguished by the best choral singing I have heard in any opera house outside Bayreuth, but by an exemplary sense of line.' *The Observer* (29 July 1956), 10.

of Iceland. The great success of these performances was indicated by the fact that although there were three performances of *Il trovatore* advertised, we had to give seven because of the great demand for seats. I had five Icelandic singers for these performances, all of them good, but a tenor, a soprano and especially a baritone, of outstanding excellence.[44] I would go so far as to say that these three singers could sing in any first-rate opera house in the world. Strange that in a town of only 60,000 people one should find such great singers.

Iceland in winter conjures up visions of icebergs, frozen rivers and snowdrifts. Such was not the case, and Reykjavík was warmer than the London I had left on the first day of November 1956. I had been told to take woolly long pants, which I did, but had no occasion to change from my summer underwear. Reykjavík, although seemingly a small town, looks like a metropolis and has every sign of being a continental town. Life can be lived to the full there, and Icelandic hospitality must be experienced to be believed.

I was anxious to see some hot springs and to learn how this hot water was harnessed and pumped into the town. I spent a very interesting afternoon walking from one 'hole' to another and went right down into the bowels of one of the pumping stations. The heat, right down below, was excessive but I was rewarded by having the mechanics of the pumping station explain to me in detail. There are numerous hot springs outside Reykjavík; the temperature of the water is mostly 100°F. Nearly every house is heated by this natural hot water, and the cost to the householder is modest, so that a bath costs something like one penny. This must be the cheapest hot water system anywhere in the world.

One aspect of life in Reykjavík is its status as a capital city. All embassies are centred there, and so is the university and the national theatre. There is quite a continental flavour about diplomatic life, and Icelanders are very proud of their place in the world. They are a very assured people and most cultured. They are proud of their ancient heritage, their 1,000-year-old parliament, and their great explorers such as Leif Erikson.[45] The USA recognized this fact by erecting a monument in the middle of Reykjavík[46] to Leif's memory; a gift to the people of Iceland. I saw this at two o'clock one morning in the glow of headlamps from several motorcars.

---

44 The cast included Þuríður Pálsdóttir (*Leonora*); Guðmunda Elíasdóttir (*Azucena*); Magnús Jónsson (*Manrico*); Guðmundur Jónsson (*Di Luna*) and Kristinn Hallsson (*Ferrando*).

45 Leif Erikson (*c.*970–*c.*1020), Norse explorer from Iceland who was the first known European to have discovered continental North America, before Christopher Columbus.

46 The statue by Alexander Stirling Calder was a gift from the United States of America in 1930, commemorating the 1000th anniversary of Iceland's parliament.

POSTLUDE
(1957–1971)

BY

ROGER FLURY

POSTLUDE (1957–1971)

At this point – and for no obvious reason – Warwick Braithwaite stopped work on his autobiography. His association with Covent Garden Opera had ended almost imperceptibly in Birmingham on 5 April 1952 with a matinée performance of *La bohème*, but was followed by a series of eleven recording sessions in London for MGM, Parlophone, EMI and RCA, mostly with the Royal Opera House orchestra.

The months following his return to England from Australia in July 1955 had been particularly lean. He had been away since January 1953 and few professional musicians, no matter how delighted they might be to tour the antipodes, would risk disappearing from London for such an extended period.

Some contract work for Associated-Rediffusion kept the wolf from the door, but it was his appointment as Musical Director for Welsh National Opera that marked not only his welcome return to a leading role in British musical life, but also a period of intense and satisfying music-making mostly, but not exclusively, in the opera house.

His return to the opera pit took place in Swansea with a performance of *Il trovatore* on 16 April 1956 and continued with some notable rarities in Verdi's *I Lombardi* and Boito's *Mefistofele*. These two operas were repeated with great success in London (as mentioned in his last chapter), and although he gives no hint of it, there would have been some personal satisfaction if his triumphs had caused even a slight sense of discomfort at Covent Garden. Later he was able to continue his passion for Russian opera by introducing Rimsky-Korsakov's *May Night* into the repertoire.

During these years, the Welsh National Opera regularly engaged the Bournemouth Symphony Orchestra to play for performances, and although the operatic schedule of seasons in Cardiff, Swansea and Llandudno left little time for formal concert engagements, Braithwaite was able to give ten concerts with the orchestra on the south coast and as far afield as Gloucester and Exeter. He also renewed his New Zealand links with a concert at the Wigmore Hall on 19 October 1956, given under the auspices of the New Zealand Music Society.[1] The programme featured music by Bach, Mozart and Finzi performed by the Jacques Orchestra with New Zealand artists Andrew Gold *(tenor)*, John McCaw *(clarinet)* and Shirley Carter *(piano)*. The only work by a composer with a New Zealand connection was Max Saunders' *Interludium*.

In addition to the highly successful performances in Reykjavík, Braithwaite also fitted in a performance of *La bohème* with the Dublin Grand Opera Society, a recording session for Columbia of Verdi arias with soprano Aase Nordmo-Løvberg accompanied by the Philharmonia Orchestra, and concert engagements with the City of Birmingham Symphony Orchestra and three BBC regional orchestras – the Scottish, Northern and Welsh. But inevitably, the strain of constant travelling between his family in London, his work in Cardiff and his engagements elsewhere, necessitated a change of strategy. The WNO, despite popular success, was experiencing financial difficulties caused, in the main, by the refusal of the Arts Council in London to increase its grant. After much politicking and wrangling behind the scenes, sufficient additional funding was found to put the company in a secure position that would enable long-term plans to be made with confidence. Those plans included the appointment of the company's first ever full-time Musical Director. Warwick Braithwaite was the obvious candidate, but he had already signalled his intention to decline any full-time appointment. Perhaps the shadow of his previous battles on behalf of the NOW made the decision easier, but without doubt he could leave Cardiff with his head held high, secure in the knowledge that WNO was about to become a significant player in the British operatic scene and that the Musical Director of the Bournemouth Symphony Orchestra, Charles Groves, was to pick up the baton.

Even so, it was a prolonged departure from the WNO. With an eye to the future, Braithwaite renewed his association with Sadler's Wells in February 1960 by conducting performances of *La bohème*, *Die Fledermaus* and *Tosca* in London, Oxford, Bristol, Manchester, Nottingham, Liverpool and on a tour of Scotland. This carried him through to June. Existing commitments to WNO required him to spend time in Llandudno in August, but September and October were again devoted to Sadler's Wells. November saw Braithwaite back again with WNO for *Madama Butterfly*, *Die Fledermaus* and *May Night*, but from January 1961 onwards he was firmly ensconced with Sadler's Wells Opera and heavily involved in its touring schedule. Except for an occasional performance of *Mefistofele* or

---

1   Co-founded by Herbert Maximillian (Max) Saunders (1903–1983). Saunders was a London-born composer whose family emigrated to Auckland in 1910. He returned to the U.K. as an orchestrator for BBC radio and television. Of this concert *The Times* critic wrote: 'The programme was completed by an introspective, elegiac *Interludium* by Max Saunders, played with great eloquence and elegance by the orchestra under the lively Mr Braithwaite.' *The Times* (20 Oct. 1956), 8.

Tosca with WNO, and two seasons of *Carmen* in Dublin, he remained with Sadler's Wells until the expiration of his contract on 15 June 1968.

With hindsight it is clear that the period 1960–1968 was a very positive time for Warwick Braithwaite. It began happily, on a personal level, with an announcement in *The Times* of 18 January 1961 signalling the engagement of Rodric Quentin Braithwaite, elder son of Mr and Mrs Warwick Braithwaite of 23 Linden Lea, Hampstead, N.2 and Gillian Mary, elder daughter of Mr and Mrs Patrick Robinson of Patchan, Oxshott, Surrey.

On a professional level, Braithwaite was spared any management responsibilities and could concentrate on what he did best – conducting. From the resumption of his work with Sadler's Wells in 1960, until his departure in 1968, he led well over 162 performances of 15 operas. If we combine these statistics with those from his earlier period with the company (1932–1940), we find that he conducted at least 541 performances of 30 operas for Sadler's Wells. I say 'at least' because many performances on tour have yet to be documented. The total could rise significantly.

A highlight of this period was his advocacy of Puccini's neglected *La fanciulla del West*. He had conducted an orchestral fantasia from the opera with the Cardiff 5WA Station Orchestra in 1924 and recorded one of Minnie's arias with Joan Hammond and the Philharmonia Orchestra in 1947, but it was Birgit Nilsson's recording of the complete opera for EMI in 1958 that convinced him of the true stature of the work. Having persuaded the Sadler's Wells management to take a risk on this opera, Braithwaite then conducted it brilliantly and, helped by outstanding performances from Elizabeth Fretwell *(Minnie)*, Donald Smith *(Johnson)* and Raimund Herincx *(Jack Rance)*, gave the opera its first foothold in the repertoire.[2]

Another significant success came with the revival of a fairly new production of Gounod's *Faust*, an opera more appreciated by O'Mara's provincial audiences than by those of swinging London in the Sixties. However, reviews made it clear that, in the right hands, Gounod's score could still reveal its secrets and move an audience.[3]

---

2   On the whole, the reviewers agreed: 'Mr Braithwaite, though, is a good Puccinian, and for the rest, he whirled his orchestra into a vibrant, dynamic account of the score, occasionally rather thin in string sonority by ideal standards, that made a powerful case for the return of *The Girl* to public favour.' *The Times* (6 December 1962), 5. A later performance on 10 January 1963, with the same principals, was broadcast by the BBC. It has appeared on several CD labels including Oriel Music OMT 877 issued in 2012.

3   Critic Philip Hope-Wallace wrote, 'Sadler's Wells' recent new *Faust* was completely transformed last night by cast changes and by the conducting of Warwick Braithwaite who has the knack (not easy) of making Gounod sound as he should. The third act cavatina could not have been better handled. The fragrant sensuous, but lightly turned music of this garden scene had its exact measure; and was heard again to deserve its great renown. The instinct for such things is not common; to sentimentalise without vulgarity is an art, if a minor one. The whole performance benefitted.' Philip Hope-Wallace, *The Guardian* (7 Feb 1965).

Despite having conducted Wagner's overture to *Der fliegende Holländer* at least 37 times during his career, it was not until 1965 that Braithwaite had the opportunity to conduct staged performances of the complete opera. The Sadler's Wells production, which toured England and Scotland, underwent many changes of cast on the seventeen occasions when Braithwaite conducted, but at certain times (when the planets were aligned) it could boast Rita Hunter *(Senta)*, Alberto Remedios *(Erik)*, and New Zealander Donald McIntyre as the Dutchman.

Braithwaite's last major assignment with Sadler's Wells was a revival of Beethoven's *Fidelio*, directed by John Blatchley, but with new dialogue by John Arden. According to Nicholas Braithwaite, this was an opera his father would have 'walked across hot coals to do.'[4] Reviews of the performance, which opened at Sadler's Wells on 7 October 1966, were mixed, but Braithwaite must have been gratified to read appreciative musical comments from Charles Reid in *The Spectator*[5] and David Cairns in *The Financial Times*.[6]

Braithwaite's contract with Sadler's Wells officially ended on 30 March 1968, but Stephen Arlen asked him to stay on and coach singers for the remaining three months of the season. It is clear from the correspondence between Braithwaite and Arlen that this was not an easy time. The conductor did not want to completely sever ties with the Wells, and he offered his services, if not to conduct, then at least to help with auditions, music rehearsals and advice based on his extensive experience in the profession. However, Sadler's Wells Opera was about to move to its new London home at the Coliseum Theatre in St Martin's Lane, and to reinvent itself as English National Opera. It had appointed Charles Mackerras as its Musical Director, and perhaps links with the past were not viewed as helpful. At about the same time, Welsh National Opera announced its new Music Director as James Lockhart. With both his 'home' companies setting forth on new adventures, Braithwaite might well have felt a little out of things, but he found some consolation in conducting the Second Orchestra at the Royal Academy of Music for a few months.

---

4   Private correspondence between Nicholas Braithwaite and Roger Flury.

5   'The thing which above all gave the night conviction and character was Warwick Braithwaite's conducting. His speeds were individually right and made sense with each other. He got a special fidelity and warmth from the strings. And he had the singers with him all the way. This for the simplest reason in the world. *He* was with the singers.' Charles Reid, *The Spectator* (14 Oct 1966), 20.

6   'Warwick Braithwaite understands the score. He seldom if ever misjudges a tempo. He gets a good sonority from the orchestra – remarkably good considering the relatively small number of players and the dryness of the acoustics. His approach is weighty but only occasionally ponderous. The plangent woodwind phrases, which are such an unforgettable heart-searching feature of Beethoven's scoring...again and again cut eloquently through the texture.' David Cairns, *Financial Times* (8 September 1966).

The January 1969 issue of *Opera* magazine contained a tribute from the editor, Harold Rosenthal, to Warwick Braithwaite on his 73rd birthday.[7] He succinctly summarized the conductor's career and highlighted his achievements. But it was the concluding paragraph that was the most telling: 'While wishing Warwick Braithwaite very many happy returns of January 9, one must express regret that his long and valuable service to British opera in general, and to Sadler's Wells in particular, has been allowed to pass unnoticed.'

The same year brought Braithwaite back to the orchestra pit for performances of Mozart's *Le nozze di Figaro* with a semi-professional company, Slough Opera. The opera would normally have been conducted by that company's Musical Director, Nicholas Braithwaite, but *his* appointment as Assistant Conductor with the Bournemouth Symphony Orchestra prompted a clever publicity-generating move to replace the son with the father. Later the same year, Braithwaite Senior conducted performances of *Madama Butterfly* in Halifax, Huddersfield and Doncaster with Yorkshire Opera. These were his last performances in the U.K.

An invitation to conduct a Beethoven bicentenary production of *Fidelio* for the Australian Opera in July 1970 was too good to refuse. A strong cast of Rosemary Gordon *(Leonore)*, Beryl Furland *(Marzelline)*, Ken Neate *(Florestan)*, Graeme Ewer *(Jaquino)*, Alan Light *(Don Pizzaro)*, and Neil Warren-Smith *(Rocco)* had been assembled, with John Copley as director. Seasons in Sydney and Melbourne were to be followed by a tour to Adelaide, Canberra and Brisbane, but disaster struck on 31 July when Her Majesty's Theatre in Sydney was severely damaged by a fire. Sets, costumes, orchestral parts and instruments were either destroyed by the flames or suffered smoke and water damage. Nine performances had been given and, undaunted by the disaster, the company gave the remaining tenth performance in concert at the Capitol Theatre.

A tired-looking Warwick Braithwaite (r) with his brother Rewi, in Hastings, 1970.

The rest of the tour went ahead, but during the Melbourne season Braithwaite became ill and was nursed back to health by Enid Alexander, a family friend. It was obvious that he needed to return home, and he did so via New Zealand (where he said goodbye to his two remaining brothers), Hawaii, Los Angeles and New York, where he spent time with his sisters-in-law Wynne

---

7   Harold Rosenthal, 'Warwick Braithwaite at 73', *Opera*, 20/1 (January 1969), 28.

and Joy, both of whom had married journalists working there. According to Nicholas Braithwaite, his father looked dreadful by the time he arrived at Heathrow Airport. An excess of socialising, and a lack of sleep had taken its toll.

He was not well over Christmas, and in early January he was admitted to the Homan Ward of Finchley Memorial Hospital.[8] Rodric Braithwaite recalls that 'at first, he was full of beans and spent his time flirting with the nurses. But things took a turn for the worse, and he died on 19 January 1971.[9] My last conversation with him was about the exultant duet between Leonore and Florestan in the second act of *Fidelio*.'[10]

Warwick Braithwaite was buried at St Peter's Church, Levington, Suffolk. His 3-year-old grandson, Mark (who died the same year), and his daughter Barbara (who died in 2002), share the same grave. Sir Rodric Braithwaite's wife, Jill (Gillian) Robinson (1937–2008), is buried in the same churchyard.

A Service of Thanksgiving was held at St Martin-in-the-Fields on 24 February 1971, officiated by the Rev. Austen Williams,[11] and attended by Arthur Trevor Campbell[12] (representing The High Commissioner for New Zealand) and a host of musical associates, friends and family. This was the church where, many years earlier, Braithwaite and Lawrance Collingwood had conducted a memorial service for Lilian Baylis.[13] Now, to honour the man who had given so many years of his life to opera, the chorus and orchestra from Sadler's Wells filled the church with music, beginning with the Prisoners' Chorus from *Fidelio*. Wales was strongly represented by the distinguished composer (and close friend of Braithwaite), Dr Daniel Jones, who read Dylan Thomas' poem *And Death Shall Have No Dominion*. Baritone Geoffrey Chard performed 'Schlummert ein' from Bach's cantata *Ich habe Genug* (BWV 82), and tenor Adrian de Peyer sang the 'Ingemisco' from Verdi's Requiem. In the hands of Barbara Walker and Robert Ferguson, the Love Duet that ends Act I of Puccini's *Madama Butterfly* must have sounded magnificent, but incongruous, in those surroundings.

The eulogy was delivered by the Administrative Director of Sadler's Wells Opera, Edward Renton:

> I am sure that the memory we all cherish most of Warwick is his immense and vital enthusiasm. It was an enthusiasm that had nothing to do with youth or age. When I first met him rehearsing at Glyndebourne in the

---

8 Ebenezer Homan was a local benefactor who bought the land on which the hospital was built. It opened in 1908. A new hospital was opened on the site in 2014.

9 According to the death certificate, the cause of death was emphysema.

10 Personal correspondence between Sir Rodric Braithwaite and Roger Flury.

11 Sidney Austen Williams (1912–2001), vicar of St Martin-in-the-Fields from 1956 to 1984.

12 Campbell was awarded an OBE later in the year for valuable services as New Zealand Public Relations Officer in London.

13 On 1 December 1937.

'30s, and rehearsing *Falstaff* at Sadler's Wells, at that time he had the same enthusiasm as he had last December about Dvorak's opera *Dimitrij* which he was then preparing for performance.[14] We shall all remember his voice saying, "What a marvellous piece!".

This enthusiasm was at the centre of his interpretive gifts. For him the work he was rehearsing was the greatest piece in the world.

After he rejoined Sadler's Wells around 1960, he drove through – against considerable opposition – *The Girl of the Golden West*. The reason that he was able to do this was because he believed at that time that it was Puccini's greatest score. I am sure that it was this conviction which enabled him to get from the cast a performance of complete conviction, which one can say of very few conductors with this work.

And this enthusiasm was totally selfless. When at Rosebery Avenue we were planning a new production of *Mastersingers*, the first at Sadler's Wells since Warwick had conducted there before the War, he inundated us with all his notes, charts, all existing timings of all the great conductors; not only that, he devoted himself for months to rehearsing a very difficult ensemble of the Masters, and indeed without all his work I doubt whether we could have got *The Mastersingers* on; and he knew that he was not going to conduct it.

This enthusiasm was not simply emotional, he was one of the most practical musicians that I ever met. I remember when he came back to Sadler's Wells and was rehearsing, as his first piece, *Bohème*, there was the first orchestral rehearsal in the London Welsh Association Hall. I seem to remember that at that time we had suffered from a superfluity of talking conductors. The orchestra, many of whom were too young to know much about Warwick, were obviously waiting to see what line of talk this new conductor would adopt. After he was introduced to the orchestra, Warwick looked rather quizzically over his glasses and said, "Act I, one in a bar," and launched into conducting.

Enthusiasm, practicality, selflessness. I would like to add courage. Not only courage in adversity, although Warwick had his lean years, and he had them at a time of life when they are hardest to bear; but through all that he had the unfailing support of his wife. But I would prefer to talk about another sort of courage – the bubbling courage which sprang from his enthusiasms; for they were not all musical. He could be enthusiastic about going to Twickenham to see the All Blacks play, or when he discovered, late in life, colour television. But one of his greatest enthusiasms was when, in the mid-sixties, he discovered that the Hillman Imp was the greatest motor car in the world. In 1965 when his son, Rodric, was at our Embassy

14 *Dimitrij* by Antonín Dvořák (1841–1904), had been premiered at the Nové České Divadlo (New Czech Theatre) in Prague on 8 October 1882. It was revised in 1885 and reorchestrated in 1892 but is rarely performed today. Braithwaite's projected performances of *Dimitrij* did not take place.

in Moscow, Warwick was going to visit him. He did not, however, as you or I would have done, climb into an aeroplane and go to Moscow - he drove 1,000 miles through Sweden, round the top of the Gulf of Bothnia near the Arctic Circle, and down to Helsinki. He did the journey alone, but of course being Warwick he made friends on the way, and he returned with an honour he certainly valued as much as any other, as Honorary Member of the Swedish Association of Racing Drivers. He was just 70.

Warwick loved children of all kinds. He regarded many of his players in this light, and to young singers he gave the greatest encouragement - you have heard two of them this morning. With his own children he had the great gift of talking to them as equals and had in return the rare joy of having them talk to him on equal terms.

It was not by chance that Warwick's greatest love was for the noblest of operas, and it was fitting that his last completed assignment was to conduct *Fidelio* in Australia, and to be able to visit from there the land of his birth, New Zealand. There is no doubt that much of his vitality stemmed from the pioneering family from which he sprang. None of his family ever seem to be able to agree whether Warwick was the 20th, 21st or 22nd child! *Fidelio* had all the qualities which were dearest to him – freedom, the unlimited devotion of a wife to her husband and that elevation of the human spirit which Beethoven made peculiarly his own.

When I was asked to talk about my old friend in this Church, on this Ash Wednesday, it was natural that I should go to the Bible. I searched the Beatitudes; some of them were singularly inappropriate - Warwick was full of humility but he was in no sense meek. But there is one which fits, and it seems to me it fits perfectly: 'Blessed are the pure in heart...'.

Edward Renton's heartfelt eulogy was followed by more music.[15] The quartet from *Fidelio*, 'Mir ist so wunderbar', was sung by Catherine Wilson, Pauline Tinsley, Adrian de Peyer and Bryan Drake.[16] The service ended with the 'Wachet auf!' chorus from Act III of Wagner's *Die Meistersinger von Nürnberg* conducted by Hazel Vivienne.

A moment of light relief occurred as the sounds of Wagner died away. An elderly woman, who had wandered into the church, said to those standing at the rear of the congregation, "That was wonderful. Does it happen every Wednesday?"

And so, the life and career of Warwick Braithwaite came to an end, but his legacy continues. His enthusiasm and passion for music must surely have carried on through the many singers and instrumentalists with whom he worked, and

---

15 Two hymns were included in the service: *Jerusalem* (Hubert Parry) and *Praise, my Soul, the King of Heaven* (John Goss).

16 Bryan Ernest Hare Drake (1925–2001), New Zealand-born baritone and teacher, associated particularly with the operas of Benjamin Britten.

subsequently through *their* influence on a new generation of artists. It also carries on through his sons. Rodric Braithwaite had a distinguished career in the Diplomatic Service, notably as Her Majesty's Ambassador in Moscow, and has written several books on aspects of Russian history. Continuing his father's association with the world of music, he has also served on the Boards of the Royal Academy of Music and English National Opera.

Nicholas Braithwaite, like his father, studied at the Royal Academy of Music, and has since established himself as a highly successful conductor. His career has often been entwined with the same organisations to which his father made significant contributions: Welsh National Opera, Sadler's Wells, Covent Garden, Australian Opera, and all the major British and Australasian orchestras. But Nicholas also forged his own path, working widely in Europe, Scandinavia and the Far East. His career has offered more substantial recording opportunities than his father enjoyed – in particular, a happy association with Lyrita which gave him the opportunity to record over 28 magnificent compact discs of neglected repertoire.

When young Warwick Braithwaite took his first tentative steps into the professional music scene as Chorus Master of the redoubtable Joseph O'Mara's Grand Opera Company in November 1919, and lifted his first conducting baton just three months later for a performance of Auber's *Fra Diavolo* at the Cork Opera House, nobody could have doubted his determination to succeed. Few, however, could have predicted the extent of that success, which would ultimately make him a seminal figure in the musical life of Britain.

He had learned the rudiments of his craft in the rough and tumble of touring opera, and experienced the politics and intrigues of working with major symphony orchestras, opera and ballet companies. His holidays and rare periods of 'resting between engagements' were spent absorbing wisdom from Hans Knappertsbusch and Bruno Walter in Germany, or breathing the operatic air of Italy. He travelled widely outside Europe, experiencing the early days of trans-world air travel to New Zealand, North America, Australia and South Africa.

He met and worked with some of the major artists of his day, including composers Elgar, Sibelius and Vaughan Williams; singers Nellie Melba, Kathleen Ferrier, Elisabeth Schwarzkopf, Kirsten Flagstad, Victoria de los Angeles, Eva Turner, Joan Hammond, Webster Booth, Tito Gobbi and Boris Christoff; dancers Margot Fonteyn, Moira Shearer and Robert Helpmann; choreographer Frederick Ashton; pianists Solomon, Frederic Lamond, Myra Hess, Harriet Cohen, Moura Lympany, Benno Moiseiwitsch, Clifford Curzon, Claudio Arrau and Arturo Benedetti Michelangeli; and violinists Isolde Menges, Melsa, Albert Sammons, Antonio Brosa and Ida Haendel.

He played a role in the expansion of talented New Zealand performers abroad. Among the familiar names in his roster of artists were Arnold Trowell, Rosina Buckman, Oscar Natzka, John Amadio, Hinemoa Rosieur, Denis Dowling, Colin Horsley, Alan Loveday, Alexander Grant, Heather Begg, Richard Farrell, Maurice Till, Andrew Gold, Rowena Jackson, Bryan Drake, John McCaw, Ronald Maconaghie, Donald McIntyre, John Hauxvell, Inia Te Wiata, Noel Mangin and Rosemary Gordon.

Yet, despite all of this, Warwick Braithwaite is virtually forgotten, both in his adopted home and in the country of his birth. But if there is any suggestion in his writings that he felt under-estimated during his lifetime, it is well hidden.

Braithwaite devoted his life to making music in every way he knew how: as performer, lecturer, teacher, author, broadcaster, recording artist, conductor, composer, arranger, répétiteur and administrator. Most of his considerable energies went into forging new ensembles, helping struggling ensembles to survive, and dragging established ensembles onto a higher plane of artistic endeavour. He made friends and enemies with equal ease, and showed little tolerance of political games or incompetence. Ultimately this may have sealed his fate on both sides of the globe, but time is a great healer (even in the arts) and it is now surely time he took another bow.

Like all of us, Warwick Braithwaite was an imperfect human being, but – unlike most of us – he was a remarkable artist, deserving of far more than a footnote in the history of music.

APPENDICES

APPENDIX 1

SOME NOTES ON THE BRAITHWAITE FAMILY

WARWICK BRAITHWAITE'S PARENTS

Joseph Braithwaite (b. Cliburn, Westmorland, England, 2 January 1848 – d. Dunedin, N.Z., 27 March 1917).

Joseph emigrated from England to Melbourne, Australia in 1852, and later from Melbourne to Dunedin, New Zealand in 1860. He established a book and stationery business in Dunedin and played a significant role in the life of the city.

He was elected a city councillor in 1901 and 1903, and subsequently became mayor from 1905–1906. He was a member of the Anglican Synod and both the City Mission Committee and the Committee of the Bible in State Schools League. He was a past grand master and life member of the Independent Order of Odd Fellows.

As vice-president of the Otago Football Association, he demonstrated a live interest in that branch of sport. In the entertainment business, he was chairman of the Empire Pictures Company.

An obituary stated, 'Mr Braithwaite displayed the finest traits of good citizenship, and, the possessor of a mind cultured and broadened by wide reading, he exerted a considerable amount of influence in the community. He took a great pride in his home life, and his familiar figure will be missed by the public at large.' *Otago Daily Times* (28 March 1917), 7.

Joseph married **Mary Ann Bellett** (b. Rotherham, England, 1856 – d. Auckland, N.Z., 1 April 1921) in Dunedin, on 2 July 1872. Although she moved to live with two of her sons in Auckland after Joseph's death, she was buried with her husband in Dunedin.

CHILDREN OF MARY AND JOSEPH BRAITHWAITE

Mabel Braithwaite (b. Dunedin, 28 September 1874 – d. Sydney, 14 June 1928).

Married William Henry John Manson (baptised 26 May 1867 – d. Sydney, 18 August 1953) in St Paul's Cathedral, Dunedin on 2 July 1895. Olive and Eric were train bearers; Kathleen was a bridesmaid, and Percy was best man.

A news item from London on 4 August 1899 announced that Mabel would study for two years with Signor Panzani in Regent Street. Mabel developed into a distinguished concert soprano and recording artist, noted particularly for her work in oratorio and ballad concerts. She appeared throughout Great Britain, and at the Promenade Concerts and other major festivals. She broadcast for the BBC and recorded under her own name as well as the pseudonyms Freda Fairchild and Elsa Sinclair.

In 1925, Mabel retired from performing, and the couple moved from London to Sydney, where he became managing director of the new HMV offices and factory. Mabel died in 1928, and William died in 1953. Both are buried in Sydney.

They had one son, William 'Willie' Braithwaite Manson, a promising composer who was born on 1 July 1896, but died in action near Gommecourt, France, on 1 July 1916. His parents had been saving to support Willie during the early years of his career, but on his death, they continued to build the fund so that when William died in 1953 there was a substantial bequest to the Royal Academy of Music. Their intention was to give other talented young composers the help which the war had denied their son.

Percy Macdonell Braithwaite (b. Dunedin, 13 September 1876 – d. Dunedin, 8 June 1959).

Married Ethel May Ellison (née Howell) on 31 July 1906. Kathleen was bridesmaid. Ethel May (b. 1874 – d. Kew, Dunedin, 6 April 1915) had previously been married to distinguished Māori All Black, Thomas Rangiwahia Ellison until his death in 1904. May died from tuberculosis.

Percy studied violin with G.H. Schacht in Dunedin. He was best man at his sister Mabel's wedding, and he worked in his father's bookshop. He was much involved in acting and singing (he sang at William Manson's farewell in June 1900), and led the popular community singing events in the 1920s. He also had an interest in sport, becoming treasurer of the Otago Football Association. He managed the Empire and Grand picture theatres in Dunedin, wrote interesting accounts for the *Otago Daily Times* of his trip to Europe via the USA in 1927, and visited his brother, Warwick, in Cardiff.

Ethel and Percy had one child, June, who became engaged to Norman Naughton in 1937. Percy married Ruby Jane St Clair Black in 1922, but they separated in 1936 and were divorced on 12 February 1940. They had three children; Ethel May, John Wharton, and Percy William. In a letter to Warwick Braithwaite, dated 28 March 1944, Percy mentions his five children – Tane, Jack, Percy, Rua, and June.

Lilian Braithwaite (b. Dunedin, 1878 – d. Dunedin, 3 April 1894) (aged 16).

Sarah Braithwaite (b. Dunedin, December 1879 – d. Dunedin, 13 January 1880) (aged 1 month).

Joseph Aubrey Braithwaite (b. birth registered in Auckland, 1881 – d. Melbourne, 24 May 1907) (aged 26).

Mary Gwendoline Braithwaite (b. Dunedin, 1882 – d. Wellington, 1 August 1928).
Married Thomas Sutcliffe on 25 April 1906.

(Jack) John Braithwaite (probably registered as Cecil James but aka Jack) (b. Dunedin, 3 January 1885 – d. Rouen, 29 October 1916).
He was court-martialled on mutiny charges and executed in 1916, but posthumously pardoned in 2000. For a detailed account visit: https://nzhistory.govt.nz/media/video/executed-five-great-war-story, accessed 23 May 2022.

Kathleen Minnie Braithwaite (b. Dunedin, 9 December 1886 – d. London, 18 November 1952).
Married William Rankin Strang in Dunedin on 28 March 1910. He was prominent in the Dunedin Operatic Society, but the couple moved to London in November 1920. They returned to Dunedin for a brief visit in December 1950.
They had two sons, both of whom had military careers; John Braithwaite Strang (b. Dunedin, 1911 – d. 3 August 1988) married Margaret Kimberley Laird on 24 July 1937 at Eastbourne, Sussex. The younger son was William Braithwaite Strang (b. Dunedin, 1913 – d. London, 12 November 1948). He married Jean Parry in 1938.

Horace Algernon Braithwaite (b. Dunedin, 13 December 1887 – d. Dunedin, 15 January 1916).
Fought with the Otago Regiment and was seriously wounded at Gallipoli in May 1915. Aged 28 years.

Eric Wharton Braithwaite (b. Dunedin, 19 October 1889 – d. Dunedin, 30 June 1955).

Married Evelyn Catherine Fell (b. Wellington, *c.*1899 – d. Auckland, 25 March 1969). They were divorced in 1921. They had two sons, Eric James (b. 1926), and Horace Neale; and two daughters Maria and Gloria.

Gunner Eric Wharton Braithwaite was reported wounded in *Otago Daily Times* (18 June 1915). He was identified as leader of an unemployed workers demonstration in Dunedin (1932) and sentenced to three months imprisonment. In 1933 he was sued for divorce and maintenance by his wife. At the time, he was managing a single unemployed men's home in Christchurch.

Olive Christabel Braithwaite (b. Dunedin, 7 December 1890 – d. Christchurch, 4 April 1967).

Married in 1916 to Richard Trembath (b. 7 February 1892 – d. 1971). They had eight children: Mary, May, Olive, Audrey, Pearl, Noel, Richard Lewis, and William.

Noel Denis Braithwaite (b. Dunedin, 2 February 1892 – d. Dunedin, 5 May 1897). (Aged 5 years).

Neville Douglas Braithwaite (b. Dunedin, 14 July 1893 – d. Levin, 9 February 1954).

Married Harriet 'Ettie' Stevenson in 1917. Divorce granted on 4 December 1935. Married Dorothy Joan Trolove in 1936. (b. N.Z., *c.*1894 – d. Levin, 18 August 1986). Owned Braithwaite's Radio Supplies on Lambton Quay, Wellington. Had two daughters, Joan and Molly.

Henry Warwick Braithwaite (b. Dunedin, 9 January 1896 – d. London, 18 January 1971).

Letters from his mother reveal that in 1919 Warwick was engaged to a girl named Lilian Smith, but the engagement had been broken off by 1921.

Warwick married Phyllis Greatrex (née Bain) – divorced wife of Cecil George Greatrex – on 9 June 1925 at Nottingham Register Office. Her details were removed from Warwick Braithwaite's passport on 5 May 1930. A divorce was granted on 17 July 1930. They had one daughter, Barbara Mary (see below).

In 1931 Warwick married Lorna Constance Davies (b. Cardiff, 21 July 1904 – d. London, 5 March 1990). They had two children, Rodric and Nicholas (see below).

John Rewi Fergusson Braithwaite (b. Dunedin, 25 September 1897 – d. Hastings, 15 January 1987).

Married to Dorothy Jacques Black (b. Studholme Junction, South Canterbury, 28 September 1905 – d. Hastings, 22 September 1984) in St Paul's

Cathedral, Wellington on 15 December 1932. Played as a defender for the national football team against Australia on six occasions during 1922–1923. Moved with Dorothy from Dunedin to Hastings and worked in the circulation department of Napier's *Daily Telegraph*. They had two daughters, Joan and Audrey.

Roderick Alistair Macdonell Braithwaite (b. Dunedin, 13 August 1901 – d. Hamilton, 3 April 1963).

Married Nora Kathleen Arey (b. Auckland, 1902 – d. Hamilton, 13 November 2000) on 21 June 1932. She was a Hamilton city councillor (1962–1974), and also served as Deputy Mayor. She was awarded the MBE in the 1963 Queen's Birthday Honours for services to the community. Roderick served two terms as Mayor of Hamilton, NZ from 1953 to 1959, and played a significant role in the establishment of the Waikato Savings Bank in 1958. He was appointed the first Chair of the Board of Trustees.

Roderick and Kathleen had three children: Warwick, David Joseph, and Marjorie Joan. David Joseph Braithwaite, was also Mayor of Hamilton (2001–2004) and was awarded the OBE in 1992 for services to the Trust Bank organisation and the community. He died in 2021.

CHILDREN OF WARWICK BRAITHWAITE

Barbara Mary Braithwaite (b. London, 5 May 1924 – d. London, February 2002).

The birth was registered as Barbara M. Greatrex in 1924, and as Barbara Mary Braithwaite in 1925, when her father was given custody. Both certificates gave the mother's maiden name as Bain.

Barbara completed her registration as a qualified nurse on 28 November 1947 at Westminster Children's Hospital (1941–1947).

Sir Rodric Quentin Braithwaite (b. London, 17 May 1932–).

In 1961 he married Gillian (Jill) Mary Robinson, an archaeologist and former diplomat (b. London, 15 September 1937 – d. London, 10 November 2008). Of their five children (Richard, Katharine, twins Julian and Mark, and David), Mark predeceased his mother in 1971.

Rodric was educated at Bedales, served in military intelligence in Vienna in 1951 and 1952, studied French and Russian at Cambridge, and joined the Diplomatic Service in 1955. He had postings in Jakarta, Warsaw, Moscow, Rome, Brussels and Washington. He was a Visiting Fellow at All Souls College, Oxford in 1972–1973. He was a member of the Sherpa team for the G7 Economic Summits (1984–1988), British Ambassador in Moscow (1988–1992), Foreign

Policy Adviser to the Prime Minister (John Major) and Chairman of the Joint Intelligence Committee (1992–1993). He was awarded the GCMG in 1994.

Since leaving government service, he has been a Governor of the English National Opera, Chairman of the Royal Academy of Music, Senior Adviser to Deutsche Bank, and has had a number of other business and not-for-profit appointments. He was a Visiting Fellow at the Wilson Center in Washington for April–June 2005.

He is a member (formerly Chairman) of the International Advisory Council of the Moscow School of Political Studies. He is a member (former Chairman) of the Programme Committee of the Ditchley Foundation and a member of its governing body. He is also an Honorary Fellow of Christ's College, Cambridge, and an Honorary Doctor and Professor of Birmingham University.

He has written three books on Russian affairs: *Across the Moscow River* (2002); *Moscow 1941: A City and its People at War* (2006); and *Afgantsy: The Russians in Afghanistan 1979–1989* (2011). His book, *Armageddon and Paranoia: The Nuclear Confrontation*, was published in 2017. He has also contributed to *The Financial Times, The Guardian, The Observer, The Sunday Times, The Evening Standard, The New Statesman, Prospect Magazine,* and *Survival.*

Nicholas Paul Dallon Braithwaite (b. London, 26 August 1939–).

He married Gillian Agnes Haggarty (August 1985) and they have two children: Felicity Anna (b. London, 1987–) and Chris (b. Australia, 2 September 1990–).

Following in his father's footsteps, Nicholas studied at the Royal Academy of Music in London. He attended masterclasses in Bayreuth, and studied with Hans Swarowsky in Vienna. He has served as associate conductor of the Bournemouth Symphony Orchestra, resident conductor at Sadler's Wells Opera (1971–1974), and music director of Glyndebourne Touring Opera (1976–1980). He has had a long association with the Manchester Camerata as principal guest conductor (1977–1984), and principal conductor (1984–1991).

In Australia, Nicholas was principal conductor of the Adelaide Symphony Orchestra (1987–1991), and held the same post with the Tasmanian Symphony Orchestra. He has also served as permanent guest conductor of the Norwegian Radio Orchestra, and musical director and chief conductor of Gothenburg's Stora Teater (1981–1984). His opera career has seen him working with the Royal Opera at Covent Garden, Welsh National Opera, Hamburg State Opera, Norwegian Opera, State Opera of South Australia, Opera Australia and New Zealand Opera. From 1988 to 1991 he served as the Dean of Music at the Victorian College of the Arts in Melbourne.

He has made many recordings with the London Philharmonic, London Symphony and Philharmonia orchestras, and has a legacy of more than forty compact discs.

APPENDIX 2

TOWARDS A NATIONAL ORCHESTRA OF WALES 'CERDDORFA GENEDLAETHOL CYMRU'

When Warwick Braithwaite was appointed musical director of the BBC Cardiff studios in 1924, the 5WA Studio Orchestra consisted of 17 permanent players. In subsequent years some players were replaced to improve standards, and in 1927 the overall size was increased to 21.

The BBC showed a commitment to local musical organisations to assist them with larger orchestral resources, as can be seen from the personnel listed in the programme for the Cardiff Musical Society's performance of Mendelssohn's *Hymn of Praise* (Lobgesang) on 15 November 1925 at Park Hall. In addition to *Lobgesang*, the orchestra contributed the Handel-Elgar *Overture in D minor*, the Bach-Elgar *Fantasia and Fugue, C minor*, and the Prelude to Act I of Wagner's *Lohengrin*.

On such occasions, the 5WA Studio Orchestra was augmented and usually renamed the 5WA Symphony Orchestra. Its players were:

Leonard Busfield (leader)

Violin I: F. Thomas; R. Swann; A.H. Struebig; F.H. Struebig; W.A. Murphy; T. Llewellyn; I. Lester; C. Poole; B. Goldstein; J. Trimnell.

Violin II: W. Donovan (principal); H. Wilmore; L. Andrews; J. Donovan; J. Leonard; W. Baker; F.M. Thomas; Miss H. Short.

Viola: Evan Walters (principal); W. Dorman; M. Webb; W.T. Hall; Miss N. Rochard.

Violoncello: Frank Whitnall (principal); D. Collier; C. Ariss; W. Bishop; Mrs Hasie; Sidney Jones.
Double Bass: F. Littlepage (principal); D. Collier; J.W. Smith; C. Taylor.
Flute: Hilary Evans; W.H. Nicholls; M. Barry (piccolo).
Oboe: H. Thorpe; G. Wallace.
Clarinet: G. Gilbert; S. Draper.
Bassoon: W.H. Lyons; R. Burns.
Trumpet: W.S. Smith; W.J. Long; J.H. Sampson.
Horn: F.T. Stephens; G.H. Francis; J. Byers; W. Cody.
Trombone: B. Walker; W.S. Porter; C. Clacy.
Tuba: A.O. Foxhall.
Timpani: J. Hughes; W.R. Wills.
Harp: Miss D. Godwin.
Pianist: Miss R. Taylor.

With the formation of the National Orchestra of Wales in 1928, the permanent ensemble was increased to 30, only eight of whom had played in the 5WA Studio Orchestra. Open auditions had been held to ensure that the best available players were recruited from throughout Britain, but although the opportunity for full-time orchestral studio and concert work drew a good response, few players were ultimately prepared to make the move to Wales. Even so, there were inevitably some voices raised in protest that a national orchestra contained some foreigners (i.e., non-Welsh) amongst its ranks and, indeed, on the conductor's podium.

The administrative structure of the National Orchestra of Wales (NOW) at the date of the inaugural concert 12 April 1928 was:

Orchestral Council Representatives
BBC: R.H. Eckersley, V.H. Goldsmith, E.R. Appleton
National Council of Music: Sir Walford Davies, Prof. David Evans (University College, Cardiff)
Cardiff City Council: The Lord Mayor, Sir John Daniel
National Museum of Wales: Dr Cyril Fox

Executive Sub-Committee: Messrs. E.R. Appleton (Chair), W. Braithwaite (Conductor), C. McLean (Secretary, NCM), R. Bonner Morgan (President, Cardiff Musical Society and representing the City Council and Listeners), and R.W. Pratt (from 5WA).

Conductor: Warwick Braithwaite
Business Manager and Secretary: Richard W. Pratt (who left us after two years

to become the orchestral manager of the BBC Symphony Orchestra in London, a position he held until 1946.

President of National Orchestra of Wales: H.R.H. The Prince of Wales (the future Edward VIII)

Leaders:
Albert Voorsanger (April 1928–April 1929)
Paul Beard (Interim, April–July 1929)
Louis Levitus (July 1929–October 1931)

1st Violins: G. Spiller; L.G. Richards; Frank Thomas*; R. Swan*
2nd Violins: T. Batty*; T.A. Russell; David Thomas
Viola: Kenneth Harding*; E. Walters*
Cello: Ronald Harding*; Bernhard Beers
Double Bass: Jeremiah Farmer; E.G. Haigh
Flute: Suzanne Stoneley; Hilary Evans*
Oboe: Frederick H. Tilsley*; Stuart Barr
Clarinet: Frederick H. Clements; G. Gilbert
Bassoon: John Wilson; W.H. Lyons
Horn: A. Holmes; F.T. Stephens
Trumpet: A.H. Trotman*; G.H. Wright
Trombone: A. Shackleton *(tenor)*; J.G. Pearson *(tenor)*; J.B. Howells *(bass)*
Timpani and Percussion.: T.J. Harris

* Indicates players who had been members of the 5WA Studio Orchestra.

The advent of a national orchestra for Wales, was greeted with enthusiasm by 'Orpheus', the music critic of the *Western Mail*:

NEW WELSH ORCHESTRA
…The orchestra, as now constituted, has been transformed from an ordinary BBC Station band of sixteen or seventeen players at Cardiff, into what Sir Walford Davies describes as, 'a compact classically complete little orchestra of thirty players, appointed no longer as merely a studio orchestra, but brought into being expressly to function both nationally and civically.' It is to play for thirty weeks in the year, giving four free performances per week in the Museum, and two symphony concerts per week in the City Hall. The players have been newly appointed after open competition; Mr Warwick Braithwaite likewise was selected as conductor on merit, and not necessarily because he already held that post at the studio. Mr

Braithwaite is entering into his task with heart and soul, and if enthusiasm can command success, the future is assured, so far as artistic results are concerned. The main essential to the efficiency of such an organisation is adequate practice to ensure perfect understanding between all the players and their conductor; and this vital factor has been secured by the provision for twelve hours' rehearsal every week... *Western Mail* (9 Apr 1928), 9

Despite the extension of support from the BBC from one to three years, and two further short reprieves in 1931, the writing was on the wall. Intensive lobbying and failed appeals for funding from the people of Wales, local politicians and businessmen, resulted in the disbanding of the NOW in October 1931.

The newly-formed BBC Symphony Orchestra had given its first concert on 22 October 1930, conducted by Adrian Boult at the Queen's Hall in London. Such was the success of this new venture that it helped seal the fate of BBC regional orchestras, although a new focus on centralization, technological advances in broadcasting, and the use of commercial recordings of music would probably have played a role in the decision.

The final three performances by the National Orchestra of Wales, conducted by Warwick Braithwaite, were:

6 October 1931 (evening); City Hall, Cardiff. Farewell Benefit Concert.
Programme selected from requests made to *Western Mail and South Wales News*.
　　Wagner: *Die Meistersinger von Nürnberg* – Overture
　　Handel: Concerto Grosso op. 3, no. 2, B flat
　　Dvořák: Symphony no. 9 'From the New World'
　　Gounod: *Faust* – Ballet Music
　　Bach: *Suite no. 3 in D* – Air (on the G String)
　　German: Welsh Rhapsody.
　　Soloists: Louis Levitus *(violin)*; Ronald Harding *(cello)*

7 October (lunchtime); National Museum of Wales. Final free NOW Concert.
　　Beethoven: Symphony no. 5

7 October (afternoon); Final 5WA Studio Broadcast.
　　Wagner: *Die Meistersinger von Nürnberg* – Overture
　　Wagner: *Tannhäuser* – O du mein holder Abendstern (O star of eve)
　　Elgar: Cello Concerto
　　Dohnányi: *Suite, F sharp minor, op. 19* – Andante with Variations
　　Liadov: Kikimora.
　　Soloists: Watcyn Watcyns *(bs-bar)*; Ronald Harding *(cello)*.

On 7 October 1931, the NOW was officially disbanded and replaced by an ensemble of nine musicians (The Western Studio Orchestra) to fulfil the needs of local broadcasting and provide free lunchtime concerts at the National Museum. Braithwaite's replacement was his former assistant Reginald Redman. The players were:

Louis Levitus *(Leader)*
Frank Thomas *(violin)*
William Donovan *(viola/violin)*
Ronald Harding *(cello)*
E.G. Haigh *(bass)*
Hilary Evans *(flute)*
Frederick H. Clements *(clarinet)*
A.H. Trotman *(trumpet)*
Hubert Pengelly *(piano)*.

The Western Studio Orchestra, and various amateur orchestras such as the Herbert Ware Orchestra, the Welsh Symphony Orchestra and the Cardiff Symphony Orchestra, filled the concert and broadcasting gap.

Redman went on to become the West of England Region's head of music. A Welsh Division was formally created on 4 September 1935 and on 1 December the same year, the Cardiff studio ensemble was increased to 20 players and broadcast as the Welsh Symphony Orchestra. The new Welsh Division's head of music was Idris Lewis, with Mansel Thomas as his deputy. Their new emphasis was to search out and promote the new generation of Welsh composers.

The BBC Welsh Orchestra folded with the outbreak of war in 1939. In 1945, the orchestra was revived and the playing size increased to 31. It steadily grew over the years, reaching 66 by 1976, at which time the orchestra's name was changed to the BBC Welsh Symphony Orchestra. However, it was not until 1987 that it reached a full symphonic complement of 88 players. To bring the story almost full circle, the orchestra was renamed the BBC National Orchestra of Wales in 1993, as it filled a dual role of public concerts and studio duties.

The BBC National Orchestra of Wales is today one of the finest orchestras in Britain. Braithwaite would have been delighted, and very proud indeed.

APPENDIX 3

WARWICK BRAITHWAITE CONDUCTS SIBELIUS

This listing of Sibelius compositions conducted by Warwick Braithwaite is arranged in chronological order, based on the dates that he first conducted the orchestras involved. A second listing of works follows in alphabetical order. In each case, the total number of performances is shown in square brackets. Italics are used to indicate when a section from a larger work is performed independently, e.g.: *King Christian II Suite* – Nocturne

BBC ORCHESTRAS (SECTIONS A, B, C, D, E) LONDON STUDIO REPERTOIRE (1924–1952)
Bard, The, op. 64 [2]
Belshazzar's Feast, Op. 51 [2]
En Saga [3]
King Christian II Suite [2]
Lemminkäinen Suite, op. 22 – The Swan of Tuonela
Pelléas et Mélisande Suite, op. 46 [2]
Romance, C, op. 42
Scènes historiques II, op. 66 – I. La chasse [4]
Scènes historiques II, op. 66 – II. Love Song [3]
Scènes historiques II, op. 66 – III. At the Drawbridge [3]
Svanevit (Swanwhite) Suite, op. 54
Symphony no. 3, C, op. 52 [2]

Symphony no. 6, D minor, op. 104
Tapiola
Two Serenatas
Valse Triste

BBC 5WA ORCHESTRA CARDIFF STUDIO REPERTOIRE (1924–1928)
Dance Intermezzo, op. 45, no. 2
Dryaden, op. 45, no. 1
En Saga
Finlandia [4]
King Christian II Suite – Musette
King Christian II Suite – Nocturne
The Tryst
Valse Lyrique, op. 96a
Valse Triste [6]

NATIONAL ORCHESTRA OF WALES CARDIFF STUDIO BROADCASTS (1928–1931)

Dance Intermezzo, op. 45, no. 2 [2]

En Saga

Finlandia [4]

Karelia Suite

Karelia Suite – Alla Marcia

King Christian II Suite – Elegy [3]

King Christian II Suite – Musette [3]

King Christian II Suite – Nocturne [3]

Lemminkäinen Suite, op. 22 – The Swan of Tuonela [4]

Nightride and Sunrise, op. 55

Pelléas et Mélisande Suite, op. 46

Scènes historiques II, op. 66 – I. La chasse

Scènes historiques II, op. 66 – II. Love Song [2]

Scènes historiques II, op. 66 – III. At the Drawbridge

Svanevit (Swanwhite) Suite, op. 54

Two Songs: Sunrise; But my bird is long homing

Valse Triste [5]

NATIONAL ORCHESTRA OF WALES CARDIFF LIVE CONCERTS (1928–1931)

Canzonetta for string orchestra

Dance Intermezzo, op. 45/2

En Saga [5]

Finlandia [8]

Finnish March

Kakastava Suite

Karelia Suite

Karelia Suite – Intermezzo

Karelia Suite – Overture [2]

King Christian II Suite [2]

King Christian II Suite – Nocturne [2]

Lemminkaïnen Suite, op. 22 – Lenninkaïnen's Return [2]

Lemminkaïnen Suite, op. 22 – The Swan of Tuonela [6]

Scènes historiques II, op. 66 – I. La chasse

Scènes historiques II, op. 66 – III. At the Drawbridge

Spring Song, op. 16

Symphony no. 1, E minor, op. 39

Symphony no. 2, D, op. 43 [2]

Symphony no. 2, D, op. 43 – Scherzo and Finale

Symphony no. 3, C, op. 52

Symphony no. 3, C, op. 52 (incomplete because of speeches)

Symphony no. 4, A minor, op. 63

Symphony no. 5, E flat, op. 82

Symphony no. 6, D minor, op. 104

Symphony no. 7, C, op. 105

Tapiola [2]

Valse Romantique

Valse Triste [14]

NATIONAL ORCHESTRA OF WALES CONCERTS OUTSIDE CARDIFF (1929–1931)

En Saga

Finlandia

Lemminkäinen Suite, op. 22 – The Swan of Tuonela

Valse Triste [2]

LONDON PHILHARMONIC ORCHESTRA (1933–1945)

En Saga [2]

Symphony no. 7, C, op. 105 [2]

Valse Triste [3]

LONDON SYMPHONY ORCHESTRA (1933–1950)

Symphony no. 2, D, op. 43

SCOTTISH ORCHESTRA (1931, 1940–1946)

Concerto, violin

En Saga [3]

Finlandia

Karelia Suite – Alla Marcia [2]

Karelia Suite – Intermezzo

King Christian II Suite

King Christian II Suite – Nocturne

Lemminkäinen Suite, op. 22 – The Swan of Tuonela [3]

Scènes historiques II, op. 66 – I. La chasse

Symphony no. 1, E minor, op. 39 [5]
Symphony no. 2, D, op. 43 [8]
Symphony no. 3, C, op. 52 [2]
Symphony no. 5, E flat, op. 82 [3]
Symphony no. 7, C, op. 105 [2]
Valse Triste [3]

BBC SYMPHONY ORCHESTRA
CONCERT AND STUDIO (1941–1951)
King Christian II Suite
Symphony no. 5, E flat, op. 82
Symphony no. 6, D minor, op. 104
Symphony no. 7, C, op. 105 [2]

BBC NORTHERN ORCHESTRA
(1941–1958)
Scènes historiques II, op. 66 – I. La chasse
Scènes historiques II, op. 66 – II. Love Song
Symphony no. 3, C, op. 52
Valse Triste

BBC SCOTTISH ORCHESTRA (1941–
1958)
En Saga
King Christian II Suite
Symphony no. 2, D, op. 43
Symphony no. 3, C, op. 52

NATIONAL SYMPHONY ORCHESTRA
(1945)
Finlandia

PHILHARMONIA ORCHESTRA
(1946–1949)
Suite Champêtre

MELBOURNE SYMPHONY
ORCHESTRA (1947, 1954)
Symphony no. 2, D, op. 43 [3]

JOHANNESBURG SYMPHONY
ORCHESTRA
(1947–1948)
Lemminkäinen Suite, op. 22 – The Swan of
Tuonela [2]
Symphony no. 1, E minor, op. 39

NATIONAL ORCHESTRA OF THE NEW
ZEALAND BROADCASTING SERVICE
(1953–1954)
Finlandia
Lemminkäinen Suite, op. 22 – The Swan of
Tuonela
Symphony no. 1, E minor, op. 39
Symphony no. 2, D, op. 45
Symphony no. 3, C, op. 52
Symphony no. 5, E flat, op. 82
Symphony no. 7, C, op. 105 (First NZ
performance)

ICELAND SYMPHONY ORCHESTRA
(1956)
Symphony no. 2, D, op. 43

ALPHABETICAL LIST OF WORKS
PERFORMED
Bard, The, op. 64 [2]
Belshazzar's Feast, Op. 51 [2]
Canzonetta for string orchestra
Concerto, violin
Dance Intermezzo, op. 45, no. 2 [4]
Dryaden, op. 45, no. 1
En Saga [16]
Finlandia [18]
Finnish March
Kakastava Suite
Karelia Suite [2]
Karelia Suite – Alla Marcia [3]
Karelia Suite – Intermezzo [2]
Karelia Suite – Overture [2]
King Christan II Suite [6]
King Christian II Suite – Elegy [3]
King Christian II Suite – Musette [4]
King Christian II Suite – Nocturne [7]
Lemminkäinen Suite, op. 22 – Lenninkaïnen's
Return [2]
Lemminkäinen Suite, op. 22 – Swan of
Tuonela [18]
Nightride and Sunrise, op. 55
Pelléas et Mélisande Suite, op. 46 [3]
Romance, C, op. 42
Scènes historiques II, op. 66 – I. La chasse [8]
Scènes historiques II, op. 66 – II. Love Song [6]

Scènes historiques II, op. 66 – III. At the Drawbridge [5]

Spring Song, op. 16

Svanevit (Swanwhite) Suite, op. 54 [2]

Symphony no. 1, E minor, op. 39 [6]

Symphony no. 2, D, op. 43 [11]

Symphony no. 2, D, op. 43 – Scherzo and Finale

Symphony no. 3, C, op. 52 [6]

Symphony no. 3, C, op. 52 (incomplete because of speeches)

Symphony no. 4, A minor, op. 63

Symphony no. 5, E flat, op. 82 [5]

Symphony no. 6, D minor, op. 104 [3]

Symphony no. 7, C, op. 105 [7]

Tapiola [3]

Tryst, The

Two Serenatas

Two Songs: Sunrise; But my bird is long homing

Valse Lyrique, op. 96a

Valse Romantique

Valse Triste [35]

APPENDIX 4

WARWICK BRAITHWAITE DISCOGRAPHY

In the twenty years between 1938 and 1958, Warwick Braithwaite made 207 recordings for HMV, Columbia, RCA Victor, Decca/London, Parlophone, and M-G-M. Many of these were of vocal excerpts from opera or oratorio with some of the finest artists of the day, but no matter how happy we are to have such examples of his work as an accompanist, it is a major source of regret that almost nothing of his core orchestral repertoire was recorded commercially, and very few of his hundreds of radio broadcast performances were preserved. The period when he was most active in the concert hall (1924–1948) was also a time when broadcasts were live and seldom preserved. Even when the technology to record on location was available, it was restricted mainly to centres such as London.

In terms of availability, the vocal recordings have fared best, thanks to the calibre of the soloists involved. Many have been reissued on compact disc and, more recently, made available as digital downloads.

To help redress the balance between vocal and orchestral recordings, an enterprising French company, Forgotten Records, has recently rescued some of Braithwaite's purely orchestral recordings and reissued them in excellent sound – including the historically important recording of a suite from Prokofiev's *Cinderella*, the British premiere of which Braithwaite conducted at Covent Garden on 23 December 1948. Some recordings of works by French composers have been digitized by the Bibliothèque National de France and can be heard on line, or downloaded free from their *Gallica Digital Library* website.

This discography consists of three sections. The first lists Braithwaite's studio recordings, including some that were not issued for one reason or another. The second section lists recordings known to exist in archives, most notably the remarkable broadcast of Puccini's *La fanciulla del West* from Sadler's Wells – a demonstration (should one be needed) of Braithwaite's exciting work in the opera house. This, along with a performance of Verdi's *I Lombardi* from Welsh National Opera, is available on compact disc, but not easily obtained. The third section lists archival recordings of Braithwaite's radio interviews.

The order of information in this discography is:

> Composer; Title of work; Title of excerpt(s)
> Soloist(s); Orchestra; Chorus; Place and date of recording
> Language of sung items (titles of French, German and Italian items are given in the original language; Russian titles are given in Latin script; Czech titles are given in English. Titles of excerpts sung in English translation are shown in brackets following the title in the original language.
> Arranger/orchestrator
> Any other notes.

Details of first issues are followed by details of subsequent issues in chronological order:

> Format; Label; Commercial issue number;
> Matrix number [in square brackets]; take number underlined if known;
> Disc size (if other than 12"); Number of discs in set;
> Issue date of recording; Album title; Coupling details for 78 and 45 rpm discs.

DISCOGRAPHY ABBREVIATIONS

+	Coupling (78 and 45 rpm discs)	EP	Extended play
45	45 rpm vinyl disc [7"]	GRC	EMI's Great Recordings of the Century series
78	78 rpm disc	HMV	His Master's Voice
a.c.	auto coupling	LP	Long-playing vinyl disc
CD	Compact disc	M-G-M	Metro Goldwyn Mayer
CS	Cassette	mx	matrix number
DL	Download (usually mp3)		

COMMERCIAL RECORDINGS

AMBROSE: One sweet solemn thought
Blanche Thebom *(mezzo)*; London Symphony Orchestra.
EMI Studio No. 1, Abbey Road, London; 10 July 1950.
Sung in English.

LP	RCA Victor LM 104 [10"] (1951) 'Fireside Favorites'
LP	RCA Victor 'Bluebird Classics' LBC 1054 (1953) 'Fireside Favorites and Beloved Hymns'
45	RCA WDM 1541 [4] 'Fireside Favorites' + My old Kentucky home; Homing; The rosary; Calm as the night; Trees; Lead kindly light; Mighty lak' a rose.
CD	Klassic Haus Restorations KHL 504 (2018) 'Fireside Favorites'

BELLINI: *Norma* – Guerrieri…Ah! del Tebro
Nicola Rossi-Lemeni *(bass)*; Chorus of the Royal Opera House, Covent Garden; Philharmonia Orchestra.
Kingsway Hall London; 5 August 1952.
Sung in Italian.

LP	HMV ALP 1074 (1953) 'Operatic Arias'
LP	Odeon (Italy) QALP 10033 (1953) 'Nicola Rossi-Lemeni nell' interpretazione di arie da opere…'
LP	HMV (France) FALP 306 (1953) 'Airs d'Opera'
LP	EMI (Italy) 3C 053-03249 (1978) 'Nicola Rossi-Lemeni interpreta Bellini, Rossini, Mozart…'
CD	Fabbri Editore 17 'Grandi Voci alla Scala 17: Nicola Rossi-Lemeni'
CD	Hamburger Archiv Arkiv CD-HB 10311 'Nicola Rossi-Lemeni Vol. 1'
CD	Phono Enterprise LV 987 (2010) 'Stelle della Lirica, Vol. VI – Nicola Rossi-Lemeni'

BELLINI: *Norma* – Ite sul colle, o Druidi
Nicola Rossi-Lemeni *(bass)*; Chorus of the Royal Opera House, Covent Garden; Philharmonia Orchestra.
Kingsway Hall London; 5 August 1952.
Sung in Italian.

LP	HMV ALP 1074 (1953) 'Operatic Arias'
LP	Odeon (Italy) QALP 10033 (1953) 'Nicola Rossi-Lemeni nell' interpretazione di arie da opere…'
LP	HMV (France) FALP 306 (1953) 'Airs d'Opéra'
LP	EMI (Italy) 3C 053-03249 (1978) 'Nicola Rossi-Lemeni interpreta Bellini, Rossini, Mozart…'
CD	Fabbri Editore 17 'Grandi Voci alla Scala 17: Nicola Rossi-Lemeni'

CD   Preiser 'Lebendige Vergangenheit' 89613 (2005) 'Nicola Rossi-Lemeni'

CD   Hamburger Archiv Arkiv CD-HB 10311 'Nicola Rossi-Lemeni Vol. 1'

CD   Phono Enterprise LV 987 (2010) 'Stelle della Lirica, Vol. VI – Nicola Rossi-Lemeni'

BELLINI: *I Puritani* – A te, o cara, amor talora

Eugene Conley *(tenor)*; New Symphony Orchestra of London.
Decca West Hampstead Studios, London; 11 September 1950.
Sung in Italian.

LP   London (USA) LL 280 [10"] (1950) 'Italian Operatic Arias'

LP   London (USA) LPS 280 [10"] (1950) 'Italian Operatic Arias'

LP   Decca LM 4534 [10"] (1951) 'Italian Operatic Arias'

CD   Preiser 'Lebendige Vergangenheit' 89574 (2003) 'Eugene Conley'

CD   Decca 480 8145 (2013) 'Most Wanted Decca Recitals'

BELLINI: *I Puritani* – Ah, per sempre io ti perdei… Or dove fuggo io mai

Paolo Silveri *(baritone)*; Philharmonia Orchestra.
EMI Studio No. 1, Abbey Road, London; 26 October 1951.
Sung in Italian.

78   Columbia LX 1509 [mx CAX 11448-3] + Gran Dio! (Verdi: *Ernani*)

CD   Preiser 'Lebendige Vergangenheit' 89573 (2003) 'Paolo Silveri, II'

BELLINI: *I Puritani* – Vieni fra questa braccia

Eugene Conley *(tenor)*; New Symphony Orchestra of London.
Decca West Hampstead Studios, London; 13 September 1950.
Sung in Italian.

LP   London (USA) LL 280 [10"] (1950) 'Italian Operatic Arias'

LP   London (USA) LPS 280 [10"] (1950) 'Italian Operatic Arias'

LP   Decca LM 4534 [10"] (1951)

CD   Preiser 'Lebendige Vergangenheit' 89574 (2003) 'Eugene Conley'

CD   Decca 480 8145 (2013) 'Most Wanted Decca Recitals'

BENEDICT: Variations de concert sur le Carnaval de Venise (The Carnival of Venice)

Marimi del Pozo *(soprano)*; Philharmonia Orchestra.
EMI Studio No. 1, Abbey Road, London; 21 July 1949.
Sung in Italian.

78   HMV C 3967 [mx 2EA 14107-1,2,3] + Ardon gl'incensi (Donizetti: *Lucia di Lammermoor*)

78   HMV (Spain) DB 4298 (1951) + Ardon gl'incensi (Donizetti: *Lucia di Lammermoor*)

LP   HMV RO 5417

BIZET: *L'Arlésienne Suite no. 2 – Intermezzo* **(arranged as Agnus Dei)**
Kirsten Flagstad *(soprano)*; George Thalben-Ball *(organ)*; Philharmonia Orchestra.
EMI Studio No. 1, Abbey Road, London; 3 July 1948.
Sung in Latin.
Note: Vocal arrangement by Ernest Guiraud of the Intermezzo from *L'Arlésienne*.
78   HMV DB 6791 [mx 2EA 13203-1,2,3] + Ombra mai fù (Handel: *Serse*)
CD   Preiser 'Lebendige Vergangenheit' 89625 (2005) 'Kirsten Flagstad, III'

BIZET: *L'Arlésienne Suite no. 2* – **Farandole**
Orchestra of the Royal Opera House, Covent Garden.
London: June 1952.
Note: Arranged by Ernest Guiraud.
LP   M-G-M (USA) E 3000 (1953)
LP   M-G-M (USA) E 3003 (1953) 'Popular Ballet Music from Great Operas'
LP   Parlophone PMC 1020 (1955)
LP   Odeon (France) ODX 146 (1956?)
LP   M-G-M Classics MCS 7007/8-3 [6] (196–?) 'Romantic Ballet Music'
CD   Forgotten Records fr 1507 (2018)

BIZET: *Carmen* – **Selections**
[Introduction; Habañera; Micaela-Don José duet; Seguidilla; Toreador's Song;
 Flower Song; March; Carmen-Escamillo duet; Finale]
Noël Eadie *(soprano)*; Nancy Evans *(contralto)*; Webster Booth *(tenor)*;
Dennis Noble *(baritone)*; Sadler's Wells Chorus and Orchestra.
Kingsway Hall, London; 21 December 1939.
Sung in English.
78   HMV C 3143 [mx 2EA 8190-1,2] and [mx 2EA 8191-1]
78   Victor 36377

BIZET: *Carmen* – **L'amour est un oiseau rebelle (Habanera)**
Winifred Heidt *(mezzo)*; New Symphony Orchestra of London.
Decca West Hampstead Studios, London; 12 September 1950.
Sung in French.
LP   Decca (unpublished)

BIZET: *Carmen* – **La fleur que tu m'avais jetée (See here thy flower'et treasured well) (Flower Song)**
Webster Booth *(tenor)*; London Philharmonic Orchestra.
Kingsway Hall, London; 12 September 1938.
Sung in English.
78   HMV C 3030 [mx 2 EA 1173-1,2] + Che gelida manina (Puccini: *La bohème*)

LP   HMV 'Treasury' HLM 7109 (1977)

CD   Heritage HTGCD 286 'Great British Tenors'

BIZET: *Carmen* – Vôtre toast je peu vous le rendre (Sirs, your toast) (Toreador's Song)

Redvers Llewellyn *(baritone)*; Philharmonia Orchestra.

EMI Studio No. 1, Abbey Road, London; 24 April 1948.

Sung in English.

78   HMV C 3800 [mx 2EA 12971] + Avant de quitter ses lieux (Gounod: *Faust*)

BIZET: *Carmen* – Vôtre toast je peu vous le rendre (Con voi ber) (Toreador's Song)

Paolo Silveri *(baritone)*; Philharmonia Orchestra.

EMI Studio No. 1, Abbey Road, London; 26 October 1951.

Sung in Italian.

78   Columbia LX 1530 [mx CAX 11450] + Greshno tait': ya skuki nye lyublyu (Borodin: *Prince Igor*)

CD   Preiser 'Lebendige Vergangenheit' 89573 (2003) 'Paolo Silveri, II'

BIZET: Jeux d'enfants: petite suite, op. 22

[Marche (Trompette et tambour); Berceuse (La poupée); Impromptu (La toupie); Duo (Petit mari, petite femme); Galop (Le bal)]

Orchestra of the Royal Opera House, Covent Garden.

London; June 1952.

LP   M-G-M (USA) E 3000 (1953)

LP   Parlophone PMC 1020 (1955)

LP   Odeon (France) ODX 146 (1956?)

LP   M-G-M Classics MCS 7007/8-3 [6] (196–?) 'Romantic Ballet Music'

CD   Forgotten Records fr 1507 (2018)

BIZET: *La jolie fille de Perth* – Danse bohémienne

Orchestra of the Royal Opera House, Covent Garden.

London; June 1952.

LP   M-G-M (USA) E 3000 (1953)

LP   M-G-M (USA) E 3003 (1953) 'Popular Ballet Music from Great Operas'

LP   Parlophone PMC 1020 (1955)

LP   Odeon (France) ODX 146 (1956?)

LP   M-G-M Classics MCS 7007/8-3 [6] (196–?) 'Romantic Ballet Music'

CD   Forgotten Records fr 1507 (2018)

BOHM: Calm as the night
Blanche Thebom *(mezzo)*; London Symphony Orchestra.
EMI Studio No. 1, Abbey Road, London; 11 July 1950.

LP   RCA Victor LM 104 [10"] 'Fireside Favorites'
LP   RCA Victor 'Bluebird Classics' LBC 1054 (1953) 'Fireside Favorites and
          Beloved Hymns'
45   RCA WDM 1541 [4] 'Fireside Favorites'
          + My old Kentucky home; Homing; The rosary; Trees; Lead kindly
          light; Mighty lak' a rose; One sweetly solemn thought.
CD   Klassic Haus Restorations KHL 504 (2018) 'Fireside Favorites'

BORODIN: *Prince Igor* – Greshno tait': ya skuki nye lyublyu (Galitsky's aria)
Nicola Rossi-Lemeni *(bass)*; Chorus of the Royal Opera House, Covent Garden;
Philharmonia Orchestra.
Kingsway Hall London; 5 August 1952.
Sung in Russian.

78   HMV DB 21559 [mx 2EA 16695-3A]
          + Chuiut pravdu (Glinka: *A Life for the Tsar*) cond. T. Beintende-Neglia
LP   HMV ALP 1074 (1953) 'Operatic Arias'
LP   HMV (France) FALP 306
LP   HMV (Italy) QALP 10033
EP   RCA Victor ERA 186
LP   EMI (Italy) 3C 053-03249 (1978?) 'Nicola Rossi-Lemeni interpreta
          Bellini, Rossini, Mozart...'
CD   Preiser 'Lebendige Vergangenheit' 89613 (2005) 'Nicola Rossi-Lemeni'
CD   Phono Enterprise LV 987 (2010) 'Stelle della Lirica, Vol. VI – Nicola
          Rossi-Lemeni'

**BORODIN: *Prince Igor* – Greshno tait': ya skuki nye lyublyu (Aihmè! Nel cor)
(Galitsky's aria)**
Paolo Silveri *(baritone)*; Philharmonia Orchestra.
EMI Studio No. 1, Abbey Road, London; 26 October 1951.
Sung in Italian.

78   Columbia LX 1530 [mx CAX 11451] + Vôtre toast je peu vous le rendre
          (Bizet: *Carmen*)
CD   Preiser 'Lebendige Vergangenheit' 89573 (2003) 'Paolo Silveri, II'

BORODIN: *Prince Igor* – Ni sna ni otdycha (No sleep, no rest)
John Hargreaves *(baritone)*; Philharmonia Orchestra.
EMI Studio No. 1, Abbey Road, London; 9 December 1946.
Sung in English.

78 HMV C 3561 [mx 2EA 11492-1,2,3] Part 1; [mx 11493-1,2,3] Part 2

CD Dutton Laboratories CDLX 7020 (1996) 'Stars of English Opera, Volume Two'

BRITTEN: *Matinées musicales, op. 24 (after Rossini)*

Orchestra of the Royal Opera House, Covent Garden.

London; 29 September 1951.

LP M-G-M (USA) E 117 [10"] (1951)

LP Parlophone PMD 1020 [10"] (1953)

LP M-G-M (USA) E 3028 (1953)

LP M-G-M (USA) E 3333 (1957)

45 M-G-M K 117 (set)

CD Forgotten Records fr 1508 (2018)

BRITTEN: *Soirées musicales, op. 9 (after Rossini)*

Orchestra of the Royal Opera House, Covent Garden.

London; 29 September 1951.

LP M-G-M (USA) E 117 [10"] (1951)

LP Parlophone PMD 1020 [10"] (1953)

LP M-G-M (USA) E 3028 (1953)

LP M-G-M (USA) E 3333 (1957)

45 M-G-M K 117 (set)

78 M-G-M 30760 'Tarantella' + Fantastic Can-Can (Respighi-Rossini: *La boutique fantasque*)

45 M-G-M K 30760 'Tarantella' + Fantastic Can-Can (Respighi-Rossini: *La boutique fantasque*)

CD Forgotten Records fr 1508 (2018)

Review: 'In this collection of fluffy movie background and ballet items, [Britten's] lighter side is agreeably presented by the Royal Opera House orchestra of Covent Garden....In all, the collector of semi-classical or light-classical music à la Strauss, Gould, Grofé, etc., should be well pleased with this set. Both the recording and performance are fine.' *The Billboard*, 2 February 1952, p. 30.

CATALANI: *La Wally* – Ebben? Ne andrò lontana

Ellabelle Davis *(soprano)*; New Symphony Orchestra.

Kingsway Hall, London; 10 February 1950.

Sung in Italian.

LP Decca LX 3008 [10"] (1950) 'Operatic and Lieder Recital'

LP London (USA) LL/LPS 181 [10"] (1950)

CHABRIER: *Suite pastorale* (orchestration by Chabrier of *10 pièces pittoresques* for piano, nos 6, 7, 4, 10)
[Idylle; Danse villageoise; Sous bois; Scherzo-valse]
Orchestra of the Royal Opera House, Covent Garden.
London; June 1952.

LP	M-G-M (USA) E 3000 (1953)
LP	Parlophone PMC 1020 (1955)
LP	Odeon (France) ODX 146 (1956?)
LP	M-G-M (USA) E 3124 (1955) (Idylle only) 'Orchestral Favorites, Vol. 3'
LP	M-G-M Classics MCS 7007/8-3 [6] (196–?) 'Romantic Ballet Music'
CD	Forgotten Records fr 1507 (2018)

CHARPENTIER: *Louise* – Depuis le jour
Joan Hammond *(soprano)*; Hallé Orchestra.
Houldsworth Hall, Manchester; 28 August 1942.
Sung in French.

78	HMV DX 1134/35 [Side 4] [mx CAX 9034-1,2,3] + Letter Scene (Tchaikovsky: *Eugene Onegin*)
78	HMV DOX 753/54 [Side 4]
CD	Testament SBT 1160 (1998) 'Dame Joan Hammond: by request'
CD	Eloquence (Australia) 4825892 [4] (2016) 'From Melba to Sutherland'

CHOPIN (orch. Gordon Jacob): *Les Sylphides* – Excerpts
[1. Prelude in A, op. 28. (no. 7); Grande valse brillante in E flat, op. 18 (Valse no. 1)]
Orchestra of the Royal Opera House, Covent Garden.
London; 16 September 1952.

LP	M-G-M (USA) E 3006 (1952) 'Nights at the Ballet'
LP	Parlophone PMC 1008 (1954) 'Nights at the Ballet'
LP	Parlophone (NZ) PMCM 1008 'Nights at the Ballet'

CIMAROSA: *Il matrimonio segreto* – Overture
Orchestra of the Royal Opera House, Covent Garden.
London; 27 November 1952.

LP	M-G-M (USA) E 3013 (1953)

Review: 'Thoroughly pleasant disc, well conducted by Braithwaite and acutely reproduced. Braithwaite's effort seems to me well worthy of the music, and the combination offering is desirable.' *The Guide to Long-Playing Records.* Irving Kolodin (N.Y.; Knopf, 1955), p. 49.

DEL RIEGO: Homing
Blanche Thebom *(mezzo)*; London Symphony Orchestra.
EMI Studio No. 1, Abbey Road, London; 11 July 1950.
Sung in English.

LP	RCA Victor LM 104 [10"] 'Fireside Favorites'
LP	RCA Victor 'Bluebird Classics' LBC 1054 (1953) 'Fireside Favorites and Beloved Hymns'
45	RCA WDM 1541 [4] 'Fireside Favorites'
	+ My old Kentucky home; Calm as the night; The rosary; Trees; Lead kindly light;
	One sweetly solemn thought; Mighty lak' a rose.
CD	Klassic Haus Restorations KHL 504 (2018) 'Fireside Favorites'

DELIBES: *Coppélia* – Excerpts
[Swanhilde's Valse (Valse lente); Czardas]
Orchestra of the Royal Opera House, Covent Garden.
London; 16 September 1952.

LP	M-G-M (USA) E 3006 (1952) 'Nights at the Ballet'
LP	Parlophone PMC 1008 (1954) 'Nights at the Ballet'
LP	Parlophone (NZ) PMCM 1008 'Nights at the Ballet'

DELIBES: *Lakmé* – Ballet Music
Orchestra of the Royal Opera House, Covent Garden.
London; 17 July 1952.

LP	M-G-M (USA) E 3003 (1953) 'Popular Ballet Music from Great Operas'
LP	Parlophone PMC 1008 (1954) 'Nights at the Ballet'
LP	Parlophone (NZ) PMCM 1008 'Nights at the Ballet'

DELIBES: *Lakmé* – C'est un rêve, une folie qui passe (O fair vision)
Webster Booth *(tenor)*; London Philharmonic Orchestra.
EMI Studio No. 1, Abbey Road, London; 3 March 1939.
Sung in English.

78	HMV (unpublished; masters destroyed May 1963) [mx 2EA 7541-1,2]

DELIBES: *Sylvia* – Suite
[Les Chasseresses (Fanfare); Pizzicato-Scherzettino]
Orchestra of the Royal Opera House, Covent Garden.
London; 16 September 1952.

LP	M-G-M (USA) E 3006 (1952) 'Nights at the Ballet'
LP	Parlophone PMC 1008 (1954) 'Nights at the Ballet'
LP	Parlophone (NZ) PMCM 1008 'Nights at the Ballet'

DONIZETTI: *La fille du régiment* – **Chacun le sait**
Patrice Munsel *(soprano)*; Orchestra of the Royal Opera House, Covent Garden (not named).
London; August 1952.
Sung in French.
Note: Soundtrack to the film *Melba*.

LP	RCA Victor LM 7012 [10"] '*Melba*: Original Soundtrack of the Motion Picture'
LP	HMV BLP 1023 [10"]
LP	HMV (Italy) QBLP 5015 [10"]
45	RCA Victor EDM 7012 [4]
CD	Flare SPEC 1025 (2006) 'On Wings of Song'
DL	Frank Bristow 'Music from the Past' EXCD 004 'A Patrice Munsel Recital'

DONIZETTI: *Linda di Chamounix* – **O luce di quest'anima**
Elda Ribetti *(soprano)*; Philharmonia Orchestra.
London; 12 December 1946.
Sung in Italian.

78	HMV C 3587 [mx 2EA 11503-2] + Caro nome (Verdi: *Rigoletto*)

DONIZETTI: *Lucia di Lammermoor* – **Ardon gl'incensi**
Marimi del Pozo *(soprano)*; Philharmonia Orchestra.
EMI Studio No. 1, Abbey Road, London; 21 July 1949.
Sung in Italian.

78	HMV C 3967 [mx 2EA 14106-1,2,3] + Carnevale di Venezia (Benedict)
78	HMV (Spain) DB 4298 (1951) + Carnevale di Venezia (Benedict)
CD	Vocal Record Collectors' Society VRCS 1994 (1994)

DONIZETTI: *Lucia di Lammermoor* – **Ardon gl'incensi**
Patrice Munsel *(soprano)*; John Cameron *(baritone)*; Chorus and Orchestra of the Royal Opera House, Covent Garden (not named).
London; August 1952.
Sung in Italian.
Note: Soundtrack to the film *Melba*.

LP	RCA Victor LM 7012 [10"] '*Melba*: Original Soundtrack of the Motion Picture'
LP	HMV BLP 1023 [10"]
LP	HMV (Italy) QBLP 5015 [10"]
45	RCA Victor EDM 7012 [4]
CD	Flare SPEC 1025 (2006) 'On Wings of Song'
DL	Frank Bristow 'Music from the Past' EXCD 004 'A Patrice Munsel Recital'

DONIZETTI: *Lucia di Lammermoor* – **Regnava nel silenzio…Quando rapita in estasi**
Elda Ribetti *(soprano)*; Philharmonia Orchestra.
London; 18 December 1946.
Sung in Italian.
78   HMV C 3616 [mx 2EA 11518-2] and [mx 2EA 11519]

DONIZETTI: *Lucia di Lammermoor* – **Tombe degl'avi miei…Fra poco a me ricovero…Tu che a dio spiegasti l'ali**
Eugene Conley *(tenor)*; New Symphony Orchestra of London.
Decca West Hampstead Studios, London; 13 September 1950.
Sung in Italian.
LP   London (USA) LL 280 [10"] (1950)
LP   London (USA) LPS 280 [10"] (1950) 'Italian Operatic Arias'
LP   Decca LM 4534 [10"] (1951)
CD   Preiser 'Lebendige Vergangenheit' 89574 (2003) 'Eugene Conley'
CD   Decca 480 8145 (2013) 'Most Wanted Decca Recitals'

DYKES: Lead, kindly light
Blanche Thebom *(mezzo)*; London Symphony Orchestra.
EMI Studio No. 1, Abbey Road, London; 10 July 1950.
Sung in English.
LP   RCA Victor LM 104 [10"] 'Fireside Favorites'
LP   RCA Victor 'Bluebird Classics' LBC 1054 (1953) 'Fireside Favorites and
          Beloved Hymns'
45   RCA WDM 1541 [4] 'Fireside Favorites'
          + My old Kentucky home; Homing; The rosary; Calm as the night; Trees;
          Mighty lak' a rose; One sweetly solemn thought.
CD   Klassic Haus Restorations KHL 504 (2018) 'Fireside Favorites'

ELGAR: Pomp and Circumstance March no. 1 in D major
London Symphony Orchestra.
Kingsway Hall, London; 9 March 1945.
78   Decca K. 1140 [mx AR 9173] + Pomp and Circumstance March no. 2
          (Elgar)
78   London LA 23 (1948) [2] (set)
LP   London LLP 30 (1949) 'March Rhythms'
LP   Decca LK 4020 (1951)
LP   Richmond (USA) B 19029 (1959) 'Symphonic Marches'

ELGAR: Pomp and Circumstance March no. 2 in A minor
London Symphony Orchestra.

Kingsway Hall, London; 9 March 1945.

78	Decca K. 1140 [mx AR 9174] + Pomp and Circumstance March no. 1 (Elgar)
78	London LA 23 [2] (1948) (set)
LP	London LLP 30 (1949) 'March Rhythms'
LP	Decca LK 4020 (1951)
LP	Richmond (USA) B 19029 (1959) 'Symphonic Marches'

ELGAR: Pomp and Circumstance March no. 3 in C minor
London Symphony Orchestra.
Kingsway Hall, London; 9 March 1945.

78	Decca K. 1141 [mx AR 9176] + Pomp and Circumstance March no. 4 (Elgar)
78	London LA 23 [2] (1948) (set)
LP	London LLP 30 (1949) 'March Rhythms'
LP	Decca LK 4020 (1951)
LP	Richmond (USA) B 19029 (1959) 'Symphonic Marches'

ELGAR: Pomp and Circumstance March no. 4 in G major
London Symphony Orchestra.
Kingsway Hall, London; 9 March 1945.

78	Decca K. 1141 [mx AR 9175] + Pomp and Circumstance March no. 3 (Elgar)
78	London LA 23 [2] (1948) (set)
LP	London LLP 30 (1949) 'March Rhythms'
LP	Decca LK 4020 (1951)
LP	Richmond (USA) B 19029 (1959) 'Symphonic Marches'

FLOTOW: *Martha* – Ach! so fromm (*M'appari*) (Safe and sure)
Webster Booth *(tenor)*; London Philharmonic Orchestra.
EMI Studio No. 1, Abbey Road, London; 3 March 1939.
Sung in English.

78	HMV (unpublished; masters destroyed May 1963) [mx 2EA 7541-1,2]

FOSTER: My old Kentucky home
Blanche Thebom *(mezzo)*; London Symphony Orchestra.
EMI Studio No. 1, Abbey Road, London; 18 July 1950.
Sung in English.

LP	RCA Victor LM 104 [10"] 'Fireside Favorites'
LP	RCA Victor 'Bluebird Classics' LBC 1054 (1953) 'Fireside Favorites and Beloved Hymns'
45	RCA WDM 1541 [4] 'Fireside Favorites'

+ Homing; Calm as the night; The rosary; Trees; Lead kindly light; Mighty lak' a rose; One sweetly solemn thought.

CD   Klassic Haus Restorations KHL 504 (2018) 'Fireside Favorites' (note: orchestra listed as LPO).

GERMAN: *Tom Jones* – **Which is my own true self?**
Gwen Catley *(soprano)*; London Symphony Orchestra.
EMI Studio No. 1, Abbey Road, London; 13 October 1950.
Sung in English.
78   HMV B 10058 [mx OEA 15121]

GOUNOD: *Faust* – **Ah! Je ris de me voir (The Jewel Song)**
Joan Hammond *(soprano)*; Philharmonia Orchestra.
EMI Studio No. 1, Abbey Road, London; 18 March 1947.
Sung in English.
78   HMV C 3674 [mx 2EA 11714-1,2] + Il était un roi de Thulé (Gounod: *Faust*)
45   HMV 7R 166 + Il était un roi de Thulé (Gounod: *Faust*)
45   HMV 7P 220 + Il était un roi de Thulé (Gounod: *Faust*)

GOUNOD: *Faust* – **Alerte! Alerte! (Trio: Then leave her)**
Joan Cross *(soprano)*; Webster Booth *(tenor)*; Norman Walker *(bass)*; Sadler's Wells Chorus; London Philharmonic Orchestra.
EMI Studio No. 1, Abbey Road, London; 3 March 1939.
Sung in English
78   HMV C 3086 [mx 2EA 7539-1,2] + Bella figlia dell'amore (Quartet) (Verdi: *Rigoletto*)
78   Victor 36235 + Bella figlia dell'amore (Quartet) (Verdi: *Rigoletto*)

GOUNOD: *Faust* – **Salut, demeure chaste et pure (All hail thou dwelling)**
Webster Booth *(tenor)*; Hallé Orchestra.
Houldsworth Hall, Manchester; 28 August 1942.
Sung in English.
78   HMV C 3309 [mx 2ER 632-1,2] + Morgenlich leuchtend (Wagner: *Die Meistersinger*)
LP   HMV 'Treasury' HLM 7109 (1977)

GOUNOD: *Faust* – **Ballet Music, Act V (Walpurgis Night Revel)**
Orchestra of the Royal Opera House, Covent Garden.
London; 17 July 1952.
LP   M-G-M (USA) E 3003 (1953) 'Popular Ballet Music from Great Operas'
LP   Parlophone PMC 1029 (1955)

LP   M-G-M (USA) E 3052 (1954) + Aurora's Wedding (Tchaikovsky: *Sleeping Beauty*)

DL   Past Classics 7964396 (2008)

Review: 'Braithwaite's effort is good, and up to standard reproductively.' *The Guide to Long-Playing Records*. Irving Kolodin (N.Y.; Knopf, 1955)

GOUNOD: *Faust* – **Avant de quitter ses lieux (Even bravest heart)**
Redvers Llewellyn *(baritone)*; Philharmonia Orchestra.
EMI Studio No. 1, Abbey Road, London; 24 April 1948.
Sung in English.
78   HMV C 3800 [mx 2EA 12970] + Vôtre toast je peu vous le rendre (Bizet: *Carmen*)

GOUNOD: *Faust* – **Avant de quitter ses lieux (Even bravest heart)**
Dennis Noble *(baritone)*; Sadler's Wells Orchestra.
Kingsway Hall, London; 8 December 1939.
Sung in English.
78   HMV C 3153 [mx 8181-1,2] + Credo in un Dio crudel (Verdi: *Otello*)
CD   Cheyne CHE 44459 'Denis Noble'
CD   Dutton Laboratories CDLX 7017 'A Tribute to Denis Noble'

GOUNOD: *Faust* – **Il était un roi de Thulé (Once there was a King of Thule)**
Joan Hammond *(soprano)*; Philharmonia Orchestra.
EMI Studio No. 1, London; 18 March 1947.
Sung in English.
78   HMV C 3674 [mx 2EA 11658-1,2] + Ah, je ris de me voir (Gounod: *Faust*)
45   HMV 7R 166 + Ah, je ris de me voir (Gounod: *Faust*)
45   HMV 7P 220 + Ah, je ris de me voir (Gounod: *Faust*)

GOUNOD: *Roméo et Juliette* – **Je veux vivre (Waltz Song)**
Patrice Munsel *(soprano)*; Orchestra of the Royal Opera House, Covent Garden (not named).
London; August 1952.
Sung in French.
Note: Soundtrack to the film *Melba*.
LP   RCA Victor LM 7012 [10"] '*Melba*: Original Soundtrack of the Motion Picture'
LP   HMV BLP 1023 [10"]
LP   HMV (Italy) QBLP 5015 [10"]
45   RCA Victor EDM 7012 [4]

CD   Flare SPEC 1025 (2006) 'On Wings of Song'
DL   Frank Bristow 'Music from the Past' EXCD 004 'A Patrice Munsel Recital'

GRAINGER: Handel in the Strand
Ernest Lush *(piano)*; Philharmonia Orchestra.
EMI Studio No. 1, Abbey Road, London; 6 January 1949.
78   Columbia DX 1660 [mx CAX 10422-1,2] + Londonderry Air (Trad. arranged by Grainger)
LP   Columbia 'Entré Series' (USA) RL 3042 (1953) 'Music of Percy Grainger'
45   EMI 'Your Kind of Music' SCD 2173 (1962) + Londonderry Air (Trad. arranged by Grainger)

GRAINGER, arr.; Irish Tune from County Derry (Londonderry Air)
Philharmonia Orchestra.
EMI Studio No. 1, Abbey Road, London; 6 January 1949.
78   Columbia DX 1660 [mx CAX 10421-1,2] + Handel in the Strand (Grainger)
45   EMI 'Your Kind of Music' SCD 2173 (1962) + Handel in the Strand (Grainger)

GRAINGER: Mock Morris
Philharmonia Orchestra.
EMI Studio No. 1, Abbey Road, London; 6 January 1949.
78   Columbia DB 2572 [mx CA 20982-1] [10"] + Molly on the Shore (Grainger)
LP   Columbia 'Entré Series' (USA) RL 3042 (1953) 'Music of Percy Grainger'

GRAINGER: Molly on the Shore
Philharmonia Orchestra.
EMI Studio No. 1, Abbey Road, London; 6 January 1949.
78   Columbia DB 2572 [mx CA 20981-1,2] [10"] + Mock Morris (Grainger)
LP   Columbia 'Entré Series' (USA) RL 3042 (1953) 'Music of Percy Grainger'

GRANADOS: Villanesca Dance no. 4
Orchestra of the Royal Opera House, Covent Garden.
London; 22 February 1951.
78   Parlophone (unpublished) [mx 2SM 142]

GRIEG: En Drøm, op. 48/6
Kirsten Flagstad *(soprano)*; Philharmonia Orchestra.
EMI Studio No. 1, Abbey Road, London; 3 April 1948.
Sung in Norwegian.

Note: Orchestrated by Arvid Kleven.

78	HMV DB 21020 [mx 2EA 12883-1] + Den Særde; Tak for dit Råd (Grieg)
LP	HMV HQM 1057 (1967) 'Golden Voice Series No. 4: Kirsten Flagstad'
LP	EMI Electrola 1C 147-01 491/92 [2] (1973) 'The Kirsten Flagstad Album'
CD	EMI 'GRC' CDH 7 63305 2 (1990) 'Kirsten Flagstad Sings Norwegian Songs'
CD	Metropolitan Opera Guild MET 222 CD (1994) 'Kirsten Flagstad - Portraits in Memory'
CD	Musikkmagasinet Ballade CM 95 (issue 3/1995) 'Norske Stemmebånd'
CD	Testament SBT 1268 (2003) 'Kirsten Flagstad – Grieg and Dørumsgaard'
CD	Preiser 'Lebendige Vergangenheit' 89625 (2005) 'Kirsten Flagstad, III'
CD	EMI Classics 50999 4 55346 2 1 [5] (2010) 'Kirsten Flagstad: The Supreme Wagnerian Soprano'

GRIEG: Eros, op. 70/1
Kirsten Flagstad (*soprano*); Philharmonia Orchestra.
EMI Studio No. 1, Abbey Road, London; 10 March 1948.
Sung in Norwegian.
Note: Orchestrated by Max Reger.

78	HMV DA 1879 [mx OEA 12788-1,2] [10"] + En svane (Grieg)
45	HMV/RCA Victor WDM 1533 [4] [7"]
LP	RCA Victor LM 99 [10"] (1952) 'Grieg Songs'
CD	EMI 'GRC' CDH 7 63305 2 (1990) 'Kirsten Flagstad Sings Norwegian Songs'
CD	Metropolitan Opera Guild MET 222 CD (1994) 'Kirsten Flagstad - Portraits in Memory'
CD	Testament SBT 1268 (2003) 'Kirsten Flagstad – Grieg and Dørumsgaard'
CD	Preiser 'Lebendige Vergangenheit' 89625 (2005) 'Kirsten Flagstad, III'
CD	EMI Classics 50999 4 55346 2 1 [5] (2010) 'Kirsten Flagstad: The Supreme Wagnerian Soprano'
CD	Membran 'Quadromania' 222215 [4] (2004) 'Fin de Siècle'
CD	Forgotten Records fr 527 (2011)

GRIEG: Fra Monte Pincio, op. 39/1
Kirsten Flagstad (*soprano*); Philharmonia Orchestra.
EMI Studio No. 1, Abbey Road, London; 10 March 1948.
Sung in Norwegian.

78	HMV (unpublished) [mx 2EA 12804-1,2]

GRIEG: Fra Monte Pincio, op. 39/1
Kirsten Flagstad (*soprano*); Philharmonia Orchestra.

EMI Studio No. 1, Abbey Road, London; 29 May 1948.
Sung in Norwegian.

78	HMV DA 1905 [mx OEA 13085-1,2] and [mx OEA 13086-1,2] [10"]
45	HMV/RCA Victor WDM 1533 [4] [7"]
EP	HMV 7EP 6011 (1955) + Våren (Grieg) Walter Süsskind *(cond)*
EP	HMV 7EB 6011 (1959) + Våren (Grieg) Walter Süsskind *(cond)*
LP	RCA Victor LM 99 [10"] (195–?) 'Grieg Songs'
LP	RCA Victor HR 228 'Treasury of Immortal Performances – Flagstad'
CD	EMI 'GRC' CDH 7 63305 2 (1990) 'Kirsten Flagstad Sings Norwegian Songs'
CD	Metropolitan Opera Guild MET 222 CD (1994) 'Kirsten Flagstad – Portraits in Memory'
CD	Testament SBT 1268 (2003) 'Kirsten Flagstad – Grieg and Dørumsgaard'
CD	Preiser 'Lebendige Vergangenheit' 89625 (2005) 'Kirsten Flagstad, III'
CD	EMI Classics 50999 4 55346 2 1 [5] (2010) 'Kirsten Flagstad: The Supreme Wagnerian Soprano'
CD	Forgotten Records fr 527 (2011)

GRIEG: Guten, op. 33/1

Kirsten Flagstad *(soprano)*; Philharmonia Orchestra.
EMI Studio No. 1, Abbey Road, London; 29 May 1948.
Sung in Norwegian.
Note: Orchestrated by Gunström.

78	HMV DA 1992 [mx OEA 13088-1,2] [10"] + Ved Rundarne (Grieg)
LP	RCA Victor LM 99 [10"] (195–?) 'Grieg Songs'
45	HMV/RCA Victor WDM 1533 [4] [7"]
CD	EMI 'GRC' CDH 7 63305 2 (1990) 'Kirsten Flagstad Sings Norwegian Songs'
CD	Testament SBT 1268 (2003) 'Kirsten Flagstad – Grieg and Dørumsgaard'
CD	Preiser 'Lebendige Vergangenheit' 89625 (2005) 'Kirsten Flagstad, III'
CD	EMI Classics 50999 4 55346 2 1 [5] (2010) 'Kirsten Flagstad: The Supreme Wagnerian Soprano'
CD	Forgotten Records fr 527 (2011)

GRIEG: Den Særde, op. 33/3

Kirsten Flagstad *(soprano)*; Philharmonia Orchestra.
EMI Studio No. 1, Abbey Road, London; 3 April 1948.
Sung in Norwegian.

78	HMV DB 21020 [mx 2EA 12882-1] + En Drøm; Tak for dit Råd (Grieg)
LP	EMI Electrola 1C 147-01 491/92 [2] (1973) 'The Kirsten Flagstad Album'
CD	EMI 'GRC' CDH 7 63305 2 (1990) 'Kirsten Flagstad Sings Norwegian Songs'

CD Testament SBT 1268 (2003) 'Kirsten Flagstad – Grieg and Dørumsgaard'
CD EMI Classics 50999 4 55346 2 1 [5] (2010) 'Kirsten Flagstad: The Supreme Wagnerian Soprano'
CD Regis RRC 1269 (2007) 'Kirsten Flagstad – Scenes and Arias'

GRIEG: En svane, op. 25/2

Kirsten Flagstad (soprano); Philharmonia Orchestra.
EMI Studio No. 1, Abbey Road, London; 10 March 1948.
Sung in Norwegian.

78 HMV DA 1879 [mx OEA 12789-1,2] [10"] + Eros (Grieg)
45 HMV/RCA Victor WDM 1533 [4] [7"]
LP HMV HQM 1057 (1967) 'Golden Voice Series No. 4: Kirsten Flagstad'
LP RCA Victor LM 99 [10"] (195–?) 'Grieg Songs'
LP EMI Electrola 1C 147-01 491/92 [2] (1973) 'The Kirsten Flagstad Album'
CD EMI 'GRC' CDH 7 63305 2 (1990) 'Kirsten Flagstad Sings Norwegian Songs'
CD Testament SBT 1268 (2003) 'Kirsten Flagstad – Grieg and Dørumsgaard'
CD Preiser 'Lebendige Vergangenheit' 89625 (2005) 'Kirsten Flagstad, III'
CD EMI Classics 50999 4 55346 2 1 [5] (2010) 'Kirsten Flagstad: The Supreme Wagnerian Soprano'
CD Membran 'Quadromania' 222215 [4] (2004) [4] 'Fin de Siècle'
CD Regis RRC 1269 (2007) 'Kirsten Flagstad – Scenes and Arias'
CD Forgotten Records fr 527 (2011)

GRIEG: Tak for dit råd, op. 21/4

Kirsten Flagstad (soprano); Philharmonia Orchestra.
EMI Studio No. 1, Abbey Road, London; 3 April 1948.
Sung in Norwegian.
Note: Orchestrated by Arvid Kleven.

78 HMV DB 21020 [mx 2EA 12883-1] + Den Særde; En Drøm (Grieg)
LP HMV HQM 1057 (1967) 'Golden Voice Series No. 4: Kirsten Flagstad'
LP EMI Electrola 1C 147-01 491/92 [2] (1973) 'The Kirsten Flagstad Album'
CD EMI 'GRC' CDH 7 63305 2 (1990) 'Kirsten Flagstad Sings Norwegian Songs'
CD Metropolitan Opera Guild MET 222 CD (1994) 'Kirsten Flagstad - Portraits in Memory'
CD Testament SBT 1268 (2003) 'Kirsten Flagstad – Grieg and Dørumsgaard'
CD Preiser 'Lebendige Vergangenheit' 89625 (2005) 'Kirsten Flagstad, III'
CD EMI Classics 50999 4 55346 2 1 [5] (2010) 'Kirsten Flagstad: The Supreme Wagnerian Soprano'
CD Regis RRC 1269 (2007) 'Kirsten Flagstad – Scenes and Arias'

GRIEG: Ved Rundarne, op. 33/9

Kirsten Flagstad *(soprano)*; Philharmonia Orchestra.
EMI Studio No. 1, Abbey Road, London; 3 April 1948.
Sung in Norwegian.
Note: Orchestrated by Arvid Kleven.

78	HMV DA 1992 [mx OEA 12881-1] [10"] + Guten (Grieg)
45	HMV/RCA Victor WDM 1533 [4] [7"]
LP	RCA Victor LM 99 [10"] (195–?) 'Grieg Songs'
CD	EMI 'GRC' CDH 7 63305 2 (1990) 'Kirsten Flagstad Sings Norwegian Songs'
CD	Metropolitan Opera Guild MET 222 CD (1994) 'Kirsten Flagstad – Portraits in Memory'
CD	Testament SBT 1268 (2003) 'Kirsten Flagstad – Grieg and Dørumsgaard'
CD	Preiser 'Lebendige Vergangenheit' 89625 (2005) 'Kirsten Flagstad, III'
CD	EMI Classics 50999 4 55346 2 1 [5] (2010) 'Kirsten Flagstad: The Supreme Wagnerian Soprano'
CD	Forgotten Records fr 527 (2011)

HANDEL: *Acis and Galatea* – Love sounds the alarm

Webster Booth *(tenor)*; orchestra.
London; 8 March 1948.
Sung in English.

78	HMV C 3796 [mx 2EA 12794] + Love in her eyes sits playing (Handel: *Acis and Galatea*)
CD	Dutton Vocalion CDLX 7032 (1998) 'Webster Booth: Handel Arias / Operatic Arias'

HANDEL: *Acis and Galatea* –Love in her eyes sits playing

Webster Booth *(tenor)*; orchestra.
London; 8 March 1948.
Sung in English.

78	HMV C 3796 [mx 2EA 12795] + Love sounds the alarm (Handel: *Acis and Galatea*)
CD	Dutton Vocalion CDLX 7032 (1998) 'Webster Booth: Handel Arias / Operatic Arias'

HANDEL: Dank sei dir, Herr

Kirsten Flagstad *(soprano)*; Sir George Thalben-Ball *(organ)*; Philharmonia Orchestra.
EMI Studio No. 1, Abbey Road, London; 3 July 1948.
Sung in German.

78	HMV (unpublished) [mx 2EA 13205-1,2]

CD   Testament SBT 1018 (1993) 'Kirsten Flagstad – Handel, Purcell, Gluck, Wagner'

HANDEL: *Judas Maccabaeus* **– How vain is man**
Heddle Nash *(tenor)*; Philharmonia Orchestra.
EMI Studio No. 1, Abbey Road; 19 November 1946.
Sung in English.
78   HMV C 3550 [mx 2EA 11420] + My arms!…Sound an alarm (Handel: *Judas Maccabaeus*)
CD   Dutton CDLX 7025 (1997) 'Stars of English Oratorio, Volume 1'

HANDEL: *Judas Maccabaeus* **– My arms!…Sound an alarm**
Webster Booth *(tenor)*; orchestra.
London; 18 March 1948.
Sung in English.
78   HMV C 3939 [mx 2EA 12796]
          + Why does the God of Israel sleep? (Handel: *Samson*) Stanford Robinson *(cond)*

HANDEL: *Judas Maccabaeus* **– My arms!…Sound an alarm**
Heddle Nash *(tenor)*; Philharmonia Orchestra.
EMI Studio No. 1, Abbey Road, London; 19 November 1946.
Sung in English.
78   HMV C 3550 [mx 2EA 11421] + How vain is man (Handel: *Judas Maccabaeus*)
LP   HMV HQM 1809 (1967) 'Golden Voice Series, No. 6: Heddle Nash'
LP   World Record Club (NZ) CO 466 (1967?)
CD   Dutton CDLX 7025 (1997) 'Stars of English Oratorio, Volume 1'
CD   Heritage HTGCD 248 (2013) 'The Voice of Heddle Nash'

HANDEL: *Messiah* **– Behold the Lamb of God**
Sadler's Wells Chorus and Orchestra.
Kingsway Hall, London; 2 November 1939.
Sung in English.
78   HMV C 3129 [mx 2EA 8177-1,2] + Hallelujah (Handel: *Messiah*)
78   Victor 11-8670 + Hallelujah (Handel: *Messiah*)

HANDEL: *Messiah* **– Comfort ye my people**
Webster Booth *(tenor)*; London Philharmonic Orchestra.
Kingsway Hall, London; 28 February 1939 .
Sung in English.
78   HMV C 3087 [mx 2EA 7369-1,2,3] + Ev'ry valley shall be exalted

(Handel: *Messiah*)

78	RCA Victor 12598 + Ev'ry valley shall be exalted (Handel: *Messiah*)
CD	Dutton Vocalion CDLX 7032 (1998) 'Webster Booth: Handel Arias / Operatic Arias'

HANDEL: *Messiah* – Ev'ry valley shall be exalted

Webster Booth *(tenor)*; London Philharmonic Orchestra.
Kingsway Hall, London; 28 February 1939.
Sung in English.

78	HMV C 3087 [mx 2EA 7370-1,2,3] + Comfort ye my people (Handel: *Messiah*)
78	RCA Victor 12598 + Comfort ye my people (Handel: *Messiah*)
CD	Dutton Vocalion CDLX 7032 (1998) 'Webster Booth: Handel Arias / Operatic Arias'

HANDEL: *Messiah* – Hallelujah

Sadler's Wells Chorus and Orchestra.
Kingsway Hall, London; 2 November 1939.
Sung in English.

78	HMV C 3129 [mx 2EA 8176-1,2] + Behold the Lamb of God (Handel: *Messiah*)
78	Victor 11-8670 + Behold the Lamb of God (Handel: *Messiah*)

HANDEL: *Samson* – Let the bright Seraphim

Isobel Baillie *(soprano)*; Arthur Lockwood *(trumpet)*; Hallé Orchestra.
Houldsworth Hall, Manchester; 18 March 1943.
Sung in English.

78	Columbia DX 1113 [mx CAX 9070-1, 2] Part 1; [mx CAX 9071-1,2,3]
78	Columbia M 780 (set)
45	Columbia SEG 7755
CS	EMI TC-RLS 7703
LP	HMV HQM 1015 (1966) 'Golden Voice Series, No. 1: Isobel Baillie'
LP	EMI 'HMV Treasury' RLS 7703 (1982) [2] 'Never Sing Louder than Lovely'
CD	Dutton Laboratories/Vocalion 9729 (2002) 'Singers to Remember – Isobel Baillie – The Unforgettable'
CD	Heritage HTGCD 273 (2014) 'The Voice of Isobel Baillie'

HANDEL: *Semele* – Where'er you walk

Webster Booth *(tenor)*; Hallé Orchestra.
Houldsworth Hall, Manchester; 28 August 1942.
Sung in English.

78	HMV C 3305 [mx 2ER 620-1,2] + Be thou faithful (Mendelssohn: *St Paul*)
LP	HMV 'Treasury' HLM 7109 (1977)
CD	Dutton Vocalion CDLX 7032 (1998) 'Webster Booth: Handel Arias / Operatic Arias'

HANDEL: *Serse* – Ombra mai fù

Kirsten Flagstad *(soprano)*; George Thalben-Ball *(organ)*; Philharmonia Orchestra.
EMI Studio No. 1, Abbey Road, London; 3 July 1948.
Sung in Italian.

78	HMV DB 6791 [mx 2EA 13204-1,2] + Agnus Dei (Bizet)
LP	EMI Electrola 1C 147-01 491/92 [2] (1973) 'The Kirsten Flagstad Album'
LP	EMI 'Références' 2902061 (1984)
CD	Testament SBT 1018 (1993) 'Kirsten Flagstad – Handel, Purcell, Gluck, Wagner'
CD	Preiser 'Lebendige Vergangenheit' 89625 (2005) 'Kirsten Flagstad, III'

JÄRNEFELT: Berceuse in G minor

Orchestra of the Royal Opera House, Covent Garden.
London; 8 June 1951.

78	HMV B 10136 [mx OEA 15693] [10"] + Praeludium (Järnefelt)
78	HMV (Finland) TG 101 [10"] + Praeludium (Järnefelt)
78	HMV (Norway) AL 3185 [10"] + Praeludium (Järnefelt)
78	HMV Electrola EG 7726 [10"] + Praeludium (Järnefelt)

JÄRNEFELT: Praeludium

Orchestra of the Royal Opera House, Covent Garden.
London; 8 June 1951.

78	HMV B 10136 [mx OEA 15693] [10"] + Berceuse (Järnefelt)
78	HMV (Finland) TG 101 [10"] + Berceuse (Järnefelt)
78	HMV (Norway) AL 3185 [10"] + Berceuse (Järnefelt)
78	HMV Electrola EG 7726 [10"] + Berceuse (Järnefelt)

KENEMAN: Kak korol' shel na voïnu = When the King went forth to war, op. 7/6

Marian Nowakowski *(bass)*; London Symphony Orchestra.
Kingsway Hall, London; 18 May 1945.
Sung in Polish.

| 78 | Decca K 1172 [mx AR 9436] + Mephistopheles' Song of the Flea (Mussorgsky) |
| CD | Pearl GEMM CD 152 (2001) 'Marian Nowakowski – The Great Polish Bass in Opera and Song' |

KERN: *Showboat* – **Ol' Man River**
Oscar Natzka *(bass)*; Orchestra and Chorus.
Kingsway Hall, London; 15 December 1939.
Sung in English.
Orchestrated by Roy Douglas.

78	Parlophone E 11433/A 4535 [mx CXE 10224-1] + Song of the Volga Boatmen (Keneman-Chaliapin)
CD	Atoll 'Treasures in Sound' ACD 400 [2] (2000) 'Oscar Natzka, The Definitive Collection v.1'
CD	Atoll ACD 801 (2004) 'Oscar Natzka: Great Recordings 1939–1950'

KETÈLBEY: In a Monastery Garden
Oscar Natzka *(bass)*; Orchestra and Chorus.
Kingsway Hall, London; 15 December 1939.
Sung in English.
Orchestrated by Roy Douglas.

78	Parlophone E 11439/A 4537 [mx CXE 10226-1] + Sanctuary of the Heart (Ketèlbey)
LP	Parlophone (Australia) 'Encore Series' PMEO 9299 (1985) 'Songs by Oscar Natzke'
CD	Ode 'New Zealand Heritage Series' CD MANU 1365 (1990) 'Oscar Natzka: A Legend in his Time'
CD	Atoll 'Treasures in Sound' ACD 400 [2] (2000) 'Oscar Natzka: The Definitive Collection v.1'
CD	Naxos 8.110848 (2002) 'The Music of Albert W. Ketelbey, Volume 2'

KETÈLBEY: Sanctuary of the Heart
Oscar Natzka *(bass)*; Orchestra and Chorus.
Kingsway Hall, London; 15 December 1939.
Sung in English.
Orchestrated by Roy Douglas.

78	Parlophone E 11439/A 4537 [mx CXE 10225-1] + In a Monastery Garden (Ketèlbey)
LP	Parlophone (Australia) 'Encore Series' PMEO 9299 (1985) 'Songs by Oscar Natzke'
CD	Ode 'New Zealand Heritage Series' CD MANU 1365 (1990) 'Oscar Natzka: A Legend in his Time'
CD	Atoll 'Treasures in Sound' ACD 400 [2] (2000) 'Oscar Natzka: The Definitive Collection v.1'

LEONCAVALLO: *Pagliacci* – Si può? (A word, allow me)
John Hargreaves *(baritone)*; Philharmonia Orchestra.
EMI Studio No. 1, Abbey Road, London; 19 November 1946.
Sung in English.
78   HMV (unpublished) [mx 2EA 11422]

LEONCAVALLO: *Pagliacci* – Si può? (A word, allow me)
Dennis Noble *(baritone)*; Sadler's Wells Orchestra.
Kingsway Hall, London; 8 December 1939.
Sung in English.
78   HMV C 3141 [mx 2EA 8179-1,2] + Largo (Rossini: *Il barbiere di Siviglia*)
78   HMV (Australia) EB 160
CD   Dutton Laboratories CDLX 7017 'A Tribute to Denis Noble'
CD   Pearl GEMM CDS 9925 (1992) 'Covent Garden on Record, Volume III, 910-1925'
CD   Greenhorn 0027 'Denis Noble Nirvana'

LISZT: Liebestraum (O dream of love)
Webster Booth *(tenor)*; with orchestra.
Kingsway Hall, London; 26 October 1939.
Sung in English.
Note: Arranged by Maurice Besly.
78   HMV C 3139 [mx OEA 8163-1,2] + Addio (Tosti)
LP   EMI 'Encore' ONCM 530 (1979) 'Music for Romance'

MALIPIERO: *La Cimarosiana* : 5 symphonic fragments by Cimarosa, re-orchestrated by Malipiero.
[Andante Grazioso; Allegro Moderato; Non Troppo Mosso; Larghetto; Allegro Vivace]
Orchestra of the Royal Opera House, Covent Garden.
London; 27 November 1952.
LP   M-G-M (USA) E 3013 (1953)
LP   M-G-M (USA) E 3333 (1957)

MASCAGNI: *Cavalleria rusticana* – Regina Cœli…Inneggiamo, il Signor non è morto (Easter Hymn)
Jeanne Dusseau *(soprano)*; Nancy Evans *(contralto)*; Sadler's Wells Orchestra and Chorus.
Kingsway Hall, London; 2 November 1939.
Sung in English.
78   HMV C 3126 [mx 2EA 8174-1,2,3] + Barcarolle (Offenbach: *Les Contes d'Hoffman*n)

78   Victor 13824 + Barcarolle (Offenbach: *Les Contes d'Hoffmann*)

45   HMV 7P 213 [7"] 'Your Kind of Music' + Barcarolle (Offenbach: *Les Contes d'Hoffmann*)

LP   HMV RLS 707 [3] (1972) 'Stars of the Old Vic and Sadler's Wells'

LP   EMI Starline MRS 5141 (1973) 'The Golden Classics'

DL   P&R (2011) 'Stars of the Old Vic and Sadler's Wells'

MASSENET: *Le Cid* – Ballet Music and Rapsodie mauresque (Moorish Rhapsody)

Orchestra of the Royal Opera House, Covent Garden.

London; 24 November 1952.

LP   Parlophone PMC 1013 (1953)

LP   M-G-M (USA) E 3016 (195–?) 'Ballet Music and Moorish Rhapsody from *Le Cid*; Scènes alsaciennes'

CD   Forgotten Records fr 1387 (2017)

Review: For a Massenet collation, the Braithwaite serving is agreeable, with the Le Cid matter including not only the seven sections also covered by Fiedler, but a "Moorish Rhapsody" from Act III. The quality of sound is about the same. *The Guide to Long-Playing Records*. Irving Kolodin (N.Y.; Knopf, 1955), p. 125.

MASSENET: Elégie (O sweet springtime)

Webster Booth *(tenor)*; Symphony Orchestra.

London; 1938.

Sung in English.

78   HMV B 8843 [OEA 6981] + Hindu Song (Rimsky-Korsakov: *Sadko*)

CD   FLAPPER PAST CD 9709 (1999) 'Moonlight & You'

MASSENET: *Hérodiade* – Celui dont la parole…Il est doux, il est bon

Joan Hammond *(soprano)*; Philharmonia Orchestra.

EMI Studio No. 1, Abbey Road, London; 13 May 1950.

Sung in French.

78   HMV (unpublished) [mx 2EA 14680]

LP   HMV 'Treasury' HLM 7042 (1974) 'Aria and Song Recital: Anthology of Unpublished Recordings'

DL   Past Classics 7888510 (2009)

MASSENET: *Scènes alsaciennes*

[Dimanche matin; Au cabaret; Sous les tilleuls; Dimanche soir]

Orchestra of the Royal Opera House, Covent Garden.

London; 24 November 1952.

LP   Parlophone PMC 1013 (1953)

LP   M-G-M (USA) E 3016 (195–?) 'Ballet Music and Moorish Rhapsody from *Le Cid*. Scènes alsaciennes'
CD   Forgotten Records fr 1387 (2017)

Review: Braithwaite works well at this music, and the sound is better than on the reverse side.
The Guide to Long-Playing Records. Irving Kolodin (N.Y.; Knopf, 1955)

MENDELSSOHN: *Elijah* – **Ye people, rend your hearts…If with all your hearts**
Webster Booth *(tenor)*; London Philharmonic Orchestra.
Kingsway Hall, London; 28 February 1939.
Sung in English.
78   HMV C 3095 [mx 2EA 7371-1,2] + Then shall the righteous (Mendelssohn: *Elijah*)
78   RCA Victor 12609 + Then shall the righteous (Mendelssohn: *Elijah*)
LP   HMV 'Treasury' HLM 7109 (1977)
CD   Dutton Laboratories 2CDAX 2004 [2] (1996)

MENDELSSOHN: *Elijah* – **Then shall the righteous**
Webster Booth *(tenor)*; London Philharmonic Orchestra.
Kingsway Hall, London; 28 February 1939.
Sung in English.
78   HMV C 3095 [mx 2EA 7372-1,2] + If with all your hearts (Mendelssohn: *Elijah*)
78   RCA Victor 12609 + If with all your hearts (Mendelssohn: *Elijah*)
CD   Dutton Laboratories 2CDAX 2004 [2] (1996)

MENDELSSOHN: *St Paul* – **Be thou faithful unto death**
Webster Booth *(tenor)*; Hallé Orchestra.
Houldsworth Hall, Manchester; 28 August 1942.
Sung in English.
78   HMV C 3305 [mx 621-1] + Where'er you walk (Handel: *Semele*)
LP   HMV HLM 7109 (1977)

MEYERBEER: *L'Africaine* – **O paradis sorti de l'onde (O paradiso, dall'onde uscito)**
Eugene Conley *(tenor)*; New Symphony Orchestra of London.
Decca West Hampstead Studios, London; 11 September 1950.
Sung in Italian.
LP   London (USA) LL 280 [10"] (1950)
LP   London (USA) LPS 280 [10"] (1950) 'Italian Operatic Arias'
LP   Decca LM 4534 [10"] (1951)

CD   Preiser 'Lebendige Vergangenheit' 89574 (2003) 'Eugene Conley'

CD   Decca 480 8145 (2013) 'Most Wanted Decca Recitals'

MOZART: *Don Giovanni* – Là ci darem la mano (Give me thy hand)

Gwen Catley *(soprano)*; Dennis Noble *(baritone)*; Hallé Orchestra.

Houldsworth Hall, Manchester; 17 March 1943.

Sung in English.

78   HMV B 9338 [mx OER 693-1,2] + The manly heart (Mozart: *Die Zauberflöte*)

CD   Dutton Laboratories CDLX 7020 (1996) 'Stars of English Opera, Volume Two'

MOZART: *Don Giovanni* – Crudele!...Non mi dir

Joan Hammond; Philharmonia Orchestra.

EMI Studio No. 1, Abbey Road, London; 12 May 1950.

Sung in Italian.

78   HMV (unpublished) [mx 2EA 14674]

LP   HMV 'Treasury' HLM 7042 (1974) 'Aria and Song Recital: Anthology of Unpublished Recordings'

DL   Past Classics 7888510 (2009)

MOZART: *Don Giovanni* – Madamina, il catalogo è questo

Oscar Natzka *(bass)*; Orchestra.

London; 29 December 1939.

Sung in Italian.

78   Parlophone A 7362 [mx CXE 10260-1] and [mx CXE 10261-1] [10"]

78   Columbia DB 2291 [mx CA 20295-1] and [mx CA 20296-1] [10"] (transferred 3 February 1947)

78   Columbia DO 3168 (1947)

LP   Columbia 33MS 6012 [10"] (196–?) 'More of Oscar Natzke' (i.e. Natzka)

CD   Ode 'New Zealand Heritage Series' CD MANU 1365 (1990) 'Oscar Natzka: A Legend in his Time'

CD   Atoll 'Treasures in Sound' ACD 400 [2] (2000) 'Oscar Natzka: The Definitive Collection, v 1'

CD   Atoll ACD 801 (2004) 'Oscar Natzka: Great Recordings 1939–50'

MOZART: *Die Entführung aus dem Serail* – (When a maiden takes your fancy)

Oscar Natzka *(bass)*; Orchestra and Chorus.

London; 29 December 1939.

Sung in English.

78   Parlophone A 4544 [mx CXE 10262-1] + Within these sacred bowers (Mozart: *Die Zauberflöte*)

78	Columbia DX 1473 [mx CAX 10006-1] (matrix renumbered 1 September 1947) + Drinking Song (Nicolai: *Die Lustigen Weiber von Windsor*) Cond. Karl Rankl
78	Columbia DOX 1019 + Drinking Song (Nicolai: *Die Lustigen Weiber von Windsor*) Cond. Karl Rankl
CD	Atoll 'Treasures in Sound' ACD 400 [2] (2000) 'Oscar Natzka: The Definitive Collection, v.1'
CD	Atoll ACD 801 (2004) 'Oscar Natzka: Great Recordings 1939–50'

MOZART: Misera, dove son!, K.369

Joan Hammond; Philharmonia Orchestra.
EMI Studio No. 1, Abbey Road, London; 12 May 1950.
Sung in Italian.

78	HMV (unpublished) [mx 2EA 14676]
LP	HMV 'Treasury' HLM 7042 (1974) 'Aria and Song Recital: Anthology of Unpublished Recordings'
DL	Past Classics 7888510 (2009)

MOZART: *Le nozze di Figaro* – Se vuol ballare (If you are after a little amusement)

Dennis Noble *(baritone)*; Hallé Orchestra.
Belle Vue Gardens, Manchester; 16 March 1943.
Sung in English.

78	HMV B 9325 [OER 688-1,2,3] + A fowler bold (Mozart: *Die Zauberflöte*)
78	HMV B 9755
45	HMV 7EG 8275 'Operatic Favourites No. 2' + A fowler bold (Mozart: *Die Zauberflöte*); I'm the factotum (Rossini: *Il barbiere di Siviglia*); Say goodbye to pastime (Mozart: *Le nozze di Figaro*).
CD	Dutton Laboratories CDLX 7020 (1996) 'Stars of English Opera, Volume Two'
CD	Greenhorn 0027 'Denis Noble Nirvana'

MOZART: *Le nozze di Figaro* – Non più andrai (Say goodbye to pastime and play)

Dennis Noble *(baritone)*; Hallé Orchestra.
Houldsworth Hall, Manchester; 29 August 1942.
Sung in English.

78	HMV C 3304 [mx 628-1,2,3] + From fair Provence (Verdi: *La traviata*)
78	HMV (Ireland) IPX 52 + From fair Provence (Verdi: *La traviata*)
45	HMV 7EG 8275 'Operatic Favourites No. 2'

+ A fowler bold (Mozart: *Die Zauberflöte*); I'm the factotum (Rossini: *Il barbiere di Siviglia*); If you are after a little amusement (Mozart: *Le nozze di Figaro*).

CD	Cheyne CHE 44459 'Denis Noble'
CD	Dutton Laboratories CDLX 7017 'A Tribute to Denis Noble'
CD	Greenhorn 0027 'Denis Noble Nirvana'

MOZART: *Le nozze di Figaro* – Voi che sapete
Patrice Munsel *(soprano)*; Orchestra of the Royal Opera House, Covent Garden (not named).
London; August 1952.
Sung in Italian.
Note: Soundtrack to the film *Melba*.

LP	RCA Victor LM 7012 [10"] '*Melba*: Original Soundtrack of the Motion Picture'
LP	HMV BLP 1023 [10"]
LP	HMV (Italy) QBLP 5015 [10"]
45	RCA Victor EDM 7012 [4]
CD	Flare SPEC 1025 (2006) 'On Wings of Song'
DL	Frank Bristow 'Music from the Past' EXCD 004 'A Patrice Munsel Recital'

MOZART: *Les petits riens*, K.299b
Orchestra of the Royal Opera House, Covent Garden.
London; 17 December 1952.

LP	M-G-M (USA) E 3034 (1952?) + *Le donne di buon umore* (D. Scarlatti-Tommasini)
CD	Forgotten Records fr 1508 (2018)

Review: Much of the lilt and rhythmic verve of these pieces is conveyed by Braithwaite in an excellent reproduction. *The Guide to Long-Playing Records*. Irving Kolodin (N.Y.; Knopf, 1955)

MOZART: *Die Zauberflöte* – Ach, ich fühls (Ah! 'tis gone)
Elisabeth Schwarzkopf *(soprano)*; Philharmonia Orchestra.
EMI Studio No. 1, Abbey Road, London; 12 April 1948.
Sung in English.

78	HMV (unpublished) [mx CAX 10218-1,2]
LP	HMV ALP 1435501 (1983)
CS	HMV TC-ALP 1435501 (1983)
CD	EMI 'Références' CDH 7 636708 2 (1990)
CD	EMI Classics 'Great Recordings of the Century' 62191679 9 (2005)
CD	EMI Classics 'Great Recordings of the Century' 76845 (2005)

CD   EMI Classics 4 40497 2 [5] (2012) 'Voices of German Opera'

CD   Istituto Discografico Italiano IDIS 6576 (2009) 'Rare Recordings 1946–1954. Vol. 2'

CD   EMI Classics 'Icon' 18459 [10] (2011) 'Elisabeth Schwarzkopf – Perfect Prima Donna'

CD   Membran Documents 223503 [10] (2011) '10 Great Sopranos'

MOZART: *Die Zauberflöte* – **In diesen heil'gen Hallen (Within these sacred bowers)**
Oscar Natzka *(bass)*; Orchestra and Chorus.
London; 29 December 1939.
Sung in English.

78   Parlophone A 4544 [mx CXE 10259-1] + Madamina, il catalogo è questo (Mozart: *Don Giovanni*)

CD   Ode 'New Zealand Heritage Series' CD MANU 1365 (1990) 'Oscar Natzka: A Legend in his Time'

CD   Atoll 'Treasures in Sound' ACD 400 [2] (2000) 'Oscar Natzka: The Definitive Collection, v.1'

CD   Atoll ACD 801 (2004) 'Oscar Natzka: Great Recordings 1939–50'

MOZART: *Die Zauberflöte* – **Ein mädchen oder Weibchen (A maiden fair and slender)**
Dennis Noble *(baritone)*; Hallé Orchestra.
Belle Vue Gardens, Manchester; 17 March 1943.
Sung in English.

78   HMV C 3520 [mx 2ER 692-1,2]
       + Yon assassin is my equal (Verdi: *Rigoletto)* Liverpool P.O. (c. Basil Cameron)

CD   Cheyne CHE 44459 'Denis Noble'

CD   Dutton Laboratories CDLX 7017 'A Tribute to Denis Noble'

MOZART: *Die Zauberflöte* – **Vogelfänger bin ich ja (A fowler bold)**
Dennis Noble *(baritone)*; Hallé Orchestra.
Belle Vue Gardens, Manchester; 17 March 1943.
Sung in English.

78   HMV B 9325 [mx 694-1,2] + If you are after (Mozart: *Le nozze di Figaro*)

EP   HMV 7EG 8275 'Operatic Favourites No. 2'
       + Say goodbye to pastime (Mozart: *Le nozze di Figaro*); I'm the factotum (Rossini: *Il barbiere di Siviglia*; If you are after a little amusement (Mozart: *Le nozze di Figaro*).

CD   Dutton Laboratories CDLX 7020 (1996) 'Stars of English Opera, Volume Two'

MOZART: *Die Zauberflöte* – **Bei Männern, welche Liebe fühlen (The manly heart)**
Gwen Catley *(soprano)*; Dennis Noble *(baritone)*; Hallé Orchestra.
Houldsworth Hall, Manchester; 17 March 1943.
Sung in English.
78   HMV B 9338 [mx OER 691-1,2,3] + Give me thy hand (Mozart: *Don Giovanni*)

MUSSORGSKY: Mephistopheles' Song of the Flea
Marian Nowakowski *(bass)*; London Symphony Orchestra.
Kingsway Hall, London; 18 May 1945.
Sung in Russian.
78   Decca K 1172 [mx AR 9437] + When the King went forth to war (Kenemann)
CD   Pearl GEMM CD 152 (2001) 'Marian Nowakowski – The Great Polish Bass in Opera and Song'

NEVIN: Mighty lak' a rose
Blanche Thebom *(mezzo)*; London Symphony Orchestra.
EMI Studio No. 1, Abbey Road, London; 10 July 1950.
Sung in English.
LP   RCA Victor LM 104 [10"] 'Fireside Favorites'
LP   RCA Victor 'Bluebird Classics' LBC 1054 (1953) 'Fireside Favorites and Beloved Hymns'
45   RCA WDM 1541 [4] 'Fireside Favorites'
          + My old Kentucky home, Homing; The rosary; Calm as the night; Trees; Lead kindly light; One sweetly solemn thought.
CD   Klassic Haus Restorations KHL 504 (2018) 'Fireside Favorites'

NEVIN: The Rosary
Blanche Thebom (mezzo); London Symphony Orchestra.
EMI Studio No. 1, Abbey Road, London; 11 July 1950.
Sung in English.
LP   RCA Victor LM 104 [10"] 'Fireside Favorites'
LP   RCA Victor 'Bluebird Classics' LBC 1054 (1953) 'Fireside Favorites and Beloved Hymns'
45   RCA WDM 1541 [4] 'Fireside Favorites'
          + My old Kentucky home; Homing; Calm as the night, Trees, Lead kindly light; One sweetly solemn thought, Mighty lak' a rose.
CD   Klassic Haus Restorations KHL 504 (2018) 'Fireside Favorites'

OFFENBACH: *Les contes d'Hoffmann* – **Barcarolle**
Jeanne Dusseau *(soprano)*; Nancy Evans *(contralto)*; Sadler's Wells Orchestra and Chorus.
Kingsway Hall, London; 2 November 1939.
Sung in English.
78   HMV C 3126 [mx OEA 8175-1,2] + Easter Hymn (Mascagni: *Cavalleria rusticana*)
78   Victor 13824 + Easter Hymn (Mascagni: *Cavalleria rusticana*)
45   HMV 7P 213 [7"] 'Your Kind of Music' + Easter Hymn (Mascagni: *Cavalleria rusticana*)

PÉREZ FREIRE: Ay, Ay, Ay (I gave all my love)
Webster Booth *(tenor)*; with orchestra.
Kingsway Hall, London; 26 October 1939.
Sung in English.
78   HMV B 9009 [mx OEA 8162-1,2] [10"] + Ideale (Tosti)

PONCHIELLI: *La gioconda* – **Cielo e mar!**
Eugene Conley *(tenor)*; New Symphony Orchestra of London.
Decca West Hampstead Studios, London; 11 September 1950.
Sung in Italian.
LP   London (USA) LL 280 [10"] (1950)
LP   London (USA) LPS 280 [10"] (1950) 'Italian Operatic Arias'
LP   Decca LM 4534 [10"] (1951)
CD   Preiser 'Lebendige Vergangenheit' 89574 (2003) 'Eugene Conley'
CD   Decca 480 8145 (2013) 'Most Wanted Decca Recitals'

PONCHIELLI: *La gioconda* – **Dance of the Hours**
Orchestra of the Royal Opera House, Covent Garden.
London; 17 July 1952.
LP   M-G-M (USA) E 3003 (1953) 'Popular Ballet Music from Great Operas'
LP   Parlophone PMC 1029 (1955)
LP   Lion (USA) CL 40006 (195–?) 'Orchestral Favorites, Volume 1'
LP   M-G-M (USA) E 3037 (195–?) 'Orchestral Favorites, Volume 1'
DL   Past Classics 7964396 (2008)

PONCHIELLI: *La gioconda* – **Suicidio!**
Joan Hammond *(soprano)*; Philharmonia Orchestra.
EMI Studio No. 1, Abbey Road, London; 6 January 1949.
Sung in Italian.
78   HMV C 3901 [mx 2EA 13533-1,2]
      + Io son l'umile ancella (Cilea: *Adriana Lecouvreur*) cond. Walter Susskind

LP   HMV HQM 1186 (1969) 'Golden Voice Series No. 16: Joan Hammond'
LP   EMI 'Connoisseur Series' CO 485
LP   World Record Club (NZ) WI 485 (1969) 'Joan Hammond'
CD   Testament SBT 1160 (1998) 'Dame Joan Hammond: by request'

PROKOFIEV: *Cinderella* **– Excerpts**
[Act I: Sewing Scene; Cinderella's Gavotte; Fairy Godmother; The Seasons. Act II: Midnight Waltz; Pas de deux; Apotheosis-Finale]
Orchestra of the Royal Opera House, Covent Garden.
London; 19 January and 9 February 1949.
Note: Selection of the music used for Sadler's Wells Ballet 1948 production, conducted by Braithwaite and choreographed by Sir Frederick Ashton.
78   Columbia DX 1562/64 [mx CAX 10437/CAX 10444] [6 sides]
78   Columbia DX 8328/30 [6 sides] [a.c.]
78   Columbia (USA) 72855/57D [6 sides]
78   Columbia (USA) MM 859 (set)
LP   Columbia (USA) ML 4229 (1949) + The Rake's Progress (Gavin Gordon) cond. Constant Lambert.
CD   Forgotten Records fr 1507 (2018)

Review: "For a change, Warwick Braithwaite was able to devote all his attention to the Royal Opera House Orchestra alone, and under his masterly direction they play superbly. It is an excellent recording in every way." *Tempo* Autumn 1949: 46

Review: '…there is excellent life and continuity in Braithwaite's performance, which is well reproduced.'
The Guide to Long-Playing Records. Irving Kolodin (N.Y.; Knopf, 1955)

PUCCINI: *La bohème* **– Che gelida manina (Your tiny hand is frozen)**
Webster Booth *(tenor)*; London Philharmonic Orchestra.
Kingsway Hall, London; 12 September 1938.
Sung in English.
78   HMV C 3030 (1938) [mx 2 EA 1172] + Flower Song (Bizet: *Carmen*)
LP   HMV 'Treasury' HLM 7109 (1977)
DL   THE ART OF SINGING '100 Greatest Tenors, Vol. 2: 1927–1940' (2014)

PUCCINI: *La bohème* **– In un coupé?…O, Mimì tu più non torni (In a coupé?…Ah Mimì, false fickle-hearted)**
Webster Booth *(tenor)*; Dennis Noble *(baritone)*; Hallé Orchestra.
Houldsworth Hall, Manchester; 29 August 1942.
Sung in English.
78   HMV C 3369 [mx 2ER 629-1,2] + Caro nome (Verdi: *Rigoletto*)

CD   Dutton Vocalion CDLX 7032 (1998) 'Webster Booth: Handel Arias / Operatic Arias'

PUCCINI: *La fanciulla del West* – **Oh, se sapeste (Oh, you've no notion)**
Joan Hammond *(soprano)*; Philharmonia Orchestra.
EMI Studio No. 1, Abbey Road, London; 29 January 1947.
Sung in English.
78   HMV B 9747 [mx OEA 11614-1,2] [10"] + Che tua madre (Puccini: *Madama Butterfly*)

PUCCINI: *Madama Butterfly* – **Sai cos'ebbe cuore…Che tua madre (Do you know my sweet?…That your mother)**
Joan Hammond *(soprano)*; Philharmonia Orchestra.
EMI Studio No. 1, Abbey Road, London; 29 January 1947.
Sung in English.
78   HMV B 9747 [mx OEA 11612-1,2] [10"] + Oh, se sapeste (Puccini: *La fanciulla del West*)

PUCCINI: *Tosca* – **Recondita armonia (Strange harmony of contrasts)**
Webster Booth *(tenor)*; London Philharmonic Orchestra.
Kingsway Hall, London; 12 September 1938.
Sung in English.
78   HMV B 8803 [mx OEA 1175] + E lucevan le stelle (Puccini: *Tosca*)
78   Victor 26483/85 [3] [10"] 'Opera in English : famous arias from Rigoletto, La bohème, La Tosca'
DL   Emerald Echoes 'Love's Old Sweet Song' (2016)

PUCCINI: *Tosca* – **Recondita armonia (Strange harmony of contrasts)**
John McHugh *(tenor)*; Philharmonia Orchestra.
EMI Studio No. 1, Abbey Road, London; 27 June 1946.
Sung in English.
78   Columbia DB 2234 [mx CA 20115-2] [10"] + E lucevan le stelle (Puccini: *Tosca*)

PUCCINI: *Tosca* – **E lucevan le stelle (When the stars were brightly shining)**
Webster Booth *(tenor)*; London Philharmonic Orchestra.
Kingsway Hall, London; 12 September 1938.
Sung in English.
78   HMV B 8803 [mx OEA 1174] + Recondita armonia (Puccini: *Tosca*)
78   Victor 26483/85 [3] [10"] 'Opera in English : famous arias from Rigoletto, La bohème, La Tosca'
45   HMV 7EG 8263 (1957)

+ Quartet (Verdi: *Rigoletto*); Lovely maid in the moonlight (*La bohème*)
Booth; Cross;
cond. Collingwood; Miserere (*Il trovatore*) Booth; Cross; cond.
Collingwood.

| CD | EMI 8 34676.2 (1995) |
| CD | EMI CDSL 8248 (1995) 'Three Great Tenors' |

PUCCINI: *Tosca* – E lucevan le stelle (When the stars were brightly shining)

John McHugh *(tenor)*; Philharmonia Orchestra.
EMI Studio No. 1, Abbey Road, London; 27 June 1946.
Sung in English.

| 78 | Columbia DB 2234 [mx CA 20116] [10"] + Recondita armonia (Puccini: *Tosca*) |

PUCCINI: *Tosca* – Vissi d'arte

Patrice Munsel *(soprano)*; Orchestra of the Royal Opera House, Covent Garden (not named).
London; August 1952.
Sung in Italian.
Note: Soundtrack to the film *Melba*.

LP	RCA Victor LM 7012 [10"] '*Melba*: Original Soundtrack of the Motion Picture'
LP	HMV BLP 1023 [10"]
LP	HMV (Italy) QBLP 5015 [10"]
45	RCA Victor EDM 7012 [4]
CD	Flare SPEC 1025 (2006) 'On Wings of Song'
DL	Frank Bristow 'Music from the Past' EXCD 004 'A Patrice Munsel Recital'

PURCELL: *Dido and Aeneas* – Thy hand Belinda...When I am laid in earth

Kirsten Flagstad *(soprano)*; Philharmonia Orchestra.
EMI Studio No. 1, Abbey Road, London; 29 May 1948.
Sung in English.

78	HMV DB 6913 [mx 2EA 13087-1,2]
	+ What is life to me? (Gluck: *Orfeo ed Eurydice*) Cond. Walter Susskind
LP	HMV HQM 1057 (1967) 'Golden Voice Series No. 4: Kirsten Flagstad'
LP	EMI Electrola 1C 147-01 491/92M (1973) 'The Kirsten Flagstad Album'
45	HMV 7P 331 + What is life to me? (Gluck: *Orfeo ed Eurydice*) Cond. Walter Susskind
45	HMV 7R 164 + What is life to me? (Gluck: *Orfeo ed Eurydice*) Cond. Walter Susskind
CD	EMI Classics 'GRC' 50999 5 09690 2 9 'Purcell: Dido and Aeneas'
CD	EMI CHS7 69741-2 (1991) 'Record of Singing, Volume 4'

CD   Testament SBT 1018 (1993) 'Kirsten Flagstad – Handel, Purcell, Gluck, Wagner'

CD   Musikkmagasinet Ballade CM 95 (issue 3/1995) 'Norske Stemmebånd'

CD   Preiser 'Lebendige Vergangenheit' 89625 (2005) 'Kirsten Flagstad, III'

CD   EMI Classics 67179 (2007) 'Sopranos in the Grand Tradition'

CD   Naxos 'Historical' 8.111264 (2007)

CD   EMI Classics 50999 4 55346 2 1 [5] (2010) 'Kirsten Flagstad: The Supreme Wagnerian Soprano'

CD   Regis RRC 1269 (2007) 'Kirsten Flagstad – Scenes and Arias'

RASBACH: Trees

Blanche Thebom *(mezzo)*; London Symphony Orchestra.
EMI Studio No. 1, Abbey Road, London; 11 July 1950.
Sung in English.

LP   RCA Victor LM 104 [10"] 'Fireside Favorites'

LP   RCA Victor 'Bluebird Classics' LBC 1054 (1953) 'Fireside Favorites and Beloved Hymns'

CD   Klassic Haus Restorations KHL 504 (2018) 'Fireside Favorites'

RESPIGHI: *La boutique fantastique* (ballet suite after Rossini) – Excerpts

[Tarantella; Scene (Andantino mosso); Can-can]
Orchestra of the Royal Opera House, Covent Garden.
London: *c.* November 1952.

LP   M-G-M (USA) E 3006 (1952) 'Nights at the Ballet'

LP   Parlophone PMC 1008 (1954) 'Nights at the Ballet'

LP   Parlophone (NZ) PMCM 1008 'Nights at the Ballet'

78   M-G-M (USA) 30760 (1953) 'Fantastic Can-Can' + Tarantella (Britten-Rossini – Soirees Musicales)

45   M-G-M (USA) K30760 (1953) 'Fantastic Can-Can' + Tarantella (Britten-Rossini – Soirees Musicales)

Review: 'This new set contains eight excerpts from popular ballets performed in warm style by the Royal Opera House Orchestra, directed by Warwick Braithwaite….It should delight all ballet fans as well as many others.' *The Billboard* 13 December 1952: 45.

RESPIGHI: *Rossiniana* – orchestral suite from Rossini's *Quelques riens*, liberally transcribed by Respighi

[Capri e Taormina; Lamento; Intermezzo; Tarantella Puro Sangue]
Orchestra of the Royal Opera House, Covent Garden.
London; 27 November 1952.

LP   M-G-M (USA) E 3013 (1953)

Review: All the problems here are well comprehended by Braithwaite, and the sound is decidedly good.
The Guide to Long-Playing Records. Irving Kolodin (N.Y.; Knopf, 1955), p. 181.

RIMSKY-KORSAKOV: *Sadko* – Chant hindou (Hindu Song)
Webster Booth *(tenor)*; Symphony Orchestra.
London; 1938.
Sung in English.
78   HMV B 8843 [mx OEA 6982] + Elégie (Massenet)
CD   FLAPPER PAST CD 9709 (1989) 'Moonlight & You'

RIMSKY-KORSAKOV: *Sadko* – Chant hindou (Hindu Song)
Joan Cross *(soprano)*; London Symphony Orchestra.
Kingsway Hall, London; 18 May 1945.
Sung in English.
78   Decca K 1272 [mx AR 9434] + Ave Maria (Schubert)
CD   Dutton CDLX 7020

RODRIGO: Cuatro madrigales amatorios
[Con qué la lavaré?; Vos me matásteis; De dónde venís, amore?; De los álamos vengo, Madre]
Marimí del Pozo *(soprano)*; Philharmonia Orchestra.
EMI Studio No. 1, Abbey Road, London; 21 July 1949.
78   HMV (unpublished) [mx 2EA 14108-1] Part 1; [mx 2EA 14109-1] Part 2
45   HMV (Spain) 7RB 1056 (1958)
DL   Bibliothèque national de France (BNF) (2016)

ROMBERG: *Maytime* – Will you remember?
Ann Ziegler *(soprano)*; Webster Booth *(tenor)*; with orchestra.
EMI Studio No. 1, Abbey Road, London; 10 June 1941.
Sung in English.
78   HMV B 9177 [mx 9366-1,2] + Love's Garden of Roses (Wood)
LP   EMI 'Encore' ONCM 530 (1980) 'Music for Romance'

ROSSINI: *Il barbiere di Siviglia* – Largo al factotum (I'm the factotum)
Dennis Noble *(baritone)*; Sadler's Wells Orchestra.
Kingsway Hall, London; 8 December 1939.
Sung in English.
78   HMV C 3141 [mx 8178-1,2] + Prologue (Leoncavallo: *Pagliacci*)
78   HMV (Australia) EB 160 + Prologue (Leoncavallo: *Pagliacci*);
EP   HMV 7EG 8275 'Operatic Favourites No. 2'
           + A fowler bold (Mozart: *Die Zauberflöte*); Say goodbye to pastime

(Mozart: *Le nozze di Figaro*); If you are after a little amusement (Mozart: *Le nozze di Figaro*).

LP	HMV 'Treasury Series' HLM 7009 (1972) 'Great British Basses and Baritones'
LP	World Record Club (NZ) CO 538 (1972?) 'Great British Basses and Baritones'
CD	Dutton Laboratories CDLX 7018 'Stars of English Opera, Volume One'
CD	Greenhorn 0027 'Denis Noble Nirvana'

ROSSINI: *Il barbiere di Siviglia* – Una voce poco fa (There's a voice within my heart)

Gwen Catley *(soprano)*; Hallé Orchestra.
Belle Vue Gardens, Manchester; 16 March 1943.
Sung in English.

78	HMV B 9323 [mx 689-1] Part 1 and [mx 690-1,2,3] Part 2
LP	HMV HLM 7066 (1977) 'Operatic and Song Recital'
CD	Dutton CDLX 7022 (1997) 'Gwen Catley: Favourite Coloratura Arias and Songs'

ROSSINI: *Il barbiere di Siviglia* – Una voce poco fa

Patrice Munsel *(soprano)*; Orchestra of the Royal Opera House, Covent Garden (not named).
London; August 1952.
Sung in Italian.
Note: Soundtrack to the film *Melba*.

LP	RCA Victor LM 7012 [10"] '*Melba*: Original Soundtrack of the Motion Picture'
LP	HMV BLP 1023 [10"]
LP	HMV (Italy) QBLP 5015 [10"]
45	RCA Victor EDM 7012 [4]
CD	Flare SPEC 1025 (2006) 'On Wings of Song'
DL	Frank Bristow 'Music from the Past' EXCD 004 'A Patrice Munsel Recital'

ROSSINI: *Guillaume Tell* – Ballet Music

Orchestra of the Royal Opera House, Covent Garden.
London; 11 February 1952.

LP	M-G-M (USA) E 149 [10"] (1952)
LP	M-G-M (USA) E 3003 (1953) 'Popular Ballet Music from Great Operas'
LP	M-G-M (USA) E 3028 (1953)
LP	Parlophone PMC 1029 (1955)
LP	M-G-M Classics MCS 7007/8-3 [6] (196–?) 'Romantic Ballet Music'
DL	Past Classics 7964396 (2008)

ROSSINI: *Guillaume Tell* – **Overture**
Orchestra of the Royal Opera House, Covent Garden.
London; 11 February 1952.
LP   M-G-M (USA) E 149 [10"] (1952)
LP   M-G-M (USA) E 3028 (1953)
LP   Parlophone PMC 1029 (1955)
LP   M-G-M Classics MCS 7007/8-3 [6] (196–?) 'Romantic Ballet Music'
DL   Past Classics 7964396 (2008)

ROSSINI: *Guillaume Tell* – **Sombre forêt**
Joan Hammond *(soprano)*; Philharmonia Orchestra.
EMI Studio No. 1, Abbey Road, London; 13 May 1950.
Sung in French.
78   HMV (unpublished) [mx 2EA 14678]

ROSSINI: *Il Signor Bruschino* – **Overture**
Orchestra of the Royal Opera House, Covent Garden.
London; 11 February 1952.
LP   M-G-M (USA) E 149 [10"]

ROSSINI: *Les soirées musicales* – **no. 6: La pastorella dell'Alpi (The Shepherdess of the Alps)**
Gwen Catley *(soprano)*; London Symphony Orchestra.
EMI Studio No. 1, Abbey Road, London; 13 October 1950.
Sung in English.
78   HMV C 4043 [mx 2EA 15119] + Skater's Waltz (Waldteufel)
CD   Dutton CDLX 7022 (1997) 'Gwen Catley: Favourite Coloratura Arias and Songs'

SAINT-SAËNS: Piano Concerto no. 2 in G minor, op. 22
Moura Lympany *(piano)*; National Symphony Orchestra.
Kingsway Hall, London; 24 July 1945.
78   Decca K.1161/63 [3] [mx AR-9579-1; AR-9580-2; AR-9581-2; AR-9582-2; AR-9583-3; AR-9584-1]
78   Decca EDA 24 [3]
CD   Pristine Audio PASC 058 (2006)
CD   Decca 'Eloquence' ELQ 4829404 [7] (2019) 'Moura Lympany: The Decca Legacy'

SAINT-SAËNS: *Samson et Dalila* – **Amour, viens aider ma faiblesse (Love from thy power)**
Winifred Heidt *(mezzo)*; New Symphony Orchestra of London.

Decca West Hampstead Studios, London; 12 September 1950.
Sung in French.
LP   Decca (unpublished)

SAINT-SAËNS: *Samson et Dalila* – **Amour, viens aider ma faiblesse (Love from thy power)**
Gladys Ripley *(contralto)*; Orchestra of the Royal Opera House, Covent Garden.
EMI Studio No. 1, Abbey Road, London; 12 October 1950.
Sung in English
78   Columbia DX 1709 [mx CAX 10413] + Mon coeur s'ouvre à ta voix
          (Saint-Saëns: *Samson et Dalila*)

SAINT-SAËNS: *Samson et Dalila* – **Mon coeur s'ouvre à ta voix (Softly awakes my heart)**
Winifred Heidt *(mezzo)*; New Symphony Orchestra of London.
Decca West Hampstead Studios, London; 12 September 1950.
Sung in French.
LP   Decca (unpublished)

SAINT-SAËNS: *Samson et Dalila* – **Mon coeur s'ouvre à ta voix (Softly awakes my heart)**
Gladys Ripley *(contralto)*; Orchestra of the Royal Opera House, Covent Garden.
EMI Studio No. 1, Abbey Road, London; 12 October 1950.
Sung in English.
78   Columbia DX 1709 [mx CAX 10416] + Amour, viens aider ma faiblesse
          (Saint-Saëns: *Samson et Dalila*)

SAINT-SAËNS: *Samson et Dalila* – **Mon coeur s'ouvre à ta voix**
Blanche Thebom *(mezzo)*; London Symphony Orchestra.
EMI Studio No. 1, Abbey Road, London; 12 July 1950.
Sung in French.
78   HMV DB 21263 [2EA 14894] + Printemps qui commence (Saint-Saëns:
          Samson et Dalila)
78   RCA Victor 12-3104 + Printemps qui commence (Saint-Saëns: *Samson et
          Dalila*)
45   RCA Victor 'Red Seal' + Printemps qui commence (Saint-Saëns: *Samson
          et Dalila*)
LP   RCA Victor 'Red Seal' LM 1148 'Treasury of Grand Opera, Volume II'
CD   Preiser 'Lebendige Vergangenheit' 89559 (2002) 'Blanche Thebom'

SAINT-SAËNS: *Samson et Dalila* – **Printemps qui commence**
Blanche Thebom *(mezzo)*; London Symphony Orchestra.

EMI Studio No. 1, Abbey Road, London; 12 July 1950.

Sung in French.

78	HMV DB 21263 [mx 2EA 14893] + Mon coeur s'ouvre à ta voix (Saint-Saëns: *Samson et Dalila*)
78	RCA Victor 12-3104 + Mon coeur s'ouvre à ta voix (Saint-Saëns: *Samson et Dalila*)
CD	Preiser 'Lebendige Vergangenheit' 89559 (2002) 'Blanche Thebom'

SCARLATTI-TOMMASINI: *Le donne di buon umore* (The Good-humoured Ladies)

[A ballet consisting of Vincenzo Tommasini's arrangements of Domenico Scarlatti's harpsichord sonatas L.388, 361, 33, 463, 385]

Orchestra of the Royal Opera House, Covent Garden.

London; 8 December 1952.

LP	M-G-M (USA) E 3034 (1953) + Les petits riens (Mozart)
CD	Forgotten Records fr 1508 (2018)

SCHUBERT: Ave Maria, D.839

Joan Cross *(soprano)*; London Symphony Orchestra.

Kingsway Hall, London; 18 May 1945.

Sung in English.

78	Decca K 1272 [mx AR 9435] + Chant hindou (Rimsky-Korsakov: *Sadko*)

SCHUBERT (arr. Clutsam): *Lilac Time* – The Flower

Ann Ziegler *(soprano)*; Webster Booth *(tenor)*; with orchestra.

EMI Studio No. 1, Abbey Road, London; 10 June 1941.

Sung in English.

78	HMV B 9202 [mx 9365-1,2] + The Golden Song (Schubert-Clutsam: *Lilac Time*)
LP	EMI 'Encore' ONCM 530 (1980) 'Music for Romance'

SCHUBERT (arr. Clutsam): *Lilac Time* – The Golden Song

Ann Ziegler *(soprano)*; Webster Booth *(tenor)*; with orchestra.

EMI Studio No. 1, Abbey Road, London; 10 June 1941.

Sung in English.

78	HMV B 9202 [mx 9364-1,2] + The Flower (Schubert-Clutsam: *Lilac Time*)
LP	EMI 'Encore' ONCM 530 (1980) 'Music for Romance'

SCHUBERT: *Rosamunde* – Excerpts

[Overture (*Die Zauberharfe*); Entracte I, B minor; Ballet I, B minor; Entracte III, B flat major; Ballet II, G minor]

Orchestra of the Royal Opera House, Covent Garden.
London; 21 February 1951.

LP	Parlophone PMD 1027 (1952?) [10"]
LP	M-G-M (USA) E 96 [10"] (195–?) 'Incidental Music to Rosamunde' (Does not include Entracte I)
LP	M-G-M (USA) K 96 (set)

SCHUMANN: *Carnival* – Excerpts

[Préambule; Reconnaissance; Pantalon et Colombine]
Orchestra of the Royal Opera House, Covent Garden.
London; 16 September 1952.
Note: Orchestrated by Anton Arensky.

LP	M-G-M (USA) E 3006 (1952) 'Nights at the Ballet'
LP	Parlophone PMC 1008 (1954) 'Nights at the Ballet'
LP	Parlophone (NZ) PMCM 1008 'Nights at the Ballet'

SIBELIUS: Finlandia, op. 26

National Symphony Orchestra.
Kingsway Hall, London; 22 March 1945.

| 78 | Decca K 1150 [mx AR 9234] |
| 78 | London T 5372 |

SMETANA: *The Bartered Bride* – Endlich allein…Wie fremd und tot

Sena Jurinac *(soprano)*; Philharmonia Orchestra.
EMI Studio No. 1, Abbey Road, London; 11 September 1950.
Sung in German.

78	HMV DB 21136 [mx 2EA 14996] and [mx 2EA 14997]
78	Columbia DX 1713 [mx CAX 10895-1,2] and [mx CAX 10896-1,2]
LP	HMV HQM 1024 (1966) 'Golden Voice Series No. 2: Sena Jurinac'
CD	EMI 'Références' CDH 7 63199 2 (1989) 'Mozart, Smetana Opera Arias; Strauss: Vier letzte lieder'
CD	Membran Documents 223503 [10] (2011) '10 Great Sopranos'
CD	Diapason DIAP 016 (March 2010)

SMETANA: *The Kiss (Hubička)* – Wiegenlied

Sena Jurinac *(soprano)*; Philharmonia Orchestra.
EMI Studio No. 1, Abbey Road, London; 11 September 1950.
Sung in German.

| 78 | HMV (unpublished) [mx 2EA 14995-1,2] |
| 78 | Historic Masters HM 187 (2007) + Alles ist schlafen (Tchaikovsky *The Queen of Spades*) L. Collingwood *(cond)* |

CD   EMI 'Références' CDH 7 63199 2 (1989) 'Mozart, Smetana Opera Arias; Strauss: Vier letzte lieder'

TCHAIKOVSKY: *Eugene Onegin* – **Tatiana's Letter Scene**
Joan Hammond *(soprano)*; Hallé Orchestra.
Houldsworth Hall, Manchester; 28 August 1942.
Sung in English.
Note: Label gives Constant Lambert as conductor, but Hammond recalls that he was too tired to conduct and Braithwaite took over.

78   Columbia DX 1134/35 [3 of 4 sides] [mx CAX 9035/37] + Side 4 Depuis le jour (Charpentier: *Louise*)
78   Columbia DOX 753/54 [3 of 4 sides] + Side 4 Depuis le jour (Charpentier: *Louise*)

TCHAIKOVSKY: *Nutcracker* – **Waltz of the Flowers**
Orchestra of the Royal Opera House, Covent Garden.
London; 26 February 1951.

LP   M-G-M (USA) E 3006 (1952) 'Nights at the Ballet'
LP   Parlophone PMC 1008 (1954) 'Nights at the Ballet'
LP   Parlophone (NZ) PMCM 1008 'Nights at the Ballet'

TCHAIKOVSKY: *Sleeping Beauty* – **Act III 'Aurora's Wedding'**
[Polonaise; Pas de quatre; Pas de caractère; The bluebird pas de deux; Aurora pas de deux; Red Riding Hood; Aurora variation; The three Ivans; Finale-Apotheosis]
Orchestra of the Royal Opera House, Covent Garden.
London; 4 July 1950.

LP   M-G-M E 524 [10"] (1950)
LP   M-G-M (USA) E 3052 (1953) + Ballet music (Gounod: *Faust*)

Review: This section from the *Sleeping Beauty* ballet is a natural hunk for the pop diskery's entry to the longhair lists. It's ballet music of the most popular variety, well-played and brilliantly recorded. *The Billboard* 9 December 1950: 32.

TCHAIKOVSKY: *Swan Lake* – **Ballet Suite**
[Act II: Scene (moderato); Danses des petits cygnes; Scene (moderato assai)]
Orchestra of the Royal Opera House, Covent Garden.
London; 16 September 1952.

LP   M-G-M (USA) E 3006 (1952) 'Nights at the Ballet'
LP   Parlophone PMC 1008 (1954) 'Nights at the Ballet'
LP   Parlophone (NZ) PMCM 1008 'Nights at the Ballet'

TOSTI: Goodbye
Webster Booth *(tenor)*; with orchestra.
Kingsway Hall, London; 26 October 1939.
Sung in English.
78   HMV C 3139 [mx OEA 8164-1,2] + Liebestraum (Liszt, arr. Besly)

TOSTI: Ideale (I love you dear)
Webster Booth *(tenor)*; with orchestra.
Kingsway Hall, London; 26 October 1939.
Sung in English.
78   HMV B 9009 [mx OEA 8165-1,2] [10"] + Ay, Ay, Ay (Pérez Freire)
DL   EMERALD ECHOES 'Love's Old Sweet Song' (2016)

TRAD.: Ĕï ukhnem (Song of the Volga Boatmen)
Oscar Natzka *(bass)*; Orchestra and Chorus.
Kingsway Hall, London; 15 December 1939.
Sung in English.
Note: Arranged by Fedor Keneman. Orchestrated by Roy Douglas.
78   Parlophone E 11433/A 4535 [mx CXE 10227-1] + Ol' Man River
        (Kern: *Showboat*)
CD   Atoll 'Treasures in Sound' ACD 400 [2] (2000) 'Oscar Natzka: The
        Definitive Collection v.1'

VERDI: *Aida* – Ballet Music (Act II, Scene 2)
Orchestra of the Royal Opera House, Covent Garden.
London; 5 November 1952.
LP   M-G-M (USA) E 3003 (1953) 'Popular Ballet Music from Great Operas'
LP   Parlophone PMC 1029 (1955)
DL   Past Classics 7964396 (2008)

VERDI: *Aida* – Ciel! Mio Padre!…Rivedrai le foreste (Heav'n, my father)
Joan Hammond *(soprano)*; Redvers Llewellyn *(baritone)*; Philharmonia Orchestra.
EMI Studio No. 1, Abbey Road, London; 18 March 1947.
Sung in English.
78   HMV C 3735 [mx 2EA 11715-1,2] and [mx 2EA 11716-1]
LP   HMV HQM 1186 (1969) 'Golden Voice Series No. 16: Joan Hammond'
LP   EMI 'Connoisseur Series' CO 485
LP   World Record Club (NZ) WI 485 (1969) 'Joan Hammond'

VERDI: *Aida* – Ritorna vincitor
Sara Menkes *(soprano)*; Philharmonia Orchestra.
London; 8 January 1951.

Sung in Italian.
78   HMV C 4078 [mx 2EA 15291]

VERDI: *Aida* – Ritorna vincitor
Aase Nordmo-Løvberg *(soprano)*; Philharmonia Orchestra.
Kingsway Hall, London; 24 April 1958.
Sung in Italian.
LP   Columbia 33CX 1651
LP   Angel (USA) 35715 (1960) 'Opera Arias'
LP   Columbia SAX 2353 (1961)
EP   Columbia ESL 6280 (1960) + Pace, pace mio Dio (Verdi: *La forza del destino*)
EP   Columbia SEL 1670 (1960) + Pace, pace mio Dio (Verdi: *La forza del destino*)

VERDI: *Un ballo in maschera* – Alzati! Là tuo figlio…Eri tu
Tito Gobbi *(baritone)*; London Symphony Orchestra.
EMI Studio No. 1, Abbey Road, London; 30 September 1950.
Sung in Italian.
78   HMV DB 21606 [mx 2EA 16795-3] and [mx 2EA 16796-3]
LP   HMV (Italy) QBLP 5056
LP   HMV RLS 738 [3] (1979) 'The Art of Tito Gobbi'
CD   EMI CDM 7 63109-2 (1989) 'Tito Gobbi – Opera Aria Recital'
CD   Regis RRC 1183 (2004) 'Tito Gobbi – Baritone Masterclass'
CD   Nimbus 'Prima Voce' NI 7946 (2007)
CD   EMI 'Icon Series' 50999 4 55378 2 0 [5] (2010)
CD   Regis RRC 3011 [3] 'Verdi: Don Carlos' (cond. Santini)

VERDI: *Un ballo in maschera* – Eri tu (It is thou)
Redvers Llewellyn *(baritone)*; Orchestra of the Royal Opera House, Covent Garden.
London; 19 February 1948.
Sung in English.
78   HMV C 3883 [mx 2EA 13586] + E sogno? (Verdi: *Falstaff*)

VERDI: *Un ballo in maschera* – Morro, ma prima in grazia
Joan Hammond *(soprano)*; Philharmonia Orchestra.
EMI Studio No. 1, Abbey Road, London; 6 January 1949.
Sung in Italian.
78   HMV C 3879 [mx 2EA 13532-1,2] + Pace, pace mio Dio (Verdi: *La forza del destino*)

VERDI: *Don Carlo* – **Nei giardin del bello Saracin**
Blanche Thebom *(mezzo)*; London Symphony Orchestra.
EMI Studio No. 1, Abbey Road, London; 12 July 1950.
Sung in Italian.

78	HMV DB 21494 [mx 2EA 14895] + O don fatale (Verdi: *Don Carlo*)
LP	RCA Victor LM-1128
CD	Preiser 'Lebendige Vergangenheit' 89559 (2002) 'Blanche Thebom'

VERDI: *Don Carlo* – **O don fatale**
Blanche Thebom *(mezzo)*; London Symphony Orchestra.
EMI Studio No. 1, Abbey Road, London; 18 July 1950.
Sung in Italian.

LP	HMV DB 21494 [mx 2EA 14938-1A]+ Nei giardin del bello Saracin (Verdi: *Don Carlo*)
CD	Preiser 'Lebendige Vergangenheit' 89559 (2002) 'Blanche Thebom'

VERDI: *Don Carlo* – **Tu che le vanità**
Aase Nordmo-Løvberg *(soprano)*; Philharmonia Orchestra.
Kingsway Hall, London; 24 April 1958.
Sung in Italian.

LP	Columbia 33CX 1651 (1959) 'Operatic Arias by Wagner and Verdi'
LP	Angel (USA) 35715 (1960) 'Opera Arias'
LP	Columbia SAX 2353 (1961)

VERDI: *Don Carlo* – **Tu che le vanità**
Ellabelle Davis *(soprano)*; New Symphony Orchestra.
Kingsway Hall, London; 10 February 1950.
Sung in Italian.

LP	Decca LX 3008 [10"] (1950) 'Operatic and Lieder Recital'
LP	London (USA) LL/LPS 181 [10"] (1950)

VERDI: *Ernani* – **Gran Dio!…O de' verd'anni miei**
Paolo Silveri *(baritone)*; Philharmonia Orchestra.
EMI Studio No. 1, Abbey Road, London; 26 October 1951.
Sung in Italian.

78	Columbia LX 1509 [mx CAX 11449] + Ah, per sempre io ti perdei (Bellini: *I Puritani*)
CD	Preiser 'Lebendige Vergangenheit' 89573 (2003) 'Paolo Silveri, II'

VERDI: *Falstaff* – **E sogno? (Am I dreaming?)**
Redvers Llewellyn *(baritone)*; Orchestra of the Royal Opera House, Covent Garden.

London; 19 February 1948.

Sung in English.

78	HMV C 3883 [mx 2EA 13587] + Eri tu (Verdi: *Un ballo in maschera*)
LP	HMV RLS 707 [3] (1972) 'Stars of the Old Vic and Sadler's Wells'
DL	P&R (2011) 'Stars of the Old Vic and Sadler's Wells'
CD	Dutton Laboratories CDLX 7018 (1995) 'Stars of English Opera, Volume One'

VERDI: *La forza del destino* – Pace, pace mio Dio

Joan Hammond *(soprano)*; Philharmonia Orchestra.

EMI Studio No. 1, Abbey Road, London; 6 January 1949.

Sung in Italian.

| 78 | HMV C 3879 [mx 2EA 13531-1,2] +Morro, ma prima in grazia (Verdi: *Un ballo in maschera*) |

VERDI: *La forza del destino* – Pace, pace mio Dio

Sara Menkes *(soprano)*; Orchestra.

London; 21 January 1951.

Sung in Italian.

| 78 | HMV (unpublished) [mx 2EA 15289] |

VERDI: *La forza del destino* – Pace, pace mio Dio

Aase Nordmo-Lövberg *(soprano)*; Philharmonia Orchestra.

Kingsway Hall, London; 24 April 1958.

Sung in Italian.

LP	Columbia 33CX 1651
LP	Angel (USA) 35715 (1960) 'Opera Arias'
LP	Columbia SAX 2353 (1961)
EP	Columbia ESL 6280 (1960) + Ritorna vincitor (Verdi: *Aida*)
EP	Columbia SEL 1670 (1960) + Ritorna vincitor (Verdi: *Aida*)

VERDI: *Macbeth* – Pietà, rispetto, amore

Tito Gobbi *(baritone)*; London Symphony Orchestra.

EMI Studio No. 1, Abbey Road, London; 30 September 1952.

Sung in Italian.

78	HMV (unpublished) [2EA 16794-1]
LP	HMV RLS 738 [3] (1979) 'The Art of Tito Gobbi'
CD	Testament SBT 1019 (1993) 'Tito Gobbi – Opera and Song'
CD	EMI 'Icon Series' 50999 4 55378 2 0 [5] (2010)

VERDI: *Otello* – Credo in un Dio crudel (Iago's Creed)

Dennis Noble *(baritone)*; Sadler's Wells Orchestra.

Kingsway Hall, London; 8 December 1939.

Sung in Italian.

78	HMV C 3153 [mx 8180-1,2] + Avant de quitter ses lieux (Gounod: *Faust*)
LP	HMV 'Treasury Series' HLM 7009 (1972) 'Great British Basses and Baritones'
LP	World Record Club (NZ) CO 538 (1972?) 'Great British Basses and Baritones'

VERDI: *Otello* – **Era più calmo?…Mia madre aveva una povera ancella… Piangea cantando…Ave Maria**

Joan Hammond *(soprano)*; Monica Sinclair *(mezzo)*; Philharmonia Orchestra.
EMI Studio No. 1, Abbey Road, London; 10 May 1950.

Sung in Italian.

78	HMV (unpublished) [mx 2EA 14667]

VERDI: *Otello* – **Era più calmo?…Mia madre aveva una povera ancella… Piangea cantando…Ave Maria**

Aase Nordmo-Lövberg *(soprano)*; Monica Sinclair *(contralto)*; Philharmonia Orchestra.
Kingsway Hall, London; 24 April 1958.

Sung in Italian.

LP	Columbia 33CX 1651 (1959) 'Operatic Arias by Wagner and Verdi'
LP	Angel (USA) 35715 (1960) 'Opera Arias'
LP	Columbia SAX 2353 (1961)

VERDI: *Rigoletto* – **Caro nome (Dearest name)**

Gwen Catley *(soprano)*; Hallé Orchestra.
Belle Vue Gardens, Manchester; 16 March 1943.

Sung in English.

78	HMV C 3369 [mx 2ER 687-1,2] + O, Mimì tu più non torni (Puccini: *La bohème*)
LP	HMV HLM 7066 (1977) 'Operatic and Song Recital'

VERDI: *Rigoletto* – **Caro nome**

Elda Ribetti *(soprano)*; Philharmonia Orchestra
London; 12 December 1946

Sung in Italian

78	HMV C 3587 [mx 2EA 11504-2] + O luce di quest'anima (Donizetti: *Linda di Chamounix*)

VERDI: *Rigoletto* – **Bella figlia dell'amore (Fairest daughter of thy graces)**

Noël Eadie *(soprano)*; Edith Coates *(mezzo)*; Webster Booth *(tenor)*; Arnold

Matters *(baritone)*; London Philharmonic Orchestra
EMI Studio No. 1, Abbey Road, London; 3 March 1939
Sung in English

78	HMV C 3086 [mx 2EA 7540-1,2] + Alerte! Alerte! (Gounod: *Faust*)
78	Victor 36235 + Alerte! Alerte! (Gounod: *Faust*)
EP	HMV 7EG 8263
	+ E lucevan le stelle (Puccini: *Tosca*); O soave fanciulla (*La bohème*) Booth; Cross;
	cond. Collingwood; Miserere (*Il trovatore*) Booth; Cross; cond. Collingwood.
CD	Dutton Laboratories CDLX 7020 (1996) 'Stars of English Opera, Volume Two'

VERDI: *La traviata* – Di Provenza il mar (From fair Provence)
Dennis Noble *(baritone)*; Hallé Orchestra.
Houldsworth Hall, Manchester; 29 August 1942.
Sung in English.

78	HMV C 3304 [mx 2ER 626-1,2] + Say goodbye to pastime (Mozart: *Le nozze di Figaro*)
CD	Dutton Laboratories CDLX 7017 'A Tribute to Dennis Noble'
CD	Greenhorn 0027 'Dennis Noble Nirvana'
CD	Cheyne CHE 4459 'Dennis Noble'

VERDI: *La traviata* – Libiamo, libiamo
Patrice Munsel *(soprano)*; Charles Craig *(tenor)*; Royal Opera House, Covent Garden Orchestra (not named).
London; August 1952.
Sung in Italian.
Note: Soundtrack to the film *Melba*.

LP	RCA Victor LM 7012 [10"] '*Melba*: Original Soundtrack of the Motion Picture'
LP	HMV BLP 1023 [10"]
LP	HMV (Italy) QBLP 5015 [10"]
45	RCA Victor EDM 7012 [4]
CD	Flare SPEC 1025 (2006) 'On Wings of Song'
DL	Frank Bristow 'Music from the Past' EXCD 004 'A Patrice Munsel Recital'

VERDI: *La traviata* – È strano…Ah! fors' è lui… Sempre libera ('Tis wondrous …Ah! Was it he?…Let me live)
Gwen Catley *(soprano)*; Hallé Orchestra.
Houldsworth Hall, Manchester; 18 March 1943.
Sung in English.

78	HMV C 3358 [mx 2ER 695-1,2] Part 1; [mx 2ER 696-1,2,3] Part 2
LP	HMV HLM 7066 (1977) 'Operatic and Song Recital'
CD	Dutton CDLX 7022 (1997) 'Gwen Catley: Favourite Coloratura Arias and Songs'

VERDI: *La traviata* – È strano…Ah! fors' è lui…Sempre libera (I love you… Ah! Was it he?… I'll enjoy the round of pleasure)
Elisabeth Schwarzkopf *(soprano)*; Philharmonia Orchestra.
EMI Studio No. 1, Abbey Road, London; 12 April 1948.
Sung in English.

78	Columbia LX 1079 [mx CAX 10219-1,2] and [mx CAX 10220-1,2]
CD	Testament SBT 2172 [2] (1999) 'Elisabeth Schwarzkopf : the Unpublished Recordings, 1946-1952'
CD	Opus Kura OPK 2111 (2015) 'Elisabeth Schwarzkopf Early Years'

VERDI: *Il trovatore* – Ai nostri monti
Winifred Heidt *(mezzo)*; Eugene Conley *(tenor)*; New Symphony Orchestra of London.
Decca West Hampstead Studios, London; 11 September 1950.
Sung in Italian.

LP	Decca (unpublished)

VERDI: *I Vespri Siciliani* – L'autunno
Orchestra of the Royal Opera House, Covent Garden.
London; 16 September 1952.

LP	M-G-M (USA) E 3006 (1952) 'Nights at the Ballet'
LP	Parlophone PMC 1008 (1954) 'Nights at the Ballet'
LP	Parlophone (NZ) PMCM 1008 'Nights at the Ballet'

WAGNER: *Lohengrin* – Einsam in trüben Tagen (Elsa's Dream)
Joan Hammond *(soprano)*; Philharmonia Orchestra.
EMI Studio No. 1, Abbey Road, London; 29 January 1947.
Sung in English.

78	HMV C 3562 [mx 2EA 11613-1,2] + Dich, teure Halle (Wagner: *Tannhäuser*)
78	HMV (Australia) EB 431 + Dich, teure Halle (Wagner: *Tannhäuser*)

WAGNER: *Die Meistersinger von Nürnberg* – Morgenlich leuchtend (Glowing with beauty) (Prize Song)
Webster Booth *(tenor)*; Hallé Orchestra.
Houldsworth Hall, Manchester; 29 August 1942.
Sung in English.

78   HMV C 3309 [mx 627-1,2] + Salut! demeure chaste et pure (Gounod: *Faust*)

CD   Dutton Vocalion CDLX 7032 (1998) 'Webster Booth: Handel Arias / Operatic Arias'

WAGNER: *Tannhäuser* – Dich, teure Halle (Elisabeth's Greeting)
Joan Hammond *(soprano)*; Philharmonia Orchestra.
EMI Studio No. 1, Abbey Road, London; 29 January 1947.
Sung in English.
78   HMV C 3562 [mx 2EA 11615-1,2] + Einsam in trüben Tagen (Wagner: *Lohengrin*)
78   HMV (Australia) EB 431 + Einsam in trüben Tagen (Wagner: *Lohengrin*)

WAGNER: *Tannhäuser* – Blick' ich umher (When I cast my eye around this noble circle)
Redvers Llewellyn *(baritone)*; Philharmonia Orchestra.
EMI Studio No. 1, Abbey Road, London; 24 April 1948.
Sung in English.
78   HMV C 3952 [mx 2EA 12968] + Wie Todesahnung (Wagner: *Tannhäuser*)

WAGNER: *Tannhäuser* – Wie Todesahnung...O du mein holden Abendstern (Like death's dark shadow...O star of eve)
Redvers Llewellyn *(baritone)*; Philharmonia Orchestra.
EMI Studio No. 1, Abbey Road, London; 24 April 1948.
Sung in English.
78   HMV C 3952 [mx 2EA 12969] + Blick' ich umher (Wagner: *Tannhäuser*)

WALDTEUFEL: *Les Patineurs, op. 183* – 'Skater's Waltz' (words by Alan Colville)
Gwen Catley *(soprano)*; London Symphony Orchestra.
EMI Studio No. 1, Abbey Road, London; 13 October 1950.
Sung in English.
78   HMV C 4043 [mx 2EA 15120] + La pastorella (Rossini)
CD   Vocal Record Collectors' Society VRCS 2000 '2000 annual issue'

WEBER: *Oberon* – Overture
National Symphony Orchestra.
Kingsway Hall, London; 22 March 1945.
78   Decca K 1322 [mx AR 9232] and [mx AR 9233]
CD   Yukihiro Okitsu (limited edition, 2002) 'A Resurrection of Dennis Brain'
DL   Beulah 1BX 117 (mp3 download)

WOOD: Love's Garden of Roses
Ann Ziegler *(soprano)*; Webster Booth *(tenor)*; Orchestra.
EMI Studio No. 1, Abbey Road, London; 10 June 1941.
Sung in English
78   HMV B 9177 [mx 9367-1,2] + Will you remember? (Romberg: *Maytime*)
CD   Symposium SYMPCD 1386 (2009)

*

ARCHIVE RECORDINGS FROM THE BBC AND RADIO NEW ZEALAND

ANON: God Save the King
National Orchestra of the NZBS
Wellington: Town Hall; 16 July 1947
Ngā Taonga Sound & Vision. Ref.: 257467

ANON: God Save the Queen
National Orchestra of the NZBS
Wellington, N.Z.; 1953?
78   Tanza (no issue number or matrix) [10"] + God Defend New Zealand
Ngā Taonga Sound & Vision. Ref.: 28652

ANON: God Save the Queen
National Orchestra of the NZBS
No date.
Ngā Taonga Sound & Vision. Ref.: 38193 (D4261b sa-d-04261-s02-pm)

ARNE: Rule Britannia
National Orchestra of the NZBS
No date.
Ngā Taonga Sound & Vision. Ref.: 38193 (D4260a sa-d-04260-s01-pm)

BEETHOVEN: Piano concerto no. 2, B flat
Hephzibah Menuhin *(piano)*; National Orchestra of the NZBS
22 October 1953
Duration: 22:09 and 9:46
Ngā Taonga Sound & Vision. Ref.: 258167 and 258160 (Disc S580 and S581)

BEETHOVEN: Symphony no. 2
National Orchestra of the NZBS
4 July 1947

Duration: 16:28
Ngā Taonga Sound & Vision. Ref.: 257464

BEETHOVEN: Symphony no. 3
National Orchestra of the NZBS
Auckland: Town Hall; 4 July 1947
Duration: 32:19
Ngā Taonga Sound & Vision. Ref.: 257465 (Disc 751 A/B)

BENJAMIN: Symphony no. 1
National Orchestra of the NZBS
[1 November 1949]
Note: Braithwaite gave the NZ premiere of this work on 8 September 1953, so this recording is either live from that date, or a studio recording made around that time.
Duration: 15:55 and 12:47
Ngā Taonga Sound & Vision. Ref.: 258155 and 258156

BORODIN: *Prince Igor* – Polovtsian Dances
National Orchestra of the NZBS
Auckland: Town Hall; 4 July 1947
Ngā Taonga Sound & Vision. Ref.: 257462 (Disc S754B)

BRAITHWAITE: Variations on an personal theme
Wellington; National Orchestra of the NZBS
Studio recording; May 1953? (the piece received its 1st NZ performance in Dunedin on 25 May 1953)
Note: The theme is missing, and Variation 1 is unfortunately overlaid with a recording of a studio nativity play.
Duration: 15:48 and 24:39
Ngā Taonga Sound & Vision. Ref.: 207206 and 207205

BRIDGE: There is a Willow Grows Aslant a Brook
National Orchestra of the NZBS
No date.
Duration: 08:17
Ngā Taonga Sound & Vision. Ref.: 38193 (D4259b sa-d-04259-s02-pm)

DELIUS: On Hearing the First Cuckoo in Spring
National Orchestra of the NZBS
Wellington: Town Hall; 16 July 1947
Ngā Taonga Sound & Vision. Ref.: 257468

DOHNANYI: Variations on a nursery theme
Maurice Till *(piano)*; National Orchestra of the NZBS
Wellington: Town Hall; 6 February 1954
Duration: 10:35, 13:49
Ngā Taonga Sound & Vision. Ref.: 258381, 258382,
Ngā Taonga Sound & Vision. Ref.: 278183, 278184, 278185
Ngā Taonga Sound & Vision. Ref.: 25022 (Russell Taberner Collection)

DOHNANYI: Wedding Waltz (from The Veil of Pierrette) (5'24")
BBC Singers Broadcast 30 July 1946
British Library. Leech Collection

FRANCHI: Rhapsody for viola and orchestra
National Orchestra of the NZBS
Recorded: 3 June 1954?
Ngā Taonga Sound & Vision. Ref.: 258162 and 258166 (Disc S899)

HANDEL: Water Music Suite
National Orchestra of the NZBS
1953
Ngā Taonga Sound & Vision. Ref.: 38193 (D4260a sa-d-04260-s01-pm) and
(D4261a sa-d-04261-s01-pm)

HARTY: Violin concerto (incomplete movements)
Albert Voorsanger *(violin)*; BBC Orchestra
Studio broadcast; 23 November 1937
BBC National Programme Daventry
British Library. Leech Collection. Ref.: 1LL0008676; 1LL0008677; 1LL0008678

IRELAND: Concerto in E flat
Ernest Jenner *(piano)*; National Orchestra of the NZBS
Christchurch: Civic Theatre; 10 July 1954
Ngā Taonga Sound & Vision. Ref.: MST7-0233

LILBURN: Symphony no. 2
National Orchestra of the NZBS
Recording: 18 December 1953?
Ngā Taonga Sound & Vision. Ref.: 258135 (Disc S904), 258162, 258166, 258163
(date given as 27 April 1950)

MACKENZIE: Benedictus
National Orchestra of the NZBS

No date.
Duration:
Ngā Taonga Sound & Vision. Ref.: 38193 (D4261b sa-d-04261-s02-pm)

MACKENZIE: Britannia (overture)
National Orchestra of the NZBS
1953
Ngā Taonga Sound & Vision. Ref.: 38193 (D4259a sa-d-04259-s01-pm)

MENDELSSOHN: Fingal's Cave
National Orchestra of the NZBS
Wellington: Town Hall; 16 July 1947
Note: Braithwaite addresses the audience at the conclusion
Ngā Taonga Sound & Vision. Ref.: 257467 and 257469

MENDELSSOHN: *A Midsummer Night's Dream* – Nocturne and Scherzo
National Orchestra of the NZBS
Auckland: Town Hall; 4 July 1947
Ngā Taonga Sound & Vision. Ref.: 257462 (Disc S754A)

MOZART: Serenade no. 13, G, K.525, 'Eine kleine Nachtmusik'
National Orchestra of the NZBS
Auckland: Town Hall; 4 July 1947
Duration: 16:11
Ngā Taonga Sound & Vision. Ref.: 257463 (Disc S753B)

MOZART: Symphony no. 35 'Haffner'
National Orchestra of the NZBS
Wellington: Town Hall; 16 July 1947
Ngā Taonga Sound & Vision. Ref.: 257467 and 257468

MUSSORGSKY: *Boris Godunov* – Monologue and Death of Boris
Yi– Kwei Sze *(bass)*; National Orchestra of the NZBS
15 November 1949
Duration: 16:17
Ngā Taonga Sound & Vision. Ref.: 258157 (Disc S584)

PUCCINI: La Fanciulla del West (The Girl of the Golden West)
London: Sadler's Wells Theatre; 10 January 1963
BBC broadcast.
Elizabeth Fretwell *(Minnie)*; Donald Smith *(Johnson)*; Raimund Herincx *(Rance)*;
Stanley Bevan *(Nick)*; John Hauxvell *(Jake Wallace)*; Eric Shilling *(Ashby)*; Derek

Hammond Stroud *(Castro)*; Neil Easton *(Sonora)*; John Delaney *(Trin)*; Howard Dyson *(Bello)*; Paul Crook *(Harry)*; Neville Griffiths *(Joe)*; Charles Draper *(Happy)*; Kenneth Fawcett *(Sid)*; David Bowman *(Larkens)*; Leigh Maurice *(Billy Jackrabbit)*; Dilys Davis *(Wokle)*; Edward Byles *(Pony Express Rider)*.
British Library. Leech Collection

CD   House of Opera CD 8930
CD   Oriel Music OMT 877 (2012)
CD   Opera Depot OD 11184-2
CD   CRQ Editions CRQ 073/074 (2017)

RACHMANINOV: Piano concerto no. 2, C minor
Jocelyn Walker *(piano)*; National Orchestra of the NZBS
New Plymouth; 16 April 1954
Ngā Taonga Sound & Vision. Ref.: 25003

RIMSKY-KORSAKOV: Scheherazade
National Orchestra of the NZBS; Vincent Aspey (leader)
Duration:
Wellington: Town Hall; Date: 16 July 1947
Note: Braithwaite addresses the audience at the conclusion
Ngā Taonga Sound & Vision. Ref.: 257469, 257466, 257470

SMYTH: The Wreckers – Excerpt (9'50")
Sadler's Wells Theatre; 22 April 1939
BBC London Regional broadcast
Morgan Jones *(Tallan)*; Rose Morris *(Jack)*; Harry Brindle *(Harvey)*; Roderick Lloyd *(Pascoe)*; John Hargreaves *(Lawrence)*; Nora Grühn *(Avis)*; Edith Coates *(Thirza)*; John Wright *(Mark)*; John Nicholson *(A Preacher)*
Orchestra of Sadler's WellsRecording Notes: Many gaps in the music. Excerpts noted from a vocal score on the tape label: Act 1, p. 16–30; Act 1, p. 46; Act 1, p. 65; Act 2, p. 87; Act 2, p. 159; Act 2, p. 172-177; the end p. 187
Duration: 35 min. 36 sec.
British Library. Leech Collection. Ref. 1LL0008783; 1LL0008784; 1LL0008785; 1LL0008786

STANFORD: *The Travelling Companion* – Ballet Music
BBC Orchestra.
BBC Regional Broadcast; 7 April 1936
Duration: 06:25
British Library. Leech Collection. Ref. ILL0008512

STANFORD: *The Travelling Companion* – Excerpts Act II, Scene 1

BBC Studio Broadcast; 17 July 1936
Duration: 10:29
Joan Cross *(The Princess)*; Arnold Matters *(The King)*; Sadler's Wells Orchestra.
Joseph Shadwick *(leader)*
British Library. Leech Collection. Ref. 1LL0008541

STRAVINSKY: *L'oiseau de feu* – **Lullaby and Episode**
National Orchestra of the NZBS
Wellington: Town Hall; 5 February 1954
RNZ ARCHIVE Ref.: 278181
Ngā Taonga Sound & Vision. Russell Taberner Collection. Ref.: 25022

VERDI: I Lombardi
Swansea: Grand Theatre; 15 April 1949
Joyce Barker *(Giselda)*; Paul Asciak *(Arvino)*; Bryan Drake *(Pagano)*; Tano
Ferendinos *(Oronte)*; Patti Lewis *(Sofia)*; Leonard John *(Pirro)*; Tegwyn Short
(Priore); Elwyn Adams *(Acciano)*
Welsh National Opera Chorus; Bournemouth Symphony Orchestra.
CD   Oriel Music OMT 880 (2012)

WAGNER: *Rienzi* – **Overture**
National Orchestra of the NZBS; Vincent Aspey *(leader)*
Wellington: Town Hall; 16 July 1947
Ngā Taonga Sound & Vision. Ref.: 257470

WALTON: Crown Imperial
National Orchestra of the NZBS
Np date.
Duration: 08:17
Ngā Taonga Sound & Vision. Ref.: 38193 (D4260b sa-d-04260-s02-pm)

WEBER: *Oberon* – **Overture**
National Orchestra of the NZBS
Auckland: Town Hall; 4 July 1947
Duration: 16:11
Ngā Taonga Sound & Vision. Ref.: 257463 (Disc S753A)

WOODS: God defend New Zealand
National Orchestra of the NZBS
Wellington, N.Z.; 1953?
Note: Arranged by Ashley Heenan.
78   Tanza (no issue number or matrix) [10"] + God Save the Queen

Ngā Taonga Sound & Vision. Ref.: 28652

WOODS: God defend New Zealand
National Orchestra of the NZBS
No date.
Duration:
Ngā Taonga Sound & Vision. Ref.: 38193 (D4261b sa-d-04261-s02-pm)

*

INTERVIEWS

Interview
Recorded and broadcast; 23 May 1953
D SERIES – This recording features an interview with the New Zealand composer
and guest conductor of the National Orchestra, Warwick Braithwaite. He talks
about the programme of the upcoming tour of New Zealand by the National
Orchestra.
Duration: 06:33
Radio New Zealand Archive. Ref.: 33988

Interview
1953
Warwick Braithwaite speaks at the conclusion of the 1953 Concert Season.
He left New Zealand in 1916 and the last time he was in this country was in 1947.
He recounts being asked to join the Royal Opera House at Covent Garden as
a staff member. He also talks about the growing appreciation by the public for
opera. He put this down to the Allied forces serving in Italy, France and Europe
gaining an appreciation of opera and beginning to demand opera in concerts.
Braithwaite mentions how luck came his way when he was in his last year at the
Royal Academy and received a cable from home "…no more money". He wrote to
Arthur Fagge, conductor of the London Choral Society, who in turn showed the
letter to Joseph O'Mara. That very day the Chorus Master of the Choral Society
had been sacked and Braithwaite got the job.
Duration: 13:39
Radio New Zealand Archive. Ref..: 23581

Interview
Canterbury Roundabout
Christchurch; 31 March 1953
Magazine-style programme which includes half a dozen questions answered by
guest of honour, Warwick Braithwaite.

Radio New Zealand Archive. Ref..: 39588

Interview
Canterbury Roundabout no. 169
Christchurch; 23 December 1954
Warwick Braithwaite speaks and farewells Christchurch at his concert with the
National Orchestra. He urges the public to support the orchestra.
Radio New Zealand Archive. Ref..: 183154

Interview (with Christopher Venning)
"Looking Backwards"
Duration: 10:29
No date.
He talks about how he became a conductor. His parents took him to opera as
a child and at the age of four he told his parents he wanted to be 'the man who
waved the stick'. He talks about studying at the Royal Academy of Music in
London, his early career, works he enjoys conducting (and those he does not),
conductors he admires and his plans to tour the United States when he leaves New
Zealand.
Radio New Zealand Archive. Ref..: 183082

APPENDIX 5

WARWICK BRAITHWAITE COMPOSITIONS

Excerpt from Symphonic Poem (Fantasia)
ATL Ref: fMS-Pappers-5136-46

The vast majority of Warwick Braithwaite's manuscript scores are held in the Alexander Turnbull Library's Archive of New Zealand Music, housed in the National Library of New Zealand. This chronological listing of identified compositions indicates if a score or set of parts is incomplete due either to missing pages, or having been left in that state by the composer. Orchestrations and durations are shown where known. All items are holographs unless otherwise indicated.

As part of his 5WA duties, Braithwaite undoubtedly made many arrangements for his studio orchestra. Few of these have survived in archives, but they may be buried in piles of salon orchestra scores and parts, discarded as unfashionable today and gathering dust in cupboards.

Composition dates followed by a question mark are those suggested by the Alexander Turnbull Library. Where these have been reassessed, a note makes that clear. Other dates are taken from information added to the manuscript by the composer, or from the earliest known date of a performance.

There is no internationally preferred method of listing instrumentation, but this catalogue has adopted the practice of many hire catalogues and should be self-explanatory.

Items held by the Alexander Turnbull Library's Archive of New Zealand Music are indicated by a reference number (e.g., ATL Ref: fMS-Papers-5136-60). Manuscript holdings can be searched using Tiaki, the Turnbull Library's catalogue of unpublished materials (https://tiaki.natlib.govt.nz). Published and unpublished material can also be accessed through the National Library of New Zealand website (https://natlib.govt.nz).

1910–c.1920	**Miscellaneous pieces composed or arranged by Warwick Braithwaite.**

Includes *Entranza*, in E flat major for violin and piano (37 bars).

Note: Manuscript music books containing early compositions and sketches of works by Warwick Braithwaite and pieces arranged by him. These include mostly pieces for piano, songs, studies and exercises.

ATL Ref.: fMS-Papers-5136-32 (6 vols).

1916	**Excerpt from 'The Passing of Arthur': for tenor, baritone, bass, SATB and piano.** Adapted from Alfred, Lord Tennyson's *Idylls of the King*.

Characters: King Arthur *(baritone)*, Gawain's Ghost's Voice *(tenor)*, Sir Bedivere *(bass)*, Chorus (SATB).

Note: A note added later on the cover of the score (in Braithwaite's hand) states that this was the composition he submitted for the Goring Thomas composition scholarship at the Royal Academy of Music. Following a long interview with the Director, Sir Alexander Mackenzie, Braithwaite was awarded the scholarship, enabling him to study for three years – until September 1919, when he joined Joseph O'Mara's touring opera company as chorus master and répétiteur.

Performance: The 'Prelude' to *The Passing of Arthur* was performed by the composer at Harry Farjeon's Invitation Concert of his Pupils' Compositions. This event, held at London's Steinway Hall, was announced in *The Daily Telegraph* (2 Feb 1918), 1, and included William Manson's Piano Trio. The score of this prize-winning work by Braithwaite's nephew has not been located.

ATL Ref.: fMS-Papers-5136-24 (score; 18 pages).

1918   **Sonata in B minor, for piano.**
Note: The manuscript score (dated 3 January 1919) indicates that the sonata was composed between 15 November and 22 December 1918.

ATL Ref.: fMS-Papers-5136-41 (score; 14 pages, 229 bars).

1920?   **Untitled compositions for piano.**
Note: These folders consist of (as yet) unidentified fragments and incomplete works for various mediums by Warwick Braithwaite.

Items include:
Upon the castle darkness falls slowly (song for tenor and piano) (49 bars).
Text taken from the prose poem *Cornet: A Tale of Love and Death* by Rainer Maria Rilke, written in 1899, revised 1906 and first published in 1912. The translation is probably by Braithwaite.

> Upon the castle darkness falls slowly.
> The turret chamber is dark. But their faces shine, each face a mirror of the other's smile. As if afraid of the dark, they press together; but they are not afraid. There is no yesterday, no tomorrow.
> He does not ask: "Your husband?"
> She does not ask: "Your name?"
> For they have found for one another a new being.

[Untitled piece] in A flat for piano (51 bars).
Berceuse in A flat for piano (78 bars).
Andante in E minor for piano 'To my Dear Father' (134 bars).

ATL Ref: fMS-Papers-5136-60.

Allegro Appassionato in E flat major, for piano (32 bars).
Allegretto e semplice in A minor, for piano (32 bars).
Gaily, in C Major, for piano (32 bars).
[Untitled piece] in G minor for piano (28 bars).

ATL Ref: fMS-Papers-5136-33.

1918–1920? **Hinemoa – a Māori legend.**
Orchestration: 2fl, 2ob, 2cl (B♭), 2bn; 4hn (F), 2tpt (B♭), 3trb+1bass trb or tuba; timp; strings.

Note: The manuscript paper of the score matches that used for the two symphonic poems written between 1918 and 1922. It is probably Braithwaite's earliest attempt to make use of the well-known Māori story of Hinemoa and Tutanekai. In 1931, he returned to Māori-themed works with *Auē – Māori tone picture* and *Legend for orchestra 'Hinemoa'*. The latter became the second movement, 'Hinemoa', of his *Symphony in E major* (14 July 1931). The manuscript of *Hinemoa – a Māori legend* ends at bar 35, but has a sketched-in 36th bar. There are no parts in the collection. The work has been computer-set by Michael Vinten with an added 37th bar to make a conclusion, but given the size of the orchestration, it is reasonable to suggest that the work was much longer.

ATL Ref.: fMS-Papers-5136-09 (incomplete score only).

1920–1921 **Symphonic poem (Fantasia); for full orchestra.**
Orchestration: 2fl+ picc, 2ob, 2cl (A), 2bn; 4hn (F), 2tpt (B♭), 3trb; timp, perc (triangle, cymbals, tam-tam, bass drum), harp; strings.

Note: Both the title page and first page of the manuscript full score are clearly dated 1918, but a note at the end states that this score was started in April 1920 at Manchester, and finished on 4 January 1921 in Liverpool.

ATL Ref.: fMS-Papers-5136-46 (score only; 57 pages).

1920–1922 **Ireland – a symphonic poem; for full orchestra.**
Orchestration: 2fl+picc, 2ob+cor ang, 2cl (A)+bass cl, 2bn+contra bn; 4hn (F), 3tpt (A), 3trb+bass trb, tuba; timp, perc

(triangle, tam-tam, side drum), harp, celeste; strings.
Duration: 25'

Note: A note at the end of the score states that the work was
composed in 1920, and the final score was started and finished in
Munich on 17 September 1922. Both the cover and title page of
the manuscript score bear the title *A Short Symphonic Poem*. The
cover has been amended to read *A Symphonic Poem 'Ireland'*, and
the title page has the word *Ireland* preceding *A Short Symphonic
Poem*. Similar confusions arise on other occasions when
Braithwaite exercises a lack of care in the naming of works (e.g.,
Legend, Auē, Hinemoa, and several Arthurian-inspired pieces.

Performances: The symphonic poem *Ireland* was performed
by The Royal Albert Hall Orchestra on the morning of 28 June
1923 as part of the Royal College of Music Patron's Fund public
rehearsal. However, Braithwaite lists the first performance of this
work at a similar concert on 31 May 1923. The reviewer of the
May event wrote:

> Five new works were on the list at the Patron's Fund rehearsal at the
> Royal College of Music, but Warwick Braithwaite's *Short Symphonic
> Poem* unfortunately had to be withdrawn for want of time. *The Era* (6
> June 1923).

Braithwaite lists the second performance as 28 June 1923. A
reviewer of this event wrote:

> No new works were heard at the Patron's Fund Rehearsal at the
> Royal College of Music on Thursday; but Mr Warwick Braithwaite's
> symphonic poem, 'Ireland', which decidedly improves with better
> acquaintance. *The Era* (4 July 1923).

This suggests that the work had either been publicly heard
(possibly on 31 May as Braithwaite claims) or at rehearsals prior
to both concerts.

ATL Ref: fMS-Papers-5136-11 (score; 75 pages).
ATL Ref: fMS-Papers-5136-12 (parts for wind and brass).
ATL Ref: fMS-Papers-5136-13 (parts for timp, perc, harp, celeste
and strings).

1924   **Romance in G**
           Romance in D minor.
           Performance: 10 September 1924. Cardiff, 5WA Studio.

           Note: Listed in the *Radio Times* schedules, these two Romances
           were to be played by the 5WA Quintet (possibly for strings) as
           part of a studio broadcast.
           Location of these scores is unknown.

1924   **St George and the Dragon (incidental music for orchestra).**
           Orchestration: 1fl, 1ob,1cl (B♭), bn; 2hn, 1tpt, 1trb; perc (side
           drum, wood blocks, bass drum); strings.

           Performance: 15 October 1924. Cardiff, 5WA Studio.
           The composition date is estimated in ATL's catalogue *Tiaki* as
           '1935?', but this incidental music was probably composed for
           a broadcast of the play *St George and the Dragon*, by S. Lyle
           Cummins which, according to *Radio Times*, was broadcast as
           'Plays for Children Old and Young' on 5WA 15 October 1924
           at 7 p.m. The cast was Richard Barron *(King)*; George Bouverie
           (Pomposo); Sidney Evans *(St George)*; Frank Nicholls *(The
           Dragon)*; Mabel Tait *(Princess Belinda)*. The Studio Orchestra
           provided the music, but no composer is identified. However, as
           part of his duties for the BBC in Cardiff, Braithwaite was required
           to provide music for radio drama.

           ATL Ref.: fMS-Papers-5136-38 (score only; 6 pages).

1925   **A Night of the Trojan War.**
           Incidental music for the play by John Drinkwater.

           Note: As part of his duties for the BBC in Cardiff, Braithwaite
           provided much music for radio drama.

           Performance: 16 January 1925. Cardiff, 5WA Studio. Performed
           by the 5WA Radio Repertory Company and the 5WA Station
           Orchestra.
           The location of these scores is unknown.

1925   **Overture – Barnaby Rudge.**
           Orchestration: 2fl, 2ob, 2cl (B♭), 2bn; 2hn (F), 2tpt (B♭), trb; timp,
           harp; strings.

Note: The composer writes on the score that *Barnaby Rudge* was 'started 1 February 1925; finished 2 February 1925.' This presumably refers to the copying out of the final score, rather than the period of composition.

Performances
7 February 1925. Cardiff, 5WA Studio. Performed by the 5WA Station Orchestra.

25 April 1927. Cardiff, 5WA Studio. Anzac Day Concert, performed by the 5WA Station Orchestra.

26 September 1927. Birmingham, BBC Studios. Performed as part of *A Charles Dickens Concert* by the Birmingham Studio Orchestra, conducted by Joseph Lewis.

7 September 1929. Cardiff, National Museum of Wales. Lunchtime concert, performed by the National Orchestra of Wales.

ATL Ref.: fMS-Papers-5136-03 (score; 32 pages, missing pages 6–7).
ATL Ref.: fMS-Papers-5136-04 (short score for filling in 2nd woodwind and brass, and complete set of orchestral parts).

1925 **Three extracts from 'The Coming of Arthur'; for orchestra.**
I Uther's Lament (composed May 1925).
Orchestration: 2fl, 2ob, 2cl (B♭), 2bn; 4hn (F), 2tpt (B♭), 2trb; timp, perc (tam-tam); harp; strings.

II Merlin (composed 15 June 1925).
Orchestration: 2fl, 2ob, 2cl (B♭), 2bn; 4hn, 2tpt (B♭), 2trb; timp, perc (glock); harp; strings.

III Arthur (composed 20-22 June 1925).
Orchestration: 2fl, 2ob, 2cl (B♭), 2bn; 4hn, 2tpt (B♭), 2trb; timp; harp; strings.

Note: These were composed between May and 22 June 1925 for the first of a proposed series of six programmes on the Arthurian Legends. The only broadcast episode was *The Wooing of Guinevere*, written by Alice M. Buckton, which aired on 28 June

1925 performed by the 5WA Radio Players and the 5WA Station Symphony Orchestra. Braithwaite provided the three pieces listed above plus a fourth piece, 'Guinevere', which was broadcast but not included with these three extracts.

The location of the score of 'Guinevere' is unknown.

Performance: 28 June 1925. Cardiff, 5WA Studio, performed by the 5WA Station Symphony Orchestra.

Uther's Lament

Performance: 14 March 1931. Cardiff City Hall Assembly Room, in a 'British Operatic Programme', performed by the National Orchestra of Wales. The composer was listed as 'Anon'.

A programme note for this concert states:

> This excerpt is taken from an unfinished opera entitled *The Coming of Arthur*, the subject of which is the first part of the Arthurian legend dealing with the love of Uther Pendragon for Igraine, the wife of Tintagil, and the subsequent drawing of the magic sword from its stone sheath by Arthur, the boy who was afterwards to become the renowned king.

> The first act of this opera opens in Uther's pavilion before Castle Terabil, where Tintagil is besieged by the forces of Uther. As the Malory book has it…'Then for pure anger and for the great love of the fair Igraine, King Uther fell sick. Then came to King Uther, Sir Ulfus, a noble knight, and asked the king why he was sick. 'I shall tell thee', said the king. 'I am sick for anger and for love of fair Igraine, that I may not be whole.' The king then proceeds to tell Sir Ulfus the events leading up to the siege; how Tintagil, after declaring a truce, 'suddenly by stealth departed in the night,' leaving the court of Uther Pendragon, breaking the truce by his action, and thus leading to further warfare. Tintagil knew that Uther had fallen deeply in love with Igraine, so he resolved that he would take her away.
>
> Uther tells Sir Ulfus of how he sought Igraine and confessed his love for her. This passage is accompanied by one solo violin.

> 'She heard my burning words, with face averted till the end;
> And cold her hand lay, lifeless in the fierce warm grip of mine.
> In a voice which trembled 'twixt her sorrowing sighs
> She told me of her loveless life in bondage
> To Tintagil's will…
> My heart, which burned before with flaming passion

> Now with pity melted,
> And although I loved this beauteous woman
> I left her and departed, determined
> When the dawn's first shaft of light
> Should sweep the purple sky of darkness
> Both she and her lord should leave in peace.'

The foregoing gives the key to the dramatic situation. The themes to note are the opening truce theme, shortly followed by one of the numerous themes to depict Igraine. Immediately there is a passionate section in which Uther tells of his first meeting with Igraine, followed by the section in which he tells of Tintagil's stealthy departure at night. Uther's vow to avenge the insult follows. Then there is the quieter section already referred to in which Uther tells of his confession of love for Igraine. The excerpt ends shortly after with two final statements of the truce theme played by muted trumpets and horns.'

Review:
For the orchestra there were Holbrooke's *Prelude* to Bronwen…
and an excerpt from an unfinished opera, *The Coming of Arthur*,
announced as by an anonymous composer. Both spoke in the
same modern style, straining all the forces of a modern orchestra
to give expression to their themes….' *Western Mail* (16 March
1931), 9.

ATL Ref.: fMS-Papers-5136-05 (full score of 'Merlin' and 'Arthur'
only).
ATL Ref.: fMS-Papers-5136-23 (parts for 'Uther's Lament' only).

1925? **Dithyramb; song for contralto and piano.**
Text:

> I will live so that my soul will nobler be
> Thou will love for thy spirit dwells in eternity.
> O give all to me and boundless as the mighty ocean
> encircling this most wondrous world
> So will be my love for ever thine.
> O love me always and I shall sing my sweetest song
> Sweeter than the rustling of the trees
> And as sweet as the mother to her blessed babe.
> The song of undying love.
> But when in death I must leave thee here alone
> Sob not with pain and anguish but know
> I await thee where'er I be my love yet deeper still.

Note: The author of the text has not been identified. A dithyramb is a Greek poetic form, but can refer to any poem in an exalted and impassioned style.

Performance: 12 February 2021, recorded by RNZ Concert in St Andrew's on the Terrace, Wellington. Performed by Sarah Court *(ms)* and Bruce Greenfield *(piano)*.
Video of performance: https://www.youtube.com/watch?v=rYx_GjfM8i8, accessed 23 May 2022.

ATL Ref.: fMS-Papers-5136-06 (score; 79 bars, 5 pages).

Published in *The Call of the Huia; a collection of early New Zealand art songs*. Compiled and edited by Michael Vinten. (Wellington, 2021). ISMN: 9790801307408.

1926	**Prelude 'Excalibur' (for orchestra).**

Orchestration: Not known.
Note: Possibly drawn from the symphonic poem *The Lady of the Lake* or extracted from *The Coming of Arthur*.

Performance: 18 February 1926, as part of a programme entitled *The Song of the Sword*. Performed by the 5WA Orchestra. The location of the score is unknown.

1926	**The Lady of the Lake: symphonic poem for full orchestra.**

Orchestration: 3fl (dbl picc), 2ob+cor ang, 2cl (B♭)+bass cl, 3bn; 4hn (F), 3tpt (B♭), 3trb, bass tuba; timp, perc (cymbal, bass drum); harp, celeste; voices *(soprano)*; strings. Duration: *c.*18′

Note: Score dated Cardiff, 1 June 1926. There is no record of any performance.

ATL Ref.: fMS-Papers-5136-14 (full score).
ATL Ref.: fMS-Papers-5136-55 (set of parts – incomplete).

1926	**Ride of the Valkyries (from Wagner's *Die Walküre*, arr. Warwick Braithwaite).**

Instrumentation: flute, clarinet, strings and piano.

Performance: 18 July 1926. Cardiff, 5WA Studio. Performed by the 5WA Station Octet.

449

Location of score and parts unknown.

1926   **Welsh Folk Song Fantasia (for small orchestra).**
Orchestration: fl, ob (dbl cor ang), cl (A), bn; 2hn (F), tpt (A), 2trb; timp, perc (side drum); piano; viola.

Performance: 12 July 1926. Cardiff, 5WA Studio. Performed by the 5WA Station Orchestra.

Note: The *Radio Times* announced that:
> Listeners will doubtless be interested in the new *Welsh Folk Song Fantasia*, written by Mr Warwick Braithwaite, Cardiff's Musical Director. The number of compositions by Welsh musicians suitable for inclusion in a programme of this kind is by no means large, and this new work will form a welcome addition to the programme. 'Cardiff News', *Radio Times*, Issue 14, vol. 12 (9 July 1926), 103.

Two excerpts from the *Welsh Folk Song Fantasia*, 'The Monk's March' and 'Once a Farmer and His Wife', were performed on 4 November 1926 by the 5WA Station Orchestra at the beginning and conclusion of a production of the one-act play *The Last Sinner* by Herbert J. Brunel Evans.

Two more excerpts, 'Over the Stone' and 'Lament' were performed as *Two Welsh Tunes* by the 5WA Station Orchestra during the broadcast, *A Welsh Medley*, on 17 August 1926.

ATL Ref.: fMS-Papers-5136-54 (score).
ATL Ref.: fMS-Papers-5136-56 (parts).
ATL Ref.: fMS-Papers-5136-58 (parts).

1927   **Poi dance; arranged by Warwick Braithwaite for orchestra and women's voices.**
Orchestration: 2fl, 2ob, 2 cl (B♭), 2bn; 4hn, 2(B♭), 3trb; harp; strings; women's voices (ad.lib.).

Performance: 20 June 1927: Cardiff, 5WA Studio, 5WA Station Orchestra (no vocal artists listed) as part of a programme entitled *Dancing Round the World*.

Note: The score is missing some final pages, and ends as the female chorus enters with the words; 'Tikina e irini kite rito harakeke'.

ATL Red.: fMS-Papers-5136-34 (score incomplete; 7 pages only).

1927?   **Ridolfo (for orchestra).**
Orchestration: 2fl, 2ob+cor ang, 2cl (B♭)+bass cl, 2bn; 3hn (F), 4tpt (F), 2trb+bass trb, tuba; timp; strings.

Note: Incomplete pencil score only (5 pages). Manuscript paper is the same brand as that used for *Welsh Fantasia* (1927).

ATL Ref.: fMS-Papers-5136-37 (incomplete pencil score only).

1927   **A Fantasia on Welsh Folk Tunes (for full orchestra).**
Orchestration: 2fl, 2ob, 2cl (A), 2bn; 4hn, 2tpt (A), 3trb+bass trb; timp, perc, celeste; harp; strings.

Note: Arranged from the version for small orchestra composed in 1926. The score is dated 20 Jul 1927.

Performances
14 May 1928. Cardiff, 5WA Studio. Performed by the National Orchestra of Wales in *A Welsh Programme*.

4 January 1930. Cardiff, 5WA Studio, in a broadcast performance by the National Orchestra of Wales, conducted by Reginald Redman.

6 April 1930. Cardiff, Park Hall, in a broadcast concert performance by the National Orchestra of Wales, conducted by Reginald Redman.

ATL Ref.: fMS-Papers-5136-07 (full score).
ATL Ref.: fMS-Papers-5136-57 (parts).

1927   **Overture [Legende] in E flat major.**
Orchestration: 2fl+picc, 2ob+cor ang, 3cl (B♭) (3rd cl ad lib.), 3bn; 4hn, 3tpt (B♭), 2trb+bass trb, tuba; timp, (cymbals, side drum, triangle, bass drum); harp, celeste; perc; strings.

Note: The word *'Legende'* is added by Braithwaite to the title at the head of the celeste part only. The ink is a different colour (blue rather than black), so it is possibly an afterthought. The full score is dated December 1927, but Braithwaite claims that it was composed in 1921.

Performance: 30 March 1929. Cardiff, City Hall Assembly Room, performed by the National Orchestra of Wales.

The programme note for the first performance contains the following information:

This work was written in 1921 and dedicated to a great friend of the composer. The title 'Legend' gives only an abstract idea of the thoughts underlying this Overture. The hearer is asked to think of the various legends of olden time, the striving after an ideal by the warriors of old, and in the later romantic era, the struggle against the forces of evil and the formation of the Round Table by King Arthur. The influence of these thoughts is easily discernible in the work.

At the commencement we are introduced to a robust and strong theme played by the horns in unison, supported by other instruments against a background of dazzling brilliance. This theme typifies the strength of a resolve to conquer against every obstacle in the way.

By itself the theme is robust and magnificently ruthless, as yet unaware of the influence of a real sense of quiet beauty. This quiet theme, the antithesis of the first, is played by the strings, and after a quiet contemplative section, the development section of the overture follows.

The main part of the middle section is given over to the natural development of the two main themes, and the climax of the whole work follows in the re-statement when the second main tune becomes more important than any other. The overture ends brilliantly after a short re-statement of the first theme.

Review

Saturday's concert…set the seal to the popularity of the National Orchestra of Wales. Two large audiences in one week, with programmes ranging from the heavy to the lighter types of music, are a good augury for the continuance of increased public support, and when the series resumes, after a brief but well-earned respite, Wales's new institution may be regarded as being firmly established on a permanent footing…

…As explained in the analytical note the title gives only an abstract idea of the thoughts underlying this overture… Mr Braithwaite seems to have been largely influenced by Wagner. There are some passages of considerable beauty. The work, which was written in 1921, was well performed. *Western Mail* (1 April 1929), 9.

ATL Ref.: fMS-Papers-5136-15 (score).
ATL Ref.: fMS-Papers-5136-16 (parts).

1927? **Quintette for strings.**
Instrumentation: Violin I and II; Viola I and II; Cello.
Two movements only:
II   Andante (E major) (10 pages; 146 bars).
III   Finale (Vigoroso) (F sharp minor) (13 pages; 197 bars).
Note: A pencil note adds the word 'Māori' to this movement.

ATL Ref.: fMS-Papers-5136-08 (score).

1929? **Sulla poppa del mio brich (from Federico Ricci's opera *La Prigione Di Edimburgo* (arr. by Warwick Braithwaite).**
Performance: 14 April 1929. Cardiff, City Hall Assembly Room, performed by Herbert Heyner *(baritone)* and the National Orchestra of Wales. A concert in the Popular Sunday Night series.

Location of score and parts not known.

1931 **Legend for orchestra 'Hinemoa'.**
Orchestration: 2fl, 2ob (dbl cor ang), 2cl (A), 2bn; 4hn, 3tpt (A), 2trb+bass trb; timp; strings. Duration: 15´

Note: Original parts dated July 1931. This work was incorporated (without alteration) into Braithwaite's *Symphony in E* as its second movement. Later sets of parts (in a different hand) are called *Hinemoa* possibly to avoid confusion with *Overture 'Legende'* which has no Māori connection.
The full score has been transcribed and computer-set by Michael Vinten as *Hinemoa*.

Performances
21 July 1931: 5WA Studio Broadcast, Cardiff. 'A Welsh Programme' performed by the National Orchestra of Wales.

5 October 1931: Cardiff, National Museum of Wales. A broadcast lunchtime concert of 'A Programme of Music by British Composers'.

21 July 1953: Dunedin, N.Z, Town Hall. Performed by National Orchestra of the New Zealand Broadcasting Service.

Review
The conductor's own tone poem 'Hinemoa' was in a different strain

from his impressive set of variations played in May. This tone poem, inspired by a well-known Māori legend, was a highly atmospheric work in which woodwind and brass frequently played the melodies to a shimmering accompaniment on the strings. Some dramatic passages were very effective and the mood of the piece turned to tranquillity at the end. Altogether it gave the impression that it would repay greater familiarity than the single performance afforded. *Evening Star* (22 July 1953), 2.

17 June 2006: Dunedin, N.Z, Town Hall at 8 p.m. Performed by Southern Sinfonia, conducted by Nicholas Braithwaite.

19 August 2015: Belfast, Ulster Hall. Performed by the Ulster Orchestra, conducted by Nicholas Braithwaite.

ATL Ref.: MS-Papers-9305 (computer-set score).
ATL Ref.: fMS-Papers-5136-10 (parts in unknown hand).
ATL Ref.: fMS-Papers-5136-17 (parts in Warwick Braithwaite's hand).

1931	**Loveliest of trees; song for tenor voice and pianoforte.**

Poem from A.E. Housman's collection *A Shropshire Lad*.
Note: Manuscript dated 1931.

ATL Ref.: fMS-Papers-5136-18 (score; 33 bars).

1931   **Meeting at night; for tenor and piano.**
Poem by Robert Browning.
Note: Manuscript dated 1931.

ATL Ref.: fMS-Papers-5136-22 (score; 31 bars).

1931   **Marie Magdalene; song for mezzo-soprano and piano.**
Poem by George Herbert.
Note: Manuscript dated December 1931.

ATL Ref.: fMS-Papers-5136-19 (score; 58 bars).

1931–1933   **Symphony in E Major.**
Orchestration: 2fl(dbl picc), 2ob+cor ang, 2cl (A and B♭), 2bn; 4hn, 3tpt (A and B♭), 2trb+bass trb; timp; strings.
I   *Adagio ma non troppo* (26 Jan 1933). Duration: 12′
II   '*Hinemoa*' (14 July 1931). Duration: 15′

III *Scherzo* (second part of score missing). Vn I and II parts complete.

IV *Finale* (original version dated 9 January 1933; incomplete. Revised version also incomplete).

Note: The holograph score of the second movement is enclosed in a Hinrichsen Edition Ltd cover. The work is given the number H.E. 207 'Hinemoa', Legend by Warwick Braithwaite. The title page of the score clearly states Symphony in E, II (Hinemoa). Most of the symphony was composed in 1932–1933, but Braithwaite's *Legend for Orchestra 'Hinemoa'* (1931) was incorporated, without alteration, into his *Symphony in E* as the second movement.

The symphony as a whole remains incomplete and unperformed, but for performances of the second movement, see *Legend for orchestra 'Hinemoa'*.

ATL Ref.: fMS-Papers-5136-47 I (28 pages); II (30 pages); III (29 pages); IV – Revised version, incomplete. (48 pages) (Full Score).
ATL Ref.: fMS-Papers-5136-48 IV – Original version. (42 pages) 'This is not the final copy of the 4th movement. It is being rewritten and the last four bars are not yet finished.'
ATL Ref.: fMS-Papers-5136-49. Parts for Violin I and II (Scherzo only).

[1931] **Auē – Māori tone picture (for orchestra).**
Orchestration: 2fl, ob+cor ang, 2cl (A), 2bn; 2hn; harp; perc (cymbals); strings.
Duration: 4.35

Performances
8 September 1931. Cardiff, 5WA Studio, performed by the National Orchestra of Wales.

9 December 1934. Cardiff, Park Hall. Composition listed as *Auē (Two Māori Folk Songs Transcribed for Orchestra)*, and performed by the Welsh Concert Orchestra. This was Braithwaite's last concert with the Cardiff Musical Society.

20 December 1939. London, Sadler's Wells Theatre. Vic-Wells Opera Company concert.

15 April 1940. London, His Majesty's Theatre. The New Zealand Centenary Concert; proceeds to be devoted to the Provision of Comforts for New Zealanders in His Majesty's Forces. Performed by the Sadler's Wells Orchestra.

30 October 1943. Glasgow, St Andrew's Hall. Performed by the Scottish Orchestra.

16 November 1943. Aberdeen, Music Hall. Performed by the Scottish Orchestra.

17 November 1943. Dundee, Caird Hall. Performed by the Scottish Orchestra.

Reviews

[Auē is] a modest work based on two Māori folk songs. It was nicely conceived and wrought. *Daily Record* (1 November 1943), 3.

Mr Braithwaite's little tone poem *Auē* is based on two Māori folk songs, and on this foundation he has built a quietly effective piece with an appealing wistfulness of mood. *The Glasgow Herald* (1 November 1943), 4.

Included in the programme was a short tone poem by the conductor, *Auē*. It is founded on two Māori folksongs – one suggesting the Bohemian composers, the other having that Sankey lilt that seems inseparable from so much South Sea music. The songs are atmospherically enfolded, and the playing was as it ought to have been. *Aberdeen Journal* (17 November 1943), 4.

One of the happiest pieces chosen was a little tone poem by Braithwaite *Aua* [sic] comprising two Māori folk-songs which imparted a curious wistfulness and breadth of melody that caught the imagination and brought the applause. *Dundee Courier* (14 November 1943), 3.

ATL Ref.: fMS-Papers-5136-01 (full score).
ATL Ref.: fMS-Papers-5136-02. (parts in WB's hand).

Another copy of the score (dated September 1931) is held in the Daniel Jones Archive, Ref. A76, at the National Library of Wales / Llyfrgell Genedlaethol Cymru, Aberystwyth.
Score and parts published by David Vine Music [DVM 146].

1934   **Solveig's slumber song from the Grieg's Peer Gynt Suite**
            (arranged for orchestra by Warwick Braithwaite).
            Orchestration: 2fl, 2ob, 2cl (A)+cor ang, 2bn; 2hn; harp; strings.

            ATL Ref.: fMS-Papers-5136-39 (score).

1935?   **Poem – Sonata in A sharp minor for pianoforte.**

            ATL Ref.: fMS-Papers-5136-40 (score; 148 bars).

1935?   **Fantaisie Sonata in G minor for pianoforte.**
            Note: The manuscript has the word 'Fantaisie' added in pencil
            before the word Sonata.

            ATL Ref.: fMS-Papers-5136-42 (score; 168 bars).

1935?   **Two preludes for piano.**
            I   D minor (30 bars).
            II   E minor (Molto tranquillo) (36 bars).

            Note: Prelude II is prefaced by the following song text taken
            from a play, *The House of Usna*, by Fiona McLeod, pseudonym of
            William Sharp (1855-1905):
                Dim face of Beauty, haunting all the world,
                Fair face of Beauty, all too fair to see.

            CD Recording
            Prelude no. 1 was recorded by William Green in 2015 on *The Young
            Pine Tree: Early New Zealand Piano Miniatures* (Organism ORG 018).

            Audio-visual Recording
            Prelude no. 1 was recorded by pianist Ludwig Treviranus
            and is available at: https://www.youtube.com/watch?time_
            continue=1921&v=_3WhIK5v4zU, accessed 23 May 2022, as part of
            a lecture given by Gillian Bibby to the Institute of Registered Music
            Teachers of NZ (IRMT) National Conference in February 2015.

            ATL Ref.: fMS-Papers-5136-35 (score).

1935?   **Piano Quartet (possibly incomplete).**
            Instrumentation: Flute; Clarinet (A); Horn (F); Bassoon;
            Pianoforte

I   Slow movement in A minor (96 bars).
II Rondo in C major (226 bars).

ATL Ref.: fMS-Papers-5136-36 (holograph; 43 pages).
Note: Revised and edited by David Vine as *Two movements for piano and wind quartet*
1 Adagio
2 Allegro Comodo
Score and parts published by David Vine Music [DVM 140].

1939–1941   **Pendragon; a grand opera in 3 acts.**
Orchestration: 3fl+picc, 2ob+ca, 2cl+bcl, 2bn+contra bn; 4hn, 3tpt, 3trb, tuba; timp, perc (tamtam, side drum, bass drum, bells, cymbal, triangle); harp; celeste; strings.
Stage: 6tpt (written in 3 parts), 2hn, 2trb, bells, perc.

Characters: King Uther Pendragon *(tenor)*; Sir Ulfus (Ulfius in Malory), his companion-in-arms *(baritone)*; Merlin *(bass)*; Duke of Tintagel *(baritone)*; Igraine *(mezzo)*; Archbishop *(high bass)*; Sir Ector, Arthur's foster-father *(baritone)*; Arthur Pendragon *(tenor)*; Sir Kay(e) *(tenor)*; a watchman *(baritone)*; a messenger *(tenor or high baritone)*; a young child *(mezzo)*; Three commoners *(TTB)*; Three barons *(TTB)*; Three knights *(TTB)*. On and off-stage chorus of people and knights *(SATB)*.

Completed 7 May 1941
Libretto entitled *The Grail* (1939-1940?)
Libretto by Henry Wharton (pseud. of Warwick Braithwaite) from Sir Thomas Malory's *Book of Merlin*.

Note: Collection contains three versions of Braithwaite's libretto (see Appendix 6).
A score was later submitted to the Arts Council of Great Britain, along with a full score of his *Variations on a Personal Theme*, as a further example of his style of orchestration. (Letter from Eric Walter White to Braithwaite, dated 1 July 1949).
It is possible that this was one of the sixty entrants in a competition for an opera to be premiered as part of the 1951 Festival of Britain.

ATL Ref.: fMS-Papers-5136-25 (full score Act I).
ATL Ref.: fMS-Papers-5136-26 (full score Act II).

ATL Ref.: fMS-Papers-5136-27 (full Score Act III; final pages missing.
Alternative endings for Acts I and II; 313 pages).
ATL Ref.: fMS-Papers-5136-28 (vocal scores, Act I and Act II; 219 pages).
ATL Ref.: fMS-Papers-5136-29 (vocal scores Act II – one copy incomplete).
ATL Ref.: fMS-Papers-5136-30 (vocal score Act I; sketches for Act II).

1944   **Variations on a personal theme (for orchestra).**
            Orchestration: 2fl+picc, 2ob (dbl cor ang), 2cl (A)+bass cl (B♭), 2bn+contra-bn; 4hn, 3tpt (A), 3trb, tuba; timp, perc (cymbals, bells); celeste; harp; strings.

            Note: Completed in Glasgow, October 1944.
            The score was submitted to the Arts Council of Great Britain, along with a score of *Pendragon*, possibly as an example of his style of orchestration. (Letter from Eric Walter White to Braithwaite, dated 1 July 1949).

            Performances and Reviews
            18 November 1944. Glasgow, St Andrew's Hall. Scottish Orchestra.

            Reviews
            > Glasgow music lovers gave spontaneous approbation to the first performance of Mr Warwick Braithwaite's Variations for Orchestra. *Daily Record* (20 November 1944), 4.

            > A warm reception was given to the first performance of Warwick Braithwaite's Variations for Orchestra. *The Scotsman* (20 November 1944), 3.

            > Mr Braithwaite's Variations for Orchestra played on Saturday for the first time, scored another success. *The Glasgow Herald* (20 November 1944), 5.

            14 March 1945: Shettleston, Public Hall. Scottish Orchestra.
            16 March 1945: Edinburgh, Usher Hall. Scottish Orchestra.

            Review
            > Mr Warwick Braithwaite's Variations for Orchestra was the other

unfamiliar work. So many derogatory things have been said about conductors' compositions that it comes as rather a surprise to find one showing genuine musical value. Mr Braithwaite has decked out his simple little theme in fine orchestral colours, but that is not all. He has shown that by thinking round it, musically and emotionally, he can convey more than the theme and its purely orchestral trappings would of themselves express. And that is the essence of good variation writing. Preoccupation with the theme itself would have led only to superficial, perhaps even tasteless trifles. The orchestra seemed none too familiar with some parts of the score, but enough came through to show that the music is worthy of further performances, and, on the whole, to be preferred to Glazunov. *The Scotsman* (17 March 1945), 4.

25 May 1953. Town Hall, Dunedin, New Zealand. National Orchestra of the New Zealand Broadcasting Service.
In a programme note for the N.Z. premiere in 1953, the composer's writes:

> The theme of these Variations is taken from the opera *Pendragon*, which was written some years ago. It is the child's song from the beginning of the Third Act and is therefore quite a simple piece of music designed so that any person could sing it without any trouble. The Variations as a whole might be considered to be an example of orchestration, for each Variation is treated differently.
> Variation 1. The first variation is a continuation of the tune and is given to the clarinet, with the strings as a harmonic background. This ends quite quietly.
> Variation 2 (Presto). This is a quick staccato string version which is repeated and in which the woodwinds join the strings.
> Variation 3. This is a background of muted strings, with the solo woodwind taking the major part.
> Variation 4. This starts off with the violoncellos and horns playing a variant of the tune in which the full orchestra eventually joins.
> Variations 5 and 6. This has, in the middle of it, the Sixth Variation, but the original variation (no. 5) is repeated at the end. Perhaps it might be of interest to note that the middle variation (no. 6) is the only part of the variation which might be considered to be personal, in that it is dedicated to the composer's mother, who was an Irish woman, and the Irish flavour of this variation will soon be perceived.
> Variation 7 (Andante con moto e misterioso). This is a quiet and quite mysterious variation in which wisps of the tune are given out by the brass and in which the strings play a background of quiet semiquavers.
> Variation 8 (Vivace). In this variation the horns come into full play,

eventually joined by the full orchestra. It is very bright and is over quite soon. This is followed immediately without a break by–
Variation 9. This is also quick and vivacious. Again, there is no break between this variation and the next one.
Variation 10. In this variation the violas have a variant of the tune, later on built up by the strings and other members of the full orchestra.
Variation 11. This has a subtitle 'Echo'. In fact, the subtitle explains the variation quite clearly, in which the strings play harmonics and the celeste joins them.
Variation 12. A solemn melody is built up by the brass instruments in which the original tune is inverted. This variation finishes quietly with the original end of the first variation.
Variation 13. The full orchestra is employed right through. The theme is played by the brass instruments, but in an enlarged form over which there are cascades of harmonics and virtuoso string playing, and it ends with the full orchestra playing fortissimo.

ATL Ref.: fMS-Papers-5136-50 (full score) (53 pages).
ATL Ref.: fMS-Papers-5136-51 (parts for wind, brass, timp).
ATL Ref.: fMS-Papers-5136-52 (parts for perc., harp, celeste, violin I and II).
ATL Ref.: fMS-Papers-5136-53 (parts for viola, cello, double bass).

Score and parts published by David Vine Music [DVM 148].

1947   **Linden Lea Wedding March (for organ)**
Note: Composed for the marriage of Miss La Valette Walker and Major Tom Arnold at Mary Magdalene Church, Rose Bay, Sydney on 19 June 1947.
According to a report in Sydney's *The Daily Telegraph* (3 May 1947), 4, Braithwaite overheard the couple in the lounge of the Australia Hotel, discussing their forthcoming marriage. He was so taken by the happy couple, that he presented them with a march for their service. It is named after his address in London.

Location of manuscript unknown.

1956   **Sonata in D for tenor trombone and pianoforte.**
Dedicated to 'Nicky' (Nicholas Braithwaite) and dated 26 August 1956.
  I   Moderato
  II Adagio 'Melody in the Classical Tradition'

461

Note: The separate score of the trombone part matches that of the piano score, but it is titled *Rhapsody* for tenor trombone and piano, and the movements are:

I   Lento
II   Melody (in olden style)

ATL Ref.: fMS-Papers-5136-43 (piano score; 12 pages, and trombone part; 4 pages).

Braithwaite arranged the second movement for trombone and medium orchestra:
Sonata in D for trombone and medium orchestra.
   II   Slow Movement (Melody in Classical Tradition).
Orchestration: 2fl, 2ob, 2cl (A), 2bn; 4hn (F), trb solo; timp; harp; strings.

ATL Ref.: fMS-Papers-5136-45 (full orchestral score).

Score and parts edited and arranged by David Vine and published as
Andante in D, for solo trombone and orchestra. [DVM 147].

Another score titled **Second Movt. Sonata for trombone and piano** is a different, or possibly alternative, slow movement.
In 3/2 time and marked *Adagio*, it begins with six bars for solo trombone.

ATL Ref.: fMS-Papers-5136-44 (piano score; 5 pages; 64 bars).

1960s?   **The Mask (The Laughing Man); opera in 3 Acts.**
Based on the novel *L'Homme qui rit* (1869) by Victor Hugo.
Libretto and music by Warwick Braithwaite.
Note: Collection contains three versions of Braithwaite's libretto (see Appendix 6).

ATL Ref.: fMS-Papers-5136-20 (musical sketches only for Acts 1 and II).
ATL Ref.: fMS-Papers-5136-21 (further musical sketches).

APPENDIX 6

WARWICK BRAITHWAITE WRITINGS

Braithwaite's autobiography makes little reference to his own musical compositions, and none whatsoever to his other literary efforts. Over the years, he contributed articles to newspapers and music journals, concert programme notes, and the occasional angry Letter to the Editor. His heartfelt and generous eulogies for other musicians appeared in newspapers if he felt that the formal obituaries had been lacking in accuracy or appreciation.

In addition to his lengthy autobiography, the Braithwaite Archive in the Alexander Turnbull Library has several manuscripts (with Braithwaite as author or contributor) which deserve to be noted.

Benton, Edward, 'Tour of German opera houses, June 1962'.
A report by Edward Benton on tours of German opera houses includes Hannover Opernhaus, Städtische Bühnen Münster, Kassel Staatstheater, Kiel Landestheater, Staatsoper Stuttgart, Hamburg Opera House, Frankfurt-am-Main Städtische Bühnen, Gelsenkirchen Städtische Bühnen, with some sketches by Warwick Braithwaite.

ATL Ref.: MS-Papers-5136-15

Braithwaite, Warwick, Autobiographical notes
Two short handwritten sections of his autobiography.
The first (2 pages) covers his trip to Milan and his meeting with Eugenio Clausetti. It is roughly equivalent to pages 124–126 of the typed manuscript.

The second section (8 pages) concerns his return to Glasgow from Germany, and is roughly equivalent to pages 205–211 of the typed manuscript.

ATL Ref.: MS-Papers-5136-11

Braithwaite, Warwick, 'Autobiography (part I)'
Comprises pages 1–103 in which Braithwaite describes his family, his introduction to music and the various steps in his progress towards becoming an international conductor. He recounts his career path which included being conductor of the O'Mara Opera Company (1919), répétiteur of the British National Opera Co (1921), with the BBC (1922), the Cardiff Musical Society and National Orchestra of Wales (until 1930), as conductor of Sadler's Wells Opera Co (1932–1940) and with the Royal Academy of Music, 1937-38. This part of the autobiography is divided into Book 1 'The Golden Shore', (pages 1–26), Book 2 (pages 27–50), Book 3 '1922 The British National Opera Company, Covent Garden, The Prinz Regenten Theatre München' (pages 51–67), and Book 4 (pages 68–103).

ATL Ref.: MS-Papers-5473-1

Braithwaite, Warwick, 'Autobiography (part II)'
Braithwaite continues his narrative with notes on opera at Sadler's Wells, his study time at La Scala Milan before the war, wartime conditions, his work in Britain where he conducted many of the important orchestras and made recordings, a spell with the Hamburg Philharmonic Orchestra (and visits to Belsen) and with the Berlin Philharmonic Orchestra in 1945. He describes broadcasting to the forces, personalities in the music world, and his visits en route to Australia and activities there prior to his visit to New Zealand. Includes news clippings of letters from Braithwaite to the 'Glasgow Herald' re the Scottish National Orchestra and one from J Barnes, secretary and manager of the Choral and Orchestral Union of Glasgow re season of the orchestra. Pages 104–117 are not included; this section therefore comprises pages 118–262.

ATL Ref.: MS-Papers-5473-2

Braithwaite, Warwick, 'Autobiography (part III)'
Braithwaite continues his narrative describing his return visit to NZ, then a tour to South Africa and his return to London and problems at Covent Garden. He writes of the disagreements in the musical scene and the difficulties of getting work, gives his opinion on homosexuality (pages 369–373). He describes various tours of Italy, Spain, France and Austria. Braithwaite discusses many of

the important people he meets, including Karl Rankl, David Webster, Herbert von Karajan, Edward J Dent, Ricardo Blamey Lafone and Vaughan Williams. Finally, he visited Finland where he met Sibelius, and had more world travels (1953–1956), visiting and working in Australia, New Zealand and the United States. (This part comprises pages 263–409).

ATL Ref.: MS-Papers-5473-3

Braithwaite, Warwick, 'The Mask (The Laughing Man): opera in 3 Acts'.
Based on the novel *L'Homme qui rit* (1869) by Victor Hugo.
Libretto and music by Warwick Braithwaite. See also Appendix 5.

ATL Ref.: MS-Papers-5136-01
ATL Ref.: MS-Papers-5136-02 (second version)
ATL Ref.: MS-Papers-5136-03 (third version, 8 August 1966–23 February 1967)

Braithwaite, Warwick, 'Notes on Puccini Mss during my stay in Milano'.
Fragmented sets of notes on textual and interpretive issues mainly in *Tosca*, but also *Il tabarro*, *Turandot*, *La bohème* and *Madama Butterfly*. During his stay in Milan, Braithwaite had access to Puccini's manuscript scores thanks to Eugenio Clausetti, an executive of the Ricordi publishing house.

The folder also contains a copy of Braithwaite's letter to Clausetti, dated 2 August 1961, which indicates that he has written an article about 'that much vexed note in *Tosca*, Act I'. He goes on to say that, 'one of these days when I have more time, I will type my article for you.' There is no typed copy of the article in the archive, and it does not appear to have been published. The letter is also significant because it shows Braithwaite's interest in viewing Puccini's 'final and altered score' of *La fanciulla del West*, an opera which was to return to the repertoire in Britain. He asks Clausetti's opinion on the idea that 'The Girl *should* be done in English (or American).'
6 items (holographs and copies of typescripts) in one folder.
Dated by WB as November 1960.

ATL Ref.: MS-Papers-5136-10

Braithwaite, Warwick, 'Nuance exercise'.
Lecture script instructing on vocal production, interpretation and characterisation. The script focuses first on Mozart, and later at length on Wagner's *Die Meistersinger*.
Typescript (16 leaves, ordered A–P; pages 45–57 'old numbering').

ATL Ref.: MS-Papers-5136-07

Braithwaite, Warwick, 'Opera – Interpretation and translation'.
A note, signed by Braithwaite, states 'Notes re. book on interpretation and translation of opera'.
Typescript with annotations. Musical examples indicated but not included. (23 pages).
1950s?

ATL Ref.: MS-Papers-5136-08

Braithwaite, Warwick, 'Opera sung in the English language'
Possibly intended as part of a larger book. There are five chapters.
Typescript, annotated (35 pages).
1950s?

ATL Ref.: MS-Papers-5136-09

Braithwaite, Warwick, 'Rimsky Korsakoff'
Script of a talk (possibly for radio) on the music of Rimsky Korsakov.
Handwritten in blue ink (13 pages; 25 sides).
Undated, but a reference to the British premiere of *Mozart and Salieri* 'a few days ago at the hands of Albert Coates', places the writing to November 1927. The performance mentioned took place at the Royal Albert Hall on 11 November 1927.
Private Collection.

Braithwaite, Warwick, 'Wilderness; a tragedy comprising 4 scenes'.
Play script, 1932.

ATL Ref.: MS-Papers-5136-12

Wharton, Henry [Warwick Braithwaite], 'The Grail'
Libretto for Braithwaite's opera, *Pendragon*. See also Appendix 5.

ATL Ref.: MS-Papers-5136-06 (The Grail, libretto).
ATL Ref.: fMS-Papers-5136-04 (composer's note and synopsis)
ATL Ref.: MS-Papers-5136-05 (libretto sketches).
ATL Ref.: fMS-Papers-5136-31 (libretto and notes; 101 pages)

Wharton, Henry [Warwick Braithwaite], [Short stories].

Short stories by Warwick Braithwaite written under his pseudonym, Henry Wharton comprise 'Jamie', 'A Strange Meeting', 'The Intelligence Test or The Stornaway [*sic*] Wonder', 'Mr Tweezling's Cure for Hiccups', 'Pleasure Before Business, (or It's Still More Dangerous to do Nothing About Dangerous Situations)'.

ATL Ref.: MS-Papers-5136-13

BIBLIOGRAPHY

Quotations cited from newspaper articles and reviews have been obtained using online resources such as the National Library of New Zealand's *Papers Past*, the British Library's *British Newspaper Archive*, the *Google Newspaper Archive*, and independent newspaper and journal subscription databases. Online resources are cited in the relevant footnotes.

In addition to the many individuals and institutions acknowledged in the Preface, the following books and journals have proved helpful in the preparation of this volume.

Arundell, Dennis, *The Story of Sadler's Wells Theatre, 1683–1964* (London: Hamish Hamilton, 1965).

Austin, Louis Daly, *LDA: LD Austin's Life in Music*, ed. Allan Thomas (Wellington: Steele Roberts, 2019).

Baillie, Isobel, *Never Sing Louder than Lovely* (London: Hutchinson, 1982).

Blom, Eric, ed., *Leslie Heward 1897–1943: A Memorial Volume* (London: J. M. Dent & Sons, 1944).

Braithwaite, Nicholas, *So What Does a Conductor Do?* (n.p.: Nicholas Braithwaite, 2017).

Braithwaite, Warwick, *The Conductor's Art* (London: Williams and Norgate, 1952).

Braithwaite, Warwick, 'Holst's Savitri', *Opera* [BNOC Magazine], 1/7, (July 1923).

Braithwaite, Warwick, 'Mendelssohn in Scotland', *Chapbook: The magazine of Scottish achievement*, 2 (March 1946), 23.

Braithwaite, Warwick, 'Opera and Symphony', *Opera News* [Metropolitan Opera Guild], 17/20 (16 March 1953), 14–15, 32.

Braithwaite, Warwick, 'Scandinavian Holiday', *Sadler's Wells Magazine*, 4 (Autumn 1966).

Braithwaite, Warwick, 'The Scottish Orchestra', *Chapbook: The magazine of Scottish achievement*, 1 (January 1946), 2-4.

Brook, Donald, *Conductors' Gallery: Biographical Sketches of Well-Known Orchestral Conductors, Including Notes on the Leading Symphony Orchestras, and a Short Biography of the Late Sir Henry Wood* (London: Rockliff, 1946).

Campbell, Margaret, *Music in Dunedin: An Historical Account of Dunedin's Musicians and Musical Societies from the Founding of the Province in 1848* (Dunedin: Charles Begg, 1945).

Cross, Joan, 'An Experiment in Opera, 1940–1945', in Eric Crozier, ed., *Opera in English: Sadler's Wells Opera Books, No. 1* (London: John Lane, 1946), 28–35.

Davies, John, *Broadcasting and the BBC in Wales* (Cardiff: University of Wales Press, 1994).

Doctor, Jennifer Ruth, *The BBC and Ultra-Modern Music, 1922–1936: Shaping a Nation's Tastes* (Cambridge: Cambridge University Press, 1999).

Donaldson, Frances, *The Royal Opera House in the Twentieth Century* (London: Weidenfeld and Nicolson, 1988).

Fawkes, Richard, *Welsh National Opera* (London: J. MacRae, 1986).

Flury, Roger. 'Out of the Shadows : the remarkable story of New Zealand's finest conductor Warwick Braithwaite', *Turnbull Library Record*, 53 (2021), 56-71.

Frankland, Noble and Charles Webster, *The Strategic Air Offensive Against Germany, 1939–1945, Volume II: Endeavour, Part 4* (London: Her Majesty's Stationery Office, 1961).

Gilbert, Susie, *Opera for Everybody: The Story of English National Opera* (London: Faber & Faber, 2009).

Grey, Dame Beryl, *For the Love of Dance* (London: Oberon Books, 2017).

Grey, Thomas S., ed., *Richard Wagner and His World* (Princeton, N.J.: Princeton University Press, 2009).

Guthrie, Tyrone, *A Life in the Theatre* (London: Hamish Hamilton, 1961).

Harrison, Frank, *Tobruk: The Great Siege Reassessed* (London: Brockhampton Press, 1999).

Hochstetter, Ferdinand von, *New Zealand: Its Physical Geography, Geology, and Natural History: With Special Reference to the Results of Government Expeditions in the Provinces of Auckland and Nelson*, tr. Edward Sauter (Stuttgart: J.G. Cotta, 1867).

Hogan, Robert Goode and Richard Burnham, *The Years of O'Casey, 1921–1926: A Documentary History* (Newark: University of Delaware Press, 1992).

Holmes, John L., *Conductors on Record* (London: Victor Gollancz, 1982).

Humphreys, Maggie and Robert Evans, *Dictionary of Composers for the Church in Great Britain and Ireland* (London: Mansell, 1997).

Inglis, Kenneth Stanley, assisted by Jan Brazier, *This is the ABC: The Australian*

Broadcasting Commission, 1932–1983 (Carlton, Vic.: Melbourne University Press, 1983).

Jensen, Owen, *The NZBC Symphony Orchestra* (Wellington, A.H. & A.W. Reed, 1966).

Lambert, Constant, *Music Ho!: A Study of Music in Decline* (London: Faber & Faber, 1934).

Langdon, Michael and Richard Fawkes, *Notes from a Low Singer* (London: J. MacRae, 1982).

Lebrecht, Norman, *Covent Garden the Untold Story: Dispatches from the English Culture War, 1945–2000* (London: Simon & Schuster, 2000).

Lew, Nathaniel Geoffrey, *Tonic to the Nation: Making English Music in the Festival of Britain* (London: Routledge, 2016).

Mercier, Anita, *Guilhermina Suggia, Cellist* (Aldershot: Ashgate, 2008).

Mitchell, Alastair, *A Chronicle of First Broadcast Performances of Musical Works in the United Kingdom, 1923–1996* (Aldershot: Ashgate, 2001).

Moore Jerrold Northrop, *Philharmonic Jubilee, 1932-1982: A Celebration of the London Philharmonic Orchestra's Fiftieth Anniversary* (London: Hutchinson, 1982).

Palmer, Jill, 'Alexander Turnbull Library: Warwick Braithwaite Collection', *Canzona*, 17/38 (1996), 39–41.

Parry, Jann, *Different Drummer: The Life of Kenneth MacMillan* (London: Faber & Faber, 2009).

Potter, Simon J., *Broadcasting Empire: The BBC and the British World, 1922–1970* (Oxford: Oxford University Press, 2012).

Proctor, Robert N., *The Nazi War on Cancer* (Princeton, N.J.: Princeton University Press, 2000).

Reid, Charles, *Thomas Beecham: An Independent Biography* (London: Gollancz, 1962).

Rodmell, Paul, *Opera in the British Isles, 1875–1918* (Aldershot: Ashgate, 2013).

Rosenthal, Harold, *Two Centuries of Opera at Covent Garden* (London: Putnam, 1958).

Ruppli, Michel and Ed Novitsky, *The MGM Labels: A Discography Vol. 3: Additional Recordings/Record and Artist Indexes* (Westport, Conn.: Greenwood Press, 1998).

Sanders, Alan, *Walter Legge: A Discography* (Westport, Conn.: Greenwood Press, 1984).

Simpson, Adrienne, *Opera's Farthest Frontier: A History of Professional Opera in New Zealand* (Auckland: Reed, 1996).

Simpson, Adrienne and Peter Downes, *Southern Voices: International Opera Singers of New Zealand* (Auckland: Reed, 1992).

Simpson, Adrienne and Geoffrey Newson, *Alex Lindsay: The Man and His*

Orchestra, Canterbury Series of Bibliographies, Catalogues, and Source Documents in Music; No. 9 (Christchurch, N.Z.: School of Music, University of Canterbury, 1998).

Stewart, H., *The New Zealand Division, 1916–1919: A Popular History Based on Official Records, Official History of New Zealand's Effort in the Great War; v. 2* (Auckland: Whitcombe and Tombs, 1921).

Stuart, Philip, *The London Philharmonic Discography* (Westport, Conn.: Greenwood Press, 1997).

Tancsik, Pamela, 'Tracing Joseph Trauneck: The Wanderings of a Persecuted Man', *Fontes Artis Musicae*, 56/ 2 (2009), 115–137.

Thomson, John Mansfield, *Biographical Dictionary of New Zealand Composers* (Wellington: Victoria University Press, 1990).

Thomson, John Mansfield, *A Distant Music: The Life and Times of Alfred Hill 1870–1960* (Auckland: Oxford University Press, 1980).

Thomson, John Mansfield, *The Oxford History of New Zealand Music* (Auckland: Oxford University Press, 1999).

Tintner, Tanya Buchdahl, *Out of Time: The Vexed Life of Georg Tintner* (Crawley, W.A.: University of Western Australia Publishing, 2011).

Tonks, Joy, *The New Zealand Symphony Orchestra: The First Forty Years* (Auckland: Reed Methuen, 1986).

Turbet, Richard, *Music Librarianship in the United Kingdom: Fifty Years of the United Kingdom Branch of the International Association of Music Libraries, Archives, and Documentation Centres* (Aldershot, Hants: Ashgate, 2003).

Walter, Bruno, *Theme and Variations* (N.Y.: Knopf, 1946).

Williams, Harcourt, *Old Vic Saga* (London: Winchester Publications, 1949).

Wilson, Conrad, *Playing for Scotland: The History of the Royal Scottish National Orchestra* (London: HarperCollins, 1993).

ABOUT THE EDITOR

Born in London and educated at Westminster City School, Roger Flury was also Head Chorister at St Margaret's Church, Westminster, and a treble soloist at the Royal Opera House, Covent Garden. A grant enabled him to study part-time as a tenor with William Parsons at the Guildhall School of Music and Drama, and although he went on to perform a number of roles with Opera Viva, he ultimately decided to pursue a career in music librarianship with Westminster City Libraries.

Emigrating to New Zealand in 1974, Flury continued his amateur musical activities, but still passionate about music libraries, he worked for 45 years in the profession, retiring as Curator, Music at the Alexander Turnbull Library (Wellington) in 2014. For much of his career he has been closely associated with the International Association of Music Libraries, Archives and Documentation Centres (IAML), serving as Secretary General, President and Historian.

He is the author of award-winning books on Mascagni and Puccini, co-editor of a volume of songs by Arturo Toscanini, co-founder of Academy Opera, writer and presenter of over 100 programmes for Radio New Zealand, and a contributor to music journals internationally.

Since his retirement and return to England, he has given talks for Opera Holland Park, the Recorded Vocal Arts Society, and the New Zealand Studies Network, and is currently collaborating with David Vine on the publication of some of Braithwaite's compositions.

INDEX

Page numbers in *italics* indicate illustrations. The letter n. refers to a footnote on that page.

CPSIA information can be obtained
at www.ICGtesting.com
Printed in the USA
BVHW092134030223
657833BV00016B/1697

9 781803 135625